An English Football Internationalists' Who's Who

1872 - 1988

by Douglas Lamming

HUTTON PRESS
1990

Published by the Hutton Press Ltd.
130 Canada Drive, Cherry Burton, Beverley
North Humberside HU17 7SB

Printed and bound by

Image Colourprint
23 Flemingate, Beverley
East Yorkshire HU17 0NT

ISBN 0 907033 93 8

To
Ray Spiller
who, in 1978, founded
the Association of Football Statisticians,
and so revolutionised researches
into our national game.

ACKNOWLEDGEMENTS

Without the pioneering exploits of that doyen of soccer statisticians, the late Morley Farror, this work would have been much more difficult to undertake. I had the privilege of knowing him for many years, a privilege that not only brought to my notice many then unknown sources of information, but also gave pointers as to the distillation and presentation of material never before made public.

Jim Creasy has been tireless in the checking and correcting of old material and the unearthing of new. Michael Featherstone and Michael Davage have again provided 'impossible' information regarding birth and death dates. The invaluable help of Malcolm Hartley and Keith Warsop has again been forthcoming, while a young relative, Damian Kerney, then at Lancing College, has obtained details of that institution's several internationalists of the Victorian era. Quite unexpectedly Peter Tymkow kindly sent the results of his in-depth investigations into several of the earliest internationalists, which fortunately arrived in time for inclusion.

I am indebted to Brendan Kerney, Garth Dykes and Sid Woodhead for help with illustrations and to Bryan Horsnell for the cover, which features items from his unique collection of soccer memorabilia.

AUTHOR'S PREFACE

England's involvement with international football now goes back well over a century. It seemed high time, therefore, that a Who's Who dealing in comprehensive detail with the 1003 England players capped to the end of season 1987/88 should be made available. Additionally it would complement that of the ancient rival, Scotland, issued in 1987.

The 1003 form an extremely varied gallery, ranging from eventual leading figures in politics, church, armed forces and the professions to so-called ordinary folk (though, it should be stressed, extraordinary in the matter of soccer skills). The gallery illustrates the game's development. How Oxbridge and the great public schools supplied most of England's players until the legalisation of professionalism quickly followed by the founding of the Football League.

The consequent dwindling number of amateurs being called upon – the last was in 1936. The great post-WW2 increase in international fixtures and possibility – and actuality – of a player winning over 100 caps.

A fascinating gallery and, although an arduous undertaking, a fascinating one to write about.

DOUGLAS LAMMING
North Ferriby.
January 1990.

England's Team against Scotland 1895
Back row: N L Jackson, L V Lodge, J Reynolds, J Reid (referee), J Holt, J W Sutcliffe, E Needham, J W Crabtree, R E Lythgoe, C J Hughes.
Seated: W I Bassett, S Bloomer, J Goodall, R C Gosling, S Smith.

NOTES ON THE TEXT

GENERAL.

In an entry's heading, the clubs mentioned are those where the player was enrolled at the time of England appearances.
The years indicate the span when caps were won (e.g. 1980-82 means season 1979/80 - 1981/82).
The final figure denotes the number of England appearances.

ABBREVIATIONS.

Apps	Appearances
cs	close season
Div.	Division
FA	The Football Association
FL	The Football League
q.v. (quod vide)	denoting a cross reference
sub	substitute
WW1	The First World War (1914-18)
WW2	The Second World War (1939-45)

POSITIONS.

Precise labelling using the classical 11-position goalkeeper to outside-left wording has been used where appropriate. Different concepts have necessitated broader terms (midfielder, defender, strike forward) being used for recent players. Similarly for the early years before the 11 positions were precisly named (and a 2-half-back system obtained) 'half-back' and 'forward' are used.

NOMENCLATURE.

Clubs are given the titles used at the time when the transfer or other event took place (e.g. Small Heath/Birmingham/ Birmingham City covers a single club's England players). Bradford refers to the defunct Bradford Park Avenue FC and Bradford City is accorded its full title throughout.

TRANSFER FEES.

Many of the fees quoted here are known to be authentic. The remainder have been taken from press reports and may be taken to be reasonably near the mark.

OTHER HONOURS recorded are for Under-21 etc international and inter-league appearances, and club honours (i.e. appearances in national and European cup finals, and qualifications for divisional championship medals). For the sake of continuity sponsors' names have been ignored (e.g. the League/Milk/Littlewood's Cup is referred to as the League or FL Cup throughout).

ABBOTT, Walter
(Everton, 1902, 1 cap)
Born Birmingham, 7th December 1877.
Died 1 February 1941.
1903: 5ft. $9^1/_2$ins.; 12st. 9lbs.

Career: Rosewood Victoria; Small Heath 1896; Everton June 1899; Burnley cs 1908; Birmingham again (the club had previously been known as Small Heath) cs 1910, retiring through injury in the ensuing season. Other honours: Football League (4 apps). (Everton) FA Cup winner 1906; finalist 1907.

Left-half/inside-left but, oddly, played centre-half in his sole international. Came to notice as a Small Heath forward, a tremendously hard worker more than usually powerful because of his fine physique. Everton moved him to left-half, where his rocket shots were still much in evidence and where he would plough through 'when even his forwards were having difficulty.' Abbott later was employed in the Birmingham motor industry and his son, Walter junior, assisted Grimsby Town during season 1919/20.

A'COURT, Alan
(Liverpool, 1958-59, 5)
Born Rainhill, Lancs. 30 September 1934.
1958: 5ft. $8^1/_4$ins.; 10st. 7lbs.

Career: Liverpool County Schools; Prescot Celtic; Prescot Cables; Liverpool September 1952; Tranmere Rovers October 1964 (£4500); Norwich City as player/coach July 1966. Subsequent administrative and coaching appointments have included those of Chester assistant manager early in 1969, Crewe Alexandra assistant manager/coach to September 1969, Stoke City coach later in the 1969/70 season, Ndola United (Zambia) coach May-July 1972 and a further spell as Crewe Alexandra's assistant manager. Other honours: England Under-23 international (7 apps).

Football League (2 apps).
(Liverpool) FL Div. 2 champions 1962.

Outside-left of the direct, no nonsense variety, showing fine speed, particularly from a standing start – and considerable shooting power. Rarely missed a game during his decade as an Anfield first-teamer, averaging about 35 League games per season. A little oddly, Alan came from a family of Rugby League fans.

ADAMS, Tony Alexander
(Arsenal, 1987-88, 14)
Born Romford, Essex,10 October 1966.
1987: 6ft. 1in; 12st. 1lb.

Career: Junior football; Arsenal apprentice, turning professional January1984. Other honours: England Youth international. England Under-21 international (5 apps). (Arsenal) FL Cup winner1987, finalist 1988.

Central defender. A major discovery of the mid-1980s, wonderfully mature for his years, revealing a centre-half's needful virtues in abundance. Has the advantage, of course, in possessing a pivot's classic proportions. Tony made his League debut on November 5, 1983, from 1983-85 collecting a haul of 18 Youth caps. His arrival at senior level caused the expensive Tommy Caton's departure to Oxford United.

ADCOCK, Hugh
(Leicester City, 1929-30, 5)
Born Coalville, Leics. 10 April 1903. Died 16 October 1975.
1927: 5ft. $5^1/_2$ ins; 10st. 2lbs.

Career: Coalville schoolboy football; Coalville Town; Loughborough Corinthians April 1921; Leicester City March 1923; Bristol Rovers July 1935; Folkestone September 1936. After retirement managed Coalville Town and coached at Whitwick College.

Other honours: Football League (1 app). (Leicester C) FL Div. 2 champions 1925.

Outside-right with the high-class diminutive winger's traditional virtues of trickery, ball skills and speed. In addition Hughie brought, in a Leicester journalist's words, "... a rather audacious habit of butting in when the defence hardly expects him to be about." And he was highly consistent, his 119th consecutive appearance on February 21, 1929 breaking the club record. Became a licensee at Sileby, Leics. after leaving the playing side before returning to Coalville and working as a maintenance engineer. Cousin of Joe Bradford (Birmingham and England).

ALCOCK, Charles William
(Wanderers, 1875, 1)
Born Sunderland, 2 December 1842. Died 26 February 1907.

Career: Forest School; Harrow School Wanderers. It was away from the playing field, however, that he made a permanent place in football history. He served in the FA Committee 1866-69, was Hon. Secretary of the FA 1870-86, Hon Treasurer 1877, Secretary 1887-95 and a Vice-President 1896-1907. He was referee of the 1875 and 1879 FA Cup finals, and was one of the people who founded this world famous competition. Other honours: (Wanderers) FA Cup winner 1872.
Forward both hard-working and consistently accurate in shooting. He captained England in his international and Wanderers for several years. Alcock, a sports journalist by profession, compiled the first 'Football Annual' (1868) and edited the 'Cricket' newspaper 1882-1905. He had a close connection with the summer game having played for Essex and crack club sides, and serving as secretary of Surrey CCC 1872 to his death. Was also chairman of the Richmond Athletic Association and vice-president of the Mid-Surrey Golf Club.

ALDERSON, John Thomas
(Crystal Palace, 1923, 1)
Born Crook, Co Durham, 28 November 1891. Died 17 February 1972.
1922: 6ft.; 13st.

Career: Crook Town; Shildon Athletic (Middlesborough on amateur forms cs 1912); Newcastle United January 1913 (£30); Crystal Palace May 1919 (£50); Pontypridd cs 1924; Sheffield United May 1925; Exeter City May 1929; Torquay United cs 1930; Crook Town again March 1931. Other honour: (Palace) FL Div. 3 champions 1921.

Goalkeeper, big, weighty and splendidly consistent. Had only 1 League appearance to his name before the Great War but clocked up 354 during the 'Twenties. When with Palace had the amazing record of saving 11 out of 12 penalties, including 2 in a single match (at Valley Parade, Bradford). Became a farmer after leaving the game.

ALDRIDGE, Albert James
(West Bromwich Albion and Walsall Town Swifts, 1888-89, 2)
Born Walsall, 13 April 1864. Died May 1891.
Career: Walsall Swifts 1882; West Bromwich Albion March 1886; Walsall Town Swifts July 1888; Aston Villa April 1889. Other honours: (WBA) FA Cup winner 1888; finalist 1887.

Right or left-back without, it would seem, any particular preference for either - his pairs of appearances in internationals and FA Cup finals found him on both flanks. Alderidge, a determined defender who gave little away, was able only to sample one early FL campaign (1889/90) before his untimely demise.

ALLEN, Albert
(Aston Villa, 1888, 1)
Born Aston, Birmingham, April 1867. Died 13 October 1899.

Career: Birmingham junior football to Aston Villa during the 1880s; retired through ill-health 1891.

Inside left. Struck up a rewarding Villa partnership with the renowned Dennis Hodgetts before his enforced retirement. Allen was a slick scorer too. For example, he notched a hat-trick inhis international, never to pull on an England shirt again. (This, though, is by no means a unique occurrence). After leaving football worked in his native city until health finally gave way.

ALLEN, Anthony
(Stoke City, 1960, 3)
Born Stoke-on-Trent, 27 November 1939.
1960: 5ft. 9ins.; 11st. 12lbs.

Career: Potteries schools football; Stoke Boys' Brigade; Stoke City amateur, turning professional November 1956; Bury October 1970 (about £10,000) - November 1971; Hellenic FC (Cape Town) February 1972-73; Stafford Rangers October 1973. Other honours: England Youth international. England Under-23 international (7 apps). Football League (2 apps). (Stoke C) FL Div. 2 champions 1963. FL Cup finalist 1964.

Left-back. Played left-half during his later FL seasons. A stylist possessing an accurate kick and crisp, effective tackle. Capped before his 20th birthday, a happening which some critics felt premature and to have affected him adversely afterwards. Became a Stoke licencee after leaving the League scene.

ALLEN, Clive Darren
(Queen's Park Rangers and Tottenham Hotspur,1984-88, 5)
Born Stepney, London, 20 May 1961.
1985: 5ft. 10ins.; 12st. 3lbs.

Career: Played for the representative sides of Havering, Essex and London Schools; Queen's Park Rangers apprentice cs 1977, turning professional September 1978; Arsenal June 1980 (£1.25m.); Crystal Palace August 1980 (in exchange for K G Sansom, q.v.) Queen's Park Rangers again May 1981 (£275,000 and another player); Tottenham Hotspur August 1984 (£700,000); Bordeaux (France) cs 1988 (£1m.). Other honours: England schoolboy international. England Youth international. England Under-21 international (3 apps). (QPR) FA Cup finalist 1982. (Spurs) FA Cup finalist 1987.

Strike forward. Has always been among the goals; registering a hat-trick on his League debut, for example, and his 1986/87 scoring feats (49 goals in League, FA and FL Cup matches). This last brought him the 1987 'Player of the year' awards for both the Football Writers and PFA. Such prolificacy is the reward for adroit positioning and timing of runs. Member of a famous football family: son of Les (Spurs & Football League) and cousin of Paul (WHU & Spurs) and Martin (QPR).

ALLEN, Henry
(Wolverhampton Wanderers, 1888-90, 5)
Born Walsall, 19 January 1866. Died 23 February 1895.
1889: 5ft. 11ins.; 11st. 12lbs.
Career: Walsall Swifts; Wolverhampton Wanderers 1886 - cs 1894 (retired). Other honours: (Wolves) FA Cup winner 1893; finalist 1889.

Centre-half classically proportioned for the job (unlike the many 'pygmy pivots' of his day). Could be a touch rash but generally quite tireless and excelling in heading and distribution. Before his early death Allen worked briefly in Wolverhampton as a licencee and coal merchant.

ALLEN, James Phillips
(Portsmouth, 1934, 2)
Born Poole, 16 October 1909.
1934: 6ft. 1in.; 12st. 10lbs.
Career: Poole schoolboy football; Poole Central; Poole Town 1927; Portsmouth February 1930; Aston Villa June 1934 (£10,775, then a record for player other than a forward); retired during WW2. Colchester United manager July 1948 - April 1953. Other honours: Football League (2 apps). (Portsmouth) FA Cup finalist 1934. (Villa) FL Div. 2 champions 1938.
Centre-half, strong and commanding. Summed up in the 'Thirties as belonging to 'the modern defensive type.' In other words, a 'stopper' pivot. Jack's move to Villa at such a fee was the sensation of the 1934 close season. Worked as a Birmingham firm's welfare officer before taking the Colchester managership and, after leaving football in 1953, became a licencee at Southsea.

ALLEN, Ronald
(West Bromwich Albion, 1952-55, 5)
Born Fenton, Staffs. 15 January 1929.

1957: 5ft. 8ins.; 10st. 9lbs.

Career: Bucknall Boys Brigade; Wellington Scouts; Northwood Misson (Handly); Port Vale on amateur form March 1944, turning professional January 1946; West Bromwich Albion March 1950 (£15,000); Crystal Palace May 1961, being player/coach 1964-65. Wolverhampton Wanderers coach March 1965, acting manager January 1966 and manager July 1966-November 1968; Atletico Bilbao (Spain) February 1969-November 1971; Sporting Lisbon manager April 1972; Walsall manager July-December 1973; West Bromwich Albion consultant January 1977, manager June 1977-January 1978, then taking appointment as manager of the Saudi Arabia national team. Other honours: England 'B' international (2 apps). Football League (1 app). (WBA) FA Cup winner 1954.

Centre-forward well capable of taking the other four forward berths. An attractive performer with an effective shot in either foot, he netted 276 goals in 638 League games for his senior clubs. His school, Hanley High, was rugger-playing and Ronnie was in the XV.

ALSFORD, Walter John
(Tottenham Hotspur, 1935, 1)
Born Edmonton, London, 6 November 1911. Died 3 June 1968.
1935: 5ft. 10½ins.; 11st. 11lbs.
Career: Tottenham Schools; London Schools; Tottenham Hotspur on amateur forms May 1929 and then developing in turn with Cheshunt and Northfleet before becoming professional August 1930; Nottingham Forrest January 1937; retired through injury May 1938.

Left-half able to take the other flank and with experience at inside-left also. A brainy and stylish performer strong in distribution and defence. After his enforced retirement he worked as a licencee at Nottingham, Brighton and Bedford.

AMOS, (Revd.) Andrew
(Old Carthusians, 1885-86, 2)
Born Southwark London, 20 September 1863. Died 2 October 1931.

Career: Charterhouse School (XI 1882); Cambridge University (Blue 1884-5-6); Old Carthusians; Corinthians 1885-90; Hitchin Town. Also represented Hertfordshire.

Half-back. Could head a ball effectively – not exactly a common accomplishment in the 1880s - and fed his attack judiciously. His appearances total for the Corinthians (45) exceeded that of most of their 'Eighties players. Andrew Amos was ordained in 1887, ministered in south-east London from 1889 until becoming Rector of Rotherhithe 1922 to his death. He served as a councillor on the Bermondsey Borough Council, later being elected an alderman.

ANDERSON, Rupet Darnley
(Old Etonians,1879, 1)
Born Liverpool, 29 April 1859. Died 23 December 1944.

Career: Eton College (XI 1878); Cambridge University (but did not win a Blue); Old Etonians.

Goalkeeper in his sole international but actually a zealous and lively forward (how marvellously versatile they were in those far off days!). Missed the 1879 FA Cup final because of injury. Worked as an orange planter in Florida for some time, residing in Staffordshire and Surrey on his return to England. In WW1 was awarded the OBE for services to the Territorial Army and Air Force.

ANDERSON, Stanley
(Sunderland, 1962, 2)
Born Horden, Co Durham, 27 February 1933.
1962: 5ft. 9ins.; 11st. 12lbs.

Career: East Durham Schools; Horden Colliery Welfare; Sunderland on amateur forms June 1949, turning professional February 1951; Newcastle United November 1963 (£19,000); Middlesbrough as player/coach November 1965 (£11,500), retired and became team manager April 1966-January 1973; AEK (Athens) manager August 1973-April 1974; Queens Park Rangers coach June 1974 and then their caretaker manager September-October 1974; Doncaster Rovers manager February 1975; Bolton Wanderers assistant manager November 1978, manager February 1980-May 1981. Other honours: England Schoolboy international. England 'B' internatioinal (1 app). England Under-23 international (4 apps). (Newcastle) FL Div. 2

champions 1955.

Right-half. Clever and strong, dispensing one of the sternest tackles of his time. Among a select quartet to have turned out for the North-east's 'Big 3' and the only one to have skippered all of them. Held Sunderland's record for senior appearences (446) which was subsequently broken by Len Ashurst during season 1969/70. Worked as an apprentice plumber until he was 21.

ANDERSON, Vivian Alexander
(Nottingham Forrest, Arsenal and Manchester United, 1979-88, 30)
Born Nottingham, 29 August 1956.
1983: 5ft.11ins.; 10st. 4lbs.

Career: Nottingham Schools; Nottingham Forest apprentice, turning professional August 1974; Arsenal July 1984 (£275,000); Manchester United May 1987 (£250,000). Other Honours: England 'B' international. England Under-21 international (1 app). (Forest) European Cup winner 1979,1980. FL champions 1978. FL Cup winner 1978; finalist 1980.(Arsenal) FL Cup winner 1987.

Right-back with an unassailable niche in England's soccer annals: the country's first coloured internationalist. By 1978 was being written of as '...arguably the most complete full-back in the game. His incisive tackling, accurate distribution and tactical awareness alone mark him as a growing prospect. Add to this his speed on the break and explosive shooting. 'Benefited subsequently by putting on poundage to over the 11st mark.

ANGUS, John
(Burnley, 1961, 1)
Born Amble, Northhumberland, 2 September 1938.
1961: 6ft.; 12st.

Career: Amble Boys Club; Burnley amateur 1954, turning professional September 1955; retired through injury May 1972. Other honours: England Youth international. England Under-23 international (7 apps). Football League (1 app). (Burnley) FL champions 1960. FA Cup finalist 1962.

Right-back capable of taking the left flank, which he did on occasion towards the end of his career. A polished back who liked an attacking sortie at a time when such a thing was not universally practiced. Tendon trouble caused his retiral. Nephew of the late John Angus (Exeter City 1930-48).

ARMFIELD, James Christopher
(Blackpool, 1959-66, 43)
Born Denton, Manchester, 21 September 1935.
1962: 5ft. 10½ins.; 12st. 12lbs.

Career: Assisted two Blackpool Youth Clubs, St Peter's and Highfield before sining amateur forms for Blackpool FC 1951, turning professional September 1954 (player/coach from February 1971). Bolton Wanderers manager May 1971; Leeds United manager October 1974-July 1978. Other honours: England Under-23 international (9 apps). Football League (12 apps).

Right-back, England's first choice for the position for 7 years, fast and sure in the tackle. Among the first backs of modern times to often go down his flank on attack. Represented Lancashire Schools at rugger while attending Arnold Grammer School, Blackpool. Since leaving club managership has been a regular soccer broadcaster on BBC radio.

ARMITAGE, George Henry
(Charlton Athletic, 1926, 1). Born Stoke Newington, London, 17 January 1898. Died 28 August 1936.
1925: 5ft. 10½ins.; 11st. 9lbs.

Career: Hackney Schools 1912/13; St Saviour's FC (Chelsea); Wimbledon; Charlton Athletic March 1924 - March 1931; Leyton from January 1931. Other honours : England amateur international (5 apps). (Charlton) FL Div. 3 (South) champions 1929.

Centre-half. A crack amateur, poised and in command of his territory, his tackling and distribution first-rate. Held his own in the professional game for some years, making 165 League appearences for Charlton. Toured South Africa with the FA party of 1929, playing twice against the South African national team. Also played in representative sides of the Surrey and London FAs.

ARMSTRONG, David
(Middlesbrough and Southampton, 1980-84, 3)
Born Durham (city), 26 December 1954.
1982: 5ft. 8ins.; 11st. 3lbs.

Career: Schoolboy football to Middlesbrough as an apprentice July 1970, turning professional January 1972; Southampton

August 1981 (£600,000, a Southampton record); AFC Bournemouth July 1987. Other honours: England 'B' internatoinal. England Under 23-international (4 apps). (Middlesbro') FL Div. 2 champions 1974.

Left-sided midfield. Marvellously consistent, a fact borne out by his once having a prodigious (and record) run of 356 consecutive senior appearances. Scorer of some memorable goals, likes to be fully involved and versatile. The fact he has averaged around 35 League outings per season over a decade and a half, is a tribute to David's fitness as well as high consistency.

ARMSTRONG, Kenneth
(Chelsea, 1955, 1)
Born Bradford, 3 June 1924. Died 13 June 1984.
1955: 5ft. 8ins.; 11st.

Career: Bradford Rovers; Army football; Chelsea December 1946; emigrated to New Zealand May 1957 where he played for Eastern Union, Gisborne City and North Shore United (Auckland), and for New Zealand's national side. Was a chief coach to the New Zealand FA. Retired from playing when aged 47! Other honours: New Zealand international (13 apps). England 'B' international (3 apps). Football League (1 app). (Chelsea) FL champions 1955.

Right-half. Could make a reasonable show at centre and inside-forward in an emergency. Very constructive half, enthusiastic and tenacious to a degree. Ken's 362 League match total for Chelsea was a club record until surpassed by Bonetti in season 1969/70. His son, Ron, appeared for New Zealand on 27 occasions.

ARNOLD, John
(Fulham, 1933, 1)
Born Cowley, Oxon. 30 November 1907. Died 3 April 1984.
1935: 5ft. 7ins.; 11st.
Career: Oxford schoolboy and junior football; Oxford City; Southampton July 1928; Fulham February 1933; retired during WW2.

Outside-left. Stocky winger displaying qualities of mobility and assertiveness. Moved to Southampton in order to obtain a residential qualification to play for Hampshire CCC (he had hitherto played Minor Counties cricket for Oxfordshire). Assisted Hants 1929-50, retiring on health grounds. Stood as a first-class umpire for some years from 1961. A 'double international' as he played in 1 Test match for England (vs. New Zealand, 1931).

ARTHUR, W(illiam) J(ohn) Herbert
(Blackburn Rovers, 1885-87, 7)
Born Blackburn, 14 February 1863. Died 27 November 1930.

Career: Lower Bank Academy (Blackburn); King's Own FC (Blackburn); Blackburn Rovers 1880/81; Southport Central cs 1890. Other honours: (Blackburn R) FA Cup winner 1884, 1885, 1886.

Goalkeeper after joining the Rovers as a right-half, the switch taking place after the player volunteered to keep goal for the reserves. He proved to be quite brilliant, cool in action and clearing his lines with despatch. Reputedly an amateur throughout his career, it seems odd to read that Blackburn gave him a benefit! Outside the game was employed as a mill furnisher and a commercial traveller (whether the jobs were synonymous and/or concurrent is not clear).

ASHCROFT, James
(Woolwich Arsenal, 1906, 3)
Born Liverpool, 12 September 1878. Died 9 April 1943.
1906: 5ft. 10½ins.; 12st.

Career: Garston Copper Works (Liverpool); Gravesend United cs 1899; Woolwich Arsenal May 1900; Blackburn Rovers May 1908; Tranmere Rovers cs 1913. Other honours: Football League (2 apps).

Goalkeeper regarded as England's best in 1906 when selected against the three home countries and for one of his inter-league appearances. Of all-round efficiency – he was equally adept with high and low shots – Ashcroft's anticipation was most marked. Losing his Blackburn place through ill-health in 1911/12 cost him a League championship medal.

ASHMORE, George Samuel Austin
(West Bromwich Albion, 1926, 1)
Born Plymouth, 5 May 1898. Died 19 May 1973.
1927: 5ft. 11ins.; 11st. 1lb.

Career: South Devon Schools; Nineveh Wesley (Handsworth League); West Bromwich Albion November 1919; Chesterfield October 1931; retired cs 1933.

Goalkeeper. Separated the Pearsons, pere et fils, as chief guardian of the West Brom. last line, clocking up 268 senior outings in so doing. An agile and daring 'keeper, the quick moving George consistently showed alertness and anticipation. A Chesterfield regular in his two Saltergate seasons.

ASHTON, Claude Thesiger
(Corinthians, 1926, 1)
Born Calcutta, India, 19 February 1901. Killed on active service, 31 October 1942.
Career: Winchester College (XI 1918-20, captain 1920); Cambridge University (Blue 1921-22, was captain in 1923 but unable to play in the 'Varsity match); Corinthians from the 1920/21 season; Old Wykehamists; retired 1933. Other honours: England amateur international (12 apps).

Centre-forward for his full international but actually a considerable utility player. Appeared in most positions for the Corinthians and thought to be best at wing-half. Shone in dribbling, tackling and marksmanship, Ashton's only real weakness was headwork. A typical amateur all-rounder of the period, he won Blues for hockey and cricket too, playing 89 matches for Essex CCC 1921-38 (he had 3 brothers who played county cricket). On leaving soccer assisted the Beckenham hockey club and played in England trials. A chartered accountant by profession, he later worked on the Stock Exchange. Lost his life in an air crash while serving as a pilot in the wartime RAF.

ASHURST, William
(Notts County, 1923-25, 5)
Born Willington, Co Durham, 4 May 1894. Died 26 January 1947.
1925: 5ft. $9^1/_2$ins.; 12st 4lbs.

Career: Willington Schools; Durham City; Leeds City cs 1919; Lincoln City October 1919 (£500); Notts County June 1920 (£1000); West Bromwich Albion November 1926 (£3100); Newark Town August 1928; retired cs 1929. Other honours: Football League (1 app). (Notts Co) FL Div. 2 champions 1923.

Right-back. A shade ponderous sometimes yet valuable as the above fees – notable by 1920s standards – illustrate. Quite intrepid and expert in tackling and placing long, powerful clearances. Was a miner together with his father and three brothers, one of whom was Eli Ashurst (Birmingham, 1922-27). The family also ran a small farm.

ASTALL, Gordon
(Birmingham City, 1956, 2)
Born Horwich, Lancs. 22 September 1927.
1957: 5ft. 9ins.; 11st. 13lbs.

Career: Horwich Schools (trial for Bolton Wanderers); Royal Marines football (Plymouth); Plymouth Argyle amateur 1947, signing professional in November of that year after his demobilisation; Birmingham City October 1953 (about £14,000); Torquay United May 1961; retired cs 1963. Other honours: England 'B' international (1 app). Football League (1 app). (Plymouth) FL Div. 3 (South) champions 1952. (B'ham C) FL Div. 2 champions 1955. FA Cup finalist 1956.

Outside-right, sometimes outside-left. A winger in the orthodox mould: a powerful runner with centering ability and a strong shot. A sturdy build gave opponents additional difficulties in stopping his progress. Employed in the insurance industry after leaving football, for a time spending part of his leisure coaching a minor Devonshire side.

ASTLE, Jeffrey
(West Bromwich Albion, 1969-70, 5)
Born Eastwood, Notts. 13 May 1942.
1969: 5ft. 11½ins., 11st. 6lbs.

Career: West Notts Schools; Holy Trinity Youth Club, Kimberley; Notts County amateur 1958, then assisted John Player FC (Nottm) until turning professional October 1959; West Bromwich Albion September 1964 (£25,000); Dunstable Town July 1974; Weymouth 1975; Atherstone Town late in 1976 (Hillingdon Borough on loan February 1977); retired later in 1977. Other honours: Football League (2 apps). (WBA) FA Cup winner 1968. FL Cup winner 1966; finalist 1967, 1970.

Centre/inside-forward of the brainy type, noted for his fine heading ability from the outset. In 393 League outings (and 2 substitutions) for his two League clubs netted 169 goals. Was the First Division's top scorer in 1969/70, two years after being named the Midlands' 'Player of the Year'.

ASTON, John snr.
(Manchester United, 1949-51, 17)
Born Manchester, 3 September 1921.
1950: 5ft. 10½ins.; 12st. 7lbs.

Career: Clayton Methodists (Manchester); Mujacs FC, Manchester United's nursery side, signing amateur forms for United May 1939, turning professional August 1946; retired on health grounds June 1955. Was on the Old Trafford staff from 1956-72, his last appointment being that of chief scout which he held from August 1970 to December 1972. Other honours: England 'B' international (1 app). Football League (2 apps). (Man. Utd) FL champions 1952. FA Cup winner 1948.

Left-back is the position with which he is associated but a splendid versatility must be mentioned. Played inside-forward and wing-half before settling at full-back to form a famed partnership with Johnny Carey. A 1970s commentator said 'Aston's remarkable versatility stemmed from his natural two-footedness. He was able to play equally well at right-back and was occasionally used as an effective emergency centre-forward.' Father of John Aston jnr., also of Manchester United and an England Under-23 internationalist.

ATHERSMITH W(illiam) Charles
(Aston Villa, 1892-1900, 12)
Born Bloxwich, Staffs. 10 May 1872. Died 18 September 1910.
1895: 5ft. 8½ins.; 11st.

Career: Bloxwich Wanderers when only 12; Unity Gas Depot (Saltley); Aston Villa

February 1891; Small Heath September 1901-1905. Grimsby Town trainer June 1907-cs 1909. Other honours: Football League (9 apps). (Villa) FL champions 1894, 1896, 1897, 1899, 1900. FA Cup winner 1895, 1897; finalist 1892.

Outside-right. A mid-'Nineties writer wrote Athersmith had '... great pace, is particularly smart and middles well.' The pace came from track experience – he had run both as an amateur and professionally with some success, in an unusual variety of distances from 100 yds. to a mile. One of the best known right-wingers of his day, Charlie's name was bracketed with Billy Bassett's.

ATYEO, P(eter) John W(alter)
(Bristol City, 1956-57, 6)
Born Dilton Marsh nr. Westbury, Wilts. 7 February 1932.
1957: 6ft.; 12st. 4lbs.

Career: Wiltshire schools and junior football; Westbury United; Portsmouth as an amateur 1950; Bristol City as a professional June 1951; retired May 1966. Other honours: England Youth international. England 'B' international (3 apps). England Under-23 international (2 apps). Football League (2 apps). (Bristol C) FL Div. 3 (South) champions 1955.

Inside-right/centre-forward. Powerfully built and powerful in performance, a fine footballer whose quickness of eye brought an untold number of goals. John holds the Bristol City records for League goals (315) and appearances (597) and in all made 645 FL and Cup appearances for the club. A schoolmaster by vocation.

AUSTIN, Samuel William
(Manchester City, 1926, 1)
Born Arnold, Notts. 29 April 1900. Died 2 April 1979.
1925: 5ft. 8½ins.; 10st. 10lbs.

Career: Arnold United (Sheffield United on trial); Arnold St Mary's; Norwich City October 1920; Manchester City May 1924 (£2000); Chesterfield December 1931; Kidderminster Harriers (his last club) cs 1933. Other honours: (Man. City) FL Div. 2 champions 1928. FA Cup finalist 1926.

Outside-right showing a clean pair of heels to many a defender and middling the ball in excellent style. Could shoot too, netting 83 goals in an aggregate 358 League appearance record. Interestingly, his Arnold St Mary's partner, Bob Dennison, also served the Canaries from 1920 and followed Sam to Maine Road in 1925 via Brighton & Hove Albion.

BACH, Philip
(Sunderland, 1899, 1)
Born Ludlow, Salop, 1872. Died 30 December 1937.

Career: Middlesbrough junior football; Middlesbrough FC; Reading cs 1895; Sunderland June 1897; Middlesbrough again April 1899; Bristol City cs 1900-1904 when he was reinstated an amateur; he did not, however, play again. Middlesbrough FC Director February 1911 (chairman July 1911)-1925, and chairman again 1931-35. FA Councillor 1925-37, serving on the international selection committee from October 1929. Served on the FL Management Committee from June 1929. Was also President of the North Eastern League for a time.

Full-back. A highly competent defender maintaining a consistently sound performance. Became a distinguished football administrator at club level and for the country's two governing bodies, his playing experience a useful adjunct in international selection duties. In private life had proprietorial hotel interests, first at Cheltenham and, latterly, at Middlesbrough,.

BACHE, Joseph William
(Aston Villa, 1903-11, 7)
Born Stourbridge, 8 February 1880. Died 10 November 1960.
1913: 5ft. $9^1/_2$ins.; 11st. 10lbs.

Career: Bewdley Victoria; Stourbridge FC; Aston Villa December 1900 (£100); Mid-Rhondda June 1919; Grimsby Town as player/coach July 1920-1921. Subsequently a coach in Germany for 4 years including a spell with Mannheim FC from October 1924, before returning and later having a period as Aston Villa's coach from August 1927. Other honours: Football League (7 apps). (Villa) FL champions 1910. FA Cup winner 1905, 1913.

Inside-left possessed of all the tricks, a goal scorer and master of the angled pass that enabled colleagues to run on to the ball and shoot. His partnership with A E Hall (q.v.) was renowned. A boiler maker by trade, Joe's surname is pronounced 'Baishe'. He was also employed as a licensee.

BADDELEY, Thomas
(Wolverhampton Wanderers, 1903-04, 5)
Born Bycars nr. Burslem, Staffs. 2 November 1874. Died 24 September 1946.
1903: 5ft. 9ins.; 12st. 2lbs.

Career: Burslem Swifts; Burslem Port Vale 1892; Wolverhampton Wanderers 1897; Bradford May 1907; Stoke 1910 for a brief spell. Other honours: Football League (4 apps).

Goalkeeper with an agility second to none, which made for a capacity to deal with any type of shot, high or low, close or long range. In 1907 was one of the newly-formed Park Avenue club's first signings and they were a well established Second Division outfit by the time he left.

BAGSHAW, J(ohn) James
(Derby County, 1920, 1)
Born Derby 25 December 1885. Died 25 August 1966.
1919: 5ft. 9ins.; 11st. 10lbs.
Career: Fletcher's Athletic; Graham Street Primitives (Derby); Derby County October 1906; Notts County February 1920 (for whom he had played during 1918/19); Watford May 1921; Grantham late 1921; Ilkeston United cs 1922. Was a Nottingham Forest trainer during WW2 and also scouted for that club and Coventry City. Other honours: England 'Victory' international 1919 (1 app). (Derby Co) FL Div. 2 champions 1912, 1915.

Right-half, sometimes centre-half. Player of stamina and perception, placing his passes accurately, sound in tackling and quick moving. Subsequently employed by Raleigh Industries, the engineering firm.

BAILEY, Gary Richard
(Manchester United, 1985, 2)
Born Ipswich, 9 August 1958.
1985: 6ft. 1in.; 13st. 2lbs.
Career: Witts University (South Africa); Manchester United January 1978; retired through injury April 1987. Other honours: England 'B' international. England Under-

21 international (14 apps). (Man. Utd) FA Cup winner 1983, 1985; finalist 1979. FL Cup finalist 1983.

Goalkeeper. Ideally proportioned being lithely built (despite his weight). Was able to throw this weight around most rapidly and with fair abandon. Gary had his critics, who doubted his ranking as England's No.2 to Shilton, but no one could deny his bravery and commitment. His premature retiral was the result of a severe knee injury sustained while training with the England squad in February 1986. A physics graduate and son of Roy Bailey, Ipswich Town's goalkeeper in 3 championship sides.

BAILEY, Horace Peter
(Leicester Fosse, 1908, 5)
Born Derby, 3 July 1881. Died 1 August 1960.

Career: Assisted Derby County reserves 1899-1902 before joining Ripley Athletic, continuing to assist the Derby reserves on occasion; Leicester Imperial to 1905; Leicester Fosse cs 1906; Derby County April 1909; Birmingham February 1911-1913. Other honours: England amateur international (8 apps).

Goalkeeper. A prominent amateur of the years immediately prior to the Great War. Bailey was not big by goalkeeping standards yet dealt with all kinds of shots capably and sometimes brilliantly. Worked in the rating department of a railway company.

BAILEY, Michael Alfred
(Charlton Athletic, 1964-65, 2)
Born Wisbech, Cambs. 27 February 1942. 1965: 5ft. 8ins.; 11st 4lbs.

Career: Gorleston schoolboy football; Gorleston Juniors; Charlton Athletic ground staff June 1958, turning professional March 1959; Wolverhampton Wanderers February 1966 (£40,000); Minnesota Kicks, USA. January 1977 (about £15,000); Hereford United player/manager August 1978. Charlton Athletic team manager October 1979, manager March 1980; Brighton & Hove Albion manager June 1981-December 1982. Other honours: England Under-23 international (5 apps). Football League (3 apps). (Wolves) Inter-Cities Fairs Cup finalist 1972 (sub). FL Cup winner 1974.

Right-half. Natural captaincy material, his driving qualities of leadership to the fore at Wolverhampton. More than pulled his weight as a player too, sporting a biting tackle and he was quite tireless. Was the Midlands' 'Footballer of the Year' for 1966/67.

BAILEY, Norman Coles
(Old Westminsters and Clapham Rovers, 1878-87, 19)
Born Streatham, London, 23 July 1857. Died 13 January 1923.

Career: Assisted at various times Westminster School, Old Westminsters, Clapham Rovers, Wanderers, Swifts, Corinthians (1886-89), and in representative matches, Surrey and London. Served on the FA Committee 1882-84 and was a Vice-President 1887-90. Other honours: (Clapham R) FA Cup winner 1880; finalist 1879.

Half-back, one of the most illustrious in the early decades. 'A very safe half-back,' the 1881 Football Annual reported, 'with plenty of dash and judgment; has both strength and pace, and never misses his kick.' He was a solicitor by profession (admitted 1880).

BAILY, Edward Francis
(Tottenham Hotspur, 1950-53, 9)
Born Clapton, London, 6 August 1925. 1953: 5ft. 7ins.; 10st. 13lbs.

Career: Hackney Schools; Middlesex Schools; Tottenham Juniors when 14; Finchley 1941; Army football (he represented the BAOR); Tottenham Hotspur as a professional during season 1945/46; Port Vale January 1956 (£8000); Nottingham Forest October 1956 (£4500); Leyton Orient December 1958; retired and became Leyton Orient coach cs 1961; Tottenham Hotspur assistant manager October 1963-September 1974; Chelsea scout October 1974 and also at this time a PTI at an Enfield school; West Ham United chief scout 1976. Other honours: England 'B' international (3 apps). Football League (6 apps). (Spurs) FL champions 1951. FL Div. 2 champions 1950.

Inside-left whose play seemed to contain a tincture of Cockney pertness that justified the commentators' tag of 'Cheeky Chappie.' He was a shrewd manipulator able to hold the ball or rapidly dribble upfield. 'Upfield' was the operative word for Eddie was of progressive, not crossfield, intention.

BAIN, John
(Oxford University, 1877, 1)
Born Bothwell, Lanarks. 15 July 1854. Died 7 August 1929.

Career: Sherborne School; Winchester College; Oxford University (Blue 1876). Other honour: (Oxford University) FA Cup finalist 1877.

Forward in his international but obviously a player of some versatility as he was at right-back for the 1877 Cup final. Possessed pace, liked to be fully involved and backed-up well. A barrister (called to the Bar 1880), he was Master of Marlborough College 1879-83 and from 1886 to his retirement in 1913.

BAKER, Alfred
(Arsenal, 1928, 1)
Born Ilkeston, 27 April 1898. Died 1 April 1955.
1927: 5ft. 8ins.; 12st. 6lbs.

Career: Ilkeston schoolboy football; Cossall St Catherine's; Long Eaton; Eastwood Rangers (guest player for Chesterfield, Crystal Palace and Huddersfield Town during WW1); RNVR football before joining Arsenal May 1919; retired May 1931. Other honours: Football League (2 apps). (Arsenal) FA Cup winner 1930; finalist 1927.

Right-back/right-half, the latter considered his 'main' position. Was actually a considerable utility man and was chosen for every outfield berth – and played goal in an emergency – while at Highbury. He had started as an outside-left and was at centre-forward for his Royal Navy side. An energetic, robust player with a fearless tackle and dangerous long range shot. Alf's brothers, Jim and Aaron, both assisted Leeds United between the wars. A one-time miner, he worked as groundsman for a London sports club after leaving the game.

BAKER, B(enjamin) Howard
(Everton and Chelsea, 1921-26, 2)
Born Aigburth, Liverpool, 13 February 1892. Died 10 September 1987.
1922: 6ft. 2ins.; 13st.

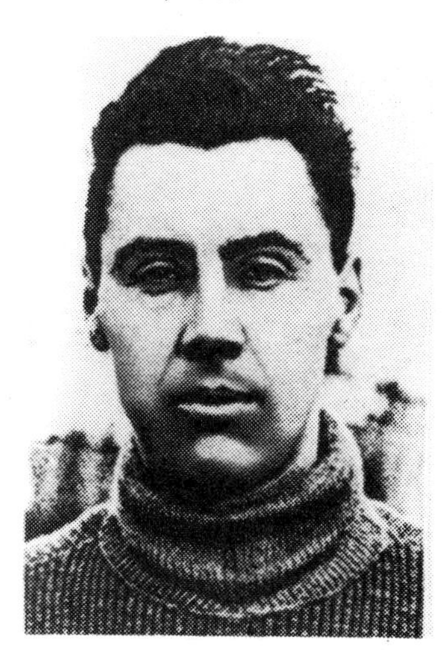

Career: Famous amateur perhaps best remembered assisting the Corinthians from season 1920/21 for more than a decade. But he was also on the books of several FL clubs: Blackburn Rovers (pre-WW1), Preston North End (December 1919), Liverpool (1920), Everton (1920/21 and 1926/27), Chelsea (October 1921-1926) and Oldham Athletic (1928/29), making 13 League appearances for Everton, 92 for Chelsea and 1 for Oldham. Early in his career he played for Marlborough Old Boys (Liverpool), Liverpool Balmoral and Northern Nomads. Other honours: England amateur international (10 apps). Football League (1 app).

Goalkeeper who earlier had been at centre-half and, indeed, represented Lancashire and had an amateur international trial in that position. An unorthodox 'keeper capable of remarkable acrobatics, owner of a prodigious kick and, in general, a colourful character. Baker was also a renowned athlete, representing Gt. Britain at the

Olympic Games of 1911 and 1920 in the high jump event – his British record (6ft. 5ins.) stood for 26 years. He also played cricket for Liverpool CC, was international standard at water polo and excelled at the hurdles and throwing the discus. An all-rounder to rank with C B Fry and Max Woosnam!

BAKER, Joseph Henry
(Hibernian and Arsenal, 1960-66, 8)
Born Liverpool, 17 July 1940
1963: 5ft. 8ins.; 11st. 7lbs.

Career: Scottish schools football; Chelsea ground staff when 15; Edinburgh Thistle; Coltness United; Armadale Thistle; Hibernian June 1956; AC Torino (Italy) May 1961 (£73,000); Arsenal July 1962 (£67,500); Nottingham Forest February 1966 (£60,000); Sunderland June 1969 (£30,000); Hibernian again January 1971 (£12,000); Raith Rovers June 1972-October 1974. Commenced spell as Fauldhouse United's manager/coach cs 1980. Other honours: Scottish schoolboy international England Under-23 international (6 apps). (Hibs) Scottish Cup finalist 1958.

Centre-forward. Scottish in everything but birth-place: born of Scottish parents, raised in Motherwell (going there as a baby), establishing his reputation and playing much of his football in Scotland. The first to play for England while with a club outside its boundaries. Not surprisingly played a game of typical Scottish craft with persistence. Had a distinctive short-stepped gait. Since leaving football, has lived in the Wishaw area and been employed as a licensee and in the building industry.

BALL, Alan James
(Blackpool, Everton and Arsenal, 1965-75, 72)
Born Farnworth, Lancs. 12 May 1945.
1970: 5ft. 7ins.; 10st.

Career: Farnworth Grammar School; Bolton Wanderers amateur 1960; Blackpool amateur September 1961, turning professional May 1962; Everton August 1966 (£110,000, a then British record); Arsenal December 1971 (£220,000, another record); Southampton December 1976 (£60,000) (assisted Philadelphia Fury and Vancouver Whitecaps during close seasons); Blackpool again as player/manager February 1980-March 1981; Southampton again March 1981-October 1982 when he went to play in Hong Kong; Bristol Rovers January 1983. Portsmouth youth coach 1983/84, manager May 1984-July 1988 after which he served as first team coach until January 1989. Other honours: England Under-23 international (8 apps). Football League (6 apps). (Everton) FL champions 1970. FA Cup finalist 1968. (Arsenal) FA Cup finalist 1972. (Soton) FL Cup finalist 1979.

Forward. The ultimate competitor, a dynamic little red head, ever resolute and never giving up. This dynamism combined with a strong character inevitably brought trouble at times, but the list of honours speaks volumes for his worth. A vital member of the 1966 World Cup side, Alan's most memorable period at club level was as part of the celebrated Everton triangle that also included Harvey and Kendall. Son of Alan Ball snr., who was also a well known player and manager.

BALL, John
(Bury, 1928, 1)
Born Hazel Grove, Stockport, 29 September 1900.
1927: 5ft. 9ins.; 12st. 7lbs.

Career: Silverwood Colliery; Sheffield United cs 1919; Bristol Rovers May 1921; Wath Athletic cs 1922; Bury May 1923 (£350); West Ham United May 1929; Coventry City May 1930; Stourbridge September 1931.

Inside-left. Thrustful and a potent link between Norman Bullock (q.v.) and Wally Amos in Bury's splendid promotion line-up of 1923/24. (A line-up, incidentally, that produced three internationalists and an inter-league 'cap'). John was no mean scorer on his own account either, netting 109 goals in his aggregate 268 League match total. This included 92 for the Shakers during his 6 years at Gigg Lane.

BALMER, William
(Everton, 1905, 1)
Born Liverpool, 1877.
1903: 5ft. 8½ins.; 11st. 9lbs.

Career: Aintree Church; South Shore; Everton 1896; Croydon Common cs 1908. Had a spell as Huddersfield Town's coach from cs 1921. Other honours: Football League (1 app). (Everton) FA Cup winner 1906; finalist 1907.

Right-back, compactly built and owner of a lusty clearance kick and rock-hard tackle. For some time partnered his younger brother, Robert, who also won an inter-league medal. Uncle of Jack Balmer (Liverpool 1935-52).

BAMBER, John
(Liverpool, 1921, 1)
Born Peasley Cross nr. St Helens, 11 April 1895. Died 1971.
1925: 5ft. 10ins.: 12st.

Career: St Helens Recreation; Heywood; Liverpool December 1915; Leicester City February 1924; Tranmere Rovers July 1927; Prescot Cables August 1930. Other honours: Football League (2 apps). (Leicester C) FL Div. 2 champions 1925.

Half-back of pronounced versatility – on the right flank with Liverpool, left at Leicester and completed his FL stint as Tranmere's pivot. Conscientious, strong in tackling and passing, it was said in 1921 he 'can now be numbered among the first three right-halves in England.' Jack, however, lost his place through injury (and for the record 'missed out' on a couple of League championship medals). In the FA touring party of South Africa, 1920, twice appearing against the national team.

BAMBRIDGE, Arthur Leopold
(Swifts, 1881-84, 3)
Born Windsor, 16 June 1861. Died 27 November, 1923.

Career: St Mark's School, Windsor (XI 1877); Upton Park (in 1879); Swifts; Clapham Rovers; Corinthians. He also represented Berkshire. Retired through injury 1884.

Back/half-back. 'Useful,' said the 1881 Football Annual, 'plays with judgment and is difficult to pass.' One of five brothers, all distinguished soccer players, the quintet including the celebrated 'Charlie Bam' and E H Bambridge below. After injury enforced A L's retirement, he journeyed abroad to study art.

BAMBRIDGE, E(dward) Charles
(Swifts, 1879-87, 18)
Born Windsor, 30 July 1858. Died 8 November 1935.

Career: Learned the game at St Mark's School, Windsor, subsequently assisting

Malvern College, Windsor Home Park, Streatham, Upton Park, Clapham Rovers, Swifts and Corinthians (1886-89) and, in representative matches for Surrey, Berkshire and London. Served on the FA Committee 1883-86 and was hon. secretary of the Corinthians 1923-32.

Outside-left, the finest of his day, who could turn in an above average game at half-back. A commentator in 1895 wrote after 'Charlie Bam' (as he was known) had retired: 'Very fast, he had splendid command over the ball, middled with great accuracy and judgment and was, to crown it all, a remarkable good shot at goal.' Brother of the Bambridges above and below.

BAMBRIDGE, Ernest Henry
(Swifts, 1876, 1)
Born Windsor, 16 May 1848. Died 16 October 1917.

Career: Windsor Home Park; Swifts; East Sheen; Corinthians. He also represented Berkshire. Served on the FA Committee 1876-82 and was a member of Corinthians' original committee in 1882.

Forward. Two years before his England appearance was noted as 'useful and hard-working.' He thrived on hard work and, once the ball was in tow, he was a tough nut to dispossess. Had four brothers who were all fine players, two of them (see above) together with E H, uniquely forming an English internationalist trio. He worked on the Stock Exchange.

BANKS, Gordon
(Leicester City and Stoke City, 1963-72, 73)
Born Sheffield, 30 December 1937.
1968: 6ft. 1in.; 13st. 6lbs.

Career: Sheffield Schools; Millspout Steel Works (Sheffield); Chesterfield September 1955; Leicester City May 1959 (£6000); Stoke City April 1967 (£52,000); retired through eye injury sustained in a road accident August 1973, becoming a club coach; Port Vale reserve team coach December 1978-December 1979; Telford United general manager January-September 1980; had spell as Stoke City specialist coach (for goalkeepers) from February 1982. Other honours: England Under-23 international (2 apps). Football League (6 apps). (Leicester) FA Cup finalist 1961, 1963. FL Cup winner 1964; finalist 1965. (Stoke C) FL Cup winner 1972.

Goalkeeper rightly placed among the very best England has produced – some critics aver the best. Superb in anticipation, reflex action and positional play, and a remarkably clean handler. The only question mark (and that arguable) was in his kicking. Awarded the OBE 1970. 'Player of the Year' 1972. Outside the game a partner in a Stoke-on-Trent plant hire firm.

BANKS, Herbert Ernest
(Millwall Athletic, 1901, 1)
Born Coventry, 1874. died 1947
1901: 5ft. 8ins.; 12st. 2lbs.

Career: Leamington junior football; Army football; Everton early in 1897; Third Lanark cs 1897; Millwall Athletic March 1899; Aston Villa April 1901; Bristol City November 1901; Watford cs 1903.

Inside-left. Not a tall man but carrying plenty of weight that nicely complemented a bustling action and hard shooting. Banks, enlisted with the Seaforth Highlanders, had tasted competitive soccer in India, his regimental team twice winning the Simla Regimental Cup out there. After leaving football he worked for a Birmingham engineering firm.

BANKS, Thomas
(Bolton Wanderers, 1958-59, 6)
Born Farnworth, Lancs. 10 November 1929.
1958: 5ft. 7½ins.; 12st.

Career: Farnworth Boys Club; Prestwich's XI; Bolton Wanderers October 1947; Altrincham cs 1961; Bangor City early in 1963. Other honours: Football League (1 app). (Bolton W) FA Cup winner 1958. (Bangor C) Welsh Cup finalist 1964.

Left-back. A natural footballer spending the whole of his first-class career at Burnden Park. Short yet weighty, fast to the tackle and an extremely solid back in general. Tommy, while with Farnworth BC, had represented both the England and Great Britain Boys Clubs, and did so for The Army while on his national service.

BANNISTER, William
(Burnley and Bolton Wanderers, 1901-02, 2)
Born Burnley, 1879. Died 26 March 1942.
1901: 5ft. 11ins.; 12st.

Career: Earley FC; Burnley 1899; Bolton Wanderers November 1901 (£75); Woolwich Arsenal January 1903; Leicester Fosse May 1904; Burnley again cs 1910; retired cs 1911. Other honours: Football League (2 apps).

Centre-half with the pivots' classical physique and especially good in defence. Not one of your eye-catching kind - something of a resolute plodder, in fact – yet a worthy team man and captain. Employed as a licensee after leaving football, first at Burnley and then Leicester.

BARCLAY, Robert
(Sheffield United, 1932-36, 3)
Born Scotswood, Newcastle-on-Tyne, 27 October 1906. Died 13 July 1969.
1936: 5ft. 7½ins.; 10st. 7lbs.

Career: Scotswood United Church; Bell's Close Juniors; Allendale; Scotswood FC; Derby County February 1927; Sheffield United June 1931; Huddersfield Town March 1937; retired during WW2. Other honours: (Sheffield U) FA Cup finalist 1936. (Huddersfield T) FA Cup finalist 1938.

Inside-forward. 'A great constructive player,' the critic rightly said, Bobby's deft footwork and thoughtful play continually emphasising the verdict. He was somewhat in the Alex James mould. Like that great Scot, he could shoot alright but some thought he should have done so more often. Even so he netted 106 goals in 369 League outings before war came.

BARHAM, Mark Francis
(Norwich City, 1983, 2)
Born Folkestone, 12 July 1962.
1983: 5ft. 7ins.; 11st.
Career: Junior football; Norwich City apprentice June 1978, turning professional April 1980; Huddersfield Town July 1987 (£25,000); Middlesbrough October 1988. Other honours: England Youth international. (Norwich) FL Div. 2 champions 1986. FL Cup winner 1985.

Wing forward whose play is informed by speed and clever dribbling that can delude the opposition. Suffered a severe knee injury in 1985/86. Son of a crack amateur golfer with another string to his sporting bow – he played roller-hockey for England.

BARKAS, Samuel
(Manchester City, 1936-38, 5)
Born Wardley Colliery, Northumberland, 29 December 1909.
1938: 5ft. 9ins.; 13st. 7lbs.

Career: Middle Dock FC (Tyneside junior club); Bradford City during the 1927/28 season; Manchester City April 1934 (£5000); retired May 1947 and appointed Workington manager. Wigan Athletic manager April -September 1957, subsequently scouting for Manchester City and Leeds United. Had spell on Bradford City's staff from 1965 running the club's pools scheme. Other honours: Football League (3 apps). (Bradford C) FL Div. 3 (North) champions 1929. (Man. City) FL champions 1937. FL Div. 2 champions 1947.

Left-back chiefly though actually a fine utility man – for example he was left-half in Bradford City's 1929 championship line-up and at inside-right for the 1936 England/Belgium match. One of four brothers who played League soccer, Sam was neatly summed-up as 'clever and stylish' with a liking for 'an occasional foray upfield.' He had worked first as a miner and then in farming. Cousin of Billy Felton (q.v.).

BARKER, John William
(Derby County, 1935-37, 11)
Born Denaby, nr. Mexborough, Yorks. 27 February 1907. Died 20 January 1982.
1935: 5ft. $10^1/_2$ins.; 12st. 7lbs.

Career: Denaby Rovers (Rawmarsh League); Denaby United for 1 season; Derby County April 1928 (£200); retired during WW2; Bradford City manager May 1946; Dundalk manager January 1947; Oldham Athletic trainer/coach November 1948-January 1949; Derby County manager November 1953-May 1955. Other honours: Football League (3 apps).
Centre-half. An attack-minded practitioner in an era of 'stopper' pivots who, nonetheless, could defend excellently as well. Few of his contemporaries had Jack's resource. He was a tough ex-miner who had experienced the terror of a pit roof subsidence.

BARKER, Richard Raine
(Casuals, 1895, 1)
Born Kensington, London, 29 May 1869. Died 1 October 1940.

Career: Repton School (XI 1887); Casuals; Corinthians 1894-1900. Other honour: (Casuals) FA Amateur Cup finalist 1894.

Wing-half capable on both right and left flanks. His placing of passes was first class, as was his kicking. However, Barker lacked pace and this defect probably limited the acquisition of honours ('much too slow for an international,' a contemporary critic bluntly remarked). An engineer by profession, he was at one time manager of the Bromley Electric Light Co.

BARKER, Robert
(Herts Rangers, 1873, 1)
Born Wouldham, Kent, 19 June 1847. Died 11 November 1915.

Career: Marlborough College (where he played rugger); Herts Rangers. Also represented Middlesex and Kent.
Utility player. 'An excellent forward sticking well to his work. As a back fairly astonished his friends at Sheffield,' reported the 1874 Annual. (The same source also credits him with an association with Westminster School and the then dominant Wanderers FC). Barker was not a fast player but his vigour and enthusiasm atoned for this, at least in part. A civil engineer by profession (MICE 1889), he was at different times Chief Assistant Engineer to the London, Chatham & Dover Railway and the South Eastern Railway.

BARLOW, Raymond John
(West Bromwich Albion, 1955, 1)

Born Swindon, 17 August 1926.
1957: 6ft.; 13st. 6lbs.

Career: Swindon schoolboy football; Garrard's FC (Swindon); West Bromwich Albion on amateur forms June 1944, turning professional the following November; Birmingham City August 1960 (originally on a month's trial); retired March 1961 but joined Stourbridge as a permit player July 1961, finally retiring cs 1962. Other honours: England 'B' international (2 apps). Football League (4 apps). (WBA) FA Cup winner 1954.

Left-half after initial success at inside-left. A hefty player who had pace, poise and elegance as well as the stamina usually associated with bodily size. Ray's class would have brought a large haul of caps in another era that did not contain the likes of Dickinson and Duncan Edwards. He later became a Stourbridge newsagent.

BARNES, John Charles Bryan
(Watford and Liverpool, 1983-88, 42)
Born Kingston, Jamaica, 7 November 1963.
1985: 5ft. 11ins.; 12st.

Career: Sudbury Court; Watford July 1981; Liverpool June 1987 (£900,000). Other honours: England Under-21 international (2 apps). (Watford) FA Cup finalist 1984. (Liverpool) FL champions 1988; FA Cup finalist 1988.

Forward. Prodigiously gifted attacker. As was well said '. . . has everything – pace, skill, strength and intelligence on the ball.' Could easily go down as one of the greatest footballers of the late twentieth century. John's father played centre-half for Jamaica. 'Player of the Year 1988' for both the PFA and the Football Writers' Association.

BARNES, Peter Simon
(Manchester City, West Bromwich Albion and Leeds United, 1978-82, 22)
Born Manchester, 10 June 1957
1980: 5ft. 10ins.; 11st.

Career: Manchester schools football; Manchester City as an associate schoolboy, apprentice July 1972, turning professional July 1974; West Bromwich Albion July 1979 (£748,000, an Albion record); Leeds United August 1981 (£930,000, again an Albion record); Real Betis (Spain) cs 1982 (£115,000); Leeds United again August 1983 (£930,000); Coventry City October 1984 (£65,000); Manchester United July 1985 (£50,000); Manchester City again January 1987 (£30,000); Bolton Wanderers (on loan) October 1987, later having spells on loan with Port Vale, Wimbledon and Hull City; joined Sunderland February 1989; Stockport County March 1989. Other honours: England Youth international. England 'B' international. England Under-21 international (9 apps).

Forward who would earlier have been precisely designated as an outside-left. A precocious talent, one commentator remarked about Peter's '. . . peculiar hurtling style, like supercharged skipping' and that he 'runs in more or less straight lines with little distracting frills. After a nominal feint simply runs through space opponent has left.' Since around 1980 his career has been uneven. Son of Ken Barnes (Manchester City 1950-61). The PFA's 'Young Player of the Year' 1975.

BARNET, Horace Hutton
(Royal Engineers, 1882, 1)
Born Kensington, London, 1855. Died 29 March 1941.

Career: Royal Engineers; was also a member of the Corinthians. Other honour: (Royal Engineers) FA Cup finalist 1878.

Forward who revealed many clever touches and lots of pace but was erratic when passing and shooting. Served with the Royal Engineers from 1875, retiring holding the rank of colonel during the 1900s. Was recalled for service in the 1914/18 War, and later lived in London.

BARRASS, Malcolm Williamson
(Bolton Wanderers, 1952-53, 3)
Born Blackpool, 13 December 1924.
1951: 5ft. $10^3/_4$ins.; 12st. 7lbs.

Career: Ford Motors (Manchester); Bolton Wanderers early in 1944; Sheffield United September 1956 (£5000); Wigan Athletic as player/manager July 1958-January 1959; Nuneaton Borough 1959/60; Pwllheli early in 1961; Hyde United trainer cs 1962. Other honours: Football League (2 apps). (Bolton W) FA Cup finalist 1953.

Centre-half after starting as an inside-left and then moving back to left-half. The typi-

cal dominating pivot, excellent in his mobility and heading skill. Son of Matt Barrass who won Second Division championship medals with both Sheffield Wednesday (1925/26) and Manchester City (1927/28).

BARRETT, Albert Frank
(Fulham, 1930, 1)
Born West Ham, 11 November 1903.
1927: 5ft. 10ins.; 11st. 5lbs.

Career: West Ham Schools; Fairbairn House Lads Club; Leytonstone 1921 (West Ham United amateur cs 1923, Southampton amateur 1924/25 making 1 League app); Fulham June 1925 as a professional; retired cs 1937. Other honours: England schoolboy international (1 app). England amateur international (4 apps). (Fulham) FL Div. 3 (South) champions 1932.

Left-half, later left-back. Nicknamed Snowball by some because of his very blond, almost white, thatch. Immensely stylish, absolutely unruffled and judicious in every action. While with Leytonstone assisted the famous amateur touring side, Middlesex Wanderers. Continued to work as an accountant after turning professional. In the years following WW2 was secretary of a Romford wholesale firm. As far as is known, not related to J W Barrett below.

BARRETT, James William ('Tiny')
(West Ham United, 1929, 1)
Born Stratford, London, 19 January 1907. Died 25 November 1970.
1929: 5ft. 11½ins.; 14st. 2lbs.

Career: West Ham Schools; Fairbairn House Lads Club; West Ham United as a professional cs 1923 when only 16; retired 1945 and had a spell in charge of West Ham's 'A' team. Other honours: England schoolboy international (2 apps).

Centre-half with extensive experience elsewhere. He appeared in every position for the Hammers' senior and reserve sides. Barrett had been a schoolboy star, scoring over 200 goals for his school team in a couple of seasons and 98 for the 1920/21 West Ham Schools side. He was able to quickly turn defence into attack and vice versa, and a prodigious bulk presented a daunting prospect to opponents. Holds the unwelcome record of the shortest recorded international career: he went off injured after only 4 minutes of his sole England match. Father of Jim Barrett jnr. (West Ham United, 1949-54). A schoolboy boxing champion.

BARRY, Leonard James
(Leicester City, 1928-29, 5)
Born Sneinton, Nottingham, 27 October 1901. Died 17 April 1970.
1927: 5ft. 8ins.; 11st.

Career: Nottingham schoolboy football; RAF football (Cranwell); Notts County on amateur forms 1921, turning professional 1923; Leicester City September 1927 (£3300); Nottingham Forest cs 1933; retired cs 1934. Other honour: England amateur international (1 app).

Outside-left in the accepted mould of his time – possessed of pace, control, centering ability and the wit to cut in and shoot. Was so enamoured with soccer as a boy he returned to his original school from a rugger-playing establishment purely on this account. Took the pro ticket soon after winning his amateur cap. After leaving the game worked on transport at RAF Chilwell and at two civilian airfields.

BARSON, Frank
(Aston Villa, 1920, 1)
Born Sheffield, 10 April 1891. Died 13 September 1968.
1921: 5ft. 11½ins.; 12st.
Career: Sheffield schoolboy football; Albion FC (Sheffield); Cammell Laird's FC (Sheffield); Barnsley 1911; Aston Villa October 1919 (£2850); Manchester United

May 1922 (£5000); Watford May 1928; Hartlepools United May 1929; Wigan Borough July 1930; Rhyl Athletic player/manager 1930/31; Stourbridge manager July 1935; Aston Villa coach October 1935 to the War; Swansea Town trainer/coach 1942-cs 1954; Lye Town trainer September 1954. Other honour: (Villa) FA Cup winner 1920.

Centre-half. A dominating, physical pivot, hard as nails and great in headwork. Often in trouble with authority, receiving suspensions of several months' duration. All the same Barson was an excellent tactician and skilled in all aspects of half-back play. By occupation, a blacksmith.

BARTON, John
(Blackburn Rovers, 1890, 1)
Born Blackburn, 5 October 1866. Died 22 April 1910.
1891: 5ft. 7ins.; 9st. 12lbs.

Career: Witton FC (Blackburn); Blackburn West End; Blackburn Rovers 1887; retired through injury late 1891. Later had spell as Preston North End's trainer. Other honours: (Blackburn R) FA Cup winner 1890, 1891.

Right-half, one of many locals in the Rovers' line-ups of the period. Said to have modelled his style on that of his great colleague, J H Forrest (he could have had no better example to follow). Barton thus emerged as a neat performer, fluent and accurate in distribution. After leaving the playing arena was a licensee in his native Blackburn.

BARTON, Percival Harry
(Birmingham, 1921 -25, 7)
Born Edmonton, London, 19 August 1895. Died October 1961.
1921: 5ft. 8ins.; 11st.

Career: North London schoolboy football; Tottenham Thursday; Sultan FC; Birmingham 1913 (guest player for Tottenham Hotspur during WW1); Stourbridge 1929. Other honour: (Birmingham) FL Div. 2 champions 1921.

Left-half, latterly left-back. A dour spoiler good at plying his attack with choice passes. A contemporary critic wrote that Percy was '... not blessed with too many inches, he yet managed to produce a good turn of speed. Recognised as one of the most persistent tacklers in the game.' His Edmonton school (Montague Road) later produced Jimmy Dimmock, the Spurs and England winger.

BASSETT, William Isiah
(West Bromwich Albion, 1888-96, 16)
Born West Bromwich, 27 January 1869. Died 8 April 1937.
1895: 5ft. $5^1/_2$ins.; 10st. 6lbs.

Career: West Bromwich schoolboy football; Oak Villa; Old Church FC; West Bromwich Strollers; West Bromwich Albion August 1886; retired April 1899. Appointed a West Bromwich Albion director in March 1905, he was chairman from September 1908 to his death. Member of the FA Council 1930-37 and of the FL Management Committee for the same period. Other honours: Football League (3 apps). (WBA) FA Cup winner 1888, 1892; finalist 1895.

Outside-right. A major name in the pre-1900 era when without a superior in his position. Orthodox as regards the time's tactics, largely keeping to the touch-line, darting runs ending with pinpoint centres. Nonetheless, his shooting after an occasional cut-in was deadly. A leading administrator subsequently. Billy was also an excellent cricketer, assisting the well known West Bromwich Dartmouth CC for 20 years.

BASTARD, Segal Richard
(Upton Park, 1880, 1)
Born Bow, London, 25 January 1854. Died 20 March 1921.

Career: Upton Park; Corinthians; also represented Essex. Served on the FA Committee 1877-82 and was referee of the 1878 FA Cup final.

Wing forward considered 'capital' by an Alcock's Annual writer, who no doubt relished the player's strength and turn of speed. Bastard assisted Essex CCC 1881-85, so was obviously one of those proliferating Victorian sports all rounders. And he must have been a man of substance, being a racehorse owner. Collapsed and died of a heart attack at Epsom station. He had been a member of the Upton Park team that won the London Senior Cup in successive seasons, 1882/83 and 1883/84. Educated at the City of London School (in rugby XV) and a solicitor in London from 1879.

BASTIN, Clifford Sydney ('Boy')
(Arsenal, 1932-38, 21)
Born Exeter, 14 March 1912.
1938: 5ft. 7³/₄ins.; 10st. 8lbs.

Career: Exeter Schools, then assisted two Exeter junior sides, St Mark's and St. James; Exeter City on amateur forms 1926, turning professional October 1928; Arsenal May 1929 (£2000); retired cs 1947. Other honours: England schoolboy international (1 app). Football League (4 apps). (Arsenal) FL champions 1931, 1933, 1934, 1935, 1938. FA Cup winner 1930, 1936; finalist 1932.

Outside-left. Took the inside berth on occasion as well. Early precocity led to the nickname 'Boy' when, even then, his main

attribute – an ice-cold temperament – had fully manifested itself. He possessed also a natural body swerve and a lethal left foot. The latter collected a rich harvest of goals that included a winger's then record 33 in 42 League games, 1932/33. Cliff played for Devon county when only 17 and became the youngest FA Cup finalist, this record standing 34 years until surpassed by Howard Kendall. Increasingly troubled by deafness at the time of leaving football, he was later employed as a Devon licensee. The subject of one of the better player biographies, 'Cliff Bastin Remembers' by Brian Glanville (Ettrick Press, 1950).

BAUGH, Richard
(Stafford Road and Wolverhampton Wanderers, 1886-90, 2)
Born Wolverhampton, 14 February 1864. Died 14 August 1929.
1889: 5ft. 9¹/₂ins.; 11st. 12lbs.
Career: Wolverhampton schools football; Rose Villa; Wolverhampton Rangers; Stafford Road; Wolverhampton Wanderers cs 1886; Walsall September 1896; retired cs 1897. Other honours: FA Cup winner 1893; finalist 1889, 1896.
Right-back. A resourceful defender prominent in Black Country soccer for a decade and a half. He was dour, resilient and efficient, clearing his lines quickly. Father of Dick jnr., also a full-back, well known with Wolves and West Bromwich Albion during the 1920s and later with Exeter City.

BAYLISS, A(bert) E(dward) James M(atthias) ('Jem')
(West Bromwich Albion, 1891, 1)

Born Tipton, Staffs. August 1863. Died 19 August 1933.

Career: Great Bridge Schools; Great Bridge Unity; Tipton Providence; Wednesday Old Athletic 1883/84; West Bromwich Albion August 1884; retired March 1892. Was an Albion director while still on the club's playing strength, eventually becoming Chairman until resigning in 1905. In June 1909 was elected a life member. Other honours: (WBA) FA Cup winner 1888; finalist 1886, 1887.

Inside-right/centre-forward, latterly wing-half. A powerful, free scoring forward, his transition to half-back (where he was capped) revealed a talent for the telling tackle also. For many years on the staff of the well known Midlands firm, Guest, Keen & Nettlefold. The nickname, Jem, derived from a transposition of his initials. A much respected man.

BAYNHAM, Ronald L.
(Luton Town, 1956, 3)
Born Birmingham, 10 June 1929.
1957: 6ft.; 12st. 2lbs.

Career: Did not play in competitive football until serving in the Army; Erdington Rovers 1946; Bromford Amateurs; Worcester City 1949; Luton Town November 1951 (£1000); retired through injury 1965. Other honours: England 'B' international (1 app). Football League (2 apps). (Luton T) FA Cup finalist 1959.

Goalkeeper. For some years vied with Bernard Streten – another England 'keeper – for the first team spot at Kenilworth Road. Baynham was very brave and showed excellent judgment, being especially good at dealing with flighted crosses. After his retirement, worked as an interior decorator in the Bedfordshire area.

BEARDSLEY, Peter Andrew
(Newcastle United and Liverpool, 1986-88, 26)
Born Longbenton, Newcastle-upon-Tyne, 18 January 1961.
1986: 5ft. 8ins.; 11st. 7lbs.

Career: Wallsend Boys Club; Carlisle United August 1979; Vancouver Whitecaps (Canada) 1981 (£27,500); Manchester United September 1982 (£250,000); Vancouver Whitecaps again 1983; Newcastle United September 1983 (£120,000); Liverpool July 1987 (£1.8m., a British record). Other honours: (Liverpool) FL champions 1988. FA Cup finalist 1988.

Strike forward. Sprang into international prominence because of a splendid rapport with Gary Lineker in England matches. Beardsley, with no physical advantages, can bore his way through most effectively and persistence makes him awkward to dispossess. His move to Anfield seemed a drawn-out affair but, at the time this is being written, looks like another Liverpool coup, the Lineker rapport evidently repeated with John Aldridge.

BEASLEY, Albert ('Pat')
(Huddersfield Town, 1939, 1)
Born Stourbridge, 16 July 1913. Died February 1986.
1938: 5ft. 8½ins.; 11st. 2lbs.

Career: Brierley Hill Schools; Cookesley; Stourbridge FC; Arsenal May 1931 (£550); Huddersfield Town October 1936; Fulham December 1945; Bristol City as player/manager July 1950, retiring from playing May 1952 and continuing as manager only to January 1958; Birmingham City joint manager February 1958, becoming sole manager September 1958 and then team manager January 1959-May 1960; Fulham scout cs 1960; Dover manager cs 1961-April 1964. Other honours: (Arsenal) FL champions 1934, 1935. (H'field T) FA Cup finalist 1938. (Fulham) FL Div. 2 champions 1949.

Outside-right/outside-left who switched to left-half late in his playing career. Pat, blessed with traditional wingman skills, added that of a marked penchant to cut in and exploit his shooting ability. Toured South Africa with the 1939 FA party, then having a couple of outings against that country's national side.

BEATS, William Edwin
(Wolverhampton Wanderers, 1901-02, 2)
Born Wolstanton, Staffs. 13 November 1871. Died 13 April 1939.
1902: 5ft. 7ins.; 10st. 12lbs.

Career: Port Hill; Port Vale Rovers 1889; Burslem Port Vale in the early 1890s; Wolverhampton Wanderers cs 1895; Bristol Rovers May 1903; Burslem Port Vale again May 1906; Reading cs 1907 as player/

trainer, playing until circa 1911. Bristol Rovers trainer cs 1911; Reading trainer 1914, retiring during WW1. Other honours: Football League (5 apps). (Wolves) FA Cup finalist 1896. (Bristol R) Southern League champions 1905.

Centre-forward. Excellent leader of the attack ('one of Wolves' cleverest'), invariably taking up advantageous positions and commendably unselfish. His ripe experience was thought to be the main factor in Bristol Rovers' winning of their 1905 championship. A Reading licensee from 1914 to his retirement in 1936, and father of Eddie Beats, an England schoolboy international who later turned professional.

BEATTIE, T(homas) Kevin
(Ipswich Town, 1975-78, 9)
Born Carlisle, 18 December 1953.
1976: 5ft. 10ins.; 12st. 2lbs.

Career: Carlisle junior football; Ipswich Town apprentice 1970, turning professional July 1971; retired through injury December 1981 but joined Colchester United July 1982; Middlesbrough November 1982-October 1983. Kongsverg (Norway) coach December 1986. Other honours: England Youth international. England Under-23 international (9 apps). (Ipswich) FA Cup winner 1978.

Left-half, sometimes left-back. Reckoned by many a good judge as England's best prospect since Duncan Edwards (with which great footballer he had many similarities). But lamentably injury caused his departure from Ipswich and subsequent attempted come-backs proved abortive. Kevin was tremendously strong in the tackle, powerful and accurate in heading, had a developed sense of when to part and when to keep possession, and a thunderous shot. An irreplaceable loss to the game.

BECTON, Francis
(Preston North End and Liverpool, 1895-97, 2)
Born Preston, Lancs. 1873. Died 6 November 1909.

Career: Preston junior football; Fishwick Ramblers; Preston North End circa 1891; Liverpool March 1895 (£100); Sheffield United October 1898; Bedminster June 1899; Preston North End again September 1900; Swindon Town cs 1901; Ashton Town cs 1903; lastly had a spell with New Brighton Tower before retiring on account of ill-health. Other honours: Football League (2 apps). (Liverpool) FL Div. 2 champions 1896.

Inside-forward of the thoughtful persuasion, his creative promptings bringing out the best from a miscellany of partners, especially Harry Bradshaw at Liverpool. Becton, best known member of a noted soccer family, was among the pre-1914 scene's most travelled players.

BEDFORD, Harry
(Blackpool, 1923-25, 2)
Born Calow nr. Chesterfield, 15 October 1899. Died 24 June 1976.
1925: 5ft. 8ins.; 12st. 4lbs.

Career: Grassmoor Ivanhoe (Chesterfield League); Nottingham Forest as an amateur 1919, turning professional in August of that year; Blackpool March 1921 (£1500); Derby County September 1925 (£3500); Newcastle United December 1930 (£4000); Sunderland January 1932 (£3000); Bradford May 1932; Chesterfield June 1933; Heanor Town player/coach August 1934. Newcastle United trainer/coach October 1937; Derby County masseur (part-time) May 1938. Had a brief spell as Heanor Town's manager in 1956. Other honours: Football League (2 apps).

Inside-right/centre-forward, initially making a big name as a centre, twice topping the Second Division scoring list (1922/23

and '23/24), and was the League's top scorer of 1923/24. His career League match figures read 486 matches, 308 goals. Was no stylist but his dash and fearlessness were qualities to be cherished. Later a licensee at Derby and Chesterfield.

BELL, Colin
(Manchester City, 1968-76, 48)
Born Hesleden, Co Durham, 26 February 1946.
1972: 5ft. 11½ins.; 11st. 12lbs.

Career: Horden Schools; East Durham Schools; Horden Colliery (trials with Sunderland and Newcastle United); Bury July 1963; Manchester City March 1966 (£47,500); retired through injury August 1979. Other honours: England Under-23 international (2 apps). Football League (4 apps). (Man. City) European Cup Winners' Cup, winner 1970. FL champions 1968. FA Cup winner 1969. FL Cup winner 1970, finalist 1974.

Right-sided midfield. A major player of his day: skilled, enthusiastic, quite tireless and chock full of running. This last caused a City manager to dub him 'Nijinsky', after the famous race-horse. Suffered grievous injuries in 1976 to a thigh and both knees, was out of the game for 2 years and eventually forced to retire. Became a restaurateur in partnership with another former player, Colin Waldron (Burnley 1967-76).

BENNETT, Walter ('Cocky')
(Sheffield United, 1901, 2)
Born Mexborough, Yorks. 1874. Died 6 April 1908.
1901: 5ft. 7½ins.; 13st.

Career: Mexborough FC; Sheffield United February 1896; Bristol City April 1905; Denaby United cs 1907. Other honours: (Sheffield U) FL champions 1898. FA Cup winner 1899, 1902 (played in first game only), finalist 1901. (Bristol C) FL Div. 2 champions 1906.

Outside right weighty in body and able to centre from any angle. Reputedly one of the hardest shots the game has seen (and said to have scored 80 goals one season for Mexborough from the outside-right position!). Brilliant on his day but apt to be temperamental. Cocky, a miner, returned to the industry after leaving Ashton Gate, losing his life when a pit roof collapsed.

BENSON, Robert William
(Sheffield United, 1913, 1)
Born Whitehaven 9 February 1883. Died 19 February 1916.
1913: 5ft. 9ins.; 14st.

Career: Swalwell FC; Newcastle United December 1902; Southampton cs 1904 (£150); Sheffield United cs 1905; Woolwich Arsenal 1913. Other honour: Football League (1 app).

Right/left-back unable to permanently break into Newcastle's senior side so moved South, there revealing his class. Did well on moving to Bramall Lane a year later, a telling tackle being a particular strong point. Bob's penalty-taking earned comment too – a colleague would place on the spot and the player would run almost the length of the field and blast the ball home. An FA tourist in South Africa 1910, playing three times against their national team. Collapsed and died during a wartime match – he had not played for almost 2 years, being engaged on munitions.

BENTLEY, Roy Thomas Frank
(Chelsea, 1949-55, 12)
Born Bristol, 17 May 1924.
1950: 5ft. 10ins.; 11st. 7lbs.

Career: Bristol Schools; Bristol Rovers amateur 1937; Bristol City ground staff 1938, turning professional August 1941; Newcastle United June 1946 (£8500);

Chelsea January 1948 (£12,500); Fulham September 1956 (£8600); Queen's Park Rangers May 1961 to Reading appointment. Reading manager January 1963-February 1969; Bradford City scout March 1969; Swansea City manager August 1969-October 1972; Reading secretary cs 1977-January 1984; Aldershot secretary December 1984. Other honours: England 'B' internatinal (2 apps). Football League (3 apps). (Chelsea) FL champions 1955.

Centre-forward. Unorthodox, elusive and apt to pop up anywhere. Experienced in several other berths: outside and inside-right, centre-half (at Craven Cottage) and, with QPR, right-back. Had been on the books of both Bristol clubs when still a boy. Roy's aggregate peacetime League record was 560 matches, 172 goals.

BERESFORD, Joseph

(Aston Villa, 1934, 1)
Born Chesterfield, 26 February 1906. Died 1978.
1935: 5ft. 5ins.; 11st. 2lbs.

Career: Assisted two sides from the Doncaster area, Askern Road WMC and Bentley Colliery, before joining Mexborough Athletic; Mansfield Town May 1926; Aston Villa May 1927; Preston North End September 1935; Swansea Town December 1937-cs 1938. Other honours: Football League (2 apps). (PNE) FA Cup finalist 1937. (Swansea) Welsh Cup finalist 1938.

Inside-forward. Canny and stocky, gave useful service wherever he went. As a Lancashire annual reported after his first Preston season: '. . . at once made his experience and astuteness felt, the big improvement in the attack being traceable to his spadework and steadying influence. Covers a lot of ground in his foraging efforts and others could draw lessons from the economy of his moves.' After leaving school worked at Bentley Colliery and in post-WW2 days ran a fish shop. Brother of Frank (Preston).

BERRY, Arthur

(Oxford University, 1909, 1)
Born Liverpool, 3 January 1888. Died 15 March 1953.
1912: 5ft. $8^1/_2$ins.; 11st. 6lbs.

Career: Oxford University (Blue 1908, 1909); Fulham cs 1909; Everton 1909/10; Oxford City from 1911; Liverpool June 1912; also assisted Wrexham and Northern Nomads; retired 1913. Other honours: England amateur international (32 apps). (Oxford C) FA Amateur Cup finalist 1913.

Outside-right/outside-left. A celebrated amateur, son of a Liverpool solicitor who was a Liverpool FC director and chairman 1904-09. His style was direct yet thoughtful and precise ('a complete art without tinsel or gaudiness,' as one writer rather elaborately described it). A barrister by profession, Berry retired from football on being called to the Bar at Gray's Inn in 1913. Educated at Denstone College where he was in the rugby XV 1904-05 and captain in the latter year.

BERRY, John J.

(Manchester United, 1953-56, 4)
Born Aldershot, 1 June 1926.
1951: 5ft. $5^1/_2$ins.; 9st. 9lbs.

Career: Aldershot schoolboy football; Aldershot YMCA; Army football; Birmingham City December 1944; Manchester United August 1951 (£25,000); retired through injuries sustained in the Munich air crash, 1958. Other honours: England 'B' international (1 app). Football League (1 app). (Man. Utd) FL champions 1952, 1956, 1957. FA Cup finalist 1957.

Outside-right, sometimes outside-left. The prototype diminutive winger – quick, full of tricks and expert in dribbling. Proved a first-rate replacement at Old Trafford for Jimmy Delaney. Johnny had at one time been an Aldershot cinema projectionist. Brother of Peter Berry (Palace and Ipswich Town, 1952-61).

BESTALL, John Gilbert

(Grimsby Town, 1935, 1)
Born Beighton nr. Sheffield, 24 June 1900. Died 11 April 1985.
1935: 5ft. 3ins.; 9st. 11lbs.

Career: Sheffield schoolboy football; Beighton Miners' Welfare; Rotherham United 1924/25; Grimsby Town November 1926 (£700); retired June 1938, becoming Birmingham's coach and chief scout; Doncaster Rovers manager March 1946-April 1949; Blackburn Rovers manager June 1949-April 1953; Nelson manager cs 1953-November 1954; Doncaster Rovers chief scout from August 1958 during which engagement he had a spell as team manager (March 1959-August 1960). Other honours: Football League (3 apps). (Grimsby Town) FL Div. 2 champions 1934.

Inside-forward (usually inside-right). A whisker shorter than the great Alex. James and reckoned the shortest inside-forward of his time, a diminutive craftsman full of guile and exceptionally constructive. Gave the Mariners outstanding service, making a club record 427 League appearances (surpassed December 1968). The recipient of a singular honour in having a Cleethorpes street named after him.

BETMEAD, Harry
(Grimsby Town, 1937, 1)

Born Grimsby, 11 April 1912. Died 26 August 1984.
1936: 6ft. $0^1/_2$in.; 12st.

Career: Grimsby schoolboy football; Hay Cross FC (Grimsby); Grimsby Town October 1930; retired December 1947. Other honour: (Grimsby Town) FL Div. 2 champions 1934.

Centre-half. Gave a magnificent service to his local club over many years, height ensuring aerial command with fine tackling equally effective on the ground. The subject of many big offers from wealthier clubs but the Grimsby management resisted them. Harry had earlier worked as a railway porter and, after leaving the game, was in business in Hertfordshire. He had played for Lincolnshire in Minor Counties cricket. Toured South Africa with the FA's 1939 party, twice appearing against the South African national team.

BETTS, Morton Peto
(Old Harrovians, 1877, 1)
Born London, 30 August 1847. Died 19 April 1914.
Career: Harrow School; Old Harrovians; Wanderers. Also represented Kent. Served on the FA Committee 1870-72 and 1881-90, and was a FA Vice-President 1890-91. Other honour: (Wanderers) FA Cup winner 1872.

Utility player, among the earliest of the versatility breed. Could play anywhere though largely engaged as a full-back or forward. In the former role his work was chiefly noted for its vigour, particularly in shoulder charging. As a forward he showed skill at dribbling. Appeared in the 1872 Cup final under a pseudonym, A H Chequer, because he had assisted another team in an earlier round. Known in the cricket world, too. Played 1 match for Middlesex (1872), 2 for Kent (1872 and '81) and was secretary of Essex CCC 1887-90.

BETTS, William
(Sheffield Wednesday, 1889, 1)
Born Sheffield, 1864. Died 8 August 1941.
1891: 5ft. 8ins.; 11st. 8lbs.

Career: Junior football to Sheffield Wednesday 1883; Lockwood
Bros. (Sheffield works team) later in 1883; Sheffield Wednesday again 1885-1895. Later was Wednesday's groundsman and,

from cs 1922, had spell as their assistant trainer. Other honours: (Wednesday) Football Alliance champions 1890. FA Cup finalist 1890.

Centre-half, occasionally wing-half. Although small in build could outwit big opposing forwards, often breaking up attacks by tackling unexpectedly. Smallnesss did not affect unduly his fine heading ability either. Betts' Wednesday service extended over many years and he was grandfather of their post-WW2 forward, Dennis Woodhead, who was on the Hillsborough club's books from season 1944/45 to cs 1955.

BEVERLEY, Joseph

(Blackburn Rovers, 1884, 3)

Born Blackburn, 12 November 1856. Died 21 May 1897.

1880: 5ft. 8ins.; 11st. 2lbs.

Career: Blackburn schoolboy football; Black Star FC; Blackburn Olympic (founder member 1876); Blackburn Rovers October 1882; Blackburn Olympic again cs 1884; Blackburn Rovers again late 1887-1889. Other honour: (Blackburn R) FA Cup winner 1884.

Full-back winning his 3 caps on the left flank and Cup medal on the right, but also a utility man able to operate in the middle and front lines also. Season 1883/84 was very much his 'peak', all the above honours accruing then. Joe was a quick mover and performed with admirable judgment. He lost his life in an accident at the Albion Mill, Blackburn, where he worked.

BIRKETT, Ralph James Evans

(Middlesbrough, 1936, 1)

Born Newton Abbot, Devon, 9 January 1913.

1938: 5ft. 9ins.; 11st. 4lbs.

Career: Dartmouth United (Plymouth & District League); Torquay United amateur 1929, turning professional March 1930; Arsenal April 1933; Middlesbrough March 1935; Newcastle United July 1938 (£5900); retired 1941. Other honours: England wartime international (1 app). Football League (2 apps).

Outside-right. Combined speed, craft and goal scoring potential. In 231 League outings before war came, he netted 63. Unable to obtain a regular first-team spot at Highbury, with Kirchen and Beasley available, Ralph's move to Middlesbrough proved beneficial. His 3 peacetime representative honours were won while there, and his FL record read 93 matches, 34 goals.

BIRKETT, Reginald Halsey

(Clapham Rovers, 1879, 1)

Born London, 28 March 1849. Died 30 June 1898.

Career: Lancing College (XI 1866-67); Lancing Old Boys; Clapham Rovers. Also represented Surrey. Other honours: (Clapham Rovers) FA Cup winner 1880; finalist 1879.

Goalkeeper for his cap and Cup final appearances but also a utility man ('as a forward or back is equally useful,' said a scribe of 1874). A fearless 'keeper and strong kicking anywhere. With C P Wilson and J W Sutcliffe forms a unique trio honoured by England at both soccer and rugger. Indeed Birkett is a name looming large in early Rugby Union annals. R H Birkett himself was a member of the original RU Committee, and his brother and son were also rugger internationals. He worked as a hide and skin broker in the City.

BIRLEY, Francis Hornby

(Oxford University and Wanderers, 1874-75, 2)

Born Chorley, Lancs. 14 March 1850. Died 1 August 1910.

Career: Winchester College; Oxford University (Blue 1874); Wanderers. Also represented Middlesex. Other honours: (Oxford University) FA Cup winner 1874; finalist 1873. (Wanderers) FA Cup winner 1876, 1877.

Half-back considered the most successful of the 1873/74 season. Strong with either foot, enthusiastic and most difficult to circumvent. An athletics Blue of 1874, he also played cricket for Lancashire (4 matches 1870-72), Surrey (1 match 1879) and Cheshire. A barrister by profession, called to the Bar January 1876.

BIRTLES, Garry
(Nottingham Forest, 1980-81, 3)
Born Nottingham, 27 July 1956.
1980: 5ft. 11ins.; 10st. 12lbs.

Career: Nottingham junior football (Aston Villa trial when 15); Long Eaton Rovers (Notts Sunday League); Long Eaton United; Nottingham Forest March 1977 (£2000); Manchester United October 1980 (£1.2m, a Forest record); Nottingham Forest again September 1982 (£250,000); Notts County June 1987. Other honours: England 'B' international. England Under-21 international (2 apps). (Forest) European Cup winner 1979, 1980. FL Cup winner 1979; finalist 1980.

Strike forward. A left-back originally, he was converted to centre-forward by Long Eaton United. Had a run at centre-half during the 1985/86 campaign. Especially strong in the heading department , deceptively quick and deft in control (as a critic put it, '. . . often holds the ball against the odds until support arrives.') Garry must be the player to have given Forest their greatest financial profit.

BISHOP, Sidney Macdonald
(Leicester City, 1927, 4)
Born Stepney, London, 10 February 1900.
Died 4 May 1949.
1927: 5ft. 11½ins.; 11st. 8lbs.

Career: London Schools; Air Force football during WW1; Ilford; Crystal Palace; West Ham United May 1920; Leicester City November 1926 (£3500, then a Leicester record); Chelsea June 1928; retired May 1933. Other honours: Football League (1 app). (WHU) FA Cup finalist 1923.

Wing-half of culture and discernment, extremely skilled in ball control and equally adroit at heading. Played centre-forward as a schoolboy and for Ilford, moving permanently to the half-back line when assisting the Palace reserves. Only the second player to be honoured by England while on Leicester's books. Known as 'Sticks' to the West Ham faithful on account of a slim build.

BLACKBURN, Frederick
(Blackburn Rovers, 1901-04, 3)
Born Mellor nr. Blackburn, Lancs. September 1879.
1904: 5ft. 6½ins.; 10st. 12lbs.

Career: Mellor FC; Blackburn Rovers 1897; West Ham United May 1905; retired cs 1913. Turned up again in a soccer context again cs 1931 when appointed Barking Town's coach. Other honour: Football League (1 app).

Outside-left. Much coveted by other clubs following a bright display in his first international, but remained a loyal Rover for another four terms. A tricky wingman, excellent in ball control, his only flaw occasional erratic shooting. Was a seafarer after WW1, hence the gap in footballing activities until the 1931 Barking Town appointment. Fred's brother, Arthur, played for Blackburn Rovers and Southampton.

BLACKBURN, George Frederick
(Aston Villa, 1924, 1)
Born Willesden Green, London, 8 March 1899. Died 3 July 1957.
1924: 5ft. 10$^1/_2$ins.; 12st.

Career: Willesden Schools; London Schools; Willesden Juniors; Hampstead Town; Aston Villa amateur December 1920, turning professional January 1921; Cardiff City cs 1926; Mansfield Town June 1931; Cheltenham Town player/coach July 1932; Moor Green coach cs 1934; Birmingham FC trainer 1937-46, afterwards joining that club's coaching staff. Other honours: (Villa) FA Cup finalist 1924. (Cardiff C) Welsh Cup winner 1927, 1930; finalist 1929.

Left-half. Spirited half, 'one of the most persistent workers in football,' reported an early 'Twenties critic. In 1919 and 1920 George represented both the London FA and Middlesex FA, and besides his England cap, was once 12th man for the Scotland fixture. The bulk of his 263 League outings were in First Division encounters.

BLENKINSOP, Ernest
(Sheffield Wednesday, 1928-33, 26)
Born Cudworth, Yorks. 20 April 1902. Died 24 April 1969.
1929: 5ft. 10$^1/_2$ins.; 11st. 8lbs.

Career: Cudworth United Methodists; Hull City October 1921 (£100); Sheffield Wednesday January 1923 ('4 figure fee'); Liverpool March 1934 (about £5000); Cardiff City November 1937; Buxton August 1939; assisted Bradford and Hurst during WW2 before retiring. Other honours: Football League (8 apps). (Wednesday) FL champions 1929, 1930. FL Div. 2 champions 1926.

Left-back likened in the 'Twenties to the legendary Howard Spencer, the commentator going on '. . . a back of polish and style, coolness in tackling, and a placer of kicks.' As a junior alternated between the left-back and inside-left positions. Latterly a licensee in Sheffield.

BLISS, Herbert
(Tottenham Hotspur, 1921, 1)
Born Willenhall, Staffs. 29 March 1890. Died 14 June 1968.
1921: 5ft. 7ins.; 11st. 2lbs.

Career: Willenhall Swifts; Tottenham Hotspur April 1912 (£10); Clapton Orient December 1922; Bournemouth and Boscombe Athletic July 1925; retired cs 1926. Other honours: (Spurs) FL Div. 2 champions 1920. FA Cup winner 1921.

Inside-left. It was recorded in 1921 that Bert was 'One of the most conscientious of players and pretty nearly the hardest shooting forward in football, his surprise efforts flashing into the net before the danger is even realised.' He was a fine dribbler too though could be faulted at times by attempting more than could be accomplished.

BLISSETT, Luther Loide
(Watford, 1983-84, 14)
1982: 5ft. 10$^1/_2$ins.; 11st 13$^1/_2$lbs.

Career: Kingfisher Youth FC (Brent Sunday League); Watford July 1975; AC Milan June 1983 (£1m); Watford again August 1984 (£550,000); AFC Bournemouth November 1988 (£60,00). Other honours: England Under-21 international (4 apps). (Watford) FL Div. 4 champions 1978.

Strike forward associated with Watford in their rapid rise to top flight status. An exciting player and a brave one, showing speed, agility and athleticism. Somewhat unkindly dubbed "Luther Missit' in some quarters because of unpredictability near goal, yet his scoring record bears scrutiny. Established records for Watford transfer fees, both selling and buying. One of the most prominent and personable of the many coloured performers to have graced our game in recent times.

BLOCKLEY, Jeffrey Paul
(Arsenal, 1973, 1)
Born Leicester, 12 September 1949.
1973: 6ft. 0$^1/_2$ins.; 12st. 5lbs.

Career: Leicestershire schoolboy football (trials with Arsenal and Leicester City); Midland Athletic (Leics); Coventry City apprentice, turning professional June 1967; Arsenal October 1972 (£200,000); Leicester City January 1975 (£100,000) (Derby County on loan January 1978); Notts County June 1978-1980. Other honours: England Under-23 international (10 apps). Football League (1 app).

Centre-half. 'A fierce tackler and very strong in the air,' read one verdict, and these were typical qualities of this sheet-anchor type pivot. An unusual case, though, in having unsuccessful trials as a youngster with two senior clubs, both of which subsequently paid hefty transfer fees to secure his services.

BLOOMER, Stephen
(Derby County and Middlesbrough, 1895-1907, 23)
Born Cradley Heath, Worcs. 20 January 1874. Died 16 April 1938.
1901: 5ft. 7ins.; 10st. 12lbs.

Career: Derby schoolboy football; Derby Swifts (Derbyshire Minor League); Derby County August 1892; Middlesbrough March 1906; Derby County again September 1910 (£750); retired 1914 thereupon a coach in Germany where he was interned until the end of WW1. Post-war served Derby County as a coach etc, a service interspersed with coaching engagements abroad including Canada April-August 1922. Irun FC (Spain) in 1924 and Rotterdam. Other honours: Football League (15 apps). (Derby Co) FL Div. 2 champions 1912. FA Cup finalist 1898, 1899.

Inside-right. A famous star from the turn of the century, 'pale and slightly built but had a terrific shot – mostly daisy cutters – and the most prolific pre-1914 scorer, 'summed up one scribe. His 28 goals for England remained a record until 1956, he headed the First Division scoring list 4 times and aggregated 352 in League matches. Assiduous practice brought about an ability to shoot unhesitatingly from any angle and any possible distance. And he employed a devastating defence-splitting pass. Father-in-law of A E Quantrill (q.v.).

BLUNSTONE, Frank
(Chelsea, 1955-57, 5)
Born Crewe 17 October 1934.
1957: 5ft. 9ins.; 10st. 7lbs.

Career: Crewe Schools; Cheshire Schools; Crewe Alexandra amateur 1951, turning professional January 1952; Chelsea February 1953 (£7000); retired through injury 1964. Chelsea's youth team trainer October 1964; Brentford manager December 1969; Manchester United youth team coach July 1973, reserve team coach August 1975; Derby County assistant manager September 1977-July 1979; Ethnikos (Greece) August 1979; Aris (Salonika, Greece) chief coach March-July 1980; later on Sheffield Wednesday's staff. Other honours: England Youth international. England Under-23 international (5 apps). Football League (2 apps). (Chelsea) FL champions 1955.

Outside-left. Thrustful, excellent in ball control and close dribbling. Twice broke a leg but managed 365 League outings (69 goals) before an enforced retirement. Frank, fifth in a family of 13, was reserve for England at schoolboy level in 1950, and represented the British Army when on national service.

BOND, Richard
(Preston North End and Bradford City, 1905-10, 8)
Born Garstang, Lancs. 14 December 1883. Died 25 April 1955.
1906: 5ft. $6^{1}/_{2}$ins.; 10st. 7lbs.

Career: Army football (Artillery); Preston North End August 1902; Bradford City May 1909; Blackburn Rovers May 1922 (£450); Lancaster Town August 1923; retired 1924 but was turning out for Garstang FC in 1926/27. Other honours: Football League (1 app). (PNE) FL Div. 2 champions 1904.

Outside-right known throughout the football world as Dicky Bond. He was a scintillating wingman, slippery as the proverbial eel, his wiry little frame withstanding two decades of League strife. Rejoined the Army for the 1914/18 conflict, finishing up as a POW. In later life ran a fried fish business in his native Garstang.

BONETTI, Peter Phillip
(Chelsea, 1966-70, 7)
Born Putney, London, 27 September 1941
1968: 5ft. 10ins.; 11st. 3lbs.

Career: Worthing RC Youth Club; Chelsea amateur cs 1958, turning professional April 1959; retired May 1979 but signed for Dundee United in July, finally retiring cs 1980. Later a Chelsea coach. Other honours: England Under-23 international (12 apps). Football League (4 apps). (Chelsea) European Cup Winners' Cup, winner 1971. FA Cup winner 1970; finalist 1967. FL Cup winner 1965; finalist 1972.

Goalkeeper extremely durable even by goalkeeping standards, with 600 League appearances for Chelsea (which was a club record but now surpassed). Known as 'The Cat' because of an outstanding agility and lightning-quick reflexes. Moved to the Isle of Mull in 1980, where he ran a guest house and worked as a postman (hence the Dundee United season), but eventually returned to London.

BONSOR, Alexander George
(Wanderers, 1873-75, 2)
Died 17 August 1907.

Career: Eton College; Wanderers; Old Etonians. Also represented Surrey. Other honours: (Wanderers) FA Cup winner 1872, 1873. (Old Etonians) FA Cup finalist 1875, 1876.

Forward, direct in style. His weighty frame combined with speed and expertise in close dribbling made him a dangerous attacker. Played little in 1873/74, when apparently 'between clubs', coming back the following season to win another cap and make further Cup final appearances. A brewer by vocation, with a firm eventually taken over by Watney's.

BOOTH, Frank
(Manchester City, 1905, 1)
Born Hyde, Cheshire, 1882. Died 22 June 1919.
1911: 5ft. 10ins.; 11st. 10lbs.

Career: Hyde FC; Glossop; Stockport County; Manchester City April 1902; Bury January 1907; Clyde June 1909; Manchester City again July 1911-cs 1912. Other honours: (Man. City) FA Cup winner 1904. (Clyde) Scottish Cup finalist 1910 (played in the final and first re-play).

Outside-left who, like another England winger, Billy Hogg, sampled the Scottish League scene of the time. Frank played the orthodox game, keeping to his touch-line and sending over centres of commendable precision. Slimly built and lively.

BOOTH, Thomas Edward
(Blackburn Rovers and Everton, 1898-1903, 2)
Born Ardwick, Manchester, 25 April 1874. Died 7 September 1939.
1903: 5ft. 10ins.; 12st.

Career: Hooley Hill; Ashton North End 1892; Blackburn Rovers May 1896; Everton April 1900; Preston North End 1908; Carlisle United November 1908; retired 1909. Other honours: Football League (4 apps).

Centre-half. Had formerly been a right-half. Booth was a reliable pivot reckoned at his peak to be the equal of any in the League. Produced no fireworks but as effective and steady as they come. Unfortunately missed the 1906 Cup final through injury and when Everton again reached the final the following year, was no longer an automatic choice.

BOWDEN, E(dwin) Raymond
(Arsenal, 1935-37, 6)
Born Looe, Cornwall, 13 September 1909.
1936: 5ft. 9½ins.; 10st. 12lbs.

Career: Looe FC; Plymouth Argyle on amateur forms cs 1926, turning professional during the next season; Arsenal March 1933 (£7000); Newcastle United November 1937 (£5000); retired September 1939. Other honours: Football League (2 apps). (Plymouth A) FL Div. 3 (South) champions 1930. (Arsenal) FL champions 1934, 1935. FA Cup winner 1936.

Inside-right/centre-forward. A graceful stylist, maker and taker of goals (137 in 321 League games before war came). He scored against Swansea Town on September 2, 1939, war was declared, and he never played competitive soccer again. During his first-class career Ray was unfortunately plagued by ankle injuries. Later employed as a sports outfitter in Plymouth, he had once been an auctioneer's clerk.

BOWER, Alfred George ('Baishe')
(Corinthians, 1924-27, 5)
Born Bromley, Kent, 10 November 1895. Died 30 June 1970.

Career: Charterhouse School (failing to get his soccer colours); Old Carthusians post-WW1; Corinthians 1919/20-1929/30; Chelsea in mid-1920s making 9 FL apps; Casuals. Served on the FA Council 1928-33. Other honours: England amateur international (13 apps).

Right/left-back. Tall, strong amateur prominent in the 'Twenties. An especially good tackler while his heading was first-rate too. Bower's calm bearing could be inspirational to colleagues, but his own game was often affected adversely if captaincy worries became onerous. After Army service worked on the Stock Exchange 1919-54 and then as welfare officer to a Croydon firm until 1960.

BOWERS, John William Anslow
(Derby County, 1934, 3)
Born Low Santon, nr. Scunthorpe, 22 Feb-

ruary 1908. Died 4 July 1970.
1934: 6ft.; 12st. 10lbs.

Career: Appleby Works (Scunthorpe); Scunthorpe United December 1927; Derby County May 1928; Leicester City November 1936 (£6000); retired and appointed coach of Notts County's colts August 1943. Returned to Derby County as assistant trainer in 1945 and was still serving in that capacity two decades later. Other honours: Football League (2 apps). (Leicester) FL Div. 2 champions 1937.

Centre-forward. Rare opportunist centre whose harassing methods and unerring marksmanship brought him 220 goals in 285 League outings before war came, an outstanding return. He cleverly introduced fellow attackers into the action, his line moving sweetly. Jack's move to Leicester is said to have ensured the Filberts' 1936/37 promotion. His son, Jack jnr., played for Derby County 1957-66.

BOWLES, Stanley
(Queen's Park Rangers, 1974-77, 5)
Born Moston, Manchester, 24 December 1948.
1975: 5ft. 10ins.; 11st. 4lbs.

Career: Manchester schoolboy football; Manchester City apprentice July 1965, turning professional January 1967; Bury (on trial) July 1970; Crewe Alexandra September 1970 (originally on month's trial); Carlisle United October 1971 (£12,000); Queen's Park Rangers September 1972 (£110,000); Nottingham Forest December 1979 (£210,000); Orient July 1980 (equalling Orient's record); Brentford October 1981 (about £40,000)-1984. Other honour: Football League (1 app).

Forward. Gave managements a few headaches because of a life style not normally associated with a professional sportsman, yet the type of ball-playing talent that brings the crowds in. 'Seems to take his dazzling ability for granted,' reported one writer, going on to say the player possessed 'a magic wand for a left foot.' The QPR crowd has for long loved a touch of the flamboyant (remember Rodney Marsh?) and Bowles admirably fitted in with this tradition.

BOWSER, Sidney
(West Bromwich Albion, 1920, 1)
Born Handsworth, Birmingham 6 April 1891. Died 25 February 1961.
1912: 5ft. 9½ins.; 12st.

Career: Birmingham schoolboy football; Astbury Richmond; Willenhall (trial with Birmingham); West Bromwich Albion July 1908; Belfast Distillery April 1913; West Bromwich Albion again February 1914; Walsall August 1924 (£1000); retired cs 1925. Other honours: Irish League (1 app). (WBA) FL champions 1920. FL Div. 2 champions 1911. FA Cup finalist 1912.

Inside-forward latterly centre-half. A resilient player of some versatility – in his three medal-winning sides above was respectively inside-right, inside-left and centre-half. He had '. . . a hefty pair of shoulders and was very strong in the leg' wrote a contemporary. A first-rate club man too. Became a licensee in 1925, working for many years at Dudley. Later managed an off-licence at Acocks Green.

BOYER, Philip John
(Norwich City, 1976, 1)
Born Nottingham, 25 January 1949.
1976: 5ft. 8ins.; 11st. 2lbs.

Career: Junior football to Derby County as an apprentice August 1965, turning professional November 1966; York City July 1968 (£3500); Bournemouth & Boscombe Athletic December 1970 (£20000); Norwich City February 1974 (£145,000, then a Norwich record); Southampton August 1977 (£125,000); Manchester City November 1980 (£220,000) (Bulovas FC, Hong Kong, on loan February 1982); Grantham July 1983, later having spells with Stamford and Shepshed Charterhouse before returning to Grantham as joint manager December 1985. Other honours: England Under-23 international (2 apps). (Norwich C) FL Cup finalist 1975. (Soton) FL Cup finalist 1979.

Strike forward. '... is nimble, on his toes all the time, hard to get the ball from and never misses a trick,' was one apt summing-up. Another remarked 'it's not often a player of such high skills is prepared to work his heart out.' Norwich's first full England cap and only the third player to make a century of League appearances for 4 different FL clubs.

BOYES, Walter Edward
(West Bromwich Albion and Everton, 1935-39, 3)
Born Sheffield, 5 January 1913. Died 16 September 1960.
1935: 5ft. 5ins.; 10st. 8lbs.

Career: Sheffield Schools; Woodhouse Mills United (Sheffield); West Bromwich Albion on amateur forms February 1931, turning professional a month later; Everton February 1938; Notts County as player/coach August 1949; Scunthorpe United August 1950; Retford Town player/manager 1953; Hyde United manager April 1958; Swansea Town trainer 1959, retiring through ill-health June 1960. Other honours: Football League (2 apps). (WBA) FA Cup finalist 1935. (Everton) FL champions 1939.

Outside-left with a fair amount of experience at left-half and the inside position. And he had led his Sheffield junior club's attack. Boyes was a splendid little player, adroit in his scheming and an effective scorer on his own account. From 1952-57 was sports master at the Oakwood Collegiate School, Sheffield.

BOYLE, Thomas Wilkinson
(Burnley, 1913, 1)
Born Hoyland, nr. Barnsley, 29 January 1888. Died 5 January 1940.
1914: 5ft. 7½ins.; 11st. 4lbs.

Career: Hoyland Star; Elsecar FC (Barnsley League); Barnsley May 1906 Burnley September 1911 (£1150) being appointed the club's player/coach cs 1922; Wrexham cs-late 1923. Coached in Germany for a spell from cs 1924. Other honours: Football League (4 apps). (Barnsley) FA Cup finalist 1910. (Burnley) FL champions 1921. FA Cup winner 1914.

Centre-half and short for the job but this was no handicap to an exceptional skipper, very vociferously inspiring his men and leading by example. As one writer put it 'he was as strong as a horse and never shirked anything.' And Boyle was masterly in headwork – the ball was invariably 'his' despite a mere 5 feet, 7½.

BRABROOK, Peter
(Chelsea, 1958-60, 3)
Born Greenwich, 8 November 1937.
1959: 5ft. 11ins.; 12st.

Career: East Ham Schools; Essex Schools; London Schools; Chelsea ground staff March 1953, turning professional March 1955; West Ham United October 1962 (£33,000); Orient July 1968; Romford August 1971. Other honours: England Youth international. England Under-23 international (9 apps). Football League (3 apps). (WHU) FA Cup winner 1964. FL Cup finalist 1966. (Orient) FL Div. 3 champions 1970.

Outside-right/outside-left, mostly the former, after originally playing inside-forward. Had stunning speed and a blistering shot at his best, but could be variable. Unusually big in physique for a wingman, a fact adding to opponents' difficulties in containment. Became proprietor of a butcher's shop.

BRACEWELL, Paul W.

(Everton, 1985-86, 3)
Born Stoke-on-Trent, 19 July 1962
1985: 5ft.8ins.; 10st.9lbs.

Career: Potteries junior football; Stoke City apprentice turning professional 1980. Sunderland June 1983 (£225,000); Everton May 1984 (£250,000). Other honours: England Under-21 international (13 apps). (Everton) European Cup Winners' Cup, winner 1985. FL champions 1985 FA Cup finalist 1985, 1986.

Midfield (left sided). Not one of your soccer greyhounds racing up and down the field for 90 minutes (and so a darling of the 'workrate' fanatics). Yet a gritty performer, first class at distribution and with much vision. Linked up admirably with Peter Reid at Goodison. Sustained a serious ankle injury in 1986 and made no appearances in Everton's 1987 championship side.

BRADFORD, Geoffrey Reginald William

(Bristol Rovers, 1956, 1)
Born Frenchay, Bristol, 18 July 1927.
1957: 6ft. 1in.; 12st. 7lbs.

Career: Bristol Schoolboy football; Soundwell FC, Bristol (trials with Blackpool and Blackburn Rovers); Bristol Rovers May 1949; retired 1964. Other honour: (Bristol Rovers) Div. 3 (South) champions 1953.

Centre/inside-forward. Forceful attacker spending the whole of his senior career at Eastville and netting a Bristol Rovers' record aggregate 245 League goals in addition to the club's record seasonal total (33 in the 1952/53 championship campaign). Geoff made 461 League appearances so averaged over a goal every 2 games, thus showing excellent consistency. Serious leg injuries did not diminish his scoring potency. On leaving football worked at Avonmouth for an oil company.

BRADFORD, Joseph

(Birmingham, 1924-31, 12)
Born Pegg's Green, Leics. 22 January 1901.
Died 6 September 1980.
1927; 5ft. 9³/₄ins.; 11st. 13lbs.

Career; Pegg's Green Victoria (Leicester Senior League) from the tender age of 12 (trials with Aston Villa and Derby County during his years with this club); Birmingham February 1920 (£125); Bristol City May 1935; retired cs 1936.Other honours: Football League (5 apps) (Birmingham) FA Cup finalist 1931.

Centre-forward, latterly inside-left. A celebrity from the inter-war years often referred to as 'Gentlemen Joe' because of his sporting attitude. A dashing attacker possessing shooting power and marksmanship, he still holds Brum's League seasonal and aggregate scoring records, and netted 5 for the Football League against the Irish League in September 1929. Cousin of Hugh Adcock (England) and brother of Billy Bradford (Walsall 1926-38). After leaving the game worked as a licensee and ran a sports shop in the Birmingham area.

BRADLEY, Warren

(Manchester United, 1959, 3)
Born Hyde, Cheshire, 20 June 1933.
1959: 5ft. 4ins.; 9st. 10lbs.

Career: Hyde Grammar School; Durham University; Durham City (Bolton Wanderers amateur); Bishop Auckland amateur 1955/56; Manchester United amateur February 1958, turning professional the following November; Bury March 1962 (around £6000); Northwich Victoria July 1963; Macclesfield November 1963; Bangor City cs 1964 – cs 1965; Macclesfield again for further spell from April 1966. Other honours: England amateur international (11 apps). (B. Auckland) FA Amateur Cup winner 1956, 1957.

Outside-right. A distinguished amateur

prior to joining the paid ranks in Manchester United's post-Munich personnel. Almost of Fanny Walden proportions yet more than held his own in the first-class game with his quick thinking, pace, control and assurance. A schoolmaster by profession.

BRADSHAW, Francis
(Sheffield Wednesday, 1908, 1)
Born Sheffield, 31 May 1885.
1912: 5ft. $9^1/_2$ins.; 11st. 10lbs.

Career: Sheffield Schools 1895-97; Sheffield Sunday school football; Sheffield Wednesday as an amateur early in 1904, turning professional the following close season; Northampton Town cs 1910 (£250): Everton November 1911 (£1250); Arsenal cs 1914; retired May 1923 when appointed Aberdare Athletic's manager to cs 1924. Other honours: Football League (4 apps).Southern League (1 app) (Sheffield W) FA Cup winner 1907.
Inside-left originally, brainy and dangerous and packing a rocket shot, then released by Wednesday as 'finished' because of serious knee injuries. However, Bradshaw confounded this view, subsequently winning 5 inter-league medals. Extremely versatile, he could literally play anywhere: at Highbury, for example, he performed at back and wing-half. A silversmith by vocation.

BRADSHAW, T(homas), Henry
(Liverpool, 1897, 1)
Born Liverpool, 24 August 1873. Died 25 December 1899.

Career: Northwich Victoria; Liverpool FC 1893; Tottenham Hotspur May 1898; Thames Ironworks cs 1899. Other honours: Football League (2 apps). (Liverpool) FL Div. 2 champions 1894, 1896.

Outside-left. A tragically short life but a not altogether uncommon circumstance among nineteenth century players. Besides outside-left, Harry also took the inside-left and centre berths at Anfield - notably in 1894/95 when he finished top scorer. But he was probably best on the left-wing, responding well to the promptings of the subtle Francis Becton who utilised Bradshaw's speed to telling effect.

BRADSHAW, William
(Blackburn Rovers, 1910-13, 4)
Born Padiham, Lancs. 1884
1910: 5ft. 8ins.: 10st. 10lbs.

Career: Padiham FC; Accrington Stanley; Blackburn Rovers May 1903 (£20); Rochdale player/manager April-September 1920. Other honours: Football League (4 apps) (Blackburn R) FL champions 1912,1914.

Left-half. One for the connoisseur spectator. As a local handbook once glowingly wrote '... the recognised artist of the intermediate line. His play, so clean, neat and skillful, is a delight to watch, and many times he is as good as a sixth forward,' Bradshaw had previously had a successful run at outside-left and was a reliable penalty-taker.

BRANN, George
(Swifts, 1886-91, 3)
Born Eastbourne, 23 April 1865. Died 14 June 1954.

Career: Ardingly College; Swifts; Slough FC; Corinthians 1886-93.

Outside/inside-right. A renowned player from the latter part of the amateurs' hey-day: strong, fast and reliable marksman. Brann was a natural games player. A Sussex county cricketer (1883-1905) who went on tours to Australia, South Africa and North America. And he was a scratch golfer who served 20 years as secretary of the Home Park Golf Club, Surbiton. He taught at his old public school, Ardingly.

BRAWN, William, Frederick
(Aston Villa, 1904, 2)
Born Wellingborough, 1 August 1878. Died 18 August 1932.
1910: 6ft. 1in.: 13st. 5lbs.
Career: Wellingborough Schools: Wellingborough FC; Northampton Town circa 1898/99; Sheffield United January 1900; Aston Villa December 1901; Middlesbrough March 1906; Chelsea late in 1907; Brentford cs 1911; retired 1913. Other honour: (Villa) FA Cup winner 1905.

Outside-right. Singularly well named given that avoirdupois and singularly well built for a wingman. On this premise alone would have posed problems to the opposing wing-half. And he had a fair turn of speed also, so must have been eye-catching when on song. Was a Brentford licensee after leaving football until his death.

BRAY, John,
(Manchester City, 1935-37, 6)
Born Oswaldtwistle, Lancs. 22 April 1909. Died 20 November 1982.
1938: 5ft. 9ins.; 10st. 9lbs.

Career: East Lancashire schoolboy football; Clayton Olympia; Manchester Central 1928; Manchester City cs 1929; retired during WW2. Watford manager February 1947 - February 1948 when he became coach to Nelson until September 1948. Other honours: Football League (5 Apps) (Man.City) FL champions 1937. FA Cup winner 1934; finalist 1933.

Left-half. Understudied,vied with and finally succeeded the great Scottish internatinal, Jimmy McMullan, at Maine Road. Well noted as 'a clever constructive player who is at his best in attack.' All his caps and inter-league honours occured in the 1935-38 period when the best left-half in England. Jack, a good class cricketer, assisted Accrington CC of the Lancashire League.

BRAYSHAW, Edward
(Sheffield Wednesday, 1887,1)
Born Kirkstall, Leeds 1863. Died 20 November 1908.

Career: Walkley All Saints (Sheffield); Sheffield Wednesday 1883; retired through injury 1891 but made a couple of League appearances for Grimsby Town during the 1892/93 season. Other honours: (Wednesday) Football Alliance champions 1890.

FA Cup finalist 1890.

Right-back. Appeared at centre-half for his international and must have performed adequately as England thrashed Ireland to the tune of 7-0. A class defender, courageous and resilient, he was said by a Wednesday historian of 1926 to have been one of the Club's ablest. Brayshaw became a Sheffield licensee, retiring in 1907 because of ill-health.

BRIDGES, Barry John
(Chelsea, 1965-66, 4)
Born Horsford nr. Norwich, 29 April 1941.
1965: 5ft. 9$^1/_4$ins.; 11st. 10$^1/_2$lbs.

Career: Norwich Schools; Chelsea ground staff July 1956, turning professional May 1958; Birmingham City May 1966 (£55,000); Queen's Park Rangers August 1968 (£50,000); Millwall September 1970 (£40,000); Brighton and Hove Albion August 1972 (£28,000); Highland Park, South Africa cs 1974; St. Patrick's Athletic, Eire, player/manager early 1976; Sligo Rovers manager early 1978. After leaving Sligo returned to his native Norfolk and managed Dereham Town, King's Lynn (for most of season 1979/80) and, from June 1980, Horsford FC (Anglian Combination). Other honours: England schoolboy international. England Youth international. Football League (1 app). (Chelsea) FL Cup winner 1965.

Outside-right/centre-forward with blistering speed - he had been a national schoolboy sprint champion. As this was combined with good ball control and marksmanship, he had to be closely watched. Scored 189 goals in his total 462 League matches (and 12 substitutions). On returning to Norfolk from Ireland had a Horsford milk round as well as keeping a stake in soccer management.

BRIDGETT, G(eorge) Arthur
(Sunderland, 1905-09, 11)
Born Forsbrook, Staffs. 1882 .
Died 1954.
1905: 5ft. 8$^1/_2$ins.; 11st. 8lbs.
Career: Potteries schoolboy football; Burslem Park; Trentham; Stoke October 1902; Sunderland January 1903; South Shields as player/manager May 1912, later becoming North Shields manager. After a long absence from playing assisted Port Vale during the 1923/24 season when in his forties. Other honours: Football League (2 apps).

Outside-left. 'Fleet of foot and accurate with his centres, Bridgett shows a marked unselfishness; as a consequence he is popular with the centre-forward of any team in which he may be playing,' an Edwardian cigarette-card tells us. He turned out to be notably durable as well, in his 1923/24 come-back making 14 Second Division appearances for Port Vale in which he netted 7 goals. Like Harold Fleming (q.v.) had religious objections to playing on Christmas Days and Good Fridays.

BRINDLE,Thomas
(Darwen, 1880, 2)
Born Darwen, Lancs. 1861. Died 15 April 1905.

Career: Junior football to Darwen. In the mid-1880s assisted Blackburn Olympic.
Left-back. Darwen had an outstanding line-up in Brindle's time. In 1879/80 the club was the first to win the coveted Lancashire Cup, defeating Blackburn Rovers by 3-0. They had two England caps besides Brindle in Marshall and Tot Rostron, and a Scot who later became a famous Blackburn Rover (Fergie Suter). Brindle was a powerful, strong-kicking back and a real work horse.('Strong back; kicks well,' said Alcock tersely).

BRITTLETON, J(ohn) Thomas
(Sheffield Wednesday, 1912-14, 5)

Born Winsford, Cheshire, 23 April, 1882.
Died 22 February 1955.
1913: 5ft. 9$^{3}/_{4}$ins.: 12st.

Career: Winsford Juniors 1896; Winsford Celtic; Winsford United; Stockport County 1902; Sheffield Wednesday September 1904; Stoke May 1920; Winsford United again as player/coach March 1925. Other honours: Football League (2 apps). (Sheffield W) FA Cup winner 1907.

Right-half came to be recognised as Tom's position although actually he was very versatile. Joining Stockport County as an outside-right, this club moved him to inside and he could also turn in a fair display at full-back. Above all, though, splendidly consistent - and over a remarkable period, not moving out of the League scene until almost 43. His son, Tom jnr., was on Villa's books between the Wars.

BRITTON, Clifford Samuel
Everton, 1935-37, 9)
Born Hanham, Bristol, 29 August 1909.
Died 1 December 1975.
1935: 5ft. 10$^{1}/_{2}$ins.; 11st.

Career: Hanham Athletic; Hanham United Methodists; Bristol St George's; Bristol Rovers as an amateur 1926, turning professional cs 1928; Everton June 1930 (4-figure fee) (guest player for Aldershot during WW2); retired October 1945 on appointment as Burnley manager; Everton manager September 1948-February 1956; Preston North End manager August 1956-April 1961; Hull City manager July 1961 until appointed that club's General manager November 1969; retired October 1971. Other honours: England wartime international (10 apps). Football League (4 Apps). (Everton) FA Cup winner 1933.

Right-half with classical skills, a natural member of Goodison's school of science whose distribution stood comparison with the best. Turned out too to have a talent for management that was particularly evident in his first appointment, steering Burnley into the First Division and a Wembley Cup final. He was a member of the FA's touring party to South Africa in 1939, thrice appearing against the country's representative side.

BROADBENT Peter Frank
(Wolverhampton Wanderers, 1958-60, 7)
Born Elvington, Kent, 15 May 1933
1959: 5ft. 9$^{1}/_{2}$ins.; 11st. 6lbs.

Career: Kent County Schools; Dover; Brentford as an amateur 1949/50 season, turning professional May 1950; Wolverhampton Wanderers February 1951 (£9000); Shrewsbury Town January 1965 (£8000); Aston Villa October 1966 (£7500); Stockport County October 1969; Bromsgrove Rovers November 1970; retired November 1971. Other honours: England 'B' international (1 app). England Under-23 international (1 app). Football

League (2 apps).(Wolves) FL champions 1954, 1958, 1959. FA Cup winner 1960.

Inside-forward. Stylish, brainy and wonderful schemer of openings for attacking colleagues. In a long career grossed 628 League appearances, scoring 138 goals himself. Wolves paid a then substantial fee for the 17-year-old Broadbent, to be handsomely rewarded with 14 years exceptional service. Became proprietor of a Halesowen children's wear shop.

BROADIS Ivan Arthur ("Ivor")
(Manchester City and Newcastle United, 1952-54, 14)
Born Isle of Dogs, Poplar, London, 18 December 1922.
1950: 5ft. 9ins.; 11st.

Career: Finchley; Northfleet (as an amateur assisted Tottenham Hotspur and Millwall during WW2); Carlisle United as player/manager. August 1946; Sunderland January 1949 (£18,000, a record fee to be received by a Northern Section club); Manchester City October 1951 (£20,000); Newcastle United October 1953 (£17,000); Carlisle United again (as player/coach) July 1955 (£3500); Queen of the South June 1959, retiring from playing 1960, coach to 1962. Other honours: Football League (3 apps).

Inside-forward possessing a rich creative vein, speed and a shot of substantial force. Commanded several transfer fees high by 1950s levels and, at 23, the youngest League club manager (and very possibly the youngest ever). A sports journalist based in Carlisle after leaving the game.

BROCKBANK John
Cambridge University, 1873, 1)
Born Whitehaven, Cumberland, 22 August 1848. Died 29 January 1904.

Career: Shrewsbury School; Cambridge University (Blue 1874-75). Represented London 1872-74.

Forward. 'In spite of a weak knee proved himself a most useful forward; is quick and dribbles well,' reported Alcock's Annual of 1874. Brockbank, like his contemporary, J P Hawtry (q.v.), was an actor by profession. A good cricketer at club level too.

BRODIE John Brant
(Wolverhampton Wanderers, 1889-91, 3)
Born Wightwick, Wolverhampton, 1862 Died 16 February 1925.
1889: 5ft. 9ins.; 12st. 3lbs.

Career: St. Luke's School, Blackenhall; founder member of Wolverhampton Wanderers 1877 (Saltley College 1880-82); retired cs 1891 after also assisting Bootle. Became a referee in 1892. A Wolverhampton Wanderers director from June 1913 onwards. Other honour: (Wolves) FA Cup finalist 1889.

Centre-forward adaptable enough to figure at wing-half and elsewhere in the attack as well. Perhaps best as a centre, his penetration being of particular value there. Noted for his exemplary conduct ('...one of the finest gentleman players in the Kingdom'). A pupil teacher after leaving Saltley College, he finished his scholastic career as a headmaster.

BROMILOW Thomas George
(Liverpool, 1921-26, 5)
Born Liverpool, 7 October 1894. Died 4 March 1959.
1922: 5ft. 9ins.; 11st. 7lbs.

Career: United West Dingle Presbyterian Club; Army football; Liverpool FC 1919; retired May 1930. Coach in Amsterdam cs 1931; Burnley manager October 1932; Crystal Palace manager July 1935-June 1936 and again from December 1936; Leicester City manager July 1939-May 1945; Newport County manager May 1946-January 1950; Leicester City scout July 1950 to his death. Other honours: Football League (6 apps). (Liverpool) FL champions 1922, 1923.

Left-half of artistic inclination who, as a 1920s scribe wrote, '...makes his passes in the way a forward likes to receive them.' A master of constructive play, Tom was not 'spotted' but asked the Anfield club for a trial, becoming an automatic first-team choice for a decade. Brother-in-law of Theo Kelly, for many years Everton's secretary and manager.

BROMLEY-DAVENPORT (General Sir) William
(Old Etonians, 1884, 2)
Born London, 21 January 1862. Died 6 February 1949.

Career: Eton College (XI 1881); Oxford University (Blue 1884); Old Etonians.

Centre-forward. At the time of his England appearances summed up as 'a hard working centre, fast and a good shot at goal; needs to pass a little more at times.' Outside the game had two distinguished careers. As a soldier won DSO in the Boer War; in the Great War was a Brigadier serving in Egypt 1916 and, 1917, assistant Director of Labour in France, As a politician he was MP for Macclesfield 1886-1906 during which period he was Financial Secretary to the War Office 1903-05. Awarded the KCB 1924. Lord Lieutenant of Cheshire 1920-49.

BROOK Eric Fred
(Manchester City, 1930-38, 18)
Born Mexborough, Yorks. 27 November 1907. Died 29 March 1965.
1933: 5ft. $6^3/_4$ins.; 11st. 6lbs.

Career: Mexborough Schools; Oxford Road YMCA; Swinton Prims; Mexborough FC; Dearne Valley Old Boys; Wath Athletic, Barnsley February 1926 (£200); Manchester City March 1928 (£4000 including Fred Tilson, q.v.); retired during WW2. Other honours: Football League (7 apps). (Man. City) FL champions 1937. FA Cup winner 1934; finalist 1933.

Outside-left. An ebullient character packing a shot of explosive velocity and giving rein to a wandering bent. Was liable to bob up anywhere, this availableness bringing him a notable goals haul – 158 in 453 League outings for Manchester City before war intervened. Eric settled in Manchester, working latterly as a crane driver.

BROOKING Trevor D.
(West Ham United, 1974-82, 47)
Born Barking, Essex, 2 October 1948.
1978: 6ft. $0^1/_2$in.; 13st. 8lbs.

Career: Ilford Schools, Essex Schools; London Schools; West Ham United apprentice July 1965, turning professional May 1966; retired May 1984. Other honours: England schoolboy international. England Youth international. England Under-23 international (1 app). Football League (1 app). (WHU) European Cup Winners' Cup finalist 1976. FL Div.2 champions 1981 FA Cup winner 1975, 1980. FL Cup finalist 1981.

Midfield. An ornament to the game for many a season: poised, graceful and with a nonchalant mastery in all aspects of his craft. The only flaw – and that minor – was a certain deficiency of killing pace at times that allowed opponents to renew a challenge. In later years has been a respected commentator in BBC radio and TV football broadcasts.

BROOKS John
(Tottenham Hotspur, 1957, 3)
Born Reading, 23 December 1931.
1957: 5ft. $9^1/_2$ins.; 11st. 9lbs.

Career: Coley Boys Club; Reading amateur February 1949, turning professional April 1949; Tottenham Hotspur February 1953 (for a fee and 2 players); Chelsea December 1959 (in exchange for another player); Brentford September 1961 (£5000); Crystal Palace January 1964; Stevenage Town October 1964, subsequently assisting Knebworth FC (Herts League). Other honour: (Brentford) FL Div. 4 champions 1963.

Inside-forward, adroit skilful and adept at creating scoring opportunity. Flawed his displays sometimes by not being sufficiently assertive. Scored 94 times in his aggregate 348 League outings. Father of Shaun Brooks, England schoolboy and Youth international, later of Palace and Orient. After leaving the first-class game Johnny became a broker's messenger in the city.

BROOME Frank Henry
(Aston Villa, 1938-39, 7)
Born Berkhamsted, Herts, 11 June 1915
1938: 5ft 7ins.; 9st. 8lbs.

Career: Berkhamsted schoolboy football; Boxmoor United; Berkhamsted Town; Aston Villa November 1934 (guest player for Wolves during WW2) Derby County September 1946; Notts County October 1949 (in exchange for another player); Brentford July 1953; Crewe Alexandra October 1953; Shelbourne February 1955. Notts County assistant trainer cs 1955, acting manager January-May 1957, then assistant manager to December 1957; Exeter City manager/coach January 1958; Southend United manager May-December 1960; Bankstown (NSW) manager/coach July 1961-October 1962; Corinthians (Sydney) manager/coach later in 1962; Melita Eagles (Sydney) part-time coach early 1967; Exeter City manager again April 1967-February 1969, then briefly coached in the Middle East. Other honours: (Villa) FL Div.2 champions 1938. (Notts Co) FL Div 3 (South) champions 1950.

Forward. Of significant versatality. Usually centre or outside-right in club games, he occupied every attack berth except inside-left for England. Was turned down as 'too small' by both Spurs and Arsenal, yet his tremendous speed and shooting prowess graced the professional scene well into his 40th year.

BROWN Anthony ('Bomber')
(West Bromwich Albion, 1971, 1)
Born Oldham, 3 October 1945
1971: 5ft. 6$^1/_2$ins.; 11st. 6lbs.

Career: Manchester Schools; Lancashire Schools; West Bromwich Albion apprentice April 1961, turning professional October 1963 (assisted New England Teaman and Jacksonville Teamen, USA during 1980 and '81'); Torquay United October 1981 (£6000)-1983; Stafford Rangers. West Bromwich Albion coach 1984-86. Other honours: Football League (2 apps) (WBA) FA Cup winner 1968. FL Cup winner 1966; finalist 1967, 1970.

Forward. Appropriately nicknamed, packing a particularly deadly right-foot shot – holder of Albion's League goals record (218) as well as that for League appearances (574). A penalty king too. Gave wonderful service at the Hawthorns, always wholehearted and equally capable in several positions. All told played 819 times in the Albion first team (312 goals)

BROWN Arthur ('Digger')
(Aston Villa, 1882, 3)
Born Birmingham. 1859. Died 1 July 1909.

Career: Florence FC (Aston); Aston Unity; Aston Villa 1881, in the mid-1880s had brief connections with Birmingham St George's and Birmingham Excelsior, returning to Villa October 1884 and continuing to play for the club until circa 1887.

Inside-right. Short and sturdy in build and reputedly 'a dour little man'. A rare opportunist, his opportunism benefiting greatly from accurate marksmanship. Able, it was said, to keep clean when performing on the muddiest of pitches (one wonders how this could be, given full involvement!). Jointly with Howard Vaughton, was Villa's first internationalist. Elder brother of Albert Brown of Villa's 1887 FA cup winning team.

BROWN Arthur Samuel
(Sheffield United, 1904-06, 2)
Born Gainsborough, Lincs. 6 April 1885. Died 27 June 1944.
1907: 5ft. 9ins.; 11st. 12lbs.

Career: Gainsborough Church Lads Brigade; Gainsborough Trintity early in 1902, originally as an amateur; Sheffield United cs 1902 (£350); Sunderland June 1908 (£1000); Fulham October 1910; Middlesbrough cs 1912-1913.

Centre-forward. Very much a boy prodigy as he was capped as a teenager and reckoned the youngest so honoured up to then. He was an outstanding opportunist, a quality enhanced by fine on-the-target shooting. Brown's career appeared to flag somewhat later, being actually disengaged when signed by Fulham. In 1907 his vocation was given as master builders' merchant and monumental mason.

BROWN George
Huddersfield Town and Aston Villa, 1927-33, 9)
Born Mickley, Northumberland, 22 June 1903. Died 10 June 1948.
1927: 5ft. 10½ins.' 11st. 2lbs.

Career: Mickley Colliery (Northern Alliance); Huddersfield Town May 1921; Aston Villa August 1929 (£5000); Burnley October 1934 (£1400); Leeds United September 1935 (£3100); Darlington as player/manager October 1936-October 1938. Other honours: Football League (3 apps) (H'field T) FL champions 1924, 1925,1926. FA Cup finalist 1928.

Inside-right/centre-forward and equally potent in both – skilful in his dribbling, possessor of a hard shot and quick to size up an opening. On leaving the game he was employed as a licensee in Birmingham. Cousin of Joe Spence (Manchester United and England).

BROWN James
(Blackburn Rovers, 1881-85, 5)
Born Blackburn, 31 July 1862. Died 4 July 1922.
1884: 5ft. 5½ins.; 9st. 10lbs.

Career: Blackburn schoolboy football; Mintholme College, Blackburn; Blackburn Law Club; Blackburn Rovers August 1879-89, playing no football subsequently. Other honours: (Blackburn R) FA Cup winner 1884, 1885, 1886; finalist 1882.

Centre-forward. Capable of taking other forward positions (e.g. he was on the left-wing for the 1884 cup final). Reckoned by many to be unique, a view borne out by an early Rovers historian. 'Brown's dribbling was so wonderful that his admirers were in the habit of saying "the ball must be tied to his bootlaces".' He was a brilliant individualist. Was employed as a solicitor's managing clerk.

BROWN John Henry
(Sheffield Wednesday, 1927-30, 6)
Born Hodthorpe, Derbys. 19 March 1899. Died 10 April 1962.
1926: 5ft. 10½ins.; 12st. 4lbs.

Career: Manton Colliery; Worksop Town 1919; Sheffield Wednesday February 1923; Hartlepools United September 1937 but, after making 1 League appearance, was released after a fortnight. Other honours: Football League (2 apps). (Wednesday) FL champions 1929, 1930. FL Div. 2

champions 1926. FA Cup winner 1935.

Goalkeeper. The sound, efficient type and utterly reliable. Signed by Wednesday shortly after a marvellous showing in a cup-tie at Tottenham when Worksop forced a sensational draw. Brown, a one-time collier, had played centre-forward as a junior, becoming a goalkeeper by chance. Made 465 League appearances for the owls. Had a sweet shop in Sheffield.

BROWN Kenneth
(West Ham United, 1960, 1)
Born Forest Gate, London, 16 February 1934.
1960: 6ft..; 13st. 1lb.

Career: Dagenham Schools; Neville United (Dagenham League); West Ham United October 1951; Torquay United May 1967; Hereford United cs 1969; Bournemouth and Boscombe Athletic trainer/coach June 1970; Norwich City assistant manager June 1970, manager October 1980 to November 1987. Other honours: (WHU) European Cup Winners; Cup, winner 1965. FL Div.2 champions 1958. FA Cup winner 1964. FL Cup finalist 1966.

Centre-half. Quiet and super-efficient ('very steady, constructive and seldom out of position,' as one writer recorded). Has brought the same quiet, capable quality into management, Norwich City having gained a Second Division championship and won a League Cup under his benevolent guidance.

BROWN William
(West Ham United, 1924,1)
Born Fence Houses, Co Durham, 22 August 1899. Died January 1985.
1923: 5ft. 7$^1/_2$ins.; 11st. 6lbs.

Career: Hetton FC (Durham); West Ham United during the 1920/21 season; Chelsea February 1924; Fulham May 1929; Stockport County July 1930; Hartlepools United September 1931. Other honour: (WHU) FA Cup finalist 1923.

Inside-right was his recognised berth in senior soccer after being something of a multi-positional player as a junior. Mainly notable for fine ball control, he did not score prolifically, making openings for the likes of Victor Watson (q.v.) Became a baths superintendent at Easington Colliery in his native North-East.

BRUTON John
(Burnley, 1928-29, 3)
Born Westhoughton nr. Bolton, 21 November 1903. Died 13 March 1986.
1929: 5ft. 8$^1/_2$ins.; 10st. 6lbs.

Career: Westhoughton Sunday School League football; Hindley Green (Lancs. Alliance) (Wigan Borough on amateur forms); Horwich RMI 1924/25; Burnley March 1925 (£125) Blackburn Rovers December 1929 (£6500); retired during WW2. Blackburn Rovers assistant secretary September 1947 and then club manager December 1947-May 1949; Bournemouth and Boscombe Athletic manager March 1950-March 1956; he then left full time involvement with football but was a part-time scout for Blackburn (appointed cs 1961) and also had spells scouting for Bournemouth and Portsmouth. Other honours: Football League (2 apps).

Outside-right. Exceptionally fast but his easy running action sometimes deluded opponents unaware of the fact. Stylish as well, while his ball control was exemplary. In an aggregate 491 League games he scored 150 goals. Jack worked as a miner prior to taking up the game professionally and for a lamp company after leaving the Bournemouth managership.

BRYANT, William Ingram
(Clapton, 1925, 1)

Born Ghent, Belgium, 1 March 1899. Died 21 January 1986.
1927: 6ft. 1in.; 12st.

Career: St Olave's Grammar School, Chelmsford; Clapton; Millwall August 1925; Clapton again May 1931; retired cs 1933. Other honours: England amateur international (7 apps). (Clapton) FA Amateur Cup winner 1924, 1925. (Millwall) FL Div. 3 (South) champions 1928.

Centre-half with service at wing-half (e.g. in the above Amateur Cup finals). It was, however, at pivot that he made a name as one of the leading inter-war amateurs. Ideally proportioned for a 'stopper' but had strong attacking inclination, scoring a dozen during Millwall's 1928 championship campaign and 30 altogether in 132 League outings with the Lions. Was later a football reporter for The Sunday Referee and a director of a wholesale seed company.

BUCHAN, Charles Murray
(Sunderland, 1913-24, 6)
Born Plumstead, 22 September 1891. Died 25 June 1960.
1921: 6ft. 1in.; 12st. 1lb.

Career: Woolwich schoolboy and junior football; Woolwich Polytechnic (signed as amateur for Woolwich Arsenal December 1908); Northfleet November 1909; Leyton as a professional March 1910; Sunderland March 1911 (£1250); Arsenal July 1925 (£4100, a fee boosted by the arrangements that £100 be paid for every goal scored during his first Highbury season); retired May 1928. Other honours: England 'Victory' international 1919 (1 app). Football League (10 apps). (Sunderland) FL champions 1913. FA Cup finalist 1913. (Arsenal) FA Cup finalist 1927.

Inside-right, sometimes centre-forward. A famous player reckoned by many the finest inside-forward of his day. Buchan was certainly masterly in every aspect, particularly with the glancing header. His subtleties were such as to bewilder colleagues as well as opponents, and this factor was said to have limited his England appearances. Went into journalism in 1928 as football and golf correspondent of the 'Daily News' and, on that paper's amalgamation, the 'News-Chronicle'. He was also a soccer commentator on BBC Radio. In 1951 became editor of the newly-launched 'Football Monthly', a magazine still in existence 38 years later. Played cricket for Durham in 1920. Wrote a most interesting book, 'A Lifetime in Football' (Phoenix House, 1955).

BUCHANAN, W. S.
(Clapham Rovers, 1876, 1)

Career: Clapham Rovers; Barnes; also represented Surrey.

Forward. Lightly built but had plenty of speed and dribbled well, though with a tendency to over-run the ball. Had possibly left Clapham Rovers by the time of the

club's FA Cup final appearances (1879 and '80).
NOTE: The player is almost certainly Walter Scott Buchanan, born Hornsey 1 June 1855. Walter Scott Buchanan died at Hammersmith on November 11, 1926.

BUCKLEY, (Major) Franklin Charles
(Derby County, 1914, 1)
Born Urmston, Manchester, 9 November 1882. Died 22 December 1964.
1912: 5ft. 11ins.; 13st. 7lbs.

Career: Junior football to Aston Villa April 1903; Brighton & Hove Albion cs 1905; Manchester United June 1906; Manchester City September 1907; Birmingham July 1909; Derby County May 1911; Bradford City May 1914; retired during WW1 because of war wounds. Norwich City manager March 1919-1920; Blackpool manager June 1923; Wolverhampton Wanderers secretary/manager May 1927; Notts County manager March 1944; Hull City manager May 1946; Leeds United manager May 1948; Walsall manager April 1953 to his retirement, June 1955. Other honour: (Derby Co) FL Div. 2 champions 1912.

Centre-half. Vigorous, attack-minded, a doughty tackler and an extremely hard grafter. Much more renowned, of course, as Major Buckley, the Wolves manager. He lifted that club from comparative obscurity to front rank status. His constant stream of discovered talent, myriad transfer deals and unusual innovations were always in the 'Thirties headlines. Commanded the famous Footballers Battn. of the Middlesex Rgt. and badly wounded on the Somme in August 1916. Brother of C S Buckley (Villa player and eventually club chairman), his partner at one time in a Redditch farm.

BULLOCK, Frederick Edwin
(Huddersfield Town, 1921, 1)
Born Hounslow, Middlesex, 1886. Died 15 November 1922.
1921: 5ft. 9ins.; 11st. 7lbs.

Career: Isleworth Schools; Hounslow Town; Ilford cs 1909; Huddersfield Town as an amateur December 1910, shortly afterwards turning professional; retired cs 1922. Represented Middlesex. Other honours: England amateur international (1 app). (H'field T) FA Cup finalist 1920.

Left-back whose work brought him to the North country and so to the ranks of Huddersfield Town. He proved a fine club man at Leeds Road, a reliable back sound in tackling and kicking. In the brief period between retirement and his passing Bullock was a licensee in Huddersfield.

BULLOCK, Norman
(Bury, 1923-27, 3)
Born Monkton, Manchester, 8 September 1900. Died 27 October 1970.
1925: 5ft. $8^1/_2$ins.; 11st. 4lbs.

Career: Salford Schools; Broughton St John's; Sedgley Park (Prestwich); Bury as an amateur 1920, turning professional February 1921, player/manager cs 1934 retiring from playing a year later; Chesterfield secretary/manager June 1938; Bury manager again July 1945; Leicester City manager December 1949-February 1955. Other honour: Football League (1 app).

Centre-forward, from circa 1928 taking other positions: inside-right, right- and centre-half. But it was leading Bury's attack that made his reputation with his quickness, stamina and power shooting. A great club man, Norman's aggregate 506 League appearances is still a Shakers' record. A competent administrator too, his 21 years in management being continuous and unbroken. (Most unusual!). Once an analytical chemist.

BURGESS, Harry
(Sheffield Wednesday, 1931, 4)
Born Alderley Edge, Cheshire, 20 August 1904.
1931: 5ft. 8ins.; 11st. 7lbs.

Career: Alderley Edge FC; signed for Stockport County who sent him to Sandbach Ramblers for development, he rejoined Stockport early in 1926; Sheffield Wednesday June 1929; Chelsea March 1935; retired during WW2. Other honour: (Wednesday) FL champions 1930.

Inside-forward. A clever dribbler, solidly built and having the solid virtue of scoring on his own account in addition to backing up others. In an aggregate peacetime League match total of 473 matches, he found the net on 173 occasions. A penalty specialist when at Stamford Bridge.

BURGESS, Herbert
(Manchester City, 1904-06, 4)
Born Openshaw, Manchester, 1883. Died 1954.
1904: 5ft. $4^3/_4$ins.; 11st. 4lbs.

Career: Assisted several junior clubs in the Manchester area – St. Francis, Gorton, Openshaw United and Moss Side – before joining Glossop in 1900; Manchester City July 1903; Manchester United January 1907 (£1400 including 4 other players); retired 1910. Subsequently coached in Spain, Italy and Hungary. In August 1921 was reported to be in Budapest holding the appointment of trainer to the Hungarian League champions. Other honours: Football League (7 apps). (Man. City) FA Cup winner 1904. (Man. Utd) FL champions 1908.

Left-back with experience on the opposite flank – he had been converted to full-back from wing-half by Glossop. Considered by one source to be the shortest back ever to play for England (which seems highly possible). Burgess, despite his lack of height, had all the required qualities: a good tackle, anticipation and accuracy in the placing of clearances.

BURNUP, Cuthbert James
(Cambridge University, 1896, 1)

Born Blackheath, Kent, 21 November 1875. Died 5 April 1960.

Career: Malvern College (XI 1893); Cambridge University (Blue 1895-98 inclusive, being captain in 1897); Old Malvernians; Corinthians 1895-1901.

Outside-left. Though having individual touches, these were not indulged to the detriment of team work. For Burnup was a whole-hearted player with belief in combination. He had dribbling skills and pace, too, and was a fair shot. In the amateur tradition of the time he also excelled at other games, being captain of cricket and racquets at Malvern. He proved a notable cricketer gaining his Blue at Cambridge and assisting Kent 1896-1907. Worked in London as a stockbroker and, later, in commerce there.

BURROWS, Horace
(Sheffield Wednesday, 1934-35, 3)
Born Sutton-in-Ashfield, Notts. 11 March 1910. Died 22 March 1969.
1935: 5ft. 9ins.; 11st. 7lbs.

Career: Notts Schools; Sutton Junction; Coventry City February 1930; Mansfield Town May 1930; Sheffield Wednesday May 1931 (£350); retired during WW2. Other honour: (Wednesday) FA Cup winner 1935.

Left-half able to take the right flank too. His crisp tackling, distribution and consistency made him a fine successor to Billy Marsden, another England cap, who had to retire injured. Horace later ran a sports outfitting business at his native Sutton-in-Ashfield, and his son, Adrian, sampled League action with Mansfield and Northampton Town 1979-84 before joining Plymouth Argyle.

BURTON, Frank Ernest
(Nottingham Forest, 1889, 1)
Born Nottingham, 18 March 1865. Died 10 February 1948.

Career: Nottingham High School; Notts County October 1886-October 1887; Nottingham Forest November 1887-November 1891.

Inside-right with a deal of experience on the extreme right too. Keen in performance, enthusiastically instigating raids into enemy territory. Became in turn manager, managing-director and chairman of Joseph Burton & Sons Ltd. This was a grocery chain founded by his father which operated in the East Midlands.

BURY, Lindsay
(Old Etonians, 1877-79, 2)
Born Withington, Manchester, 9 July 1857. Died 30 October 1935.

Career: Eton College (XI 1875-76); Cambridge University (Blue 1877-78); Old Etonians. Served on the FA Committee 1878. Other honour: (Old Etonians) FA Cup winner 1879.

Full-back adept on both flanks and reckoned the strongest of his period. Very certain in his kicking and, moreover, the kicks were well judged as regards length. A triple Blue: soccer, cricket (1877) and athletics (1878-9-80) specialising in throwing the hammer and sprints. In 1877 played once for Hampshire CCC. Later an orange planter in Florida.

BUTCHER, Terence Ian
(Ipswich Town and Rangers, 1980-88, 54)
Born Singapore, 28 December 1958.
1984: 6ft. 4ins.; 14st. 5lbs.

Career: Lowestoft Schools; Ipswich Town August 1976; Rangers August 1986 (£725,000, an Ipswich record). Other honours: England 'B' international. England Under-21 international (7 apps). (Ipswich) UEFA Cup winner 1981. (Rangers) Scottish League champions 1987. Scottish League Cup winner 1987.

Central defender. A giant of a man not unpredictably known as 'Big Tel' up in Glasgow, where he has earned fresh kudos skippering a resurgent Rangers side. Terry is a tremendous competitor besides being skilled, and opponents find him most difficult to outwit. Favours the left flank, the reason said to be a scalded right foot as a youngster.

BUTLER, John Dennis
(Arsenal, 1925, 1)
Born Colombo, Ceylon, 14 August 1894. Died 5 January 1961.
1927: 5ft. 11$^{1}/_{2}$ins.; 11st. 5lbs.

Career: West London Schools; Fulham on amateur forms 1913, playing with their Thursday XI: Dartford as a professional during the 1913/14 season; Arsenal May 1914; Torquay United May 1930-1932.

Coach to Daring FC, Brussels, 1932-39; Leicester City coach October 1940-1946 and briefly coached in Copenhagen before appointment as Torquay United manager June 1946; Crystal Palace manager cs 1947; Daring FC manager May 1949; Colchester United manager June 1953-January 1955. Other honour: (Arsenal) FA Cup finalist 1927.

Centre-half. Brought up in London and originally played inside-right and centre-forward before conversion to a pivot. Tall and willowy in build, which aided his heading. And a critic of the period said Jack was '. . . exceptionally quick to recover and had excellent 'feeding' ideas.'

BUTLER, William

(Bolton Wanderers, 1924, 1)
Born Atherton nr. Bolton, 27 March 1900. Died 11 July 1966.
1923: 5ft. 7ins.; 10st. 10lbs.

Career: Howe Bridge FC; Army football during WW1; Atherton Collieries; Bolton Wanderers May 1921; Reading June 1933; retired May 1935. Reading manager August 1935-February 1939; Guildford City manager June 1939 and throughout the War; Torquay United manager cs 1945-May 1946 when he emigrated to South Africa. There he managed Johannesburg Rangers and coached for the Pietermaritzburg & District FA. Subsequently went to Rhodesia and was a coach to that country's FA. Other honours: (Bolton W) FA Cup winner 1923, 1926, 1929.

Outside-right. Played centre-forward for the Army and was signed by Bolton for that position. Eventually, though, thought too small for League exposure and when Andy Donaldson, the Scotland right-winger, moved to Sunderland, Butler was tried there with excellent results. His great pace and improved ball control led to 11 seasons as first choice at Burnden Park (and, incidentally, to a trio of Cup winners' medals). Said to be the League's then youngest manager on his Reading appointment.

BYRNE, Gerald

(Liverpool, 1963-66, 2)
Born Liverpool, 29 August, 1938.
1965: 5ft. 10ins.; 12st. 6lbs.

Career: Liverpool schoolboy football; Liverpool FC on amateur forms, turning professional August 1955; retired through injury December 1969 and later served on Liverpool's coaching staff. Other honours: England Under-23 international (1 app). (Liverpool) European Cup Winners' Cup finalist 1966. FL champions 1964, 1966. FL Div. 2 champions 1962. FA Cup winner 1965.

Right/left-back whose career blossomed after Bill Shankly took over at Anfield, developing into a thoughtful, ball playing defender and an ideal partner for Chris Lawler. A very brave one also, famously playing 117 minutes of the 1965 'extra-time' Cup final with a broken collar bone. An extraordinary feat.

BYRNE, John J.

(Crystal Palace and West Ham United, 1962-65, 11)
Born West Horsley, Surrey, 13 May 1939.
1964: 5ft. $8^1/_2$ins.; 11st. 7lbs.

Career: Epsom Town; Guildford City Youth; Crystal Palace amateur 1955, turning professional May 1956; West Ham United March 1962 (£58,000 and another player, a then record fee between English clubss); Crystal Palace again February 1967 (£45,000); Fulham March 1968 (£18,000); Durban City, South Africa, May 1969, retiring circa 1971 and becoming Durban City's manager. Other honours: England Youth international. England Under-23 international (7 apps). Football League (4 apps). (WHU) FA Cup winner 1964. FL Cup finalist 1966.

Inside-right/centre-forward. A star of the 'Sixties, a clever striker (dubbed 'the English Di Stefano' by his West Ham manager) and a dangerous one. Netted 171 goals in an aggregate 410 League matches (and 2 substitutions). Known as 'Budgie' at Upton Park. Johnny was also employed as a tyre company representative while with Durban City.

BYRNE, Roger William

(Manchester United, 1954-58, 33)
Born Manchester, 8 February 1929. died in the Munich air crash, 6 February 1958.
1950: 5ft. 9ins.; 11st. 7lbs.

Career: Manchester schools football; Ryder Brow Boys Club (Gorton, Manchester); Manchester United March 1949. Other honours: England 'B' international (3 apps).

Football League (6 apps). (Man. Utd) FL champions 1952, 1956, 1957. FA Cup finalist 1957.

Left-back after early experience at outside-left. His exceptional speed, revealed as a winger, was no less important in defence and he became one of the fleetest full-backs ever. Had ball control too and was a reliable penalty-taker. Succeeded Johnny Carey as United's skipper, leading the side to two championships and a Wembley final.

CALLAGHAN, Ian Robert
(Liverpool, 1966-78, 4)
Born Liverpool, 10 April 1942.
1972: 5ft. 7ins.; 11st. 1lb.

Career: Liverpool Schools; Liverpool FC ground staff 1957, turning professional March 1960; Swansea City September 1978-January 1981, later that season assisting Cork United and Soudifjord (Norway); Crewe Alexandra October 1981-February 1982. Other honours: England Under-23 international (4 apps). Football League (2 apps). (Liverpool) European Cup winner 1977. European Cup Winners' Cup finalist 1966. EUFA Cup winner 1973, 1976. FL champions 1964, 1966, 1973, 1976, 1977. FL Div. 2 champions 1962. FA Cup winner 1965, 1974; Finalist 1971, 1977 (sub). FL Cup finalist 1978.

Midfield after a decade or so of senior football at outside-right – he had been converted to the latter from wing-half in his early Anfield days. 'A thinking player of honest endeavour and at all times a gentleman . . .' recorded a local sports writer. And an outfield player of extraordinary durability: over 20 years in the Football League and holder of the Reds' appearance record (over 840 senior games). The Football Writers' 'Player of the Year' 1974 and awarded the MBE in 1975. In 1981 opened a restaurant at Rainford, Lancs.

CALVEY, John
(Nottingham Forest, 1902, 1)
Born South Bank, Middlesbrough, 23 June 1875. Died January 1937.
1902: 5ft. 9ins.; 12st. 12lbs.

Career: South Bank Juniors; Millwall Athletic 1895/96 as a professional; Nottingham Forest May 1899; Millwall Athletic again cs 1904. Other honour: Football League (1 app).

Centre-forward. A proven goal scorer, the player using his muscular frame to good effect. Calvey's spell with Forest was thought to be somewhat disappointing (which seems strange considering both his England cap and inter-league medal were won during City Ground days). Later a dock worker.

CAMPBELL, Austen Fenwick
(Blackburn Rovers and Huddersfield Town, 1929-32, 8)

Born Hamsterley, Co Durham, 5 May 1901. Died 8 September 1981.
1931: 5ft. 9ins.; 11st. 7lbs.

Career: Spen Black & White; Leadgate Park; Coventry City 1919/20; Leadgate Park again June 1921; Blackburn Rovers February 1923; Huddersfield Town September 1929; Hull City November 1935-cs 1936. Other honours: Football League (5 apps). (Blackburn) FA Cup winner 1928. (H'field T) FA Cup finalist 1930.

Left-half. An unflagging half of forceful disposition, strongly into the tackle. Had a liking for occasionally dribbling through himself to test the 'keeper – a dangerous ploy to opponents as Austen could hit a ball tremendously hard. In early working life was a pit boy. Cousin of Alan Brown (Burnley & Football League and subsequent well known club manager).

CAMSELL, George Henry
(Middlesbrough, 1929-36, 9)
Born Framwellgate Moor near Durham, 27 November 1902. Died 7 March 1966.
1930: 5ft. 9ins.; 11st. 12lbs.

Career: Durham chapel team 1921, a few months later joining Esh Winning; Tow Law Town; Durham City as an amateur 1923, turning professional June 1924; Middlesbrough October 1925 (£800); retired from playing during the War serving Middlesbrough as coach, chief scout and (from October 1956) assistant secretary in succession until retiring December 1963. Other honours: Football League (1 app). (Middlesbro') FL Div. 2 champions 1927, 1929.

Centre-forward. One-time pit boy who did not take up soccer seriously until aged 18. A few years later sensationally broke the League scoring record with 59, only 1 fewer than Dixie Dean's all time record. Strongly built, Camsell was hard to shake off and his 1926/27 total was no flash in the pan. In 444 League matches for Durham City and Middlesbrough he notched 344 goals.

CAPES, Arthur John
(Stoke, 1903, 1)
Born Burton-upon-Trent, 23 February 1875. Died 26 February 1945.
1903: 5ft. 8½ins.; 12st. 3lbs.

Career: Burton Wanderers; Nottingham Forest cs 1896; Stoke cs 1902; Bristol City May 1904; Swindon Town cs 1905 – 1906. Other honours: Football League (1 app). (Forest) FA Cup winner 1898.

Inside-left. Had no claims to being a stylist but was a worthy artisan, a good club man and revealed a fair eye for goal chances. For example, he netted (and before half-time) 2 of the 3 goals that sank Derby County in the 1898 cup final. His brother, Adrian also assisted Burton Wanderers and Forest. Arthur was popularly known as 'Sailor'.

CARR, John
(Middlesbrough, 1920-23, 2)
Born South Bank, Middlesbrough, 26 November 1892. Died 10 May 1942.
1921: 5ft. 8ins.; 11st. 8lbs.

Career: South Bank schoolboy and junior football; South Bank FC; Middlesbrough January 1911; Blackpool May 1930; Hartlepools United as player/coach July 1931 and then that club's manager April 1932-April 1935; Tranmere Rovers manager May 1935; Darlington manager October 1938. Other honours: Football League (3 apps). (South Bank) FA Amateur Cup finalist 1910. (Middlesbro') FL Div. 2 champions 1927, 1929.

Outside-right/inside-forward. Versatility was only one of this craftsman's virtues. His subtle skills aided a succession of international attackers at Ayresome Park – Elliott, Andy Wilson, Camsell, Pease et al – in exploiting their goal-scoring proclivities. Jackie came from a noted local footballing family. Two brothers William (1910-24) and George (1919-24) also being 'Boro players, the latter a member also of Leicester's 1925 championship side.

CARR, John
(Newcastle United, 1905-07, 2)
Born Seaton Burn, Northumberland, 1876. Died 17 March 1948.
1910: 5ft. 9½ins.; 12st. 8lbs.

Career: Seaton Burn FC; Newcastle United December 1899; retired 1912 and joined Newcastle's training staff, remaining for 10 years; Blackburn Rovers team manager February 1922 and then their secretary/manager September 1925–December 1926. Other honours: Football League (1 app). (Newcastle) FL champions 1905, 1907. FA Cup winner* 1910; finalist 1905, 1900s. * Played in re-play only.

Left-back. Member of the Newcastle squad that was so outstanding in 1990s Cup and League competition. Carr, an excellent team man, scorned the use of dubious tactics, and was sound and judicious. A good cricketer too, assisting Northumberland besides class club sides in Lancashire and the North-East.

CARR, William Henry
(Sheffield Club, 1875, 1)
Born Sheffield, 1848. Died 22 February 1924.
Career: Besides Sheffield Club he also assisted other clubs in the area – Walkley, Wednesday and Owlerton – and, indeed, at the time of his international, was Secretary of the last-named. Also represented the Sheffield FA.

Goalkeeper. Much respected during the first international decade, as Alcock's Annual of 1874 relates. Carr 'has again and again vindicated his right to the first place among custodians of the goal.' (A delightful phrase, 'custodians of the goal'!) Being tall aided his goalkeeping talents which included composure and the capacity to judge shots. Could perform efficiently in outfield positions too.

CARTER, Horatio Stratton ('Raich')
(Sunderland and Derby County, 1934-47, 13)
Born Hendon, Sunderland, 21 December 1913.
1938: 5ft. 8ins.; 10st. 6lbs.

Career: Sunderland Schools; Whitburn St. Mary's; Esh Winning; Sunderland Forge; Sunderland FC on amateur forms November 1930, turning professional November 1931; Derby County December 1945 (£8000) after being a guest player for that club during WW2; Hull City as player/assistant manager March 1948 (£6000) becoming player/manager the following May, resigning the managership September 1951 and continuing to play until April 1952; Cork Athletic January-May 1953. Leeds United manager May 1953-June 1958; Mansfield Town manager February

1960; Middlesbrough manager January 1963-February 1966. Other honours; England schoolboy international (4 apps). England wartime international (8 apps). Football League (4 apps). (Sunderland) FL champions 1936. FA Cup winner 1937. (Derby Co) FA Cup winner 1946. (Hull City) FL Div. 3 (North) champions 1949. (Cork Ath.) FA of Ireland Cup winner 1953.

Inside-forward among the greatest the game has known. Superb inball control, a powerful marksman and, above all, a master tactician. A fine cricketer, he played for Durham and, in 1946, made 3 appearances for Derbyshire.

CARTER, Joseph Henry
(West Bromwich Albion, 1926-29, 3)
Born Aston, Birmingham, April 1901. Died 21 January 1977.
1930: 5ft. 11ins.; 11st. 4lbs.

Career: Birmingham schoolboy football; Westbourne Celtic (Handsworth League); West Bromwich Albion April 1921 (signed for Sheffield Wednesday February 1936 but deal cancelled 6 days later because of a domestic accident); Tranmere Rovers June 1936; Walsall November 1936; Vono Sports player/manager 1937; retired cs 1940. Other honours: Football League (1 app). (WBA) FA Cup winner 1931; finalist 1935.

Inside-right. Lasted a long while, especially for an inside man. His footballing longevity owed much to a tough wiry frame. A good dribbler – in which connection a fine body swerve was a major contribution – and he supplied his quota to the score sheet. Later a Handsworth licensee.

CATLIN, A(rthur) Edward
(Sheffield Wednesday, 1937, 5)
Born South Bank, Middlesbrough, 11 January 1910.
1935: 5ft. 10ins.; 10st. 10lbs.

Career: Middlesbrough Schools; South Bank FC; Sheffield Wednesday October 1930 (guest player for Charlton Athletic during WW2); retired through injury late in the war. Other honours: Football League (1 app). (Wednesday) FA Cup winner 1935.

Left-back. A worthy successor at Hillsborough to the immaculate Ernie Blenkinsop (q.v.). Ted, of the rather gangling build, put thought into his play: wise in positioning,

tackling well timed with clearances judiciously placed. A knee injury caused a retirement that took place some time after appearing for Wednesday in the League's 1943 wartime North Cup final. Later employed as a licensee.

CHADWICK, Arthur
(Southampton, 1900, 2)
Born Church, Lancs. 1875. Died 21 March 1936
1910: 5ft. 8ins.; 12st.

Career: Church FC; Accrington; Burton Swifts 1895; Southampton cs 1897; Portsmouth May 1901; Northampton Town cs 1904; Accrington again cs 1906; Exeter City cs 1908; retired cs 1910 when appointed the last-named club's manager to December 1922. Reading manager January 1923; Southampton manager October 1925-April 1931. Other honours: (Soton) Southern League champions 1898, 1899, 1901. FA Cup finalist 1900. (Portsmouth) Southern League champions 1902.

Centre-half. A Lancashire player who made his name in the South, an efficient pivot defensively and in attack. Did not relish being 'run at' by dribbling specialists but generally coped. Cousin of the England winger, Edgar Chadwick, he died while watching a match at Exeter City's ground.

CHADWICK, Edgar Wallace
(Everton, 1891-97, 7)
Born Blackburn, 14 June 1869. Died 14

February 1942.
1895: 5ft. 6ins.; 10st. 7lbs.

Career: Little Dots FC 1884; Blackburn Olympic 1886/87; Blackburn Rovers cs 1887; Everton July 1888; Burnley cs 1899; Southampton August 1900; Liverpool cs 1902; Blackpool May 1904; Glossop cs 1905; Darwen cs 1906 afterwards having spells coaching in Germany and Holland. Other honours: Football League (3 apps).(Everton) FL champions 1891.FA Cup finalist 1893, 1897. (Southampton) Southern League champions 1901. FA Cup finalist 1902.
Inside-left, the best known member of a distinguished and numerous footballing family that included his cousin, Arthur Chadwick above. Fast and shrewd, constantly in the action, Edgar and the outside-left, Alfred Milward, probably made up the finest forward wing of the pre-1914 era. Chadwick was a baker by trade.

CHAMBERLAIN, Mark V.
(Stoke City, 1983-85, 8)
Born Stoke-on-Trent, 19 November 1961.
1984: 5ft. 81/2ins.; 10st. 7lbs.
Career: Potteries junior football; Port Vale apprentice, turning professional April 1979; Stoke City August 1982 (£125,000); Sheffield Wednesday September September 1985 (£350,000); Portsmouth August1988 (£200,000). Other honours: England schoolboy international. England Under-21 international (4 apps).
Forward who made a sensational entry into First Division football in 1982, his brilliance earning England selection within a few months. At his best is capable of scintillating performance with his trickery and ball skills but a tendency towards inconsistency is a flaw. Mark's brother, Neville, has also been on the books of Port Vale and Stoke City.

CHAMBERS, Henry ('Smiler')
(Liverpool, 1921-24, 8)
Born Willington Quay, Northumberland, 17 November, 1896. Died 29 June 1949.
1922: 5ft. 9$^1/_2$ins.; 13st.

Career: Tynemouth Schools; Willington United Methodists; North Shields Athletic; Liverpool April 1915 (guest player for Belfast Distillery and Glentoran during WW1); West Bromwich Albion March 1928; Oakengates Town as player/manager July 1929, continuing to play into middle age. Other honours: England schoolboy international (2 apps). Football League (5 apps). (Liverpool) FL champions 1922, 1923.
Centre-forward/inside-left. Who moved to centre-half at West Bromwich. Perhaps best at inside-left. Harry had go-ahead notions backed by a hefty frame, deftly dribbling at speed and employing a left-foot shot of considerable force. The last was even more

deadly because of an ability to swerve the ball. Before turning professional he had been a shipyard worker.

CHANNON, Michael Roger
(Southampton and Manchester City, 1973-78, 46)
Born Orcheston, Wilts, 28 November 1948.
1975: 6ft. $0^1/_2$ins.; 12st. 4lbs.

Career: Amesbury Schools; Wiltshire Schools; Southampton as an associate schoolboy 1963/64, apprentice March 1964, turning professional December 1965; Manchester City July 1977 (£300,000); Southampton again September 1979 (£200,000); Caroline Hills FC (Hong Kong) cs 1982; Newcastle United September 1982; Bristol Rovers October 1982; Norwich City December 1982; Portsmouth August 1985 - 1986. Other honours: England Under-23 international (9 apps). Football League (2 apps). (Soton) FA Cup winner 1976. (Norwich C) FL Cup winner 1985.

Strike forward of footballing longevity whose infectious enthusiasm for the game has refreshed many a jaded palate. Once aptly described as 'a fearless front runner' and a 'power propelled striker who can destroy even the most tight defence when in full flight.' and he is the Saints' champion scorer. Proprietor of butchers', hairdressing and sports goods shops, Mike has often appeared on TV match broadcasts.

CHARLTON, John
(Leeds United, 1965-70, 35)
Born Ashington, Northumberland, 8 May 1935.
1967: 6ft. $1^1/_2$ins.; 12st. $7^1/_2$lbs.

Career: Ashington YMCA; Ashington Welfare; Leeds United Amateur 1950/51, turning professional May 1952; retired May 1973. Middlesbrough manager May 1973-May 1977; Sheffield Wednesday October 1977-May 1983; Middlesbrough caretaker manager briefly March 1984; Newcastle United manager June 1984-1985; manager of the Eire national team, appointed February 7, 1986. Other honours: Football League (6 apps). (Leeds U) Inter-Cities Fairs Cup winner 1968, 1971; finalist 1967. FL champion 1969. FL Div. 2 champions 1964. FA Cup winner 1972; finalist 1965, 1970. FL Cup winner 1968.

Centre-half. Sheet anchor stalwart of England's 1966 World Cup side, brother of Bobby and related to the Milburns, famed Ashington footballing family. Jack arrived late on the international scene and was almost 30 at the time of his first cap. Besides being so fine defensively, he had an attacking flair, scoring 70 goals in the course of 629 League outings (a Leeds' appearance record, by the way). Nicknamed 'The Giraffe' because of a long neck, so useful in aerial clashes. Successful in management too, and outside the game a TV personality through angling programmes. Awarded the OBE in 1974. 'Footballer of the Year' 1967.

CHARLTON, Robert
(Manchester United, 1958-70, 106)
Born Ashington, Northumberland, 11 October 1937.
1964: 5ft. 9ins.; 11st. 2lbs.

Career: East Northumberland Schools; Manchester United amateur January 1953, turning professional October 1954; retired April 1973. Preston North End manager June 1973-August 1975 and played for that club during the whole of season 1974/75. Later a director of Wigan Athletic, running the team in 1983 prior to a new manager being appointed. A Manchester United director from June 1984. Other honours: England schoolboy international. England Youth International. England Under-23 international (6 apps). Football League (8 apps). (Man. Utd) European Cup winner 1968. FL champions 1957, 1965, 1967. FA Cup winner 1963; finalist 1957, 1958.

Centre and inside-forward/outside-left. A world class performer from modern times, universally revered for his sportsmanship. An exponent of dribbling and other attacking skills, he latterly played deep but still scored goals. These were often obtained by long range thunderbolt shooting, as spectacular as any in living memory. In September 1968 signed an 8-year contract with Manchester United, the longest in FL history. Was 'Footballer of the Year' for both England and Europe in 1966. Awarded the OBE in 1969. Worked for a travel firm after leaving Preston, later running a football school. Brother of Jack (above).

CHARNLEY, Raymond O.
(Blackpool, 1963, 1)
Born Lancaster, 29 May 1935.

1963: 5ft. 11$^3/_4$ins.; 11st. 12lbs.

Career: Bolton-le-Sands FC (Preston North End Amateur); Morecambe; Blackpool May 1957 (£750); Preston North End December 1967 (£11,000); Wrexham July 1968 (£10,000); Bradford January 1969 (in exchange for another player); Morcambe again cs 1970.

Centre-forward. Thrustful and fast moving leader, his admirable physique aiding performance. Returned the useful figure of 217 goals in an aggregate 464 League games (and 1 substitution). The major contribution, of course, came from the Blackpool decade, the return there 193 goals in 363 appearances.

CHARSLEY, Charles Christopher
(Small Heath, 1893, 1)
Born Leicester, 7 November 1864. Died 10 January 1945.
1891: 5ft. 11$^1/_4$ins.

Career: Stafford schoolboy football; Stafford Town 1881; Stafford Rangers (during which spell he was a guest player for Aston Villa); Small Heath 1886; West Bromwich Albion August 1891 (1 FL app); Small Heath again December 1891; retired cs 1893 but came out of retirement to assist Small Heath in the 1894 Test matches. Other honour: (Small Heath) FL Div. 2 champions 1893.

Goalkeeper. An outstanding amateur of high competence, occasionally brilliant, and the first chronologically of Brum's several capped custodians. Charsley joined the Birmingham City police force in 1884, subsequently serving as Chief Constable of Coventry 1899-1918, when he retired. He then moved to Weston-super-Mare and was a borough councillor from 1933 to his death (Deputy Mayor 1939-40).

CHEDGZOY, Samuel
(Everton, 1920-25, 8)
Born Ellesmere Port, Cheshire, 27 January 1889. Died 15 January 1967.
1925: 5ft. 8ins.; 11st.

Career: Birnell's Ironworks (Ellesmere Port); Everton December 1910; New Bedford, USA, May 1926-1930, subsequently assisting Carsteel FC (Montreal) until around 1940 when he had turned 50. Other honours: Football League (5 apps). (Everton) FL champions 1915.

Outside-right possessing speed and dribbling and centering ability who disdained a robust approach. Was responsible for a change in the game's laws – his introduction of dribbling corner-kicks was soon countered by the rule that the taker may only play the ball once. His son, Sidney, was a well known outside-right in the 'Thirties with Millwall and other clubs. Sam died in Montreal.

CHENERY, Charles John
(Crystal Palace, 1873-74, 3)
Born Lambourn, Berks. 1 January 1850.
Career: Crystal Palace (the original club of that name); Barnes; Wanderers. Also represented Surrey and London. Secretary of the Wanderers 1871.
Forward. One of the earliest dribbling specialists and one who played at full stretch all the time. A Surrey cricketer (12 matches 1872-73), he also assisted Northants before the club's elevation to first-class county status. Thought to have gone abroad circa 1877. Educated Marlborough Grammer School.

CHERRY, Trevor John
(Leeds United, 1976-80, 27)
Born Huddersfield, 23 February 1948.
1978: 5ft. 10ins.; 11st. 6lbs.
Career: Huddersfield Schools; Huddersfield YMCA; Huddersfield Town July 1965; Leeds United June 1972 (£99,000); Bradford

City as player/manager December 1982 (£10,000)-1985; continuing as manager to January 1987. Other honours: Football League (1 app). (H'field T) FL Div. 2 champions 1970. (Leeds U) European Cup Winners' Cup finalist 1973. FL champions 1974. FA Cup finalist 1973. (Bradford C) FL Div. 3 champions 1985.

Full-back/midfield. Played left-half at Huddersfield, left-back (as well as midfield) for Leeds and was at right-back in the 1985 Bradford City promotion side. Cherry's main contribution lay in a capacity to win the ball and inspire colleagues with his spirited, no surrender attitude. He skippered Leeds for some years.

CHILTON, Allenby C.
(Manchester United, 1951-52, 2)
Born South Hylton, Co Durham, 16 September 1918.
1951: 6ft. 1in.; 12st.

Career: Sunderland Schools; Seaham Colliery; Manchester United November 1938 (guest player for Charlton Athletic during WW2); Grimsby Town player/manager March 1955, retired from playing October 1956 and continued as manager until April 1959; Wigan Athletic manager May 1960; Hartlepools United scout 1961/62 and manager July 1962-May 1963. Other honours: (Man. Utd) FL champions 1952. FA Cup winner 1948. (Grimsby T) FL Div. 3 (North) champions 1956.

Centre-half. Had only one League game before WW2 (in the abandoned 1939/40 season) but subsequently appeared in 2 wartime cup finals: for Charlton in 1944 and his own club, Manchester United, the following season. Was an Old Trafford regular when peace returned, dominating in defence with excellent headwork and precise ground passing. Steered the Mariners to promotion in his first season at Blundell Park.

CHIPPENDALE, Henry
(Blackburn Rovers, 1894, 1)
Born Blackburn, 2 October 1870. Died 29 September 1952.

Career: Nelson; Blackburn Rovers cs 1891-cs 1897. Later served as a FL linesman to November 1908.

Outside-right. Big physically for the position, making his forceful play that much more difficult to contain. Had a good turn of speed and was accurate in centring and shooting. Was partnered by a club colleague, Jimmy Whitehead, in his solitary international. Harry was employed at Hornby's Brookhouse Mill, Blackburn, later rising to the rank of manager with the firm.

CHIVERS, Martin Harcourt
(Tottenham Hotspur, 1971-74, 24)
Born Southampton, 27 April 1945.
1973: 6ft. 1in.; 13st. 12½lbs.
Career: Southampton schoolboy football; CPC Sports (Soton); Southampton FC amateur early in 1962, turning professional in September of that year; Tottenham Hotspur January 1968 (£125,000, then a record); Servette (Geneva) July 1976 (£80,000); Norwich City July 1978 (£20,000); Brighton & Hove Albion March 1979 (£15,000); Dorchester Town player/manager early 1980 to following December; later had a spell with Barnet, retiring in December 1982. Other honours: England Under-23 international (17 apps). Football League (1 app). (Spurs) Inter-Cities Fairs Cup winner 1972; finalist 1974. FL Cup winner 1971, 1973.

Centre-forward with much experience at inside-right. Massively built but extremely nimble all the same, and hard to dispossess when boring his way through. High promise at Southampton was amply fulfilled at White Hart Lane where he thrived on the promptings of Gilzean, Peters and other Tottenham stars. Latterly a licensee in Herts and Sussex.

CHRISTIAN, Edward
(Old Etonians, 1879, 1)
Born Malvern, Worcs. 14 September 1858. Died 3 April 1934.
Career: Eton College; Cambridge University (no Blue); Old Etonians. Did not play after 1881. Other honour: (Old Etonians) FA Cup winner 1879.

Full-back. 'A fine back,' Alcock tells us, 'kicking well with either foot.' This two-footedness is borne out by his appearing on the right flank in the above Cup final and on the left in the Scotland match of that year. Was in Ceylon from 1881 to 1904, the long exile, of course, ending Christian's soccer-career.

CLAMP, H(arold) Edwin
(Wolverhampton Wanderers, 1958, 4)
1958: 5ft. 11in.; 11st. 10lbs.
Born Coalville Leicster. 14 September 1934.
Career: Coalville Schools; Wolverhampton Wanderers amateur cs 1950, turning professional April 1952; Arsenal November 1961 (£34,500); Stoke City September 1962 (£14,000); Peterborough United October 1964 (£5000); Worcester City August 1965-cs1966, then out of football until spell with Lower Gornal FC from September 1967. Other honours: England schoolboy international. Football League (1 app). (Wolves) FL champions 1958, 1959. FA Cup winner 1960. (Stoke C) FL Div. 2 champions 1963.

Wing-half of proven efficiency on either flank. Really came to fruition in the mid-1950s as an acknowledged Wolves' first-teamer, going on to international rank and winning championship and FA Cup medals. Forceful and vigorous, Eddie owned a tackle both lusty and well judged.

CLAPTON, Daniel Robert
(Arsenal, 1959, 1)
Born Aldgate, London, 22 July 1934. Died June 1986.
1969: 5ft. 9ins.; 10st. 2lbs.
Career: Hackney Schools; Leytonstone; Arsenal August 1953; Luton Town September 1962 (£6000)-cs 1963; went to Australia late in 1964 and assisted Corinthians FC, Sydney. Other honour: Football League (1 app).

Outside-right. A typical dashing wingman – dash which persisted throughout the whole game – and exhibiting lots of tricks. Had been a Smithfield meat porter prior to turning professional. His younger brother, Dennis, an England Youth international, was a colleague at Highbury.

CLARE, Thomas
(Stoke, 1889-94, 4)
Born Congleton, Cheshire, 1865. Died 27 December 1929.
1897: 'about 6ft.; 13st.'
Career: Talke FC (Staffs); Goldenhill Wanderers; Stoke 1883 (the club's first professional); Burslem Port Vale as coach cs 1897, later becoming manager. Played many times for Staffordshire. Other honours: Football League (1 app). (Stoke) Football Alliance champions 1891.

Right-back. 'A capital man in club games but seldom shows his true form in international matches. A steady going back, who is always reliable and works hard,' remarked a critic in 1893. Clare, together with Rowley and Underwood (q.v.) formed, of course, one of the most renowned of club defences.

Fast despite his size. Emigrated to Canada before the Great War and died there at Vancouver.

CLARKE, Allan John
(Leeds United, 1970-76, 19)
Born Short Heath nr. Willenhall, Staffs, 31 July 1946.
1973: 6ft.; 10st. 13lbs.

Career: Birmingham Schools; South-East Staffordshire Schools; Walsall apprentice 1961, turning professional August 1963; Fulham March 1966 (£35,000); Leicester City June 1968 (£100,000); Leeds United June 1969 (£165,000); Barnsley as player/manager May 1978 (£45,000, then a Barnsley record), retiring from playing January 1980 and manager only to the following September; Leeds United manager September 1980-June 1982; Scunthorpe United manager (also became a director) February 1983-August 1984; Barnsley manager again July 1985. Other honours: England Under-23 international (6 apps). Football League (2 apps). (Leicester) FA Cup finalist 1969. (Leeds U) European Cup finalist 1975. Inter-Cities Fairs Cup winner 1971. FL champions 1974. FA Cup winner 1972; finalist 1970, 1973.

Strike forward of slim build but deadly with head and foot near the enemy citadel. This nose for goals earned him at his peak the sobriquet of 'Sniffer'. Something of an individualist at first, he linked up at Leeds with Mick Jones (q.v.) to form an outstanding club spearhead. Allan is from a noted footballing family; one of his brothers is Wayne, of Everton's 1987 championship side.

CLARKE, Henry Alfred
(Tottenham Hotspur, 1954, 1)
Born Woodford Green, Essex, 23 February 1923.
1950: 6ft. 3ins.; 12st. 8lbs.

Career: Woodford Schools and then played in junior soccer in that area; RAF football during wartime service, representing his Command; Lovell's Athletic (Newport, Mon) 1946; Tottenham Hotspur March 1949 (£1000 or £1500); Llanelly as player/manager February 1959; Romford manager for a long spell from March 1962. Other honours: England 'B' international (1 app). (Lovell's Ath) Welsh Cup winner 1948. (Spurs) FL champions 1951. FL Div. 2 champions 1950.

Centre-half. A deceptive player in that he appeared to make tardy challenges when actually length of leg sped him to interceptions 'on time'. Was naturally dominant in the air, of course. Harry arrived at White Hart Lane from Lovell's Athletic with a glowing record – besides the above Welsh Cup medal he had participated in successive Welsh League championships.

CLAY, Thomas
(Tottenham Hotspur, 1920-22, 4)
Born Leicester, 19 November 1892. Died 21 February 1949.
1921: 5ft. 10ins.; 11st. 10lbs.

Career: Belvoir Street Sunday School, Leicester; Leicester Fosse cs 1911; Tottenham Hotspur January 1914; Northfleet (then Spurs' nursery club) as player/coach July 1929; St Albans City coach for a spell from cs 1931. Other honours: Football League (1 app). (Spurs) FL Div. 2 champions 1920. FA Cup winner 1921.

Right-back in the classic tradition. A supreme strategist which enabled him to avoid being pulled out of position (and thereby concealing a certain lack of pace). Tommy's low skimming clearances were always de

liberately aimed at a colleague. He was a bricklayer by trade and, after leaving football, returned to the building industry in the Southend area.

CLAYTON, Ronald
(Blackburn Rovers, 1956-60, 35)
Born Preston, Lancs. 5 August 1934.
1958: 5ft. 10ins.; 11st. 4lbs.

Career: Preston Schools; Lancashire Youths; Blackburn Rovers on amateur forms July 1949, turning professional August 1951; Morecambe as player/manager July 1969-August 1970, joining Great Harwood later that year. Other honours: England 'B' international (1 app). England Under-23 international (6 apps). Football League (10 apps.). (Blackburn R) FA Cup finalist 1960.

Right-half of exceptional worth, master of all wing-half facets and captain of both club and country. Started young too, senior debut at 17, and in 1952 said to be the youngest player ever to appear in a Cup semi-final. Ronnie's total of League matches for Blackburn stood as a club record for 17 years. Brother of Ken Clayton (Blackburn Rovers 1949-61). Outside the game has been employed as a newsagent and as a representative for a tie manufacturing firm.

CLEGG, (Sir) John Charles
(Sheffield Club, 1872, 1)
Born Sheffield, 15 June 1850. Died 26 June 1937.

Career: Assisted clubs in Sheffield other than the above – Sheffield Wednesday, Norfolk and Perseverance. Subsequently a first-class referee (his engagements included 2 FA Cup finals, 1882 and 1892, and the England vs. Scotland match of 1886). Became one of the greatest administrators the game has known. Served on the FA Committee from 1885, Chairman 1889, Vice-President 1889-1923 and President 1923 to his death. Also served as President of the Sheffield & Hallamshire FA and at different times as director and chairman of both Sheffield United and Sheffield Wednesday. Knighted in 1927 for services to football.

Forward. 'Very fast with the ball, passing it with great judgment and, when within sight of the enemy's goal-posts, an unerring kick', said the Football Annual for 1874. Did not confine his sporting activities to soccer, winning some 120 prizes on the running track and returning excellent times in 100 and 440 yard events. And he also played rugger and won many tennis tournaments. A solicitor by profession and brother of W E Clegg below.

CLEGG, (Sir) William Edwin
(Sheffield Club, 1873-79, 2)
Born Sheffield, 21 April 1852. Died 22 August 1932.

Career: Besides Sheffield Club he played for other clubs in the area, viz. Sheffield Wednesday, Perseverance, Sheffield Albion and Norfolk. He also assisted Sheffield FA in representative matches. Retired through injury January 1880. Later a director of both Sheffield United and Sheffield Wednesday.

Half-back of good all-round quality and noted for the certainty of his kicking. Like his brother (J C Clegg above) achieved success on the running track. A solicitor by profession (admitted 1874), he was knighted in 1906. Was Lord Mayor of Sheffield 1893-99. Awarded the OBE in 1918 for work on the Sheffield Munitions Tribunal.

CLEMENCE, Raymond Neal
(Liverpool and Tottenham Hotspur, 1973-84, 61)
Born Skegness, Lincs. 5 August 1948.
1978: 5ft. 11½ins.; 12st. 9lbs.

Career: Skegness schools football; Skegness Youth Club (trial with Notts County); Scunthorpe United August 1965; Liverpool June 1967 (£18,000); Tottenham

Hotspur August 1981 (£300,000). Other honours: England Under-23 international (4 apps). Football League (2 apps). (Liverpool) European Cup winner 1977, 1978, 1981. UEFA Cup winner 1973, 1976. FL champions 1973, 1976, 1977, 1979, 1980. FA Cup winner 1974; finalist 1971, 1977. FL Cup winner 1981; finalist 1978. (Spurs) FA Cup winner 1982; finalist 1987. FL Cup finalist 1982.

Goalkeeper of world class status whose rich haul of England caps would possibly have been doubled and more but for his contemporary and friend, Peter Shilton. Hard to flaw technically with his concentration, positional sense, immaculate handling and wonderful reflexes. A vocal boss of his goal area. Supplemented his Scunthorpe wages by close season work as a deck chair attendant on Skegness beach. Awarded the MBE in the 1987 Birthday Honours List.

CLEMENT, David T.
(Queen's Park Rangers, 1976-77, 5)
Born Battersea, London, 2 February 1948. Died 31 March 1982.
1976: 5ft. 10ins.; 11st. 5lbs.
Career: South London Schools; Queen's Park Rangers on schoolboy forms circa 1963 and, though never an apprentice, turned professional July 1965; Bolton Wanderers June 1979 (£170,000); Fulham October 1980; Wimbledon October 1981. Other honour: England Youth international.

Right-back. Had a long and distinguished partnership at Loftus Road with Ian Gillard, both gaining England honours and making over 400 League appearances for Rangers. Clement was quick to sense danger, moved intelligently into tackles and parted with the ball to useful purpose.

CLOUGH, Brian Howard
(Middlesbrough, 1960, 2)
Born Middlesbrough, 21 March 1935.
1960: 5ft. 10½ins.; 11st. 1lb.
Career: Great Broughton FC (North Yorks); Middlesbrough as an amateur November 1951, professional May 1953; Sunderland July 1961 (£45,000); retired through injury November 1964 and joined Sunderland's coaching staff. Hartlepools United manager October 1965; Derby County manager July 1967-October 1973; Brighton & Hove Albion manager November 1973; Leeds United manager July-September 1974; Nottingham Forest manager January 1975. Other honours: England 'B' international (1 app). England Under-23 international (3 apps). Football League (2 apps).

Centre-forward. Quite dynamic, a direct strike forward ever hungry for goals. His scoring record bears comparison with the very best: in 274 League games for his two senior clubs he netted no fewer than 251, a phenomenal total. And they were scored in record time. Has won even more fame in management, steering clubs to many high honours (including 2 Forest European Cup wins). A fame compounded by TV appearances, his forthright views expressed with a pungency made disarming by a ring of complete honesty. Father of Nigel Clough (Forest & England Under-21).

COATES, Ralph
(Burnley and Tottenham Hotspur, 1970–71, 4)
Born Hetton-le-Hole, Co. Durham, 26 April 1946.
1970: 5ft. 7¼ins.; 11st. 7lbs.

Career: Lambton & Hetton District Schools; County Durham Schools; Hetton Juniors; Burnley amateur October 1961, turning professional April 1963; Tottenham Hotspur May 1971 (£190,000); played in Australian football cs 1978 before joining Orient the following October until 1981. Other honours: England Under-23 international (8 apps). Football League (4 apps). (Spurs)

Inter-Cities Fairs Cup winner 1972; finalist 1974. FL Cup winner 1973 (sub).

Inside-forward/outside-left. An adaptable forward excellent in foraging and distribution qualities. No great goal scorer (52 in his aggregate 463 League games and 17 substitutions), his team work and the chances made for colleagues more than atoned for this.

COBBOLD, William Nevill
(Cambridge University and Old Carthusians, 1883-87, 9)
Born Long Melford, Suffolk, 4 February 1863. Died 8 April 1922.

Career: Charterhouse School; Cambridge University (Blue 1883-4-5-6, being captain in the final two years); Corinthians 1885-88.

Forward labelled 'The Prince of Dribblers,' his facility in this respect outstanding as it was combined with great speed. Played rugger at his first school (Cranbrook), taking up soccer at Charterhouse. The Football Annual for 1881 remarked on Cobbold's brilliant dribbling. He also represented Cambridge University at tennis and was a useful cricketer, playing a single game for Kent in 1887. He was an MA (Cantab) and a private tutor by profession.

COCK, John Gilbert
(Huddersfield Town and Chelsea, 1920, 2)
Born Hayle, Cornwall, 14 November 1893. Died 19 April 1966.
1922: 5ft. 11ins.; 12st.

Career: West Kensington United 1908; Forest Gate; Old Kingstonians December 1912 (Brentford as amateur March 1914); Huddersfield Town cs 1914, originally as an amateur; Chelsea October 1919 (£2650); Everton January 1923; Plymouth Argyle March 1925; Millwall November 1927; Folkestone July 1931; Walton (Surrey Senior League) as a permit player October 1932. Millwall manager November 1944-August 1948. Other honours: England 'Victory' international 1919 (1 app). Football League (2 apps). (Millwall) FL Div. 3 (South) champions 1928.

Centre-forward. Athletic, fast, had ball control and scored his goals using head and feet with equal facility. A somewhat flamboyant character, the best dressed footballer of his day, who had showbiz connections in films and 'on the halls' (Jack possessed a fine tenor voice). In the Great War rose to the rank of Sgt.major and won the MM and the DCM. Was a licensee at New Cross latterly. His brother Donald, also a centre-forward, commanded some hefty fees by the standards of the 'Twenties.

COCKBURN, Henry
(Manchester United, 1947-52, 13)
Born Ashton-under-Lyne, Lancs. 14 September 1923.
1950: 5ft. 6ins.; 10st. 4lbs.

Career: Manchester area schoolboy football; Gosling's FC (Manchester); Manchester United on amateur forms 1943, turning professional August 1944; Bury October 1954 (£3000); Peterborough United July

1956; Corby Town July 1959; Sankey's FC (Wellington) cs-December 1960. Oldham Athletic assistant trainer February 1961; Huddersfield Town assistant trainer/coach September 1964, then senior coach 1969-cs 1975. Other honours: England 'B' international (1 app). Football League (1 app). (Man. Utd) FL champions 1952. FA Cup winner 1948.

Left-half, little and good, fast and tenacious. 'One of the most astute ball players in the game today,' wrote a 1949 commentator, while his heading was astonishing. By dint of much practice, Henry could jump for the high ball with the best of 'em.

COHEN, George Reginald
(Fulham, 1964-68, 37)
Born Kensington, London, 22 October 1939.
1966: 5ft. 10ins.; 12st. 7lbs.

Career: West London Schools; London Schools; Fulham amateur 1955, turning professional October 1956; retired through injury March 1969. Fulham's youth team manager January 1970-June 1971, later having spell as manager of Tonbridge FC from March 1974. Other honours: England Under-23 international (8 apps). Football League (4 apps).

Right-back. A member of the 1966 World Cup-winning side and so automatically a celebrity. An intelligent reader of a game and fast moving. Speed was useful for his overlap sorties, at which device he was an early practitioner. Fulham received a then record sum in compensation when George was forced into retirement with knee trouble. He was proprietor of a sports goods shop until 1971. In later life overcame serious illness.

COLCLOUGH, Henry
(Crystal Palace, 1914, 1)
Born Meir nr. Longton, Staffs. 1891. Died 1941.
Circa 1912: 5ft. 8ins.; 11st. 5lbs.

Career: Junior football to Crewe Alexandra August 1910 (originally on trial); Crystal Palace June 1912; retired through injury during WW1, the injury sustained while playing in Army football. Other honours: Southern League (3 apps).

Left-back. Attained international rank in his second first-class season (Crewe was not in Colclough's time a member of the Football League). So his was a rapid rise. A most solid defender, kicking and tackling in fine style. A great pity about the Great War injury – he would have been only 30 at the time of Palace's 1921 promotion.

COLEMAN, Ernest Herbert
(Dulwich Hamlet, 1921, 1)
Born Steyning, Sussex, 19 October 1889. Died 15 June 1958.
1921: 5ft. $9^1/_2$ ins.; 12st. 8lbs.

Career: Croydon Amateurs; Dulwich Hamlet 1912; retired 1925 (captained the team 1921-23). Represented Surrey 1913 and London 1913 and 1920. Served on the Dulwich Hamlet committee for many years, also as a selector and member of their Finance committee. Later was the club's Hon. Assistant Treasurer, retiring on health grounds in 1956, whereupon he was made a Life Member. Other honours: England amateur international (4 apps). (Dulwich H) FA Amateur Cup winner 1920.

Goalkeeper. A verdict that there was '. . . nothing eccentric about his goalkeeping – he is just a safe and sound custodian' perhaps errs on the side of understatement, for he could be brilliant as well. Anyway, his success came from a profound study of required techniques. Served Dulwich Hamlet for over 40 years, a colourful personality of the amateur game. By profession, Coleman was an accountant.

COLEMAN, John George ('Tim')
(Woolwich Arsenal, 1907, 1)
Born Kettering, 26 October 1881. Died 20 November 1940.
1900s: 5ft. $6^1/_2$ins.; 11st. 4lbs.

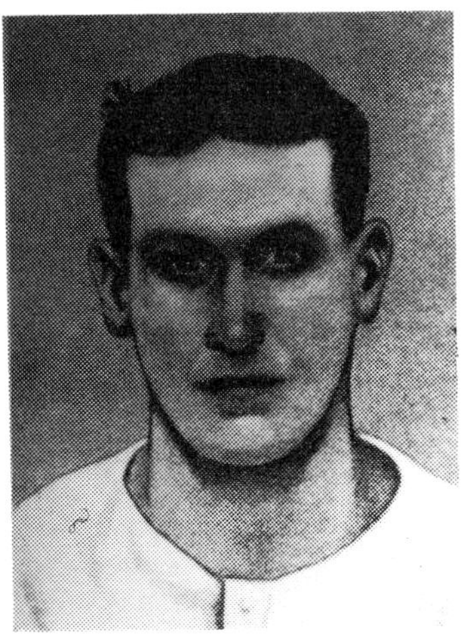

Career: Kettering FC; Northampton Town cs 1901; Woolwich Arsenal May 1902; Everton February 1908; Sunderland May 1910; Fulham June 1911; Nottingham Forest cs 1914; retired during WW1 but, in 1920, was reported to be assisting Tunbridge Wells Rangers. Other honours: Football League (3 apps).

Inside-forward, mostly inside-right. A prominent name from the Edwardian era and associated with several leading clubs during that time. Tim was highly skilled in ball control and in the deft provision of scoring opportunities for his attack's sharp-shooters. Like many fine players he 'missed out' on the acquisition of club League and Cup honours.

COMMON, Alfred
(Sheffield United and Middlesbrough, 1904-06, 3)
Born Sunderland, 25 May 1880. Died 3 April 1946.
1903: 5ft. 8ins.; 13st.

Career: Jarrow 1897; South Hylton Juniors; Sunderland cs 1900; Sheffield United November 1901 (£325); Sunderland again cs 1904 (£520, a record); Middlesbrough February 1905 (£1000, a record); Woolwich Arsenal cs 1910 (£250); Preston North End December 1912 (£250)-1914. Other honours: Football League (1 app). (Sheffield U) FA Cup winner 1902. (PNE) FL Divs. 2 champions 1913.

Inside-right/centre-forward. Holds a permanent place in the game's annals, of course, for being the subject of the first 4-figure transfer fee. What is less well known is that he was involved in the first deal over £500 also. Powerful and aggressive in style, a constant menace to opposing defences, but a jovial humorous character off the field. After leaving football was for many years a Darlington licensee.

COMPTON, Leslie Harry
(Arsenal, 1951, 2)
Born Woodford, Essex, 12 September 1912. Died 27 December 1984.
1949: 6ft. $1^1/_4$ins.; 13st. 6lbs.

Career: Hendon schools football; Bell Lane Old Boys (Hendon); Hampstead Town when 17; Arsenal on amateur forms cs 1931, turning professional February 1932 (Army football during WW2); retired July 1935 and joined Arsenal's coaching staff, leaving February 1956. Other honours: England wartime international (7 apps). Football League (1 app). (Arsenal) FL champions 1948. FA Cup winner 1950.

Centre-half latterly after playing full-back pre-war and then centre-forward circa 1940. He took the pivotal position during army service. Extremely strong, never giving an inch, hard in tackles and dominant in the air. Up to the War was deputy to Male and Hapgood, the Gunners' England backs, getting only 67 League outings in 7 seasons. Elder brother of Denis Compton, the famous Middlesex and England cricketer and an Arsenal colleague. Les himself played for that county 1938-56 (272 matches). Worked as a wine company representative after leaving football. Has the distinction of being England's oldest debutant (but see the entry for A Morten).

CONLIN, James
(Bradford City, 1906, 1)
Born Consett, Co Durham, 6 July 1881. Killed in action 23 June 1917.
1906: 5ft. 5ins.; 9st. 1lb.

Career: Captain Colt's Rovers (Lanarkshire League); Cambuslang; Hibernian; Falkirk; Albion Rovers; Bradford City cs 1904; Manchester City cs 1906; Birmingham September 1911; Airdrieonians cs 1912. Other honours: Football League (2 apps). (Man. City) FL Div. 2 champions 1910.

Outside-left. The archetypal diminutive winger ('fast on the ball and a wonderful dodger and dribbler') – in Conlin's case very diminutive given his jockey weight. Also truly described as 'a honorary Jock' for, like the great Jock Simpson (q.v.), he had spent much of his early life over the border. Lost his life in Flanders while serving with the 15th Highland Light Infantry.

CONNELLY, John Michael
(Burnley and Manchester United, 1960-66, 20)
Born St Helens, Lancs. 18 July 1938.
1962: 5ft. 8ins.; 11st. 2lbs.

Career: St Helens schools football; St Teresa's Old Boys (St Helens); Southport 'A' (when 15); St Helens Town; Burnley as a professional November 1956 after signing amateur forms a month before; Manchester United April 1964 (£56,000); Blackburn Rovers September 1966 (£40,000); Bury June 1970; retired May 1973. Other honours: England Under-23 international (1 app). Football League (8 apps). (Burnley) FA champions 1960. FA Cup finalist 1962. (Man. Utd) FL champions 1956.

Outside-right/outside-left more associated with the right flank although a proportion of his England appearances were on the left. Splendidly two-footed, direct and a keen snapper-up of goal opportunities. He scored 180 in 571 League matches (and 2 subs) for his four senior clubs – an excellent return for a wingman. On his retirement John opened a fish and chip shop at Brierfield near Burnley.

COOK, Thomas Edwin Reed
(Brighton & Hove Albion, 1925, 1)
Born Cuckfield, Sussex, 5 February 1901. Died 15 January 1950.
1927: 5ft. $8^1/_2$ins.; 11st. 4lbs.

Career: Sussex junior football; RN football during WW1; Cuckfield FC, Brighton & Hove Albion 1921-cs 1929, then a cricket coach in South Africa, returning to join Northfleet September 1930; Bristol Rovers October 1931; retired cs 1933. Brighton & Hove Albion manager 1946-1947.

Centre-forward unusually selected for England when a Third Division player (nor, indeed, did he ever appear in any other League tourney than the Third South). Tommy, however, was a centre of a high order: constructive, an accurate shot and inspiration to colleagues. Equally well known as a Sussex cricketer, 1922-37, when he undertook another coaching engage-

ment in South Africa. He joined that country's Air Force when war broke out and in 1943 was seriously injured in an accident at a South African air school.

COOPER, Norman Charles
(Old Brightonians, 1893, 1)
Born Long Ditton, Surrey, 12 July 1870. Died 30 July 1920.

Career: Brighton College (XI 1887-8-9, captain 1889); Cambridge University (Blue 1891-2-3, captain 1893); Old Brightonians; Corinthians 1891-95. Also represented Sussex.

Wing-half numbered among the many accomplished top-class amateurs of Victorian times. Cooper's was a neat style. He specialised in cleverly timed interventions, shrewdly parting with the ball to his side's advantage. A useful cricketer too – he assisted Cambridge University 1891-92 and also Surrey, but played in no first-class matches for the latter.

COOPER, Terence
(Leeds United, 1969-75, 20)
Born Brotherton nr. Castleford, Yorks. 12 July 1944.
1972: 5ft. 7$^1/_2$ins.; 10st. 9lbs.

Career: Ferrybridge Amateurs (trial for Wolverhampton Wanderers 1961); Leeds United apprentice May 1961, turning professional July 1962; Middlesbrough March 1975 (£50,000); Bristol City July 1978 (£20,000); Bristol Rovers as player/coach June 1979 and then manager 1980-October 1981; Doncaster Rovers (as player) November 1981; Bristol City as player/manager May 1982, making a last League appearance (as sub) October 6, 1984. He left the club in March 1988. Other honours: (Leeds U) Inter-Cities Fairs Cup winner 1968, 1971; finalist 1967. FL champions 1969. FA Cup finalist 1970. FL Cup winner 1968.

Left-back following early experience at outside-left, bringing wing qualities to the defence. This was especially so in the manner of modern overlapping – there has never been a better exponent with his speed and intricate dribbling. A badly broken leg in 1972 cost Cooper both representative and club honours (Leeds was then in a great run). He again broke a leg in his first game for Bristol City in 1978. Was an apprentice fitter in a coal mine after leaving school. Became England's first club player/director (for Bristol City).

COOPER, Thomas ('Snowy')
(Derby County, 1928-35, 15)
Born Fenton, Staffs. 1904. Died 25 June 1940.
1929: 5ft. 9ins.; 12st.

Career: Trentham FC (Cheshire League); Port Vale August 1924 (£20); Derby County March 1926 (£2000); Liverpool December 1934 (£7500). Other honours: Football League (5 apps).

Right-back ranking with the best: splendid in the tackle, possessing a lovely clean kick and superb in anticipation. His sole blemish – and this was relative – was occasionally in heading. Lined up with another England notable, Ernie Blenkinsop, at Anfield, both having turned 30, the pair showing how full-back play at club level should be performed. Tom lost his life through a motor-cycle accident while serving with the Military Police.

COPPELL, Stephen James
(Manchester United, 1978-83, 42)
Born Liverpool, 9 July 1955.
1980: 5ft. 7$^1/_2$ins.; 11st. 1lb.

Career: Liverpool University; Tranmere Rovers amateur June 1973, turning professional January 1974; Manchester United February 1975 (£30,000); retired through injury October 1983. Crystal Palace manager June 1984. Other honours: England Under-23 international (1 app). (Man. Utd) FA Cup winner 1977; finalist 1976, 1979. FL Cup finalist 1983.

Midfield/forward. Perhaps this incisive player's best role was in the old outside-right slot. Described by a commentator (who apparently wanted a fresh simile!) as '. . . a footballing ant whose every journey has a purpose'. Steve certainly gave full value: his imagination, energy, variations of pace and two-footed power were valued by club and country. Lost a two year fight against a bad knee injury to become the League's then youngest manager. Had a spell as Chairman of the Players' Union. A B Sc (Econ) of Liverpool University.

COPPING, Wilfred
(Leeds United and Arsenal, 1933-39, 20)
Born Barnsley, 17 August 1907. Died 1980.
1936: 5ft. 7ins.; 10st. 13lbs.

Career: Dearne Valley Old Boys; Middlecliffe Rovers (Barnsley); Leeds United March 1929 as amateur, professional 1930; Arsenal June 1934 (£6000); Leeds United again March 1939; retired during WW2. Coach in Belgium 1945-46; Southend United trainer cs 1946; Bristol City trainer July 1954; Coventry City trainer November 1956-May 1959. Other honours: Football League (2 apps). (Arsenal) FL champions 1935, 1938. FA Cup winner 1936.

Left-half. Grim visaged, dark jowled performer, probably the most famous 'hard man' of them all. Wilf's juddering tackle was legendary and his shoulder charging earned equal respect. There was, of course, much more to him than hardness, his distribution being both astute and accurate, while he could achieve great distance with throws. Originally a miner.

CORBETT, Bertie Oswald
(Corinthians, 1901, 1)
Born Thame, Oxon. 15 May 1875. Died 30 November 1967.

Career: Thame Grammar School; Oxford University (Blue 1896-97); Corinthians 1897-1906 (secretary 1902-04). Assisted Reading and Slough in 1906/07 while teaching in the area.

Outside-left. An amateur of note (he represented Oxfordshire when only 15) whose clever dribbling was enhanced by pace and a natural body swerve. Played cricket for Buckinghamshire and appeared once for Derbyshire (in 1910). Editor of 'Annals of the Corinthian Football Club' (Longmans, 1906). A schoolmaster by profession (BA (Oxon)), he taught at Brighton College and in Derbyshire before becoming proprietor of a Dorset preparatory school. Brother of R Corbett below.

CORBETT, Reginald ('Rex')
(Old Malvernians, 1903, 1)
Born Thame, Oxon. 1879. Died 2 September 1967.
Career: Malvern College (XI 1898); Old Malvernians; Corinthians 1902-05. Other honour: (Old Malvernians) FA Amateur Cup winner 1902.

Inside/outside-left, more associated with the latter berth. Inclined to be erratic he could, however, turn in a quite brilliant performance at times, and his name regularly appeared on the score-sheet. Brother of B O Corbett above and, like him, a schoolmaster by profession.

CORBETT, Walter Samuel
(Birmingham, 1908, 3)
Born Wellington, Salop. 26 November 1880. Died 1955.

Career: King Edward Grammar School, Birmingham; Astbury Richmond; Bournbrook; Aston Villa; Birmingham cs 1907-1911 (1 app for Queen's Park Rangers September 1907); also assisted Wellington Town from April 1909. Other honours: England amateur international (18 apps).

Full-back of infinite resource and splendid speed. He was a leading amateur in his day and consequently much honoured at amateur international level.

CORRIGAN, Joseph Thomas

(Manchester City, 1976-82, 9)
Born Manchester, 18 November 1948.
1979: 6ft. 4½ins.; 14st.

Career: Sale FC; Manchester City amateur September 1966, turning professional January 1967; Seattle Sounders, USA, March 1983 (£30,000); Brighton & Hove Albion September 1983-1985 (Norwich City on loan September 1984, Stoke City on loan October-December 1984); retired through injury February 1985. Other honours: England Under-23 international (1 app). England Under-21 international (3 apps). England 'B' international. (Man. City) European Cup Winners' Cup winner 1970. FA Cup finalist 1981. FL Cup winner 1970, 1976.

Goalkeeper of unusually hefty physique (his weight sometimes hovered over the 15st mark) whose progress to a regular senior spot at Maine Road was halting. In fact inconsistency delayed this outcome until the mid-'Seventies. From then on until his departure, however, Joe reigned unchallenged, his considerable presence and often brilliant goalkeeping universally recognised. Made 476 League appearances for Manchester City, 310 of them in the 1975-83 segment. The 310 included 4 consecutive campaigns as an 'ever-present'.

COTTEE, Anthony Richard

(West Ham United, 1987-88, 3)
Born West Ham, 11 July 1965.
1987: 5ft. 8ins.; 11st. 4lbs.

Career: Essex Schools; Chase Cross United; West Ham United apprentice May 1981, turning professional September 1982; Everton July 1988 (2m.). Other honours: England Youth international. England Under-21 international (7 apps).

Forward following on in the long tradition of Hammers' local developments that dates from the club's Thames Ironworks days. Sturdy and muscular, he seized his opportunity when stand-in for an injured Paul Goddard (q.v.), the latter eventually moving on to Newcastle. Tony had scored freely in West Ham's youth and reserve sides and continued to do so for the first team (102 in 202 League and Cup games and 9 subs to the end of season 1986/87). Formed a fine spearhead with Frank McAvennie after the Scot's arrival at Upton Park in 1985. 'Young Player of the Year' 1986.

COTTERILL, George Huth

(Cambridge University and Old Brightonians, 1891-93, 4)
Born Brighton, 4 April 1868. Died 1 October 1950.
Height: over 6ft. 3ins.

Career: Brighton College (XI 1882-86, captain 1884-86); Cambridge University (Blue 1888-9-90-91, captain 1890); Old Brightonians; Corinthians 1887-98); also assisted Weybridge and Burgess Hill and played in representative matches for Surrey and Sussex.

Centre-forward of immensely powerful build and fast with it plus dribbling and shooting skills for good measure. A typical example of the Victorian games all-rounder. At cricket he played for Cambridge University 1888-89 (without getting a Blue) and Sussex 1886-90. Richmond for 2 seasons and Surrey (twice) had his services at rugger. And he was a multi-event athlete – track, field and rowing. MA (Cantab).

COTTLE, Joseph Richard

(Bristol City, 1909, 1)
Born Bedminster, Bristol, 1886. Died 3 February 1958.
1909: 5ft. 8ins.; 10st.

Career: Eclipse FC (Bristol); Dolphin FC (Bristol & District League); Bristol City cs 1904; retired cs 1911. Other honours: (Bristol C) FL Div. 2 champions 1906. FA Cup finalist 1909.

Left-back found by Bristol City on their own doorstep to star in the club's most successful period. A dashing defender, he was quite fearless and played with a refreshing enthusiasm. Cottle retired remarkably early – before his 25th birthday – and apparently not because of injury. He then became a Bristol licensee until his death.

COWAN, Samuel
(Manchester City, 1926-31, 3)
Born Chesterfield, 10 May 1901. Died 4 October 1964.
1926: 5ft. $10^1/_2$ins.; 13st.

Career: Adwick le Street Park; Adwick Juniors; Bullcroft Colliery; Denaby United; Doncaster Rovers cs 1923; Manchester City December 1924; Bradford City October 1935 (£2000); Mossley July 1937. Brighton & Hove Albion coach June 1938; Manchester City manager November 1946-June 1947. Other honours: Football League (1 app). (Man. City) FL Div. 2 champions 1928. FA Cup winner 1934; finalist 1926, 1933.

Centre-half. Developed quickly after a late start (reputedly not taking up the game until 17). Hefty and enthusiastic, Sam spent much of his career as a club captain. He loved to attack, once scoring a hat-trick from the pivotal position in a League match. Had a physiotherapy practice at Brighton and was masseur to the Sussex CCC and several MCC touring sides. Died while refereeing a soccer match at Hayward's Heath.

COWANS, Gordon Sidney
(Aston Villa and Bari, 1983-86, 9)
Born in County Durham, 27 October 1958.
1984: 5ft. $7^1/_2$ins.; 10st. $5^1/_2$lbs.

Career: Dukeries Miners' Welfare (from the age of 11); Aston Villa apprentice, turning professional September 1976; Bari FC (Italy) June 1985 (£850,000 including another player); Aston Villa again June 1988 (£250,000). Other honours: England Youth international. England 'B' international. England Under 21 international (5 apps). (Villa) European Cup winner 1982. FL champions 1981. FL Cup winner 1977.

Midfield, usually on the left though naturally right-footed: assiduous practice made his left equally dexterous. A complete player, 'all action' and quite instinctive, coping wonderfully with any kind of situation. Sustained a double fracture of the right leg in a Spanish pre-season tournament, August 1983, and was out of football for a long time.

COWELL, Arthur
(Blackburn Rovers, 1910, 1)
Born Blackburn 20 May 1886. Died 12 February 1959.
1910: 5ft. $7^1/_2$ins.; 10st. 10lbs.

Career: Blackburn St Peter's (a Sunday school side); Nelson 1904; Blackburn Rovers May 1905; retired cs 1920. He then became Blackburn Rovers trainer until May 1937, shortly afterwards being appointed Wrexham's trainer; Wrexham manager August 1938-early 1939. Other honours: Football League (1 app). (Blackburn R) FL champions 1912, 1914.

Left-back. 'Though built on slender lines, he is a masterful back, using resource as an aid to skill,' a 1910 handbook records. Cowell complemented the play of his distinguished partner, Bob Crompton, perfectly with doggedness and polish. Cousin of 'Kelly' Houlker (Blackburn Rovers & England). Ran newsagencies at Kirkham and Darwen after leaving football.

COX, John
(Liverpool, 1901-03, 3)
Born Blackpool, 21 November 1876.

1901: 5ft. 9ins.; 11st. 7lbs.

Career: South Shore Standard (Blackpool); South Shore FC; Blackpool cs 1897; Liverpool February 1898 (£150); Blackpool again (as player/manager) cs 1909; retired cs 1911. Other honours: Football League (3 apps). (Liverpool) FL champions 1901, 1906. FL Div. 2 champions 1905.

Outside-left was the position in which his honours were won although one source says 'generally an outside-right', and the inside-left slot was certainly not unknown to him. The first Blackpool sojourn, less than a year long, quickly revealed his potential to the Anfield club. Extremely fast and a regular scorer, Cox sometimes inclined to self-indulgence in unnecessarily tricking an opponent twice.

COX, John Davies
(Derby County, 1892, 1)
Born Spondon, Derbys. 1870. Died June 1957.
1891: 5ft. 7ins.; 11st. 2lbs.

Career: Spondon FC; Long Eaton Rangers; Derby County cs 1891; emigrated to Canada 1900. Other honours: (Derby Co) FA Cup finalist 1898, 1899.

Right-half. Skilful wing-half invariably parting with the ball to advantage and tackling tenaciously. One of only five Rams to participate in both the 1898 and '99 Cup finals. The club was undergoing an unusually quick turn-round of players it would seem. He died in Toronto.

CRABTREE, James William
(Burnley and Aston Villa, 1894-1902, 14)
Born Burnley, 23 December 1871. Died 18 June 1908.
1895: 5ft. 10in.; 12st. 3lbs.

Career: Burnley Royal Swifts 1885 (during which spell he assisted Burnley's reserves); Rossendale cs 1890; Heywood Central cs 1891; Burnley cs 1892; Aston Villa August 1895 (£250); Plymouth Argyle January 1904, retiring later that year. Other honours: Football League (9 apps). (Villa) FL champions 1896, 1897, 1899, 1900. FA Cup winner 1897.

Full-back/half-back. A versatile celebrity probably best at left-half. He was an unusually gifted ball juggler, sometimes overdoing the pattern-weaving, yet could also reveal orthodox qualities in abundance. Said to be extremely sensitive to criticism.

CRAWFORD, John Forsyth
(Chelsea, 1931, 1)
Born Jarrow, Co. Durham, 26 September 1896. Died 27 September 1975.
1930: 5ft. 2ins.; 8st. 6lbs.

Career: Palmer's Works FC (Jarrow) before WW1 service in the Royal Navy; Jarrow Town; Hull City December 1919; Chelsea May 1923 (£3000); Queen's Park Rangers May 1934; retired cs 1937 and became a QPR coach to 1939. Post-war coached Maldon Town (Essex) in his spare time.

Outside-right/outside-left. Of Fanny Walden proportions yet to be feared almost as much as that little genius. Crawford had speed, tricks in plenty and his centres produced goals galore, although he wasn't a prolific scorer himself. Started on the left-wing, moving to the right at Hull to accommodate David Mercer (q.v.). Did similarly at Stamford Bridge for Alex. Jackson, and was then the sole English cap in an all-international forward-line. A factory worker during WW2.

CRAWFORD, Raymond
(Ipswich Town, 1962, 2)
Born Portsmouth, 13 July 1936.
1962: 5ft. 10in.; 11st. 10lbs.

Career: Portsmouth junior football; Portsmouth FC amateur June 1954, turning professional the following December; Ipswich Town September 1958 (£6000); Wolverhampton Wanderers September 1963 (£42,000); West Bromwich Albion February 1965 (£35,000); Ipswich Town again March 1966 (£15,000); Charlton Athletic March 1969 (£12,500); Kettering Town October 1969; Colchester United June 1970 (£3000); Durban City (South Africa) August-October 1971. Brighton & Hove Albion coach 1971-72, later having spells coaching with Eden FC (New Zealand) and Portsmouth in the mid-1970s, leaving the latter during season 1977/78. Other honours: Football League (3 apps). (Ipswich T) FL champions 1962. FL Div. 2 champions 1961, 1968.

Centre-forward, occasionally inside-right. A leader of thrust and scoring proclivity outstandingly illustrated during the peak period of the first Ipswich spell – 142 League goals in 197 matches. Such fecundity might have been less pronounced elsewhere but he still finished with highly creditable League figures of 289 in 475 League games. And he netted a splendid 228 in his two-spell all matches 354 at Portman Road.

CRAWSHAW, Thomas Henry
(Sheffield Wednesday, 1895-1904, 10)
Born Sheffield, 27 December 1872. Died 25 November 1960.
1901: 5ft. 10ins.; 12st.

Career: Park Grange (Sheffield); Attercliffe (Sheffield); Heywood Central for one season; Sheffield Wednesday 1894; Chesterfield Town cs 1908. Subsequently had a brief spell as secretary of Glossop FC. Other honours: Football League (8 apps). (Wednesday) FL champions 1903, 1904. FL Div. 2 champions 1900. FA Cup winner 1896, 1907.

Centre-half. A fine Wednesday servant whose Hillsborough days coincided with one of the club's great eras. Played a hard game for the whole 90 minutes, tackled well, was unselfish, and dextrous in headwork. Had a newsagency in Sheffield.

CRAYSTON, W(illiam) John
(Arsenal, 1936–38, 8)
Born Grange-over-Sands, Lancs. 9 October 1910.
1938: 6ft. 0$^1/_4$ins.; 13st. 4lbs.

Career: Barrow-in-Furness schoolboy football; Ulverston Town; Barrow August 1928; Bradford May 1930; Arsenal May 1934 (£5250, a then Park Avenue record); retired through injury 1943, becoming Arsenal's assistant manager. Arsenal manager December 1956-May 1958; Doncaster Rovers manager June 1958, secretary/manager March 1959-June 1961. Other honours: Football League (1 app). (Arsenal) FL champions 1935, 1938. FA Cup winner 1936.

Right-half. Played at centre-half also for Barrow and Bradford. A graceful performer, height giving dominance in the air and systematic in his approach to a game. For some years from 1961 ran a newsagency at Streetly near Birmingham.

CREEK, F(rederick) Norman S(mith)
(Corinthians, 1923, 1)
Born Darlington, 12 January 1898. Died 26

July 1980.
1922: 5ft. 8½ins.; 11st. 4lbs.

Career: Darlington Grammar School, where he captained the XI; Cambridge University (Blue 1920 and '22 – he was unfit in 1921); Corinthians from 1919/20 into the 1930s; Darlington on amateur forms April 1922 (2 FL apps 1922-24). Worked for the FA from January 1954-October 1963, managing the England amateur international side and the Olympic Games team. Other honours: England amateur international (5 apps).

Inside-right/centre-forward. A great Corinthian who devoted a lifetime to soccer. As a player, a keen forward outstandingly prolific in the matter of scoring. For the Corinthians up to the end of 1931/32 he had amassed a remarkable 120 goals in 103 matches, and he netted 4 in his England amateur international debut, a feat not equalled until 1964. Awarded the MC in WW1 and the MBE in 1943. A schoolmaster (BA Cantab) at Dauntsey's School, Wilts, for many years, during which time he played cricket for Wiltshire. Later a Daily Telegraph football writer for nearly 20 years. Author of 'A History of the Corinthian FC' (Longmans, 1933).

CRESSWELL, Warneford
(South Shields, Sunderland and Everton, 1921-30, 7)
Born South Shields, 5 November 1897. Died 20 October 1973.
1925: 5ft. 9ins.; 10st. 13lbs.

Career: South Shields Schools; South Shields junior football (assisted Morton, Heart of Midlothian and Hibernian of the Scottish League during WW1); South Shields FC cs 1919; Sunderland March 1922 (£5500); Everton February 1927 (about £7000); retired and became Port Vale coach May 1936, later serving as manager; Northampton Town manager April 1937-September 1939. Other honours: England schoolboy international 1911 (1 app). Football League (5 apps). (Everton) FL champions 1928, 1932. FL Div. 2 champions 1931. FA Cup winner 1933.

Right/left-back in the classic mould, his finest attribute probably being a marvellous sense of anticipation. A contemporary wrote that Warney '. . . kicks a fine length, is a resolute tackler and a fine all-round defender.' His brother, Frank, was also a schoolboy international and his son, Corbett, won many amateur international caps. Warney served in both World Wars (a POW in WW1) and was employed as a licensee after WW2.

CROMPTON, Robert
(Blackburn Rovers, 1902-14, 41)
Born Blackburn, 26 September 1879. Died 15 March 1941.
1907: 5ft. 10½ins.; 13st. 10lbs.

Career: Blackburn schoolboy football; Trinity (Sunday School League); Blackburn Rovers September 1896; retired May 1920. A Blackburn Rovers' director June 1921-March 1931 during which period he acted as team manager December 1826-February 1931; Bournemouth & Boscombe Athletic Manager June 1935-February 1936; Blackburn Rovers honorary manager April 1938 to his death. Other honours: Football League (17 apps). (Blackburn R) FL champions 1912, 1914.

Right-back. Among the most famous players of his time, an England stalwart for a dozen years, member of the celebrated Hardy/Crompton/Pennington defence. A robust performer – well equipped physically for this predilecton! – he was nonetheless scrupulously fair and notably quick in recovery. Held the records for the number of England caps (surpassed by Billy Wright Post-WW2) and for the period spent with one League club. A plumber by trade, he was later involved in a motor business. His son, Wilf, assisted Blackburn Rovers in the 1930s.

CROOKS, Samuel Dickinson

(Derby County, 1930-37, 26)
Born Bearpark, Co Durham, 16 January 1908. Died 5 February 1981.
1929: 5ft. 7½ins.; 10st. 9lbs.

Career: Bearpark Collery (when only 15); Brandon Juniors; Tow Lawn Town; Durham City as an amateur cs 1926, turning professional during the ensuing season; Derby County April 1927 (£300); retired cs 1947 and joined Derby's coaching staff to August 1949. Retford Town manager August 1949; Shrewsbury Town manager December 1949-June 1954; later in the 1950s managed Gresley Rovers (2 spells), Burton Albion and Heanor Town; Derby County chief scout June 1960 – May 1967, subsequently working as a free-lance scout. Other honours: Football League (5 aps).

Outside-right. A famous figure of the inter-war years, a sprightly goal scoring winger who netted 111 in 445 League and FA Cup encounters for the Rams. Sammy was fast and direct in style, centreing with pinpoint exactitude. He came from a family numbering 17 and was once a miner. Missed the 1946 Cup final through injury.

CROWE, Christopher

(Wolvehampton Wanderers, 1963, 1)
Born Newcastle-upon-Tyne, 11 June 1939.
1963: 5ft. 7ins.; 11st.

Career: Edinburgh Schools; Edinburgh junior football; Leeds United amateur October 1954, turning professional June 1956; Blackburn Rovers March 1960 (£25.000); Wolverhampton Wanderers January 1962 (£30.000); Nottingham Forrest August 1964 (£30,000); Bristol City January 1967 (£15,000); Auburn FC (Sydney) May 1969 (£4,000); Walsall September 1969 (£1,000); retired 1970 but in Febrauary 1971 joined Bath City for a spell. Other honours: Scottish schoolboy international. England Youth internatoinal. England Under-23 international (4 apps).

Outside-right/inside-forward. Like Joe Baker (q.v) a year later, achieved Scottish schoolboy honours before representing England at more than one level. Crowe, compactly built, was an adaptable forward, a judicious passer of the ball and thoughtful. Around 1970 was a Leeds licensee for a time, later working as a newsagent in Bristol.

CUGGY, Francis

(Sunderland, 1913-14, 2)
Born Walker, Northumberland, 16 June1889. Died 27 March 1965.
1913: 5ft. 8¾ins; 11st.4lbs.

Career: Willingham Athletic; Sunderland March 1909; Wallsend as player/manager May 1921 – cs 1922. Coach in Spain November 1923 on a 5-year contract. Other Honours: Football League (3 apps). (Sunderland) FL champions 1913. FA Cup finalist 1913.

Right-half. Together with the John Mordue/Charlie Buchan forward wing formed one of soccer's most celebrated triangles, the trio's understanding becoming legendary. Cuggy himself was a cool precise performer with no hint of the physical. After leaving the game was employed as a shipyard worker.

CULLIS, Stanley
(Wolverhampton Wanderers, 1938-39, 12)
Born Ellesmere Port, Cheshire, 25 October 1916
1939: 5ft. 10ins.; 11st. 8lbs.

Career: Ellesmere Port Schools; Ellesmere Port Wednesday; Wolverhampton Wanderers February 1934-August 1947 when appointed the club's assistant manager. Wolves' secretary/manager June 1948-September 1964; Birmingham City manager December 1965 – March 1970. Other honours: England wartime international (17 apps). Football League (3 apps). (Wolves) FA Cup finalist 1939.

Centre-half, one of the finest England has produced. Had a degreeof aggression, preferred the attacking game was masterly at providing through balls. Rose quickly from junior ranks – when working as a grocer's assistant to international status. After leaving football became managing-director of a Wolverhampton photographic agency. Appointed to the Midlands Sports Council in May 1972.

CUNLIFFE, Arthur
(Blackburn Rovers, 1933. 2)
Born Blackrod, Lancs. 5 February 1909. Died 28August 1986.
1930: 5ft. $7^1/_2$ins.; 10st. 8lbs.

Career: Adlington when only 14; Chorley 1927; Blackburn Rovers January 1928; Aston Villa May 1933; Middlesborugh December 1935; Burnley April 1937; Hull City June 1938; Rochdale cs 1946; retired July 1947 and appointed Rochdale's trainer. Bournemouth & Boscombe Athletic trainer July 1950 and then that club's physiotherapist 1971 – cs 1974, when he retired.

Outside-left was where he made his reputation following a deal of experience on the opposite extreme flank. Had astonishing speed yet exhibited complete ball control and he could manoeuvre in a confined space. Scored his share of the goals too. Cousin of J N Cunliffe (Everton & England). Once a cotton mill worker.

CUNLIFFE, Daniel
(Portsmouth, 1900, 1)
Born Bolton, 1875. Died 28 December 1937.
1903: 5ft. 8ins.; 11st. 7lbs.

Career: Little Lever; Middleton Borough; Oldham County; Liverpool cs 1897; New Brighton Tower cs 1898; Portsmouth cs 1899; New Brighton Tower again May 1900; Portsmouth again May 1901; New Brompton May 1906; Millwall Athletic cs 1907; Heywood September 1909-April 1912;

Rochdale cs 1912 – 1914. Other honour: (Portsmouth) Southern League champions 1902.

Inside-right, one of the games's early wanderers, favouring fairly equally with his presence both North and South. His stocky frame made dispossession difficult and an admirable persistence brought many goals.

CUNLIFFE, James Nathaniel
(Everton, 1936, 1)
Born Blackrod, Lancs. 5 July 1912. Died 21 November 1986.
1938: 5ft. 10ins.; 11st. 3lbs.

Career Haslingden; Adlington; Everton May 1930; Rochdale September 1946 for a short while in the first post-war season.

Inside-right. A performer of some versatility, taking at some time all the attack positions except outside-right. A 1930s commentator wrote that Cunliffe '... can be of the dashing type, but always a reliable forward, helping to get as many goals as he actually scores.' A cousin of the England winger, Arthur Cunliffe, he had earlier worked as an apprentice plater, and he became a scratch Crown Green bowls player.

CUNNINGHAM, Lawrence Paul
(West Bromwich Albion and Real Madrid,1979-81, 6)
Born St Mary's Archway, London, 8 March 1956. Died 15 July 1989.
1978: 5ft. 8ins.; 10st 13lbs.

Career: Haringey Schools; South-East Counties Schools; Orient apprentice August 1972, turning professional March 1974; West Bromwich Albion March 1977 (£110.000); Real Madrid June 1979 (£995,000, then an Albion record) (Manchester United on loan March 1983); Olympique Marseilles (Leicester City on loan October 1985-May 1986); Sporting Gijon (Spain), later joining the Belgian club, Charleroi. and Wimbledon. Other honours: England Under-21 international (6 apps). England 'B' international. (Real Madrid) European Cup finalist 1981. Spanish League champions 1980. Spanish Cup winner 1980.

Forward operating on the wing, usually the left. A live wire at his peak and tremendously popular with his deft footwork, speed and poise. The first coloured player to be capped by England in a match of the importance of Under-21 level (in 1977). Laurie's career was blighted in latter years by injuries. He was killed in a car accident.

CURREY, Edmund Samuel
(Old Carthusians , 1890, 2)
Born Lewes, Sussex, 28 June 1868. Died March1920. Died 12 March 1920.

Career: Charterhouse School (XI 1885-86); Oxford University (Blue 1888-9-90, captain 1890); Old Carthusians; Corinthians 1888-91. Also represented Sussex.

Inside-forward. Had Plenty of aggresion and attacking flair in the customary style. And he was very much a scoring ace, slotting in a couple against Wales at Wrexham March 15, 1890, and a splendid 25 in an aggregate 30 games for the Corinthians. Currey was a solicitor by profession (admitted 1895) and practised in London.

CURRIE, Anthony Williams
(Sheffield United and Leeds United, 1972-79,17)
Born Edgware, Middlesex, 1 January 1950.
1975: 5ft 10½ins.; 12st. 10lbs.

Career: Hendon Schools (trials with Chelsea and Queen's Park Rangers); Watford amateur September 1965 and then an apprentice February 1966, turning professional May 1967; Sheffield United February 1968 (£26.500); Leeds United June 1976 (£240,000); Queen's Park Rangers August 1979 (£450,000); Chesham United (Isthmian League) August 1983; Torquay United March 1984 – 1985; Hendon September 1985; Goole Town player/coach October1987. Other honours: England Youth initernational. England Under-23 interna–

tional (13 apps). Football League (3 apps). (QPR) FA Cup finalist 1982.

Midfield, usually left-sided. A personality among the best ball players of recent times. Spirited yet composed and the subject of two hefty transfer fees. Interestingly four of his five clubs after leaving Watford were Uniteds (Not that this has any significance, of course!).

CURSHAM, Arthur William
(Notts County, 1876-83, 6)
Born Wilford, Notts. 14 March 1853. Died 24 December 1884.

Career; Oakham School; Nottingham Law Club; Notts County 1875-84; Sheffield Club.

Forward, mostly right-wing. 'Very fast and energetic,' said a contempoary writer, and these characteristics were always much in evidence. He also captained his country against Scotland. Cursham was a colliey proprietor (near Ambergate, Derbyshire) and played cricket for that county 1879-80 and Notts, 1876-78. Cursham emigrated to Florida in 1884, dying there at the end of that year of yellow fever. Elder brother of H A Cursham (below).

CURSHAM, Henry Alfred
(Notts County, 1880-84, 8)
Born Wilford, Notts. 27 November 1859. Died 6 August 1941.

Career: Repton School; Notts County from circa 1880, appearing during the first FL seasons, 1888-90 Corinthians 1882–86 (member of that club's original committee); Grantham FC; Thursday Wanderers (Sheffield).

Forward. 'Very fast and clever left-wing forward,' was a nutshell summing-up of 1881, intimating that the player at least shared pace with his brother (above). H. A. Cursham made a couple of appearances for Notts CCC which are worthy of recording as 24 years separated them (1880 and 1904). He was an insurance broker by profession.

DAFT, Harry Butler
(Notts County, 1889-92, 5)
Born Radcliffe-on-Trent, Notts. 5 April 1866. Died 12 January 1945.
1895: 5ft. 9ins.; 11st. 7lbs.

Career: Played a little soccer at school (Trent College) and joined Notts County after leaving during the 1880s; Nottingham forest January 1893; Notts County again August 1893; Newark December 1894. Assisted the Corinthians 1887-90 and appeared for Nottinghamshire in representative matches. Served on the FA Committee 1884-85. Other honours: Football League (2 apps). (Notts Co) FA Cup winner 1894; finalist 1891.

Outside-left. A splendid amateur. 'Fast on the ball and ready to pass when required, he has most of the requirements for a wing player,' opined a writer in 1895. Daft was a first-class performer at other sports – a lacrosse player good enough to be England reserve and a Notts cricketer 1885-99. His father and uncle were also well known Notts cricketers. Was later connected with the Oxford University CC, umpiring at many of their matches up to WW1.

DANKS, Thomas
(Nottingham Forest, 1885, 1)
Born Nottingham, 30 May 1863. Died 27April 1908.
Career: Junior football to Nottingham forest December 1882 – February 1889. Also assisted Notts County for a spell from 1884 and Burslem Port Vale from September 1888.
Inside-right. A Forest notability of the years just prior to the Alliance and Football League inaugurations. He did not shine in his international (vs. Scotland at the Kennington Oval) – 'somewhat outclassed' it was said. But at club level he had a reputation as an industrious and unselfish forward. Worked as an ironmonger in his native Nottingham .

DAVENPORT, J(ames) Kenyon ('Kenny')
(Bolton Wanderers, 1885-90, 2)
Born Bolton, 23 March 1862. Died 27 September 1908.

Career: Gilnow Rangers (Bolton); Bolton Wanderers 1883; Southport Central during season 1892/93. Represented Lancashire on a number of occasions.

Outside and inside-right for his internationals, and a versatile player appearing for the Trotters in a variety of positions. Fast and tricky, the diminutive Kenny impressed the selectors before receiving his first cap by representing his county 6 times between 1883 and '85. He was the very first Bolton Wanderer to be capped and is thought to be the first native Boltonian so honoured. A fitter by trade.

DAVENPORT, Peter
(Nottingham Forest, 1985, 1)
Born Birkenhead, 24 March 1961.
1985: 5ft. 11ins.; 11st. 3lbs.

Career: Cammell Laird (Birkenhead League)(Everton Amateur); Nottingham Forest January 1982; Manchester United March 1986 (£570,000); Middlesbrough November 1988 (£700,000).

Strike-forward. Successfully introduced by Forest to the senior game, his quick and thrustful play producing a commendable 54 goals in 118 League outings for the Nottingham club. He accordingly attracted a large fee on moving to Old Trafford, where the goals did not flow quite so readily.

DAVIS, George Henry
(Derby County, 1904, 2)
Born Alfreton, Derbys. 5 June 1881. Died 28 April 1969.
1903: 5ft. 6½ins.; 10st. 12lbs.

Career: Alfreton Town; Derby County December 1899 - cs 1909. Subsequently went to Canada where he had a big hand in developing the game in Vancouver and Alberta. He assisted Calgary Hillhurst for a number of years, winning with that club a Canadian Cup-winners' medal as late as 1922. Later coached in Manitoba. Other honour: (Derby Co) FA Cup finalist 1903.
Outside-left. Stocky wingman, purposeful and virile. Said to be a model player, training diligently and never giving a ha'p'orth of trouble. Unfortunate with injuries, however. Was still in Canada during the 1950s, later returning to England and retiring to the Nottingham area. He had been a very successful hotelier and, in early life, an England trialist at lacrosse. At one time an Alfreton potato merchant.

DAVIS, Henry
(Sheffield Wednesday, 1903, 3)
Born Wombwell nr. Barnsley, 1880.
1903: 5ft. 4ins.; 11st. 10lbs.

Career: Ardsley Parish 1895; Barnsley cs 1897 (£5); Sheffield Wednesday January 1900 (£200 and another player); broke a leg during season 1906/07 and played little thereafter, becoming Wednesday's assistant trainer. Other honours: Football League (1 app). (Wednesday) FL champions 1903, 1904. FL Div. 2 champions 1900.

Outside-right said in the early 1900s to be the First Division's smallest forward. He was, though, no light-weight (see above). Harry was extremely popular at both Oakwell and Owlerton, leaving the Barnsley club only because it was impecunious. He had tremendous acceleration and an explosive shot. The first Barnsley FC development to reach the highest class. A noted penalty taker, he later became a Sheffield newsagent.

DAVISON, J(ohn) Edward
(Sheffield Wednesday, 1922, 1)
Born Gateshead, 2 September 1887. Died 1971.
1921: 5ft. 7ins.; 11st. 10lbs.

Career: Gateshead St. Chad's; Sheffield Wednesday April 1908; Mansfield Town as player/manager June 1926. Chesterfield secretary/manager December 1927; Sheffield United Secretary/manager June 1932-August 1952 when he became Chesterfield's manager again to May 1958, then becoming the club's chief scout.

Goalkeeper reckoned to be England's shortest ever. Teddy, though, more than compensated for lack of inches with his unusual agility. And these brilliant acrobatics did not affect reliability and were fearlessly carried out. Made a big contribution to Sheffield soccer – 18 years a Wednesday player and 20 as United's secretary/manager.

DAWSON, Jeremiah
(Burnley, 1922, 2)
Born Holme nr. Burnley, 18 March 1888. Died 8 August 1970.
1921: 5ft. 10$^1/_2$ins.; 11st 5lbs.

Career: Portsmouth Rovers (Todmorden); Holme FC; Cliviger FC (Burnley); Burnley February 1907; retired cs 1929. Later scouted for Burnley. Other honours: Football League (4 apps). (Burnley) FL champions 1921. He also received a FA Cup winner's medal in 1914 after missing the final because of injury.
Goalkeeper. whose quick eye, long reach and general excellence place him in the vanguard of his craft. Jerry, however, was unfortunately contemporary with that nonpareil, Sam Hardy, hence his meagre return in representative honours. His total peacetime League appearances (530) is still a Burnley record. To this formidable total can be added 39 FA Cup-ties, and the overall aggregate for the club is said to be around 700. Early in life was apprenticed to a blacksmith.

DAY, Samuel Hulme
(Old Malvernians. 1906, 3)
Born Peckham Rye, London, 29 December 1878. Died 21 February 1950.
1906: 5ft. 10$^1/_2$ins.; 11st.

Career: Malvern College (XI 1896-98, captain '98); Cambridge University (Blue 1901); Corinthians 1902-12 (brief spell as club secretary); Old Malvernians. Other honours: English amateur international (1 app). Amateur FA international (5 apps). (Old Malvernians) FA Amateur Cup winner 1902.

Inside-forward. Skilled amateur: neat, quick moving and a sure marksman. Also a renowned cricketer, a Cambridge blue for 4 consecutive seasons, 1899-1902, and for Kent 1897-1919. He had two brothers who also assisted Kent. A schoolmaster by profession who taught at Westminster 1902-13 and then became headmaster of a Berkshire preparatory school. MA Cantab.

DEAN, William Ralph ("Dixie")
(Everton, 1927-33, 16)
Born Birkenhead, 22 January 1907. Died 1 March 1980
1930: 5ft. 10$^1/_2$ins.; 12st. 7lbs.

Career: Birkenhead Schools; Moreton Bible Class; Heswall; Pensby United; Tranmere

Rovers November 1923, originally as an amateur; Everton March 1925 (£2500); Notts County March 1938 (£3000) Sligo Rovers January 1939; Hurst cs 1939; retired during WW2. Other honours: Football League (6 apps). (Everton) FL champions 1928, 1932. FL Div. 2 champions 1931. FA Cup winner 1933. (Sligo R) FA of Ireland Cup finalist 1939.

Centre-forward. A soccer immortal, holder of the Football League seasonal scoring record (60 in 1927/28). Altogether he netted 379 in 437 League outings. This prolific return was achieved by dashing play, powerful marksmanship and unsurpassed skill in headwork. Dixie's progress was unblighted by a bad motor-cycle accident in 1926. He was obliged by ill-health to give up his employment as a Chester licensee in 1962, after which he worked for a pools firm. Somehow it seems a poetic justice that Dixie actually died at Goodison following an Everton/Liverpool derby match.

DEELEY, Norman Victor
(Wolverhampton Wanderers, 1959, 2)
Born Wednesbury, Staffs. 30 November 1933.
1959: 5ft. $4^3/_4$ins.; 10st. 3lbs.

Career: South-East Staffs. Schools; Wolverhampton Wanderers amateur cs 1948, turning professional November 1950; Leyton Orient February 1962 (£13,000); Worcester City July 1964; Bromsgrove Rovers cs 1967; Darlaston August 1971. Other honours: England schoolboy international. (Wolves) FL champions 1958, 1959. FA Cup winner 1960.

Outside-right/outside-left after sound displays at right-half and inside-forward. Very small but, from the start, this seemed no great handicap (note he was capped as a schoolboy). Shrewd, plucky and no stranger to the score sheet: he netted 76 in the course of his 279 League games for Wolves and the Orient.

DEVEY, John Henry George
(Aston Villa, 1892-94, 2)
Born Birmingham, 26 December 1866. Died 11 October 1940
1895: 5ft. $8^1/_2$ins.; 11st. 6lbs.

Career: Excelsior FC; Aston Unity; Mitchells St. George's; Aston Villa March 1891-April 1902. An Aston Villa director from later in 1902-September 1934. Other honours: Football League (4 apps). (Villa) FL champions 1894, 1896, 1897, 1899, 1900. FA Cup winner 1895, 1897; finalist 1892.

Inside-right/centre-forward. Relied on skill and dexterity (the converse of a long servicing successor, Harry Hampton). Had the trick of suddenly pivoting on his heel and shooting for the corner of the enemy goal. A Warwickshire cricketer 1894-1907 after playing in the Minor Counties team 1888-93, he also shone at baseball and cycling. By vocation John Devey was a sports outfitter at Lozells, Birmingham.

DEVONSHIRE, Alan Ernest
(West Ham United, 1980-84, 8)
Born Park Royal, London, 13 April 1956.
1982: 5ft. $10^1/_2$ins.; 11st.

Career: Middlesex Schools; London Schools; Southall; West Ham United September 1976 (£5000).
Other honours: England 'B' international. (WHU) FL Div. 2 champions 1981. FA Cup winner 1980. FL Cup finalist 1981.

Midfield. A most attractive player with the unfashionable (or perhaps the word should be 'forbidden') attribute of running the ball round opponents in a sinuous dribble, having the balance to withstand crude tackling. A bad knee injury early in 1984 came at a time when he was in view for regular England selection. Once worked as a fork-lift truck driver for Hoover's. Alan had an 18-month association with Crystal Palace when 16, after which he was out of football for 2 years. Son of Les Devonshire (Crystal Palace, 1951-55).

DEWHURST, Frederic
(Preston North End, 1886-89, 9)
Born Preston, Lancs. 16 December 1863. Died 21 April 1895.
1889: 5ft. $10^1/_2$ins.; 12st. 7lbs.

Career: Preston junior football; Preston North End 1882 – 1891. Also assisted the Corinthians 1886-89. Other honours: (PNE) FL champions 1889. FA Cup winner 1889; finalist 1888.

Inside-left. A leading amateur. It would seem he and Dr. Mills-Roberts were the unpaid brigade's sole contributions to the famous Invincibles' line-up. Dewhurst, splendidly proportioned and diligent in performance, excelled in footwork and passing. Scored 12 times in his 28 matches for the Corinthians, so consistent in this aspect. He was a master at Preston Catholic Grammar School.

DEWHURST, Gerald Powys
(Liverpool Ramblers, 1895, 1)
Born London, 14 February 1872. Died 29 March 1956.
Career: Repton School (XI 1889-90); Cambridge University (Blue 1892-3-4); Liverpool Ramblers; Corinthians 1892-95.

Inside-forward. A heavy build but fast nonetheless, weight making his shooting additionally powerful. His fault – as with so many pre-1914 amateurs – lay in a tendency to hog the ball. He maintained a good scoring rate, e.g. 18 goals in 32 games for the Corinthians. By calling a cotton merchant based in Liverpool. In the 1930s was living at Llandegla near Wrexham.

DICKINSON, James William
(Portsmouth, 1949-57, 48)
Born Alton, Hants. 24 April 1925. Died 9 November 1982.
1950: 5ft. 10ins.; 11st.

Career: Hampshire schools football; Alton Youth Club; Portsmouth as an amateur 1943, turning professional January 1944. Portsmouth FC scout and PRO on retirement as a player, April 1965, secretary July 1968 and manager April 1977-May 1979 when he retired on medical advice. Other honours: England 'B' international (3 apps). Football League (11 aps). (Portsmouth) FL Champions 1949, 1950. FL Div. 3 champions 1962.

Left-half the main berth but also played right-half for England and, late in his career, at centre-half and left-back for Pompey. Not a spectacular performer but one whose quiet, super efficient skills graced the game for 19 peacetime campaigns. The ultimate in one clubmanship: 764 League appearances (establishing an all-time FL record, since surpassed) and 36 years association on and off the field. Said to have been coached by Eddie Lever, a Portsmouth player and subsequent manager, from the age of 8. Awarded the MBE in the 1964 Birthday Honours List.

DIMMOCK, James Henry
(Tottenham Hotspur, 1921-26, 3)
Born Edmonton, London, 5 December 1900. Died 23 December 1972
1921: 5ft. $9^1/_2$ins.; 11st. 9lbs.

Career Edmonton schoolboy football; Park Avenue FC; Gothic Works; registered with Tottenham Hotspur when 17 and assisted Clapton Orient and Edmonton Ramblers during WW1, becoming a Spurs' professional May 1919; Thames August 1931; Clapton Orient September 1932; Ashford March 1934; retired cs 1934. Other honours: (Spurs) FL Div. 2 champions 1920. FA Cup winner 1921.

Outside-left. Emerged after the Great war as a leading left-winger and a major star of Spurs' great 1919-22 period. Jimmy was extremely elusive, had innate ball control and shot strongly when on the run, Worked in the road haulage industry on leaving the game.

DITCHBURN Edwin George
(Tottenham Hotspur, 1949-57, 6)
Born Gillingham, Kent, 24 October 1921.
1950: 6ft. 0$^{3}/_{4}$in.; 12st. 12lbs.

Career: Northfleet schoolboy football; Northfleet Paper Mills; Tottenham Hotspur amateur cs 1937 (sent to Spurs' nursery side, Northfleet FC, for development 1938), turning professional cs 1939 (during WW2 service in RAF was a member of the Tommy Walker X1 which toured the Far East); Romford April 1959-1965, acting as player/manager July 1959-March 1962; Brentwood August 1965. Other honours: England wartime international (2 apps). England 'B' international (2 apps). Football League (6 apps). Spurs FL champions 1951. FL Div. 2 champions 1950.

Goalkeeper. Son of a Kent heavy-weight boxing champion, Ted himself nearly took up the noble art seriously. Fortunately for Spurs, however, it was soccer that claimed his allegiance. Quite brilliant – and consistent as well – he threw his big frame around in acrobatic fashion aided by hands large enough to be in the Frank Swift class. Ted's 418 League outings included a consecutive run of 247. Later a Romford sports outfitter.

DIX, Ronald William
(Derby County, 1939, 1)
Born Bristol, 5 September 1912.
1938: 5ft. 8$^{1}/_{2}$ins.; 12st.

Career: Bristol Schools; Bristol Rovers 1927, originally as an amateur; Blackburn Rovers May 1932 (£3000); Aston Villa May 1933; Derby County February 1937; Tottenham Hotspur June 1939 (guest player for Blackpool during WW2); Reading November 1947; retired cs 1949. Other honours: England Schoolboy international (2 apps). Football League (1 app).

Inside-forward, mostly inside-left. Earned a mammoth reputation as a schoolboy star and much coveted as a consequence. Made his League debut at 15 years, 173 days and, on scoring a week later (March 3, 1928), was said to be the youngest scorer ever in a FL match. Ronnie was clever and highly constructive with an important added quality of consistency.

DIXON, John Auger
(Notts County, 1885, 1)
Born Grantham, 27 May 1861. Died 8 June 1931.

Career: Played soccer at his three schools (Grantham Grammar, Nottingham High and Chigwell Grammar) and assisted Notts County from the middle of season 1884/85. In this season he played also for the Corinthians. Retired on health grounds circa 1886.

Left-wing forward who played a serious game, spirited and unstinting in effort. A county cricketer for Notts. 1882-1905, captaining the side for 11 seasons from 1889. Was a member of the Notts. CCC committee from 1895 to his death and memorial gates were erected at the main entrance of the Trent Bridge ground in 1933. Was partner in a firm of manufacturing clothiers and a JP.

DIXON, Kerry M.
(Chelsea, 1985-87, 8)
Born Luton, 24 July 1961.
1986: 6ft.; 13st.

Career: Cheshunt; Tottenham Hotspur apprentice; Dunstable Town 1979; Reading July 1980 (£20,000); Chelsea August 1983 (£175,000). Other honours: England Under-21 international (1 app). (Chelsea) FL Div. 2 champions 1984.

Strike-forward. A consistent goal scorer throughout his career, the 52 netted while with Dunstable inducing Reading to provide a League debut. Has an ideal build, is athletic and possessing main attributes of pace and heading ability. After leaving school was apprenticed as a tool-maker.

DOBSON, Alfred Thomas Carrick
(Notts County, 1882-84, 4)
Born Basford, Nottingham, 1859. Died 22 October 1932.

Career: Downside School; Notts County; Corinthians.

Right-back defined in 1884 as 'a hard working and reliable back'. He was also very fast and tackled most effectively. Was not unduly handicapped by weak eyesight. Brother of Charles Dobson below, the pair both being engaged in the family's fabric business in Nottingham.

DOBSON, Charles Frederick
(Notts County, 1886, 1)
Born Basford, Nottingham, 9 September 1862. Died 18 May 1939.

Career: Junior football to Notts County (making his final senior appearance in season 1888/89); Corinthians 1885-86.

Half-back. Had his variable moments but for the most part a capable half. Plied his forwards with useful passes and took a full role in defence. Played his first and last League match for Notts County against Aton Villa on December 8, 1888, which turned out to be his final senior appearance for the club. Younger brother of Alf Dobson (q.v.) with whom he worked in the family's Nottingham fabric business.

DOBSON, J(ohn) Martin
(Burnley and Everton, 1974-75, 5)
Born Blackburn, 14 February 1948.
1975: 5ft. 10ins.; 11st. 6lbs.

Career: Lancashire Youth; Bolton Wanderers July 1966; Burnley August 1967; Everton August 1974 (£300,000 – a record); Burnley again August 1979 (£100,000); Bury as player/manager March 1984, from 1986 serving as manager until March 1989. Other honours: England Under-23 international (1 app). Football League (1 app). (Burnley) FL Div. 2 champions 1973. (Everton) FL Cup finalist 1977. (Burnley) FL Div. 3 champions 1982.

Midfield. Possessor of admirable technique 'with the capacity of the best 'W' formation wing-halves not only to win tackles but to drive forward into attack.' 'In modern terms, both a ball winner and creator – a rarity these days,' wrote another commentator. Represented England Grammar Schools at both soccer and cricket. Martin made no League appearances for Bolton, who gave him a free transfer after a single season, and nearly gave up the game disillusioned, but fortunately Burnley stepped in.

DOGGART, A(lexander) Graham
(Corinthians, 1924, 1)
Born Bishop Auckland, 2 June 1897. Died 7 June 1963.
1922: 5ft. 8ins.; 12st.

Career: Darlington Grammar School; Bishop's Stortford School (XI 1912-16); Cambridge University (Blue 1921-22); Corinthians for many seasons from 1920/21; Darlington April 1922. playing in 2 League matches before the season ended; Bishop Auckland. Served on the FA Council 1932-50, was vice-President 1950-61 and President from May 1961 (he collapsed and died at the 1963 AGM). He was acting Chairman 1961-62 when the holder was indisposed. Other honours: England amateur international (4 apps).

Inside-left. A leading amateur of his day, expert at close dribbling and ball control, and owner of a blistering left-foot shot. The Corinthians' champion marksman – up to the end of 1931/32 had scored an amazing 160 in 170 appearances. Head of a famous cricketing family: he himself played for Cambridge (Blue 1921-22), Durham and Middlesex, and one of his sons (Hubert) appeared in 2 Tests for England. Graham Doggart was a chartered accountant.

DORRELL, Arthur Reginald
(Aston Villa, 1925-26, 4)
Born Small Heath, Birmingham. 30 March 1896. Died 13 September 1942.
1924: 5ft. $6^1/_2$ins.; 10st. 2lbs.

Career: Leicester Schools; Carey Hall (Leicester Sunday School side); Army football; Aston Villa May 1919; Port Vale June 1931; retired cs 1932. Other honours: Football League (2 apps). (Villa) FA Cup winner 1920; finalist 1924.

Outside-left. Mainly notable for speed and the ability to middle the ball accurately when going full tilt. Ice-cool in any situation, he formed a famous wing with Billy Walker (q.v.) Arthur was a son of William Dorrell, Aston Villa of the 'Nineties, who represented the Football League. He served throughout the Great War, giving a false age on enlisting in 1914.

DOUGLAS, Bryan
(Blackburn Rovers, 1958-63, 36)
Born Blackburn, 27 May 1934.
1960: 5ft. 5ins.; 9st. 10lbs.

Career: Blackburn Schools; Blackburn Youth; Lancashire Youth; Lower Darwen Youth Club; Blackburn Rovers on amateur forms 1950, turning professional April, 1952; Great Harwood June 1969. Other honours: England 'B' international (1 app). England Under-23 international (5 apps). Football League (4 apps). (Blackburn R) FA Cup finalist 1960.

Outside-right/inside-forward. A ball artist of the first rank who, like so many of his kind, was unorthodox in his wanderings, which made for much entertainment value. A one-club man – as regards the senior game – and for his local club too, Bryan scored 102 goals in 438 League matches for the Rovers. Wonderfully consistent over his 19 years on the Ewood books.

DOWNS, John Thomas ('Dicky')
(Everton, 1921, 1)
Born Middridge, Co. Durham, 13 August 1886. Died 24 March 1949.
1921: 5ft. $6^1/_2$ins.; 12st.

Career: Crook; Shildon Athletic September 1907; Barnsley May 1908; Everton March 1920 (£2500); Brighton and Hove Albion August 1924; retired through injury May 1925. Afterwards coached in Europe. Other honours: Football League (2 apps). (Barnsley) FA Cup winner 1912; finalist 1910.

Right-back. Short but weighty back celebrated for hefty acrobatic kicking and as an exponent – some said inventor – of the sliding tackle. Something of a joy to cartoonists as well, with his bandy, heavily muscled legs. Certainly a personality to relish.

DOYLE, Michael
(Manchester City, 1976-77, 5)
Born Manchester, 25 November 1946.
1976: 6ft.; 11st. 9lbs.

Career: Stockport Schools; Manchester City ground staff May 1962, turning professional May 1964; Stoke City June 1978 (£50,000); Bolton Wanderers January 1982; Rochdale August 1983 – 1984. Other honours: England Under-23 international(8 apps). Football League (2 apps). (Man. City) European Cup Winners' Cup, winner 1970. FL champions 1968. FL Div. 2 champions 1966. FA Cup winner 1969. FL Cup winner 1970, 1976; finalist 1974.

Right-half. Tall and powerful, a stalwart throughout Manchester City's great decade from 1965. Mick's was a determined style with an incisive tackle that brooked no argument. In all he made 551 appearances (and 7 substitutions) in senior competition while at Maine Road, in which he scored 40 goals.

DRAKE, Edward Joseph
(Arsenal, 1935-38, 5)
Born Southampton, 16 August 1912.
1936: 5ft. 10ins.; 11st. 12lbs.

Career: Southampton Schools; Winchester City; Southampton FC November 1931; Arsenal March 1934 (£6000); retired through injury 1945. Became Hendon FC manager before appointment as Reading manager June 1947; Chelsea Manager June 1952-September 1961; Barcelona assistant manager January-June 1970; later in the 1970s a full-time Fulham scout into the 1980s. Other honours: (Arsenal) FL Champions 1935, 1938. FA Cup winner 1936.

Centre-forward. In 'Forward Arsenal!', his Highbury colleague, Bernard Joy, graphically wrote 'There was no finesse about Drake. He went for the ball in a blunt, uncompromising way. A human dynamo, big hearted and well-built, he had great speed and a powerful shot.' These vigorous tactics brought him many injuries but also many goals. His 42 in the League, 1934/35, remains an Arsenal record, and he netted 7 against Villa during the following season, 14 December 1935. He worked as a gas meter inspector when with Southampton, and between managerial appointments were periods as a bookmaker and salesman. Ted played for Hampshire CCC 1931-36, and his son, Bob, was a Fulham full-back in the 'Sixties.

DUCAT, Andrew
(Woolwich Arsenal and Aston Villa, 1910-21, 6)
Born Brixton, London, 16 February 1886, Died 23 July 1942.
1910: 5ft.10ins; 11st. 11lbs.

Career: Southend schoolboy football; Westcliff Athletic (Southend); Southend Athletic; Woolwich Arsenal February 1905;

Aston Villa June 1912 (£1500) Fulham May 1921 (£2000); retired May 1924 then becoming their manager to May 1926. He was then reinstated as an amateur and joined the Casuals. Other honour: (Villa) FA Cup winner 1920.

Right-half, cultured and unflurried, a master of positional play. Had formerly played centre-forward and, as a schoolboy, at full-back. A noted Surrey cricketer (1906-31) with one Test appearance for England. Outside his sporting activities Ducat at different times had differing jobs which included sports outfitting, hotel management and journalism. He died at the wicket at Lords in a wartime cricket match.

DUNN, Arthur Tempest Blakiston
(Old Etonians, 1883-92, 4)
Born Whitby, 12 August 1860. Died 20 February 1902.

Career: Eton College; Cambridge University (Blue 1883-84); Old Etonians; Granta; Corinthians 1886-92. Also represented Cambridgeshire and Norfolk. Other honours: (Old Etonnians) FA Cup winner 1882; finalist 1883.

Centre-forward at the outset but obviously a utility man as he played elsewhere in the attack and, for his two internationals of' 92, appeared at right-back. The Alcock annual for 1884 says Dunn was 'a good centre, rather light, but has plenty of pluck, and is a sure shot at goal'. A schoolmaster, he founded Ludgrove School, New Barnet, 1892. an establishment which subsequently had W J Oakley and G O Smith (q.v.) as joint headmasters. The well known 'Old Boys' trophy, the Arthur Dunn Cup, was donated by R C Gosling (q.v.) in his memory. His daughter, Mary Dunn, born 1900, became a noted satirical writer.

DUXBURY, Michael
(Manchester United, 1984-85, 10)
Born Accrington, 1 September 1959.
1984: 5ft. 9½ins.; 11st. 2lbs.

Career: Lancashire schoolboy football; Manchester United apprentice 1975 turning professional October 1976. Other honours: England Under-21 international (7 apps). (Man. Utd) FA Cup winner 1983, 1985 (sub). FL Cup finalist 1983.

Right-back chiefly though possessing a versatility that can cope with any defensive or midfield berth. An inconspicuous reserve until blossoming in the 1980/81 campaign, gaining England Under-21 status that very season. Is very resilient and plucky and has a dogged spirit well demonstrated in tackling. No slouch either, a useful quality when raiding down the touch-line.

EARLE, Stanley George James
(Clapton and West Ham United, 1924-28, 2)
Born Stratford, London, 6 September 1897. Died 26 September 1971.
1927: 6ft. 1in.; 12st. 1lb.

Career: West Ham Schools; Clapton (Arsenal on amateur forms March 1922, making 4 Div.1 appearances and scoring 3 goals 1921/22-23/24); West Ham United as an amateur August 1924, signing professional the following year; Clapton Orient May 1932; retired cs 1933. Later Leyton Manager (resigned October 1946) and Walthamstow Avenue's coach. Other honours: England schoolboy international (1 app). England amateur international (2 apps). (Clapton) FA Amateur Cup winner 1924.

Inside-right. It was said he made the change to professional status, aged nearly 28, with some reluctance, but the Hammers certainly had no cause to repine. Tall, immensely constructive, creating and scoring goals, Stanley was first choice at Upton Park for 6 of his 8 campaigns there. Son of Harry Earle, pre-WW1 goalkeeper for Millwall Athletic and other clubs.

EASTHAM, George Edward
(Arsenal, 1963-66, 19)
Born Blackpool, 23 September 1936.
1965: 5ft. 7½ins.; 9st. 12½lbs.

Career: Ards (Northern Ireland) amateur, turning professional May 1956; Newcastle United later in May 1956 (£9000); Arsenal November 1960 (£47,500); Stoke City August 1966 (£30,000); Hellenic FC (Cape Town) as player/manager February-August 1971; Stoke City again October 1971, assistant manager also December 1972, retiring from playing February 1975; Stoke City manager May 1977 (after 3 months as caretaker) to January 1978. Other honours: England Under-23 international (6 apps.) Football League (3 apps) (Stoke C) FL Cup winners 1972.

Inside-right for the major part of his career. Like his father (George snr., below) an extremely deft ball player and graceful with it. Preferred a creative rather than a goal-scoring role. When at Newcastle instigated a famous High Court action that led to the removal of the maximum wage and changes in the retain and transfer system. Awarded the OBE in 1973.

EASTHAM, George Richard
(Bolton Wanderers, 1935, 1)
Born Blackpool, 13 September 1913.
1938: 5ft 8ins.; 10st. 2½lbs.

Career: Cambridge Juniors (Blackpool); South Shore Wednesday (Blackpool); Bolton Wanderers 1932; Brentford June 1937; Blackpool November 1938 (£7000); Swansea Town August 1947; Rochdale June 1948; Lincoln City January 1949; Hyde United 1950. Ards player/manager July 1953-55, continuing as manager to October 1958, when appointed Accrington Stanley manager; Belfast Distillery manager June 1959-March 1964; Ards manager again late 1964-March 1970; Hellenic FC (South Africa) manager late 1971 after spell scouting for Stoke City; Glentoran manager for a spell late 1972.

Inside-forward. A superlative close dribbler and master of the delayed pass. Sometimes called 'Diddler' by the press, which was highly appropriate in view of the way opponents were mesmerised. He originally worked in a Blackpool bakery. Father of George jnr. (above) – when the latter was first capped in 1962/63, it was the first time a father and son had won full England caps.

ECKERSLEY, William
(Blackburn Rovers, 1950-54, 17)
Born Southport, 16 July 1925. Died 25 October 1982.
1950: 5ft. 6ins.; 10st. 1lb.

Career: High Park FC (Southport); Blackburn Rovers as an amateur November 1947, turning professional March 1948; retired through injury February 1961. Other honours: England 'B' international (3 apps). Football League (6 apps.)

Left-back. Slight and light yet his tackling was good and effective. Other easily discerned qualities were composure and clearances so accurately judged that few were wasted. Bill worked as a private car driver latterly.

EDWARDS, Duncan
(Manchester United, 1955-58, 18)
Born Dudley, Worcs. 1 October 1936. Died 21 February 1958 as a result of injuries sustained in the Munich air crash.
1957: 5ft. 11ins.; 13st.

Career: Dudley Schools when only 11; Manchester United on amateur forms May 1952, turning professional October 1953. Other honours: England schoolboy international (9 apps). England Youth international. England 'B' international (4 apps). England Under-23 international (6 apps). Football League (4 apps). (Man. Utd.) FL champions 1956, 1957. FA Cup finalist 1957.

Left-half. Of all the many valuable lives lost through the Munich air crash, none was a greater loss than that of Duncan Edwards. Like a young Colossus he had bestrode the game as the complete footballer when astonishingly youthful; courageous and mightily skilled in every facet of ball play. Duncan was among the youngest of schoolboy caps and the youngest debutant for club and country. There are two stained glass windows to his memory at St Francis Church, Dudley. Cousin of Dennis Stevens (Bolton Wanderers & England Under-23).

EDWARDS, John Hawley
(Shropshire Wanderers, 1874, 1)
Born Shrewsbury, 1850. Died 14 January 1893.

Career: Shropshire Wanderers; Wanderers, Shrewsbury FC. Was the first Treasurer of the FA of Wales on its formation in 1876. Other honours; Welsh international 1876 (1 app). (Wanderers) FA Cup winner 1876.

Forward. Hard working and unselfish. Dribbled strongly but occasionally overran the ball. Came into the England side as a late replacement for J G Wylie and showed excellent form 'in spite of the disadvantages under which he laboured from being a stranger to most of his own team.' (One wonders if the fact his birth was registered at Shrewsbury accounts for the selection). A solicitor by profession (admitted September 1871), he was Clerk to the Shrewsbury magistrates for 19 years until his death. Played cricket for Shropshire in the early 1870s and had a spell as the club's secretary.

EDWARDS, Willis
(Leeds United, 1926-30, 16)
Born Newton, Derbys. 28 April 1903. Died 27 September 1988.
1927: 5ft. 8ins.; 11st. 9lbs.

Career: Newton Rangers; Chesterfield cs 1922; Leeds United March 1925 (£1500); retired during WW2 becoming the club's trainer, serving until June 1960. This long spell was interrupted by his year as United's manager (May 1947-April 1948). Other honours: Football League (11 apps).

Right-half, possibly the best of the inter-war era. The complete wing-half yet quite unspectacular – calm, superb on control and positional play, and deceptively quick. 'Rolled his passes through the gaps with the

cool precision of a billards player', reported one scribe. A great performer.

ELLERINGTON, William
(Southampton, 1949, 2)
Born Southampton, 30 June 1923.
1949: 6ft.; 12st. 3lbs.

Career: Sunderland Schools; Fatfield Juniors (Sunderland FC amateur); Southampton on amateur forms 1940, turning professional 1945; retired cs 1961. Subsequently had spell in charge of Southampton's colts. Other honours: England schoolboy international. England 'B' international (1 app). Football League (1 app).

Right-back. A star from his school days, physically commanding and highly proficient in tackling and positional play. Billy's first-class career was interrupted by a serious bout of pneumonia in the late 1940s, and it was by no means certain he would be able to resume. Happily he recovered to give the Saints many more years of service. Son of Billy Ellerington snr., well known Middlesbrough half-back of the 'Twenties.

ELLIOTT, George Washington
(Middlesbrough 1913-20, 3)
Born Sunderland, 1889. Died 27 November 1948.
1921: 5ft.9ins.; 11st. 8lbs.

Career: Middlesbrough schools football; Redcar Crusaders; South Bank; Middlesbrough FC May 1909 (guest player for Celtic during WW1); retired August 1925. Other honours: Football League (3 apps).

Centre-forward. (Played inside for Middlesbrough after the return of the

Scottish cap, A N Wilson, cs 1921). A contemporary critic said it was '. doubtful whether England has possessed a more competent centre-forward but he is not always at his best in representative matches.'He was, the critic went on,'the brainy type, holding wings together in finished style. perhaps would have been even more successful if more go-ahead.' Subtle head and footwork also brought forth praise. He came from a long established shipping family, and he himself was employed as a cargo superintendent at Middlebrough Docks.

ELLIOTT, William Henry
(Burnley, 1952-53, 5)
Born Bradford, 20 March 1925.
1951: 5ft. 7ins.; 10st. 7lbs.

Career: Bradford schoolboy and junior football; Bradford FC amateur 1939/40, turning professional March 1942; Burnley August 1951 (£23,000); Sunderland June 1953 (£26,000); Wisbech Town July 1959-61; national coach to Libyan FA 1961-63; Sheffield Wednesday scout 1963-64; coach to US forces in Germany 1964-66; Daring FC (Brussels) trainer July 1966; Sunderland coach January 1968-June 1973; Brann FC (Norway) coach 1974-78; Sunderland caretaker manager December 1978-May 1979; Darlington manager June 1979 – June 1983. Other honours: Football League (4 apps).

Outside-left. was where his reputation was made, later moving in turn to left-half and left-back. Correctly summed up 'fast and incisive; Billy was no great goal scorer (58 in a total 443 League matches) but he 'made' a myriad. Garnered a rich cosmopolitan variety of coaching and managerial appointments after giving up playing.

EVANS, Robert Ernest
(Sheffield United, 1911-12, 4)
Born Chester, 21 November 1885. Died 28 November 1965.
1913: 5ft. 11ins.; 11st. 5lbs.

Career: Saltney Ferry; Wrexham cs 1905; Aston Villa early in 1906; Sheffiel;d United 1908; retired during WW1. Other honours: Welsh international (10 apps). (Sheffield U.) FA Cup winner 1915.

Outside-left. A lithe winger, unusually tall for the position, whose raking stride left many an opponent floundering. In addition, was a dangerous marksman. Born of Welsh parents and an established international for the Principality until the England selectors discovered he actually hailed from Chester. Evans later worked for the Shell-Mex oil company at Ellesmere Port and turned out for their soccer team.

EWER, Frederick Harold
(Casuals, 1924-25, 2)
Born West Ham, 30 September 1898. Died 29 January 1971.

Career: Casuals; Corinthians from the 1922/23 season into the 1930s. Other honours: England amateur international (14 apps).

Wing-half. Adept on both flanks, Ewer was among the leading inter-war amateurs: a resolute, gritty performer persistently coming back in the face of many injuries. His peak occurred in the 1923-30 period when all his caps, full and amateur, were won. One of a select number to have played in a 100 and more matches for the Corinthians (at the end of 1931/32, his total stood at 142). A member of the Stock Exchange.

FAIRCLOUGH, Percy
(Old Foresters, 1878, 1)
Born Mile End, London, 1 February 1858. Died 22 June 1947.

Career: Forest school (X1 1876-77); Old Foresters; Corinthians. Also represented Essex and London.

Forward. Somewhat ponderous yet a powerful attacking player exploiting a strong (if often wayward) kick. Like many of the pioneers, made an ally of the robust shoulder charge. Was a partner in a stockbroking firm and member of the Stock Exchange for 40 years. Lost his life as a result of a road accident.

FAIRHURST, David Liddle
(Newcastle United, 1934, 1)
Born Blyth, Northumberland, 20 July 1906. Died 26 October 1972.
1932: 5ft. 8ins.; 11st. 13lbs.

Career: New Delaval Villa; Blyth Spartans; Walsall June 1927; Newcastle United March 1929 (£1750); retired May 1946. Was Birmingham City's trainer from July 1946 for a time. Other honour: (Newcastle) FA Cup winner 1932.

Left-back. Sturdily built and quite reliable. Maintained a fair level of performance for Newcastle, being first choice for 6 of his 10 peacetime seasons, never dropping below 28 League outings in the sequence. Came from a soccer family: his father assisted Blyth Spartans and his brother, William, Shaw Fairhurst, also a full-back, played for Nelson, Northampton Town and Southport during the inter-war period. A former mines and shipyard worker.

FANTHAM, John
(Sheffield Wednesday, 1962, 1)
Born Sheffield, 6 February 1939.
1962: 5ft. $7^{1}/_{4}$ins.; 11st. $2^{1}/_{2}$lbs.

Career: Sheffield Schools; Yorkshire Schools; Sheffield YMCA; Sheffield Wednesday amateur 1954, turning professional October 1956; Rotherham United October 1969 (£5000); Macclesfield cs 1971. Other honours: England Under-23 international (1 app). Football League (3 apps). (Wednesday) FL Div.2 champions 1959. FA Cup finalist 1966.

Inside-forward. Sturdily proportioned, combining in his play tenacious foraging and regular goal-getting to some purpose. Scored 167 in 426 senior matches (and 9 substitutions) whilst at Hillsborough. A successful business man after leaving football, Johnny was a son of J T Fantham, a well known professional with Rotherham United and other clubs in the 'Thirties. He shone also at cricket (represented Yorkshire Schools) and golf.

FELTON, William
(Sheffield Wednesday, 1925, 1)
Born Heworth nr. Gateshead, 1 August 1900. Died 22 April 1977.
1926: 5ft. 9ins.; 12st.

Career: Pelaw Albion; Pandon Temperance; Wardley Colliery; Jarrow; Grimsby Town January 1921; Sheffield Wednesday January 1923 (£1500); Manchester City March 1929; Tottenham Hotspur March 1932; Altrincham cs 1935. Other honour:(Wednesday) FL Div.2 champions 1926.

Right-back, who often took the left flank also. 'A powerful and robust defender, quick to tackle and recover. Just a little excitable,' averred a mid-'Twenties critic after praising Felton's heartiness and brilliance. Skippered Spurs' promotion team of 1932/33. Cousin of Sam Barkas (q.v.)

FENTON, Michael
(Middlesbrough, 1938, 1)
Born Stockton-on-Tees, 30 October 1913.
1938: 5ft. 9ins.; 11st.

Career: Stockton Schools; South Bank East End; Middlesbrough March 1933, appointed player/coach January 1949, retiring as a player cs 1951 and continuing as a club coach until cs 1966.

Centre-forward. was where the reputation was made, later demonstrating he could take an inside berth with equal facility. Micky was outstandingly quick, even from a standing start, a two-footed marksman and strong enough to withstand buffetings. A member of the 1939 FA touring party to South Africa, he played against the national team 3 times. Apart from football, ran a Stockton newsagency.

FENWICK, Terence W.
(Queen's Park Rangers, 1984-88, 20)
Born Camden, Co. Durham, 17 November 1959.
1985: 5ft. 11ins.; 11st. 1lb.

Career: Junior football; Crystal Palace apprentice, turning professional December 1976; Queen's Park Rangers December 1980 (£100,000); Tottenham Hotspur December 1987 (£550,000). Other honours: England Youth international. England Under-21 international (11 apps). (Palace) FL Div.2 champions 1979. (QPR) FL Div.2 champions 1983. FA Cup finalist 1982. FL Cup finalist 1986

Defender. Built on slender lines, quick and incisive in the challenge and one dispensing the ball to profitable purposes. Has turned out, too, to be a good skipper at Loftus Road. Terry has been much among both representative and club honours since gaining a Youth cap in 1978.

FIELD, Edgar
(Clapham Rovers, 1876-81, 2)
Born Wallingford, Berks. 29 July 1854. Died 11 January 1934.

Career: Lancing College (XI 1870-71); Reading during the mid-1870s; Clapham Rovers. Also assisted Berks and Bucks in representative matches. Other honours: (Clapham Rovers) FA Cup winner 1880; finalist 1879.

Full-back. Mostly on the left but took the right-hand berth for his 1881 international. That year's football Annual described him as a 'powerful but somewhat erratic kick' and that 'he charges well but is rather slow.' (Some writers have always believed in a 'warts and all' approach it seems). Field was a chartered accountant by profession. With Reading he partnered J R Morgan, a Cambridge Blue and subsequent holder of 10 Welsh caps.

FINNEY, Thomas
(Preston North End, 1947-59, 76)
Born Preston, Lancs. 5 April 1922.
1950: 5ft. 7 $^{1}/_{2}$ins.; 10st. 6lbs

Career: Preston Schools, Preston North End on amateur forms 1937, turning professional January 1940 (while serving with Tank Corps during WW2 played with the British Services XI, the Wanderers, in the Middle East); retired April 1960. Later on the PNE board. Other honours: England 'B' international (1 app). Football League (17 apps). (PNE) FL Div.2 champions 1951. FA Cup finalist 1954.

Outside-right principally – though a natural left-footer – with substantial and successful spells at centre-forward and outside-left also. By general acknowledgement, a genius of a player, effortlessly flitting through defences to release a scoring shot. Awarded the OBE in the 1961 Birthday Honours List and twice 'Footballer of the year' (1954 and '57). In an aggregate 569 first-class matches, scored 249 goals: he never played in North End's reserve side. Vice-President of PNE cs 1973 and President during season 1975/76. Head of a Preston plumbing and electrical contracting firm.

FLEMING, Harold John
(Swindon Town, 1909-14, 11)
Born Downton nr. Salisbury, 30 April 1887. Died 23 August 1955.
1909: 5ft. 10ins.; 11st. 7lbs.
Career: Swindon junior football; Swindon Town October 1907; retired August 1924. Other honours: Southern League (6 apps).

Inside-right. whose greatness was the biggest factor in Swindon Town's pre-WW1 FA Cup runs. A brilliant player, splendid in dribbling and shooting and, moreover, extremely consistent. Twice a member of FA touring parties, playing twice against South Africa's national side in that of 1910. Fleming was a man of religious principle – son of a clergyman and himself a local preacher – who refused to play on Christmas Days and Good Fridays. He became a

successful business man in Swindon and played Minor Counties cricket for Wiltshire on occasion. Proprietor of a football boot factory in Swindon.

FLETCHER, Albert Thomas
(Wolverhampton Wanderers, 1889-90, 2)
Born Wolverhampton, 4 June 1867. Died 1940.
1889: 5ft. $10^1/_2$ins.; 12st. 1lb.

Career: Willenhall Pickwick; Wolverhampton Wanderers 1885; retired through injury cs 1891, thereupon being appointed Wolves' assistant trainer, a post he held until cs 1920. Other honour: (Wolves) FA Cup finalist 1889.

Right-half. A hard worker and an efficient one whose play benefited from the possession of an ideal build. The flaw was a tendency towards premature commitment. A real Wolves loyalist, though, with 35 years continuous service at Molineux on and off the arena.

FLOWERS, Ronald
(Wolverhampton Wanderers, 1955-66, 49)
Born Edlington nr. Doncaster, 28 July 1934.
1960: 5ft. 11ins.; 12st. 11lbs.

Career: Doncaster area schools football; Yorkshire Schools; Doncaster Rovers Juniors; Wath Wanderers; Wolverhampton Wanderers as a professional July 1952; Northampton Town September 1967, player/manager May 1968-May 1969; Telford United player/coach July 1969-October 1971. Other honours: England Under-23 international (2 apps). Football League (13 apps) (Wolves) FL champions 1954, 1958, 1959. FA Cup winner 1960.

Left-half. A notable Wolf for many seasons, solid and industrious with a crisp tackle and apparently boundless stamina. Loved to go on attack and try a shot himself – he packed a hard one. In an England appearance (October 1959) Ron was the side's senior member – at 25! – establishing a home championship record. His feat in scoring in 4 consecutive internationals (May and June 1962) established another England record (for a non-forward).

FORMAN, Frank
(Nottingham Forest, 1898-1903, 9)
Born Aston-on-Trent, Derbys. 23 May 1875. Died 4 December 1961.
1902: 6ft.; 12st. 4lbs.

Career: Aston-on-Trent FC; Beeston Town; Derby County as an amateur circa 1894; Nottingham Forest February 1895; retired cs 1905. A member of the Nottingham Forest committee 1903-61. Other honours: Football League (2 apps). (Forest) FA Cup winner 1898.

Right/Centre-half with early experience on the left flank. A classic half-back and born leader. Had generalship of a very high order and was composed in the tightest of tight situations. Later in business was a building contractor with his brother-in-law, J H Linacre (q.v.). Brother of F R Forman below. Served a remarkably long time on the Forest committee.

FORMAN, Frederick Ralph
(Nottingham Forest, 1899, 3)
Born Aston-on-Trent, Derbys 8 November 1873. Died 14 June 1910.
1903: 5ft. 11ins.; 11st. 6lbs.

Career: Aston-on-Trent FC; Beeston Town;

Derby County as an amateur; Nottingham Forest cs 1894; retired cs 1903.

Outside-right. was reckoned to be his position but caps were won on the opposite flank. And good versatility was proven as he had performed at half-back and inside-forward also (his height would certainly have been useful in these roles). A competent player, Fred's little failing was an occasional lapse towards lethargy. J H Linacre of Forest and England married his sister while Frank Forman (above) was a younger brother. A railway draughtsman by vocation.

FORREST, James Henry
(Blackburn Rovers, 1884-90, 11)
Born Blackburn, 24 June 1864. Died 30 December 1925.
1880s: 5ft. 7ins.; 10st. 4lbs.

Career: Imperial United; Witton FC 1880; King's Own FC (Blackburn); Blackburn Rovers January 1883; retired cs 1895 but joined Darwen the following October to 1896. A Blackburn Rovers director 1906 to his death. Other honours: (Blackburn R) FA Cup winner 1884,1885,1886,1890,1891.

Left-half with much first-class experience at centre-half despite a slight physique. Forrest was an early 'great', elusive to opponents and marvellous in his clean kicking and precision passing. Holder of several distinctions: shares with Lord Kinnaird and C H R Wollaston the record of the most FA Cup winners's medals won (5); he was the first professional to play for England, and but 19 years of age at the time of his international debut. His son, James Henry jnr., was on Blackburn's books in the 'Twenties.

FORT, John
(Millwall Athletic, 1921, 1)
Born Leigh, Lancs. 15 April 1888. Died 23 November 1965.
1923: 5ft. 8ins.; 12st. 6lbs.

Career: St. Andrew's Mission (Bolton and District League) when 14; Atherton (Lancashire Combination) as a professional 1907; Exeter City cs 1911; Millwall Athletic cs 1914; retired cs 1930 and was subsequently employed in a variety of posts on Millwall's back-room staff – coach, trainer, scout and groundman. He was working as a part-time groundsman to within a few days of his death. Other honours: Southern League (1 app). (Millwall) FL Div.3 (South) champions 1928.

Right-back- Sturdiness personified. A 1920s commentator tells of his '. . . good positional play, uncommonly keen sense of anticipation and strong tackling.' Worked as a miner before taking up soccer full-time. Jack's long association with Millwall which exceeded half a century when including WW1 Army service, places him in the vanguard of outstanding Lions.

FOSTER, Reginald Erskine ('Tip')
(Oxford University and Corinthians, 1900-02, 5)
Born Malvern, Worcs. 16 April 1978. Died 13 May 1914.

Career: Malvern College (XI 1896); Oxford University (Blue 1898-99); Old Malvernians; Corinthians 1899-1902. Other honours: (Old Malvernians) FA Amateur Cup winner 1902.

Inside-forward, with a preference for inside-right, and an emergency goalkeeper. A richly gifted amateur – long in limb, subtle, fine in ball control and shooting and with boundless resource. An Oxford (Blue 1897-1900), Worcestershire and England cricketer (8 Tests), he had six brothers who also assisted Worcester and thus caused the county to be nicknamed 'Fostershire'. He also represented Oxford University at rackets and golf. A stockbroker by profession, his early demise was the result of diabetes.

FOSTER, Stephen B.
(Brighton and Hove Albion, 1982, 3)
Born Portsmouth, 24 September 1957.
1982: 6ft.; 12st. 8lbs.

Career: Junior football to Southampton as an apprentice; Portsmouth October 1975; Brighton and Hove Albion July 1979 (£130,000); Aston Villa March 1984 (£150,000 and another player); Luton Town November 1984 (£70,000). Had a spell as Luton's player/coach to August 1988. Other honours: England Under-21 international (1 app). (Brighton) FA Cup finalist 1983. (Luton Town) FL Cup winner 1988.

Central-defender. A striker originally, rejected by Southampton and converted to the defence while at Fratton Park. Is actually a centre-half of the old school, dominating in challenges for high balls, adept at marshalling his defence and by no means averse to attacking forays. Prominent on the field by reason of a headband that keeps his flowing locks in subjection.

FOULKE, William Henry ('Tiny')
(Sheffield United, 1897, 1)
Born Dawley, Salop, 12 April 1874. Died 1 May 1916.
1892: 6ft. 2ins.; 15st. 1901: 6ft. 2½ins.; 21st.

Career: Alfreton FC; Blackwell Colliery; Sheffield United cs 1894; Chelsea May 1905; Bradford City April 1906; retired November 1907. Other honours: Football League (2 apps). (Sheffield U) FL champions 1898. FA Cup winner 1899, 1902; finalist 1901.

Goalkeeper and the Colossus of the fraternity as the above sets of dimensions illustrate. By the Chelsea days his impressive weight exceeded 22 stones. Not surprisingly Tiny's clearance kicks were both forceful and lengthy, while he could fist a ball an astonishing distance too. Later ran a Penny-a-Penalty sideshow on Blackpool sands – if beaten he paid the successful marksman 3d. Made 4 appearances for Derbyshire CCC in the 1900 season.

FOULKES, William Anthony
(Manchester United, 1955, 1)
Born St Helens, 5 January 1932.
1957: 5ft. 11ins.; 12st. 4lbs.

Career: Whiston Boys Club (St Helens); Manchester United amateur March 1950, turning professional August 1951; retired cs 1970. He thereupon joined United's coaching staff, later in the 1970s holding coaching appointments with New York Cosmos, Chicago Sting and Tulsa Roughnecks. Returning to England he managed Witney Town to March 1980 before going back later in 1980 to coach San José Earthquake for a year or so. Following this he managed two Norwegian clubs, Stenjkoe and Lillestrom. Other honours: England Under-23 international (2 apps). Football League (2 apps). (Man. Utd) European Cup winner 1968. FL champions 1956, 1957, 1965, 1967. FA Cup winner 1963; finalist 1957, 1958.

Right-back/centre-half. An Old Trafford servant into his 39th year: authoritative, efficient and quite dependable, and once holder of the club appearance record. Grandson of a Rugby League international and son of a former New Brighton goalkeeper, Bill himself at one time played soccer on Saturdays and rugger on Sundays. An excellent golfer too, good enough to play for Cheshire.

FOX, Frederick Samuel
(Gillingham, 1925, 1)
Born Highworth nr. Swindon, 22 November 1898. Died 1968.
1925: 5ft. 10ins.; 12st. 4lbs.

Career: Junior football to Swindon Town during WW1; Abertillery; Preston North End cs 1921; Gillingham July 1922; Millwall May 1925; Halifax Town June 1927; Brentford March 1928-1931.

Goalkeeper. The Gills' solitary England cap and that fairly rare phenomenon, a man so honoured while in the ranks of a Third Division club. Fox, however, was a brilliant custodian, boasting a safe pair of hands and excellent anticipation. Apart from 3 appearances for Preston in 1921/22, all his League service was in the Third Divisions, North and South.

FRANCIS, Gerald Charles James
(Queen's Park Rangers, 1975-76, 12)
Born Hammersmith, London, 6 December 1951.
1975: 5ft. 10ins.; 12st. 3lbs.

Career: Chiswick Sunday League football; Queen's Park Rangers apprentice 1968, turning professional June 1969; Crystal Palace May 1979 (£462,000); Queen's Park Rangers again February 1981 (£150,000); Coventry City February 1982 after a month's trial (£150,000); Exeter City player/manager July 1983-May 1984; Cardiff City September 1984; Swansea City October 1984; Portsmouth November 1984-May 1985; Wimbledon later in 1985; Bristol Rovers September 1985, manager July 1987 with seat on the board. Other honours: England Under-23 international (6 apps).

Midfielder of strong attacking instinct, starting attacks from a distance and taking part again in their later stages. Able to lay off the ball at any height or angle, troubling opponents with subtle variations in pace. Unfortunately Gerry's career was marred by injury when he was establishing himself as England's skipper. Son of George Francis (Brentford, 1953-62).

FRANCIS, Trevor John
(Birmingham City, Nottingham Forest, Manchester City and Sampdoria, 1977-86, 52)
Born Plymouth, 19 April 1954.
1981: 5ft. 10ins.; 11st. 7lbs.

Career: Plymouth Schools; Birmingham City apprentice cs 1969, turning professional April 1971; Nottingham Forest February 1979 (£1.1m., Britain's first million-pound fee); Manchester City September 1981 (£1m.); Sampdoria (Genoa) July 1982 (£6-700,000); Atalanta (Bergamo) July 1986; Rangers August 1987 (£75,000); Queen's Park Rangers March 1988, player/manager December 1988. Other honours: England Youth international. England Under-23 international (5 apps). (Forest) European Cup winner 1979. FL Cup finalist 1980. (Rangers) Scottish League Cup winner 1988 (sub).

Forward with outstanding flair for goals (hence the kind of transfer fees he has attracted). Made his senior debut at 16 and hit the headlines by scoring 12 goals in 8 matches. His success has been due to split-second recognitions of opportunity, great acceleration and confidence in his own ability. Trevor's FL record before decamping to Italy read 373 matches, 3 subs, 158 goals.

FRANKLIN, Cornelius ('Neil')
(Stoke City, 1947-50, 27)
Born Stoke-on-Trent, 24 January 1922.
1950: 5ft. 10½ins.; 11st. 4lbs.

Career: Potteries schools football; Stoke Old Boys; Stoke City ground staff 1936, turning professional January 1939 (guest player for Gainsborough Trinity during WW2); Santa Fe, Bogota May 1950; Hull

City February 1951 (£22,500); Crewe Alexandra February 1956 (£1250); Stockport County October 1957 (£1250); Wellington Town as player/coach July 1959; Sankey's FC (Wellington) July 1960, acting as player/manager for a year, 1961-62; retired December 1962. Coach to Appoel FC (Nicosia, Cyprus) February-November 1963; Colchester United manager November 1963-May 1968. Other honours: England wartime international (3 apps). England 'B' international (1 app). Football League (5 apps).

Centre-half. Brilliant star of the immediate post-war era with every requirement: in heading, positioning, marshalling the defence, distribution and ever-stubborn. Some thought he might have been even better in a more creative berth! This stems from his ball mastery. Became an Oswaldtwistle licensee.

FREEMAN, Bertram Clewley

(Everton and Burnley, 1909-12, 5)
Born Handsworth, Birmingham October 1885. Died 11 August 1955.
1909: 5ft. $9^1/_2$ins.; 11st. 12lbs.

Career: Birmingham schoolboy football; Gower Street Old Boys (Aston); Aston Manor; Aston Villa April 1904; Woolwich Arsenal 1905; Everton 1907; Burnley April 1911 (£800 including another player); Wigan Borough September 1921-cs 1922; Kettering Town during season 1923/24, finally retiring cs 1924. Other honours: Football League (4 apps). (Burnley) FA Cup winner 1914.

Centre-forward. 'One of the great marksmen of all time,' wrote a 1919 commentator, and justifiably because Freeman's tally of 38 in a season 1908/09 was then still the record. And it wasn't equalled until 1920/21 or surpassed until 1924/25. Bert, unlike so many contemporaries, was not overly robust, was graceful in action and a schemer who placed his shots rather than blasting them. Had the controlling interest in a cutlery business.

FROGGATT, Jack

(Portsmouth, 1950-53, 13)
Born Sheffield, 17 November 1922.
1951: 5ft. 8ins.; 12st 4lbs.

Career: RAF football; Portsmouth amateur 1945, turning professional in September of that year; Leicester City March 1954 (£15,000); Kettering Town as player/coach November 1957 (£5000), player/manager from January 1958 and player only September 1961-cs 1963. Other honours: Football League (4 apps). (Portsmouth) FL champions 1949, 1950. (Leicester) FL Div. 2 champions 1957.

Centre-half/outside-left; disparate positions yet capped in both, an ultimate test in versatility. Was wont to surge down his wing powerfully and the power was more apparent still as a pivot, his tackling a potent asset. Cousin of Redfern Froggatt (q.v.). After leaving Kettering Jack was employed as a licensee in the Portsmouth area.

FROGGATT, Redfern

(Sheffield Wednesday, 1953, 4)

Born Sheffield, 23 August, 1924.
1950: 5ft. 11ins.; 11st. 1lb.

Career: Sheffield YMCA; Sheffield Wednesday as an amateur before turning professional July 1942; Stalybridge Celtic May 1962. Other honours: England 'B' international (1 app). Football League (1 app). (Wednesday) FL Div. 2 champions 1952, 1956, 1959.

Inside-forward. Spent the whole of a long first-class career at Hillsborough, an astute and constructive inside man. Adept at switching the point of attack with one cross-field pass. His allegience to Wednesday is not surprising as his father was an 'ever-present' in, and the skipper of, the club's 1926 Division Two championship team. Cousin of Jack Froggatt (above). Redfern subsequently worked as the representative of a fuel oil firm.

FRY, Charles Burgess
(Corinthians, 1901, 1)
Born Croydon, Surrey, 25 April 1872. Died 7 September 1956.
1903: 5ft. 10ins.; 11st. 13lbs.

Career: West Kent FC when only 12; Repton School (XI 1888-91, captain '91); Casuals before going to Oxford University (Blue 1892-95, captain '94); Old Reptonians; Corinthians 1892-1903; Southampton 1900-02; Portsmouth 1902-03. Player soccer until 1904. Other honour: (Soton) FA Cup finalist 1902.

Right-back, highly efficient and dependable, but whose not inconsiderable footballing feats were dwarfed by his claims to be the greatest sports all-rounder of all time. An Oxford Blue at cricket (1892-95, captain '94), he also played for Surrey, Sussex, Hampshire and England (26 Tests). He was an athletics Blue (President 1894) specialising in sprints and the long jump, establishing a world record in the latter event. Played rugger for Oxford University (missing his Blue through injury), Blackheath, Barbarians and Surrey. A brilliant scholar – he won a First at Oxford – who taught at Charterhouse 1896-98 and then went into journalism (with the Daily Express and founding, in March 1904, C B Fry's magazine). He then took over the naval training ship, Mercury, in 1908, remaining until retiring in 1950. Was an unsuccessful candidate for parliament as a Liberal. Father of Stephen Fry (Hampshire CCC, 1922-31). An interesting biography of an amazingly gifted and unusual man – who was, by the way, once offered Albania's throne! – is 'C B: a Life of Charles Burgess Fry,' by Clive Ellis (Dent, 1984).

FURNESS, William Isaac
(Leeds United, 1933, 1)
Born New Washington, Co. Durham, 8 June 1909. Died 29 August 1980.
1938: 5ft. 8½ins.; 11st. 6lbs.

Career: Usworth Colliery; Leeds United August 1928 (£50) Norwich City June 1937 (£2750); retired 1947, being then appointed Norwich's assistant trainer, later serving as head trainer until May 1955. Later still was physiotherapist for 8 years, thus completing a quarter of a century with Norwich City.

Inside-forward. A chunky build made him hard to dispossess and a natural aggression brought a fair return in the matter of goals. Assisted Norwich during WW2 while on war work in electrical engineering. Besides his last Carrow Road stint, Billy practised generally as a physiotherapist.

GALLEY, Thomas
(Wolverhampton Wanderers, 1937, 2)
Born Hednesford, Staffs. 4 August 1915.
1935: 5ft. 11ins.; 10st. 12lbs.

Career: Hednesford Schools; Cannock Town (Notts County on amateur forms, later turning professional with Cannock); Wolverhampton Wanderers April 1934; Grimsby Town November 1947; Kidderminster Harriers cs 1949; Clacton Town as player/coach May 1950. Later managed a Cannock junior side. Other honours: Football League (1 app). (Wolves) FA Cup finalist 1939.

Right-half and inside-right mainly, and more than adequate at centre-half and centre-forward – and a first rate utility man in other words. A regular in Major Buckley's fine Wolves line-up of the late 'Thirties, a rangy build giving aerial command and powerful play in other aspects. Father of John Galley, a prominent centre-forward of the 1960s and 70s.

GARDNER, Thomas
(Aston Villa, 1934-35, 2)
Born Huyton, Liverpool, 28 May 1910. Died May 1970.
1934: 5ft. $9^1/_2$ins.; 11st. 4lbs.

Career: Orrell FC (Liverpool); Liverpool on amateur forms 1928, turning professional the following year; Grimsby Town May 1931; Hull City May 1932; Aston Villa February 1934 (£4500); Burnley April 1938 (guest player for Blackpool during WW2); Wrexham December 1945; Wellington Town August 1947; Oswestry Town player/manager before becoming that club's player/coach January 1952; Chester assistant trainer cs 1954-May 1967. Other honour: (Hull City) FL Div. 3 (North) champions 1933.

Right-half. Vied with his contemporary, Sam Weaver (q.v.), as a long throw specialist. In this aspect, Tom won a 1932 competition with a throw of 32 yards, 2 inches. He played an enthusiastic game, preferring the ground pass when parting. Served Wrexham, his last League club, at outside-right. After leaving football was steward at a Chester club.

GARFIELD, Ben Walter
(West Bromwich Albion, 1898, 1)
Born Burton-on-Trent, 4 April 1872. Died 1942.
1903: 5ft. 7ins.; 10st. 3lbs.

Career: Kettering Burton Wanderers 1893 West Bromwich Albion May 1896; Brighton and Hove Albion May 1902 – 1905. Other honour: (Brighton) Southern League Div. 2 champions 1903.

Outside-left. Like many others a slight build was more than compensated for by liveliness and an all-action style. Tremendously popular at the Hawthorns as a consequence, a popularity made the more so because he was a colourful personality as well. Had a good scoring record for a wingman (e.g. 39 goals in 115 senior outings for the Throstles).

GARRATY, William
(Aston Villa, 1903, 1)
Born Saltley, Birmingham, 6 October 1878. Died 6 May 1931.
1905: 5ft. 9ins.; 12st.

Career: Birmingham Schoolboy football; Highfield Villa; Aston Shakespeare; Aston Villa cs 1897; Leicester Fosse September 1908; West Bromwich Albion October 1908; Lincoln City November 1910; retired 1911.

Other honours: (Villa) FL champions 1900. FA Cup winner 1905.

Inside-right/centre-forward able to perform usefully at right-and centre-half also. 'Not polished but a clever, hard working, never-say–die player,' was a typical verdict. Slotted in the goals too, heading the League's scoring list for 1899/1900. From 1923 to his death worked as a driver for a brewery firm.

GARRETT, Thomas H.
(Blackpool, 1952-54, 3)
Born Sunderland, 28 February 1927.
1951: 5ft. 10¼ins.; 12st.

Career: Horden Colliery; Blackpool amateur 1942, turning professional 1946; Millwall May 1961; Fleetwood August 1962; Mayfield United (Newcastle, NSW) cs 1963. Other honours: Football League (3 apps). (Blackpool) FA Cup winner 1953; finalist 1951.

Full-back mainly associated with the left flank. A defender in the classic tradition: confident, fast and resolute. Specialised in keeping his opposing wingman quiet by confining the player's activities to the touchline. Made over 300 League appearances for Blackpool but only a dozen in Millwall's championship side of 1961/62.

GATES, Eric Lazenby
(Ipswich Town, 1981, 2)
Born Ferryhill, Co Durham, 28 June 1955.
1981: 5ft. 6ins.; 10st. 4lbs.

Career: Junior football; Ipswich Town apprentice, turning professional October 1972; Sunderland August 1985 (£150,000). Other honours (Ipswich) UEFA Cup winner 1981.(Sunderland) FL Div. 3 champions 1988.

Forward. At Ipswich played close behind the front runners, pulling opponents out of position. Able to retain the ball when needful and also indulge in shooting surprisingly powerful for one so slight. Brother of the England Youth international, Bill Gates (Middlesbrough 1961-74).

GAY, Leslie Hewitt
(Cambridge University and Old Brightonians, 1893-94, 3)
Born Brighton, 24 March 1871. Died 1 November 1949.

Career: Brighton College (XI 1889); Cambridge University (Blue 1892); Old Brightonians; Corinthians 1891-94.

Goalkeeper. Very skilled and quite fearless. Liked to take the ball early, a liking usually fulfilled because of a keen alertness. A distinguished cricketer (wicket-keeper) who assisted Cambridge University (Blue 1892-93), Hampshire, Somerset and England (1 Test). Also a good golfer, he represented Devon. A land agent by profession, he had also worked as a coffee planter in Ceylon during the 'Nineties.

GEARY, Fred
(Everton, 1890-91, 2)
Born Hyson Green, Notts. 23 January 1868. Died 8 January 1955.

Career: Notts. schoolboy football; Balmoral FC; Notts Rangers with whom he had 3 separate spells due to brief engagements with Grimsby Town (in 1887) and Notts County; Everton cs 1889; Liverpool May 1895 (£60); retired 1899. Other honours: Football League (2 apps). (Everton) FL champions 1891. (Liverpool) FL Div. 2 champions 1896.

Centre-forward, noted for 'his electric runs, trickery and lightning shooting.' Geary's success at Goodison owed not a little to an association with the superb Chadwick/Milward wing, a debt the player himself admitted. He was for many years a Liverpool licensee, including 28 years at one hostelry, retiring in 1946. Latterly too an excellent bowls player good enough to represent Lancashire.

GEAVES, Richard Lyon
(Old Harrovians, 1875, 1)
Born in Mexico, 6 May 1854. Died 21 March 1935.

Career: Harrow School (XI 1872); Cambridge University (Blue 1874); Clapham Rovers; Old Harrovians.

Wing-forward. A hard worker and quite tireless. His speed and clever dribbling made him a difficult man to dispossess. Joined the 14th (Bucks) Prince of Wales Regiment in 1875, retiring with the rank of captain in 1881.

GEE, Charles William
(Everton, 1932-37, 3)
Born Stockport, 6 April 1909. Died 1981.
1938: 5ft. 11ins.; 12st. 6lbs.
Career: Stockport Schools; Reddish Green

Wesleyans; Stockport County October 1928; Everton July 1930 (£3000); retired May 1940. Other honours; Football League (1 app). (Everton) FL champions 1932. FL Div.2 champions 1931.

Centre-half. Of orthodox bent – strong and constructive, plying his forwards with precise ground passes. Deservedly popular with the Goodison crowd because he was a born trier, always in good heart and never gave up. Was side-lined for a cartilage operation in 1932 and was not in Everton's 1932/33 FA Cup-winning side.

GELDARD, Albert
(Everton, 1933-38, 4)
Born Bradford, 11 April 1914.
1935: 5ft. 8ins.; 11st.

Career: Bradford Schools, Manningham Mills; Bradford on amateur forms cs 1928, turning professional 1930; Everton November 1932; Bolton Wanderers June 1938 (£6500); retired cs 1947 but came out of retirement November 1949 to have a spell with Darwen. Other honours: England schoolboy international (3 apps). Football League (1 app). (Everton) FA Cup winner 1933.

Outside-right. Entered the record books early when reputedly becoming the youngest peacetime FL debutant at the tender age of 15 years 156 days. This followed a glittering career in schoolboy football. Albert was blessed with a blistering turn of speed and was wont to cut in and deliver a testing shot. Later worked in sports journalism and was involved in a successful dry-cleaning business.

GEORGE, Charles Frederick
(Derby County, 1977, 1)
Born Islington, London, 10 October 1950.
1977: 5ft. 11ins.; 11st. 9lbs)

Career: Islington Schools; Arsenal apprentice May 1966, turning professional February 1968; Derby County July 1975 (£80,000); Southampton December 1978 (£400,000 then a Southampton record) (Nottingham Forest on loan January-February 1980); Bulova FC (Hong Kong) cs 1981; AFC Bournemouth March 1982; Derby County again March 1982 (Dundee United on trial September 1982, Coventry City on trial cs 1983); retired 1983. Other honours; England Under-23 international (5 apps). (Arsenal) FL champions 1971. FA Cup winner 1971.

Strike-forward. Renowned for explosive shooting backed up by pace and an ice-cool temperament. A big factor in Arsenal's 'Double" triumph of 1971, Charlie was subsequently plagued by a knee injury, playing but 22 times in a Southampton League line-up. He later became a Winchester licensee.

GEORGE, William
(Aston Villa, 1902, 3)
Born Shrewsbury, 29 June 1874. Died 4 December 1933.
1902: 6ft. 1$^1/_2$ins.; 13st. 7lbs.

Career: Woolwich Ramblers; Army football (Trowbridge); Trowbridge Town; Aston Villa October 1897; Birmingham as trainer July 1911 (1 FL app season 1911/12). Other honours: Football League (1 app). (Villa) FL champions 1899,1900. FA Cup winner 1905.

Goalkeeper, whose substantial build was no hindrance to exceptional agility. A keen eye also contributed to George's success and his clearances were thoughtfully placed. Played first-class cricket for Warwickshire 1901-06 and also assisted Wiltshire and Shropshire. After leaving football worked at the Austin Motor Works, Longbridge.

GIBBINS, W(illiam) Vivian T(albot).
(Clapton, 1924-25, 2)
Born Forest Gate, London, 10 August 1901. Died 21 November 1979.
1925: 6ft.; 11st. 10lbs.

Career: Clapton 1919; West Ham United December 1923; Brentford February 1932; Bristol Rovers cs 1932; Southampton September 1933; Leyton 1933/34, subsequently assisting Catford Wanderers, ending playing career in 1939 when his school was evacuated. Other honours: England amateur international (12 apps). (Clapton) FA Amateur Cup winner 1924, 1925. (Leyton) FA Amateur Cup finalist 1934.

Centre/inside-forward. Crack amateur never prevailed upon to take a professional ticket. A schemer and sound tactician, he eventually adapted well to demands of the first-class game scoring, for example, 64 goals in 138 League and FA Cup outings for the Hammers. Was a schoolmaster in East London 1922-67.

GIDMAN, John
(Aston Villa, 1977, 1)
Born Garston, Liverpool, 10 January 1954.
1977: 5ft. 11ins.; 11st. $12^1/_2$lbs.

Career: Liverpool Schools (Liverpool FC amateur); Aston Villa apprentice 1970, turning professional August 1971; Everton October 1979 (£550,000 plus another player valued at £100,000: an Everton record); Manchester United July 1981 (£50,000 and another player); Manchester City October 1986; Stoke City August 1988. Other honours: England Youth international. England 'B' international. England Under-23 international (4 apps). (Villa) FL Cup winner 1977. (Man. Utd) FA Cup winner 1985.

Right-back, on the injured list for more than his fair share of time (and thus missing a few club honours), but a resilient character, returning to play as doughtily as ever. No back has ever been more willing to race down his flank on attack, and he dispenses a tackle of stunning effectiveness.

GILLARD, Ian Terry
(Queen's Park Rangers, 1975-76, 3)
Born Hammersmith, London, 9 October 1950.
1975: 6ft.; 12st. 8lbs.

Career: London schoolboy football (Tottenham Hotspur on associate schoolboy forms when 16); Queen's Park Rangers apprentice March 1967, turning professional October 1968; Aldershot July 1982, later serving as player/coach. Other honours: England Under-23 international (5 apps).(QPR) FA Cup finalist 1982.

Left-back. For years formed a splendid full-back duo with the late Dave Clement (q.v.), each of them tall and lithe in physique. Ian Gillard in that time was justly admired for his skill and composure. He made over 400 League appearanceswhile at Loftus Road.

GILLIAT, (Revd.) Walter, Evelyn
(Old Carthusians, 1893, 1)
Born Stoke Poges, Bucks. 22 July 1869. Died 2 January 1963.
Career: Charterhouse School (XI 1887-88); Oxford University (Blue 1892); Old Carthusians; Woking. A member of the Corinthians but did not turn out for that club.

Inside-forward whose brilliant dribbling was considered at the time to be second only to that of the wizard W N Cobbold. Slight of frame, Gilliat sustained several injuries, but could vie with the best when fully fit. He could size up and capitalise on a goal chance, scoring a hat-trick in his lone international. Played cricket for Bucks. Ordained in 1895, he served as curate at Woking and Tunbridge Wells, Vicar of Iver 1901-21 and Rector of Sevenoakes 1921-29, then lived at Woking in retirement. Grandfather of R M C Gilliat who captained Oxford University at both soccer and cricket, and Hampshire CCC 1971-78 after assisting the county from 1966.

GODDARD, Paul
(West Ham United, 1982, 1)
Born Harlington, Middlesex, 12 October 1959.
1982: 5ft $9^1/_2$ ins.; 11st. 5lbs.

Career: Junior football; Queen's Park

Rangers as an associate schoolboy December 1972, apprentice July 1976, professional July 1977; West Ham United August 1980 (£800,000, a West Ham record); Newcastle United November 1986 (£432,000, again a West Ham record); Derby County July 1988 (£425,000). Other honours: England Under-21 international (8 apps). (WHU) FL Div.2 champions 1981. FL Cup finalist 1981.

Strike-forward, strong in combination and capable of boring his way through with perseverance and no little skill, and who scores his goals' quota. Hence, of course, the considerable fees paid for him. Known as 'Sarge' to colleagues at his London clubs through an association with the Boys Brigade. Was unlucky to lose his place at Upton Park because of injury.

GOODALL, F(rederick) Roy.
(Huddersfield Town, 1926-34, 25)
Born Dronfield, Yorks. 31 December 1902. Died 19 January 1982.
1930: 5ft. 11½ins.; 11st. 8lbs.

Career: Dronfield Woodhouse FC; Huddersfield Town January 1921; retired May 1937 when appointed Nottingham Forrest's trainer to 1944; Mansfield Town secretary/manager 1945 until his return to Huddersfield Town as trainer August 1949 and then as assistant trainer October 1964-July 1965. Other honours; Football League (8 apps).(H'field T) FL champions 1924,1925,1926. FA Cup finalist 1928,1930.

Right-back. In his early Leeds Road years had as partner the great Sam Wadsworth, the pair forming as strong a club full-back duo as the game has seen. Roy, a master of positional tactics, possessed speed, a magnificent first-time tackle, a vigorous shoulder charge and a confidence that revelled in the big occasion. Skippered England during his later appearances.

GOODALL, John
(Preston North End and Derby County, 1888-98, 14)
Born Westminster London, 19 June 1863. Died 20 May 1942.
1903: 5ft. 9ins.; 11st. 12lbs.

Career: Kilmarnock Burns: Kilmarnock Athletic 1880; Great Lever 1883; Preston North End during the 1885/86 season; Derby County May 1889; New Brighton Tower cs 1899; Glossop cs 1900; Watford as player/manager cs 1903. Played for Maerdy vs. Swansea Town in January 1913 when in his 50th year, this was his last appearance. Other honours: Football League (4 apps). (PNE) FL Champions 1889. FA Cup winner 1889; finalist 1888. (Derby Co) FA Cup finalist 1898.

Inside-right /centre-forward. One of the most illustrious names from the late 19th century, a superb leader controlling his forwards and fine marksmanship making him highly dangerous anywhere near the opposing goal. His feats included scoring 9 for Preston against Dundee Strathmore and 16 in their famous 26-0 annihilation of Hyde FC. Son of Scottish parents, his father a corporal in the Scottish Fusiliers, John had a brother and sister respectively born in Belfast and Edinburgh. The former was Archie Goodall (Derby County, Glossop and Ireland). John played cricket professionally for Derbyshire (2 matches) and Hertfordshire, and he had a shop in Watford.

GOODHART, Harry Chester
(Old Etonians, 1883, 3)
Born Wimbledon, 17 July 1858. Died 21 April 1895.

Career: Eton College (XI 1877); Cambridge University (no Blue); Old Etonians.
Other honours: (Old Etonians) FA Cup winner 1879, 1882; finalist 1881, 1883.
Forward. Received the approbation of Alcock's Annual (1881) – 'a very good forward, dribbles well and unselfishly; always in front of goal when required.' A good team man, obviously. He was a lecturer at Cambridge 1884-90 and Professor of Humanities at Edinburgh University 1890-95.

GOODWYN, Alfred George
(Royal Engineers, 1873, 1)
Born in India, 1849 or '50. Died 14 March 1874.

Career: Royal Military Academy, Woolwich 1870; Royal Engineers.
Other honour: (Royal Engineers) FA Cup finalist 1872.

Full-back/half-back, excellent at both. Kicked confidently and well, more often than not divined the intentions of an oppo-

nent and was generally very skilled. At the time of the 1872 cup final he held the rank of lieutenant. Died while serving in the East Indies, he had been with the RE's less than 3 years (joined August 1871).

GOODYER, Arthur Copeland
(Nottingham Forest, 1879. 1)
Born Stamford, Lincs 1854. Died 8 January 1932.

Career: Junior football; Nottingham Forest November1877 – 1880.

Winger with an assertive bent. A good shot, he scored 10 goals in 10 FA Cup -ties for Forest – a tally that would flatter any centre-forward, never mind a wingman. He had a reputation as a middle- distance runner. Goodyer's time in first-class soccer was brief: he played his first match for Forest in November 1878 and the last in March 1880. In 1888 he emigrated to the States where he died 44 years later as the result of a car accident. Was employed in the lace trade.

GOSLING, Robert Cunliffe
(Old Etonians, 1892-95, 5)
Born Farnham, Essex, 15 June 1868. Died 18 April 1922.
1890s: 6ft.; 13st.

Career: Eton College (XI 1887, which he captained); Cambridge University (Blue 1890); Old Etonians; Corinthians 1889-1900.

Inside forward. 'With plenty of weight, as well as pace, he takes a lot of stopping. He usually plays centre or inside-right, and as he is a good shot and also passes well, he plays the game so thoroughly that he is bound to be of use to any side,' wrote a commentator in 1895. Eldest of five brothers , all at Eton at the same time during the late 1880s, when they were known as max, ma, mi, min and quint. Donor of the Arthur Dunn Cup. An excellent cricketer, Gosling played for Cambridge University (Blue 1888-89-90) and Essex 1894-96.

GOSNELL, Albert Arthur
(Newcastle United, 1906, 1)
Born Colchester, 10 February 1880. Died 6 January 1972.
1910; 5ft 10ins.; 12st.

Career; The Albion FC (Colchester), cs 1898; Colchester Town (during which spell he represented Essex); New Brompton cs 1901; Chatham cs 1902; Newcastle United May 1904; Tottenham Hotspur July 1910; Darlington cs 1911; Burslem Port Vale circa 1912. Worked in Newcastle during WW1, ran a successful works side, then, when peace returned, was employed on Newcastle United's staff until appointed Norwich City manager January 1921, retaining this post until March 1926. Later that year became coach to Colchester Town. Other honours: (Newcastle) FL champions 1905, 1907. FA Cup finalist 1905, 1906.

Outside-left, big for the berth and lively, possessor of appreciable shot. Despite these estimable qualities, however, Gosnell was never a Gallowgate favourite – because he had supplanted the ball-juggling Bobby Templeton, and his own sometimes indifferent passing. The player 'had to endure much barracking. Was a licensee after leaving the game.

GOUGH, Harold
(Sheffield United, 1921. 1)
Born Chesterfield, 31 December 1890. Died. 1970.
1921: 5ft. 10ins. 12st. 6lbs.

Career: Spital Olympic; Castleford Town; Bradford cs 1910; Castleford Town again August 1911; Sheffield United April 1913 (£30); Castleford Town for a third time January 1925; Harrogate October 1926; Oldham Athletic February 1927 (£500); Bolton Wanderers December 1927; Torquay United June 1928; retired through injury 1930. Other honour: (Sheffield Utd) FA Cup winner 1915.

Goalkeeper earning the description of 'cool, collected and very tough', ('Keepers had to be tough in those days when forwards could legally bundle them over the goal-line). Harold's speciality was in dealing with high shots, and his bravery and daring were renowned. He actually left Bramall Lane through taking over, against club rules, a Castleford public house, and was suspended from close season to December 1924. Member of the FA touring side to South Africa 1920, twice appearing against the national side.

GOULDEN, Leonard Arthur
(West Ham United, 1937-39, 14)
Born Hackney, London, 16 July 1912.
1938: 5ft 8ins.; 10st. 21bs.

Career; West Ham Schools; West Ham United on amateur forms 1931, then 'farmed out' to Chelmsford and, cs 1932, Leyton for development, becoming a West Ham professional April 1933 (guest player for Chelsea during WW2); Chelsea December 1945 (£5000); retired cs 1950 and joined Chelsea's training staff. Watford manager November 1952-July 1956 (which spell included period as general manager, October 1955-February 1956); returned to Watford as a coach July 1959-cs 1962; later coached in Libya for 2 years before returning to manage Banbury United for a similar period to March 1967; Oxford United trainer/coach for a spell from January 1969. Other honours: England schoolboy international (2 apps). England wartime international (4 apps). Football League (2 apps)

Inside-left. A major star from the 'Thirties, a strategist and master of the attack-switching crossfield pass. Outside the game has worked as a postmaster and at a Northants USAF base. His son, Roy, also became a schoolboy international.

GRAHAM, Leonard
(Millwall, 1925, 2)
Born Leyton, Essex, 20 August 1901. Died 21 December 1962.
1925: 5ft. 8ins.; 10st. 11lbs.

Career: Leyton Schools; Capworth United (Walthamstow League); Leytonstone 1922/23 (toured with Middlesex Wanderers); Millwall Athletic amateur cs 1923, turning professional the following October; retired through injury 1934. FA coach 1934-36; coach in The Hague, Holland 1936-39. Other honours: Football League (1app). (Millwall) FL Div. 3 (South) champions 1928.

Left-half, well defined as 'an excellent ball player, quick to appraise a tactical situation, he was adept at turning defence into attack with a clever feint and a shrewd pass. He was always at his best in these attacking roles.' Len was also a useful cricketer – on the Essex ground staff for 3 years, twice appearing in first-class matches 1926 and later a coach at Merchant Taylors' School, Northwood. Was a London licensee before and after Army service in WW2, later going into business.

GRAHAM, Thomas
(Nottingham Forest, 1931-32, 2)
Born Hamsterley, Co Durham, 12 March 1905. Died 29 March 1983.
1930: 5ft 8ins.; 11st.

Career: Hamsterley Swifts; Consett Celtic (North-Eastern League) (trial with Newcastle United) ; Nottingham Forest May 1927 (£50, originally on two months trial); retired 1944 and became Forest's trainer to January 1961, then served as chief scout and youth adviser until March 1969, from which date he was a part-time scout until finally retiring July 1970. Other honours: Football League (2 apps).

Centre-half with junior (and subsequent) experience at left-half. Short for a pivot but a constructive stylist of the first rank, combining attack and defence in an outstandingly cultured way. Having clocked up approaching half a century's service at the City Ground, Tommy has claims to being the greatest Forest loyalist of all time.

GRAINGER, Colin
(Sheffield United and Sunderland, 1956-57, 7)
Born Havercroft, West Yorks. 10 June 1933. 1957: 5ft. 9ins.; 10st. 12lbs.

Career: South Elmsall; Wrexham ground staff 1949, turning professional October 1950; Sheffield United June 1953 (£2,500); Sunderland February 1957 (£7000 and another player); Leeds United July 1960 (£13,500); Port Vale October 1961 (£6000); Doncaster Rovers August 1964; Macclesfield cs – October 1966. Other honour: Football League (3 apps).

Outside-left of incisive intent – 'fast moving and keen to score' as one writer recorded in the mid-'Fifties. He did so, in fact, on 57 occasions in his total 325 League outings. From a famous soccer family: brother of Jack (Rotherham & England 'B'), uncle of Edwin Holliday (q.v.) brother-in-law of Jim Iley (England Under-23) and he had two cousins with FL clubs. After leaving football was employed as regional manager for a cash register company and then as representative for a firm of wine merchants. Made a reputation, too, as a professional singer.

GREAVES, James Peter
(Chelsea and Tottenham Hotspur, 1959-67, 57)
Born Poplar, London, 20 February 1940. 1963: 5ft. 8ins.; 10st. 8lbs.

Career: Represented Dagenham, Essex and London Schools; Lakeside Manor Boys Club; Chelsea Juniors 1955; Chelsea as a professional May 1957; AC Milan June 1961 (£80,000); Tottenham Hotspur November 1961 (£99,999); West Ham United March 1970 (in part exchange for Martin Peters, q.v.); retired May 1971 but later in the 1970s assisted Chelmsford City and Barnet. Other honours: England Youth international. England Under-23 international (12 apps) Football League (10 apps). (Spurs) European Cup winners' Cup, winner 1963. FA Cup winner 1962, 1967.

Inside-forward opportunist extraordinary, finishing his FL record with 357 goals in 514 matches (and 2 substitutions). He was the first to score 100 goals in senior football before his 21st birthday (the second century was reached at 23 years, 290 days). Also had the remarkable record of scoring on his debuts with England, England Under-23, Chelsea, AC Milan, Spurs and West Ham. Later had business interests in road haulage, packaging and sports goods. Has found fame in more recent years as a soccer commentator on commercial TV, especially in partnership with his old Scotland contemporary, Ian St John. 'The Saint and Greavsie Show' with its backchat and quick wit , is reminiscent of an old time variety act.

GREEN, Frederick Thomas
(Wanderers, 1876, 1)
Born 21 June 1851. Died 6 July 1928.

Career: Winchester College; Oxford University (there prior to the institution of the 'Varsity match); Wanderers; also represented Middlesex Other honours: (Oxford University) FA Cup winner 1874. (Wanderers) FA Cup winner 1877, 1878.

Half-back of quality, annexing a fair clutch of FA Cup medals (as did so many gifted amateurs in Green's day). He was a sure-footed player, resolved always and dependable to a degree. A barrister (called to the bar 1877), he left the legal profession and from 1880, was employeed as an Inspector of Schools.

GREEN, George Henry
(Sheffield United, 1925-28, 8)
Born Leamington, Warwicks. 2 May 1901. Died 1980.
1925: 5ft. 9½ins.; 12st. 4lbs.

Career: Leamington junior football; Nuneaton (Bimingham League); Sheffield United May 1923; Leamington Town July 1934. Other honours: Football League (3 apps). (Sheffield U) FA Cup winner 1925.

Left-half, latterly left-back. A 1927 critique of Green was worded '. . .is of hefty build and knows how to use his weight to the best advantage. He is, however, not merely a spoiler, but plays a game of football that is a pleasure to watch.' Played at right-half for Nuneaton, during which time he represented the Birmingham FA against Scotland in a junior international. and was much coveted by senior clubs. A turner and fitter by trade.

GREENHALGH, Ernest Harwood
(Notts County, 1873, 2)
Born Mansfield, 1849.

Career: Notts County 1867 – 1883, after which he was secretary of Greenhalgh's FC (Mansfield).

Full-back. 'A very fair back,' observed The Football Annual for 1874, "Has managed the football at Nottingham with great success", this last statement a tribute to Greenhalgh's pioneering soccer work in that city. As a player he was robust, originally with individualistic leanings but later adapted to the team game. Appeared in England's first two internationals and accordingly is Notts County's first cap by some years. Proprietor of the Field Mill at Mansfield, at the rear of which the firms's team played. This ground still bearing the name 'Field Mill', has been the home of Mansfield Town since 1905, immediately prior to which it had been occupied by Mansfield Mechanics FC.

GREENHOFF, Brian
(Manchester United and Leeds United, 1976-80, 18)
Born Barnsley, 28 April 1953
1978: 5ft. 10ins.; 11st. 8lbs.

Career: Yorkshire Schools; Manchester United apprentice August 1968, turning professional June 1970; Leeds United August 1979 (£350,000) (Hull City on trial November 1983); Rochdale as a non-contract player later in November 1983; retired 1984. Other honours: England 'B' international. England Under-23 international (4 apps). (Man.Utd) FL Div.2 champions 1975. FA Cup winner 1977; finalist 1976.

Central defender became his recognised berth as a senior, but he had been a full-back, made his debut in midfield and, in emergencies, could take a forward role and even go in goal. A performer quick in thought and movement, and an excellent team man. Younger brother of Jimmy Greenhoff, also an England Under-23 cap, who had a spell at Old Trafford in Brian's time, and with whom Brian linked up again at Rochdale where Jimmy was manager.

GREENWOOD, Doctor Haydock
(Blackburn Rovers, 1882, 2)
Born Blackburn, 31 October 1860. Died 3 November 1951.

Career: Malvern College (XI 1878-79); Blackburn Rovers. Was a member of the Corinthians, and on that club's committee on its formation in 1882.

Full-back. Strong kicking, robust defender. Tended to be slow sometimes otherwise good to have on your side. Member of a prominent Blackburn family which had much to do with the successful introduction of soccer to the area. The Greenwoods supplied two other players to Rovers' ranks including the club's first skipper. D H who went into agriculture, missed the 1882 Cup final because of injury. His first name was actually Doctor and did not stand for a medical or other learned qualification.

GREGORY, John C.
(Queen's Park Rangers, 1983-84, 6)
Born Scunthorpe, 11 May 1954.
1983: 6ft. 1in.; 11st. 5lbs.

Career: Junior football; Northampton Town apprentice, turning professional January 1973; Aston Villa June 1977 (£40,000); Brighton and Hove Albion July 1979 (£250,000); Queen's Park Rangers June 1981 (£300,000); Derby County November 1985 (£100,000) to 1988. Portsmouth assistant coach 1988, chief coach January 1989. Other honours: (QPR) FL Div. 2 champions 1983. FA Cup finalist 1982. (Derby Co.) FL Div. 2 champions 1987.

Midfield. A solid, dependable and worthy performer whose career took off after a decade as a professional. His displays acquired a lustre absent hitherto, not least in the art of getting into attack and scoring himself. John's father, J E Gregory, played for West Ham, Scunthorpe and Aldershot during the 'Fifties.

GRIMSDELL, Arthur
(Tottenham Hotspur, 1920-23, 6)
Born Watford, 23 March 1894. Died 12 March 1963.
1921: 5ft. $10^1/_2$ins.; 12st. 8lbs.

Career: Watford Schools; Watford St Stephen's; Watford FC as an amateur 1909, turning professional November 1911; Tottenham Hotspur March 1912 (£350); Clapton Orient as player/sec-manager cs 1929 – 1930. Watford FC director 1945-51. Other honours: England schoolboy international 1908. England 'Victory' international 1919 (2 apps). Football League (1 app). (Spurs) FL Div. 2 champions 1920. FA Cup winner 1921.

Left-half. One of the greatest captains of all time besides being a leading man in his position. Aggressive, dominating and unorthodox, he was tantamount to a sixth forward, loving to burst through and score (he netted 14 in Spurs' record-breaking 1920 championship side, establishing a record for a half-back). Grimsdell was a sports outfitter in his native Watford, a brother of the English amateur international, E F Grimsdell, and a Hertfordshire cricketer (wicket-keeper) 1922-47.

GROSVENOR, A(rthur) Thomas
(Birmingham, 1934, 3)
Born Netherton nr. Dudley, Worcs. 22 November 1908. Died 31 October 1972.
1938: 6ft. $1^1/_4$ins.; 12st 1lb.

Career: Tippity Green Vics; Vono Works (Cradley Heath League); Stourbridge; Birmingham March 1928; Sheffield Wednesday February 1936; Bolton Wanderers May 1937; retired during WW2. Other honour: Football League (1 app).

Inside-right, lithely built, his lofty height giving considerable aerial command. Though not a prolific scorer, Tommy was an excellent forager and provider of opportunities. Brother of Percy Grosvenor, Leicester City wing-half 1933-41.

GUNN, William (Notts County, 1884, 2)
Born Nottingham, 4 December 1858. Died 29 January 1921.
Height: 6ft. $4^1/_2$ins.

Career: Nottingham Forest (1 app, November 1881); Notts. County 1881-90. In September 1890 reinstated as an amateur and played in Nottingham area junior football. Later a Notts County director and at the time of his death was Vice-President of the club.

Outside-left. Would have been conspicuous anywhere given his great height, but his presence on the extreme left must have presented a unique sight. Quite brilliant, though, cutting through the opposition at great speed, and renowned – before the law changed – for massive one- armed throws. A minor fault was an occasional failure to part soon enough. A great cricketer for Notts (1880-1904) and England (11 Tests). Co. founder in 1885 of the well known sports good firm, Gunn & Moore.

GURNEY, Robert
(Sunderland, 1935, 1)
Born Silksworth, Co Durham, 13 October 1907.
1935: 5ft. 8½ins.; 10st. 3lbs.

Career: Hetton Juniors; Seaham Harbour; Bishop Auckland; Sunderland as a professional May 1925; retired and joined Sunderland's training staff May 1946. Horden Colliery FC Manager FC manager 1947; Peterbrough United manager February 1950; Darlington manager March 1952 – October 1957, then a scout for Leeds United before a second spell as Horden Colliery's manager 1960-63; Hart; Hartlepools United manager April 1963 – January 1964. Other honours: (Sunderland) FL champions 1936. FA Cup winner 1937.

Centre-forward. Sometimes inside-left. Possessed of a consistent goal touch, registering 228 in 388 Div. 1 and FA Cup outings for Sunderland. The tally included a 5 against Bolton Wanderers in December 1935 and he once notched 9 for the reserves. This in spite of bad injuries (he broke both legs while at Roker). A roamer, speedy and brave. Latterly a representative for a wine and spirit firm.

HACKING, John
(Oldham Athletic, 1929, 3)
Born Blackburn, 22 December 1897. Died 31 May 1955.
1929: 6ft.; 12st. 7lbs.

Career: Blackburn Co-op (also assisted Blackburn Rovers reserves); Blackpool December 1919; Fleetwood cs 1925; Oldham Athletic early 1926; Manchester United March 1934; Accrington Stanley as player/manager May 1935, retiring from playing October 1935; Barrow secretary/ manager May 1949 to his death. Other honours: Football League (2 apps).

Goalkeeper. A fitful start, making his senior debut in 1921/22 and grossing only 33 FL games at Blackpool before leaving the League scene. On returning a year later gained an inter-league medal in 1927/28, repeating this feat in '28/29, a season in which he was capped against the three home countries. 'Alert and resourceful with a long reach,' was a 'Twenties judgment that pithily summed up his goalkeeping. Jack's first employment was as a shop assistant in a Blackburn Co-operative store.

HADLEY, Harold
(West Bromwich Albion, 1903, 1)
Born Barrow-in-Furness, 1877
1907: 5ft. 10ins.; 12st. 7lbs.

Career: Colley Gate United; Halesowen 1895/96; West Bromwich Albion February 1897; Aston Villa February 1905; Nottingham Forest April 1906; Southampton cs 1907; Croydon Common cs 1908; Halesowen again February 1910. Well known as a manager during the inter-war period, having four spells as Merthyr Town's manager between May 1919 and September 1931. Other managerial appointments included Chesterfield (April-August 1922); Aberdare Athletic (November 1927-April 1929); Gillingham (April 1929-1930) and Bangor City (July 1935 to his retirement in 1936). Other honour: (WBA) FL Div. 2 champions 1902.

Left-half. Able to take the other half back positions too. An enthusiastic performer though not 'over the top' in this respect, his game tempered with judgement and composure. A minor weakness was a tendency to balloon the ball occasionally. He was a button maker by trade.

HAGAN, James
(Sheffield United, 1949, 1)
Born Washington, Co. Durham, 21 January 1918.
1949: 5ft. 8ins.; 10st. 10lbs.

Career: Washington Schools; Liverpool as an amateur January 1932; Derby County as an amateur cs 1933, turning professional cs 1936; Sheffield United November 1938 (£2500); retired March 1958. Peterborough United manager August 1958-October 1962; West Bromwich Albion manager April 1963-May 1967; Manchester City scout 1967/68; Benfica (Portugal) manager/trainer March 1970-September 1973; coach in Kuwait 1974-76; spell as manager of Sporting Club de Portugal (Lisbon) from 1976. Other honours: England schoolboy international (2 apps). England wartime international (15 apps). Football League (3 apps). (Sheffield U) FL Div. 2 champions 1953.

Inside-forward. Unlucky in that his playing days coincided with those of Carter, Mannion and Mortensen, his England appearance thus much restricted. Jimmy was a master craftsman, his unobstrusive subtleties and tactical awareness able to change the course of a game. Son of Alf Hagan, who was on the books of Newcastle, Cardiff and Tranmere in the 'Twenties.

HAINES, John T W
(West Bromwich Albion, 1949, 1)
Born Wickhamford Nr. Evesham, Worcs. 24 April 1920. Died 19 March 1987.
1949: 5ft. 9ins.; 10st. 11lbs.

Career: Evesham schoolboy football; Evesham Town; Cheltenham Town; Liverpool 1937/38; Swansea Town cs 1939 (representative football for the RAF while serving in WW2); Leicester City June 1947; West Bromwich Albion March 1948 (in exchange for another player); Bradford December 1949 (nearly £10,000); Rochdale September 1953 (£2000); Chester July 1955; Wellington Town cs 1957; Kidderminster Harriers cs 1958; Evesham Town again October 1958; retired 1959/60.

Inside-forward whose senior debut was delayed by the war. He then moved around the League circuit to some purpose, in the decade from 1946/47 appearing in 340 FL matches, scoring 94 goals in the process. Had ball command and shot hard and well but unfortunate with injuries. Scored twice in his sole international.

HALL, Albert Edward
(Aston Villa, 1910, 1)
Born Wordsley, Staffs. 1882 Died 17 October 1957.
1914: 5ft. 9ins.; 11st. 8lbs.

Career: Stourbridge; Aston Villa cs 1903; Millwall Athletic late 1913; retired during WW1. Other honours: Football League (2 apps).(Villa) FL champions 1910. FA Cup winner 1905.

Outside-left. Virile, difficult to subject and a danger man in front of goal. Responded admirably to the promptings of his Villa partner, the celebrated Joe Bache. Hall became an enamel ware manufacturer at Stourbridge for some years until ill-health forced retirement. He had been badly gassed during the Great War, in which he served with the 5th South Staffordshire Rgt.

HALL, G(eorge) William
(Tottenham Hotspur, 1934-39, 10)
Born Newark, Notts. 12 March 1912. Died 22 May 1967.
1938: 5ft. $6^1/_2$ins.; 11st. 9lbs.

Career: Notts Schools; Ransome and Marles FC (Newark); Notts County November 1930; Tottenham Hotspur December 1932 (fee included extra £500 for England appearance); retired through injury 1944. Clapton Orient manager/coach August-December 1945, resigning through ill-health; Chingford Town manager briefly from December 1949. Other honours: England wartime international (1 app). Football League (3 apps).

Inside-forward. Famed in England annals for scoring 5 goals in succession against Northern Ireland, 16 November 1938, the first 3 in the space of $3^1/_2$ minutes. Despite this Billy was, in truth, more of a provider for others, his dexterous control and dribbling contributing to such a team role. Latterly employed as a licensee, he became seriously ill, both his legs having to be amputated in the mid-1940s. Uncle of the England amateur international, Harry Parr (Lincoln City).

HALL, Jeffrey James
(Birmingham City, 1956-57, 17)
Born Scunthorpe, 7 September 1929. Died 4 April 1959.
1957: 5ft. $7^1/_2$ins.; 11st. 4lbs.

Career: Bingley (West Yorks) area schoolboy football; St. Anne's (Keighley); Wilsden; Bank Top; Army Football (Bradford amateur); Birmingham City as a professional May 1950. Other honours: England 'B' international (1 app). Football League (4 apps). (B'ham C) FL Div. 2 champions 1955. FA Cup finalist 1956.

Right-back. Stocky back, commendably tenacious and always game. Had occupied a variety of other positions earlier. Started at centre-forward, was on Bradford Park Avenue's books as an outside-right and signed by Brum as a wing-half after representing the Army. Jeff died tragically young through poliomyelitis, an event that caused a tremendous wave of sympathy at the time.

HALSE, Harold James
(Manchester United, 1909, 1)
Born Leytonstone, Essex, January 1886. Died April 1951.
1909: 5ft. 6ins.; 10st. 5lbs.

Career: Wanstead schoolboy football; Newportians FC (Leyton); Wanstead FC; Barking Town; Clapton Orient; Southend United cs 1906; Manchester United cs 1907; Aston Villa July 1912; Chelsea May 1913; Charlton Athletic July 1921; retired cs 1923. Other honours: Football League (5 apps).(Man. Utd) FL champions 1911. FA Cup winner 1909. (Villa) FA Cup winner 1913. (Chelsea) FA Cup finalist 1915.

Inside-right/centre-forward. Described as 'a skilful dribbler able to get the best out of partners' but that 'a lack of inches prevented outstanding success as a centre-forward.' Admittedly the honours listed above were won as an inside-right, yet he did once score 6 in succession in a Charity Shield match. And as a junior he once netted an astonishing 125 in a season. A dangerous attacker over a long period.

HAMMOND, Henry Edward Denison
(Oxford University, 1889,1)
Born Priston Nr. Bath, 26 November 1866. Died 16 June 1910.
Career: Lancing College (XI 1883-85, captain 1885); Oxford University (Blue 1888-89); Lancing Old Boys; Corinthians 1889-90.
Right-half. Noticeably athletic in action (not surprisingly because he won a Blue for athletics in 3 of his Oxford years, 1886-7-9). Maintained consistency, too, with his powerful play. Assisted Somerset CCC in 1889 before the County achieved first-class status. He was a master at Blair House School (1889) and Edinburgh Academy 1890-99 before becoming Director-General of Education for Rhodesia from 1900. He acted as superintendent of the British Education Section at the Paris Exhibition of 1899.

HAMPSON, James
(Blackpool, 1931-33, 3)
Born Little Hulton Nr. Bolton, 23 March 1906. Died 10 January 1938.
1935: 5ft. 7ins.; 11st 5lbs.

Career: Walkden Park; Little Hulton St. John's (trial with Manchester United); Nelson cs 1925; Blackpool October 1927 (£1250) to his death. Other honours: Football League (4 apps). (Blackpool) FL Div. 2 champions 1930.

Centre-forward. Experienced in the inside berths too. Took to League soccer from the start, registering 3 consecutive hat-tricks for Nelson in the very first season. His 45 for Blackpool, 1929/30, remains a club record. A feared marksman, Jimmy had ball control and a natural swerve to back up his goal scoring. Lost his life through drowning when the yacht in which he was sailing collided with a trawler off Fleetwood. His brother, Harold, was a Southport and Sheffield United forward.

HAMPTON, Harry
(Aston Villa, 1913-14, 4)
Born Wellington, Salop, 21 April 1885. Died 15 March 1963.
1913: 5ft. 8½ins.; 11st. 3lbs.

Career: Shifnal Juniors; Wellington Town; Aston Villa May 1904 (guest player for Stoke during WW1); Birmingham February 1920; Newport County September 1922; retired cs 1923 but rejoined Wellington Town January 1924. Had spells as Preston North End's coach from June to December 1925 and Birmingham's third team coach from 1934. Other honours: Football League (3 apps). (Villa) FL champions 1910. FA Cup winner 1905, 1913. (Birmingham) FL Div. 2 champions 1921.

Centre-forward. Played right-half also latterly. The prototype of the 'through a brick wall' centre-forward category, utterly fearless, tremendously fast and a terror to goalkeepers. Gave plenty of hard knocks but had to take plenty in return. Subsequently lived for many years at Rhyl, where he had catering interests and where he died.

HANCOCKS, John
(Wolverhampton Wanderers, 1949-51, 3)
Born Oakengates, Salop, 30 April 1919.
1950: 5ft. 4in.; 9st. 5lbs.

Career: Oakengates Town; Walsall August 1938 (represented The Army during wartime service); Wolverhampton Wanderers May 1946 (£4000); Wellington Town as player/manager July 1957, relinquished managership late in 1959 and continued as player only until December of that year; Cambridge United January 1960; Oswestry cs 1960; Sankey's FC (Wellington) December 1960. Other honours: Football League (2 apps). (Wolves) FL champions 1954. FA Cup winner 1949.

Outside-right. Could play on the other far flank too. A small man with a big heart. Brave, a rapid mover and especially renowned for blistering shooting despite taking a mere Size 2 in footwear. Scored 158 goals in 343 FL outings for Wolves, a truly prodigious return for a wingman.

HAPGOOD, Edris Albert
(Arsenal, 1933-39, 30)
Born Bristol, 24 September 1908. Died 20 April 1973.
1934: 5ft. 9ins.; 11st.

Career: Bristol junior football (Bristol Rovers amateur when 18); Kettering Town cs 1927; Arsenal October 1927 (£750); (guest player for Luton Town and Chelsea during WW2); retired 1944. Blackburn Rovers manager on release from war service with RAF June 1946-February 1947; Shrewsbury Town player/coach August 1947; Watford manager February 1948; Bath City manager March 1950-February 1956. Other honours: England wartime international (9 apps). Football League (4 apps). (Arsenal) FL champions 1931, 1933, 1934, 1935, 1938. FA Cup winner 1930, 1936; finalist 1932.

Left-back, justly counted among the greatest ever. Not dissimilar in style to his illustrious England predecessor, Blenkinsop, with his superbly judged clearances and tackles and overall polish. Early a milk roundsman and latterly employed by the YMCA.

HARDINGE, Harold Thomas William
(Sheffield United, 1910, 1)
Born Greenwich, 25 February 1886. Died 8 May 1965.
1910: 5ft. 6$^1/_2$ins.; 10st. 13$^1/_2$lbs.

Career: Maidstone United; Newcastle United May 1905; Sheffield United December 1907; Woolwich Arsenal May 1913 (£500); retired cs 1921. Had a spell as Spurs' reserve team coach from 1935.

Inside-left. Unable to claim a regular place in Newcastle's then brilliant team, he shone at Bramall Lane. A tricky performer with a penchant for lying back and drawing defences –a ploy more fashionable in the period after Hardinge's retiral. A Kent cricketer for 31 years (1902-33) with 1 Test appearance for England, he was a director of John Wisden & Co, the sports outfitting and publishing firm.

HARDMAN, Harold Payne
(Everton 1905-08, 4)
Born Kirkmanshulme, Manchester, 4 April 1882. Died 9 June 1965.
1907: 5ft. 6$^1/_2$ins.; 9st. 13lbs.

Career: Played in Blackpool schoolboy football and junior football in that area and in Manchester and also for Northern Nomads before joining Blackpool FC cs 1900; Everton cs 1903; Manchester United cs 1908; Bradford City January 1909; Stoke cs 1910; retired cs 1913 but played as a guest for Stoke during WW1. It should be mentioned he assisted Northern Nomads on occasion while with FL clubs. Appointed a Manchester United director November 1912-1931 and again from 1934, being Chairman 1951 to his death. Was a member of the FA Council, treasurer of the Lancashire FA (awarded a long service medal in 1949 after 21 years in the post) and also served as Chairman and as Chairman of the Central League. Other honours: England amateur international (10 apps). Football League (1 app). (Everton) FA Cup winner 1906; finalist 1907.

Outside-left. A distinguished amateur later an equally distinguished administrator. A diminutive physique proved no great handicap to Hardman for he had speed, elusiveness and style in plenty. A solicitor by profession (admitted December 1907) who practised in Manchester.

HARDWICK, George Francis M.
(Middlesbrough, 1947-48, 13)
Born Saltburn, Yorks. 2 February 1920.
1949: 5ft. 9$^1/_2$ins.; 12st.

Career: Cleveland schoolboy football; South Bank East End 1934; Middlesbrough on amateur forms 1935, turning professional May 1937 (guest player for Chelsea during WW2); Oldham Athletic as player/manager November 1950 (£15,000), resigned and retired as a player April 1956. Coach to US Army team in Germany August 1956; Eindhoven FC (Holland) coach June 1957-cs 1959; Middlesbrough FC coaching staff August 1961-November 1963; Sunderland manager November 1964-May 1965; Gateshead manager 1968-February 1970. Other honours: England wartime international (12 apps). Football League (3 apps). (Oldham A) FL Div. 3 (North) champions 1953.

Left-back reckoned the best looking footballer of his day. But, more importantly in this context, a cool and cultured stylist effective in all aspects of defence. Played forward at school and during his Oldham tenure. Employments outside the game have included garage management and the chairmanship of a steel firm.

HARDY, Henry
(Stockport County, 1925, 1)
Born Stockport, 14 January 1895. Died 17 February 1969.
1927: 5ft. 9ins.; 11st. 8lbs.

Career: Brentnall Street Sunday School (Stockport Sunday Schools League); Alderney Edge FC; Stockport County early in 1920; Everton October 1925 (£2350); Bury July 1929-1931. Other honours: Football League (2 apps). (Stockport) FL Div. 3 (North) champions 1922.

Goalkeeper. Although not then engaged in First Division football, Hardy was recognised in the early 'Twenties as belonging to the top flight of 'keepers. A deft handler, superb in judgment and ever cool. Toured Australia with the 1925 FA party, twice

appearing against that country's national side. An excellent oboist, he was a professional musician for 13 years, later working as a caretaker in Stockport.

HARDY, Sam
(Liverpool and Aston Villa 1907-20, 21)
Born Newbold, Chesterfield, 26 August 1883. Died 24 October 1966.
1913: 5ft. $9^1/_4$ins.; 12st.

Career: Newbold White Star; Chesterfield Town April 1903; Liverpool cs 1905 (£500); Aston Villa May 1912 (guest player for Nottingham Forest during WW1); Nottingham Forest August 1921; retired cs 1925. Other honours: England 'Victory' international 1919 (3 apps). Football League (10 apps). (Liverpool) FL champions 1906. (Villa) FA Cup winner 1913, 1920. (Forest) FL Div. 2 champions 1922.

Goalkeeper with strong claims to the title of the best of all time. A measure of the claim is that he was England's first choice at a time when great practitioners such as Jerry Dawson and Tim Williamson were at their peak. Hardy, always unspectacular and seemingly always in form, had superb anticipation that made his saves appear simple and he was as good as ever when turned 40. A life-long resident of Chesterfield where he was a hotel proprietor.

HARFORD, Michael G.
(Luton Town, 1988, 1)
Born Sunderland, 12 February 1959.
1988: 6ft. 2ins.; 12st. 9lbs.

Career: Lambton Street Boys Club (Sunderland); Lincoln City July 1977; Newcastle United December 1980 (£216,000, a Lincoln and Div. 4 record fee); Bristol City August 1981 (£160,000); Birmingham City March 1982 (£100,000); Luton Town December 1984 (around £270,000, a Luton record). Other honour: (Luton Town) FL Cup winner 1988.

Strike-forward. After commanding a series of substantial fees, Mick has emerged as a leading striker valued in the 6-figure bracket (if reports concerning other clubs' bids are correct). Brave, deft in footwork, powerful in heading and excellent in combination. Was actually transferred briefly back to Newcastle in March 1982 to get cash owed by a then financially stricken Bristol City.

HARGREAVES, Frederick William
(Blackburn Rovers, 1880-82, 3)
Born Blackburn, 16 August 1858. Died 5 April 1897.

Career: Malvern College (XI 1877); Blackburn Rovers. Also represented Lancashire. Other honour: (Blackburn R) FA Cup finalist 1882.

Half-back. One of three ex-Malvern public schoolboys assisting Rovers in the club's early seasons – another was Hargreaves's brother, John (below). Fred was an excellent half-back, quick to effectively tackle, a worker and judicious. A useful cricketer, he played once for Lancashire CCC in 1881. A son of the Blackburn coroner.

HARGREAVES, John
(Blackburn Rovers, 1881, 2)
Born Blackburn, 13 December 1860. Died 13 January 1903.

Career: Malvern College (XI 1878-79); Blackburn Rovers 1878-84. Also represented Lancashire. Other honours: (Blackburn R) FA Cup winner 1884; finalist 1882.

Winger equally adept on both flanks. He was fast and parted with the ball accurately and to advantage. Younger brother of F W Hargreaves above. A solicitor by profession (admitted 1884) practising in his native Blackburn until his early death.

HARPER, Edward Cashfield
(Blackburn Rovers, 1926, 1)
Born Sheerness, Kent, 22 August 1901. Died 22 July 1959.
1925: 5ft. 10½ins.; 11st. 10lbs.

Career: Kent junior football; Sheppey United; Blackburn Rovers May 1923; Sheffield Wednesday November 1927 (£4700); Tottenham Hotspur March 1929; Preston North End December 1931 (£5000 including another player); Blackburn Rovers again November 1933 (£1300); retired May 1935 and was employed on Blackburn's training staff from then until May 1948.

Centre-forward, strong and quick moving, among the most consistent scorers of the inter-war period – 264 goals in his aggregate 327 League games. Did not start playing until aged 16, two years later establishing a Kent junior record with 102 goals in a single season. In 1925/26 broke Bert Freeman's FL record (43 in 37 matches) and so did Ken McDonald (43) and Jimmy Cookson (44). Was an apprentice shipwright, joining Blackburn on the apprenticeship's completion. Worked for English Electric from 1948 to his death.

HARRIS, Gordon
(Burnley, 1966, 1)
Born Worksop, Notts. 2 June 1940.

1966: 5ft. 9½ins.; 13st. 1lb.
Career: Worksop Schools; Firbeck Colliery; Burnley January 1958; Sunderland 1968 (£65,000); South Shields July 1972. Other honours: England Under-23 international (2 apps). Football League (2 apps). (Burnley) FA Cup finalist 1962.

Outside-left later making successful switches to inside-left and left-half. A lively player, fast and incisive. Gordon's name was no stranger to the score sheet: in all he notched 85 goals in 382 League matches (and 1 substitution) for his two senior clubs.

HARRIS, Peter Philip
(Portsmouth, 1950-54, 2)
Born Southsea, Portsmouth, 19 December 1925.
1950: 5ft. 7ins.; 10st. 2lbs.
Career: Portsmouth schools football; De Haviland's Works FC; Havant Juniors; Gosport Borough; Portsmouth as an amateur 1944; turning professional in November of that year; retired on health grounds December 1959. Other honours: Football League (5 apps). (Portsmouth) FL champions 1949, 1950.
Outside-right. A goal scoring winger – 209 in 508 League and Cup games for Pompey – able to show a clean pair of heels to most opponents as well. Completed his apprenticeship as a woodworker before taking the professional plunge and, after leaving the game, became a restaurateur at Hayling Island in partnership with Cyril Rutter (Portsmouth, 1951-63).

HARRIS, Stanley Shute
(Cambridge University and Old Westminsters, 1904-06, 6)
Born Clifton, Bristol, 19 July 1881. Died 4 May 1926.
1904: 6ft.; 13st.

Career: Westminster School (XI 1900-01); Cambridge Unviersity (Blue 1902-03-04, captain 1904); Old Westminsters; Casuals; Worthing; Corinthians 1904-10; Portsmouth 1905-07; also represented Surrey.
Other honour: England amateur international (1 app).

Inside-left. A splendidly built amateur, adroit in dribbling and shooting. Excellent, too, in passing thanks to the dexterity of his footwork. A useful cricketer who played for Cambridge University 1902-04 (no Blue), Surrey (1 match 1904), Gloucestershire (1 match 1902) and Sussex (3 matches 1919). BA (Cantab) and headmaster of a Worthing preparatory school 1904-26.

HARRISON, Alban Hugh
(Old Westminsters, 1893, 2)
Born Bredhurst, Kent, 30 November 1869. Died 15 August 1943.

Career: Westminster School (XI 1887-88); Cambridge University (Blue 1889 and '91, captain 1891); Old Westminsters; Corinthians 1891-94.

Right-back. The 1893 Athletic News annual said of Harrison 'very much like A. M. Walters in his clever and accurate kicking, particularly in half-volleying. He does not, however, charge or hustle in such determined fashion as the Walters, and this may be put down as his weak point.' To be bracketed with the celebrated Walters brothers was naturally high praise despite the criticism as to lack of vigour. Soccer then was still in thrall to the muscular amateur and quiet subtleties not always appreciated.

HARRISON, George ('Jud')
(Everton, 1921-22, 2)
Born Church Gresley, Derbys. 18 July 1892. Died 12 March 1939.
1926: 5ft. 8ins.; 12st. 7lbs.

Career: Gresley Rovers; Leicester Fosse cs 1910; Everton April 1913; Preston North End November 1923; Blackpool November 1931; retired cs 1932. Other honour:

(Everton) FL champions 1915.

Outside-left, owner of one of the hardest shots in the game's history. This ability was put to profitable use with penalty kicks and it was said he missed only 9 in an exceptionally long career. These misses were said to have either hit goalkeeper or woodwork. Harrison himself confessed to deliberately aiming at the 'keeper knowing evasive action would be taken!. He was also admirably consistent while a powerful, stocky frame made his persistence most difficult to contain. Later a licensee in Preston.

HARROW, Jack Harry
(Chelsea, 1923, 2)
Born Beddington, Surrey, 8 October 1888.
Died 19 July 1958.
1922: 5ft. 8ins.; 11st. 6lbs.

Career: Mill Green Rovers; Croydon Common as a professional after playing a few games as an amateur; Chelsea April 1911 (£50); retired cs 1926 and continued to serve Chelsea on their training staff until 1938. Other honours: Football League (1 app). (Chelsea) FA Cup finalist 1915.

Left-back following many seasons in other positions – first centre-forward, then left-half (for which berth he joined Chelsea) and right-back. Quick to tackle and possessing powers of recovery, Harrow was good in dead-ball situations both in taking free-kicks and penalties. A hard facial blow by the ball in December 1924 affected his eyesight and thus his displays thereafter. On leaving football worked for the Mitcham local authority until retiring in 1956.

HART, Ernest Arthur
(Leeds United, 1929-34, 8)
Born Overseal, Derbys. 3 January 1902.
Died 21 July 1954.
1930: 5ft. 10ins.; 11st. 10lbs.

Career: Overseal schoolboy and junior football; Woodlands Wesleyans (Doncaster); Leeds United December 1919; Mansfield Town August 1936-May 1937. Later in that close season appointed a Coventry City scout; Tunbridge Wells player/manager July 1938. Other honours: Football League (3 apps). (Leeds Utd) FL Div. 2 champions 1924.

Centre-half. For more than a decade and a half a Leeds linchpin, joining the re-born club shortly before his 18th birthday. Had the skill, strength and tactical nous to safely bridge the transition between the attacking and 'stopper' eras that pivots underwent. Toured South Africa with the FA 1929, thrice appearing against the national side. Latterly engaged in a haulage and bus business in the Doncaster area.

HARTLEY, Frank
(Oxford City, 1923, 1)
Born Shipton-under-Wychwood, Oxon. 20 July 1896. Died 20 October 1965.
1928: 5ft. 10ins.; 11st. 10lbs.

Career: Oxford City; Tottenham Hotspur on amateur forms November 1922; Corinthians 1924-28; Tottenham Hotspur as a professional February 1928-1931. Other honours: England amateur international (7 apps).

Inside-forward. Should really be classified

as a highly talented amateur, joining the paid ranks in his 32nd year and thereafter playing only half a dozen League games. A member of an Oxfordshire farming family, Hartley's exploits for Oxford City won him the Gamage Annual 'Player of the Year' award for 1923. 'A fine close dribbler and grand shot, and one moreover who is not easily knocked off the ball, the Oxford City inside-left shines in any company,' the citation read. A typical amateur all-rounder too – an Oxfordshire cricketer who represented the Minor Counties and an England trialist at hockey (his brother, Ernest, was an England hockey internationalist).

HARVEY, A
(Wednesbury Strollers, 1881, 1)
Career: Junior football to Wednesbury Strollers. Also represented Staffordshire.

Full-back. 'A clever, hard-working back; dodges well,' observed Alcock in his 1881 Annual. (The 'dodges well' rather indicates that Harvey was not averse to a dribble, hardly a typical ploy for defenders then). The first player from a Black Country club to be capped by England.

HARVEY, J(ames) Colin
(Everton, 1971, 1)
Born Liverpool, 16 November 1944.
1968: 5ft. 7ins.; 11st.

Career: Liverpool junior football; Everton amateur 1961/62 and then an apprentice before turning professional October 1962; Sheffield Wednesday September 1974 (£70,000); retired through injury early in 1976. Everton youth coach 1976 and then reserve team coach before appointment as joint first team coach November 1983. Was the club's chief coach/assistant manager at the time of his promotion to the managership June 1987. Other honours: England Under-23 international (5 apps). Football League (3 apps). (Everton) FL champions 1970. FA Cup winner 1966; finalist 1968.

Midfield. A stylist who (somewhat unusually) combined culture and a phenomenal work rate, pushing himself to the limit. Formed a famous Goodison triangle with Alan Ball and Howard Kendall. On leaving school worked as a clerk in the National Health Service.

HASSALL, Harold William
(Huddersfield Town and Bolton Wanderers, 1951-54, 5)
Born Tyldesley nr. Bolton, 4 March 1929.
1950: 5ft. 11ins.; 11st. 8lbs.

Career: Astley & Tyldesley Collieries (Bolton Combination); Huddersfield Town September 1946; Bolton Wanderers January 1952 (£25,000); retired through injury December 1955. Subsequently a distinguished coach:FA staff coach at Lilleshall, member of the FIFA panel of coaches from 1966, coach of the Malayan national side in 1968. Also had spells as manager of the England youth team and, from February 1971, as a Preston North End scout. Other honours: Football League (3 apps). (Bolton W) FACup finalist 1953.

Inside-left. Long striding, powerful and a marksman, unfortunateley side-lined at 26 when in his prime. But he put plenty back into the game afterwards with his coaching activities. Became a lecturer on PT at the Padgate College of Education (Warrington)1962 and from 1966, senior lecturer.

HATELEY, Mark Wayne
(Portsmouth AC Milan, and Monaco, 1984-88, 31)
Born Liverpool, 7 November 1961.
1984: 6ft. 1in.; 11st. 7lbs.

Career: Sefton (Liverpool) schools and junior football; Coventry City apprentice August 1978, turning professional the following November; Portsmouth June 1983 (£190,000); AC Milan June 1984 (£915,000); Monaco (France) June 1987 (£1m.) Other honours: England Youth international England Under-21 international (10 apps). (Monaco) French League champions 1988.

Strike forward whose successful entry into full international football caused a rapid rise in transfer value. Pompey received from wealthy AC Milan a fee almost five times that expended a mere year before. Rangy and athletic, Mark's main stock in trade is his exceptional heading ability which can be directed with awesome power. It is hereditary too, for it was the chief asset of his father, Tony Hateley, a leading centre-forward 1958-73.

HAWKES, Robert Murray
(Luton Town, 1907-08, 5)

Born Breachwood Green, Herts. 18 October 1880. Died 12 September 1945.
1907: 5ft. 8½ins.; 10st. 8lbs.

Career: Played in Luton schoolboy soccer and for junior clubs in that town (Stanley, Victoria and Clarence) before becoming a Luton Town amateur cs 1901, turning professional 1911. Made his final appearance for Luton Town in season 1919/20 then saw out the rest of the campaign with Bedford Town before retiring. Represented Hertfordshire on four occasions. Other honours: England amateur international (22 apps).

Left-half, reputedly the country's best around the mid-1900s. Had superb ball control and was a penalty specialist said never to have missed. It was also said he wore a metal plate under his auburn hair, this accounting for an apparent disinclination to head the ball. Skippered Luton from 1905 to the Great War. Appropriately reported to be a straw-hat manufacturer by vocation.

HAWORTH, George
(Accrington, 1887-90, 5)
Born Accrington, 17 October 1864.

Career: Christ Church FC 1878; Accrington FC 1883 and served the club until 1892, the period being broken by a brief spell with Blackburn Rovers (on loan ?) that tookin the 1885 Cup final. He re-signed for Accrington in the close season of 1885. Other honour: (Blackburn R) FA Cup winner 1885.

Right-half / centre-half. His 5 caps included 3 against Scotland – a sure measure of the player's worth. Indeed, some years after the tireless Haworth had hung up his boots, the great James Crabtree said that he and J H Forrest were the best tacklers and most judicious performers he (Crabtree) had ever seen. NOTE. It should be pointed out that in some sources the surname is given as Howarth. Confusion between the names is common. Bob Haworth, well known member of Bolton's Cup-winning sides of the 'twenties, often had his surname mis-spelled.

HAWTREY, John Purvis
(Old Etonions, 1881, 2)
Born Eton, Bucks. 19 July 1850. Died 17 August 1925.

Career: Old Etonians; Remnants. Also represented London and Berks & Bucks FAs. Other honour: (Old Etonians) FA Cup winner 1879.

Goalkeeper apt to be variable although brilliant at his best. Won his caps following one of his 'on' days playing for London against Birmingham in February 1881 ('the fine goalkeeping of Hawtrey contributed greatly to their success') but he let 6 through against Scotland the following month. He did not play football at his schools (Eton 1857-64 and Clifton College from '64). Taught at his father's school (Aldin House, Slough) for some time but when his younger brother, Charles, found fame as an actor, he too went on the stage and became a playwright under the name of John Trent-Hay. In later years he ran the journal 'Sporting World'.

HAYGARTH, Edward Brownlow
(Swifts, 1875, 1)
Born Cirencester, Glos. 26 April 1854. Died 14 April 1915.

Career: Lancing College; Wanderers; Swifts; Reading (in that club's initial season, 1871/72). Also represented Berkshire.

Full-back, formidably built, intrepid in his play and powerful with his kicking. Useful at cricket too: turned out for Gloucestershire (2 matches 1883), Hampshire (1 match 1875) and Berkshire. Haygarth actually came from a cricketing family, his brother being an Oxford Blue and a cousin assisted the MCC 1844-61, Middlesex and Sussex. A solicitor (admitted August 1876), he practised in his native Cirencester.

HAYNES, John Norman
(Fulham, 1955-62, 56)
Born Kentish Town, London, 17 October 1934.

1959: 5ft. 9 $^1/_2$ ins.; 11st.10lbs.

Career: Edmonton Schools; Middlessex Schools; London Schools; Fulham ground staff July 1950, developing with Feltham United, Wimbledon and Woodford Town until turning professional May 1952, briefly Fulham's caretaker manager November-December 1968; Durban City August 1970; Wealstone November 1972; later returned to South Africa and assisted 3 Durban clubs - City, United and Celtic. Other honours: England schoolboy international. England Youth international. England 'B' international (5 apps). England Under23 international (8 apps). Football League (13 apps).

Inside-forward. A megastar of the 'Fifties, a brilliant ball player, stylish and cool. Most renowned, though, for superb distribution, hitting the ball from any angle or distance and finding his man unerringly. Johnny was the first player to be capped at six levels and the first to be paid £100 per week (at least in Britain).

HEALLESS, Henry
(Blackburn Rovers, 1925-28, 2)
Born Blackburn, 10 February 1893. Died 11 January 1972.
1928: 5ft. 9$^1/_2$ins.; 12st.

Career: Blackburn Athletic; Victoria Cross (Blackburn); Blackburn Trinity; Blackburn Rovers as an amateur 1914/15 season, turning professional May 1919; retired April 1933. Coach to Almelo Club, Holland, September 1935-October 1937 when he returned to England, was reinstated an amateur and assisted Haslingden Grane FC. After WW2 was still playing in Blackburn junior football (at full-back) when in his fifties. Other honours: Football League (1 app). (Blackburn R) FA Cup winner 1928.

Centre/wing-half. Dour, stong tackling and efficient in any half-back possition. As a local reporter related 'his capable generalship often pulled the Rovers through when things seemed to be going badly against them. He could last through the most arduous game, and the team often derived encouragement from the fact that he never seemed to tire!' For long the club's skipper, a period that took in the momentous 1928 Wembley Cup victory.

HECTOR, Kevin James
(Derby County, 1974, 2)
Born Leeds, 2 November 1944.
1974: 5ft. 9ins.; 10st. 9lbs.

Career: South Leeds; Bradford July 1962; Derby County September1966 (£34,000); Vancouver Whitecaps (Canada) January 1978 (£100,000) (spent the English seasons with Boston United and then Burton Albion); Derby County again October 1980; Shepshed Charterhouse August 1982, later assisting Belper Town. Other honours: Football League (3 apps). (Derby Co) FL champions 1972,1975. FL Div. 2 champions 1969.

Inside-left. A rare opportunist whose opportunisim flourished in the top flight as well as in the lower divisions. Scored 113 League goals in 176 outings for Park Avenue before going on to register 201 first-team goals on Derby's behalf, a total surpassed only by the legendary Steve Bloomer. Kevin did, however, annex the club's record for FL appearences (486). He was poised, fast and blessed with a character that made him deservedly popular.

HEDLEY, George Albert
(Sheffield United, 1909, 1)
Born South Bank, Middlesbrough, 20 July 1876. Died 16 August 1942.
1901: 5ft. 10ins.; 11st. 7lbs.

Career: South Bank FC; Sheffield United as an amateur 1897/98 season, turning professional May 1898; Southampton May 1903; Wolverhampton Wanderers May 1906 – 1913. Bristol City manager April 1913 – WW1. Other honours: Football League (1 app).(Sheffield U) FA Cup winner 1899, 1902; finalist 1901. (Soton) Southern

League champions 1904. (Wolves) FA Cup winner 1908

Centre-forward. An advocate, and a practising one, of the open game: a robust, aggressive opportunist. His tactics were ideally suited to knock-out competitions and he appeared in 4 FA Cup finals in a decade, claiming winners' medals in 3 of them. Was for many years – until 1941 – a Bristol licencee, then not long before his death returned to Wolverhampton to take over a boarding-house.

HEGAN, (Lieut.) Kenneth Edward
(Corinthians and the Army, 1923-24, 4)
Born Coventry, 24 January 1901.
1924: 5ft. 7½ins.; 9st. 4lbs.

Career: Bablake School; RMC, Sandhurst; Army football when serving with the 1st Dublin Fusiliers and RASC, also appearing many times in the Army's representative side; Corinthians from 1919/20 into the 1930s. Other honours: England amateur international (23 apps).

Outside-right/outside-left. An inter-war ornament of the amateur game, slight in build and, in 1924, reckoned the fastest player around. 'Pace, control and accurate centering are his chief assets,' was another report. A regular Corinthian, his record for that club to the end of 1931/32 was 37 goals in 138 matches. Retired from the Army July 1949 with the rank of Lt-Colonel. Awarded the OBE during WW2.

HELLAWELL, Michael Stephen
(Birmingham, City, 1963, 2)
Born Keighley, Yorks. 30 June 1938.
1963: 5ft. 11ins.; 11st. 6lbs.

Career: Salts FC (Huddersfield Town amateur for 1 year); Queen's Park Rangers August 1955; Birmingham City May 1957 (for fee and another player); Sunderland January 1965 (£27,500); Huddersfield Town September 1966 (£15,000); Peterborough United November 1968 (£4000); Bromsgrove Rovers August 1969. Other honour: (Birmingham City) FL Cup winner 1963.

Outside-right, flame haired and displayed a liveliness to match this natural attribute. His main asset was tremedous speed. Represented Division 3(South) against Division 3(North) in his early senior days. A good cricketer – professional to the Walsall CC and in 1962 played one match for Warwickshire. Mike's brother, John, assisted Bradford City and other League clubs during the 1960s.

HENFREY, Arthur George
(Cambridge University and Corinthians, 1891-96, 5)
Born Wellingborough, 1868. Died 17 October 1929.

Career: Wellingborogh Grammar School; Cambridge University (Blue 1890-91); Finedon FC; Corinthians 1890-1903. Also represented Northamptonshire.

Half-back/forward. Hard working amateur, a utillity player of value. Strong and brave in the tackle, and judicious in distribution. Best in the intermediate line because a natural spoiler. Shone at cricket too, playing for Cambridge University (no Blue) and

Northants 1886-99 (Captain 1893 and '94).

HENRY, Ronald Patrick
(Tottenham Hotspur, 1963, 1)
Born Shoreditch, London, 17 August 1934.
1963: 5ft. 10ins.; 11st. 13lbs.

Career: Harpenden Schools; Hertfordshire Schools; Harpenden Town; RA Depot, Woolwich; Redbourne FC (Herts) (Luton Town amateur); Tottenham Hotspur January 1955; retired cs 1969. Later worked part time with Spurs' training staff. Other honours: (Spurs) European Cup winners' Cup, winner 1963. FL champions 1961. FA Cupwinner 1961, 1962.

Left-back after turning professional following periods at outside-left and left half. Highly consistent, first class in anticipation and reliable, a valued member of Spurs' great 1961 'Double' side. Combined his job as a White Hart Lane backroom boy with that of a Hertfordshire nurseryman.

HERON, C(harles) Francis W(illiam)
(Wanderers, 1876, 1)
Born Uxbridge, 1853. Died 23 October 1914.

Career: Mill Hill School; Uxbrige; Swifts; Wanderers; Windsor. Other honour : (Wanderers) FA Cup winner 1876.

Forward. 'Always useful . . . will make one of the best forwards of the day, ' opined the Football Annual for 1874, anticipating future honours. Heron had expertise in dribbling, and elusiveness was essential because his light build was unsuited to vigorous contemporary tactics. Brother of G H H Heron below, whom he partnered in the 1876 Cup final, and like him a wine merchant.

HERON, G(eorge) Hubert H(ugh)
(Uxbridge and Wanderers, 1873-78, 5)
Born Uxbridge, 30 January 1852. Died 5 June 1914.
Career: Mill Hill School; Uxbridge; Wanderers; Swifts. Also represented Middlesex. Served on the FA Committee 1873-76. Other honours: (Wanderers) FA Cup winner 1876, 1877, 1878.
Forward. At the outset of his cap-winning career a journalist wrote '. . . seems, if possible, to improve every season.' And so it proved, with 5 appearances against England's main foe, Scotland, in 6 years, and 3 Cup-winners' medals in consecutive campaigns. He was a fast, dexterous and sometimes brilliant dribbler flawed a little by a tendancy towards keeping possesion too long. A younger brother of Frank Heron (Wanderers & England) and later a Bournemouth wine merchant.

HIBBERT, Wiliam
(Bury, 1910, 1)
Born Golborne nr. Wigan, 21 September 1884. Died 16 March 1949.
1911: 5ft. 17$^1/_2$ins.; 10st. 10lbs.

Career: Golbourne school and junior football; Newton-le-Willows (Lancashire Combination) when 16; Brynn Central for 1 season; Bury May 1906; Newcastle United October 1911 (£1950, then a record); (guest player for Leeds City during WW1); Bradford City May 1920 (£700); Oldham Athletic May 1922. To USA as coach July 1923 where he also managed Coats FC, Rhode Island; coach in Spain June 1927; Wigan Borough trainer 1929. Other honours:Football League (3 apps).

Inside-right. In junior days played centre-forward. Had brilliance in spite of his small frame, skill and enthusiasm producing a fair crop of goals. Billy's eye for openings was never more in evidence than when touring South Africa with the FA party in 1910 – he notched 6 in one match and 5 in another. In 1938 went to live and work at Blackpool, where he died.

HIBBS, Henry Edward
(Birmingham, 1930-36, 25)
Born Wilnecote, Staffs. 27 May 1906. Died 23 April 1984.
1931: 5ft. 9$^1/_2$ins.; 12st. 2lbs.

Career: Wilnecote Holy Trinity; Tamworth Castle; Birmingham May 1924; retired April 1940. Walsall manager August 1944 – June 1951; was a permit player for de Havilands February 1953 – cs 1954 when in his late 40s; his last job in football was as manager/ coach of Ware FC (Delphian League) for a few months from August 1960. Other honours: Football League (3apps) (Birmingham) FA Cupfinalist 1931.

Goalkeeper rightly categorised with the previous generation's Sam Hardy. Hibbs' superb anticipation enabled him to get his body behind the hardest shot, while overall reliability was pronounced. Member of the touring party to South Africa 1929, making an appearance against the national team. Originally a plumber's apprentice, he was at Welwyn, Herts, after leaving the professional game.

HILL, Frederick
(Bolton Wanderers, 1963, 2)
Born Sheffield, 17 January 1940.
1963: 5ft. $10^3/_4$ins.; 11st.11lbs.

Career: Sheffield Schools; Bolton Wanderers March 1957 Halifax Town July 1969 (£5000); Mancherster City May 1970 (£13,000); Peterborough United August 1973 (£5000) – 1975; Droylsden 1976. Other honours: England Under-23 international (10 apps). Football League (2 apps). Peterbo') FL Div. 4 champions 1974.

Inside-forward exhibiting ball manipulation of a high order and, like so many others of similar dexterity, always seemed to have plenty of time to carry out his manoeuvres. Was of pronounced two-footed ability too. Finished with a League record of 499 matches plus 10 substitutions and 87 goals. Cousin of the late Brian Hill (Sheffield Wednesday, 1955-66).

HILL, Gordon Alec
(Manchester United, 1976-78, 6)
Born Sunbury-on-Thames, Middlesex, 1 April 1954.
1977: 5ft. 7ins.; 10st. 12lbs.

Career: Sunbury schoolboy football; Ashford Youth Club (Middlesex) when 15 (trials with Queen's Park Rangers and Southend United); Staines Town; Southall; Millwall as a professional January 1973; Manchester United November 1975 (£80,000); Derby County April 1978 (£250,000); Queen's Park Rangers November 1979 (£150,000) went to North America in 1981, first assisting Montreal Manic and then Chicago Sting early 1982 and other clubs. Stafford Rangers on his return; later Northwich Victoria's player/coach to October 1988. Other honours: England Youth international. England amateur international. England 'B' international. England Under-23 international (1 app). (Man. Utd) FA Cup winner 1977; finalist 1976.

Outside-left must be his positional definition in spite of post-'66 World Cup realignments. For Hill was an out-and-out left-sided wingman: attack minded, prone to cut in for a crack at a goal and not to rush back into defence. Went to Old Trafford the same year as Steve Coppell, the pair being respective wingers in a 4-2-4 combination.

HILL, John Henry
(Burnley and Newcastle United,1925-29, 11)
Born Hetton-le-Hole, Co Durham, 2 March1897. Died April 1972.
1928: 6ft. 3ins.; 12st. 11lbs.

Career: Junior football to Durham City as a professional during season 1919/20; Plymouth Argyle September 1920; Burnley May 1923 (£5450); Newcastle United October 1928 (£8100); Bradford City June 1931 (£600); Hull City November 1931 (in part exchange for another player); retired April 1934 on appointment as Hull City manager – January 1936. Hull City scout 1948-55 and in charge of the Scarborough FC Pools Scheme until retiring in August 1963. Other honours: Football League (3 apps). (Hull City) FL Div. 3 (North) champions 1933.

Centre-half, occasionally right-half. A

combination of red hair and tall stature made him conspicious on the field. Quite dominating in the air, shrewd and constructive generally and a rare spoiler of opponents' raids. Sometimes referred to as 'Hill 60', a once notorious eminence that wartime troops had to storm.

HILL, Richard Henry
(Millwall,1926, 1)
Born Mapperley, Notts. 26 November 1893. Died April 1971.
1925: 5ft.11ins.; 11st. 6lbs.

Career:Army football (Grenadier Guards); Millwall Athletic cs 1919; Torquay United July 1930; Newark Town August 1931. Mansfield Town trainer August 1932; Coventry City trainer cs 1935; Torquay United trainer July 1950. Other honour: (Millwall) FL Div. 3 (South) champions 1928.

Left-back 'spare of frame and tall in stature', as one writer recorded. For a decade the left flank half of a noted Lions' full-back partnership, his speed and dexterous kicking an exellent foil to the stolid Jack Fort (q.v.). Served many years as a trainer, his long stint at Coventry taking in both sides of the 1939/45 War.

HILL, Ricky Anthony
(Luton Town, 1983-86, 3)
Born Paddington, London, 5 March 1959.
1986: 5ft. 10$^1/_2$ins.; 13st.

Career: North London schools football; Luton Town on schoolboy forms, apprentice 1976, full professioal May 1976. Other honours: England Youth international. (Luton T) FL Div. 2 champions 1982. FL Cup winner 1988.

Midfield. Precocious as a youngster, making a League debut at 16 and justifying his early promise subsequently. Has natural control, a strong physique and can shoot from any angle. Considering Hill's all-round skills, it is suprising to many that more honours have not come his way. Be that as it may, he has proved a model professional and is highly regarded as a person.

HILLMAN, John
(Burnley, 1899, 1)
Born Tavistock, Devon, 1871. Died 1 August 1955.
1903: 6ft.; 14st.

Career; Junior football to Burnley late in 1891; Everton February 1895 (£150); Dundee June 1896 (£150) Burnley again March 1898 (£225); Manchester City January 1902; Millwall Athletic January 1907; Burnley trainer 1921-22. Other honours: Football League (1 app). (Man. City) FL Div. 2 champions 1903. FA Cup winner 1904.

Goalkeeper hefty by later standards so even more so in pre-WW1 days when they were often around the five-and-a-half ft. mark. Hillman was remarkably (and naturally) agile despite his size, and shone in all goalkeeping aspects. For long had a sweet-shop in Burnley, reputedly as late as the early 1950s. Played cricket for Forfarshire when a young man.

HILLS, Arnold Frank
(Old Harrovians, 1879, 1)
Born Lambeth, London,12 March 1857. Died 7 March 1927.

Career: Harrow School (XI 1875-76, captain 1876); Oxford University (Blue 1877-78); Old Harrovians. Other honour: (Oxford University) FA Cup finalist 1877.

Forward. Extremely fast and needed watching on that account, but tended to be variable and was prone to overrun the ball. A noted athlete, Hills was a Blue for 4 successive years, 1877-80, and was President of the University Athletic Club for the final year. He was the AAA mile champion of 1878. Later became managing-director of Thames Ironworks and founder of the soccer club of that name, from which, as is well known, emerged the famous West Ham United FC.

HILSDON, George Richard
('Gatling Gun')
(Chelsea, 1907-09, 8)
Born Bow, London, 10 August 1885. Died 10 September 1941.
1911: 5ft. 8$^1/_2$ins.; 12st. 2lbs.

Career: East Ham Schools; South-West Ham FC; Clapton Orient; Luton Town cs 1902; West Ham United 1903; Chelsea May 1906; West Ham United again cs 1912; Chatham cs 1919. Other honours: Football League (2 apps).

Centre-forward. Owed his nickname to lethal shooting with both feet, a quality aided by an acute positional sense. Scored

with fine consistency throughout his first-class career. A notable tally was netting 6 for Chelsea in a cup-tie. January 1908. On returning to Upton Park made a big contribution to the development of another England cap, Syd Puddefoot. Badly gassed during WW1, Hilsdon had theatrical connections and was reported to be touring with Fred Karno's company in the mid-1920s.

HINE, Ernest William
(Leicester City, 1929-32, 6)
Born Smithy Cross nr. Barnsley, 9 April 1901. Died 1974.
1930: 5ft. 7½ins.; 11st. 1lb.

Career: Staincross Station (Barnsley Nelson League); Barnsley FC as an amateur April 1921, turning professional January 1922; Leicester City January 1926 (£3000); Huddersfield Town May 1932; Manchester United February 1933; Barnsley again December 1934; retired May 1938. Other honours: Football League (5 apps).

Inside-forward. 'A full 90 minutes player; a deadly shot; speedy and ever on the look out for a 'snap' chance,' reported a 1927 annual, neatly summing-up this fine performer. Figured in 17 of the 20 inter-war seasons, scoring 287 goals in 600 plus League outings. The most unassuming of footballers too, the epitome of a model player.

HINTON, Alan Thomas
(Wolverhampton Wanderers and Nottingham Forest, 1963-65, 3)
Born Wednesbury, Staffs, 6 October 1942.
1964: 5ft. 9½ins.; 11st. 5lbs.
Career: South-East Staffs. Schools; Wolverhampton Wanderers ground staff 1958, turning professional October 1959; Nottingham Forest January 1964 (in exchange for another player); Derby County September 1967 (£29,500); retired from the first-class game May 1976 and assisted Barrowash Victoria (E Midlands Regional League) from August 1976. Later went to the States and coached Tulsa Roughnecks to 1979/80 and Seattle Sounders 1980. Other honours: England Youth International. England Under-23 international (7 apps). (Derby Co.) FL champions 1972. FL Div. 2 champions 1969.

Outside-left. An excellent example of the top grade orthodox winger. Shattering pace in short bursts, control and ability to cut in and shoot. Additionally – a personal quirk – had a disconcerting shuffle. In America Alan won the 1980 'Coach of the Year' award.

HITCHENS, Gerald Archibald
(Aston Villa and Inter-Milan, 1961-62, 7)
Born Rawnsley, Staffs. 8 October 1934.
Died 13 April 1983.
1960: 5ft. 10½ins.; 12st. 2lbs.

Career: Highley Youth Club; Highley Miners Welfare; Kidderminster Harriers; Cardiff City January 1955 (£1000); Aston Villa December 1957 (£22,500); Internazionale Milan June 1961 (£80,000); Torino November 1962 (in exchange for another player); Atalanta of Bergamo June 1965; Cagliari (Sardinia) cs 1967; Worcester City November 1969; Merthyr Tydfil 1970/71 retiring May 1971 after 6 appearances. Other honours: England Under-23 international (1 app). Football League (1 app). (Cardiff C) Welsh Cup winner 1956. (Villa) FL Div. 2 champions 1960.

Centre-forward. Also appeared at inside-right for Villa. An exciting player to watch with his aggression, courage and resolution, ever in contention for the ball. Gerry scored in the first minute of his international debut and, for Cardiff and Villa, netted 118 goals in a total 227 League matches. Was able to adjust his game to meet Italian demands. After leaving football was director of a Pontypridd firm.

HOBBIS, Harold Henry Frederick
(Charlton Athletic, 1936, 2)
Born Dartford, 9 March 1913.
1938: 5ft. 9ins.; 11st 5½lbs.

Career: Kent Schools; Brent School Old Boys (Dartford); Bromley; Charlton Athletic on amateur forms February 1931, turning professional the following month; Tonbridge as player/manager November 1948. Later a scout for Crystal Palace and Wolverhampton Wanderers. Other honour: (Charlton) FL Div. 3 (South) champions 1935.

Outside-left. A major member of the Charlton team that sensationally rose from Third Division to First in successive seasons. Hobbis, lively and with distinctive gait, often appeared on the score-sheet. In 251 peacetime League matches for the South Londoners he netted 76 goals. Had been at left-half as a schoolboy. Latterly a Charlton Licensee.

HODDLE, Glenn
(Tottenham Hotspur and Monaco, 1980-88,53)
Born Hayes, Middlesex, 27 October 1957.
1984: 6ft.; 11st. 6lbs.

Career: Harlow Schools; Essex Schools; Tottenham Hotspur apprentice April 1974, turning professional April 1975; Monaco (France) June 1987 (£750,000). Other honours: England Youth international. England 'B' international. England Under-21 international (12 apps). (Spurs) FA Cup winner 1981, 1982; finalist 1987. FL Cup finalist 1982. (Monaco) French League champions 1988.

Midfield. Probably the most naturally gifted performer of recent years. Has great vision and ball control and is master of the weighted pass as well as the delicate variety. Liable at any time to score a brilliant goal from long range. Some critics have questioned his work rate but, all in all, Glenn's is a talent for every connoisseur onlooker to enjoy. 'Young Player of the Year' 1980.

HODGE, Stephen Brian
(Aston Villa and Tottenham Hotspur, 1986-87, 15)
Born Nottingham, 25 October 1962.
1987: 5ft. 8ins.; 9st. 11lbs.

Career: South Notts Schools; Nottingham Forest apprentice, turning professional October 1980; Aston Villa August 1985 (£400,000); Tottenham Hotspur December 1986 (£650,000); Nottingham Forest again August 1988 (£550,000). Other honours: England Under-21 international (8 apps). (Spurs) FA Cup finalist 1987.

Midfield. operating mainly on the left. A fast performer with a rare sense of the creative possibilities of space and scoring opportunity. Won golden opinions on his elevation to full international status.

HODGETTS, Dennis
(Aston Villa, 1888-94, 6)
Born Birmingham, 28 November 1863. Died 26 March 1945.

Career: Birmingham St. George's (service there interrupted by a brief spell with Great Lever); Aston Villa 1886; Small Heath October 1896; retired cs 1898. Was elected an Aston Villa Vice-President in June 1930. Other honours: Football League (1 app).

(Villa) FL champions 1894, 1896. FA Cup winner 1887, 1895; finalist 1892.

Inside/outside-left. A great solo player especially dangerous because of the ability to shoot from any angle. And he had the size and weight to be forceful. Individualism did not mar his accurate passing and centring. Employed as a licensee when playing days were over.

HODGKINSON, Alan
(Sheffield United, 1957-61, 5)
Born Laughton, Rotherham, 16 August 1936.
1959: 5ft. 9ins.; 11st. $4^1/_2$lbs.

Career: Rother Valley Schools; Thurcroft Youth Club; Worksop Town; Sheffield United on amateur forms January 1953, turning professional the following August; retired cs 1971. Sheffield United assistant trainer/coach January 1971; Gillingham assistant manager November 1975, subsequently holding coaching appointments which have included Birmingham City (part-time, late 1981) and two specially for goalkeepers: Coventry City (August 1981) and Scotland (August 1986). Other honours: England Under-23 international (7 apps). Football League (1 app).

Goalkeeper. A long serving Blade who clocked up 637 League and Cup appearances for the club. Rewarded after 15 years (September 1968) with a Lord Mayor's civic dinner and testimonial match. Wonderfully consistent and sound throughout his career. Represented the Army while on national service. Alan was a student of his craft and this brought coaching jobs aimed exclusively at custodians.

HODGSON, Gordon
(Liverpool, 1931, 3)
Born Johannesburg, South Africa, 16 April 1904, of English parents.
Died 14 June 1951.
1930: 6ft. $0^1/_4$in.; 13st. 5lbs.

Career: Transvaal FC (South Africa); Liverpool December 1925; Aston Villa January 1936 (£3000); Leeds United March 1937; retired during WW2 and became a Leeds United coach; Port Vale manager October 1946 to his death. Other honours: South African amateur international. Football League (1 app.)

Inside-right. Sometimes centre-forward. Heavily built and powerful, his vigour making him a force to be reckoned with. Established Liverpool seasonal and aggregate League scoring records that remained until broken by Roger Hunt (q.v.) many years after WW2. Came to England with a South African touring party in 1924/25; another member being Arthur Riley, for many seasons Liverpool's regular goalkeeper. Hodgson played cricket for Lancashire 1928-33 and Forfarshire 1934-36. He was an excellent baseball player too.

HODKINSON, Joseph
(Blackburn Rovers, 1913-20, 3)
Born Lancaster, 1889. Died 18 June 1954.
1919: 5ft. 8ins.; 10st. 7lbs.

Career: Lancaster St. Mary's; Lancaster Town; Glossop cs 1909; Blackburn Rovers January 1913 (£1000); Lancaster Town again April 1923; retired January 1925. Other honours: Football League (2 apps). (Blackburn) FL champions 1914.

Outside-left. 'A remarkable footballer, either individually or in combination, his centres are perfect,' reported a Lancashire handbook in 1913. And post-war his feet had not lost their cunning, the same source telling us in 1920 that Hodkinson was '. one of the cleverest and fastest wingers in the League. His centres are invariably accurate and well timed.' In the late 1920s became a licensee in his native Lancaster.

HOGG, William
(Sunderland, 1902, 3)
Born Newcastle-upon-Tyne, 29 May 1879. Died 30 January 1937.
1902: 5ft. 9ins.; 11st. 11lbs.

Career: Willington Athletic; Sunderland October 1899; Rangers May 1909 (£100); Dundee May 1913; Raith Rovers player/manager appointed cs 1914 but on the outbreak of war returned to Sunderland to work in an engineering works. Post-war assisted Montrose when in his early 40s. Sunderland FC coach October 1927 – 1934. Other honours: Football League (3 apps). (Sunderland) FL champions 1902. (Rangers) Scottish League champions 1911, 1912, 1913.

Outside-right. At Ibrox also figured at inside-right partnering the Scottish cap, Alec Bennett. Above everything else a veritable speed merchant, though this is not to denigrate his skills in dribbling and middling the ball. For some years a licensee in the Sunderland area and elsewhere.

HOLDCROFT, G(eorge) Henry
(Preston North End, 1937, 2)
Born Burslem, Stoke-on-Trent, 23 January 1909. Died 17 April 1983.
1938: 5ft. 11$^1/_2$ins.; 11st. 2lbs.

Career: Biddulph FC (Staffs); Norten Druids (Burslem); Whitfield Colliery; Port Vale September 1926; Darlington August 1928; Everton August 1931; Preston North End December 1932 (£1500 including another player); Barnsley November 1945, retiring through injury shortly afterwards. He did, however, subsequently assist Leyland Motors, Morecambe and Chorley. Other honours: Football League (1 app). (PNE) FA Cup winner 1938.

Goalkeeper. Composed and finely attuned as regards anticipation. His agility was even more pronounced by not possessing

any excess poundage. Harry had not enjoyed all that much first-team exposure before going to Deepdale – under 100 League outings in fact, with none for Everton where Coggins and Ted Sagar held sway. However, he more than repaid Preston for a 4-figure outlay (289 League and FA Cup matches). Missed the 1937 Cup final because of a broken figure.

HOLDEN, Albert Douglas
(Bolton Wanderers, 1959, 5)
Born Manchester, 28 September 1930
1959: 5ft. 8$^1/_2$ins.; 10st. 8$^1/_2$lbs.

Career: Manchester schoolboy football; Manchester YMCA; Bolton Wanderers amateur 1948, turning professional May 1949; Preston North End November 1962 (£8000); emigrated to Australia cs 1965 and played there Hakoah FC, Sydney, until 1968. Was Hakoah's coach from 1968-69 and held a similar post with another Sydney club, Auburn, 1969-70. Returned to England November 1970 and had a spell on

Grimsby Town's training staff from January 1971. Other honours: England Youth international. Football League (1 app). (Bolton W) FA Cup winner 1958; finalist 1953. (PNE)FA Cup finalist 1964.

Outside-right/outside-left. Had all the wingman's requirements speed, control, a repertoire of tricks and, moreover, was equally capable on either flank. Totalled 509 League appearances (53 goals) of which the Bolton share was 419 (40).

HOLDEN, George Henry
(Wednesbury Old Athletic, 1881-84, 4)
Born West Bromich, 6 October 1859. Died in the 1920s.

Career: Wednesbury Old Park; Wednesbury St James 1877; Wednesbury Old Athletic 1878; West Bromwich Albion May 1886; Wednesbury Old Athletic again cs 1887; Derby Midland 1888.

Outside-right. An early Black Country star: besides his 4 England caps he represented the Birmingham FA and Staffordshire on literally dozens of occasions. Described at various times as 'an extremely fast player' and a 'pretty player', his style is maybe best encapsulated by The Football Annual of 1881. 'Clever and useful right forward; is small but has plenty of pace, and dribbles well.'

HOLDEN-WHITE, Charles Henry
(Swifts, 1888, 2)
Born 1869. Died 14 July 1948.

Career: Brentwood School; Clapham Rovers; Corinthians 1882-91; Swifts. Served on the FA committee 1883-85.

Left-half. C B Fry wrote in the first Corinthians history (1906) 'C Holden-White was a very polished half-back – just the half-back a clever inside forward would be likely to become'. For the player had earlier partnered that notable forward, George Brann (q.v.). He turned out to be an even better middle-line man, fast moving and certain in his crisp tackling. Holden-White had the honour of being the Corinthians' very first captain and served on the club's original committee. He was a business man in the City.

HOLFORD, Thomas
(Stoke, 1903, 1)
Born Hanley, 28 January 1878. Died 6 April 1964.
1921: 5ft. $6^1/_2$ins.; 10st. 8lbs.

Career: Granville's Night School, Stoke; Cobridge; Stoke FC cs 1898; Manchester City April 1908; Port Vale as player/manager 1914 (guest player for Nottingham Forest during WW1), remaining on Port Vale's playing strength until 1924 and acting as trainer also from July 1923. Served Port Vale in various capacities as coach, trainer, team manager again (cs 1933-September 1935) and latterly as scout until retiring in 1950. Other honour: (Man City) FL Div. 2 champions 1910.

Centre/left-half chiefly but a super utility man (described as 'a capable natural footballer') who could take any berth. Capped in the pivotal position despite his short stature. Enjoyed a career of extraordinary length, making his last League appearances in season 1923/24 when in his mid-forties. The Potteries clubs have had no better servant.

HOLLEY, George H.
(Sunderland, 1909-13, 10)
Born Seaham Harbour, Co. Durham. 20 November 1885. Died 27 August 1942.
1909: 5ft. 9ins.; 12st.

Career: Seaham Athletic; Seaham Villa; Seaham White Star 1903/04; Sunderland November 1904; Brighton & Hove Albion July 1919; retired cs 1920. Sunderland coach later in 1920; Wolverhampton Wanderers trainer July 1922; Barnsley trainer August 1932. Other honours: Football League (5 apps). (Sunderland) FL champions 1913. FA Cup finalist 1913.

Inside-forward. Usually inside-left. A ball artist of the first rank, enthralling spectators with his consummate skills. And consistent with it besides contributing his share of goals. Member of the FA touring party to South Africa in 1910, playing 3 times against the national team. Became a very experienced trainer/coach with his long stints at Wolverhampton and Barnsley. Father of Tom Holley (Leeds United 1936-49) and once worked as a plater.

HOLLIDAY, Edwin
(Middlesbrough, 1960, 3)
Born Leeds, 7 June 1939.
1960: 5ft. 9ins.; 10st. 12lbs.

Career: Barnsley Schools; Middlesbrough on amateur forms 1955, turning professional June 1956; Sheffield Wednesday March 1962 (£27,000); Middlesbrough again June 1965; Hereford United July 1966; Workington February 1968; Peterborough United July 1969; retired through injury September 1970. Other honours: England Under-23 international (5 apps). Football League (1 app).

Outside-left. A thrustful, powerful attacker calling on a repertoire of tricks and shooting hard with both feet. Nephew of Colin Grainger (Sheffield United, Sunderland & England). Edwin broke a leg in November 1969 and did not appear again in the first-class game. Scored 38 times in the course of his 280 FL outings (and 4 substitutions).

HOLLINS, John William
(Chelsea, 1967, 1)
Born Guildford, 16 July 1946.
1967: 5ft. 7½ins.; 11st. 5lbs.

Career: Guildford Schools; Guildford junior football; Chelsea amateur September 1961, turning professional July 1963; Queen's Park Rangers July 1975 (£80,000)' Arsenal July 1979 (£75,000); Chelsea again May 1983 as player/assistant coach (he played during season 1983/84); Chelsea manager June 1985–March 1988. Other honours: England Youth international. England 'B' international. England Under-23 international (12 apps). Football League (3 apps). (Chelsea) FL Div. 2 champions 1984. FA Cup winner 1970; finalist 1967. FL Cup winner 1965; finalist 1972. European Cup Winners' Cup, winner 1971. (Arsenal) European Cup winners' Cup, finalist 1980.

Midfield (right-half), but was right-back for his playing swansong – member of the Chelsea 1983/84 Div. 2 championship side. A perky little player, energetic and purposeful, over 20 years in the first-class game. In all made 736 League appearances plus 7 subs (62 goals). Son of a professional and one of his brothers, David was a Welsh cap.

HOLMES, Robert
(Preston North End, 1888-95,7)
Born Preston, 23 June 1867. Died 17 November 1955.
1889; 5ft. 8ins.; 11st. 7lbs.

Career: Preston Olympic; Preston North End 1884-1901. Reinstated as an amateur May 1901 and placed on the Football League referees' list. Served as trainer of Bradford City (May 1904 – 1905) and Blackburn Rovers (January 1909-November 1913) besides coaching at several public schools. Other honours: Football League (3 apps). (PNE) FL champions 1889,1890. FA Cup winner 1889; finalist 1888.

Right/left-back. Played at right-half in the 1888 Cup final. A very popular performer; energetic, courageous and capable of kicking from any angle, while his heading and tackling were first-rate. Represented Lan-

cashire when still in North End's reserves and it was said in the mid–'Nineties he held a remarkable record of having never been on the losing side in a representative match.

HOLT, John
(Everton and Reading, 1890-1900, 10)
Born Church, Lancs. 10 April 1865.
1890s: 5ft. 4$^1/_2$ins.; 10st. 2lbs.

Career: King's Own FC (Blackburn); Blackpool St. John's; Church; Bootle circa 1885; Everton 1888; Reading October 1898; retired 1902. Elected a Reading director in that year, Holt was unable to take up the appointment because the FA refused to reinstate him as an amateur. He subsequently returned to Liverpool and scouted for Reading in the Merseyside area until 1914. Other honours: Football League (2 apps). (Everton) FL champions 1891. FA Cup finalist 1893, 1897.

Centre-half. A prime example of the midget pivots who flourished during the early professional era. Sir Frederick Wall, secretary of the FA, described Holt as '... a Jack-in-the-box, a regular spring-heeled Jack rising for the ball and tackling his enemy unawares.' By some printed accounts he was also a master of the sly minor foul. (One can imagine the libel actions resulting from such comments a half-century and more later!).

HOPKINSON, Edward
(Bolton Wanderers, 1958-60, 14)
Born Wheatley Hill, Co Durham, 29 October 1935.
1959: 5ft. 8$^3/_4$.; 11st. 7lbs.

Career: Royton (Oldham) schoolboy football; Lancashire Schools; Haggate Lads Club (represented Lancashire Youth); Oldham Athletic amateur 1951; Bolton Wanderers amateur cs 1952,turning professional the following November; retired cs 1970 and joined Bolton's coaching staff; Stockport County assistant manager in the mid-1970s (briefly acting manager August 1975); Oldham RLFC trainer on a voluntary basis February 1977. Other honours: England Under-23 international (6 apps). Football League (2 apps). (Bolton W) FA Cup winner 1958.

Goalkeeper. Mere average height was no bar to brilliance for this daring 'keeper and he was consistent with it. Made well over 500 league appearances for the Trotters. Eddie represented Lancashire at water polo and his son, Paul, was a Stockport County player in the mid-'Seventies.

HOSSACK, Anthony Henry
(Corinthians, 1892-94, 2)
Born Walsall, 2 May 1867. Died 24 January 1926.

Career: Chigwall School (XI 1882-85, captain 1885); Cambridge University (Blue 1890); Corinthians 1891-94.

Right-half. Able to take the left-half berth too. Was an accomplished middle-line player notable for his outstanding speed. Played cricket for Cambridge University in 1889 (though not awarded a Blue) and Essex from 1891 before the county gained first-class status. A solicitor (admitted May 1897), Hossack practised at Dawlish, Devonshire.

HOUGHTON, W(illiam) Eric ('Coog')
(Aston Villa, 1931-33, 7)
Born Billingborough, Lincs. 29 June 1910.
1938: 5ft. 8$^1/_4$ins.; 11st. 10lbs.

Career: Donington Grammar School, Lincs; Billingborough FC; Boston Town; Aston Villa on amateur forms August 1927, turning professional August 1928; Notts County December 1946; retired May 1949. Notts County manager May 1949-August 1953; Aston Villa manager September 1953-November 1958; Nottingham Forest chief scout July 1959-November 1960; Rugby Town manager February 1961 (secretary/ manager from cs 1961)-March 1964; Walsall scout 1965, later joining that club's board; Aston Villa director September 1972-

December 1979; served Walsall again as general secretary in the early 1980s. Other honours: Football League (4 apps).(Villa) FL Div. 2 champions 1938.

Outside-left. Able to take the other wing too. Extremely fast and packed a whizzbang shot in either foot. Very likely the hardest dead ball shot of his generation. This quality led naturally to penalty specialisation and he is reputed to have a career record of converting 72 out of a possible 79. Played cricket for Warwickshire (1946-47) and Lincolnshire, and in 1971 was awarded the MCC's advanced coaching certificate.

HOULKER, Albert Edward ('Kelly')
(Blackburn Rovers, Portsmouth and Southampton, 1902-06, 5)
Born Blackburn, 27 April 1872. Died 27 May 1962.
1902: 5ft. $6^1/_2$ins.; 10st. 5lbs.

Career: Blackburn schoolboy football and then assisted several junior clubs in that town's district (Blackburn Hornets, Oswaldtwistle Rovers, Cob Wall and Park Road) before joining Blackburn Rovers in the 1893/94 season; Portsmouth May 1902; Southampton May 1903; Blackburn Rovers again cs 1906; retired cs 1907 but signed for Colne FC October 1909. In an emergency played a wartime game for Blackburn Rovers when within 3 months of his 46th birthday (January 1918). Other honours: Football League (1 app). (Soton) Southern League champions 1904.

Left-half summed up as 'dour and diminutive'. Tenacious, too, never knowing when he was beaten, his plucky displays making him popular everywhere. On leaving football was overlooker at a Blackburn mill, then ran a coal and haulage business in the town until retiring in 1947. Cousin of the England cap, Arthur Cowell.

HOWARTH, Robert Henry
(Preston North End and Everton, 1887-94, 5)
Born Preston, Lancs. 20 June 1865. Died 20 August 1938.
1889: 5ft. $11^1/_2$ins.; 13st.

Career: Preston junior football; Preston North End during the 1880s (probably 1884); Everton November 1891; Preston North End again cs 1894-1895. Other honours: Football League (2 apps). (PNE) FL champions 1889, 1890. FA Cup winner 1889; finalist 1888. (Everton) FA Cup finalist 1893.

Right-back, who brought a daunting physique to bear. This, though, was not the outstanding footballing facet of an immaculate full-back. Howarth tackled with a confidence bred of success and was always composed in demeanour. A lawyer's clerk at the time of joining North End originally, he eventually qualified himself (admitted a solicitor January 1908) and practised in his native town. His brother, Sir Alfred Howarth, was once Town Clerk of Preston.

HOWE, Donald
(West Bromwich Albion, 1958-60, 23)
Born Wolverhampton, 12 October 1935.
1959: 5ft. 11ins.; 10st. 13lbs.

Career: Wolverhampton Schools; West Bromwich Albion as an amateur December 1950, turning professional November 1952; Arsenal April 1964 (about £45,000); broke a leg March 1966 and had to retire. Subsequently joined the Arsenal staff becoming chief coach November 1967 and assistant manager March 1969; West Bromwich Albion manager July 1971-April 1975; Galatasaray FC (Turkey) coach; Leeds United coach October 1975; Arsenal coach again August 1977, caretaker manager December 1983 and manager April 1984-March 1986. Has also been coach to the England team for some years. Wimbledon assistant manager August 1987. Other honours: England 'B' international (1 app). England Under-23 international (6 apps). Football League (6 apps).

Right-back. Clever in positional play, confident with his kicking and tackling. Did well in the way of representative honours but – like many another internationalist – won no medals at club level. Is regarded as being one of the best coaches of modern times.

HOWE, John Robert
(Derby County, 1948-49, 3)
Born West Hartlepool, 7 October 1915. Died 5 April 1987.
1951: 5ft. 11ins.; 12st. 10lbs.

Career: Hartlepools junior football; Hartlepools United June 1934; Derby County March 1936 (guest player for Aberdeen, Hearts, Falkirk and St. Mirren during WW2 while serving with the Cameron Highlanders); Huddersfield Town October 1949; King's Lynn player/manager July 1951; Long Sutton FC player/manager August 1955 and he also assisted Wisbech Town. Other honour: FA Cup winner 1946.

Full-back. Mostly found on the left flank though notably two-footed, kicking hard and accurately with both. Built on powerful lines, Jack could exert natural dominance and went without hesitation into any tackle. One of the first footballers to play in contact lenses. For some time was a King's Lynn licensee.

HOWELL, Leonard Sidgwick
(Wanderers, 1873, 1)
Born Dulwich, 6 August 1848. Died 7 September 1895.

Career: Winchester College; Wanderers. Also represented Surrey. Other honour: (Wanderers) FA Cup winner 1873.

Full-back/half-back expert in both roles, his kicking much admired. The 1874 Annual considered he had, perhaps, been playing'. . .better than ever in the position of back' at the beginning of season 1873/74, but injury prevented him appearing thereafter. Howell turned out for Surrey at cricket 1869-80 (13 matches) and was a malt factor by vocation.

HOWELL, Raby
(Sheffield United and Liverpool, 1895-99, 2)
Born Wincobank, Sheffield, 12 October 1869. Died 1937.
1896: 5ft. $5^1/_4$ins.; 9st. 8lbs.

Career: Ecclesfield; Rotherham Swifts 1889 as a professional; Sheffield United cs 1890; Liverpool April 1898 (£200) Preston North End cs 1901; retired through injury late 1903. Other honour: (Sheffield United) FL champions 1898.

Right-half. Converted to the position by Sheffield United after earlier being a (very diminutive) pivot. A quick mover and tireless in performance. Broke a leg 26 September 1903, this ending his career. Howell was a gypsy, born in a caravan and said to probably be the only British gypsy to earn a cap. (This compiler, however, can think of another pre-1914 England international who might well have been of that people). Uncle of Colin Myers, a much travelled professional of the 'Twenties.

HUSDON, Alan Anthony
(Stoke City, 1975, 2)
Born Chelsea, 21 June 1951.
1974: 5ft. $10^1/_2$ins.; 12st 1lb.

Career: Chelsea FC originally on schoolboy forms, becoming an apprentice 1966 and full professional June 1968; Stoke City January 1974 (£240,000); Arsenal December 1976 (£180,000); Seattle Sounders (USA) October 1978 (£100,000); Chelsea again August 1983; Stoke City again January 1984. Other honours: England Under-23 international (10 apps). (Chelsea) European Cup Winners' Cup, winner 1971. FL Cup finalist 1972. (Arsenal) FA Cup finalist 1978.

Midfield. Soon recognised as a practitioner possessing talents well above the norm. This particularly so in distribution, his passes models of accuracy. Alan has been the victim of many injuries, an early one causing him to miss the 1970 FA Cup final (and consequently a winners' medal).

HUDSON, John
(Sheffield Club, 1883, 1)
Born Sheffield, 1860. Died November 1941.

Career: Sheffield Heeley; Sheffield Club; Shefield Wednesday (was club secretary for a spell) 1880-83; Blackburn Olympic; Sheffield United (took part in their first match).

Half-back. Very prominent in Sheffield soccer during the immediate pre-Football League years, making the rounds of the steel city's premier clubs. A resilient half particularly able in defence, and a tenacious tackler. By trade, an engraver. After leaving the playing side (through injury) he was Wednesday's trainer/coach for a time.

HUDSPETH, Francis Carr
(Newcastle United, 1926, 1)
Born Percy Main, Northumberland, 20 April 1890. Died 8 February 1963.
1924: 5ft. $8^3/_4$ins.; 11st. $8^1/_2$lbs.

Career: Scotswood; Newburn; Clare Vale; North Shields Athletic; Newcastle United March 1910 (£100); Stockport County January 1929; Crook Town December 1930. Rochdale trainer July 1933; Burnley assistant trainer 1934-45 when he left football. Other honours: England 'Victory' international 1919 (1 app). (Newcastle) FL champions 1927. FA Cup winner 1924.

Left-back. Among the most durable of outfield performers – he skippered Newcastle to FA Cup and League championship wins at 34 and 37 respectively (an 'ever present' in the latter). And one of the oldest England debutants. He was actually third choice for the '26/27 Ireland game, both the original selections being compelled to withdraw. All the same, a most worthy footballer; intelligent in positioning, safe in kicking and wonderfully consistent.

HUFTON, A(rthur) Edward
(West Ham United, 1924-29, 6)
Born Southwell, Notts. 25 November 1892. Died 2 February 1967.
1928: 5ft. $10^1/_2$ins.; 12st.

Career: Atlas and Norfolk Works (Sheffield); Sheffield United cs 1912; West Ham United cs 1919 (£350) after being a guest player for the club during WW1; Watford June 1932 – 1933. Other honour: (WHU) FA Cup finalist 1923.

Goalkeeper. Of spectacular bent and legendary bravery. Ted's several consequent injuries included breaking an arm in one of the England appearances. Highly popular at Upton Park, where he served as press steward after WW2. He worked in the motor trade on leaving the playing arena. Accidents in 1963, when knocked down by a motor scooter, and, a few months later, by a car, marred his last years.

HUGHES, Emlyn Walter
(Liverpool and Wolverhampton Wanderers, 1970-80, 62)
Born Barrow-in-Furness, 28 August 1947.
1975: 5ft. $10^1/_2$ins.; 11st. 13lbs.

Career: North Lancashire Schools, Roose FC (Blackpool); Blackpool September 1964; Liverpool February 1967 (£65,000); Wolverhampton Wanderers August 1979 (£90,000); Rotherham United as player/manager July 1981; Hull City March 1983; Mansfield Town August 1983; Swansea City September-October 1983. Became a Hull City director during the 1988/89 season. Other honours: England Under-23 international (8 apps). Football League (4 apps). (Liverpool) European Cup winner 1977, 1978. EUFA Cup winner 1973, 1976. FL champions 1973, 1976, 1977, 1979. FA Cup winner 1974; finalist 1971, 1977. FL Cup finalist 1978. (Wolves) FL Cup winner 1980.

Full-back/midfield. A long career marked by many honours. Displayed infectious enthusiasm throughout and combined this with no little skill, and he scored some spectacular goals. Came of sporting stock: son of a Rugby League international, a brother and an uncle also played that game professionally while an Aunt played hockey for England. Emlyn was awarded the OBE in 1980.

HUGHES, Lawrence
(Liverpool, 1950, 3)
Born Waterloo, Liverpool, 2 March 1924.
1950: 6ft.; 12st. 4lbs.

Career: Merseyside schoolboy and junior football; Tranmere Rovers as an amateur

1942; Liverpool as a professional February 1943; retired May 1960. Other honours: England 'B' international (1 app). (Liverpool) FL champions 1947. FA Cup finalist 1950.

Centre-half. Occasionally wing-half. Prominent Anfielder of the immediate post-WW2 period. As the 'A-Z of Mersey Soccer' said in 1973: 'For sheer consistency Big Lol took some beating and his other assets included good positional sense and outstanding heading ability.' Grossed over 300 peacetime League appearances for Liverpool despite spending much of seasons 1948/49 and '52/53 on the injured list. Later went into business.

HULME, Joseph Harold Anthony
(Arsenal, 1927-33, 9)
Born Stafford, 26 August 1904.
1928: 5ft. 8½ins.; 10st. 11lbs.

Career: Stafford YMCA; York City as a professional 1923; Blackburn Rovers February 1924 (£250)' Arsenal February 1926 (£3500); Huddersfield Town January 1938, retiring the following close season. Tottenham Hotspur assistant secretary February 1944 and then that clubs manager October 1945 – May 1949. Other honours: Football League (5 apps). (Arsenal) FL champions 1931. FA Cup winner 1930, 1936; finalist 1927, 1932. (H'field T) FA Cup finalist 1938.

Outside-right reputedly the fastest player of his time, his fleetness of foot a byword. Added to this major asset trickery, accurate centering and shooting abilities, and we had a complete winger. Joe played regularly for Middlesex CCC 1929-39. After leaving the Spurs managership he worked as a sports journalist until retiring in 1965.

HUMHREYS, Percy
(Notts County, 1903, 1)
Born Cambridge, 3 December 1880. Died 13 April 1959.
1903: 5ft. 7ins.; 11st 6lbs.
Career: Cambridge St. Mary's; Queen's Park Rangers cs 1900; Notts County cs 1901; Leicester Fosse June 1907; Chelsea February 1908; Tottenham Hotspur December 1909; Leicester Fosse again October 1911; Hartlepools United as player/manager cs 1912. Other Honour: Football League (1 app).

Inside-right who could take the other inside berth and lead the attack also. Short and strongly built, Percy could dribble and unleash a telling shot. Being enthusiastic, he pleased his managers by maintaining a good work-rate. Represented Cambridgeshire during his amateur days.

HUNT, George Samuel
(Tottenham Hotspur, 1933, 3)
Born Mexborough nr. Rotherham, 22 February 1910.
1933: 5ft. 8ins.; 11st. 4lbs.

Career: Regent Street Congregationals (Barnsley) (trials with Barnsley and Sheffield United); Chesterfield September 1929; Tottenham Hotspur June 1930; Arsenal October 1937; Bolton Wanderers March 1938; Sheffield Wednesday November 1946; retired May 1948. Bolton Wanderers staff May 1948-September 1968, in this long spell serving as coach, scout and assistant trainer. Other honour: (Arsenal) FL champions 1938.

Inside-right/centre-forward. Became a star in 1932/33, when he won his 3 caps and led Spurs' attack in a promotion season. A persistent, courageous forward and a fine goal scorer, George hit 124 in the course of 185 League outings while at White Hart Lane. One of the very few to have made the short journey from Tottenham to Highbury or visa versa. Grandson of a former Barnsley player.

HUNT, (Revd.) Kenneth Reginald Gunnery
(Leyton, 1911, 2)
Born Oxford, 24 February 1884. Died 28 April 1949.
1910: 6ft.; 12st. 10lbs.

Career: Trent College (XI 1901-04, captain 1903 and '04); Oxford University (Blue 1905-6-7-8); Corinthians 1906-07 and 1920-23; Wolverhampton Wanderers; Leyton; Crystal Palace; Oxford City. Served on the FA Council 1946-49. Other honours: England amateur international (20 apps). Football League (1 app). (Wolves) FA Cup winner 1908. (Oxford City) FA Amateur Cup finalist 1913.

Wing or centre-half. A famous amateur, the muscular parson personified. Fast and quite without fear, he gloried in a hard game and was well able to hold his own in the best company. Ordained in 1909 and a schoolmaster (MA Oxon.) who taught at Highgate School 1908-45.

HUNT, Roger
(Liverpool, 1962-69, 34)
Born Golborne, Lancs. 20 July 1938.
1965: 5ft. 9ins.; 11st. 10lbs.

Career: Lancashire schools football; Croft Youth Club, Merseyside; Stockton Heath (Mid-Cheshire League); Liverpool amateur 1958, turning professional July 1959; Bolton Wanderers December 1969 (£31,000); retired cs 1972. Other honours: Football League (5 apps). (Liverpool) European Cup Winners' Cup finalist 1966. FL champions 1964, 1966. FL Div. 2 champions 1962. FA Cup winner 1965.

Inside-right in England's 1966 World Cup-winning side and holder of Liverpool's League scoring records: seasonal (41 goals in 1961/62) and aggregate (245). All of which gives a measure of the man in question. Virile, full of running and always determined, Roger was an ace clincher of scoring opportunity. Played for The Army when on national service, during this period assisting Devises Town also. Has been engaged with a family haulage business since leaving the game.

HUNT, Stephen K.
(West Bromwich Albion, 1984, 2)
Born Witton, Birmingham, 4 August 1956.
1984: 5ft. 7ins.; 10st. 10lbs.

Career: Birmingham junior football; Aston Villa apprentice, turning professional January 1974; New York Cosmos, USA, 1977 (£35,000); Coventry City August 1978 (£40,000); West Bromwich Albion March 1984 (£100,000); Aston Villa again March 1986 (for fee and another player); retired through injury November 1987.

Midfield. Really made his reputation in the States, Coventry being pleased to get his signature after a year over there. They were rewarded by nearly six seasons of enter-

prising and resolute displays (178 League games, 7 substitutions and 26 goals) before transferring him to West Brom. at a tidy profit. Returned to Villa as an established player – he had only 7 FL outings in his initial professional seasons with the club.

HUNTER, John
(Sheffield Heeley, 1878-82, 7)
Born Sheffield, 1852. Died 13 April 1903.

Career: With Sheffield Heeley from 1870, assisting other Sheffield teams from time to time including Providence, Wednesday and Sheffield Albion; Blackburn Olympic 1882; Blackburn Rovers 1887 for a short spell, remaining as assistant trainer and groundsman. Other honour: (Blackburn Olympic) FA Cup winner 1883.

Half-back among the best of his time. 'Very good; works hard throughout and kicks with judgment as well as vigour,' an ancient annual remarks. Played full-back too but not so effective there. Had been a noted runner during his early sporting life. Latterly was also engaged as a licensee in Blackburn. In Sheffield was first employed as a butcher and later as a silver cutler.

HUNTER, Norman
(Leeds United, 1966-75, 28)
Born Eighton Banks nr. Newcastle, 29 October 1943.
1970: 5ft. 11½ins.; 12st. 8lbs.

Career: Birtley Juniors; Leeds United November 1960; Bristol City October 1976 (about £40,000); Barnsley June 1979-1983, manager September 1980; West Bromwich Albion assistant manager/coach February 1984; Rotherham United manager June 1985-December 1987; subsequently a Leeds United coach to October 1988; appointed a Bradford City coach March 1989. Other honours: England Under-23 international (3 apps). Football League (6 apps). (Leeds Utd) European Cup finalist 1970, 1975. European Cup Winners' Cup finalist 1973. Inter-Cities Fairs Cup winner 1968; 1971; finalist 1967. FL champions 1969, 1974. FL Div. 2 champions 1964. FA Cup winner 1972; finalist 1965, 1970, 1973. FL Cup winner 1968.

Left-half famed for a tackle of massive strength made, of course, not one jot less shattering because the executant was usually smiling. Did most work with a marvellous left foot though not one-footed. At Elland Road throughout the club's greatest years as the above list of honours shows.

HURST, Geoffrey Charles
(West Ham United, 1966-72, 49)
Born Ashton-under-Lyne, Lancs. 8 December 1941.
1969: 5ft. 11½ins.; 12st. 9lbs.

Career: Chelmsford Schools; Essex Schools; West Ham United ground staff 1958, turning professional April 1959; Stoke City August 1972 (£80,000); West Bromwich Albion August 1975 (£20,000)-January 1976; Cork Celtic February 1976; Telford United player/manager later in 1976-cs 1979; Chelsea coach July 1979, caretaker manager September 1979 and manager October 1979-April 1981. Had a spell as assistant coach to the England squad from August 1977. Other honours: England Youth international. England Under-23 international (4 apps). Football League (7 apps). (WHU) European Cup Winners' Cup, winner 1965. FA Cup winner 1964. FL Cup finalist 1966.

Centre-forward/inside-left after an amount of experience at wing-half. Had been competent enough in the latter role but was a revelation as a striker. This climaxed with his hat-trick in the '66 World Cup final, a feat that brought wide fame. A brave player, wholehearted and absolutely unselfish, a pioneer in the new tactic of attacking without wingers. Geoff, son of an ex-pro, played cricket for Essex in 1962. He had interests in Midlands licensed premises during the 1970s and, since leaving Chelsea, has been involved in motor insurance.

IREMONGER, James
(Nottingham Forest, 1901-02, 2)
Born Norton, Yorks. 5 March 1876. Died 25 March 1956.
1901: 6ft. 1in.; 13st. 7lbs.

Career: Wilford FC (Notts); Jardine's FC (Nottingham); Nottingham Forest early in 1896; retired cs 1910. Notts County trainer cs 1919-May 1927. Other honours: Football League (4 apps).

Right/left-back of considerable proportions – his brother Albert (Notts County's goalkeeper 1904-26) was actually over 4 inches taller!. James was a doughty defender, strong in both feet, but his rushes were ill-

timed on occasion. A distinguished Notts cricketer, 1899-1914, he was a member of the MCC's touring side to Australia 1911/12 and a Notts CCC coach 1921-38.

JACK, David Bone Nightingale
(Bolton Wanderers and Arsenal, 1924-33, 9)
Born Bolton, 3 April 1899. Died 10 September 1958.
1930: 5ft. 10½ins.; 11st. 10lbs.

Career: Southend Schools; Plymouth Argyle Juniors (circa 1916) and Royal Navy football during WW1, also during the war 'guesting' for Chelsea; Plymouth Argyle cs 1919; Bolton Wanderers December 1920 (£3000); Arsenal October 1928 (£10,890, the first 5-figure fee); retired May 1934. Southend United, Sec/manager May 1934-August 1940; Middlesbrough manager September 1944-April 1952; Shelbourne manager August 1953-April 1955. Other honours: Football League (5 apps). (Bolton W) FA Cup winner 1923, 1926. (Arsenal) FL champions 1931, 1933, 1934. FA Cup winner 1930; finalist 1932.

Inside-right, sometimes centre-forward. Well outlined as 'an opportunist, with a watchful eye and cool brain, he took advantage of any slip made by the opposition to put in a first-time, deadly shot.' Scorer of Wembley's first-ever Cup final goal, he came of footballing stock. Son of Bob Jack (Plymouth's manager, 1910-38) and he had brothers who played professionally. His son, David jnr., became a well known soccer journalist. A wonderful footballer.

JACKSON, Elphinstone
(Oxford University, 1891, 1)
Born Calcutta, 9 October 1868. Died December 1945.

Career: Lancing College (XI 1886-87, captain 1887); Oxford University (Blue 1890-91); Corinthians 1889-90. Founder member of the India FA in 1893.

Full-back. 'A very good back, but cannot head. Tackles fairly well, and is a safe kick,' said the Athletic News in 1891 with its refreshing candour. A lack of heading ability was not, of course, an uncommon flaw in Victorian times, especially in the thriving amateur sector. Jackson, son of a High Court judge in Calcutta, returned to India after leaving university. He obviously retained a love for soccer with the above-mentioned part in the founding of India's ruling body.

JARRETT, (Revd.) Beaumont Griffith
(Old Harrovians, 1876-78, 3)
Born London, 18 July 1855. Died 11 April 1905.

Career: Harrow School; Cambridge University (Blue 1876-7-8, captain 1877); Old Harrovians; Grantham FC. Served on the FA Council 1876-78.

Half-back. A fast mover and often quite brilliant in ball control. Moreover, unlike so many ball artists who take a languid approach, he was tireless. Jarrett could really be faulted in only one respect - he was a little given to showing-off his skills. Ordained in 1878 he spent the remainder of his life in Lincolnshire following his calling.

JEFFERIS, Frank
(Everton, 1912, 2)
Born Fordingbridge, Hants. 3 July 1884. Died 21 May 1938.
1912: 5ft. 8½ins.; 11st. 4lbs.

Career: Fordingbridge Turks; Southampton circa 1905; Everton March 1911 (£750); Preston North End January 1920 (£700); Southport as player/coach June 1923; retired cs 1925. Re-engaged as Southport's trainer/coach May 1926, he actually played 2 League games for the club in an emergency during the 1926/27 campaign; Millwall trainer May 1936 to his death which actually occurred at their New Cross ground.

Other honours: (Everton) FL champions 1915. (PNE) FA Cup finalist 1922.

Inside-right. 'Never a great scorer but the way he drew opponents before passing was an object lesson,' declared one critic, and in 1920 another wrote he was 'a finished craftsman who knows the game as few forwards do.' Fair comments on a subtle schemer who was also the 'brainbox' of Everton's 1915 League championship line-up.

JEZZARD, Bedford A. G.
(Fulham, 1954-56, 2)
Born Clerkenwell, London, 19 October 1927.
1957: 5ft. 10$^1/_2$ins.; 13st. 4lbs.

Career: Croxley Green School (Herts); Croxley Green Juniors (Watford FC amateur); Fulham on amateur forms cs 1948, turning professional the following October; retired through injury August 1957. Fulham coaching staff later in 1957, team manager June 1958 and lastly general manager October-December 1964. Other honours: England 'B' international (3 apps). Football League (3 apps). (Fulham) FL Div. 2 champions 1949.

Centre-forward/inside-left with thrust and speed and most difficult to repulse. Had a nose for the goals too, hitting 154 in his 292 League outings for Fulham. Worked on the staff of the Old Merchant Taylors' sports ground before turning pro, and as a Hammersmith licensee after leaving Craven Cottage.

JOHNSON, David Edward
(Ipswich Town and Liverpool, 1975-80. 8)
Born Liverpool, 23 October 1951.
1976: 5ft. 10ins.; 11st.

Career: Liverpool Schools; Everton apprentice May 1967, turning professional April 1969; Ipswich Town October 1972 (in exchange for another player); Liverpool August 1976 (£200,000); Everton again August 1982 (£100,000) (Barnsley on loan February 1984); Manchester City March 1984, then had a brief spell with Tulsa Roughnecks before assisting Preston North End during season 1984/85. Other honours: England Under-23 international (9 apps). (Liverpool) European Cup winner 1981. FL champions 1977, 1979, 1980. FA Cup finalist 1977.

Strike forward with the unusual record of scoring in four competition debuts for Everton - Central League, Football League, FA Cup and European Cup. And he scored the club's quickest goal (after 5 seconds in a Youth Cup match) and in his 'derby' debut against Liverpool. David was not one of the 'super craftsman' breed but often surprised, seemingly having a quiet game and then unexpectedly creating an opening that changed the complexion of things.

JOHNSON, Edward
(Saltley College and Stoke, 1880-84, 2)
Born Stoke-on-Trent 1860. Died 30 June 1901.

Career: Junior football before assisting Saltley College (Birmingham) 1880-81; Stoke from 1880 for several years, eventually retiring through injury. Also represented the Birmingham FA. After giving up playing was closey connected with the administration of Stoke St Peter's FC, and for many years a member of the Staffordshire FA before being compelled to resign on health grounds in 1898.

Forward. A wingman of parts, fine in dribbling but, like so many of his kind, liable to keep the ball too long. When he did part, however, the pass was invariably precisely placed and his speed was an asset also. Johnson's retiral from the playing-field was not the result of an injury sustained there but from an accident that occurred when he fell from a horse-drawn vehicle.

JOHNSON, Joseph Alfred
(Stoke City, 1937, 5)
Born Grimsby, 4 April 1911. Died 8 August 1983.

1938: 5ft. 7½ins.; 10st. 8lbs.

Career: Grimsby junior football; Scunthorpe United; Bristol City May 1931; Stoke City April 1932 (£150); West Bromwich Albion November 1937; Northwich Victoria August 1946; Hereford United November 1946-1948. Other honour: (Stoke City) FL Div. 2 champions 1933.

Outside-left. Penetrative little wingman, scorer of 77 goals in 246 League outings before war came. Joe's skilful, swerving runs could be bewildering. He had only 7 League games to his name before joining Stoke where he starred in a burgeoning side that was just bringing out the legendary Stanley Matthews on the opposite flank. A fishmonger before turning professional.

JOHNSON, Thomas Clark Fisher ('Tosh')
(Manchester City and Everton, 1926-35, 5)
Born Dalton-in-Furness, Lancs. 19 August 1900. Died 28 January 1973.
1932: 5ft. 9¾ins.; 11st 11lbs.

Career: Dalton Athletic; Dalton Casuals; Manchester City February 1919, originally as an amateur; Everton March 1930 (£6000); Liverpool March 1934; Darwen August 1936. Other honours: Football League (3 apps). (Man City) FA Cup finalist 1926. FL Div. 2 champions 1928. (Everton) FL champions 1932. FL Div. 2 champions 1931. FA Cup winner 1933.

Inside Left. With a deal of experience at centre-forward too. A strong forward, prominent throughout a lengthy period (as the above club honours' list demonstrates) and consistent withal. Well summed up as 'a combination of a technician and finisher.' Tommy is still holder of Manchester City's seasonal and aggregate League goal total records.

JOHNSON, William Harrison
(Sheffield United, 1900-03, 6)
Born Ecclesfield nr. Sheffield, 4 January 1876. Died 17 July 1940.
1901: 5ft. 9ins.; 12st 1lb.

Career: Atlas and Norfolk Works (Sheffield) for a brief spell; Ecclesfield Church; Sheffield United 1895; retired through injury cs 1909 and appointed the club's assistant trainer, remaining on the training staff until the mid-1930s. Other honours: Football League (1 app). (Sheffield U) FA Cup winner 1899, 1902; finalist 1901.

Wing-half as a senior after playing at centre-half for Ecclesfield Church. Quite tireless and with a distinct attacking bent, being able to both shoot well and middle the ball accurately. His sons, Harry and Tom, were Sheffield United stalwarts too, each appearing in a Wembley Cup final in the inter-war period.

JOHNSTON, Henry
(Blackpool, 1947-54, 10)
Born Droylsden, Manchester, 26 September 1919. Died 12 October 1973.
1951: 5ft. 11ins.; 12st 4lbs.

Career: Manchester Schools; Lancashire Schools; Droylsden Athletic; Blackpool amateur June 1935, turning professional 1936; retired November 1955. Reading manager November 1955-January 1963; Blackpool chief scout April 1967, afterwards having two spells as caretaker manager before leaving the club in 1972. Other honours: Football League (4 apps). (Blackpool) FA Cup winner 1953; finalist 1948, 1951.

Centre/wing-half. An established League player before WW2, Harry resumed to become a leading half-back of the first post-war decade: constructive, composed, brainy and an exceptionally good club captain.' Footballer of the year' for 1951. Worked as a sports journalist after leaving Reading as well as running a Blackpool newsagency.

JONES, Alfred.
(Walsall Town Swifts and Great Lever, 1882-83, 3)

Born Walsall, 1861.

Career: Junior football to Walsall Town Swifts; Great Lever 1882; Walsall Town Swifts again cs 1883; Aston Villa during season 1885/86.

Right/left-back strong in both feet but apparently favouring the left flank, all three England appearances being played there. Steady and reliable in performance, sporting an effective tackle and parting thoughtfully. The first Walsall player to be capped (the club had a couple of internationalists before the Great War, the other was W Taggart for Ireland, 1898/99).

JONES, Harry
(Nottingham Forest, 1923, 1)
Born Blackwell, Derbys. 24 May 1891.
1919: 5ft. 9½ins.; 12st 7lbs.

Career: Blackwell Boys Brigade when aged 11; Blackwell Wesley Guild; Blackwell Colliery; Notingham Forest cs 1911; retired through injury cs 1924 but joined Sutton Town the following December. Other honours: Football League (1 app). (Forest) FL Div. 2 champions 1922.

Left-back consistently lauded by the Nottingham press. A typical sample (this in 1923): '. . .absolutely fearless and unexcelled for dash and resolution.' And in 1922: '. . .has no nerves, will face anything and always plays the same resolute, dashing game.' One of the few players of those days to suffer a broken leg and to return absolutely unimpaired.

JONES, Herbert ('Taffy')
(Blackburn Rovers, 1927-28, 6)
Born Blackpool, 3 September 1896. Died 11 September 1973.
1927: 5ft. 8ins.; 11st.

Career: South Shore Strollers Army football; Fleetwood 1920; Blackpool FC cs 1922; Blackburn Rovers December 1925 (£3850); Brighton & Hove Albion June 1934; Fleetwood again cs 1935. Other honours: Football League (3 apps). (Blackburn R) FA Cup winner 1928.

Left-back. Fast and fearless, he performed thoughtfully which led to excellent positional play. Came to the first-class game comparitively late and won his first cap when turned 30. The nickname appears to derive merely from the possession of a Welsh surname.

JONES, Michael David
(Sheffield United and Leeds United, 1965-70, 3)
Born Worksop, Notts. 24 April 1945.
1967: 5ft. 10½ins.; 11st 11lbs.

Career: Worksop Schools; Rotherham Schools; Dinnington Miners Welfare; Sheffield United as an apprentice April 1961, turning professional November 1962; Leeds United September 1967 (£100,000); retired through injury August 1975. Other honours: England Under-23 international (9 apps). (Leeds U) European Cup Winners' Cup finalist 1973. Inter-Cities Fairs Cup winner 1968, 1971. FL champions 1969, 1974. FA Cup winner 1972; finalist 1970, 1973.

Centre-forward. Involved in the bulk of Leeds' great decade, when his 'courage and raw strength' (as a commentator aptly defined it) blended so well with Allan Clarke's differing skills. Courage also brought its toll in injuries and it was a knee problem that finally caused retirment. Employed in a cycle factory on leaving school, Mick worked as representative of a sports goods firm after leaving football, later running his own shop.

JONES, William
(Bristol City, 1901, 1)
Born Brighton, 6 March 1876. Died circa 1908.
1901: 5ft. 8ins.; 11st. 8lbs.
Career: Heaton Rovers (Newcastle-upon-Tyne); Willington Athletic; Loughborough Town 1896; Bristol City cs 1897; Tottenham Hotspur May 1906; Swindon Town

May 1907. Other honour: (Bristol C) FL Div. 2 champions 1906.

Right-half after making a name as a centre-forward, showing fine qualities of interception and distribution. Skippered Bristol City for 3 seasons, becoming the club's first internationalist. Known as 'Bristol' Jones when at Tottenham, to distinguish him from the Welsh cap, J L Jones. His early demise was the result of typhoid.

JONES, William H.
(Liverpool, 1950, 2)
Born Whaley Bridge, Derbys. 13 May 1921
1951: 5ft. 11ins.; 13st. 1lb.

Career: Hayfield St Matthew's (Derbyshire); Liverpool September 1938; Ellesmere Port Town as player/manager May 1954. Did some scouting for Liverpool in the 1960s and later. Other honours: England 'B' international (1 app) Football League (1 app). (Liverpool) FL champions 1947. FA Cup finalist 1950.

Centre-half for his two full caps but actually a man of unusual adaptability, taking a full-back or forward role with the same assurance as that of half-back. The 1947 championship season found him in 6 different berths. Always gave maximum effort and was skilled in all aspects. Bill won the MM during his wartime Army service and went into business after giving up playing.

JOY, Bernard
(Casuals, 1936, 1)
Born Fulham, 29 October 1911. Died 18 July 1984.
1938: 6ft. 1in.; 12st. 6lbs.

Career: London University; Casuals (signed as amateur for Southend United and Fulham FC, 1 FL app for latter 1933/34); Corinthians in the mid-1930s; Arsenal May 1935-cs 1947 (last senior appearance 19.10.46.); Casuals again cs 1947; retired cs 1948. Other honours: England wartime international (1 app). England amateur international (12 apps).(Casuals) FA Amateur Cup winner 1936. (Arsenal) FL champions 1938.

Centre-half. The last amateur to win a full England cap. Big, powerful pivot able to hold his own with the leading pros of his day. In style developed into a typical 'third back' in the mode of Arsenal's Herbie Roberts (q.v.). Originally employed as a schoolmaster, Joy became a football writer with the London newspapers, 'Star' and 'Evening Standard', retiring October1976 after 31 years in journalism. Author of 'Forward, Arsenal!' a club history that is a model of its kind. (Phoenix House, 1952).

KAIL, Edgar Isaac Lewis
(Dulwich Hamlet, 1929, 3)
Born Camberwell, London, 26 November 1900. Died early in 1976.

Career: South London Schools; Dulwich Hamlet 1915-34; also represented Surrey. Signed amateur forms for Chelsea, March 1930 (no FL apps). Served on the Dulwich Hamlet committee for a period to 1956. Other honours: England schoolboy international (2 apps). England amateur international (21 apps). (Dulwich H) FA Amateur Cup winner 1920, 1932.

Inside-right. One of the inter-war period's most illustrious amateurs. His senior career really commenced in 1919 and, within 2 years, had 2 amateur caps and an Amateur Cup-winners' medal to his name. Kail possessed all the required inside-forward skills. If at times he attempted too much, the reason was over-confidence. Represented the Isthmian League on 24 occasions, held cups and medals for all competitions entered by the Hamlet club, and was thrice a reserve for full England internationals. Employed as a traveller for a wine and spirit firm, retiring in 1966.

KAY, Anthony Herbert
(Everton, 1963, 1)
Born Attercliffe, Sheffield, 13 May 1937.
1963: 5ft. 7½ins.; 12st.
Career: Sheffield junior football; Sheffield

Wednesday ground staff 1952, turning professional May 1954; Everton December 1962 (£55,000, a then record for a half-back) – April 1965. Other honours: England Under-23 international (7 apps). Football League (4 apps). (Wednesday) FL Div. 2 champions 1959. (Everton) FL champions 1963.

Left-half. Often referred to as 'flame haired' and his ginger thatch was in keeping with his play. For Kay's biting tackles won the ball more often than not, and then it was released by a well directed pass. Only of small stature but solidly proportioned.

KEAN, Frederick William
(Sheffield Wednesday and Bolton Wanderers, 1923-29, 9)
Born Sheffield 10 December 1898. Died 28 October 1973.
1925: 5ft. 8½ins.; 12st.

Career: Sheffield Hallam; Portsmouth cs 1919; Sheffield Wednesday cs 1920; Bolton Wanderers September 1928 (£5500); Luton Town June 1931; Sutton Town as player/coach November 1935. Other honours: Football League (4 apps). (Wednesday) FL Div. 2 champions 1926. (Bolton W) FA Cup winner 1929.

Right or centre-half. Earlier an inside-forward and, after moving to the intermediate line, still had attacking ideas and indulged in the occasional pop at goal. Kean was a skilled performer, dour in tackling and fine with heading. Noticeable on the field with his fair hair and upright carriage.

KEEGAN, J(oseph) Kevin
(Liverpool, SV Hamburg and Southampton, 1973-82, 63)
Born Armthorpe nr. Doncaster, 14 February 1951.
1976: 5ft. 8ins.; 10st. 10lbs.
Career: Doncaster area schools football; Lonsdale Hotel FC (Doncaster Sunday League); Scunthorpe United apprentice December 1967, turning professional December 1968; Liverpool May 1971 (£33,000); SV Hamburg June 1977 (£500,000); Southampton July 1980 (£400,000); Newcastle United August 1982 (£100,000); retired May 1984. Other honours: England Under-23 international (5 apps). (Liverpool) European Cup winner 1977. UEFA Cup winner 1973, 1976. FL champions 1973, 1976, 1977. FA Cup winner 1974; finalist 1977. (Hamburg) Bundesliga champions 1979. European Cup finalist 1980.

Forward or Midfield. (Originally designated as an outside-right). An outstanding figure of his time and the supreme example of the 'self made' player where diligence and hard work achieve both honours and rich financial reward. Quite dynamic in performance-sharp, creative, maker and taker of goals. For some time England's captain. Won 5 'player of the year' awards; in England 1976 and '82, European 1978 and '79, West Germany 1978. Awarded the OBE 1982.

KEEN, Errington Ridley Liddell
(Derby County, 1933-37, 4)
Born Walker, Newcastle-upon-Tyne, 4 September 1910. Died July 1984.
1937: 5ft. 8ins.; 10st. 6lbs.

Career: Newcastle Schools; Nun's Moor (Northern Amateur League); Newcastle Swifts 1926; Newcastle United September 1927; Derby County December 1930 (in an exchange deal involving Harry Bedford, q.v.); Chelmsford City May 1938; Hereford United player/manager July 1939; Leeds United December 1945; Bacup Borough July 1946; later coached in Hong Kong. Other honour: Football League (1 app).

Left-half. Stylish blond half, fast to the tackle and sure of foot. Prompted his attack admirably. Made but a single League appearance for Newcastle (and that, oddly enough, against Derby), thanks to that club's then half-back strength. Known as Ike at St James Park, his first name was subsequently, and conveniently, abbreviated to Eric by the cognoscenti.

KELLY, Robert
(Burnley, Sunderland and Huddersfield Town, 1920-28, 14)
Born Ashton-in-Makerfield, Lancs. 16 November 1893.
Died 22 September 1969.
1925: 5ft. 7ins.; 10st.

Career: Ashton White Star; Ashton Central; Earlestown (Liverpool County Combination) 1912; St Helens Town August 1913; Burnley November 1913 (£275); Sunderland December 1925 (£6550, then a record); Huddersfield Town February 1927 (£3500); Preston North End July 1932; Carlisle United as player/manager March 1935, retiring from playing midway through the ensuing season. Stockport County manager November 1936-March 1939. After the War had spells as S C de Portugal's trainer from August 1946 and Barry Town's manager from December 1960. Other honours: Football League (7 apps). (Burnley) FL champions 1921. (Huddersfield) FA Cup finalist 1928, 1930.

Outside/inside-right, mostly inside. An ornament to the game for a generation with a deadly shot in either foot and consummate dribbling skills. Of the latter a particular one was a capacity to suddenly go through and score himself, employing an individual swerve in so doing. A swerve, incidentally, said to compare with Charlie Buchan's.

KENNEDY, Alan Phillip
(Liverpool, 1984, 2)
Born Sunderland, 31 August 1954.
1980: 5ft. 9ins.; 10st. 7lbs.

Career: Junior football to Newcastle United as an apprentice July 1971, turning professional September 1972; Liverpool August 1978 (£330,000); Sunderland September 1985 (£100,000); Hartlepool cs-November 1987 when he moved to Beerschot FC (Belgium); Wigan Athletic (on trial) December 1987. Other honours: England 'B' international. England Under-23 international (6 apps). (Newcastle) FA Cup finalist 1974. FL Cup finalist 1976. (Liverpool) European Cup winner 1981, 1984; finalist 1985. FL champions 1979, 1980, 1982, 1983, 1984. FL Cup winner 1981, 1982, 1983, 1984.

Left-back noticeably courageous in tackling and obviously a believer in the maxim about fortune favouring the brave. Also the possessor of attacking flair, the scorer of some vital goals. Alan was actually selected for a full cap 9 years before the honour materialised, having to call off through injury. Brother of Keith Kennedy (Bury 1972-82).

KENNEDY, Raymond
(Liverpool, 1976-80, 17)
Born Seaton Delaval, Northumberland, 28 July 1951.
1978: 5ft. 11ins.; 13st. 4lbs.

Career: South Northumberland Schools (trial with Port Vale when 15); New Hartley Juniors (Seaton Delaval); Arsenal apprentice May 1968, turning professional November 1968; Liverpool July 1974 (£180,000); Swansea City January 1982 (£160,000)-October 1983; Hartlepool United November 1983-1985. Sunderland first team coach April 1987 after being a part-time coach from February 1987. Other honours: England Under-23 international (6 apps). (Arsenal) FL champions 1971. FA Cup winner 1971; finalist 1972 (sub). (Liverpool) European Cup winner 1977,

1978, 1981. EUFA Cup winner 1976. FL champions 1976, 1977, 1979, 1980, 1982. FA Cup finalist 1977. FL Cup winner 1981; finalist 1978. (Swansea) Welsh Cup winner 1982, 1983.

Inside-forward, later midfield. Extremely powerful performer with the physique and motivation to impress his stamp on a game. Was always attack-minded, even when positioned in midfield, scoring important goals and often employing a blistering shot to do so. Later a licensee in his native North-East.

KENYON-SLANEY, (Rt. Hon.) William Stanley
(Wanderers, 1873, 1)
Born Rajkot, Gujarat, India, 24 August 1847. Died 24 April 1908.

Career: Eton College; Oxford University (prior to the 'Varsity match); Old Etonians; Wanderers. Other honours: (Wanderers) FA Cup winner 1873. (Old Etonians) FA Cup finalist 1875 (first game only), 1876.

Forward. Lively, dashing attacker, among the best of the 1870s. Maintained his form over several seasons. Kenyon-Slaney was also a good cricketer. He played for the MCC 1869-80 and Shropshire, and was on the MCC Committee for 8 years. Served with the Grenadier Guards 1867-88, attaining the rank of colonel. Was MP for Newport, Salop, 1886-1908 and a Privy Councillor from 1904.

KEVAN, Derek Tennyson
(West Bromwich Albion, 1957-61, 14)
Born Ripon, 6 March 1935.
1959: 5ft. 11ins.; 12st. 13lbs.

Career: Harrogate & District Schools; Ripon City; Ripon YMCA (trial with Sheffield United); Bradford October 1952; West Bromwich Albion July 1953 (£3000); Chelsea March 1963 (£45,000); Manchester City August 1963 (£40,000); Crystal Palace July 1965; Peterborough United March 1966; Luton Town December 1966; Stockport County March 1967 (£2000 and another player); Macclesfield Town August 1968; Boston United October 1968; Stourbridge 1968/69; Ancell's FC 1969 then retired. Other honours: England Under-23 international (4 apps). Football League (1 app). (Stockport) FL Div. 4 champions 1967.

Centre/inside-forward with the build and stamina to bull-doze his way through, which he did frequently. Not one for the purist perhaps but mightily effective all the same. Derek served many clubs though he spent a decade with West Brom. for whom he notched 173 goals in 291 League and Cup games. Worked for a brewery for some years before, in 1982, joining the Albion's commercial office.

KIDD, Brian
(Manchester United, 1970, 2)
Born Manchester, 29 May 1949.
1970: 5ft. 10ins.; 11st. 6lbs.

Career: Manchester Schools; Manchester United apprentice August 1964, turning professional June 1966; Arsenal July 1974 (£110,000); Manchester City July 1976 (£100,000); Everton March 1979 (£150,000); Bolton Wanderers May 1980 (£110,000)-January 1982; went to America later in '82 and played for Lauderdale Strikers and Atlanta Chiefs before returning to manage Barrow; Swindon Town assistant manager April 1985, later that year taking similar post with Preston North End, becoming the latter's manager (after 2 months as 'caretaker') January-March 1986. Other honours: England Youth international. England Under-23 international (10 apps). Football League (1 app). (Man. Utd) European Cup winner 1968.

Strike forward possessing an abundance of attacking know-how, the subject of 4 6-figure fees. Came to notice very early, winning a coveted European Cup winners' medal at 19. (As was said, a real 'Roy of the Rovers' happening!). Perhaps oddly, in view of such a start – and the clubs he played for – Brian did not pick up any further club honours.

KING, (Canon) Robert Stuart
(Oxford University, 1882, 1)
Born Leigh-on-Sea, Essex, 4 April 1862. Died 4 March 1950.

Career: Felsted School (XI 1878-79-80, captain 1880); Oxford University (Blue 1882-3-4-5, captain 1885); Upton Park; Grimsby Town (in 1887). Also represented Essex.

Half-back. Calm, dependable and tough (obviously a typical Victorian muscular parson or, in this instance, future parson).

Also had the then fairly uncommon attribute of heading skills, enabling him to as accurately direct the ball as with his feet. Ordained in 1887 and was Rector of Leigh-on-Sea for an extraordinary 58 years, 1892 to his death.

KINGSFORD, Robert Kennett
(Wanderers, 1874, 1)
Born Sydenham, Kent, 23 December 1849. Died 14 October 1895.

Career: Marlborough College; Old Marlburians; Wanderers; Crystal Palace. Also represented Surrey. Had spell as secretary of the Wanderers club, succeeding C W. Alcock in 1874. Other honour: (Wanderers) FA Cup winner 1873.

Forward. Mobile and dangerous. Had '... a happy knack of putting the ball between the posts,' as a contemporary recorded. The knack was greatly in evidence in the 1873/74 season when he headed the country's scoring list and scored England's only goal in his international. Played 3 matches for Surrey CCC during the 1872-74 period. Kingsford, a one time law student, went to Australia where he died in Adelaide.

KINGSLEY, Matthew
(Newcastle United, 1901, 1)
Born Turton, Lancs. 1875. Died 27 March 1960.
1901: 5ft. 10½ins.; 13st. 4lbs.

Career: Edgworth; Turton FC; Darwen 1896; Newcastle United April 1898; West Ham United May 1904; Queen's Park Rangers cs 1905 for a season and then out of the game for a year until joining Rochdale October 1907. He also assisted Barrow. Other honours: Football League (3 apps).

Goalkeeper. Newcastle United's first internationalist whose other distinction was a habit of constantly swinging his arms when not in action. (Maybe he wanted to be more involved?). A proficient performer despite this peccadillo (if such it was), with the ability to fist a ball a prodigious distance. His weight – which in 1903 was recorded as 14st. 4lbs. – contributed mightily to the fisting.

KINSEY, George
(Wolverhampton Wanderers and Derby County, 1892-96, 4)
Born Burton-on-Trent, 1867. Died 1911.

Career: Burton Crusaders; Burton Swifts; Mitchell St George's; Wolverhampton Wanderers cs 1891; Aston Villa June 1894; Derby County July 1895; Notts County March 1897; Bristol Eastville Rovers cs 1897-1900; reinstated as an amateur August 1904. Other honour: (Wolves) FA Cup winner 1893.

Left-half. Made a tour of the 1890s Midlands' circuit before heading off West to Bristol. George was a capable wing-half, determined in attitude, who could always be relied upon to pull his full weight.

KIRCHEN, Alfred John
(Arsenal, 1937, 3)
Born Shouldham, Norfolk, 26 April 1913.
1938: 5ft. 11½ins.; 12st. 1lb.

Career: King's Lynn Schools; King's Lynn Old Boys; Shouldham FC; Norwich City on amateur forms October 1933, turning professional the following month; Arsenal March 1935 (£6000); retired through injury 1943. Later a Norwich City director. Other honours: England wartime international (3 apps). (Arsenal) FL champions 1938.

Outside-right. Unusually hefty for a winger and this physique, combined with dash and speed, made him a tough nut to contain. Consistent in scoring also, his League record at the outbreak reading 46 goals in 109 matches. A farmer in his native Norfolk subsequently.

KIRTON, William John
(Aston Villa, 1922, 1)
Born Newcastle-on-Tyne, 2 December 1896. Died 27 September 1970.
1924: 5ft. 7ins.; 11st. 4lbs.

Career: North Shields 1913/14; Pandon Temperance 1917; Leeds City May 1919; Aston Villa October 1919 (£400); Coventry City September 1928; Kidderminster Harriers September 1930; Leamington Town October 1930. Other honours: (Villa) FA Cup winner 1920; finalist 1924.

Inside-right. Had a solitary League appearance to his name before Villa bought him at the celebrated Leeds City 'auction'. He proved an excellent investment, splendidly linking up with right-wingman Dicky York and inside partners besides netting valuable goals himself. One of them was famous – it won Villa the Cup of 1920, going in off the back of Billy's neck from a corner-kick.

KNIGHT, Arthur Egerton
(Portsmouth, 1920, 1)
Born Godalming, Surrey, 7 September 1887. Died 10 March 1956.
1919: 5ft. 11ins.; 12st.

Career: King Edward VI Grammar School, Guildford, and junior football; Portsmouth 1909-22; Corinthians 1921-31. Other honours: England 'Victory' international 1919 (1 app). England amateur international (30 apps). (Portsmouth) Southern League champions 1920.

Left-back. A stalwart amateur for long a pillar of Pompey's defence and playing top-class amateur soccer into his mid-40s. Expert in tackling and heading, a deficiency of pace was masked by adroit positioning. He was a useful batsman and played a few matches for Hampshire 1913-23. Knight served with the Border and Hampshire regiments during the Great War, rising to the rank of captain.

KNOWLES, Cyril Barry
(Tottenham Hotspur, 1968, 4)
Born Fitzwilliam nr. Pontefract, Yorks. 13 July 1944.
1968: 6ft.; 11st. 13½lbs.

Career: South Elmsall Schools; Manchester United ground staff for 1 season; Hemsworth FC (trial with Blackpool); Monkton Colliery (Wolves' nursery side); Middlesbrough amateur 1962, turning professional in October of that year; Tottenham Hotspur May 1964 (£42,500); retired through injury May 1976. Hertford Town manager cs 1976; returned to Yorkshire 1977 and after scouting for Spurs was Doncaster Rovers coach 1977-81; Middlesbrough reserve team coach cs 1981, first team coach February 1982; Darlington manager May 1983-March 1987; Torquay United manager June 1987. Other honours: England Under-23 international (6 apps). Football League (1 app). (Spurs) Inter-Cities Fairs Cup winner 1972. FA Cup winner 1967. FL Cup winner 1971, 1973.

Right/left-back. Tall, long legged defender, incisive in the tackle. Was wont to lope down the wing to float over a seductive centre. He had first been an outside-left and switched to the defence at Middlesbrough. Brother of Peter Knowles (Wolves' Youth and Under-23 international). This writer has a notion Cyril was the original subject of the catch phrase 'Nice one, Cyril'. (But is willing to be contradicted).

LABONE, Brian Leslie
(Everton, 1963-70, 26)
Born Liverpool, 23 January 1940.
1966: 6ft. 0½in.; 12st. 11lbs.

Career: Liverpool schoolboy football (during which period he represented Lancashire Grammar Schools); Everton July 1957; retired through injury June 1972.Other honours: England Under-23 international (7 apps). Football League (5 apps). (Everton) FL champions 1963, 1970. FA Cup winner 1966; finalist 1968.

Centre-half who 'stayed put', concentrating on a purely defensive role. Used his natural advantages effectively, particularly in headwork, and was cultured in approach. An exemplary character, Brian was a Goodison fan from boyhood, going on to play 533 senior games in the famous blue shirt and to skipper the side. After leaving

soccer ran an electrical contracting concern and worked in insurance.

LAMPARD, Frank R. G.
(West Ham United, 1973-80, 2)
Born West Ham, 20 September 1948 .
1972: 5ft. 10ins.; 12st. 1lb.

Career: East London schoolboy football; West Ham United apprentice July 1964, turning professional September 1965; Southend United as player/coach cs 1985-February 1986. Other honours: England Youth international. England Under-23 international (4 apps). (WHU) European Cup Winners; cup finalist 1976. FL Div. 2 champions 1981. FA Cup winner 1975, 1980. FL Cup finalist 1981.

Left-back. For two decades a Hammers' stalwart, grossing 665 League and Cup encounters (22 goals) in that period. Very mobile and possessing a clean kick, Frank overcame severe injuries to eventually resume valuable as ever. It almost goes without saying – a remarkable clubman.

LANGLEY, E(rnest) James
(Fulham, 1958, 3)
Born Kilburn, London, 7 February 1929.
1958: 5ft. 9ins.; 11st 5lbs.

Career: London schoolboy football; Yiewsley; Hounslow Town; Uxbridge; Hayes (Brentford on amateur forms); Ruislip; Guildford City 1947; Leeds United June 1952; Brighton & Hove Albion July 1953 (£1500); Fulham February 1957 (£12,000); Queen's Park Rangers June 1965 (£4000); Hillingdon Borough as player/manager September 1967-May 1971. Crystal Palace trainer/coach August 1971; Hillingdon Borough manager again late in 1973. Other honours: England 'B' international (3 apps). Football League (1 app.) (QPR) FL Div. 3 champions 1967. FL Cup winner 1967.

Left-back with attacking notions, pre-dating the type commonplace a little later. Jim had the speed to resume his defensive position after upfield forays. Scored 57 goals in 584 League games (and 1 substitution), which beats the records of most full-backs.

LANGTON, Robert
(Blackburn Rovers, Preston North End and Bolton Wanderers, 1947-51, 11)
Born Burscough, Lancs. 8 September 1918.
1949: 5ft. 6ins.; 10st. 10lbs.

Career: Burscough Victoria; Blackburn Rovers September 1938 (during WW2 represented The Army while on service in India and later a guest player for Glentoran); Preston North End August 1948 (for fee an another player); Bolton Wanderers November 1949 (£22,250); Blackburn Rovers again September 1953 (£2500); Ards June 1956; Wisbech Town July 1957; Kidderminster Harriers cs 1959 (on trial);

Wisbech Town again September 1959 – December 1959; Colwyn Bay October 1960. King's Lynn trainer/coach July 1962; Wisbech Town coach cs 1963, later having several years as Burscough Rangers manager. Other honours: England 'B' international (4 apps). Football League (9 apps). (Blackburn R) FL Div. 2 champiopns 1939. (Bolton W) FA Cup finalist 1953. (Glentoran) Irish Cup finalist 1945.

Outside-left who enjoyed a long and varied career extending into his forties. He combined fleetness and cleverness with precision centreing. Had spell as a Wisbech licensee from 1961.

LATCHFORD, Robert D.
(Everton, 1978-79, 12)
Born Birmingham, 18 January 1951.
1977: 6ft.; 12st.

Career: Junior football to Birmingham City as an apprentice, turning professional August 1968; Everton February 1974 (for about £80,000 and 2 players); Swansea City July 1981 (£125,000); NAC Breda (Holland) February 1984; Coventry City June 1984; Lincoln City July 1985; Newport County January 1986, leaving the following close season; Merthyr Tydfil 1986/87. Other honours: England Youth international. England Under-23 international (6 apps). Football League (1 app). (Everton) FL Cup winner 1977. (Swansea) Welsh Cup winner 1982, 1983. (Merthyr) Welsh Cup winner 1987.

Strike forward reminiscent of previous eras, his power and bustle bringing substantial goal tallies. A specialist in capitalising on chances apparently slim, often from 'impossible' angles. Early doubts concerning Bob's seeming lack of pace were mistaken.

LATHERTON, Edwin Gladstone ('Pinky')
(Blackburn Rovers, 1913-14, 2)
Born Grangetown nr. Middlesborough, 1887. Killed in action 14 October 1917.
1907: 5ft. 5ins.; 10st. 8lbs.

Career: Grangetown FC; Blackburn Rovers March 1906 (£25) to his death. Other honours: Football League (5 apps). (Blackburn R) FL champions 1912, 1914.

Inside-forward known as Pinky because of his complexion and reddish hair. Well under

average height but possessing dazzling footwork that created openings for fellow forwards besides himself. Lost his life while serving with the Royal Field Artillery.

LAWLER, Christopher
(Liverpool, 1971-72, 4)
Born Liverpool, 20 October 1943.
1971: 6ft.; 12st. 10lbs.

Career: Liverpool Schools; Liverpool FC on amateur forms May 1959, turning professional October 1960; Portsmouth October 1975; Stockport County August 1977; Bangor City cs 1978. Later coached in Norway and (from October 1981) had spell as Wigan Athletic's assistant manager before joining Liverpool's coaching staff. Other honours: England schoolboy international. England Youth international. England Under-23 international (4 apps). Football League (2 apps). (Liverpool) EUFA Cup winner 1973. European Cup Winners' Cup finalist 1966. FL champions 1966, 1973. FA Cup winner 1965; finalist 1971.

Right-back from 1964/65 after service as a reserve centre-half. A real cool number, cultured and super-efficient, known to some – with typical Scouse wit – as 'The Silent Knight'. Chris's greatest distinction must be in goal scoring: 61 in 546 senior matches while at Anfield. Surely a full-back record, and they weren't from penalties either. Remarkable.

LAWTON, Thomas
(Everton, Chelsea and Notts County, 1939-49, 23)
Born Bolton, 6 October, 1919.
1947: 5ft. 11ins.; 12st.

Career: Bolton schoolboy football; Lancashire Schools; Hayes Athletic; Rossendale

United (Lancashire Combination) when only 15, at which age he had signed amateur forms for Bolton Wanderers and Sheffield Wednesday; Burnley as an amateur May 1935, signing professional October 1936; Everton January 1937 (£6500) (guest player for Aldershot and Morton during WW2); Chelsea November 1945 (£11,500); Notts County November 1947 (£20,000 plus another player); Brentford March 1952 (£12,000) being player/manager from January 1953; Arsenal September 1953 (£10,000 plus another player); Kettering Town player/manager February 1956 (£1000)-April 1957. Notts County manager May 1957-July 1958; Kettering Town manager November 1963-April 1964 when appointed a club director; Notts County coach and chief scout October 1968-April 1970. Other honours: England wartime international (15 apps). Football League (3 apps). (Everton) FL champions 1939. (Notts. Co) FL Div. 3 (South) champions 1950.

Centre-forward among the most illustrious in British football history. His immense promise as a juvenile was fully realised in the first-class game. In brief, Tommy had everything – superlative in the air with matching ability on the ground (the latter despite having flat feet). His distribution was magnificent and, when at a magnificent best, was almost uncontainable. Became the youngest player to score a FL hat-trick (4 days after his 17th birthday).

LEACH, Thomas ('Tony')
(Sheffield Wednesday, 1931, 2)
Born Wincobank, Sheffield, 23 September 1903. Died 1970.
1930: 5ft. 10$^1/_2$ins.; 11st. 9lbs.

Career: Wath Athletic cs 1924; Sheffield Wednesday 1926; Newcastle United June 1934 (£1100); Stockport County July 1936 (£300); Carlisle United February 1937; Lincoln City September 1938; retired cs 1939. Other honours: Football League (1 app). (Wednesday) FL champions 1929, 1930. (Stockport) FL Div. 3 (North) champions 1937.

Centre-half. Strange, Leach and Marsden, members of Wednesday's 1929 and '30 championship half-back line, were all originally forwards and all were honoured by England. Leach developed into a fine defensive pivot astute in distribution. Later skippered Newcastle.

LEAKE, Alexander
(Aston Villa, 1904-05, 5)
Born Small Heath, Birmingham, 11 July 1871. Died 29 March 1938.
1904: 5ft. 8$^1/_2$ins.; 12st. 1lb.

Career: Birmingham schoolboy football and then assisted a couple of junior clubs in the area (Hoskins & Sewell's FC and King's Heath) before his first professional engagement with Old Hill Wanderers 1893/94; Small Heath cs 1894; Aston Villa June 1902; Burnley December 1907; Wednesbury Old Athletic cs 1910. Crystal Palace trainer cs 1913 – cs 1915; Merthyr Town trainer October 1919-cs 1920. His full-time involvement with football then ceased but he did a little coaching (including a spell with Walsall from September 1932). Other honours: Football League (1 app). (Villa) FA Cup winner 1905.

Centre/left-half tremendous in stamina and fine defensively. Extremely popular, probably the more so for never 'showing off', and a great humorist. A seasoned player by the time of the Villa signing, Alec had captained Small Heath for the bulk of his time there. A blacksmith by trade.

LEE, E(rnest) Albert
(Southampton, 1904, 1)
Born Bridport, Dorset, 1879. Died 14 January 1958.
1903: 5ft.11ins. 12st. 8lbs.

Career: Poole FC; Southampton cs 1900; Dundee May 1906; Southampton again cs 1911, becoming player/trainer 1913; retired from playing during WW1 and remained as the club's trainer to 1935. Other honours: (Soton) Southern League champions 1901, 1903, 1904. FA Cup finalist 1902. (Dundee) Scottish Cup winner 1910.

Right-half. A long-time Saints' servant with some 30 years service at The Dell. Bert's play was a useful amalgam of dash and shrewdness heightened, of course, by a commanding physique. Skippered Dundee to their 1910 Scottish Cup triumph and was one of several Anglos in that fine line-up. On leaving football worked as a salesman with his son's radio firm.

LEE, Francis Henry
(Manchester City, 1969-72, 27)

Born Westhoughton, Lancs. 29 April 1944. 1970: 5ft. 7½ins.; 12st. 2lbs.

Career: Lancashire Schools; Bolton Wanderers amateur July 1959, turning professional May 1961; Manchester City October 1967 (£60,000); Derby County August 1974 (£110,000); retired May 1976. Other honours: England Youth international. Football League (1 app). (Man. City) European Cup Winners' Cup, winner 1970. FL champions 1968. FA Cup winner 1969. FL Cup winner 1970; finalist 1974. (Derby Co) FL champions 1975.

Outside-right/centre and inside-forward. Short, sturdy, spirited forward, scorer of 229 goals in a total 499 FL matches, a fine total enhanced by penalty-kick expertise. Made his senior debut at 16, always a first-teamer thereafter and never came on as a sub (at any rate in League matches). During his career Franny became a prosperous business man, a sure sign of this prosperity occurring in the mid-1980s with his emergence as a racehorse owner/trainer.

LEE, Jack
(Derby County, 1951, 1)
Born Sileby, Leics. 4 November 1920.
1949: 6ft.; 12st. 2lbs.

Career: Quorn Methodists (Leicestershire Senior League); Leicester City February 1941; Derby County June 1950 (£18,500); Coventry City November 1954 (£5000) – cs 1955. Other honour: (Leicester C) FA Cup finalist 1949.

Inside-right/centre-forward. Free scoring forward who combined bustle with good control. Could shoot from any angle, distance being no object. Plagued with knee injuries throughout his first-class career which necessitated several operations. Jack was a useful cricketer and played in a match for Leicestershire during the 1947 season – a memorable occasion in that he took a wicket with the very first ball he bowled.

LEE, Samuel
(Liverpool, 1983-84, 14)
Born Liverpool, 7 February 1959.
1983: 5ft. 7ins.; 10st. 1lb.

Career: Liverpool schoolboy football; Liverpool FC apprentice 1975, turning professional April 1976; Queen's Park Rangers August 1986 (£200,000); Osasuna (Spain) July 1987 (£200,000). Other honours: England Youth international. England Under-21 international (6 apps). (Liverpool) European Cup winner 1981, 1984. FL champions 1982, 1983, 1984. FL Cup winner 1981, 1982, 1983, 1984.

Midfield. A busy little player who never lets up, strong in his tackling and beautifully accurate in distribution. Won a clutch of club and representative honours after gaining a regular place at Anfield in 1980 but a loss of form during the campaign of 1984/85 eventually brought a departure to pastures new.

LEIGHTON, John Edward
(Nottingham Forest, 1886, 1)
Born Nottingham, 26 March 1865. Died 15 April 1944.

Career: Nottingham schoolboy and junior football; Nottingham Forest 1884-88; Corinthians 1885-89.

Outside-left. In the words of J A H Catton ('Tityrus') '... that feather-weight of international fame ... who was a swift dribbler and most artful dodger.' Leighton had a notable partnership for Forest with the equally well known Sam Widdowson. He was a wholesale stationer and paper merchant with premises at Clinton Street, Nottingham. And an avid Forest follower, rarely missing a match at the City Ground be it first team, reserve or colts. He actually died at the ground.

LILLEY, Henry E.
(Sheffield United 1892, 1)
Born Staveley, Derbys. 1873.
Career: Staveley FC; Sheffield United cs 1890; Gainsborough Trinity cs 1894.

Left-back. Another of those teenage caps that proliferated in home countries' selections during Victorian times. Lilley's one and only appearance was at Wrexham, March 3, 1892, when he made his contribution to a 2-0 victory. He was a sound performer, owning a good kick and showing much vitality. Shares with Michael Whitham the distinction of being Sheffield United's first cap – England put out two teams that day, each containing one Blade.

LINACRE, J(ames) Henry
(Nottingham Forest, 1905, 2)

Born Aston-on-Trent, Derbys. 1880. Died 11 May 1957.
1903: 5ft. 11in.; 11st. 2lbs.

Career: Loughborough Grammar School; Aston-on-Trent FC; Draycott Mills; Derby County December 1898; Nottingham Forest August 1899 – cs 1909. Other honours: Football League (1 app). (Forest) FL Div. 2 champions 1907.

Goalkeeper, undisputed first choice at Forest for a decade, with 331 League and FA Cup encounters to his credit. Advantaged by a long reach and instinctive reflex action, he was quite brilliant. Brother-in-law of the Forman brothers (q.v.) – he married their sister – and was in business with Frank of that ilk in a building contractors firm.

LINDLEY, Tinsley
(Cambridge University, Nottingham Forest and Corinthians, 1886-91, 13)
Born Nottingham, 27 October, 1865. Died 31 March 1940.
1892: 5ft. 9ins.; 10st. 9lbs.

Career: Nottingham High School; Cambridge University (Blue 1885-6-7-8, captain '88); Nottingham Forest 1883-92; Corinthians 1885-94; he also assisted on occasion the Casuals, Notts County, Crusaders and Swifts, and made a single appearance for Preston North End in February 1892.

Centre-forward. An amateur among the greatest centres of the early days, amateur or professional. Adept at passing and shooting, and kept his line moving very judiciously. Most useful at other games too. Played cricket for Cambridge University (no Blue) 1885 and Notts 1888; and rugby for his Cambridge college (Caius), the Old Leysians and Notts. A barrister by profession (LL.D. and BA (Cantab)) called to the Bar 1889, he lectured on law at Nottingham University and eventually became a County Court judge. Awarded the OBE in 1918 for his work as chief officer of the Nottingham Special Constabulary.

LINDSAY, Alec
(Liverpool, 1974, 4)
Born Bury, Lancs. 27 February 1948.
1974: 5ft. 9½ins; 11st.
Career: Junior football; Bury FC apprentice, turning professional March 1965; Liverpool March 1969 (£67,000); Stoke City on loan August 1977, signing permanently the following month (£20,000); Oakland (USA) March 1978. Came out of retirement late 1982 to assist Newton FC (North-West Counties League). Other honours: England Youth international. (Liverpool) EUFA Cup winner 1973. FL champions 1973. FA Cup winner 1974; finalist 1971.

Left-back at Anfield after playing wing-half and inside-forward for Bury. A fast performer, Lindsay naturally took to the modern overlap ploy while his strong left foot was much in evidence in all aspects. 'Also a rough handful when wingers try to "take the mickey",' observed a contemporary critic. Outside the game has worked as a scrap metal merchant, had a fried fish shop and been a licensee.

LINDSAY, William
(Wanderers, 1877, 1)
Born in India, 3 August 1847. Died 15 February 1923.

Career: Winchester College; Old Wykehamists; Wanderers. Also represented Surrey. Other honours: (Wanderers) FA Cup winner 1876, 1877, 1878.

Full-back chiefly though a valuable utility player who could shine at half-back and as a forward as well. A sure kick, plucky and a first-rate team man. Played cricket for Surrey 1876-82 (33 matches). Employed in the India Office 1865-1900.

LINEKER, Gary Winston
(Leicester City, Everton and Barcelona, 1984-88, 35)
Born Leicester, 30 November 1960.
1985: 5ft. 10ins.; 12st. 5lbs.

Career: Leicester junior football; Leicester City apprentice July 1977, turning professional November 1978; Everton June 1985 (£800,000 plus percentage of profit on transfer to Barcelona: an Everton and Leicester record); Barcelona July 1986 (£2.75m., an Everton record). Other honours: (Leicester C) FL Div. 2 champions 1980. (Everton) FA Cup finalist 1986.

Strike forward, a superstar of the 1980s, 'Player of the Year' 1986 for both the Football Writers and PFA. Has acceleration, correctly described as 'exhilarating', which outdistances most opponents, and an awareness when nearing the enemy citadel that has resulted in outstanding goals. Obviously a soccer addict from the start – a Leicester City season-ticket holder from the age of 8.

LINTOTT, Evelyn Henry
(Queen's Park Rangers and Bradford City, 1908-09, 7)
Born Godalming, Surrey, 2 November 1883. Killed in action 1 July 1916.
1908: 5ft. 10ins.; 12st.

Career: St. Luke's Training College, Exeter 1905; Woking (when he also represented Surrey); Plymouth Argyle 1906; Queen's Park Rangers as an amateur September 1907, turning professional May 1908; Bradford City November 1908; Leeds City June 1912. Other honours: England amateur international (5 apps). Football League (1 app). (QPR) Southern League champions 1908.

Left-half (was on the other flank in QPR's 1908 championship side). A distinguished graduate from the amateur ranks – skilful, robust and exercising fine judgment in his tackling and distribution. A school teacher by vocation, Lintott had a spell as chairman of the Players Union until January 1911. Lost his life on the Somme while serving with the 1st Yorkshire Regiment.

LIPSHAM, Herbert Broughall
(Sheffield United, 1902, 1)
Born Chester, 29 April 1878. Died in Canada 1932 (in a train accident).
1901: 5ft. 9ins.; 11st.

Career: King's School, Chester, then assisted two clubs in the district (St. Oswald's and Chester SA) before joining Crewe Alexandra cs 1898; Sheffield United February 1900; Fulham 1907/08; Millwall Athletic cs 1910 (player/manager cs 1913). West Norwood coach August 1921; Northfleet manager cs 1922 – early 1923 when he emigrated to Canada. Other honours: Football League (2 apps). Southern League (2 apps). (Sheffield U) FA Cup winner 1902; finalist 1901.

Outside-left, dedicated and enthusiastic. A formidable marksman whose strength of kick when employed in centering sometimes overshot his inside-forwards. Had the misfortune to lose a hand in a Canadian sawmill accident.

LITTLE, Brian
(Aston Villa 1975, 1)
Born Peterlee, Co. Durham, 25 November 1953.
1975: 5ft. 8ins.; 11st. 2lbs.

Career: North Eastern schools football; Aston Villa apprentice April 1969, turning professional March 1971; retired through injury March 1981. Subsequently joined Villa's backroom staff and worked for the commercial department's travel club and was the youth team coach until January 1986; Wolverhampton Wanderers caretaker manager August-October 1986, later joining Middlesbrough's staff as reserve team coach to February 1989 when he was appointed Darlington's manager. Other honours: (Villa) FL Cup winner 1975,1977.

Forward. An extremely fine ball player and a nippy one unfortunately lost to the game when only 27. At his retiral Brian had logged 242 League games and 5 substitutions and scored 60 goals during them in an Aston Villa shirt. His brother Alan, a colleague at Villa Park, later had good runs with Southend United and other FL clubs.

LLOYD, Laurence Valentine
(Liverpool and Nottingham Forest, 1971-80, 4)
Born Bristol, 6 October 1948.
1975: 6ft. $2^{1}/_{2}$ins.; 14st. $3^{1}/_{2}$lbs.

Career: Bristol schools and junior football; Bristol Rovers amateur, turning professional July 1967; Liverpool April 1969 (£50,000); Coventry City August 1974 (£225,000); Nottingham Forest November 1976 (about £60,000 following a month on loan, September-October 1976); Wigan Athletic player/manager March 1981; Notts County team manager July 1983-October 1984. Other honours: England Youth international. England Under-23 international (8 apps). (Liverpool) EUFA Cup winner 1973. FL champions 1973. FA Cup finalist 1971. (Forest) European Cup winner 1979, 1980. FL champions 1978. FL Cup winner 1978, 1979.

Centre-half of awesome proportions, the sheet anchor pivot in excelsis. Very determined with it and, of course, dominated in aerial duals. Won a fair old clutch of medals at club level too, his spells at Anfield and Nottingham coinciding with vintage seasons.

LOCKETT, Arthur
(Stoke, 1903, 1)
Born Alsagers Bank nr. Stoke-on-Trent, 1875. Died 1957.
1903: 5ft. 8ins.; 11st. 7lbs.

Career: Alsagers Bank FC; Crewe Alexandra; Stoke May 1900; Aston Villa April 1903 (£400); Preston North End September 1905; Watford cs 1908-1912. Other honour: Football League (1 app).

Outside-left. Greatly talented and possessing tremendous speed. Like many of his kind, though, had an inclination to bamboozle the same opponent twice, thus holding up an attack. Attracted a sizeable fee by 1900s standards from Villa.

LODGE, Lewis Vaughan
(Cambridge University and Corinthians, 1894-96, 5)
Born Aycliffe, nr. Darlington, 21 December 1872. Died 21 October 1916.

Career: Durham School; Cambridge University (Blue 1893-4-5, acting captain '95); Corinthians 1894-98; Casuals. Other honour: (Casuals) FA Amateur Cup finalist 1894.

Right/left-back. All his international appearances, except one, were on the right flank, and he played at right-back in the '94 Amateur Cup final. Energetic and courageous, certain in his tackling and kicking, a fault was a proneness to premature commitment. Vaughan was also a useful cricketer, playing for Durham and making 3 appearances for Hampshire in 1900. Besides learning soccer at Durham School he was in its rugger XV. A schoolmaster by profession, he taught at a Newbury school from leaving Cambridge to his death.

LOFTHOUSE, Joseph Morris
(Blackburn Rovers and Accrington, 1885-90, 7)
Born Witton, Blackburn, 14 April 1865. Died 10 June 1919.
1891: 5ft. 8ins.; 11st. 12lbs.

Career: Blackburn schoolboy football; King's Own FC (Blackburn); Blackburn Rovers 1882; Accrington cs 1887; Blackburn Rovers again cs 1889; Darwen cs 1892; Walsall December 1893. Coach to the Magyar Athletic Club, Budapest, February 1902; New Brompton trainer during season 1902/03; Everton assistant trainer August 1903. Other honours: (Blackburn R) FA Cup winner 1884, 1885, 1890, 1891.

Outside-right. Uncommonly fast and particularly dangerous because speed was allied to consummate ball control. Bigger physically than the average winger. An early 'missionary' to the continent, even if the mission lasted but a matter of months. (Perhaps his Hungarian, like the compiler's Serbo-Croat, was rusty).

LOFTHOUSE, Nathaniel
(Bolton Wanderers, 1951-59, 33)
Born Bolton, 27 August 1925.
1957: 5ft. $9^{3}/_{4}$ins.; 12st. 2lbs.

Career: Bolton Schools; Lomax's FC (Bolton); Bolton Boys Federation; Bolton Wanderers amateur September 1939, turning professional 1942/43; retired cs 1961. Subsequently occupied a succession of posts for the Wanderers: reserve team trainer July 1961, chief coach June 1967, caretaker manager August 1968, manager December 1968, general manager November 1970, chief scout August 1971-June 1972. Was later in charge of the executive club at Burnden Park and had a further, if very brief, spell as manager December 1985. Was Arsenal's Lancashire scout for a time from September 1973. Other honours: England 'B' international (1 app). Football League (15 apps). (Bolton W) FA Cup winner 1958; finalist 1953.

Centre-forward. A major post-war star and super club man. Dash and resolution cost him many injuries but he still recorded a splendid 255 goals in 452 League encounters. Bravery earned Nat the title of 'The Lion of Vienna' after the match with Austria in 1952. 'Player of the Year' 1953.

LONGWORTH, Ephraim
(Liverpool, 1920-23, 5)
Born Halliwell, Bolton, 2 October 1887. Died 7 January 1968.
1925: 5ft. 8½ins.; 11st. 3lbs.

Career: Bolton Schools; Bolton St Luke's (Lancashire Combination); Hyde St George's as a professional; Bolton Wanderers June 1907; Leyton late in 1908; Liverpool May 1910; retired cs 1928 and thereupon served on the Liverpool staff for some time, first as a coach. Other honours: England 'Victory' international 1919 (2 apps). Football League (6 apps). (Liverpool) FL champions 1922, 1923. FA Cup finalist 1914.

Right-back. The first Liverpool player to captain England and for decades a notable Anfield servant on and off the field. Fine tactically and his strong clearances with either foot were cannily designed to start attacks. Something of an attraction to cartoonists for, as one writer said, his '. . . bowed legs rivalled Dicky Downs' and Joe Mercer's.' Toured South Africa with the FA party in 1920, playing against the national side on three occasions.

LOWDER, Arthur
(Wolverhampton Wanderers, 1889, 1)
Born Wolverhampton, 1863. Died 4 January 1926.
1889: 5ft. 8ins.; 10st.6lbs.

Career: Wolverhampton schoolboy football; Wolverhampton Wanderers from the early 1880s – late 1891. Was a coach in Cologne in the 1920s untill shortly before his death. Other honour: (Wolves) FA Cup finalist 1889.

Left-half. Like several other distinguished colleagues was a product of that fine nursery, St Luke's at Blakenhall. Lowder, with Albert Fletcher and Harry Allen, formed an all international half-back line, and was its 'lightweight' member. But lightweight only in the sense of poundage, his play being marked by judgement, persistence and control.

LOWE, Edward
(Aston Villa, 1947, 3)
Born Halesowen, Worcs. 11 July 1925.
1949: 5ft. 11ins.; 11st. 3lbs.

Career: Napier Aircraft Co (Millwall amateur); Kynoch's (Birmingham works side); Finchley; Aston Villa June 1945; Fulham May 1950 (£15,000 including his brother, Reg.) Notts County player/manager May 1963-April 1965. Had a spell as Plymouth Argyle's Midlands scout from September 1965.

Left-half. Long legged performer included among the strongest attacking wing-halves of his day. Gave a splendid 13 season's service at Craven Cottage in which he averaged 36 league outings per campaign, a confirmation of excellent consistency. And the aggregate created a club record (since surpassed). Eddie's father was once on Villa's books as a goalkeeper, while his brother, mentioned above, was with him at Finchley as well as Villa and Fulham. After leaving football was employed as purchasing manager for an international boiler company.

LUCAS, Thomas
(Liverpool, 1922-26, 3)
Born St Helens, Lancs. 20 September 1895.
Died 11 December 1953.
1925: 5ft. 6½ins.; 11st.4lbs.

Career: Sherdley Villa; Sutton Commercial; Heywood United; Peasley Cross; Eccles Borough (trial with Manchester United); Liverpool cs 1916; Clapton Orient July 1933; retired cs 1934 and was briefly in charge of Orient's nursery club, Ashford FC (Kent). Other honours: Football League (4 apps). (Liverpool) FL champions 1922.

Right/left-back. Doughty little defender, notably two-footed and ultra-reliable. He had been a forward until conversion to full-back during his Eccles period. Proved an admirable stand-in for both Longworth (q.v.) and McKinlay, the veteran internationalist, playing in so many matches as to deemed a 'regular'. (He aggregated 341 peacetime League appearances for the Reds) Tommy was a licencee at Stoke Mandeville, Bucks, for 18 years to his death.

LUNTLEY, Edwin
(Nottingham Forest, 1880, 2)
Born Croydon, Surrey 1857. Died 1 August 1921.

Career: Nottingham Castle FC; Nottingham Forest November 1878-January 1883.

Right-back. The most distinguished of 3 Luntleys who turned out for Forest during the club's first decades. One of the others (W Luntley) was also a full-back and appeared 1878-83. Edwin, courageous and a quick mover, was a lace manufacturer by calling. He was interested in other sports, being an early exponent of lacrosse and a founder member of the Chilwell Manor Golf Club.

LYTTELTON, Hon. Alfred
(Old Etonians, 1877, 1)
Born Westminster, London, 7 February 1857. Died 5 July 1913.

Career: Eton College (captain of XI 1875); Cambridge University (Blue 1876-7-8); Old Etonians; Hagley FC (Worcs). Other honour: (Old Etonians) FA Cup finalist 1876.

Forward. Summed up in 1881 as 'a very strong and fast forward and a splendid shot at goal.' In addition he was not averse to using his weight and was difficult to dispossess. His ball control, however, left something to be desired. From a famous cricketing family, with 5 brothers in the first-class game, he played for Cambridge University (Blue 1876-7-8-9), *Worcestershire, Middlesex (1877-87) and England (4 Tests). President of the MCC 1898. He also represented Cambridge University at Real Tennis, rackets and athletics. A barrister and KC. he was MP for Warwick 1895-1906, and St George's Hanover Square, 1906 to his death, serving as Secretary for the Colonies 1902-05. Brother of Edward Lyttelton (below) and father of Lord Chandos, who also attained government office.*

LYTTELTON, Revd. the Hon. Edward
(Old Etonians, 1878, 1)
Born Westminster, London 23rd July 1855. Died 26 January 1942.

Career: Eton College; Cambridge University (no Blue); Old Etonians; Hagley FC (Worcs). Other honour: (Old Etonians) FA Cup finalist 1876.

Full-back. A redoubtable defender presenting a substantial barrier and exploiter of a considerable kick. One of a family of 6 brothers (including Alfred above) who played first-class cricket, he turned out for Cambridge University (Blue 1875-6-7-8) and Middlesex (13 matches 1878-82) and also Hertfordshire and, before elevation to first-class status, Worcestershire. He was a master at Wellington College (18880-82) and Eton (1882-89) before appointments as Headmaster of Haileybury (1890-1905) and Eton (1905-16), thereafter serving in various clerical appointments to his death.

MABBUTT, Gary Vincent
(Tottenham Hotspur, 1983-88, 13)
Born Bristol, 23 August 1961.
1985: 5ft. 9ins.; 10st. 10lbs.

Career: Bristol Schools; Bristol Rovers apprentice 1977, turning professional January 1979; Tottenham Hotspur July 1982 (£150,000). Other honours: England Youth international. England Under-21 international (7 apps). (Spurs) EUFA Cup winner 1984. FA Cup finalist 1987.

Defender/midfield. A performer of unusual adaptability able to display his talents anywhere, midfield or rear, and could doubtless do so in the attack as well. Is especially praiseworthy because, despite being a diabetic, has reached the highest class, and so ranks with Scotland's Danny McGrain. Capable in all aspects, his headwork is probably the most noticeable quality, being able to outjump much taller oppo-

nents. Gary comes from soccer stock: son of Ray Mabbutt (Bristol Rovers 1956-69) and brother of Kevin, England schoolboy and Youth international.

McCALL, Joseph
(Preston North End, 1913-21, 5)
Born Kirkham Lancs. 6 July 1886. Died 3 February 1965.
1919: 5ft. 8½ins.; 11st. 12lbs.

Career: Kirkham FC; Preston North End as an amateur 1905/06, turning professional July 1906; retired May 1925. Other honours: England 'Victory' international 1919 (2 apps). Football League (2 apps). (PNE) FL Div. 2 champions 1913. FA Cup finalist 1922.

Centre-half, to be numbered among the best – stylish, always in position yet giving full vent to an attack-minded disposition. Never wasted a ball, serving his wingers with long raking passes. An excellent cricket professional for Lancashire clubs for many years, also coaching at Stoneyhurst College. Was a smallholder and poultry farmer at Wrea Green near Kirkham.

MACAULAY, Reginald Heber
(Old Etonians, 1881, 1)
Born Hodnet, Salop, 24 August 1858. Died 15 December 1937.

Career: Eton College (XI 1878); Cambridge University (Blue 1881-82); Old Etonians. Other honours: (Old Etonians) FA Cup winner 1882; finalist 1881, 1883.

Forward. Alcock's Annual (as so often) had reservations. 'Heavy centre-forward. Can make a good run, has plenty of pace but over-runs the ball and is not clever in close quarters.' Macaulay, however, despite any soccer shortcomings, was a fine and versatile athlete. He represented Cambridge University 1879-82, winning the high jump 1879-80 and the quarter-mile 1880-1-2. He was the AAA high jump champion of 1879. Worked in India 1884-1901 and was subsequently a merchant in the City.

McDERMOTT, Terence
(Liverpool, 1978-82, 25)
Born Kirkby, Liverpool, 8 December 1951.
1980: 5ft. 9ins.; 12st. 13lbs.

Career: Liverpool schoolboy football; Bury apprentice, turning professional October 1969; Newcastle United February 1973 (£22,000); Liverpool November 1974 (£170,000); Newcastle United again September 1982 (£100,000)-September 1984; Cork City January 1985 for 5 matches, subsequently joining Apoel FC (Cyprus). Other honours: England 'B' international (1 app). England Under-23 international (1 app). (Newcastle) FA Cup finalist 1974. (Liverpool) European Cup winner 1977, 1978, 1981. FL champions 1977, 1979, 1980, 1982. FA Cup finalist 1977. FL Cup winner 1981, 1982; finalist 1978.

Midfield. Became renowned for telling surges from deep positions, these often resulting in spectacular goals. A hard running player, McDermott did not attain 'regular' status at Anfield until 1977/78, but then made up for lost time by winning a rich crop of medals. Was 'Player of the Year' for both PFA and Football Writers in 1980, the first time this had been done.

McDONALD, Colin Agnew
(Burnley, 1958-59, 8)
Born Summerseat nr. Bury, Lancs. 15 October 1930.
1958: 6ft.; 12st.

Career: Bury Technical College; Hawkshaw St. Mary's; Burnley amateur August 1948, part-time professional October 1948 (Headington United on loan 1950/51 while on national service), Burnley full time profesional July 1952; retired through injury cs 1961. Wycombe Wanderers coach August 1961; Bury chief scout October 1961; Altrincham as a player January 1965; Bury chief scout again May 1967; Bolton Wanderers chief scout October 1968; Bury administrative manager August 1969, general manager May 1970; subsequently had youth coaching posts with Oldham

Athletic and Tranmere Rovers, leaving the latter February 1987. Other honours: Football League (3 apps)

Goalkeeper. Rightly described as 'safe, sure and brilliant', his lithe performances a spectators' delight. Colin's untimely retiral came from an injury sustained three years before, during March 1958: a broken leg whilst representing the Football League.

MACDONALD, Malcolm Ian
(Newcastle United, 1972-76, 14)
Born Fulham, London, 7 January 1950.
1974: 5ft. $10^1/_2$ins.; 13st. $4^1/_2$lbs.

Career: Knole Juniors (Sevenoaks League); Tonbridge July 1967; Fulham August 1968; Luton Town July 1969 (£17,500); Newcastle United May 1971 (£180,000); Arsenal July 1976 (£333,333); retiring through injury August 1979. Fulham commercial manager September 1979, manager November 1980 (director also from November 1981) – April 1984; Huddersfield Town manager October 1987 – May 1988. Other honours: England Under-23 international (4 apps). Football League (1 app). (Newcastle) FA Cup finalist 1974. FL Cup finalist 1976. (Arsenal) FA Cup finalist 1978.

Centre-forward. Now part of Tyneside soccer lore as 'Supermac', who led United's attack with a brash assurance that captivated the fans. Malcolm had a blistering left-foot shot, was good at heading and devastated defenders with electrifying bursts down the middle. After leaving the Fulham managership became a Worthing licensee.

McFARLAND, Roy Leslie
(Derby County, 1971-77, 28)
Born Liverpool, 5 April 1948.
1974: 5ft. 11ins.; 11st. 2lbs.

Career: Edge Hill Boys club (Liverpool); Tranmere Rovers July 1966; Derby County August 1967 (£24,000); Bradford City as player/manager May 1981; Derby County team manager November 1982, reverting to assistant manager after Arthur Cox's arrival in June 1984. Other honours: England Under-23 international (5 apps). Football League (6 apps). (Derby Co.) FL Champions 1972. FL Div. 2 champions 1969.

Centre-half. Among the best of the post-WW2 vintage: skilled, uncompromising and maintaining a high level of performance. Dogged by injuries latterly, particularly one to an achilles tendon that cost him a 1975 League championship medal. On his return from Bradford Roy was a non-contract player for the Rams, making 3 full and 5 sub. appearances in 1983/84. He was a 'hot property' in the managerial sense after steering Bradford City to promotion.

McGARRY, William Harry
(Huddersfield Town, 1954-56, 4)
Born Stoke-on-Trent, 10 June 1927.
1957: 5ft. 8ins.; 11st.

Career: Northwood Mission (Hanley); Port Vale 1945; Huddersfield Town March 1951 (£10,000); Bournmouth & Boscombe Athletic as player/manager March 1961 (£2000). Watford Manager June 1963; Ipswich Town manager September 1964; Wolverhampton Wanderers manager November 1968-May 1976; Saudi Arabia national coach June 1976 – October 1977; Newcastle United manager November 1977-August 1980; later a Brighton & Hove Albion scout and then coached in Africa, briefly interrupting the latter to have a very brief second spell as Wolves' manager (September-November 1985), immediately returning to Bophathatswana. Other honours: England 'B' international (1 app). Football League (1 app).

Right-half. Had figured at inside-right earlier. A solid and competent performer, not given to fireworks but reliability personified. Said to have been something of a disciplinarian as a manager (which, of course, can be no bad thing, particularly in permissive times).

McGUINNESS, Wilfred
(Manchester United, 1959, 2)

Born Manchester, 25 October 1937.
1959: 5ft. 8ins.; 10st. 10lbs.

Career: Manchester Schools; Lancashire Schools; Manchester United apprentice June 1953, turning professional November 1954; retired through injury December 1961 (made abortive attempt at a come-back during 1966-67 but this was 'only a gesture'). Thereupon became Manchester United's youth team manager folowed by appointments as chief coach June 1969, team manager August 1970 and reserve team trainer/coach December 1970-March 1971; Aris Salonika (Greece) manager July 1971-73, then managed another Grecian side, Panaraiki, before returning late 1974 to scout for Everton; York City manager February 1975-October 1977; Hull City 1st team coach July 1978- December 1979; Bury reserve team coach August 1980, later taking posts of assistant manager and physiotherapist with that club. Was trainer (part-time) of the England Youth team 1963-69. Other honours: England schoolboy international. England Youth international. England Under-23 international (4 apps). Football League (1 app).

Left-half. A career that started so rich in promise and ended by a badly broken leg in a reserves' match that took place 2 years before the announcement of definite retirement. McGuinness was a thrustful, skilled wing-half imbued with strong attacking instincts. At the outset of his professional years had the job of understudying Duncan Edwards and, when that great player died, had but another 2 playing years himself. So he grossed only 81 League games.

McINROY, Albert
(Sunderland, 1927, 1)

Born Walton-le-Dale nr. Preston, Lancs. 23 April 1901. Died 7 January 1985.
1930: 5ft. 10ins.; 13st. 21lbs.

Career: Preston schoolboy football; Upper Walton (Preston & District League) 1919; Cuppull Central (West Lancashire League) (signed amateur forms for Preston North End 1921/22); Great Harwood; Leyland cs 1922; Sunderland May 1923; Newcastle United October 1929 (£2750); Sunderland again June 1934; Leeds United May 1935; Gateshead June 1937; retired during WW2 during which period he made occasional appearances for Stockton and other North-East clubs.
Other honour: (Newcastle) FA Cup winner 1932.

Goalkeeper of great durability who made 496 League appearances in 16 senior seasons, thus averaging a splendid 31 per campaign. The soul of consistency and very agile, his leaps and springs being described as cat-like. Played outside-left as a boy. For many years a Geordieland licensee.

McMAHON, Stephen
(Liverpool, 1988, 4)
Born Liverpool, 20 August 1961.
1987: 5ft. 7ins.; 10st. 9lbs.

Career: Liverpool schools football to Everton on 'S' forms when 14, apprentice december 1977, professional August 1979; Aston Villa May 1983 (£350,000); Liverpool September 1985 (£350,000). Other honours: England Under-21 international (6 apps). (Liverpool) FL champions 1986, 1988. FA Cup finalist 1988. FA Cup finalist 1987.

Midfield. His total involvement and rugged tackling won him a regular first team spot at Goodison when only 19. Refusal to renew his contract resulted in a transfer to Villa. After two years Steve returned to his native heath to win international and club honours as an integral part of the successful Anfield line-up.

McNAB, Robert
(Arsenal, 1969, 4)
Born Hudderfield, 20 July 1943.
1969: 5ft. 9ins. 11st 6lbs.

Career: Huddersfield schools football; Mold Green Civic Youth Club (Huddersfield); Huddersfield Town amateur 1961, turning professional April 1962; Arsenal October

1966 (£40,000); Wolverhampton Wanderers July 1975. Barnet 1976. Other honours: Football League (1 app). (Arsenal) Inter-Cities Fairs Cup winner 1970. FL champions 1971. FA Cup winner 1971; finalist 1972. FL Cup finalist 1968, 1969.

Left-back. Member of the Arsenal line-up in one of the club's great periods, a quick tackling defender good at starting attacks. The fee paid by the Gunners was then a record for a full-back. Bob was a joiner by trade but in the 1970s was reported to have two betting shops.

McNEAL, Robert
(West Bromwich Albion, 1914, 2)
Born Hobson nr. Stanley, Co Durham, 15 January 1891. Died 15 May 1956.
1912: 5ft. 6ins.; 10st. 10lbs.

Career: Hobson Wanderers; West Bromwich Albion June 1910 (guest player for Port Vale and Middlesbrough during WW1); retired throuth injury May 1926. Later had a spell as part time Albion coach. Other honours: Football League (5 apps). (WBA) FL champions 1920. FL Div. 2 champions 1911. FA Cup finalist 1912.

Left-half. Short, sturdy half-back, a fine feeder of the left-wing attackers who fronted him. Stylish, confident, shrewd and a penalty specialist. Subsequently a West Bromwich licencee until his death.

McNEIL, Michael
(Middlesbrough, 1961-62, 9)
Born Middlesbrough, 7 February 1940.
1962: 5ft. 11ins.; 12st. 2lbs.

Career: Middlesbrough Technical College; Cargo Fleet FC (Middlesbrough); Middlesbrough FC on amateur forms June 1954, turning professional February 1957; Ipswich Town June 1964 (about £15,000) Cambridge City June 1972. Other honours: England Under-23 international (9 apps). Football League (1 app).

Left-back. Also played left half for Ipswich. Made use of his handy physique, being good in the air, and he employed a stern tackle. In all made 319 League appearances (plus 5 substitutions), scoring 8 goals. Became proprietor of a number of sports shops in East Anglia.

MACRAE, Stuart
(Notts County, 1883-84, 5)
Born Port Bannatyne, Isle of Bute, 1856. Died 27 January 1927.

Career: Edinburgh Academy (where he played rugger); Notts County; Corinthians 1883-90; Newark FC.

Half-back ranking high in the 1880s. Extolled in the middle of the decade as follows '. . .one of the most reliable half-backs; tackles well and is very quick as well as a good kick. Very difficult to pass.' Macrae was a good rugger player too, a member of the Edinburgh Academy XV 1872-73 and then team captain for the final year. A maltser by vocation employed by a Newark firm.

MADDISON, Frederick Brunning
(Oxford University, 1872, 1)
Born 1850. Died 25 September 1907.

Career: Marlborough Grammar School; Oxford University (no Blue); Wanderers; Crystal Palace. Other honours: (Oxford University) FA cup winner 1874; finalist 1873. (Wanderers) FA Cup winner 1876.

Utility player of note, shining in full-back, half-back and forward positions. Fearless, virile and a worker not averse to a good shoulder charge. Was a barrister (called to the Bar 1876) but disbarred October1884 at his own request to become a solicitor (admitted December 1884). He was originally known as Frederick Patey Chappell, assuming the names at the head of this entry in 1873.

MADELEY, Paul Edward
(Leeds United, 1971-77, 24)
Born Beeston, Leeds, 20 September 1944.
1974: 6ft.; 12st. 13lbs.

Career: Leeds Schools; Farsley Celtic; Leeds United May 1962; retired May 1981. Other honours: England Youth international.

Football League (1 app). (Leeds U) European Cup finalist 1975. European Cup Winner's Cup finalist 1973. Inter-Cities Fairs Cup winner 1968, 1971. FL champions 1969, 1974. FL champions 1969. 1974. FA Cup winner 1972; finalist 1970, 1973. FL Cup winner1968.

Utility player ranking among the most versatile the game has known, appearing for Leeds in all 10 outfield positions – he did so in 9 during the course of a single season. And he was no mere stopgap but he did well everywhere. Always composed, expert in control, unselfish and a thorough sportsman. As a schoolboy had been an England reserve and he was also a sprint champion. In business he is associated with his family's well known chain of DIY shops.

MAGEE, Thomas Patrick
(West Bromwich Albion, 1923-25, 5)
Born Widnes, Lancs. 6 May 1898. Died 4 May 1974.
1925: 5ft. 3ins.; 10st. 10lbs.

Career: Played Rugby League football originally, then soccer for Penksett Albion (1914), Widnes Juniors and Widnes Athletic. While serving with a Labour Battn. during WW1 his form was so good he was recommended to West Bromwich Albion, signing as an amateur January 1919 and professional the following May. Crystal Palace as player/coach May 1934; Runcorn as player/manager May 1935-cs 1937, later serving that club as manager and coach until 1947. Other honours: (WBA) FL champions 1920. FA cup winner 1931.

Right-half with early experience in both right-wing forward berths. Thought to be the shortest half-back ever capped. A wonderful midget – tenacious, constructive, consistent and having a capacity for enjoying his game. A great little player, maybe Britain's best right-half around the mid-1920s.

MAKEPEACE, J(oseph) W(illiam) Henry
(Everton, 1906-12, 4)
Born Middlesbrough, 22 August 1881. Died 19 December 1952.
1910: 5ft. 7ins.; 10st. 12lbs.

Career: Liverpool Schools; Queens Road Misson FC (Stoneycroft) Bootle Amateurs; Everton 1902; retired January 1919. When peace returned he coached in Holland and was an Everton coach, and in the 1930s coached the well-known amateur side, Marine Crosby. Other honours: Football League (5 apps). (Everton) FL champions 1915. FA Cup winner 1906; finalist 1907.

Wing-half, a quiet man of character off the field, on it exhibiting a tackle decribed as 'fearsome' and a high capability for precision passing. Achieved fame at cricket too, playing for Lancashire 1906-30 and England in 4 tests. He was a Lancashire coach 1931-51. Harry moved to Merseyside at the age of 10, hence his formative years in that area's soccer and cricket teams.

MALE, George Charles
(Arsenal, 1935-39, 19)
Born West Ham, 8 May 1910. 1935: 5ft. 11½ins.; 12st. 2lbs.

Career: West Ham Schools; Clapton; Arsenal on amateur forms November 1929, turning professional the following May; retired cs 1948. Subsequently Arsenal's chief scout after being a club coach. Other honours: Football League (2 apps). (Arsenal) FLchampions 1933, 1934, 1935, 1938. FA Cup winner 1936; finalist 1932.

Right-back after originally playing half-

back – he was Clapton's pivot and left-half in the 1932 Cup final. Took over as the Gunners' right-back in 1932/33, an inspired move in anticipation of Tom Parker's retiral. His excellent positional play and factors stemming from an ideal physique blended perfectly with the talents of Eddie Hapgood for both club and country. Before turning professional he had worked as a bank messenger.

MANNION, Wilfred J.
(Middlesbrough, 1947-56, 26)
Born South Bank, Middlesbrough, 16 May 1918.
1950: 5ft. 5ins.; 11st.

Career: South Bank St Peter's; Middlesbrough on amateur forms September 1936, turning professional January 1937 (Army football during WW2); retired June 1954 but joined Hull City the following December (£5000); Poole Town September 1955-March 1956; Cambridge United August 1956; King's Lynn May 1958; Haverhill Rovers (Suffolk) October 1958-cs 1959; Earlestown (Lancashire Combination) as player/manager October 1962. Other honours: England wartime international (4 apps). England ' B' international (3 apps). Football League (7 apps).

Inside-forward dubbed by journalists 'The Golden Boy of Soccer,' a title acknowledging both the subject's blond hair and brilliant play. Performed an orthodox game but with a most unusual facility in the way of ball control and passing skills. Worked at Vauxhall Motors, Luton, between the Haverhill and Earlestown engagments, returning to live in the Teeside area after the latter.

MARINER, Paul
(Ipswich Town and Arsenal, 1977-85, 35)
Born Bolton , 22 May 1953.
1981: 6ft.; 12st. 2lbs.

Career: Chorley St Gregory's; Chorley FC; Plymouth Argyle May 1973 (£5000); Ipswich Town October 1976 (£130,000 and two other players) Arsenal February 1984 (£150,000); Portsmouth cs 1986 – May 1988; Colchester United commercial manager July 1988. Other honours: England 'B' international. (Ipswich T) UEFA Cup winner 1981. FA Cup winner 1978.

Centre-forward. Picked out as having '. . .more poise and better balance than most' and as '. . .giving the impression of being able to look beyond the milling throng around him.' Be that as it may Mariner has proved a durable figure in the first-class game and scored his fair share of goals. His transfer to Plymouth was interesting: £1200 down plus £1800 after he had played 20 first team games, plus another £2000 after 50.

MARSDEN, Joseph Thomas
(Darwen, 1891, 1)
Born Darwen, Lancs. 1868. Died 18 January 1897.

Career: Junior football to Darwen FC; Everton cs 1891, played in the first League match of 1891/92 (vs. West Bromwich Albion, 5 September 1891) and then left the game.

Right-back described in 1891 as 'a back on the light size, but wonderfully clever and possesses great judgement'. The last – by a decade – of Darwen FC's four England caps. And, on a sad note, yet another of the early internationalists to die at a young age.

MARSDEN, William
(Sheffield Wednesday, 1930, 3)
Born Silksworth, Co Durham, 10 November 1901. Died 1983.
1930: 5ft. 9ins.; 11st. 3lbs.
Career: Silksworth Colliery; Sunderland October 1920; Sheffield Wednesday May 1924; retired through injury 1930. Had short spell as Gateshead's trainer from cs 1934 then to Holland until the War as a club coach and he was also assistant coach to the Netherlands FA; Doncaster Rovers man-

ager April 1944 – January 1946; Worksop Town manager for a spell from May 1953. Other honours: Football League (1 app) (Wednesday) FL champions 1929, 1930. FL Div. 2 champions 1926.

Left-half. A Hillsborough conversion of an erstwhile inside-right. Marsden was naturally right-footed, assiduous practice with his left resulting in the making of an outstanding half. 'Tackles shrewdly and passes discreetly' a 1926 writer reported in a flattering pen picture. A severe spinal injury sustained in England's match against Germany in May 1930 brought an abrupt halt to a fine career.

MARSH, Rodney William
(Queen's Park Rangers and Manchester City, 1972-73, 9)
Born Hatfield, Herts. 11 October 1944.
1972: 6ft. 1in.; 13st. 2lbs

Career: Hackney Schools; Alexander Boys Club (West Ham United amateur); Fulham October 1962; Queen's Park Rangers March 1966 (£15,000); Manchester City March 1972 (£200,000); Tampa Bay Rowdies, Florida, January 1976 (£45,000) (Fulham again by arrangement, August 1976-February 1977); retired September 1979, continuing to manage the Tampa Bay club. Other honours: England Under-23 international (2 apps). (QPR) FL Div. 3 champions 1967. FL Cup winner 1967. (Man. City) FL Cup finalist 1974.

Forward. Gifted ball player and marvellous entertainer whose machinations brought great popularity. The QPR fans' chant 'Rod . . . ney' reverberated round the grounds during his peak period with the club. Has become a successful business man in the States since going over there.

MARSHALL, Thomas
(Darwen,1880-81, 2)
Born Withnell, Lancs. 12 September 1858.
Died 29 April 1917.
1884: 5ft. 8ins.
Career: Junior football to Darwen 1878; Blackburn Olympic briefly in 1886 and then retired.

Outside-right. 'Shows to advantage with his own club,' it was reported, and form at this level brought him a couple of caps. Marshall was a fast winger having the ability to pass the ball accurately when going full tilt. Played twice against Wales and on the second occasion – the venue , nearby Blackburn – he was partnered by club-mate Tot Rostron. He had been a professional sprinter and worked in a cotton mill.

MARTIN, Alvin Edward
(West Ham United, 1981-87, 17)
Born Bootle, 19 July 1958.
1984: 6ft. 1in.; 13st. 3lbs.

Career: Merseyside juvenile football; West Ham, United apprentice 1974, turning professional July 1976. Other honours : England Youth international. England 'B'international. (WHU) FL Div. 2 champions 1981. FA Cup winner 1980. FL Cup finalist 1981.

Central defender with the classic centre-half build and of the dominating variety. Like the old time pivots too in his love of going upfield, thus registering more goals than is usual for a defender. This trait is perhaps the more unusual as some critics have detected a lack of speed. However the alleged flaw must surely be only relative.

MARTIN, Henry
(Sunderland, 1914, 1)
Born Selston, Notts. 5 December 1891.
1913: 5ft. $10^1/_4$ins.; 12st.

Career: Sutton Junction 1909; Sunderland January 1912; (guest player for Nottingham Forest during WW1); Nottingham Forest May 1922; Rochdale June 1925 - cs 1929, when he became club trainer (1 FL appearance 1930/31). Mansfield Town Manager December 1933 – March 1935; Swindon Town trainer cs 1936, remaining on their staff into the 1950s. Other honours: England 'Victory' international 1919 (2 apps). Football League (3 apps). (Sunderland) FL champions 1913. FA Cup finalist 1913.

Outside-left. A daunting proposition for any defence and made more so by such unusually hefty dimensions for a wingman. Moreover a raking stride carried him down the flank at speed and he was able to middle the ball accurately at full tilt. Capped during his second full season as a senior.

MASKREY, Harry Mart
(Derby County, 1908, 1)
Born Unstone nr. Dronfield, Derbys. 8 October 1880. Died 21 April 1927.
1908: 6ft. 1ins. 13st. 2lbs.

Career: Ripley Athletic; Derby County December 1902; Bradford City October 1909; Ripley Town cs 1911; Burton All Saints; Derby County again briefly September-December 1920, adding another 5 League appearances to his tally before returning to Burton All Saints; retired December 1922. Other honour: Football League (1 app).

Goalkeeper. Agile despite his weight and quick to sense danger. Harry, once a miner, soon made the Rams' senior team, proving both courageous and consistent and clocking up over 200 League and Cup appearances before departing to Valley Parade. Went into business in Derby after leaving football.

MASON, Charles
(Wolverhampton Wanderers, 1887-90, 3)
Born Wolverhampton, 1 April 1863. Died 3 February 1941.
1889: 5ft. 10ins.; 11st. 13lbs.

Career: St. Luke's School, Blakenhall; founder member of Wolverhampton Wanderers 1877; retired cs 1892. During his playing days appeared on occasion as a guest player for West Bromwich Albion. Other honour: (Wolves) FA Cup finalist 1889.

Left-back. Utterly fearless, this ideally built defender gave Wolves splendid service for many years and was their very first internationalist. Really made his mark in the Cup matches of 1886/87 against Aston Villa (the eventual winners) which went to two replays. Charlie played brilliantly and was rewarded by his first cap before the season ended.

MATTHEWS, Reginald D.
(Coventry City, 1956-57, 5)
Born Coventry, 20 December 1932.
1957: 5ft. 11ins.; 11st. 7lbs.

Career: Coventry Schools; Coventry City ground staff in 1947 when only 14, and assisting the club's nursery side, Modern Machine Tools, turning professional May 1950; Chelsea November 1956 (£22,500); Derby County October 1961 (about £10,000); Rugby Town as player/manager August 1968. Other honours: England 'B' international (3 apps). England Under-23 international (4 apps). Football League (2 apps).

Goalkeeper. Capped as a Third Division player, a not unique occurrence though comparatively rare just the same. But to win 5 when so categorised recognised Matthews's talent. He was superb in anticipation and extremely courageous. He attended a rugby playing school and captained its XV, nonetheless taking to soccer and deemed good enough to represent the city's schools side. After leaving football he worked in a tractor factory.

MATTHEWS, (Sir) Stanley
(Stoke City and Blackpool, 1935-57, 54)
Born Hanley, Stoke-on-Trent, 1 February 1915.
1949: 5ft. 10ins.; 11st. 8lbs.

Career: Hanley Schools; Stoke St. Peter's; Stoke City amateur September 1930, turning professional February 1932 (guest player for Morton, Blackpool and other clubs during WW2); Blackpool May 1947 (£11,500); Stoke City again October 1961 (£2500); retired 1965. Port Vale general manager July 1965-July 1968 then acted in honorary advisory capacity; Hibernian FC (Malta) manager April 1970; coach in

Soweta, South Africa 1974-76. Other honours: England schoolboy international. Football League (13 apps). (Stoke C) FL Div. 2 champions 1933, 1963. (Blackpool) FA Cup winner 1953; finalist 1948, 1951.

Outside-right. Arguably the most famous name British football has produced. 'The Wizard of Dribble' enchanted spectators for well over a generation with his swerving, side stepping, dribbling magic. The Football Writers' 'Player of the Year' 1948 and '63 (and if that 15-year interval is noteworthy, how about the interval between his Division 2 championship medals?). Football's first knight (1965), he was also its first CBE (1957). Received an honorary degree at Keele University June 1987. Since 1969 has lived abroad in Malta and Canada.

MATTHEWS, Vincent
(Sheffield United, 1928, 2)
Born Oxford, 15 January 1896. Died 15 November 1950.
1928: 6ft.; 13st.

Career: St. Frideville FC; Oxford City; Bournemouth & Boscombe Athletic; Bolton Wanderers January 1923 (£1000); Tranmere Rovers cs 1925; Sheffield United cs 1927; Shamrock Rovers May 1931; Oswestry Town player/manager; Shrewsbury Town June 1935, Other honours: (Shamrock Rovers) FAI Cup winner 1932, 1933.

Centre-half. The traditional rugged pivot, well advantaged phsically and bringing these natural assets to bear. Something of a late developer – League debut at 27 and 32 when capped. Returned to Oxford in 1944, worked for Morris Motors at Cowley and coached the works team from 1948 until his death.

MAYNARD, William John
(1st Surrey Rifles, 1873-76, 2)
Born Camberwell, London, 18 March 1853. Died 2 September 1921.

Career: 1st Surrey Rifles; Wanderers 1880-81. Represented Surrey in 1877.

Goalkeeper/forward. Kept goal in the very first international and was possibly pressed into duty there because Alex. Morten, an original choice, was unable to play. We do know, however, about Maynard's prowess as a forward. He played on the wing, was fast and hard working, but at times delayed making his centres. Was District Registrar of Durham from 1903 to his death. His son, Alfred Frederick Maynard, who lost his life in the Great War, was an England RU internationalist.

MEADOWS, James
(Manchester City, 1955, 1)
Born Bolton, 21 July 1931.
1957: 6ft.; 12st. 1lb.

Career: Bolton YMCA; Southport amateur October 1948, turning professional February 1949; Manchester City March 1951; retired through injury October 1957. Manchester City training staff late 1959, head trainer August 1960-April 1965; Stockport County trainer/coach December 1965, manager October 1966-March 1969; Bury assistant manager July-September 1969; Blackpool assistant trainer October 1969, caretaker manager October 1970, assistant manager December 1970; Bolton Wanderers manager January-April 1971; Southport manager May 1971-December 1973; Stockport County manager May 1974-August 1975; subsequently had spells with Blackpool again (twice), coaching in Sweden and an appointment as assistant manager with the Kuwait Sporting Club. Other honours: Football League (1 app). (Man. City) FA Cup finalist 1955.

Right-back following early service at outside-right and centre-forward, and it was as a back that he made his international and

Cup final appearances. A direct, enthusiastic player, his speed was a bonus in defence as it had been in the attack. Sustained a bad knee injury in the 1955 final that eventually forced his retiral when only 26.

MEDLEY, Leslie Dennis
(Tottenham Hotspur, 1951-52, 6)
Born Lower Edmonton, London, 3 September 1920.
1951: 5ft. 7ins.; 11st. 3lbs.

Career: Edmonton Schools; Tottenham Hotspur amateur cs 1935, turning professional February 1939; emigrated to Canada October 1946 where he assisted Toronto Greenbacks and Ulster United (Toronto); returned to Spurs February 1948, remaining until May 1953 when he went back to Canada. Was player/coach to Randfontein FC, Johannesburg, 1958-61. Other honours: England schoolboy international. Football League (1 app). (Spurs) FL champions 1951. FL Div. 2 champions 1950.

Outside-left. Of the wandering kind, apt to show up anywhere. Possessed a good shot that was often exercised and formed a nifty wing with Eddie Baily (q.v.). Served in Canada with the RAF during WW2, where he met his wife, hence the journeyings between England and Canada.

MEEHAN, Thomas
(Chelsea, 1924, 1)

Born Harpurhey, Manchester, 1896. Died 18 August 1924.
1919: 5ft. 5ins.; 10st. 7lbs.

Career: Newtown; Walkden Central; Rochdale January 1917; Manchester United cs 1917 (during his time at Old Trafford went on loan to Atherton and also had a few more games for Rochdale); Chelsea December 1920 (£3300). Other honours: Football League (2 apps).

Left-half. Played on the other flank while on loan to Atherton. Tommy was constructive and stylish, a small bundle of energy undaunted by a slight physique, and extremely popular. His sadly untimely demise was the result of sleeping sickness.

MELIA, James
(Liverpool, 1963, 2)
Born Liverpool, 1 November 1937.
1963: 5ft. 8½ins.; 10st. 12lbs.

Career: Liverpool Schools; Liverpool FC ground staff 1953, turning professional November 1954; Wolverhampton Wanderers March 1964 (£55,000); Southampton December 1964 (£30,000); Aldershot player/coach November 1968 (£9000), player/manager April 1969-January 1972; Crewe Alexandra player/manager May 1972-December 1974; Southport manager July-September 1975; later that year was coaching in the Middle East then scouted for California Lasers, USA, subsequently working in a like capacity for Brighton & Hove Albion before serving as their manager March-October 1983. He afterwards managed a club in Portugal and then Stockport County July-November 1986. Other honours: England schoolboy international. England Youth International. Football League (1 app). (Liverpool) FL champions 1964. FL Div. 2 champions 1962.

Inside-left, latterly midfield. Both a schemer and a goal scorer when a forward, later putting his craft to good use as a half-back. Had stamina and always played at full stretch. Jimmy was fifth in a family of eleven. His brief Brighton managership took in the club's 1983 FA Cup final appearance.

MERCER, David William
(Sheffield United, 1923, 2)
Born St Helens, Lancs. 20 March 1893. Died 4 June 1950.
1925: 5ft. 7½ins.; 11st. 3lbs.

Career: Prescot Athletic; Skelmersdale; Hull City January 1914; Sheffield United December 1920 (£4500, then a record); Shirebrook November 1928; Torquay United June 1929; retired cs 1930. Other honours: Football League (1 app). (Sheffield U) FA Cup winner 1925.

Outside-right. Came into prominence in wartime soccer during an unbroken run of 200 games for Hull City (April 1914-April 1920), scoring impressively. David exhibited dazzling footwork and was a thorough craftsman. Partnered his brother, Arthur, during the Bramall Lane period and was father of Arthur jnr. (Torquay United, 1946-49).

MERCER, Joseph
(Everton, 1939, 5)
Born Ellesmere Port, Cheshire, 9 August 1914.
1939: 5ft. 9ins.; 11st.

Career: Ellesmere Port Schools; Cheshire Schools; Elton Green FC (Ince); Shell-Mex FC (Liverpool County Combination); Ellesmere Port Town (trials with Chester and Blackburn Rovers and played a few games for Runcorn); Everton on amateur forms 1931/32, turning professional September 1932 (guest player for Aldershot during WW2); Arsenal November 1946 (£7000); retired through injury cs 1955. Sheffield United manager August 1955; Aston Villa manager December 1958-July 1964; Manchester City manager July 1965 and then general manager October 1971; Coventry City general manager June 1972, and served as a director April 1975-July 1981. Other honours: England wartime international (19 apps). Football League (1 app). (Everton) FL champions 1939. (Arsenal) FL champions 1948, 1953. FA Cup winner 1950; finalist 1952.

Wing-half. A great personality with his infectious smile, spindly legs and, of course, massive footballing talent. Liked to take the ball through, releasing it unexpectedly; and defending strongly, employing a crisp tackle. The famous legs suffered some bad injuries and a double-fracture forced retirement (when nearly 41)

MERRICK, Gilbert Harold
(Birmingham City, 1952-54, 23)
Born Sparkhill, Birmingham, 26 January 1922.
1951: 6ft. 1in.; 13st.

Career: Birmingham Schools; Fenton Rovers; Shirley Juniors; Olton Sports; signed amateur forms for Solihull Town August 1939, later that month becoming a Birmingham professional; retired May 1960. Birmingham City manager June 1960-April 1964; Bromsgrove Rovers part-time manager early 1967; in the 1970s was managing Atherstone Town. Other honours: Football League (11 apps). (B'ham C) FL Div. 2 champions 1948, 1955. FA Cup finalist 1956.

Goalkeeper said to have styled himself on his illustrious Brum predecessor, Harry

Hibbs, and could hardly have had a better model. The result was a composed 'keeper whose quiet efficiency made his duties look simple. From 1964 was employed as the personnel manager of a Midlands stores group.

METCALFE, Victor
(Huddersfield Town, 1951, 2)
Born Barrow-in-Furness, 3 February 1922.
1951: 5ft. 8ins.; 11st.

Career: West Riding schoolboy football; Ravensthorpe Albion; Huddersfield Town amateur January 1940, turning professional December 1945; Hull City June 1958; retired February 1960. Huddersfield Town youth coach 1961-October 1964; Halifax Town coach/scout December 1964, manager June 1966-November 1967. Other honours: Football League (2 apps).

Outside-left. A Huddersfield wartime development who went on to play 434 peacetime League games for the club, scoring 87 goals in the course of them. Vic was a slippery customer with dexterous footwork and a potent shot. His father had played rugger for Yorkshire.

MEW, John William
(Manchester United, 1921, 1)
Born Sunderland, 30 March, 1889. Died 1963.
1922: 5ft. 9½ins.; 12st.

Career: Sunderland schoolboy football; Blaydon United (Northern Alliance) for 2 seasons, during which spell he was offered terms by Sunderland FC when 18; Marley Hill Colliery; Manchester United October 1912 after a month's trial; Barrow September 1926-cs 1927. Subsequently coached in Belgium and South America. Other honour: Football League (1 app).

Goalkeeper who had studied his craft to goodly effect, becoming expert in the narrowing of angles and a sound handler aided by strength of arm and wrist. Jack's studies had been long for he started as his school team's 'keeper when only 9. Conceded 15 goals only during the two Blaydon United campaigns. Toured South Africa with the 1920 FA party, playing once against their national team. He worked in a Manchester factory after leaving football. In the mid-1920s he was in a business partnership with Cecil Parkin, the Lancashire and England cricketer.

MIDDLEDITCH, Bernard
(Corinthians, 1897, 1)
Born Highgate, London, 1871. Died 3 October 1949.

Career: Cambridge University (Blue 1895); Corinthians 1895-1905.

Right-half. Educated privately and probably had some junior club experience before achieving the accolade of a Blue at Cambridge. The bulk of his 82 appearances for the Corinthians were made in the later 1890s when together with fellow England caps, C.Wreford-Brown and A. G. Henfrey, he formed a fine middle line. Middleditch, a shrewd half, worked hard, feeding his front line commendably. He was a schoolmaster by profession, holding appointments at University School, Hastings, 1895-1900, and then at two public schools, Malvern 1900-03 and Harrow from 1903 until his retirement in 1932.

MILBURN, John Edward Thompson
(Newcastle United, 1949-56, 13)
Born Ashington, Northumberland, 11 May 1924. Died 8 October 1988.
1951: 5ft. 11½ins.; 12st. 9lbs.

Career: Ashington ATC; Newcastle United August 1943; Linfield player/manager June 1957 (in exchange for another player); Yiewsley November 1960, appointed player/manager the following month; part time Reading coach cs 1962; Ipswich Town manager appointed January 1963 with effect from the following April-September 1964; had spell as Gateshead manager from November 1965. Other honours: Football League (3 apps). (Newcastle) FA Cup winner 1951, 1952, 1955. (Linfield) Irish Cup winner 1960; finalist 1958.

Outside-right/centre-forward. 'Wor Jackie', as he was universally known, will always be associated with Newcastle's FA Cup exploits of the 'Fifties. A tall, elegant player with blistering pace – a Powderhall sprinter – and shooting power, he was a right-winger until moved to the centre in 1947/48. Ulster's 'Footballer of the Year' 1958 and a Freeman of the City of Newcastle. Became a sports journalist in 1964. Remembering his speed, how appropriate the word formed by Jackie's initials!. A Tyneside folk hero, his passing was much lamented and received attention from the national media.

MILLER, G(eorge) Brian
(Burnley, 1961, 1)
Born Hapton nr. Burnley, 19 January 1937.
1961: 6ft. 0½ins.; 12st. 10lbs.

Career: Blackburn Schools; Burnley February 1954; retired through injury April 1968 and joined the club's coaching staff. Within a short time was appointed first team trainer, eventually becoming manager October 1979-January 1983. Began a second managerial spell July 1986, reverting in January 1989 to post of chief scout. Other honours: England Under-23 international (3 apps). Football League (2 apps). (Burnley) FL champions 1960. FA Cup finalist 1962.

Left-half and long time Turf Moor loyalist, able to take the other two half-back berths. A solid, hard tackling midfielder, excellent in backing-up his attack. Served an apprenticeship as a marine engineer in early senior days when a part time professional.

MILLER, Harold Sydney
(Charlton Athletic, 1923, 1)
Born Watford, 20 May 1902.
1924: 5ft. 7ins.; 10st. 6lbs.

Career: St Albans City; Charlton Athletic as an amateur January 1922, turning professional December 1922; Chelsea June 1923; Northampton Town cs 1939; retired during WW2.

Inside-left who successfully switched to left-half during season 1933/34, a thoughtful little player neat in style. Was a source of possible goal chances if no great scorer himself. Had two elder brothers, H E and R B Miller, both well known St Albans City performers and on Watford's books as amateurs, the former also being an English amateur internationalist.

MILLS, George Robert
(Chelsea, 1938, 3)
Born Deptford, London, 29 December 1908.
Died 15 July 1970.
1938: 6ft.; 12st. 9lbs.

Career: South-East London Schools; Emerald Athletic; Bromley; Chelsea on amateur forms November 1929, turning professional February 1930; retired during WW2 subsequently serving as Chelsea's 'A' team coach.

Inside-right/centre-forward. Enthusiastic and direct, he maintained an even level of goal scoring. For Chelsea netted 123 in 239 League and FA Cup encounters. Scored a hat-trick on his international debut (vs. Northern Ireland at Belfast, October 1937). Mills had to battle for a first-team place at Chelsea due to the club's several important inside- and centre-forward signings, and his highest seasonal League appearance total was only 32. Worked for a City printing firm.

MILLS, Michael Denis
(Ipswich Town, 1973-82, 42)
Born Godalming, Surrey, 4 January 1949.
1978: 5ft. 6ins.; 10st. 8lbs.

Career: Schoolboy football to Portsmouth's ground staff; Ipswich Town amateur August 1965, apprentice later that year and turning professional February 1966; Southampton November 1982 (£50,000); Stoke City player/manager July 1985. Other honours: England Youth international. England Under-23 international (5 apps). Football League (2 apps). (Ipswich) EUFA Cup winner 1981. FA Cup winner 1978.

Right/left-back. Sturdy little back, 17 years an Ipswich stalwart, released by Pompey when they dispensed with their reserve side. Needless to say, much to Ipswich's benefit, ever-reliable Mick for so long skippering club and country with quiet authority. His 588 League appearances (plus 3 substitutions) is a record for the Suffolk club. Awarded the MBE in the 1984 New Year's Honours list.

MILNE, Gordon
(Liverpool, 1963-65, 14)
Born Preston, Lancs. 29 March 1937.
1964: 5ft. $7^1/_2$ins.; 11st. 3lbs.

Career: Preston Amateurs; Morecambe; Preston North End January 1956; Liverpool August 1960 (£16,000); Blackpool May 1967 (£30,000); Wigan Athletic player/manager January 1970, also acting as the England Youth manager/coach from 1971; Coventry City manager June 1972, executive manager May 1981; Leicester City manager August 1982, general manager June 1986-1987; Besiktas FC (Turkey) manager later in 1987. Other honours: Football League (2 apps). (Liverpool) European Cup Winners' Cup finalist 1966. FL champions 1964, 1966. FL Div. 2 champions 1962.

Right-half. An ever-busy, compactly built midfielder of high skills. Much sought after in the managerial field after a successful introduction to the admin. side at Wigan. Gordon missed the 1965 FA Cup final through injury, a misfortune that had beset his father, Jimmy Milne of Preston North End, 27 years before.

MILTON, C(lement) Arthur
(Arsenal, 1952, 1)
Born Bedminster, Bristol, 10 March 1928.
1951: 5ft. $8^1/_2$ins.; 10st.

Career: Bristol schools football; Arsenal on amateur forms 1945, turning professional July 1946; Bristol City February 1955 for £4000, £2000 of which was refunded on his retirement the following July. Other honour: (Arsenal) FL champions 1953.

Outside-right pithily summed up as 'blond, fast and persistent'. He was certainly all of these things and his retiral when only 27 seemed premature to say the least. But perhaps the demands of cricket prevailed, for Arthur was a star of the summer game. He played for Gloucestershire 1948-74 (585 matches) and England (6 Tests, scoring a century in his first innings), and had a spell as Gloucester's skipper. Subsequently employed as a postman.

MILWARD, Alfred Weatherell
(Everton, 1891-97, 4)
Born Great Marlow, Bucks, 12 September 1870. Died 10 November 1934.
1895: 5ft. $8^1/_2$ins.; 12st.

Career: Sir William Borlase's Grammar School; Old Borlasians; Marlow; Everton 1888; New Brighton Tower cs 1897; Southampton May 1899; New Brompton cs 1901; retired 1903. Other honours: Football League (1 app). (Everton) FL champions 1891. FA Cup finalist 1893, 1897. (Soton) Southern League champions 1901. FA Cup finalist 1900.

Outside-left, half of the famed Chadwick/Milward wing that shone in the Saints' 1901 championship win in addition to the Goodison years. Alf, hefty as wingmen go, had skill and pace in plenty but his great attribute was an indomitable spirit – no cause seemd lost to him.

MITCHELL, Clement
(Upton Park, 1880-85, 5)
Born Cambridge, 20 February 1862. Died 6 October 1937.

Career: Felsted School (XI 1877-8-9, captain 1879); Upton Park; also represented Essex and London. A member of the Corinthians.

Centre-forward who scored prolifically thanks to fine shooting and positional know-how. And was not lacking in control or distribution skills either ('. . . but apt to play selfishly,' admonishes the Alcock Annual with its usual frankness). Mitchell was a competent cricketer – 8 matches for Kent 1890-92, after spending some years in India where, the 'Who's Who of Cricketers' records, 'he was a noted cricketer in Calcutta in the 1880s.'

MITCHELL, James Frederick
(Manchester City, 1925, 1)
Born Manchester, 18 November 1897. Died 30 May 1975.
1925: 6ft. 1in.; 13 st. 4lbs.

Career: Arnold Grammar School, Blackpool; Blackpool FC 1914/15; Northern Nomads; Manchester University; Preston North End October 1920; Manchester City May 1922; Leicester City October 1926-27. Other honours: England amateur international (6 apps). (PNE) FA Cup finalist 1922.

Goalkeeper. Big amateur famed in the 'Twenties not only for his goalkeeping but also because he played wearing spectacles. Employed a massive clearance kick and was notably athletic in action. This last is accounted for by athletic prowess: he represented England at the 1920 Olympics in the high jump event. For a time Mitchell was a master at his old school above, later joining the staff of the footwear chain, Stead & Simpson. HIs father was the amateur billiards champion of 1894.

MOFFAT, Hugh
(Oldham Athletic, 1913, 1)
Born Congleton, Cheshire, January 1885. Died 14 November 1952.
1911: 5ft. 10½ins.; 12st. 4lbs.

Career: Junior football to Burnley 1903; Oldham Athletic late in 1910. Other honours: Football League (2 apps).

Wing-half. On the left at Burnley and right for Oldham, this last to accommodate the long serving skipper and Scottish cap, David Wilson. Hugh could also turn in capable displays at full-back. But the middle line was his forte, where he showed accomplished attacking and defensive qualities in equal measure.

MOLYNEUX, George
(Southampton, 1902-03, 4)
Born Liverpool, 1875. died 14 April 1942.
1902: 5ft. 10ins.; 12st. 1lb.

Career: Kirkdale FC (Liverpool Junior League); Third Grenadiers; South Shore; Wigan County; Stoke 1897/98; Everton cs 1898; Southampton cs 1900; Portsmouth May 1905; Southend United cs 1906, subsequently assisting Colchester Town. Other honours: (Soton) Southern League champions 1901, 1903, 1904. FA Cup finalist 1902.

Left-back. In his day among the best headers of a ball in senior soccer. Had an ideal physique and all-round ability, especially in the quickness of his tackling. During a successful stint at The Dell had a number of partners – one of them was the celebrated C B Fry (q.v.).

MOON, William Robert
(Old Westminsters, 1888-91, 7)
Born Maida Vale, London, 27 June 1868. Died 9 January 1943.

Career: Westminster School (XI 1884-85); Old Westminsters; Corinthians 1886-1901. Also represented the London FA.

Goalkeeper without a superior in his heyday: resourceful, confident, courageous and quick with hands and feet. A useful wicket-keeper/batsman who twice assisted Middlesex in 1891, he would have made a bigger name at cricket if able to devote more time to the game. A solicitor by profession (admitted 1891) and partner in a firm practising in Bloomsbury. Brother of the Middlesex and England cricketer, L. J. Moon.

MOORE, Henry Thomas
(Notts County, 1883-85, 2)
Born Nottingham, 27 June 1861. Died 24 September 1939.

Career: Junior football to Notts County, for which club he played 1881-88.

Full-back, one of Notts County's several locally-born early caps. Stalwart in defence, quite reliable, sound tactically and confident with his kicking. Ran an off-licence in Nottingham, eventually retiring to Sudbury, Middlesex, where he died. His son, W H Moore, was on Notts County's books at the turn of the century. He, however, was more notable as a cricketer – on the Lords' ground staff and coach at St Paul's School 1909-14.

MOORE, James
(Derby County, 1923, 1)
Born Birmingham, 11 May 1889.
1925: 5ft. 6ins.; 10st. 6lbs.

Career: Quebec Albion (Handsworth, Birmingham); Glossop cs 1911; Derby County October 1913 (£1500); Chesterfield March 1926; retired cs 1927 but came out of retirement to assist Mansfield Town from November 1927 to the end of season 1927/28, and Worcester City from March 1929. Other honour: (Derby Co) FL Div. 2 champions 1915.

Inside-forward, mainly on the left but was inside-right in the Rams' 1914/15 championship line-up. Could be cited as a typical diminutive inside man with a complement of ball skills and a setter-up of goal chances. Jimmy, however, scored on his own account too, on one memorable occasion (vs. Crystal Palace, Christmas Day, 1922) netting 5.

MOORE, Robert Frederick Chelsea
(West Ham United, 1962-74, 108)
Born Barking, Essex, 12 April 1941.
1968: 6ft.; 12st. 13lbs.

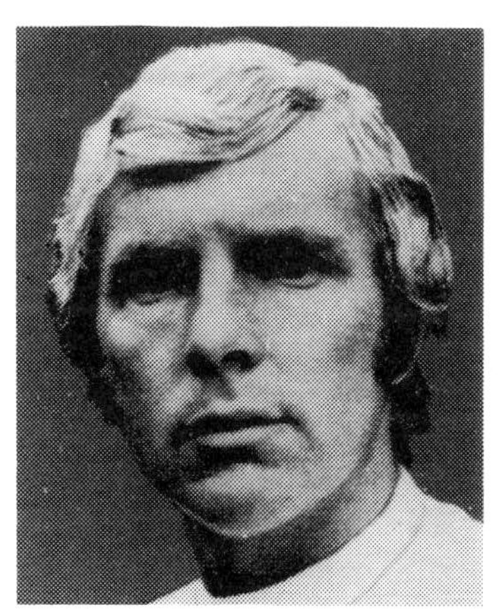

Career: Barking Schools; Leyton Schools; Woodford Youth Club; West Ham United amateur before turning professional June 1958; Fulham March 1974 (£25,000); retired May 1977, but had spell as player/

coach with Herning FC (Denmark) from February 1978. Oxford City manager December 1979-May 1981; Southend United chief executive August 1983, manager June 1984-April 1986. Other honours: England Youth international. England Under-23 international (8 apps). Football League (12 apps). (WHU) European Cup Winners' Cup, winner 1965. FA Cup winner 1964. FL Cup finalist 1966. (Fulham) FA Cup finalist 1975.

Left-half. One of the undying names, captaining his country to the 1966 World Cup triumph and among the greatest of English defensive players ever: ice-cool and a master strategist. A natural leader, he for long skippered both club and country and is said to be England's youngest. Bobby's list of achievements also include a record 18 caps for the England Youth team, the then record for West Ham senior appearances (642 League and Cup) and being 'Footballer of the Year' for 1964. His business interests include mens wear, sports goods and journalism. He was awarded the OBE in 1967.

MOORE, William Grey Bruce
(West Ham United, 1923, 1)
Born Newcastle-upon-Tyne, 6 October 1894. Died 26 September 1968.
1923: 5ft. 7ins.; 10st.

Career: Seaton Delaval; Sunderland as an amateur November 1912, turning professional during WW1; West Ham United May 1922; retired cs 1929, then becoming West Ham's assistant trainer, appointed head trainer 1932 and holding this appointment until his retirement May 1960. Other honours: England amateur international (4 apps). (WHU) FA Cup finalist 1923.

Inside-left. Made the vital link between two other celebrated Hammers – his partner, Jimmy Ruffell, and Vic Watson in the centre. Billy, a clever executant, set up countless openings for the pair. And he himself was not amiss in the scoring line, totalling 48 in 202 League and FA Cup encounters for the Upton Park club. His aggregate Hammers' service totted up to a meritorious 38 years.

MORDUE, John
(Sunderland, 1912-13, 2)
Born Edmondsley, Co Durham 1887. Died 14 December 1957.
1913: 5ft. 7ins.; 10st. 8lbs.

Career: Sacriston FC; Spennymoor United; Barnsley October 1906; Woolwich Arsenal April 1907 (£450); Sunderland May 1908; Middlesbrough May 1920; Durham City player/manager February 1923-February 1924. Other honours: Football League (3 apps). (Sunderland) FL champions 1913. FA Cup finalist 1913.
Outside-right/outside-left, his best known assignment in the former, partnering Charlie Buchan with Frank Cuggy, at right-half, completing a famous triangle. Jackie had great pace and his distribution commendably accurate. The most distinguished member of a noted North-Eastern soccer family, he later became one of the world's finest fives players.

MORICE, Charles John
(Barnes, 1872, 1)
Born Kensington, London, 27 May 1850. Died 17 June 1932.

Career: Harrow School; Harrow Chequers;

Barnes FC. Served on the FA Committee 1873-77.

Forward. 'Is wanting in weight, but there is little other fault to be found in his forward play,' the Football Annual for 1874 remarks. Which is borne out by other critics who favourably commented on Morice's speed and distributive skills. He was a member of the Stock Exchange.

MORLEY, Anthony William
(Aston Villa, 1982-83, 6)
Born Ormskirk, Lancs. 26 August 1954.
1982: 5ft. 8½ins.; 11st. 8½lbs.

Career: Junior football to Preston North End as an apprentice, turning professional September 1972; Burnley February 1976 (around £100,000); Aston Villa June 1979 (£220,000); West Bromwich Albion December 1983 (£70,000). Other honours: England Youth international. England 'B' international. England Under-23 international (1 app). (Villa) European Cup winner 1982. FL champions 1981.

Forward who has commanded big fees. Would likely have been labelled an outside-left in previous times. A very mobile and skilled player, able to take goal chances. Tony's most profitable spell, of course, was at Villa Park, with European Cup and League championship medals won, responding to the service of the gifted Gordon Cowans.

MORLEY, Herbert
(Notts County, 1910, 1)
Born Kiveton Park, Sheffield, October 1882. Died 15 July 1957.
1908: 6ft. 1in.; 13st. 4lbs.

Career: Kiveton Park FC; Grimsby Town August 1904; Notts County March 1907; retired during WW1 after which he scouted for Notts County. Other honour: (Notts Co) FL Div. 2 champions 1914.

Right-back. A fearless, dashing defender, the dash in no way lessened by a particularly large physique. Was extremely skilled and powerful with his headwork too. Is said to have actually been the innovator of the notorious offside trap that is generally ascribed to Bill McCracken (Newcastle United, 1904-23).

MORREN, Thomas
(Sheffield United, 1898, 1)
Born Sunderland, 1871. Died 31 January 1929.
1896: 5ft. 5¼ins.; 10st. 4lbs.

Career: Middlesbrough Victoria; Middlesbrough Ironopolis; Middlesbrough FC; Barnsley St Peter's; Sheffield United early 1896-cs 1904. Other honours: Football League (2 apps). (Middlesbro') FA Amateur Cup winner 1895. (Sheffield U) FL champions 1898. FA Cup winner 1899; finalist 1901.

Centre-half. A leading example of the diminutive first-class pivots who proliferated in pre-Great War days. Morren, tenacious and insistent, did his work well despite a disposition towards wandering. After leaving football was a Sheffield newsagent until his death.

MORRIS, Frederick
(West Bromwich Albion, 1920-21, 2)
Born Tipton, Staffs. 27 August 1893. Died 4 July 1962.
1922: 5ft. 8ins.; 11st. 7lbs.

Career: Staffordshire schoolboy football; Bell Street Primitives; Tipton Victoria; Redditch; West Bromwich Albion May 1911 (guest player for Fulham and Watford during WW1); Coventry City August 1924; Oakengates Town cs 1925; retired 1930. Other honours: Football League (1 app). (WBA) FL champions 1920.

Inside-left. A noted hard shooting marksman, he headed the League's scoring list in 1919/20 with 37 goals. Was brave, fast and neat in ball control. After leaving the game, worked in his native Tipton, where he died.

MORRIS, John
(Derby County, 1949-50, 3)
Born Radcliffe nr. Manchester, 27 September 1923.
1950: 5ft. $7^3/_4$ins.; 10st. 8lbs.

Career: Sunday school football; Mujacs FC, Manchester United's nursery side, August 1939, later turning professional (guest player for Charlton Athletic and Bolton Wanderers during WW2); Derby County March 1949 (£23,850, then a record); Leicester City October 1952 (£20,000); Corby Town as player/manager June 1958; Kettering Town cs 1961; Great Harwood manager cs 1964; Oswestry Town manager October 1967. Other honours: England 'B' international (1 app). Football League (5 apps). (Man. Utd) FA Cup winner 1948. (Leicester C) FL Div. 2 champions 1954, 1957.

Inside-right, later right-half also. An excellent dribbler difficult to dispossess because, although no heavyweight, he had a certain hardness. An aptitude for opening up a game was perhaps even more in evidence when at right-half. A nephew of Eddie Quigley, whose fee on joining Preston surpassed that paid by Derby for Johnny. Became a tyre salesman after leaving football.

MORRIS, William Walter
(Wolverhampton Wanderers, 1939, 3)
Born Handsworth, Birmingham, 26 March 1913.
1939: 5ft. 10ins.; 11st. 7lbs.

Career: Handsworth Schools; Handsworth Old Boys (trials with West Bromwich Albion): Halesowen Town; Wolverhampton Wanderers May 1933; retired cs 1947. Other honour: (Wolves) FA Cup finalist 1939.

Right-back eventually after being Wolves' centre-half until the emergence of Stan Cullis. Morris was in a fact a super utility man. He had made a reputation as a schoolboy outside-right, a position retained up to, and including the first stages of, a connection with Wolves 'A' team. There he appeared everywhere except in goal. A most resilient and mobile performer.

MORSE, Harold
(Notts County, 1879, 1)

Career: Initially played rugger for Derby Wanderers, later turning to soccer and assisting Notts County and Notts Rangers.

Left-back. A defender both strong and fast who utilised a hefty kick. The clearances, however, were not always well placed, their strength over-shooting his forwards. The Football Annual of 1881 reported that Morse 'used to play back, but played centre-foward last season and did not show to so much advantage in that position.'

NOTE: Is possibly Harold Morse whose birth was registered in Birmingham during the first quarter of 1860. If this is, in fact, the England cap, he was honoured as a teenager.

MORT, Thomas
(Aston Villa, 1924-26, 3)
Born Kearsley nr. Bolton, 1 December 1897. died 6 June 1967.
1924: 5ft. 8ins.; 11st. $9^1/_2$lbs.

Career: St Stephen's (Bolton), a Sunday School side; Newton Lads after leaving school; Army football during WW1; Altrincham 1918/19; Rochdale cs 1919; Aston Villa April 1922; retired cs 1935. Other honour: (Villa) FA Cup finalist 1924.

Left-back. Reliable, no believer in taking undue risks and owner of a particularly effective sliding tackle. Had a renowned partnership of many years with Tom Smart (q.v.), Mort's mobility ideally complementing the style of the more ponderous Smart. Mort's Great War service was with the Lancashire Fusiliers and he played for his battalion's team.

MORTEN, Alexander
(Crystal Palace, 1873, 1)

Career: N N (Kilburn) circa 1863-66; Crystal Palace (the original club) circa 1865-74. Wanderers circa 1865-72. He also represented Middlesex and London in the county matches. Served on the FA Committee 1874.

Goalkeeper in the year of his England appearance reputedly without a rival. Fine in temperament, withstanding the severest pressure with equanimity. The following year was said to be 'now almost retired from active service on the field, but as umpire is still held in the highest esteem.'

NOTE: He is thought to be the Alexander Morten who was born in Middlesex in 1831 or '32, and who died at Earl's Court on February 24, 1900, a Stock Exchange broker. If this is so, he easily claims the distinction of being England's oldest debutant.

MORTENSEN, Stanley Harding
(Blackpool, 1947-54, 25)
Born South Shields, 26 May 1921.
1950: 5ft. $9^1/_2$ins.; 11st. 7lbs.

Career: South Shields Ex-Schoolboys after local schools football; Blackpool April 1937 (guest player for Aberdeen during WW2); Hull City November 1955 (£2000); Southport February 1957; Bath City July 1958; retired May 1959 but came out of retirement to join Lancaster City November 1960, finally retiring March 1962. Blackpool manager February 1967-April 1969. Other honours: England 'B' international (1 app). England wartime international (2 apps). Football League (5 apps). (Blackpool) FA Cup winner 1953; finalist 1948, 1951.

Centre/inside-forward. A leading personality of the immediate post-war years. Famous for electrifying bursts of speed, the astonishing height reached when heading, and marksmanship. Appeared as a substitute for Wales in a wartime international. Served in the RAF as a bomber pilot during WW2 and after a crash it was thought he would never play football again. Happily for the game he recovered to accomplish great things. Later went into business in Blackpool.

MORTON John
(West Ham United, 1938, 1)
Born Sheffield, 26 February 1914. Died 8 March 1986
1938: 5ft. 9ins.; 10st. 4lbs.

Career: Sheffield schoolboy football; Woodhouse Alliance FC (Sheffield); Gainsborough Trinity as a professional cs 1931; West Ham United December 1931 (£600); retired during WW2. Other honour: Football League (1 app).

Outside-right/outside-left. Occasionally inside-forward. Snapped up by West Ham at 17 after a few months Midland League fare and as a professional, In some quarters it was felt he might be too frail for the big time but such misgivings were unfounded. John had plenty of tricks and was an excellent shot. After leaving football worked as a bookmaker in the East End.

MOSFORTH, William
(Sheffield Wednesday and Sheffield Albion, 1877-82, 9)
Born Sheffield, 1858. Died 11 July 1929.
Career: Assisted 3 Sheffield clubs (Hallam, Heeley and Providence) before joining Sheffield Wednesday from Ecclesfield; Sheffield Albion 1878; Sheffield Wednesday again cs 1880; Sheffield United cs 1889. Represented the Sheffield FA.

Outside-left. Billy, said that ace journalist, J A H Catton, was 'the pocket Hercules of his day, who used to rush along the wing with tongue protruding from the left corner of his mouth ... possibly no Sheffielder has earned such fame.' This was written in 1897 and several footballers hailing from the steel city have earned equal renown since. But there is little doubt Mosforth was unusually gifted with his wily dribbles and wonderful 'screw' kick. Is said to have figured in Sheffield United's very first line-up.

MOSS, Frank
(Arsenal, 1934-35, 4)
Born Leyland, Lancs. 5 November 1909.
Died 7 February 1970.
1932: 5ft. 9½ins.; 11st. 6lbs.

Career: Lostock Hall; Leyland Motors; Preston North End on amateur forms October 1927, turning professional February 1928; Oldham Athletic May 1929; Arsenal November 1931 (£3000); retired through injury cs 1936. Heart of Midlothian manager March 1937 – 1940 when called up for war service. Other honours: Football League (2 apps). (Arsenal) FL champions 1933, 1034, 1935. FA Cup finalist 1932.

Goalkeeper. As the 1952 club history ('Forward, Arsenal!') said 'agile and fearless, he had a splendid sense of anticipation'. The same paragraph concluded the title of best-ever Arsenal 'keeper 'might undeniably be his if a shoulder injury had not ended his career prematurely.' At the time of his death Moss was employed as a licensee at Chorley, Lancs. He had once worked as a driller at Leyland Motors.

MOSS, Frank
(Aston Villa, 1922-24, 5)
Born Aston, Birmingham, 17 April 1895.
Died 15 September 1965.
1920: 5ft. 11ins.; 11st. 4lbs.

Career: Birmingham Schools; Walsall when only 15; Aston Villa February 1914 (£250); Cardiff City January 1929; Bromsgrove Rovers as player/manager cs 1929, subsequently playing 2 seasons with Worcester City before retiring. Other honours: Football League (2 apps). (Villa) FA Cup winner 1920; finalist 1924.

Wing-half. A king-pin on both flanks in the early 'Twenties, skippering club and country finely. Stood out with his blond hair, athletic bearing and easy mastering of half-back arts. Latterly licensee of a Worcester hostelry for 35 years. His two sons, Frank jnr. and Amos, played for Villa, the former making around 300 senior peacetime appearances, 1938 – 56.

MOSSCROP, Edwin
(Burnley, 1914, 2)
Born Southport, 16 June 1892. Died 14 March 1980.
1914: 5ft. 7ins.; 9st. 10lbs.

Career: Blowick FC (Southport); Shepherd's Bush (during which spell he represented Middlesex); Southport YMCA; Southport Central; Burnley on amateur forms cs 1912, signing professional September 1912 (guest player for Reading during WW1); retired on health grounds November 1922. Other honours: Football League (2 apps). (Burnley) FL champions 1921. FA Cup winner 1914.

Outside-left. Only small and light yet a polished forward showing speed and guile. 'A crafty winger, he adds to the tone of the game, and his skill is most marked,' a local reporter wrote a few months prior to Mosscrop's retirement. (Regarding this retiral and its reason, it is interesting to note the player attained a grand old age). A school teacher by profession, employed in Manchester and then his native town.

MOZLEY, Bert
(Derby County, 1950, 3)
Born Derby, 21 September 1923.
1950: 5ft. 9ins.; 12st. 2lbs.

Career: Derby Schools; Shelton United (Nottingham Forest amateur early in 1944); Derby County March 1945; emigrated to Canada January 1955. Other honour: Football League (1 app).

Right-back and a speedy one, reckoned to be almost as quick as Laurie Scott (q.v.). Speed did not adversely affect other necessary qualities for he was cool and steady too, and had high distributive skills. Toured Canada with the 1950 FA party. (Which influenced Bert's later permanent removal to the land of the maple leaf?)

MULLEN, James
(Wolverhampton Wanderers, 1947-54, 12)
Born Newcastle-upon-Tyne, 6 January 1923. Died October 1987.
1950: 5ft. 10ins.; 11st 4lbs.

Career: Newcastle Schools; Wolverhampton Wanderers' ground staff July 1937, turning professional January 1940; retired cs 1960. Other honours: England schoolboy international. England wartime international (2 apps) England 'B' international (3 apps). Football League (1 app). (Wolves) FL champions 1954, 1958, 1959. FA Cup winner 1949.

Outside-left. Originally a boy prodigy with First Division appearances at 16, and thought to be the youngest ever to play in a Cup semi-final (not long after his 16th birthday). Jimmy, big for a wingman and fast moving, loved to cut in and exercise his marksmanship. Scored 99 goals for Wolves in the course of 448 League outings. Became a sports shop proprietor in Wolverhampton.

MULLERY, Alan Patrick
(Tottenham Hotspur, 1965-72, 35)
Born Notting Hill, London, 23 November 1941.
1968: 5ft. 9ins.; 12st. 4lbs.

Career: Middlesex Schools; London Schools: Fulham ground staff June 1957, turning professional December 1958; Tottenham Hotspur March 1964 (£72,500); Fulham again, on loan March-April 1972, signing permanently July 1972 (£65,000);

retired May 1976. Brighton & Hove Albion manager July 1976-June 1981; Charlton Athletic manager July 1981; Crystal Palace manager June 1982-May 1984; Queen's Park Rangers manager June-December 1984; Brighton & Hove manager again 1986-January 1987. Other honours: England Under-23 international (3 apps). Football League (2 apps). (Spurs) Inter-Cities Fairs Cup winner 1972. FA Cup winner 1967, FL Cup winner 1971. (Fulham) FA Cup finalist 1975.

Right-half. Of all-round excellence – brainy, an incisive tackler with attacking flair, and a tactician. 'Footballer of the year' 1975 and awarded the MBE in 1976. After leaving the Brighton managership for the second time took an appointment with an insurance company and additionally, in August 1987, became part-time manager of Southwick FC (Sussex), leaving two months later.

NEAL, Philip George
(Liverpool, 1976-84, 50)
Born Irchester, Northants. 20 February 1951.
1980: 5ft. 11ins.; 12st. 2lbs.

Career: Irchester FC; Northampton Town apprentice July 1967, turning professional December 1968; Liverpool October 1974 (£66,000); Bolton Wanderers as player/manager December 1985. Other honours: (Liverpool) European Cup winner 1977, 1978, 1981, 1984; finalist 1985. UEFA Cup winner 1976. FL champions 1976, 1977, 1979, 1980, 1982, 1983, 1984. FA Cup finalist 1977. FL Cup winner 1981, 1982, 1983, 1984; finalist 1978.

Right-back. Extraordinarily consistent – and injury-free – missing only one League match in the 10 seasons 1975/76 to 1984/85, the solitary absence occuring in 1983/84. Phil became an integral part of a great club side, the essence of soundness and a master of the attacking full-back game.

NEEDHAM, Ernest ('Nudger')
(Sheffield United, 1894-1902, 16)
Born Newbold Moor, Chesterfield, 21 January 1873. Died 8 March 1936.
1901: 5ft. 5$^{1}/_{2}$ins.; 10st. 8lbs.

Career: Waverley FC (Staveley); Staveley Wanderers 1889; Staveley Town 1890/91; Sheffield United April 1891; retired 1913. Other honours: Football League (10 apps). (Sheffield U) FL champions 1898. FA Cup winner 1899, 1902; finalist 1901.

Left-half. A great pre-1914 player, called 'the prince of half-backs', and indeed one of the greatest of all time. Short yet solidly built and blessed with immense stamina, he was fast, resolute and brave. Had a brother and nephew who also were professionals. A Derbyshire cricketer 1901-12 who once scored 2 centuries in a match (vs. Essex at Leyton in 1908). Later a steel worker.

NEWTON, Keith Robert
(Blackburn Rovers and Everton, 1966-70, 27)
Born Manchester, 23 June 1941.
1968: 5ft. 11ins; 11st. 2lbs.

Career: Manchester Schools 'B'; Ryder Brow Boys Club (Gorton); Spurley Hey Youth Club (Manchester); Blackburn Rovers amateur, turning professional October 1958; Everton December 1969 (£80,000); Burnley June 1972; retired May 1978 but subsequently played in non-League football. Other honours: England Under-23 international (3 apps). Football League (5 apps). (Burnley) FL Div. 2 champions 1973.

Right/left back, occasionally wing-half. Could take either full-back berth with equal facility, a creative defender never lacking in resolution. Hit a bad patch in the season prior to leaving Goodison but shone brightly again for Burnley. In fact he made over 200 League appearances while at Turf Moor, still a 'regular' into his mid-thirties.

NICHOLLS, John
(West Bromwich Albion, 1954, 2)
Born Wolverhampton, 3 April 1931.
1957: 5ft. 9ins.; 11st.

Career: Wolverhampton schoolboy football; Heath Town Wesley; Heath Town United (Wolverhampton Wanderers amateur); West Bromwich Albion amateur August 1950, turning professional August 1951; Cardiff City May 1957; Exeter City November 1957 (about £4000); Worcester City June 1959; Wellington Town February 1961; Oswestry Town cs 1961; Sankey's FC (Wellington) 1961/62, finishing his career with H Meadows FC and Red Dragon (West Bromwich League). Other honours: England 'B' international (1 app). England Under-23 international (1 app). (WBA) FA Cup winner 1954.

Inside-forward. Chiefly noted for goal poaching proclivities, the player instinctively arriving on the right spot at the right time. This attribute brought him 83 goals in an aggregate 195 League matches (his time in the first-class game was only 8 years). Johnny's best spell – at The Hawthorns – took in a fine spearhead partnership with Ronnie Allen (q.v.)

NICHOLSON, William Edward

(Tottenham Hotspur, 1951, 1)
Born Scarborough, 26 January, 1919.
1951: 5ft. 9ins.; 11st. 8lbs.

Career: Scarborough Working Men's Club Juniors; Tottenham Hotspur amateur March 1936, developing with Northfleet and signing as a professional August 1938 (guest player for Sunderland, Middlesbrough and Newcastle United during WW2); retired 1955. There followed a succession of appointments with Spurs: coaching staff 1955, assistant manager August 1957 and manager October 1958-August 1974; West Ham United consultant August 1975; returned to Spurs in an administrative role July 1976. Other honours: England 'B' international (4 apps). Football League (1 app). (Spurs) FL champions 1951. FL Div. 2 champions 1950.

Right-half mainly though he played a fair game as pivot, was inside-right at Scarborough and left-back in pre-war League games. An ultra-reliable performer, hard though fair, while his length of service at Tottenham shows a super club man. Bill found more fame behind the scenes. Under his managership Spurs won a League championship, the FA Cup three times, the League Cup twice and two European competitions. He paid large transfer fees but rarely made a poor deal, achieving blends that delighted crowds besides winning trophies.

NISH, David John

(Derby County, 1973-74, 5)
Born Burton-on-Trent, 26 September 1947.
1972: 5ft. 11ins.; 11st. 3lbs.

Career: Coalville Junior Boys; Measham Imperial; Leicester City July 1966; Derby County August 1972 (£225,000, then a British record); Tulsa Roughnecks, USA February 1979 (£10,000); Seattle Sounders, USA, 1980; Shepshed Charterhouse (Midland League) April 1982, later joining Middlesbrough as youth team coach. Other honours: England Youth international. England Under-23 international (10 apps). Football League (5 apps). (Leicester) FL Div. 2 champions 1971. FA Cup finalist 1969. (Derby Co.) FL Champions 1975.

Left-back with a delicacy unusual in a back, finding his man in skilled fashion by a glancing or direct pass, either variety unerringly placed. His Derby period was clouded by illness and operations on a knee. Led Leicester at Wembley in 1969 when only 21, and regarded as the youngest FA Cup final skipper ever.

NORMAN, Maurice

(Tottenham Hotspur, 1962-65, 23)
Born Mulbarton, Norfolk, 8 May 1934.
1963: 6ft. 1ins.; 12st. 2lbs.

Career: Norfolk Schools; Mulbarton FC; Wymondham Minors; Norwich City on amateur forms 1951, turning professional September 1952; Tottenham Hotspur November 1955 (£17,250 plus another player); retired through injury 1967. Other honours: England Under-23 international (3 apps). Football League (1 app). (Spurs) European Cup Winners Cup, winner 1963. FL champions 1961. FA Cup winner 1961, 1962.

Centre-half was where the honours were won but he had a substantial spell at right-back too. Tall, commanding and unflurried, Norman naturally shone at headwork and loved to join in an attack. After his enforced retirement was assistant manager at a north London garage, later, with his wife, opening a wool etc. shop at Frinton-on-Sea, and also working as a gardener there.

NUTTALL, Henry
(Bolton Wanderers, 1928-29, 3)
Born Bolton, 9 November 1897. Died April 1969.
1926: 5ft. $8^3/_4$ins.; 10st. 8lbs.

Career: Bolton St. Mark's (a Sunday school side); Fleetwood; Bolton Wanderers December 1920; Rochdale May 1932; Nelson August 1933. Joined Bolton Wanderers' staff 1935, serving in various capacities (e.g. was assistant trainer for some time from July 1946) until retiring in 1964. Other honours: (Bolton W) FA Cup winner 1923, 1926, 1929.

Wing-half. Thoughtful, consistent half-back – '. . . a master of positional play and a student of football moves' in the words of a 1929 annual. Shone in attacking manoeuvres. Harry was the most loyal of Trotters too, serving the club some 40 years, and he was actually born in a cottage within Burnden Park's confines. Son of Jack Nuttall, once Bolton Wanderers' trainer, who held a like appointment with Manchester United at one time.

OAKLEY, William John
(Oxford University and Corinthians, 1895-1901, 16)
Born Shrewsbury, 27 April 1873. Died 20 September 1934.
1901: 6ft.; 11st. 7lbs.

Career: Shrewsbury School (XI 1887-92, captain '92'); Oxford University (Blue 1893-4-5-6); Corinthians 1894-1903 (co-secretary 1898-1902); Casuals.

Right/left-back. Strong in both feet and among the speediest defenders of his day. Not the least useful trait was a capacity for the acrobatic clearance. Also famous in athletics. President of the Oxford University Athletic Club 1895, represented the University 1893-96, won the AAA long jump 1894 and represented England vs. USA in 1895 at this event and in the hurdles. A school master by profession (MA (Oxon)), he was joint headmaster from 1902 with G O Smith (q.v.) of the Ludgrove Preparatory School, the pair also sharing the Corinthians' secretaryship and the writing of a book, 'Association Football'. Oakley rowed for Shrewsbury School and at Oxford appeared in the trial eights. Lost his life as a result of a motor accident.

O'DOWD, J(ames) Peter
(Chelsea, 1932-33, 3)
Born Halifax, 26 February 1908. Died 8 May 1964.
1932: 6ft.; 11st. 6lbs.

Career: Bradford schoolboy football; Apperley Bridge (Bradford League); Selby Town (Bradford on amateur forms late 1926); Blackburn Rovers as a professional December 1926; Burnley March 1930 (£3000); Chelsea November 1931 (£5250, then reported a record for a centre-half); Valenciennes FC, France, September 1935 (nearly £3000); Torquay United March 1937, retiring soon afterwards through breaking a leg in a trial match. Other honour: Football League (1 app).

Centre-half. With a fair experience at wing-half too. A fine natural talent – cool, skilful, always it seemed having time to spare and extremely intelligent. Among the most prominent of British players attracted to French football in the 'Thirties. Around this time Peter had a drapery business in Weybridge.

OGILVIE, Robert Andrew Muter Macindoe
(Clapham Rovers, 1874, 1)
Born London, 1852. Died 7 March 1938.

Career: Brentwood School; Upton Park 1871-73; Clapham Rovers. Served on the FA Committee 1874-81 and 1884-86. Other honours: (Clapham Rovers) FA Cup winner 1880; finalist 1879.

Full-back. 'Fair back; not always certain; works hard throughout,' reported Alcock's Football Annual with its usual pithy 'warts and all' comment. Ogilvie sometimes appeared as a half-back. He was a member of

Lloyds, chairman of the Institute of Lloyds Underwriters 1910-11 and underwriter of the Alliance Assurance Coy. to 1914. Served with the War Risks Department 1914-19.

O'GRADY, Michael
(Huddersfield Town and Leeds United, 1963-69, 2)
Born Leeds, 11 October 1942.
1966: 5ft. 9ins. 11st.

Career: Leeds schoolboy football: Huddersfield Town amateur, turning professional October 1959; Leeds United October 1965 (£20-30,000); Wolverhampton Wanderers September 1969 (£80,000) (Birmingham City on month's loan February 1972); Rotherham United November 1972 (about £5000)-1974. Other honours: England Under-23 international (3 apps). Football League (3 apps). (Leeds U) Inter-Cities Fairs Cup winner 1968; finalist 1967. FL champions 1969.

Outside-left. Later as successful on the opposite wing and, for Wolves, played inside too. Quickly came to notice as a youngster, his pace and incisiveness making for a crowd-pleasing performer. Not surprisingly, the son of an Irish father.

OLIVER, Leonard Frederick
(Fulham 1929, 1)
Born Fulham, 1 August 1905. Died August 1967.
1925: 5ft. 9ins. 11st. 2lbs.

Career: Fulham Schools; Alma Athletic 1920; Tufnell Park early in 1924; Fulham on amateur forms cs 1924, turning professional cs 1925; retired cs 1935. Cliftonville (Belfast) coach 1937 to the War; Arlesey Town (Herts) coach for a spell from 1947. Other honour: (Fulham) FL Div. 3 (South) champions 1932.

Right-half, occasionally centre-half. A highly efficient performer and a consistent one, averaging 37 League games per season in his 11 years at Craven Cottage. In 7 of these he clocked in 40 or more and for a like number of campaigns was skipper. Len served as an Army PTI during WW2, after which he lived at Letchworth, Herts, for the rest of his life. Before taking up football full time, he had been employed as a clerk in a West End store.

OLNEY, Benjamin Albert
(Aston Villa, 1928, 2)
Born Holborn, London, 30 March 1899. Died September 1943.
1929: 6ft. 1in.; 13st. 12lbs.

Career: Fairley's Athletic (Birmingham works team) before and after WW1 during which he played Army football: Aston Park Rangers (in this spell signed amateur forms for Brierley Hill Alliance); Stourbridge as a semi-professional; Derby County April 1921 (£900); Aston Villa December 1927; Bilston United July 1930; Walsall August 1931; Shrewsbury Town August 1932 – cs 1933. Later with Moor Green.

Goalkeeper. Secured by Derby following an impressive display for the Birmingham FA in a 'junior international' against Scotland. Powerfully built, possessing fine anticipation and consistent to a degree. Moved to the Birmingham area when 10, hence the early connection with West Midlands minor soccer.

OSBORNE, Frank Raymond
(Fulham and Tottenham Hotspur, 1923-26, 4)

Born Wynberg, South Africa, 14 October 1896. Died 8 March 1988.
1925: 5ft. 11½ins.; 10st. 7lbs

Career: Bromley 1919; Fulham as a professional November 1921; Tottenham Hotspur January 1924; Southampton June 1931; retired cs 1933. A Fulham director from March 1935, he became that club's manager September 1948, general manager 1950 and retiring October 1964.

Outside-right/centre-forward. A slim physique seemed to accentuate the grace of this stylish player, who came to England in 1911 when a teenager. Netted 96 goals in his 292 League outings with Fulham, Spurs and Southampton. Elder brother of Reg. Osborne below, their father was an officer in the RAMC.

OSBORNE, Reginald
(Leicester City, 1928, 1)
Born Wynberg, South Africa, 23 July 1898. Died 1977.
1927: 5ft. 10½ins.; 11st. 2lbs.

Career: Army football (RAMC); Watling Street Boot Coy. FC (Leicester); Leicester City on amateur forms February 1923, shortly afterwards turning professional; retired cs 1933 but joined Folkestone the following November. Other honours: England amateur international (2 apps). (Leicester C) FL Div. 2 champions 1925.

Left-back. An all-round defender ('. . . fearless in his tackling, speedy in recovery, and a sure kick'). Played for the Army in representative matches which brought him to the notice of the England amateur selectors. He had joined the Army as a boy and served throughout the 1914/18 War. Brother of Frank Osborne above.

OSGOOD, Peter Leslie
(Chelsea, 1970-74)

Born Windsor, 20 February 1947.
1972: 6ft. 2ins.; 12st. 10lbs.

Career: Spital Old Boys (Windsor); Windsor Corinthians; Chelsea amateur March 1964, turning professional the following August; Southampton March 1974 (£240,000) (Norwich City on month's loan November 1976); Philadelphia Fury, USA, December 1977 (about £50,000); Chelsea again December 1978 (£25,000); retired September1979. Other honours: England Youth international. England Under-23 international (6 apps). Football League (3 apps).(Chelsea) European Cup winners' Cup, winner 1971.FA Cup winner 1970. FL Cup finalist 1972. (Soton) FA Cup winner 1976.

Centre-forward. Very gifted player, a two-footed marksman excellent in ball control and a personality. Roamed to some effect. Originally a bricklayer, since leaving the game Peter has been employed as a Windsor licencee, a coach at Butlin's Holiday Camps and, from June 1986, Portsmouth FC's youth coach.

OSMAN, Russell Charles
(Ipswich Town, 1980-84, 11)
Born Repton, Derbys. 14 February 1959.
1982: 6ft.; 11st. 10lbs.

Career: Juvenile football; Ipswich Town apprentice 1974, turning professional March 1976; Leicester City July 1985 (£220,000); Southampton June 1988 (£325,000). Other honours: England Youth international. England 'B' international. England Under-21 international (7 apps). (Ipswich T) UEFA Cup winner 1981.

Central defender. Two-footed, quick to intercept and sound tactically. At Ipswich operated on the right side, his friend, Terry Butcher, taking the left. Once deemed too casual but this foible was obviated by maturity. Skippered England Schools at rugby – he was then at a rugger-playing institution, Burton-on-Trent Grammar School. Son of Rex Osman, himself a Youth international and at one time on the books of Derby County.

OTTAWAY, Cuthbert John
(Oxford University, 1873-74, 2)
Born Dover, 20 July 1850. Died 2 April 1878.

Career: Eton College; Oxford University (Blue 1874 when he was captain); Old Etonians. Served on the FA Committee 1872-73. Other honours: (Oxford University) FA Cup winner 1874; finalist 1873. (Old Etonians) FA Cup finalist 1875 (first game only).

Forward. 'Is an excellent forward, being fast and very skilful in piloting the ball,' observed Alcock in 1874. Ottaway was also an examplar of the gifted multi-sport amateur that later brought celebrity to C B Fry, Max Woosnam et al. He was a cricket Blue 1870-73, also assisting Kent and Middlesex. He won the Public Schools rackets doubles championship 1868 and '69, a sport at which he represented Oxford University, as he did at Real Tennis and Athletics. Despite all this sporting activity, he left Oxford with a First to become a barrister (called to the Bar 1876). It is hard to imagine anyone achieving more in such a tragically brief life. 'He whom the gods favour dies young.'

OWEN, (Revd.) John Robert Blayney
(Sheffield Club, 1874, 1)
Born Reading, 1848. Died 13 June 1921.

Career: Queen's College, Oxford (before the institution of the 'Varsity match); Sheffield Club; Maldon FC (Essex). Also represented the Sheffield Association, Nottinghamshire and Essex.

Forward. Received unstinted praise at the time of his international – e.g. 'a wonderfully fine forward in every respect, and when playing with his own club invariably scores well.' Showed plenty of pace but was no individualist, best responding to strong support. Owen was ordained in 1876 and held the following scholastic appointments: Second Master of Trent College 1872-81, Master of Hawkshead Grammar School 1881-83 and Headmaster of Trent College 1883-90. He then gave up academic life and was Vicar of Toftrees, Norfolk, 1890-1905 and Rector of Bradwell-on-Sea, Essex, 1905-21.

OWEN, Sydney William
(Luton Town, 1954, 3)
Born Birmingham, 29 September 1922.
1957: 6ft.; 11st. 10lbs.

Career: Birmingham junior football; Birmingham City October 1945; Luton Town June 1947 (£1500); retired May 1959. Luton Town manager April 1959-April 1960; Leeds United coach May 1960-October 1975; Birmingham City assistant manager October 1975-September 1977; Hull City first team coach December 1977-February 1978; Manchester United youth coach May 1978-cs 1981, rejoining that club August 1982 as part-time scout etc. Other honours: Football League (2 apps). (Luton T) FA Cup finalist 1959.

Centre-half. A conversion from left-half not long after transferring to Luton. A commanding pivot, naturally commanding in the air, and an inspiring captain. Proved a wonderful servant at Kenilworth Road, clocking up 388 League appearances. 'Footballer of the Year' 1959, he went on several FA tours abroad. Turned out a first-class coach also, his work having a considerable bearing on Leeds United's rise to eminence in the 1960s. A fitness zealot and man of character.

PAGE, Louis Antonio
(Burnley, 1927-28, 7)
Born Kirkdale, Liverpool, 27 March 1899.
Died 12 October 1959.
1927: 5ft. 7½ins.; 11st 9lbs.

Career: Liverpool City Schools; Sudley Juniors; South Liverpool; Stoke cs 1919; Northampton Town cs 1922; Burnley May 1925 (a transfer that involved Jack Tresadern, q.v., moving to Northampton); Manchester United March 1932; Port Vale October 1932; Yeovil & Petters United player/manager July 1933-cs 1935. Newport County manager June 1935-September 1937; Glentoran trainer/coach December 1938; Swindon Town manager July 1945-May 1953; Chester manager June 1953-June 1956; subsequently a Leicester City scout. Other honour: Football League (1 app).

Outside-left. A potent force able to take the inside and centre-forward berths too. In his first outing leading the attack (vs. Birmingham, 4 April 1926) sensationally scored a double hat-trick, 3 goals in each half. 'Is very speedy, being a winger who moves near goal dangerously, and makes the most of his opportunities,' a critic of 1926 reported. Louis had three brothers, all soccer pros, and was a baseball internationalist.

PAINE, Terence Lionel
(Southampton, 1963-66, 19)
Born Winchester, 23 March 1939.
1966: 5ft. 8ins.; 10st. 6lbs.

Career: Winchester Schools; Winchester Corinthians; Winchester City (trials with Arsenal and Portsmouth); Southampton amateur August 1956, turning professional February 1957; Hereford United as player/coach July 1974; retired 1977. Cheltenham Town manager 1977-79. Went briefly to South Africa April 1980 to coach Johannesburg schoolboys, and he later returned to continue coaching there. Other honours: England Under-23 international (4 apps). Football League (5 apps). (Soton) FL Div. 3 champions 1960. (Hereford) FL Div. 3 champions 1976.

Outside-right, sometimes inside-right. Fast, strong in both feet and a schemer. And of outstanding durability: he passed Jimmy Dickinson's FL match total in October 1975 and eventually aggregated 815 plus 9 substitutions (168 goals). Has had a number of interests outside the game. Was a Conservative town councillor for Southampton 1969-71, proprietor of a cafe and a greengrocery business, a property owner and a Cheltenham licensee. Awarded the MBE in 1977.

PALLISTER, Gary A.
(Middlesbrough, 1988, 1)
Born Ramsgate, 30 June 1965.
1988: 5ft. 10ins.; 11st. 11lbs.

Career: Billingham Town; Middlesbrough 1985 (Darlington on loan October-November 1985).

Central defender. A leading light in the remarkable Middlesbrough rise from relegation (and possible extinction) to Division 3 to top flight status in the space of 2 years. Gary, too, had a notable personal rise by gaining England selection in less than 3 years from making his League debut. As the England manager, Bobby Robson, remarked in April 1988, Gary is '. . . quick on his feet, good in the air and has the right temperament.'

PANTLING, H(arry) Harold
(Sheffield United, 1924, 1)
Born Leighton Buzzard, Beds. 1891. Died 21 December 1952.
1925: 5ft. 8½ins.; 11st.

Career: Junior football to Watford as an amateur 1908, turning professional cs 1911; Sheffield United March 1914; Rotherham United cs 1926; Heanor Town November 1927. Other honour: FA Cup winner 1925.

Right-half excelling in distribution, his long and short passes, nicely weighted, reaching the intended colleague with telling precision. Consistent with his capabilities too, averaging 35 League outings for Sheffield United in the first half-dozen post-WW1 seasons. After leaving football, Pantling was a Sheffield licensee to his death.

PARAVICINI, Percy John de
(Old Etonians, 1883, 3)
Born London, (Kensington) 15 July 1862. Died 11 October 1921.

Career: Eton College (XI 1880-81); Cambridge University (Blue 1883); Old Etonians; Windsor; Corinthians 1884/85 season. Also represented the Berks & Bucks FA. Served on the FA Committee 1885. Other honours: (Old Etonians) FA Cup winner 1882; finalist 1883.

Full-back dexterous with each foot – was on the left flank for the above Cup finals and the right in his three internationals. This facility, together with great speed, made him one of the 1880s' best defenders. A first-rate cricketer: Cambridge Blue 1882-3-4-5, Middlesex (62 matches 1881-92) and Buckinghamshire. His brother, H F de Paravicini, assisted the MCC 1882-85. P J de Paravicini was created a MVO in 1908 and a CVO in the year of his death.

PARKER, Thomas Robert
(Southampton, 1925, 1)
Born Peartree Green, Southampton, 19 November 1897. Died 1 November 1987.
1927: 5ft. 10$^1/_4$ins.; 12st. 6lbs.

Career: Assisted two Sholing (Southampton) sides, Rangers and Athletic, before joining Southampton FC in 1918; Arsenal March 1926; retired March 1933. Norwich City manager March 1933; Southampton manager February 1937-May 1943; Norwich City manager again April 1955-March 1957; subsequently Southampton's chief scout. Other honours: (Soton) FL Div. 3 (South) champions 1922. (Arsenal) FL champions 1931. FA Cup winner 1930; finalist 1927, 1932.

Right-back. An outstanding Arsenal skipper and steadfast defender, his positional sense compensating for a certain slowness. Always appeared composed (although Bernard Joy says he suffered from pre-match nerves). Tom, a fine man of character, had worked in the Southampton shipyards.

PARKES, Philip B. F.
(Queen's Park Rangers, 1974, 1)
Born Sedgeley, Staffs. 8 August 1950.
1974: 6ft. 3ins.; 14st. 7lbs.

Career: West Midlands schools football, joined Walsall's ground staff and sent to Brierley Hill Alliance for development, returning to Walsall as a professional January 1968; Queen's Park Rangers June 1970 (£18,500); West Ham United February 1979 (£560,000, a then world record for a goalkeeper). Other honours: England 'B' international (1 app). England Under-23 international (6 apps). England Under-21 international (1 app). (WHU) FL Div. 2 champions 1981. FA Cup winner 1980. FL Cup finalist 1981.

Goalkeeper possessing remarkable consistency as well as brilliance, making full use of height and reach. A superb handler too. Commanded an extraordinary fee on moving to Upton Park especially, some thought, for one in his 29th year. But goalkeepers can last long without deterioration. Think of Shilton and Clemence, contemporaries of Phil's, whose presence has denied him many England caps.

PARKINSON, John
(Liverpool, 1910, 2)
Born Bootle, September 1883. died 13 September 1942.
1910: 5ft. 9ins.; 12st.

Career: Assisted Merseyside junior clubs, Hertford Albion and Valkyrie, before signing amateur for Liverpool during season 1901/02, turning professional 1903; Bury cs 1914; retired during WW1. Other honours: Football League (3 apps). (Liverpool) FL Div. 2 champions 1905.

Centre-forward, sometimes inside-left. Earned a reputation as a youngster ('the terror of junior goalkeepers') with his speed and scoring powers. He continued with scoring feats in the first-class game but, through injury and so on, was not always an automatic choice (It will be noted he did not qualify for a 1906 championship medal nor was he selected for the 1914 Cup final). After leaving football, Jack had two newsagent/tobacconist shops in Liverpool.

PARR, Percival Chase
(Oxford University, 1882, 1)
Born Widmore, Bromley, Kent, 2 December 1859.
Died 3 September 1912.

Career: Winchester College (XI 1877); Oxford University (Blue 1880-1-2, captain 1882); West Kent. Also represented Kent county.

Goalkeeper/centre-forward, occupying the latter for his international and, incidentally, registering a goal in that match. (In those pioneering days, goalkeeping was not considered an exclusive art, players happily performing both there and in the outfield). Parr brought to each berth bravery and coolness. A barrister by profession (called to the Bar 1885). He was obviously a man of parts, being a director of the publishing firm. W H Allen & Co, and editor of the journals, 'National Observer' and 'Ladies Field'.

PARRY, Edward Hagarty
(Old Carthusians, 1879-82, 3)
Born Toronto, Canada, 24 April 1855. Died 19 July 1931.

Career: Charterhouse School (XI 1872-3-4, captain '73 and '74); Oxford University (Blue 1875-6-7, captain 1877); Old Carthusians; Swifts, Remnants; Stoke Poges; Windsor. Also represented Berks & Bucks FA. Served on the FA Committee 1881. Other honours: (Oxford University) FA Cup finalist 1877. (Old Carthusians) FA Cup winner 1881.

Forward. A fast dribbler showing persistence and utilising a fair shot, but he did not relish the then universally prevalent charging. Parry's fine captaincy had much to do with the Old Carthusians' 1881 Cup triumph. A schoolmaster, he taught at Felsted 1879-80 and Stoke House School, Slough 1881-92, then serving as Headmaster there until his retirement in 1918.

PARRY, Raymond Alan
(Bolton Wanderers, 1960, 2)
Born Derby, 19 January 1936.
1958: 5ft. 8½ins.; 10st. 8lbs.

Career: Derby Schools; Bolton Wanderers amateur September 1950, turning professional January 1953; Blackpool October 1960 (£20,000); Bury October 1964 (£6000), player/coach September 1970, playing until 1972. Other honours: England schoolboy international. England Youth international. England Under-23 international (4 apps). Football League (2 apps). (Bolton W) FA Cup winner 1958.

Inside/outside-left with what the jollier reporters used to term 'an educated left foot'. Ray's was certainly powerful for a slight man and valuable to one of thrustful bent and a penalty specialist. He had been a juvenile star, winning 9 schoolboy caps and captaining the side. This prowess transferred naturally to the senior game. Younger brother of Jack Parry (Derby County, 1948-67).

PATCHITT, Basil Clement Alderson
(Corinthians, 1923, 2)
Born 12 August 1900.

Career: Charterhouse School (XI 1917-19, captain 1919); Cambridge University (Blue 1922); Corinthians during seasons 1921/22 and 1922/23; Castleford Town late 1923.

Full-back/half-back. A sound amateur especially good in defence. He had a degree of versatility, appearing at back in his 'Varsity match and later as a pivot and wing-half. The recipient of two full caps yet never so honoured at amateur international level – an unusual occurrence. Later lived in South Africa, at Johannesburg.

PAWSON, (Revd.) Francis William
(Cambridge University, 1883-85, 2)
Born Sheffield, 6 April 1861. Died 4 July 1921.

Career: Sheffield Collegiate School; Cambridge University (Blue 1882-3-4, captain 1884); Swifts; Sheffield Club; Casuals; Corinthians 1885-89. Also represented Surrey. Served on the FA Committee 1882-83.

Forward. The adaptable type – for instance, occupied the outside-right and centre positions for his internationals. Accurate with his shooting and passing and he moved smartly. Broke a leg in 1886 when playing for the Corinthians against Cambridge University on colliding with their goalkeeper. Ordained 1886, curate of Battersea (1886-90) and Bexhill (1890-99) before becoming Rector of Lewes 1900-03 and Vicar of Ecclesfield, Sheffield, 1903-21.

PAYNE, Joseph
(Luton Town, 1937, 1)
Born Brimington Common nr. Chesterfield, 17 January 1914. Died 22 April 1975. 1938: 5ft. 11ins.; 12st.

Career: Bolsover Colliery; Biggleswade Town; Luton Town cs 1934; Chelsea March 1938 (£5000); West Ham United December 1946 (in exchange for another player and a fee); Millwall September 1947; retired through injury during the 1947/48 season but signed for Worcester City October 1952, not having played in the interim. Other honour: (Luton) FL Div. 3 (South) champions 1937.

Centre-forward. Often referred to as 'Ten Goal Payne' because of the League record he established (10 for Luton vs. Bristol Rovers, 13 April 1936). It was a record made the more sensational as it came in Joe's very first game leading the attack – he had hitherto been a reserve wing-half. 'Good in the air, strong with both feet and a marvellous eye for the ball,' was one verdict. Played Minor Counties cricket for Bedfordshire in 1937.

PEACOCK, Alan
(Middlesbrough and Leeds United, 1962-66, 6)
Born Middlesbrough, 29 October 1937.
1964: 6ft.; 11st. 4lbs.

Career: Middlesbrough schools and junior football; Middlesbrough FC amateur, turning professional November 1954; Leeds United February 1964 (£60,000); Plymouth Argyle October 1967 (£10,000); retired through injury March 1968. Other honours: England Youth international. (Leeds U) FL Div. 2 champions 1964. FA Cup finalist 1965.

Centre-forward/inside-left. Occupied the latter berth for his home town club at first, moving to the centre following Brian Clough's transfer to Sunderland. Alan, a shrewd and clever forward, had a good scoring record (153 goals in a total 284 League matches). His career was marred by injury in its later stages and he took over a Middlesbrough newsagency.

PEACOCK, John ('Joe')
(Middlesbrough, 1929, 3)
Born Wigan, 15 March, 1897. died 4 March 1979.
1929: 5ft. 9ins.; 11st. 7lbs.

Career: Wigan Recreation; Atherton; Everton cs 1919; Middlesbrough cs 1927; Sheffield Wednesday May 1930; Clapton Orient June 1931. Coach in Sweden March 1933; appointed Wrexham trainer July 1939. Other honour: (Middlesbrough) FL Div. 2 champions 1929.

Wing-half with very useful utility value in having experience of pivotal and the three inside-forward berths also. A sound performer, excellent in ball control. Apparently signed by Wednesday as a *helpmate* for *their youngsters, he left after a year to clock up over 50 Southern Section appearances for Clapton Orient before hanging up his boots.*

PEARCE, Stuart
(Nottingham Forest, 1987-88, 5)
Born Shepherd's Bush, London, 24 April 1962.
1987: 5ft. 10ins.; 12st. 9lbs.

Career: Wealdstone; Coventry City October 1983 (£25,000); Nottingham Forest June 1985 (£450,000 including another player). Other honour: England Under-21 international (1 app).

Left-back. Gained full international recognition, deputising for an injured Kenny Sansom, after a single Under-21 appearance and less than four seasons' League experience. A capable defender, intelligent in covering and a good user of the ball. Has succeeded to the Forest captaincy on the departure of Johnny Metgod to Tottenham. An electrician by trade.

PEARSON, Harold Frederick
(West Bromwich Albion, 1932, 1)

Born Tamworth, Staffs. 7 May 1908.
1931: 6ft. 1in.; 12st. 6lbs.

Career: Tamworth Schools; Glascote United Methodists; Belgrave WMC; Tamworth Castle; Bromsgrove Rovers; West Bromwich Albion on amateur forms April 1925, turning professional the following month; Millwall August 1937; retired during WW2. Other honours: (WBA) FA Cup winner 1931; finalist 1935. (Millwall) FL Div. 3 (South) champions 1938.

Goalkeeper whose forte was soundness rather than the spectacular. Ideally built, his reach a natural advantage and massive clearance kicks a feature. Very much of goalkeeping stock. Son of Hubert Pearson (West Bromwich Albion 1906-26, who twice represented the Football League), and his cousins included the great Harry Hibbs (q.v.) and Horace Pearson of Blackpool's 1930 championship-winning side. A plumber by trade.

PEARSON, J(ames) Stuart
(Manchester United, 1976-78, 15)
Born Hull, 21 June 1949.
1977: 5ft. 9ins.; 12st. 7lbs.

Career: East Riding schools and junior football; Hull City on amateur forms May 1966, turning professional July 1968; Manchester United May 1974 (£170,000 and another player); West Ham United August 1979 (£220,000); retired through injury 1982. Subsequently became manager of Northwich Victoria and, in November 1987, joined West Bromwich Albion's coaching staff, assistant manager November 1988. Other honours: England Under-23 international (1 app). (Man. Utd) FL Div. 2 champions 1975. FA Cup winner 1977; finalist 1976. (WHU) FA Cup winner 1980. FL Cup finalist 1981 (sub).

Centre-forward. A determined, tenacious attacker possessed of no little skill. Could always be relied up on to pull his full weight. Later ran a ceramic business in Manchester.

PEARSON, John Hargreaves
(Crewe Alexandra, 1892, 1)
Born Crewe, 25 January 1868. Died 22 June 1931.

Career: Juvenile football to Crewe Alexandra when only 13½ years of age, remaining with the club until injury forced his retirement around the time of his international appearance. Became a referee in 1893 eventually gaining first-class status and remaining on the Football League list until 1914. He refereed the FA Cup final of 1911.

Inside-right. Crewe Alexandra's first (and sole English) internationalist, a fast and mobile forward. A touch too individualistic sometimes but, without doubt, a highly skilled performer. For long on the staff of the London & North Western Railway, which became on the 1923 amalgamations the LMS, he retired in December 1930.

PEARSON, Stanley C.
(Manchester United, 1948-52, 8)
Born Salford, 15 January 1919.
1950: 5ft. 8½ins.; 11st.

Career: Adelphi Lads Club (Manchester & District Amateur League); Manchester United on amateur forms 1935, turning professional May 1936; Bury February 1954; Chester October 1957; retired May 1959. Chester manager April 1959-November 1961. Other honours: England 'B' international (1 app). Football League (1 app). (Man. Utd) FL champions 1952. FA Cup winner 1948. (Chester) Welsh Cup finalist 1958.

Inside-forward, a key figure of the first great Busby team. Stan was a stylist able to create and take goals with like facility. His shot was, as they say, lethal. After leaving Chester ran a Prestbury newsagency/post office and coached the local East Cheshire League side.

PEASE, Willie Harold
(Middlesbrough, 1927, 1)
Born Leeds, 30 September 1899. Died 2 October 1955.

1930: 5ft. 9½ins.; 11st. 5lbs.

Career: Army football; Leeds City as an amateur 1918/19; Northampton Town as a professional October 1919; Middlesbrough May 1926; Luton Town June 1933; retired through injury January 1935. Other honours: (Middlesbrough) FL Div. 2 champions 1927, 1929.

Outside-right. Extremely quick forward, direct in style, whose judged centres when running full tilt created many a goal. Scored prolifically himself in winger's terms, especially in the above promotion seasons when he netted 23 and 27 respectively. Played rugby at school, taking up soccer during wartime service with the Northumberland Fusiliers. Toured South Africa with the FA party of 1929, twice appearing against the host country's national side. After leaving the game was employed as a licensee in the Middlesbrough district.

PEGG, David
(Manchester United, 1957, 1)
Born Doncaster, 20 September 1935. Died in the Munich air crash, 6 February 1958.
1957: 5ft. 9½ins.; 11st. 11lbs.

Career: Doncaster Schools; Manchester United amateur 1951, turning professional September 1952. Other honours: England schoolboy international. England 'B' international (1 app). England Under-23 international (3 apps). (Man. Utd) FL champions 1956, 1957. FA Cup finalist 1957.

Outside-left with sparkle, deft footwork and a fine line in elusiveness. Had been inside-left in United's Youth Cup-winning side of 1953. Scored 24 goals in 127 League outings for the club and it is quite likely he would have risen to greater heights.

PEJIC, Michael
(Stoke City, 1974, 4)
Born Chesterton, Staffs. 25 January 1950.
1974: 5ft. 6½ins.; 11st.

Career: Potteries schoolboy football; originally joined Stoke City when 14, later becoming an apprentice and turning professional January 1968; Everton February 1977 (£135,000); Aston Villa September 1979 (£250,000); retired through illness March 1981. Port Vale first team coach 1988. Other honours: England Under-23 international (8 apps). (Stoke C) FL Cup winner 1972.

Left-back. Short in stature but solidly built, owner of a tackle reckoned to be perhaps the fiercest ever seen at Goodison. Had a robust approach generally and apt to make attacking sorties down the flank. Mike's untimely retiral was the result of a pelvic disorder that started in 1978. He played only 10 League games for Villa. Son of a Yugo-Slav immigrant.

PELLY, Frederick Raymond
(Old Foresters, 1893-94, 3)
Born Upminster, Essex, 11 August 1868. Died 16 October 1940.
1895: 6ft.; 15st.

Career: Forest School (XI 1882-86); Old Foresters; Corinthians 1891-98; Casuals. Also represented Essex and the London FA.

Left-back. Given the above physique it comes as no surprise to read he was 'a very awkward man to get past.' And, for his size, he possessed a good turn of speed and was reliable to a degree. Qualities of leadership were much in view also – he skippered Old Foresters and the Casuals for around a decade, and Essex for 5 years. Engaged in commercial life, he finished as senior partner of a well known firm.

PENNINGTON, Jesse
(West Bromwich Albion, 1907-20, 25)
Born West Bromwich, 23 August 1883. Died 5 September 1970.
1910: 5ft. 8ins.; 11st. 7lbs.

Career: Smethwick schoolboy football; Summit Star (a junior side he helped to found); Smethwick Centaur; Langley Villa (during which spell he signed amateur forms for Aston Villa); Langley St Michael's; Dudley Town; West Bromwich Albion April 1903, originally as an amateur; retired August 1922 and served as a club coach during the ensuing season; Kidderminster Harriers coach to 1925, then scouted for Albion until 1960. In the late 1960s was made a life member of the club. Other honours: Football League (9 apps). (WBA) FL champions 1920. FL Div. 2 champions 1911. FA Cup finalist 1912.

Left-back. A famous back who, with Sam Hardy and Bob Crompton, formed the renowned England defence of 1907-14. A wonderful club servant too: 17 years an Albion player (interrupted briefly in 1910 following a pay dispute), followed by many years 'back stage'. On the field was not all that conspicuous but tremendously effective nonetheless: immaculate positionally, an accurate kicker and employer of a perfectly timed tackle. His 494 League and FA Cup appearances remained an Albion record for 56 years. Rightly dubbed 'Peerless'. Worked as a poultry farmer.

PENTLAND, Frederick Beaconsfield
(Middlesbrough, 1909, 5)
Born Wolverhampton, 1883. Died 16 March 1962.
1909: 5ft. 9ins.; 11st. 11lbs.

Career: Birmingham area junior football; Small Heath August 1900; Blackpool cs 1903; Blackburn Rovers 1903/04; Brentford May 1906; Queen's Park Rangers May 1907; Halifax Town as player/manager cs 1912; Stoke later in 1912. Coach in Europe 1914 (interned) and after WW1 into the 1930s; Brentford staff 1936; Barrow manager January 1938 to WW2. Other honour: (QPR) Southern League champions 1908.

Outside-right. Speedy, a dexterous ball player and expert in precision centering. His blemish was a tendency towards over elaboration. In the 1920s was extraordinarily successful as Bilbao's manager/coach, steering them to 5 Spanish League championships in 7 years. Had a second spell there from May 1933 and he also coached Spain's national side.

PERRY, Charles
(West Bromwich Albion, 1890-93, 3)
Born West Bromwich, January 1866. Died 2 July 1927.
1895: 5ft. 10ins.; 12st. 4lbs.

Career: West Bromwich schoolboy football; West Bromwich Strollers; West Bromwich Albion June 1884; retired through injury May 1896, serving as an Albion director 1898-1902. Other honours: Football League (1 app). (WBA) FA Cup winner 1888, 1892; finalist 1886, 1887.

Centre-half of parts, polished in action and, as a captain, adroit in marshalling his forces.

Particularly fine defensively. Had four brothers who likewise assisted Albion in the club's early years, the quartet including Tom below. Worked for a brewery, eventually becoming a director of the firm.

PERRY, Thomas
(West Bromwich Albion, 1898, 1)
Born West Bromwich 1871. Died 18 July 1927.
1903: 5ft. 10ins.; 12st.

Career: West Bromwich schoolboy football; Christ Church FC (W. Bromwich); Stourbridge; West Bromwich Albion July 1890; Aston Villa October 1901; retired cs 1903. Other honours: Football League (3 apps). (WBA) FA Cup finalist 1895.

Right-half generally though capable of switching to inside-forward, outside-left or full-back on demand, so thoroughly versatile. Wholehearted and efficient, Tom was one of five brothers who turned out for the Albion. They included another internationalist, Charlie (above), who predeceased Tom by 16 days.

PERRY, William
(Blackpool, 1956, 3)
Born Johannesburg, South Africa, 10 September 1930.
1957: 5ft. 8ins.; 10st. 7lbs.

Career: Johannesburg Rangers; Blackpool October 1949; Southport June 1962; Hereford United July 1963; South Coast United (Australia) July 1964 for a few months; Holyhead Town April 1966. A director of Fleetwood FC cs 1967-february 1970. Other honours: England 'B' international (2 apps). Football League (1 app). (Blackpool) FA Cup winner 1953, finalist 1951.

Outside-left qualified for England by reason of an English father. An assertive forward always hungry for the ball and highly dangerous in front of goal. The last-mentioned aspect is revealed by his aggregate Blackpool figures – 120 goals from 394 League outings, excellent for a winger. (Especially when later centres of great repute never reach 20 in a season and are often with single-figure totals).

PERRYMAN, Stephen John
(Tottenham Hotspur, 1982, 1)
'Born Ealing, London, 21 December 1951.
1980: 5ft. 8ins.; 10st. 10lbs.
Career: Middlesex Schools; London Schools; Tottenham Hotspur apprentice July 1967, turning professional January 1969; Oxford United March 1986; Brentford as player/assistant manager November 1986, player/manager January 1987. Other honours: England schoolboy international. England Youth international. England Under-23 international (17 apps). (Spurs) Inter-Cities Fairs Cup winner 1972. UEFA Cup winner 1984; finalist 1974. FA Cup winner 1981, 1982. FL Cup winner 1971, 1973; finalist 1982.

Midfield, latterly defender. Highly competent in all aspects of his craft. Noted, of course, for his long period at White Hart Lane, being club skipper for most of it and establishing the Spurs' appearances record (655 in the League the main element). Awarded the MBE in the Birthday Honours List of 1986.

PETERS, Martin Stanford
(West Ham United and Tottenham Hotspur, 1966-74, 67)
Born Plaistow, London, 8 November 1943.
1970: 6ft. $0^1/_2$ins.; 11st. $10^1/_2$lbs.

Career: Played for the representative school teams of Dagenham, Essex and London before becoming a West Ham United apprentice May 1959, turning professional November 1960; Tottenham Hotspur March 1970 (£125,000 plus Jimmy Greaves); Norwich City March 1975 (£50,000); Sheffield United as player/coach July 1980, ceased playing January 1981 on appointment as team manager to June 1981. Other honours: England schoolboy international. England Youth international. England Under-23 international (5 apps). Football League (6 apps). (WHU) European Cup Winners' Cup, winner 1965. FL Cup finalist 1966. (Spurs) Inter-Cities Fairs Cup winner 1972. UEFA Cup finalist 1974. FL Cup winner 1971, 1973.

Midfield was the usual printed designation but Martin was in fact a 'play anywhere' specialist. Famed for the much quoted Sir Alf Ramsey remark of his being '10 years ahead of his time', that was inspired by outstanding tactical awareness and general intelligence. Awarded the MBE in 1978. Since leaving football has been employed by fruit machine and insurance companies.

PHILLIPS, Leonard H.
(Portsmouth, 1952-55, 3)
Born Hackney, London, 11 September 1922.
1951: 5ft. 7$^1/_2$ins.; 11st.

Career: Royal Marines (Portsmouth) football; Hillside Youth Club; Portsmouth amateur 1944, turning professional February 1946; retired through injury May 1956 but ('defying doctors' orders') joined Poole Town the following August and subsequently assisted Chelmsford City (July 1959) and Bath City (May 1963). Other honours: Football League (2 apps). (Portsmouth) FL champions 1949, 1950.

Inside-left, later right-half. As a forward was fast and incisive, showing poise and control. These factors were still in evidence at wing-half, a move which, incidentally, demonstrated Phillips's two-footedness. From 1959 worked as a machine operator with a Portsmouth engineering firm.

PICKERING, Frederick
(Everton, 1964-65, 3)
Born Blackburn, 19 January 1941.
1965: 5ft. 11ins.; 12st. 7$^1/_2$lbs.

Career: Blackburn junior football to Blackburn Rovers as an amateur, turning professional January 1958; Everton March 1964 (£82,000); Birmingham City August 1967 (£50,000); Blackpool June 1969 (£45,000) Blackburn Rovers again March 1971 (£10.000); Brighton & Hove Albion on 2 months trial February 1972. Other honours: England Under-23 international (3 apps) Football League (1 app).

Centre-forward. Originally a full-back, he found his true vocation leading the attack before joining Everton. Used an ideal physique to potent effect, surging power making him a feared striker. In all registered 168 goals in 353 League matches and he scored a hat-trick on his international debut. Fred was awarded a 1966 FA Cup winners' medal although he missed the final owing to injury.

PICKERING, John
(Sheffield United, 1933, 1)
Born Mortomley, Yorks. 18 December 1908. Died 10 May 1977.
1934: 5ft. 10$^1/_2$ins.; 11st.
Career: Barnsley Grammar School; Mortomley St Saviour's; Sheffield United May 1925; retired cs 1948, then becoming Poole Town's manager/coach. Other honours: Football League (1 app). (Sheffield U) FA Cup finalist 1936.

Inside-left. A craftsman, lithe physically whose lengthy stride was deceptively fast. Could shoot powerfully with either foot. On Sheffield United's books a remarkable 23 years, reputedly the longest span with a single club of any forward in the first-class game. An accountant by profession, Jack held United's record for first-team appearances until surpassed by Joe Shaw (1948-66).

PICKERING, Nicholas
(Sunderland, 1983, 1)
Born Newcastle-upon-Tyne, 4 August 1963.
1983: 6ft.1in.; 11st. 11lbs.

Career: North Shields Schools; Sunderland apprentice, turning professional August 1981; Coventry City January 1986 (£120,000); Derby County July 1988 (£250,000). Other honours: England Youth international. England Under-21 international (15apps). (Sunderland) FL Cup finalist 1985. (Coventry C) FA Cup winner 1987.

Defender/midfield, found on the left side as behoves the possessor of a trusty left foot. A wholehearted performer and quick of movement. Reputedly at 21 the youngest skipper ever for a Wembley final (for Sunderland in 1985). Played a notable part in Coventry's successful visit to that celebrated arena 2 years later.

PIKE, Thelwell Mather
(Cambridge University, 1886, 1)
Born Andover, Hants. 17 November 1866. Died 21 July 1957.

Career: Malvern School (XI 1884-85); Cambridge University (Blue 1886 and '88); Old Malvernians; Crusaders; Brentwood; Swifts; Thanet Wanderers; Corinthians 1886-91.

Winger usually associated with the right flank but was at outside-left for his international. An extremely fast player whose centres were beautifully judged. A Worcestershire cricketer 1886-95. Held scholastic appointments on the South coast and Edinburgh before becoming headmaster of Weybridge Preparatory school 1897-1906, then was head of Thanet School, Margate until his retirement.

PILKINGTON, Brian
(Burnley, 1955, 1)
Born Farington nr. Leyland, Lancs. 12 February 1933.
1957:5ft. 5ins.; 10st.

Career: Leyland Motors; Burnley April 1951; Bolton Wanderers February 1961 (around £25,000); Bury February 1964 (£5,000); Barrow January 1965; Chorley late in 1967; retired through injury January 1968 but joined Leyland Motors August 1969, becoming that side's manager 1970. Other honours: England 'B' international (2 apps) Football League (2 apps). (Burnley) FL champions 1960.

Outside-left. Fast little forward, direct in style and always liable to score on his own account. Totalled 84 goals in 487 League appearances (and 1 substitution) for his 4 senior clubs. Played a deal of football during his national service, representing the RAF on 16 occasions, 1952-54.

PLANT, John
(Bury, 1900 1)
Born Bollington, Cheshire, 1871.
1903: 5ft.8ins.; 12st. 4lbs.

Career: Denton FC; Bollington FC; Bury April 1890; Reading cs 1898; Bury again cs 1899 – cs 1907. Other honours: (Bury) FL Div. 2 champions 1895. FA Cup winner 1900, 1903.

Outside-left. Beefy as wingers go – and so made his presence felt that bit more – and owner of noted and deadly shot. Surely his 16 seasons with Bury, admittedly in two instalments, makes Plant the club's longest serving player, and the period embraced its greatest years. He made 319 League appearances while at Gigg Lane (55 goals) – it will be appreciated League status was not attained until 1894, i.e. Plant's fifth season as a Shaker. An incisive, valuable performer.

PLUM, Seth Lewis
(Charlton Athletic, 1923, 1)
Born Edmonton, London, 15 July 1899. Died 29 November 1969.
1925: 5ft. $7^1/_2$ins.; 10st. 5lbs.

Career: Tottenham schoolboy football; Mildway Athletic 1912/13; Tottenham Park Avondale; Barnet; Charlton Athletic as an amateur cs 1922 turning professional August 1923; Chelsea March 1924; Southend United cs 1927 – 1928.

Wing-half of slight build. From his earliest days had been good in interception, tackling and anticipating moves excellently. Later, on improving passing skills, became an all-round performer. Plum's Charlton period was his best, failing to win regular spots at Stamford Bridge and Southend. Afterwards lived and worked in his native North London.

POINTER, Raymond
(Burnley, 1962, 3)
Born Cramlington, Northumberland, 10 October 1936.
1962: 5ft. 9ins.; 10st.10bs.

Career: Northumberland Schools; Northumberland Youth; Cramlington Welfare (represented the BAOR while on national service); Dudley Welfare; Burnley August 1957; Bury August 1965 (£8,000); Coventry City December 1965 (£20,000); Portsmouth January 1967 (in part exchange for another player), player/coach from 1971. Blackpool training staff August 1973-May 1976. Other honours: England Under-23 international (5 apps). Football League (2 apps) (Burnley) FL champions 1960. FA Cup finalist 1962.

Centre-forward later playing at inside-forward and on the wing. A force to be respected in his prime with a non-stop style and scoring potential. Altogether netted 179 goals in 416 League games (and 4 substitutions) of which the Burnley share was 118 in 222. A bad knee injury caused Ray to miss the bulk of season 1964/65.

PORTEOUS, Thomas Stoddard
(Sunderland, 1891, 1)
Born Newcastle-upon-Tyne, 1865. Died 23 February 1919.
1894: 5ft. $9^1/_4$ins.; 11st. 10lbs.

Career: Heart of Midlothian; Kilmarnock 1884; Sunderland cs 1889; Rotherham Town June 1894; Manchester City cs 1895. Other honours: (Sunderland) FL champions 1892, 1893.

Right-back. Member of Sunderland's celebrated 'Team of all the talents'. Not the most prominent star in that constellation but valuable all the same, playing with efficiency and steadiness. Possibly related to William Porteous (Hearts & Scotland) but this has not been proven.

PRIEST, Alfred Ernest ('Fred')
(Sheffield United, 1900, 1)
Born Guisborough, North Yorks. 1875. Died 5 May 1922.
1901: 5ft. 8ins.; 12st. 12lbs.

Career: Darlington; South Bank; Sheffield United cs 1896; Middlesbrough as player/assistant trainer cs 1906; Hartlepools United player/manager 1908. Other honours: (Sheffield United) FL champions 1898. FA Cup winner 1899, 1902; finalist 1901.

Inside/outside-left. 'A splendid player and marksman,' recalled a critic writing in the 1920s. An accurate judgment, for Priest scored vital goals and was a vital cog in the great Sheffield United side of the turn of the century. Originally on their left wing, he moved inside when Bert Lipsham arrived and had a big part in 'bringing out' that fine forward. Appeared at left-back during the 1904/05 season and was a West Hartlepool licensee at the time of his death.

PRINSEP, James Frederick McLeod
(Old Carthusians, 1879, 1)
Born in India, 27 July 1861. Died 22 November 1895.

Career: Charterhouse School (XI 1877-78); Old Carthusians; Clapham Rovers. Also represented Surrey. Other honours: (Clapham Rovers) FA Cup finalist 1879. (Old Carthusians) FA Cup winner 1881.

Half-back. The Football Annual for 1881 described Prinsep as 'a splendid half-back; can kick the ball in any position and passes it admirably to his forwards.' A regular soldier, he served in the Essex Regt. from May 1882 (Sudan campaign 1884-85) and the Egyptian Army 1885-90 (involved in operations around Suakin, Sudan, 1888). Transferred to the Egyptian Coastguard Service 1890, becoming Sub-Inspector General. In 1884 was awarded the Albert Medal for saving a man of his regiment from drowning.

PUDDEFOOT, Sydney Charles
(Blackburn Rovers, 1926, 2)
Born Limehouse, London, 17 October 1894. Died 2 October 1972.
1926: 5ft. 10½ins.; 12st.

Career: East London schoolboy football; Conder Athletic; Limehouse Town; West Ham United as an amateur 1912/13, turning professional the following season (Falkirk as a guest player during WW1); Falkirk February 1922 (£5000, then a record); Blackburn Rovers February 1925 (£4000); West Ham United again February 1932; retired cs 1933. Coach in Turkey with Fenerbahce (Istanbul) 1933/34 and Galatia Seray 1934/35; Northampton Town manager March 1935 – March 1937; returned to Turkey later in 1937 and coached in Istanbul until 1940. Other honours: England 'Victory' international 1919 (3 apps). Football League (2 apps). Southern League (1 app). (Blackburn) FA Cup winner 1928.

Inside-right/centre- forward. A most attractive player, dashing and unorthodox, a big name in his day. Combined well despite his unorthodoxy. The 1922 move to Falkirk created a sensation (it was said West Ham quoted a fee thought impossible for the Scottish club to meet). 'Puddy', a good cricketer, made 8 appearences for Essex in the 1922-23 period. Later a civil servant, he retired in 1963, then had a spell on Southend United's staff.

PYE, Jesse
(Wolverhampton Wanderers, 1950, 1)
Born Treeton nr. Rotherham, 22 December 1918. Died 1984.
1950: 5ft. 10ins.; 11st. 7lbs.

Career: Catliffe; Treeton FC; Sheffield United as an amateur 1938, later becoming a part-time professional; Notts County August 1945; Wolverhampton Rovers May 1946 (£10,000); Luton Town July 1952 (more than £9000); Derby County October 1954 (about £5000); Wisbech Town July 1957, becoming their player/manager March 1960, resigned managership 1966. Other honours: England 'B' international (3 apps). Football League (1 app). (Wolves) FA Cup winner 1949.

Centre/inside-forward of beguiling elegance, mixing subtlety and incisiveness in his game to telling effect. Shone in all three berths equally. Jesse netted 145 goals in 209 League matches for Wolves, Luton and Derby, a splendid record. Later the proprietor of a Blackpool private hotel.

PYM, Richard Henry ('Pincher')
(Bolton Wanderers, 1925-26, 3)
Born Topsham, Devon, 2 February 1893.
Died September1988.
1926: 5ft.11½ins.; 12st.

Career: Topsham schoolboy and junior football; Exeter City February 1911, first as an amateur; Bolton Wanderers June 1921 (£2000); Yeovil & Petters United May 1931. In 1934 was coaching Topsham FC and even played occasionally. Had spell as Exeter City's assistant trainer from August 1937 and another scouting for Bolton Wanderers. Other honours; Football League (2 apps). (Bolton W) FA Cup winner 1923, 1926, 1929.

Goalkeeper. Cool under the severest pressure and blessed with such excellent anticipation as to make goalkeeping appear simple. Consistent also – at Exeter once had a run of 186 concecutive appearences ended only by injury. Well known as a deep sea fisherman, carrying this on as a hobby in his Bolton decade but it had been his living.

QUANTRILL, Alfred Edward
(Derby County, 1920-21, 4)

Born in the Punjab, India, 22 January 1897. died 19 April 1968.
1925: 5ft.9½ins.; 11st.8lbs.

Career: Boston Swifts (Lincs); Derby County August 1914; Preston North End June 1921 (£4000); Chorley August 1924; Bradford September 1924; Nottingham Forest May 1930; retired cs 1932. Other honour: (Bradford) FL Div. 3 (North) champions1928.

Outside-left. Established a big reputation in the early 'Twenties. 'Always gets the ball under immediate control,and can beat his man in little room. Finishes strongly with either foot. . .,' wrote a contemporary who also said Alf was then 'probably the fleetest left-winger in the country.' son-in-law of Steve Bloomer (qv.), a skilled boxer and, latterly, a successful insurance broker.

QUIXALL, Albert
(Sheffield Wednesday, 1954-55, 5)
Born Sheffield, 9 August 1933.
1957: 5ft. 7¾ins.; 11st. 5lbs.

Career: Sheffield Schools; Meynell Youth Club (Sheffield); Sheffield Wednesday on amateur forms cs 1948, turning professional August 1950; Manchester United September 1958 (£45,000, a then British record); Oldham Athletic September 1964 (£7000); Stockport County July 1966; retired through injury February 1967 but joined Altrincham late that year for a spell. Other honours: England schoolboy international. England 'B' international (3 apps). England Under-23 international (1 app). Football League (4 apps). (Wednesday) FL Div. 2 champions 1952, 1956. (Man. Utd) FA Cup winner 1963.

Inside-forward. Perennially boyish looking – as was that earlier Wednesday star, Ernie Blenkinsop – and the introducer (it would seem) of the now universal brief shorts. These things, however, are of small consequence besides Albert's playing qualities, which were invention, first-class distribution and the exploiting of a cunning body swerve. Went into business as a Manchester scrap metal merchant.

RADFORD, John
(Arsenal, 1969-72, 2)
Born Hemsworth, Yorks. 22 February 1947.
1970: 5ft. 11ins.; 11st. 11lbs.

Career: Hemsworth Schools; Hemsworth

Youth Club; Arsenal apprentice October 1962, turning professional February 1964; West Ham United December 1976 (£80,000); Blackburn Rovers February 1978 (£20,000)-cs 1979; Bishop's Stortford October 1979, later their coach. Other honours: England Under-23 international (4 apps). Football League (2 apps). (Arsenal) FL champions 1971. FA Cup winner 1971; finalist 1972. FL Cup finalist 1968, 1969. Inter-Cities Fairs Cup winner 1970.

Centre/inside-forward with considerable attacking flair, his forceful directness posing threats on the ground and in the air. Became a licensee in Essex and Hertfordshire. Joined Arsenal 24 hours after signing amateur forms for Bradford City.

RAIKES, (Revd.) George Barkley
(Oxford University, 1895-96, 4)
Born Carleton-Forehoe, Norfolk, 14 March 1873. Died 18 December 1966.
1895: 6ft. 2ins.

Career: Shrewsbury School (XI 1890-92); Oxford University (Blue 1893-4-5-6); Corinthians 1893-96; Wymondham FC (Norfolk). Also appeared in Norfolk's county team. Retired from first-class football in 1896 after leaving university.

Goalkeeper of commanding stature, as a writer emphasised in 1895 – 'with height in his favour, he has great physical advantages for goalkeeping as he is very quick with his hands as well as his feet . . .' Also a noted cricketer. After prominence at Shrewsbury he assisted Oxford University 1893-95 (Blue 1894 and '95) and Norfolk, and played 9 matches for Hampshire 1900-02. Ordained in 1897, he was curate at Portsea to 1903, chaplain to the Duke of Portland 1905-20 and Rector of Bergh Apton, Norfolk, 1920 to his retirement in 1936.

RAMSEY, (Sir) Alfred Ernest
(Southampton and Tottenham Hotspur, 1949-54, 32)
Born Dagenham, Essex, 22 January 1920.
1950: 5ft. $8^1/_4$ins.; 12st. 8lbs.

Career: Essex Schools; Five Elms FC; Army football (signed as amateur for Portsmouth); Southampton on amateur forms 1943, turning professional August 1944; Tottenham Hotspur May 1949 (£21,000); retired August 1955. Ipswich Town manager August 1955; England's team manager April 1963-May 1974. In the mid-1970s had spell on the Birmingham City board during which he acted as consultant, resigning March 1978. Other honours: England 'B' international (1 app). Football League (6 apps). (Spurs) FL champions 1951. FL Div. 2 champions 1950.

Right-back. An imperishable name in the annals because England won the World Cup under his shrewd managership, a feat for which he was awarded a knighthood in 1967. Of 113 matches under his aegis, England won 69 and lost only 17. This followed an Ipswich spell that took in a League and 2 divisional championships. A deep thinker, too, as a player – unflurried and placing clearancess judiciously, a slowness of turn countered by intelligent positioning.

RAWLINGS, Archibald
(Preston North End, 1921, 1)

Born Leicester, 2 October 1891. Died 11 June 1952.

1922: 5ft. 11½ins.; 12st.

Career: Wombwell; Shirebrook; Northampton Town early in 1908; Barnsley 1911-cs 1913; Rochdale cs 1914; Dundee 1919; Preston North End June 1920 (£1500); Liverpool March 1924; Walsall June 1926; Bradford February 1927; Southport July 1928; Dick, Kerr's FC (Preston) December 1928; Burton Town cs 1931. Later in the 1930s served as Preston North End's assistant trainer. Other honour: (PNE) FA Cup finalist 1922.

Outside-right exceptionally large as wingers go (or went) and exceptionally long-lasting for a forward – over two decades as a professional. The direct type, spelling danger with his great pace and powerful shooting. Father of Syd Rawlings, also an outside-right (Millwall and other FL clubs during the 'Thirties).

RAWLINGS, William Ernest
(Southampton, 1922, 2)
Born Andover, Hants. 3 January 1896. Died 25 September 1972.
1925: 5ft. 10ins.; 11st. 10lbs.

Career: Andover FC and Army football; Southampton as an amateur 1918, turning professional May 1919; Manchester United March 1928; Port Vale November 1929-1930. Other honour: (Soton) FL Div. 3 (South) champions 1922.

Centre-forward. It was said 'no footballer is a more deadly goal-getter' while another contemporary wrote Rawlings 'knows how to open out the game but is best as an individualist. Moreover he can shoot well with either foot.' He netted 155 in 294 FL games for the Saints, this including 29 in 38 during the 1921/22 championship campaign.

RAWLINSON, John Frederick Peel
(Old Etonians, 1882, 1)
Born New Alresford, Hants. 21 December 1860. Died 14 January 1926.

Career: Eton College; Cambridge University (Blue 1882-83); Old Etonians; Corinthians (on club's original committee 1882). Served on the FA Committee 1885-86. Other honours: (Old Etonians) FA Cup winner 1882; finalist 1881, 1883.

Goalkeeper. A sound, cool custodian, although the coolness seemed at times to border on casualness. A barrister by profession (called to the Bar 1884) and a QC from 1897. Was Recorder of Cambridge 1898-1926 and MP for Cambridge University 1906-26..

RAWSON, Herbert Edward
(Royal Engineers, 1875, 1)
Born Port Louis, Mauritius, 3 September 1852. Died 18 October 1924.

Career: Westminster School (XI 1869-71, captain 1871); Royal Engineers; Royal Military Academy, Woolwich. Also represented Kent. Other honours: (Royal Engineers) FA Cup winner 1875; finalist 1874.

Forward. A hard worker, skilled dribbler and accurate marksman, qualities that place him among the leading centres of the 1870s. Served in the Royal Engineers 1872-1909, retiring with the rank of colonel. In 1873 played on one occasion for Kent CCC, further first-class cricket opportunities being lost because of a posting overseas the following year. Brother of W S Rawson (q.v.).

RAWSON, William Stepney
(Oxford University, 1875-77, 2)
Born Cape Town, South Africa, 14 October 1854. died 4 November 1932.

Career: Westminster School (XI 1872-73, captain 1873); Oxford University (Blue 1874-5-6-7, captain 1876); Old Westminsters; Wanderers. Served on the FA Committee 1876-77 and 1879. Referee of the 1876 FA Cup final. Other honours: (Oxford University) FA Cup winner 1874; finalist 1877.

Half-back, stocky in build, playing a telling game with touches of brilliance. Had strength in both feet, judicious in tactics and of cool temperament. Good at other games, he played for his Oxford college (Christ Church) 4 seasons and, in 1889 and 1899 represented the South vs. the North at lacrosse. MA (Oxon.) and brother of H E Rawson above.

READ, Albert
(Tufnell Park, 1921, 1)
Born Ealing, London, 1899.
1922: 5ft. 9ins.; 12st.

Career: Tufnell Park; Queen's Park Rangers as a professional May 1921; Reading July 1922, released cs 1923. Other honours:

England amateur international (2 apps). (Tufnell P) FA Amateur Cup finalist 1920.

Right or centre-half, quietly effective in all phases of half-back play, his shrewd passes generally made on the ground. Acquired a reputation in top-grade London amateur soccer. Sustained a serious knee injury in Reading's third League match of the 1922/23 campaign and did not play again until the following April, when he had a run out with the club's reserves. It seems highly possible the injury forced his retirement from the first-class game.

READER, Josiah
(West Bromwich Albion, 1894, 1)
Born West Bromwich, 27 February 1866.
Died 8 March 1954.
1900: 6ft.; 12st.

Career: West Bromwich schools and junior football, joining West Bromwich Albion from Carters Green FC January 1885; retired on health grounds April 1901. Later served Albion as trainer and coach, and then as a steward at The Hawthorns, his association with the club totalling a remarkable 65 years. Other honours: Football League (3 apps). (WBA) FA Cup winner 1892; finalist 1895.

Goalkeeper. An outstanding Throstles' loyalist whose innumerable brave exploits included a memorable occasion when he played with an arm in a sling. Clean in handling, superb in reflex action and (somewhat unusually) with his feet, it is surprising England called on Joe only once.

REANEY, Paul
(Leeds United, 1969-71, 3)
Born Fulham, 22 October 1944.
1970: 5ft. 9ins.; 11st. 1lb.

Career: Leeds Schools; joined Leeds United ground staff when 16, assisting South Leeds FC before turning professional October 1961; Bradford City June 1978; Newcastle U B United (NSW, Australia) January 1980, subsequently returning to England. Other honours: England Under-23 international (5 apps). Football League 3 apps). (Leeds U) European Cup finalist 1975. Inter-Cities Fairs Cup winner 1968, 1971; finalist 1967. European Cup Winners' Cup finalist 1973. FL champions 1969, 1974. FL Div. 2 champions 1964. FA Cup winner 1972; finalist 1965, 1973. FL Cup winner 1968.

Right-back. Yorkshire in everything but birth-place (of Yorks. parentage and moved to Leeds when but a few weeks old), Paul graced United's line-up for most of the club's vintage years. Was very fast, a trait 'made' for an attacking sortie and extremely consistent. Was an apprentice motor mechanic before turning pro. Australia's 'Player of the Year' during his New South Wales stint.

REEVES, Kevin Philip
(Norwich City and Manchester City, 1980, 2)
Born Burley, Hants. 20 October 1957.
1980: 5ft. 10ins.; 11st. 4lbs.

Career: Wessex schools football; AFC Bournemouth as an associate schoolboy when 16, later becoming an apprentice before turning professional July 1975; Norwich City February 1977 (£50,000); Manchester City March 1980 (£1.25m.); Burnley July 1983 (£125,000); retired because of an arthritic hip cs 1985 but assisted Barrow the following November and, later the same month, Yeovil Town; subsequently with Boston before joining Birmingham

City's coaching staff February 1986. Other honours: England Youth international. England 'B' international. England Under-21 international (10 apps). (Man. City) FA Cup finalist 1981.

Forward. Virile performer, the subject of one of Britain's largest transfer fees. Before his enforced retirement he had scored 103 goals in 327 League games (and 6 substitutions). John Bond was the manager who signed him for each of his 4 FL clubs and engaged him for the Birmingham appointment. Could be Reeves's No 1 fan.

REGIS, Cyrille
(West Bromwich Albion and Coventry City, 1982-88, 5)
Born Maripiasoula, French Guyana, 9 February 1958.
1983: 6ft.; 13st. 4lbs.

Career: Harlesden Schools; Mosley FC (trial with Chelsea); Hayes; West Bromwich Albion May 1977 (£5000); Coventry City October 1984 (£300,000). Other honours: England 'B' international. England Under-21 international (6 apps). (Coventry) FA Cup winner 1987.

Centre-forward. A very muscular striker whose athleticism is evidently a family trait (a cousin ran for Britain in the World Games of 1987). Cyrille has devastating speed, control, a blistering shot and is especially strong when heading. Established an unusual record by scoring on his debuts for Albion in five different competitions. The PFA's 'Young Player of the Year' for 1979.

REID, Peter
(Everton, 1985-88, 13)
Born Huyton, Liverpool, 20 June 1956.
1986: 5ft. 8ins.; 10st. 7lbs.

Career: Huyton Schools; Bolton Wanderers apprentice July 1971, turning professional May 1974; Everton December 1982 (£60,000), appointed player/coach June 1987; Queen's Park Rangers February 1989. Other honours: England Under-21 international (6 apps). (Bolton W) FL Div. 2 champions 1978. (Everton) European Cup Winners' Cup winner 1985. FL champions 1985, 1987. FA Cup winner 1984; finalist 1985, 1986. FL Cup finalist 1984.

Midfield. Has endured a horrendous catalogue of injury that includes a broken kneecap, serious ligament and cartilage troubles, Achilles tendon damage and a broken leg. But such was his spirit that he came fighting back to be a vital link in Everton's magnificent spell of the mid-1980s. No speed merchant but his enthusiasm, ball winning capacity and ability to set up and keep involved in attacking moves are unsurpassed. In 1980 Everton offered a fee many times the figure that eventually was paid. 'Player of the Year' 1985.

REVIE, Donald George
(Manchester City, 1955-57, 6)
Born Middlesbrough, 10 July 1927.
Died 26 May 1989.
1957: 5ft. 11ins.; 12st. 9lbs.

Career: Middlesbrough schools football; Newport Boys Club (Middlesbrough); Middlesbrough Swifts; Leicester City August 1944; Hull City November 1949 (£20,000); Manchester City October 1951 (£13,000 and another player); Sunderland November 1956 (£23,000); Leeds United November 1958 (£14,000), player/manager March 1961, gave up playing cs 1963 and remained as manager to April 1974; England team manager April 1974-July 1977; coach to the United Arab Emirates July 1977-May 1980; subsequently coached in Egypt. Other honours: England 'B' international (1 app). Football League (2 apps). (Man. City) FA Cup winner 1956; finalist 1955.

Wing-half/centre and inside-forward. A coveted player from wartime days, thoughtful and deliberate in control and distribution. The major figure of Manchester City's successful 'Revie Plan' involving a deep-lying centre-forward (i.e. Revie), a tactic copied from the great contemporary Hungary side. Equally in the limelight in management, raising a near-moribund Leeds

United into a power, followed by an England spell that ended in a sensational departure. 'Footballer of the Year' 1955. Awarded the CBE 1970.

REYNOLDS, John
(West Bromwich Albion and Aston Villa, 1892-97, 8)
Born Blackburn, 21 February 1869. Died 12 March 1917.
1895: 5ft. 5ins.; 12st.

Career: After moving to Ireland when a boy returned to Blackburn at 15 and assisted local sides (Park Road, Witton and Blackburn Rovers reserves) before joining the East Lancashire Rgt. in 1886 and playing in the regimental team. Was posted to Ireland the following year and there wore the colours of Belfast Distillery and Ulster (joined cs 1890). Subsequently with West Bromwich Albion March 1891 (guest player for Droitwich FC 1891/92); Aston Villa May 1893; Celtic cs 1897; Southampton 1897/98; Bristol St George's cs 1898 (New Zealand as a coach early in 1902); Stockport County cs 1903; Willesden Town cs-October 1904, retiring from the game around that time. Other honours: Irish international (5 apps). Football League (4 apps). (Ulster) Irish Cup finalist 1891. (WBA) FA Cup winner 1892. (Villa) FL champions 1894, 1896, 1897. FA Cup winner 1895, 1897.

Right-half, short yet weighty. Substantial in performance too with his speed, skilled footwork, marksmanship and tenacity. Won 5 Irish caps before it was discovered he was an Englishman. Latterly a collier in the Sheffield district.

RICHARDS, Charles Henry
(Nottingham Forest, 1898, 1)
Born Burton-on-Trent, 9 August 1875.
1898: 5ft. 6ins.; 11st. 11lbs.

Career: Gresley Rovers; Notts County 1895; Nottingham Forest January 1896; Grimsby Town December 1898; Leicester Fosse June 1901; Newton Heath 1901/02-1903. Other honours: (Forest) FA Cup winner 1898. (Grimsby Town) FL Div. 2 champions 1901.

Inside-right with a stocky build. Not one of your spectacular performers, his virtues lying in team work, foraging and exploiting a sharp eye for goal chances. Struck up fruitful partnerships at Nottingham with the Scottish international, Tommy McInnes, and at Grimsby alongside the League 'cap', Harry Fletcher.

RICHARDS, George Henry
(Derby County, 1909, 1)
Born Castle Donington, Leics. 10 May 1880. Died 1 November 1959.
1911: 5ft. $8^3/_4$ins.; 11st. 5lbs.
Career: Whitwick White Star; Derby County April 1902; retired during WW1. Other honours: (Derby Co) FL Div. 2 champions 1912. FA Cup finalist 1903.

Left-half/inside-left, starting in the latter position and taking the left-half berth regularly during the 1907/08 campaign. Very popular at the Baseball ground – a 1911 description read 'a capable and industrious half-back, and a skilful dribbler, who was reserve for the England v. Scotland match two years ago.' Despite several mishaps George logged 309 League and Cup appearances for Derby. An FA tourist in South Africa during the 1910 close season, he then twice played against the national team.

RICHARDS, John Peter
(Wolverhampton Wanderers, 1973, 1)
Born Warrington, 9 November 1950.
1973: 5ft. $9^1/_2$ins.; 11st. 5lbs.

Career: Lancashire Schools; Wolverhampton Wanderers July 1969 (Derby County on loan, November 1982-February 1983); Maritimo FC (Portugal) August 1983. Other honours: England 'B' international. England Under-23 international (6 apps). England Under-21 international (2 apps). Football League (1 app). (Wolves) Inter-Cities Fairs Cup finalist 1972. FL Div. 2 champions 1977. FL Cup winner 1974, 1980.

Centre/Inside-forward of intelligence, taker and maker of opportunities, and a first-rate club man at Molineux. Aggregate League figures: 375 matches, 20 subs, 146 goals. 'Young Footballer of the Year' 1973. After leaving the game was appointed the Wolverhampton local authority's sport and recreation officer.

RICHARDSON, James Robert
(Newcastle United, 1933, 2)
Born Ashington, 8 February 1911. Died 28 August 1964.
1932: 5ft. $7^1/_2$ins.; 10st. 9lbs.

Career: East Northumberland Schools;

Blyth Spartans 1925 when only in his 15th year; Newcastle United April 1928 (£200); Huddersfield Town October 1934 (£4000); Newcastle United again October 1937 (£4500); Millwall March 1938 (£4000); Leyton Orient player/coach January 1948, later serving as assistant trainer and then trainer June 1951-June 1955; Millwall assistant trainer November 1956 for a short period before being compelled to retire on health grounds. Other honours: England schoolboy international (2 apps). Football League (1 app). (Newcastle) FA Cup winner 1932.

Inside-forward (usually inside-right). A work horse though a skilled one, the ball under instant control following a lightning burst to win it. Was involved in the notorious 1932 Cup final goal ('was it over the line?') that sank Arsenal. Richardson had a varied career, sampling for instance, all three Divisions in season 1937/38. Once a motor mechanic.

RICHARDSON, William
(West Bromwich Albion, 1935, 1)
Born Framwellgate Moor nr. Durham, 29 May 1909.
Died 29 March 1959.
1931: 5ft. 8in.; 10st. 12lbs.

Career: Durham schoolboy football; Horden Wednesday; United Bus Co FC (Hartlepool); Hartlepools United originally as an amateur, signing professional during the 1928/29 season; West Bromwich Albion June 1929 (£1000); Shrewsbury Town November 1945. Later Albion's assistant trainer and was still on their training staff at the time of his death. Other honours: FA Cup winner 1931; finalist 1935.

Centre-forward with the goal touch, netting 217 in 350 League outings, which included some impressive match performances (e.g. 4 in 5 minutes at West Ham, November 1931). Always alert, specialising in the conversion of low, hard-driven centres. Appeared on Albion's team sheets as W G Richardson – the 'G' standing for Ginger – to distinguish him from their centre-half who was also named William Richardson. The Framwellgate Moor air must have been beneficial for centre-forwards – the great George Camsell also hailed from there.

RICKABY, Stanley
(West Bromwich Albion, 1954, 1)
Born Stockton-on-Tees, 12 March 1924.
1951: 6ft.; 13st.
Career: Stockton Schools; South Bank; Middlesbrough 1941/42; West Bromwich Albion February 1950 (£7500); Poole Town as player/manager July 1955-July 1959, continuing as a player in the ensuing season; Weymouth cs 1960 for a season; Newton Abbot Spurs August 1963 for a season and then retired. Other honour: Football League (1 app).
Right-back. A Middlesbrough reserve who prospered on moving to The Hawthorns, developing into a class back with tackling and kicking reliability and an acute positional sense. A bad thigh injury that occurred during the 1954 FA Cup semi-final shortened his senior career (and cost him a winners' medal). After employment with a life assurance firm in the Birmingham area, Rickaby emigrated to Australia in 1969.

RIGBY, Arthur
(Blackburn Rovers, 1927-28, 5)
Born Chorlton, Manchester, 7 June 1900.
Died 25 March 1960.
1928: 5ft. 81/2ins.; 11st.

Career: Manchester district football; Stockport County; Crewe Alexandra 1919; Bradford City February 1921; Blackburn Rovers April 1925 (£2500); Everton November 1929 (£2000); Middlesbrough May 1932; Clapton Orient August 1933; Crewe Alexandra again August 1935; retired cs 1937. Other honours: Football League (1 app). (Blackburn R) FA Cup winner 1928. (Everton) FL Div. 2 champions 1931. (Crewe A) Welsh Cup winner 1936.
Inside/outside-left. All his England appear-

ances were at inside-left but it was as a winger that most of his club football was played. A shrewd performer exercising immaculate control and an accurate shot. He also lasted a long time in the first-class game, his aggregate 467 League outings encompassing 17 of the 20 inter-war campaigns. Started as a goalkeeper and was an electrician by trade.

RIMMER, Ellis James
(Sheffield Wednesday, 1930-32, 4)
Born Birkenhead, 2 January 1907. Died 16 March 1965.
1930: 5ft. 10ins.; 11st. 7lbs.

Career: Birkenhead Schools; Parkside FC; Northern Nomads (during which spell he assisted Everton 'A'); Whitchurch September 1923; Tranmere Rovers 1924; Sheffield Wednesday February 1928 (£3000); Ipswich Town August 1938; retired February 1939. Other honours: (Wednesday) FL champions 1929, 1930. FA Cup winner 1935.
Outside-left appreciably taller than the usual winger. Had all the requirements: speed, trickiness, marksmanship and the ability to middle the ball accurately. After leaving the game was a licensee.

RIMMER, J(ohn) James
(Arsenal, 1976, 1)
Born Southport, 10 February 1948.
1976: 6ft. 1in.; 13st. 2lbs.
Career: Schools football; Manchester United apprentice 1963, turning professional May 1965 (Swansea City on loan October 1973-February 1974); Arsenal March 1974 (£40,000) after a month on loan; Aston Villa August 1977 (£65,000); Swansea City July 1983 (£35,000); Luton Town October 1986. Other honours: (Villa) European Cup winner 1982. FL Champions 1981.

Goalkeeper notably durable even though those occupying the position are more liable to be long-lasting than their outfield brethren. Jimmy, a brave 'keeper, has taken the eye for a score of years, hurling a big frame around his goal area to splendid effect.

RIX, Graham
(Arsenal, 1981-84, 17)
Born Doncaster, 23 October 1957.
1982: 5ft. 9ins.; 11st.

Career: Doncaster schools football; Arsenal apprentice 1974, turning professional January 1975. (Brentford on loan December 1987); Caen (France) cs 1988. Other honours: England 'B' international. England Under-21 international (7 apps) (Arsenal) European Cup Winners' Cup finalists 1980. FA Cup winner 1979; finalist 1978 (sub), 1980.

Midfield, left side. Akin to the old time outside-lefts with his speed, clever intricate footwork and goal scoring capibility. Has been a long-serving Gunner, quickly obtaining a regular first team place after getting full professional status, and eventually having a spell as team skipper. Not so prominent when a new wave of Arsenal youngsters captured the headlines in 1986/87.

ROBB, George
(Tottenham Hospur, 1954, 1)
Born Finsbury Park, London , 1 June 1926.
1954:5ft. 7$^1/_2$ins.; 11st 12lbs.

Career: North London schools football; Finchley 1942; Tottenham Hospur as an amateur December 1951, turning professional June 1953; retired through injury May 1960. Other honours: England amateur international (18 apps). England 'B' international (3 apps) football League (1 app).
Outside-left. Took the professional ticket at 27 after years as a top amateur. A direct, hard-shooting wingman, George scored 52 goals in 182 League games for Tottenham. Was sports master at Christ's College, Finchley, 1952-64 and then at the Sussex public school, Ardingly, from 1964 where he also taught English.

ROBERTS, Charles
(Manchester United, 1905, 3)
Born Rise Carr, Darlington, 6 April 1883.
Died 7 August 1939.
1909: 5ft. 11½ins.; 12st. 7lbs.

Career: Darlington St Augustine's; Bishop Auckland; Grimsby Town May 1903 ;Manchester United April 1904 (£700); Oldham Athletic August 1913 (£1300); retired January 1919. Oldham Athletic manager July 1921 – December 1922. Other honours: Football League (9 apps). (Man. Utd.) FL champions 1908, 1911. FA Cup winner 1909.

Centre-half whose meagre haul of caps does not indicate his true ranking. (Besides having to compete with the great Billy Wedlock, Charlie, it is thought, was 'victimised' because of union activites). He was, in fact, an all time master pivot, strong in every particular and in reading a game. A founder member of the Players' Union and later its Chairman until September 1921. Was the owner of stationery and newsagents' shops in the Manchester area and uncle of the three well known Hooper brothers of Darlington FC.

ROBERTS, Frank
(Mancherster City, 1925, 4)
Born Sandbach, Cheshire, 3 April 1893.
Died 23 May 1961.
1925: 5ft. 8ins.; 12st.

Career: Sandbach Villa; Sandbach Ramblers; Crewe Alexandra; Bolton Wanderers August 1914; Mancherster City October 1922 (£3400); Manchester Central June 1929; Horwich RMI July 1930. Other honours: Football league (1 app). (Man. City) FL Div. 2 champions1928. FA Cup finalist 1926.

Inside-right/centre-forward. No dispenser of the subtle touch or delicate dribble but a rare marksman and opportunist. His aggregate League match total (373, 1914-29) brought him a very respectable 195 goals. Bolton Wanderers had no wish to lose Frank's services, the player's persistent wish to become mine host of a local hotel causing the rift. Was employed as a licensee, too, after leaving the game.

ROBERTS, Graham Paul
(Tottenham Hotspur, 1983-84, 6)
Born Southampton, 3 July 1959.
1983: 5ft. 10ins.; 12st 12lbs.

Career: Junior football (trials with Southampton, AFC Bournemouth and Portsmouth); Weymouth; Tottenham Hotspur May 1980 (£35,000, a record receipt for a non-League club); Rangers December 1986 (£450,000). Chelsea August 1988 (£470,000). Other honours: (Spurs) UEFA Cup winner 1984. FA Cup winner 1981, 1982. (Rangers) Scottish League champions 1987. Scottish League Cup winner 1988.

Central-defender. They don't come much harder than this well known battler. Nor do they come any braver, his indomitable spirit producing memorable goals (sometimes personally scored) as well as memorable last-ditch recoveries the other end. Was a fitter's mate in a shipyard prior to taking up the game full-time.

ROBERTS, Henry
(Millwall, 1931, 1)
Born Barrow-in-Furness, 1 September 1907.

Died October 1984.
1930: 5ft. 8½ins.; 11st 8lbs.

Career: Lancashire Schools; Barrow Wireworks; Barrow FC December 1925; Chesterfield June 1926; Lincoln City August 1928; Port Vale June 1930 (£100); Millwall April 1931 – 1935; Sheffield Wednesday (on trial) October 1935.

Inside-right, with service at centre-forward too. Thickset in build and bustling in style but not lacking in subtle touches – a rather unusual combination. Harry spent much of his career in the Third Divisions and never did sample First Division football. Scored 65 goals in his 207 aggregate League appearances.

ROBERTS, Herbert ('Policeman')
(Arsenal, 1931, 1)
Born Oswestry, Salop, 19 February 1905. Died 19 June 1944.
1931: 6ft.; 11st. 10lbs.

Career: Oswestry Town; Arsenal December 1926 (£200); retired through injury during the 1937/38 season and briefly acted as Margate's trainer before returning to join the Arsenal training staff cs 1938. Other honours: (Arsenal) FL champions 1931, 1933, 1934, 1935. FA Cup winner 1936; finalist 1932.

Centre-half. Called Policeman Roberts because, on manager Herbert Chapman's instructions, he became the first of the 'stopper' pivots, staying put and never being drawn upfield. An unpopular style at the time but effective in counteracting the changed offside law introduced in 1925. Roberts died from erysipelas while on wartime service with the Royal Fusiliers, the illness said to have been caused by the injury which ended his playing career. Before going to Highbury in 1926 he had been employed as a gunsmith (which seems highly appropriate given Arsenal's nickname).

ROBERTS, Robert John
(West Bromwich Albion, 1887-90, 3)
Born West Bromwich, April 1859. Died 28 October 1929.
Height: 6ft. 4ins.

Career: West Bromwich schoolboy football; Salter's Works (W. Bromwich); West Bromwich Albion September 1879; Sunderland Albion May 1890; West Bromwich Albion again May 1891; Aston Villa May 1892; retired 1893. Other honours: (WBA) FA Cup winner 1888; finalist 1886, 1887.

Goalkeeper of prodigious height and presumably of prodigious weight too (he took a size 13 boot). Blessed with an ideal temperament, he handled the ball well and easily withstood the hefty shoulder charges of opponents that were common currency in Roberts' day. Originally played in several outfield berths. After retiring worked as a plasterer in Sunderland. He was West Brom's first internationalist.

ROBERTS, W(illiam) Thomas
(Preston North End, 1924, 2)
Born Handsworth, Birmingham, 29 November 1898. Died 13 October 1965.
1922: 5ft. 10½ins.; 12st.

Career: Soho Villa (Birmingham); Leicester Fosse (guest player for Southport Vulcan during WW1); Preston North End May 1919 (£400); Burnley October 1924

(£4600); Preston North End again July 1926 (£1500); Tottenham Hotspur May 1928 (£1000); Dick, Kerr's FC (Preston) August 1929; Chorley October 1930. Other honours: Football League (2 apps). (PNE) FA Cup finalist 1922.

Centre-forward. A dynamic leader in the 'Twenties, full of dash and a goal-threatening menace anywhere near the opposing citadel. Consistent scoring while a Southport Vulcan wartime guest brought him to notice, and he maintained this form in the First Division on moving to Deepdale. An aggregate 277 League and FA Cup matches there produced 179 goals. He suffered a broken pelvis while at Burnley that probably affected his later career. Tommy was a Preston licensee for some 30 years.

ROBINSON, John ('Jackie')
Sheffield Wednesday, 1937-39, 4)
Born Shiremoor, Northumberland, 10 August 1917. Died 1979.
1938: 5ft. 9½ins.; 10st.

Career: Northumberland junior football; Sheffield Wednesday 1935; Sunderland October 1946 (£5000); Lincoln City October 1949 – 1950 (broke a leg after a few games and left League football). Other honour: Football League (1 app).

Inside-right. A major discovery of the 'Thirties, a much talented, graceful prodigy. A writer of the time tells of Jackie 'revealing brilliant natural talents as a boy'. And that 'in the development of his play he has always shown remarkable assurance and exceptional ease and certainty in his ball control'. Was a Wednesday regular long before his 20th birthday.

ROBINSON, John William
(Derby County, New Brighton Tower and Southampton, 1897-1901, 11)
Born Derby, 22 April 1870. Died 28 October 1931.
1901: 5ft. 10ins.: 13st 4lbs.

Career: Derby Midland: Lincoln City; Derby County cs 1891; New Brighton Tower August 1897; Southampton May 1898 (£400) Plymouth Argyle May 1903; Exeter City late in 1905; Millwall Athletic November 1905; Green Waves FC (Plymouth) cs 1907; Exeter City again September 1908; Stoke May 1909 – 1912. Other honours: (Soton) Southern League champions 1899, 1901, 1903. FA Cup finalist 1900, 1902.

Goalkeeper. Possessing great crowd appeal, his brilliant displays garnished with sensational saves brought about by agility and speed of movement. Emigrated to the States in October 1912, returning to live at Turnditch near Derby shortly before his death.

ROBSON, Bryan
(West Bromwich Albion and Manchester United, 1980-88, 69)
Born Chester-le-Street, Co Durham, 11 January 1957.
1984: 5ft. 10½ins.; 11st 11½lbs.

Career: Chester-le-Street Schools (trials with Burnley, Coventry City and Newcastle United); West Bromwich Albion, originally on schoolboy forms September 1972, later an apprentice, turning professional August 1974; Manchester United October 1981 (£1.5m., a then British record). Other honours:England Youth international. England 'B' international. England Under-21 international (7 apps). (Man. Utd.) FA Cup winner 1983, 1985.

Midfield. Thought by many sound judges the most complete midfielder in Britain (and possibly Europe) since WW2. Aggressive, brave, extremely skilled and an inspiring captain of both club and country. Has not been deterred by a series of injuries (starting with three broken legs in 1976/77) that would have deterred many – perhaps, most – people. His brother, Gary, followed him to The Hawthorns.

ROBSON, Robert William
(West Bromwich Albion,1958-62, 20)
Born Langley Park, Co. Durham, 18 February 1933.
1960: 5ft. 9½ins.; 11st. 10lbs.

Career: Chester-le-Street junior football; Langley Park Juniors; Fulham May 1950; West Bromwich Albion March 1956 (£25,000); Fulham again August 1962 (£20,000); Vancouver Royals (Canada) player/coach May 1967-January 1968. Fulham manager January-November 1968; Ipswich Town manager January 1969; England team manager appointed July 1982 with effect from the following September. Other honours: England Under-23 international (1 app). Football League (5 apps).

Right-half. After a deal of experience at inside-right, the former the position in which his caps were won. As a forward, partnering the England men, Jezzard and Haynes, he proved a dangerous raider, ever on the look-out for goals. At wing-half his tireless and confident play was even more effective. Following a lengthy and successful managerial spell with Ipswich, Bobby is much in the limelight as his country's supremo.

ROSE, William Crispin
(Swifts, Preston North End and Wolverhampton Wanderers, 1884-91, 5)
Born St. Pancras, London, 1861. Died 4 February 1937.
1895: 5ft. 11$^1/_2$ins.; 12st. 12lbs.

Career: Small Heath; Swifts; Preston North End February 1885; Stoke; Wolverhampton Wanderers 1888/89; Loughborough Town May 1894; Wolverhampton Wanderers again cs 1895; retired cs 1896. Other honour: (Wolves) FA Cup winner 1893.

Goalkeeper. 'At his best had few superiors,' summed up a contemporary scribe after commenting on the player's abilities to deal with hard shooting and to clear with foot and fist. In early career played in representative matches for Wiltshire, London and Birmingham. Rose, in October 1893, issued a circular letter that was instrumental in launching the Players' Union. After leaving football was employed as a licensee in Birmingham and Wolverhampton and as a tobacconist at Bordesley. His brother, A C Rose, was a well known athlete in his day.

ROSTRON, Thurston ('Tot')
(Darwen, 1881, 2)
Born Darwen, Lancs. 21 April 1863. Died 3 July 1891.
1884: 5ft. 5ins.

Career: Helmshore FC; Old Wanderers; Darwen FC; Great Lever during season 1883/84; Darwen again 1885, around this period assisting Blackburn Rovers also. Represented Lancashire.

Forward. 'small but clever forward with plenty of pace, good screw kick and works hard,' reported the 1881 Football Annual. Only a teenager when he played for his country (his debut international took place at nearby Blackburn). But also, lamentably among the band of top Victorian notables who met an early death. A sprinter of note, he was employed first as a weaver and then as a bowling green keeper.

ROWE, Arthur Sydney
(Tottenham Hotspur, 1934, 1)
Born Tottenham, 1 September 1906.
1935: 5ft. 9ins.; 12st. 8lbs.

Career: Schools football (Chestnut, Herts) and junior football before signing amateur forms for Tottenham Hotspur 1923, develping with their nursery club, Northfleet, before turning professional May 1929; retired through injury cs 1939, then becoming a coach in Hungary. Chelmsford City manager July 1945; Tottenham Hotspur manager May 1949-May 1955 when he left on health grounds; West Bromwich Albion chief scout August 1957; Crystal Palace assistant manager October 1958, manager April 1960 later becoming a director and continuing to work on Palace's staff until May 1971; employed by Football's 'Hall of

Fame' (an exhibition) from about that time to December 1971; Orient FC consultant January 1972-cs 1978; Millwall consultant for a time from June 1978.

Centre-half. The thoughtful kind, cleverly turning defence into attack and trying always to distribute accurately. Won more fame as Spurs' manager when architect of the celebrated 'push-and-run' style. This entailed a player quickly passing the ball along the ground and running into an open space to receive a return pass or decoy an opposing defender. The system brought Spurs the Second and First Division championships in consecutive seasons.

ROWLEY, John Frederick
(Manchester United, 1949-52, 6)
Born Wolverhampton, 7 October 1920.
1950: 5ft. 9ins.; 12st.

Career: Dudley Old Boys; Wolverhampton Wanderers November 1935 (on loan to Cradley Heath October 1936 and then Bournemouth & Boscombe Athletic, February 1937); Manchester United October 1937 (£3500); Plymouth Argyle as player/manager February 1955, retired as a player cs 1957 and manager only to March 1960; Oldham Athletic manager July 1960-July 1963; Ajax FC (Amsterdam) coach August 1963-July 1964; Wrexham manager January 1966; Bradford general manager April 1967; Oldham Athletic manager again October 1968-December 1969. Other honours; England wartime international (1 app). England 'B' international (1 app). Football League (2 apps). (Man Utd) FL champions 1952. FA Cup winner 1948.

Forward. Of great versatility: he actually appeared for England in four of the five forward positions, the exception being outside-right. Jack's aggression, power and searing shooting caused him to become known as 'The Gunner' (despite, it may be remarked, having no connection with Arsenal FC). Brother of Arthur Rowley (Leicester City and England 'B')

ROWLEY, William
(Stoke, 1889-92, 2)
Born Hanley.

Career: Hanley Orion (assisted Stoke's reserves during season 1883/84); Burslem Port Vale; Stoke cs 1887-1896 when he became club secretary. Leicester Fosse secretary August 1898 but the FA would not accept the registration and he was suspended October 1898. Played many times for Staffordshire. Other honours: Football League (1 app). (Stoke) Football Alliance champions 1891.

Goalkeeper after turning out at centre-forward for Hanley Orion. In J A H Catton's opinion '. . . one of the cleverest men who ever stood between the posts. He was always judicious and wonderfully cool.' Sustained a number of serious injuries including, in 1890/91, a broken breastbone, yet his nerve was never affected. Member of one of football's most celebrated defensive triumvirates (Rowley, Clare and Underwood) and, together with Tommy Clare, played in 17 consecutive matches for Staffordshire, 1884-90.

ROYLE, Joseph
(Everton and Manchester City, 1971-77, 6)
Born Liverpool, 8 April 1949.
1974: 6ft. 1ins.; 12st. 1lb.

Career: Liverpool Schools; Everton apprentice July 1964, turning professional August 1966; Manchester City December 1974 (£200,000); Bristol City December 1977 after a month on loan; Norwich City August 1980 (£60,000); retired through injury April; 1982. Oldham Athletic manager July 1982. Other honours: England Youth international. England Under-23 international (10 apps). Football League (1 app). (Everton) FL Champions 1970. FA Cup finalist 1968. (Man. City) FL Cup winner 1976.

Centre-forward. Occasionally played elsewhere in the attack. Quickly to the fore, becoming Everton's youngest senior debu-

tant (in 1966) and proceeding to give a good account of himself. Used physical advantage wisely and was brilliant in the air. Suffered injury problems with his back but it was a knee injury that caused the retiral.

RUDDLESDIN, Herod
(Sheffield Wednesday, 1904-05, 3)
Born Birdwell nr. Barnsley, 1876. Died 26 March 1910.
1905: 5ft. 7ins.; 11st. 2lbs.

Career: Birdwell FC; Sheffield Wednesday cs 1898; retired on health grounds December 1906. In 1908 made an abortive attempt at a come-back with Northampton Town. Other honours: (Wednesday) FL Champions 1903, 1904. FL Div. 2 champions 1900.

Wing-half. Won his international and club honours on both flanks, an adroit and scrupulously clean performer. Displayed no hint of showiness or affectation despite possessing extreme cleverness. It was lamentable that one with such admirable qualities was lost to the game prematurely. A 7-handicap golfer. Had once been a collier.

RUFFELL, James William
(West Ham United, 1926-30, 6)
Born Barnsley, 8 August 1900. Died 5 September 1989
1923: 5ft. $7^1/_2$ins.; 10st. 2lbs.

Career: Fuller's FC; Chadwell Heath United; Manor Park Albion; Wall End United (East Ham); West Ham United March 1920; Aldershot June 1938; retired through injury during the ensuing season. Other honours: Football League (3 apps). (WHU) FA Cup finalist 1923.

Outside left. Exceptionally fast and unleasher of thunderbolt shots, Jimmy was a winger who warranted the closest of close marking. Gave the hammers wonderful service, setting up a club League appearance record (506 matches, 159 goals) that stood until 1973. Moved to London as a child, hence the early connection with metropolitan area junior soccer. After leaving the game was an Essex licensee until retiring early in 1966.

RUSSELL, Bruce Bremner
(Royal Engineers, 1883, 1)
Born Kensington, London, 25 August 1859. Died 13 May 1942.

Career: Royal Military College, Woolwich; Royal Engineers.

Left-back. Blossoming at soccer too late for the Royal Engineers' FA Cup final exploits of the 1870s, Russell had played rugger at his public school (Cheltenham). He exercised a nice judgment in his kicking and was quite dependable. His service in the RE's extended from 1878 to 1907, when he retired holding the rank of Colonel. He returned to serve in the 1914/18 War.

RUTHERFORD, John ('Jock')
(Newcastle United, 1904-08, 11)
Born Percy Main, Northumberland, 12 October 1884. Died 21 April 1963.
1911: 5ft. 9ins.; 11st. 6lbs.

Career: Percy Main schoolboy football; Willington Athletic 1900; Newcastle United January 1902 (£75); Woolwich Arsenal October 1913 (£800) (guest player for Chelsea during WW1), was briefly Stoke's manager, March-August 1923, returning to

Arsenal the following month; retired cs 1925 but re-registered by Arsenal January 1926; Clapton Orient August 1926; finally retired cs 1927. Later coach of Tufnell Park FC. Other honours: Football League (1 app). (N'castle U) FL champions 1905, 1907, 1909. FA Cup winner 1910; finalist 1905, 1906, 1908, 1911.

Outside-right of extreme durability, especially for a forward. Scored 88 as Percy Main School's centre-forward in season 1897/98 and notched some vital goals from the wing in the first-class game. Tremendously fast with good control and inch-perfect at centering. Had two brothers who were professionals – one was Sep of Portsmouth's 1934 Cup final side – while his son, John James Rutherford, made his League debut in November 1925, some time prior to Jock's eventual retirement. He (Jock) became a London licensee.

SADLER, David
(Manchester United, 1968-71, 4)
Born Yalding, Kent, 5 February 1946.
1970: 6ft.; 12st. 3lbs.

Career: Maidstone junior football; Maidstone United; Manchester United on amateur forms November 1962, turning professional February 1963; Preston North End November 1973 (£20,000); retired through injury May 1977. Other honours: England Youth international. England amateur international (2 apps). England Under-23 international (3 apps). Football League (2 apps). (Man. Utd) European Cup winner 1968. FL champions 1967.

Utility player of great adaptability, taking roles in defence, midfield and attack with equal efficiency. He won his 2 amateur caps at inside-right and was later to be found at centre-forward, centre-half and elsewhere, solid and reliable without any ostentation. David's first employment was as junior in a Maidstone bank. After leaving the game he became a branch manager for a building society.

SAGAR, Charles
(Bury, 1900-02, 2)
Born Daisy Hill, Edgworth, Lancs. 28 March 1878. Died 4 December 1919.
1903: 5ft. $11^1/_2$ins.; 11st. $0^1/_2$lb.

Career: St Anne's (Turton Sunday school side) 1895; Edgworth Rovers; Turton FC; Bury cs 1898; Manchester United cs 1905-07. Joined Haslingden FC early in 1909. Other honours: Football League (4 apps). (Bury) FA Cup winner 1900, 1903.

Centre-forward/inside-left spreading his England and Cup final appearances evenly: one England and one Cup final in each position. Not an ultra-consistent performer but, when in form, revealed much craftsmanship, particularly in the way of skilled footwork. A tall, lithe physique came in handy when leading the attack.

SAGAR, Edward
(Everton, 1936, 4)
Born Moorends, Doncaster, 7 February 1910. Died 16 October 1986.
1936: 5ft. 10ins.; 10st. 8lbs.

Career: Thorne Colliery (Doncaster Senior League) (trial for Hull City November 1928); Everton March 1929; retired May 1953. Other honours: Football League (5 apps). (Everton) FL champions 1932, 1939. FA Cup winner 1933.

Goalkeeper in the record books on two counts: his 24 years at Goodison constitute the longest period any professional has spent with a single FL club, and his 463 peacetime League match total is an Everton record. Slim and light as 'keepers go, Ted was utterly fearless, his displays marked with aerial athleticism and superb handling. In later years was employed as an Aintree licensee.

SANDFORD, Edward A.
(West Bromwich Albion, 1933, 1)
Born Handsworth, Birmingham, 22 October 1910.
1935: 5ft. 9½ins.; 11st. 4lbs.

Career: Birmingham schoolboy football; Tantany Athletic; Overend Wesley; Birmingham Carriage Works; Smethwick Highfield; West Bromwich Albion on amateur forms October 1929, turning professional May 1930; Sheffield United March 1939; retired 1943. Later an Albion coach and he also scouted for the club. Other honours: (WBA) FA Cup winner 1931; finalist 1935.

Inside-left, latterly centre-half (he had played half-back when a junior). A subtle inside man of the quieter kind, his work never showy, and an excellent marksman. Won a Cup winner's medal at 20 in his first pro season, reputedly the youngest Throstle to do so. Later owned a cafe near The Hawthorns.

SANDILANDS, Rupert Renorden
(Old Westminsters, 1892-96, 5)
Born Thrapston, Northants. 7 August 1868. Died 20 April 1946.

Career: Westminster School (XI 1885-87); Old Westminsters; Casuals; Corinthians 1889-97. Also represented London and Kent.

Outside-left well delineated in the mid-'Nineties as follows. 'For the Old Westminsters and the Corinthians he has done excellent service during the last few years, and no XI of late would have been fully representative of London without him. Fast on the ball and an excellent dribbler as well as a safe shot at goal, he is bound to be dangerous at all times. On his day there are few better forwards in the South.' He was on the staff of the Bank of England.

SANDS, John
(Nottingham Forest, 1880, 1)
Born 1859. Died 29 February 1924.

Career: Junior football to Nottingham Forest whom he assisted 1878-83.

Goalkeeper deemed 'very good' by that demanding critic, C W Alcock, who was mindful of Sands' agility and soundness. The player first appeared for Forest in November 1878 and had his last match on January 13, 1883, and during that period had taken part in 13 FA Cupties. One of three Forest stalwarts to be honoured by England that season.

SANSOM, Kenneth Graham
(Crystal Palace and Arsenal, 1979-88, 86)
Born Camberwell, London, 26 September 1958.
1983: 5ft. 6ins.; 11st. 8lbs.

Career: London Schools; Crystal Palace apprentice, turning professional December 1975; Arsenal August 1980 (in exchange for Clive Allen, q.v.); Newcastle United December 1988 (about £300,000). Other honours: England schoolboy international. England Youth international. England 'B' international. England Under-21 international (8 apps). (Palace) FL Div. 2 champions 1979. (Arsenal) FL Cup winner 1987.

Left-back. A much capped Londoner. Around the time of the first full honour it was written his '. . . secret is his dedication allied to sharpness, control, agility and a fine soccer brain.' Small yet sturdy and purveyor of one of the longest throws in the modern game.

SAUNDERS, Frank Etheridge
(Swifts, 1888, 1)
Born Brighton, 26 August 1864. Died 14 May 1905.

Career: Repton School (XI 1882-83); Cambridge University (Blue 1885-6-7); Swifts; Corinthians 1885-91; St Thomas's Hospital. Also represented Sussex.

Centre/wing-half. Equally comfortable in all three half-back positions. Saunders was a tough opponent, well endowed physically and unrelenting when challenging and tackling. He was a licentiate of the Society of Apothecaries, emigrated to South Africa and died there at Fricksburg, Orange River Colony (later the Orange Free State).

SAVAGE, A. H.
(Crystal Palace, 1876, 1)
Career: Crystal Palace; also represented Surrey.

Goalkeeper. A sound custodian and reliable. Had a remarkably hefty kick but the advantage this gave to clearances was nullified somewhat by indiscrimate placing.

NOTE. Savage has proved to be the most intractable of the early difficult entries from a researcher's point of view. He was alleged to have been educated at Rugby, but this cannot be established. He *could* be the Alfred Henry Savage born at Reading in 1854 (birth registered in the second quarter of that year). Another possibility is Arthur Harold Savage, of the English & Oriental Hotel, Penang, who died in Penang on August 4, 1930. A third suggestion, received as the book was going to press, is Arthur Henry Patrick Savage, born Sydney, Australia, 18 October 1850, who died in Bayswater on August 15, 1905. He is a valid candidate as some match reports list the player as A H P Savage.

SAYER, James
(Stoke, 1887, 1)
Born Mexborough, Yorks. 1862. Died 1 February 1922.

Career: Mexborough FC; Sheffield Heeley; Sheffield Wednesday; Stoke.

Outside-right. Counted among the fastest wingers of his day, a fact relished by Stoke supporters who dubbed him 'The Greyhound'. Speed was backed by an all-round ability. Represented the Sheffield FA in district matches when based in the steel city. Sayer was secretary of a Stoke pottery firm, eventually becoming a company director.

SCATTERGOOD, Ernald Oak
(Derby County, 1913, 1)
Born Riddings, Derbys. 29 May 1887. Died 2 July 1932.
1911: 5ft. 8ins.; 12st. 9lbs.

Career: Alfreton junior football; Riddings St James; Ripley Athletic; Derby County August 1907 (£11); Bradford October 1914; retired cs 1925. Other honour: (Derby Co.) FL Div. 2 champions 1912.

Goalkeeper. Succeeded another England 'keeper (Maskrey) for both Ripley Athletic and Derby. Scattergood was of moderate height for the position but agile, a clean handler and had no superiors at hefty punching. Having a strong kick, he took penalties for both the Rams and Bradford. His son, Ken, also a custodian, played for Stoke City and Derby during the 'Thirties.

SCHOFIELD, Joseph Alfred
(Stoke, 1892-95, 3)
Born Hanley, Stoke-on-Trent, 1 January 1871. Died 29 September 1929.

Career: Potteries junior football to Stoke 1891; retired through injury cs 1899. Between other employments had a spell on Stoke's secretarial staff and was Port Vale's secretary/manager from February 1920 to his death. Other honours: Football League (2 apps).

Outside-left. The Athletic News Editor, J A H Catton, in 1897 gave the following account of Schofield. 'He has a very nice turn of speed, coupled with rare command over the ball and fine shooting abilities. Although lacking in that reckless bravado which at times achieves so much, Schofield is remarkably clever, and on his day leads the opposing half-back and back a rare dance.' Outside football the player worked at various times as a school teacher and Poor Law officer.

SCOTT, Lawrence
(Arsenal, 1947-49, 17)
Born Sheffield, 23 April 1917.
1948: 5ft. $9^1/_2$ins.; 11st. 8lbs.

Career: Junior football to Bradford City as an amateur 1931, turning professional 1934; Arsenal February 1937; Crystal Palace player/manager October 1951, retiring from playing August 1953 and continuing as manager until September 1954; Hendon FC manager later in 1954-cs 1957; Hitchin Town manager for a spell from August 1957. Other honours: England wartime international (10 apps). England 'B' international (4 apps). Football League (5 apps). (Arsenal) FL champions 1948. FA Cup winner 1950.

Right-back reputed to be the fastest of his time. Tackled powerfully, positioned himself well and placed clearances with consummate accuracy. Outside the game, Laurie was employed as a sales representative.

SCOTT, William Reed
(Brentford, 1937, 1)
Born Willington Quay, Northumberland, 6 December 1907. Died 18 October 1969.
1938: 5ft. 7ins.; 11st.

Career: Howden Bridge British Legion; Middlesbrough cs 1927; Brentford May 1932 (£1500 including 2 other players); Aldershot August 1947; Dover August 1948. Other honours: (Brentford) FL Div. 3 (South) champions 1933. FL Div. 2 champions 1935.

Inside-forward, usually inside-left for the Bees but equally adept on the right. Regarded as the mastermind behind their powerful forward play of the Thirties, his machinations contributing greatly to the scoring exploits of Jack Holliday and Dave McCulloch. And he netted a fair number of goals himself. Held the Brentford FL appearance record for some years.

SEDDON, James
(Bolton Wanderers, 1923-29, 6)
Born Bolton, 20 May 1895. Died 21 October 1971.
1925: 6ft. $1^1/_4$ins.; 11st. 11lbs.

Career: Bolton Schools; Hamilton Central, Chorley (West Lancashire League); Bolton Wanderers as an amateur 1912/13, turning professional, June 1919; retired cs 1932. Dordrecht FC (Holland) coach cs 1932; Altrincham trainer June 1935; Southport trainer cs 1936; after WW2 had spell on Liverpool's training staff. Other honours: (Bolton W) FA Cup winner 1923, 1926, 1929.

Centre-half without elaboration using a pivot's ideal physique to good – and fair – effect. Linch-pin in three Bolton FA Cup triumphs, being skipper in the last of them (1929). After leaving football was assistant manager of a Southport hotel. His son, K J Seddon, was on Liverpool's books, later becoming well known as a referee on the first-class list.

SEED, James Marshall
(Tottenham Hotspur, 1921-25, 5)
Born Blackhill, Co Durham, 25 March 1895. Died 16 July 1966.
1925: 5ft. $10^1/_2$ins.; 11st. 9lbs.

Career: Whitburn; Sunderland April 1914; Mid-Rhondda 1919; Tottenham Hotspur

February 1920 (about £350); Sheffield Wednesday August 1927 (for another player plus a fee); retired early 1931. Clapton Orient manager April 1931; Charlton Athletic sec/manager May 1933-September 1956; Bristol City consultant January 1957; Millwall manager January 1958-July 1959, remaining in an advisory capacity and appointed a director January 1960, keeping this directorship until his death. Other honours: (Spurs) FA Cup winner 1921. (Sheffield W) FL champions 1929, 1930.

Inside-right. 'Tireless and thrustful, subtle, and a schemer with few superiors for stamina . . .' wrote one critic in 1925. A fair summing-up and for a player who, after being gassed in the Great War, had been considered 'finished' as regards the first-class game. Had a remarkable playing swan song, captaining Wednesday to successive League championships. And famous as a manager too, leading Charlton from Third to First Divisions in 2 years. A clever football caricaturist, his work appeared widely in the 1920s sports pages but he ceased this activity on entering management. His autobiography, 'The Jimmy Seed Story' (Phoenix Sports Books), appeared in 1957 and his brother, Angus, managed Aldershot 1927-37 and Barnsley 1937-53.

SETTLE, James
(Bury and Everton, 1899-1903, 6)
Born Millom, Cumberland, 1875.
1902: 5ft. 6ins.; 11st.

Career: Bolton junior football; Bolton Wanderers cs 1894; Halliwell Rovers cs 1895; Bury January 1897; Everton April 1899 (£400); Stockport County May 1908; retired cs 1909. Other honours: Football League (4 apps). (Everton) FA Cup winner 1906; finalist 1907.

Inside/outside-left more often in the inside berth. Diminutive forward whose speed in thought and action placed him among the most dangerous goal poachers of his day. And induced Everton to pay a very high fee by 1890s standards. Jimmy required little space in which to trick an opponent. His faults lay in an occasional selfishness and lapse in work-rate.

SEWELL, John
(Sheffield Wednesday, 1952-54, 6)
Born Kells, Whitehaven, 24 January 1927.
1957: 5ft. 8ins.; 11st. 4lbs.

Career: Whitehaven Schools; Kells Miners' Welfare Under-18; Whitehaven Town (guest player for Workington and Carlisle United during WW2); Notts County amateur 1942, turning professional October 1944; Sheffield Wednesday March 1951 (£34,500, then a record); Aston Villa December 1955 (£18,000); Hull City October 1959 (£5000); Lusaka City (Zambia) as player/coach September 1961, and was also Zambia's national coach until his return to England May 1973. Other honours: Football League (5 apps). (Notts Co) FL Div. 3 (South) champions 1950. (Wednesday) FL Div. 2 champions 1952, 1956. (Villa) FA Cup winner 1957.

Inside-forward star of the immediate post-WW2 years – mobile, a live wire and consistently on the score-sheet (he finished with 227 goals in a total 510 League games). Jackie was the subject of much transfer talk as a Notts County player. The fee forthcoming from Sheffield Wednesday created a furore at the time.

SEWELL, W(alter) Ronald
(Blackburn Rovers, 1924, 1)
Born Middlesbrough, 19 July 1890. Died 4 February 1945.
1925: 5ft. $11^1/_2$ins.; 12st. 8lbs.

Career: Wingate Albion (North-Eastern League); Gainsborough Trinity cs 1911; Burnley February 1913 (£1800 including 2 other players); Blackburn Rovers February 1920; Gainsborough Trinity again September 1927. Other honour: (Burnley) FA Cup winner 1914.

Goalkeeper. 'Has a "cap", immense optimism, heaps of experience, a classical physique, and is one of the personalities of the side,' said a local annual in 1926. The same source had in previous years commented on this cool and resourceful 'keeper's humour, which was a dressing-room tonic. His transfer to Burnley had caused a sensation, the entire Gainsborough defence going to Turf Moor following a cup-tie between the clubs. He played in the 1914 Final because Jerry Dawson was injured. Ronnie, a one-time seafarer, was a Lincoln licensee for a long time up to his death.

SHACKLETON, Leonard Francis
(Sunderland, 1949-55, 5)
Born Bradford, 3 May 1922.
1950: 5ft. 7½ins.; 11st. 5lbs.

Career: Bradford Schools; Kippax United; Arsenal ground staff August 1938 (loaned to London Paper Mills and Enfield for development); returned home at the outbreak of war, signing for Bradford as a professional December 1940 (guest player for Bradford City during WW2); Newcastle United October 1946 (£13,000); Sunderland February 1948 (£20,050); retired through injury September 1957. Other honours: England schoolboy international (3 apps). England 'B' international (2 apps). Football League (2 apps).

Inside-forward dubbed 'The Clown Prince of Soccer' because of his sorcerer's brilliance in trickery (so brilliant he sometimes mystified colleagues too). This tag also served as the title for Shack's book, a work so irreverent it scandalised the football establishment. E.g. a page devoted to 'what the average director knows about soccer' which was blank except for the caption. Played cricket on occasion for Northumberland. Later a sports journalist based in the North-East. Had spell as a Fulham director from 1976.

SHARP, John
(Everton, 1903-05, 2)
Born Hereford, 15 February 1878. Died 28 January 1938.
1905: 5ft. 7ins.; 11st. 7lbs.
Career: Hereford Thistle (Bristol League); Aston Villa cs 1897; Everton cs 1899; retired cs 1910. Served as an Everton director from 1923. Other honours: Football League (3 apps). (Everton) FA Cup winner 1906; finalist 1907.

Outside-right gifted with a powerful stocky build and the orthodox qualities of pace and centering ability. Additionally – and fairly uncommon in his day – he was wont to cut inside. Famous, too, as a cricketer for Lancashire (1899-1925) and England (3 Tests in 1909), he played as a professional to 1914 and as an amateur from 1919. He also assisted Herefordshire occassionally. Sharp's brother Bert, a full-back, was a colleague at Hereford Thistle, Villa and Everton, and his son also became an Everton director. Founder of a well-known sports outfitting firm which the aforementioned son eventually took over.

SHAW, George Edward
(West Bromwich Albion, 1932, 1)
Born Swinton nr. Rotherham, 13 October 1899. Died March 1973.
1931: 5ft. 10in.; 11st. 3lbs.

Career: South Yorks. school and junior football; Gillingham 1920/21; Rossington Main Colliery 1921; Doncaster Rovers cs 1922; Huddersfield Town February 1924; West Bromwich Albion December 1926 (£4100, then an Albion record); Stalybridge Celtic May 1938; Worcester City player/manager March 1939; post-war managed and coached Floriana FC (Malta) 1948-51. Other honours: Football League (1 app). (WBA) FA Cup winner 1931; finalist 1935.

Right-back occasionally appearing on the opposite flank. An all-round defender, strong in heading, a safe kick – particularly adept with the volley – and a penalty taker. Went on two FA tours: to Europe 1929 and Canada 1931. Brother of Wilf Shaw (of Doncaster's 1935 Northern Section championship side) but was not related to Cecil Shaw (Albion back, 1936-47).

SHAW, Graham L.
(Sheffield United, 1959-63, 5)
Born Sheffield, 9 July 1934.
1961: 5ft. 8ins.; 11st.

Career: Sheffield schoolboy football; Oaks Fold; Sheffield United July 1951; Doncaster Rovers September 1967; Scarborough player/manager March 1968-January 1969. Other honours: England Under-23 international (5 apps). Football League (4 apps). (Sheffield U) FL Div. 2 champions 1953.

Left-back. Strong in tackling, quite dependable and intelligent in use of the ball when passing or clearing. A regular first-teamer at Bramall Lane for many seasons, making 442 League appearances for the Blades. Shone at boxing as a boy and was an ABA schools champion.

SHEA, Daniel
(Blackburn Rovers, 1914, 2)
Born Wapping of Irish parents, 6 November 1887. Died 25 December 1960.
1923: 5ft. 7ins.; 11st. 7lbs.

Career: Pearl United; Manor Park Albion; West Ham United November 1907; Blackburn Rovers January 1913 (for a record £2000 of which the player received £550) (guest player for West Ham and Nottingham Forest during WW1); West Ham United again May 1920 (£1000); Fulham November 1920; Coventry City cs 1923; Clapton Orient March 1925; Sheppey United October 1926, where he finished his playing career. Other honours: England 'Victory' international (2 apps). Football League (2 apps). Southern League (3 apps). (Blackburn) FL champions 1914.

Inside-right. A subtle schemer with, it was stated, 'twinkling feet' and 'a slow deliberate style and fine ball control.' In contrast to this dribbling delicacy Danny would wheel suddenly when nearing the opposing goal to deliver a thunderbolt of a shot. In the 1930s was running a sub-post office in West Ham.

SHELLITO, Kenneth J.
(Chelsea, 1963, 1)
Born East Ham, London, 18 April 1940.
1963: 5ft. $9^3/_4$ins.; 12st. 12lbs.

Career: Essex Schools; London Schools; Chelsea amateur May 1956, turning professional April 1957; retired through injury January 1969. Chelsea coaching staff cs 1969, manager July 1977-December 1978; Queen's Park Rangers coach/assistant manager May 1979-80; Crystal Palace coaching staff 1980/81; Preston North End assistant manager July-December 1981; Crystal Palace assistant manager cs 1982-November 1983; Wolverhampton Wanderers first team coach January 1985; Cambridge United manager March-December 1985. Other honour: England Under-23 international (1 app).

Right-back. A fast, bold and aggressive performer whose enforced retiral when only 28 was a loss to the game. Ken had bravely struggled for six years and undergone four operations to his left knee – the injury had been sustained in October 1963. Has since held a variety of managerial and coaching jobs on the League circuit.

SHELTON, Alfred
(Notts County, 1889-92, 6)
Born Nottingham, 11 September 1865. Died 24 July 1923.

Career: Notts Rangers; Notts County cs 1888; Loughborough Town cs 1896; Heanor Town August 1897; reinstated as an amateur cs 1898. Notts County director October 1908-1911. Had spell as Preston North End's trainer from cs 1912. Other honours: (Notts Co) FA Cup winner 1894; finalist 1891.

Left-half. An Athletic News comment of 1891 – 'a steady half-back who uses his head a great deal' – rather understated his value. A value underlined, of course, by his award of 6 caps in 3 seasons. He was a cool, hardworking performer and the referred-to 'use of head' applied to both heading ability and general shrewdness. Brother of Charles Shelton below, Alf was latterly employed at Cammell Laird's works in Nottingham, and lost his life there in a crane accident.

SHELTON, Charles
(Notts Rangers, 1888, 1)
Born Nottingham, 22 January 1864. Died 1899.

Career: Junior football to Notts Rangers; Notts County cs 1888-1892.

Left-half for his international but generally at centre-half for Notts County. Played a robust game and always pulled his full weight. Elder brother of Alf Shelton (England) whose continuous service at left-half for Notts County probably accounts for Charlie's regular appearances as their pivot.

SHEPHERD, Albert
(Bolton Wanderers and Newcastle United, 1906-11, 2)
Born Great Lever, Lancs. 10 September 1885. Died 8 November 1929.
1910: 5ft. 8ins.; 12st. 6lbs.

Career: Bolton Schools; Bolton St Mark's (Sunday school side); Bolton Temperance (signed as amateur for both Blackburn Rovers and Bolton Wanderers); signed amateur forms again for Bolton cs 1902 then assisted Bolton St Luke's before becoming a Bolton professional cs 1904; Newcastle United November 1908 (£850); Bradford City July 1914 (£1500); retired during WW1. Other honours: Football League (2 apps). (N'castle U) FL champions 1909. FA Cup winner 1910.

Centre-forward renowned for dash and devastating shooting. Fast, too, and able to bring the wings into play with nice judgment. His style naturally courted injury, the knock which caused him to miss the 1911 Cup final being said to have shortened his career. Latterly a licensee in Bolton.

SHILTON, Peter Leslie
(Leicester City, Stoke City, Nottingham Forest, Southampton and Derby County 1971-88, 100)
Born Leicester, 18 September 1949.
1979: 6ft.; 12st. 10lbs.

Career: Leicester Schools; Leicester City apprentice June 1965, turning professional September 1966; Stoke City November 1974 (£325,000); Nottingham Forest September 1977 (£270,000); Southampton August 1982 (£300,000); Derby County June 1987 (£90,000). Other honours: England schoolboy international. England Youth international. England Under-23 international (13 apps). Football League (3 apps). (Leicester) FL Div. 2 champions 1971. FA Cup finalist 1969. (Forest) European Cup winner 1979, 1980. FL champions 1978. FL Cup winner 1979; finalist 1980.

Goalkeeper. Latest in the long line of England 'keepers par excellence, starting in first-class soccer as Leicester's youngest debutant at 16 and still his country's first choice at 39. Supremely assured, master of all goalkeeping arts and unusually dedicated. 'Footballer of the Year' 1978 and awarded the MBE in 1986.

SHIMWELL, Edmund
(Blackpool, 1949, 1)
Born Wirksworth, Derbys. 27 February 1920. Died October 1988.
1949: 5ft. $10^3/_4$ins.; 12st. 6lbs.

Career: Wirksworth FC; Sheffield United 1939; Blackpool December 1946 (£7500); Oldham Athletic May 1957; Burton Albion player/manager July 1958; retired December 1958. Other honours: (Blackpool) FA Cup winner 1953; finalist 1948, 1951.

Right-back. Solidly built and solid in performance, one of a quartet who played in each of Blackpool's FA Cup finals (fellow England caps, Johnston, Matthews and Mortensen, were the others). Eddie kicked hard and true with either foot. Later a Matlock licensee.

SHUTT, George
(Stoke, 1886, 1)
Born Stoke-on-Trent, 1861. Died 1936.
Career: Junior football; Stoke until 1889; a Football League referee from circa 1891.

Centre-half. A highly competent pivot and difficult one to outwit, his tackling was assured and reliable. An occasional blemish was a tendency to mis-kicking. Has the distinction of being Stoke's first-ever internationalist (18 of the club's players were honoured prior to the Great War.) Shutt had left the Potters before they carried off the 1890/91 Football Alliance championship, by which time he must have been one of the youngest referees on the FL list.

SILCOCK, Jack
(Manchester United, 1921-23, 3)
Born New Springs, Wigan, 15 January 1898.
Died 28 June 1966.
1922: 5ft. 10ins.; 12st. 6lbs.

Career: Aspull Juniors; Atherton; Manchester United as an amateur April 1916, turning professional September 1917; Oldham Athletic on trial May 1934, retiring later that year. However, he signed for Droylsden United (Manchester) July 1936 for a spell in minor soccer. Other honours: Football League (3 apps).

Left-back. 'Sturdy and sure-kicking' was a typical 1920s verdict and, indeed, Silcock's kicking was his principle feature. He was especially expert at the volley, the ball arriving precisely at the colleague intended. To Jack's aggregate 449 peacetime League and FA Cup outings may be added a wartime figure of over 100, confirming his status as an all-time Old Trafford loyalist. Later a licensee in the Manchester area, he had originally worked as a miner.

SILLETT, R(ichard) Peter
(Chelsea, 1955, 3)
Born Southampton, 1 February 1933.
1955: 6ft. $1^1/_2$ins.; 12st. 7lbs.

Career: Salisbury schoolboy football; No man's Land FC (Salisbury); Southampton June 1950; Chelsea May 1953 (£10,000 plus a further £1000 on being capped); Guildford City June 1962; Ashford Town as player/manager July 1965. Other honours: England Youth international. England Under-23 international (3 apps). England 'B' international (1 app). Football League (1 app). (Chelsea) FL champions 1955.

Right-back. Built more like a centre-half. Could boot a ball a phenomenal distance, tackling sternly and well. Son of Charlie Sillett (Southampton of the 1930s) and brother of John (Chelsea and Football League) who had so much to do with Coventry City's lifting of the FA Cup in 1987. Like Peter, both were full-backs.

SIMMS, Ernest
(Luton Town, 1922, 1)
Born South Shields, 23 July 1891. Died 1971.
1922: 5ft. 9ins.; 12st. 7lbs.

Career: South Shields Adelaide; Murton Colliery; Barnsley; Luton Town cs 1913; South Shields March 1922; Stockport County January 1924; Scunthorpe United cs 1926; York City February 1928. Later assisted Vauxhall Motors (Luton).

Centre-forward. Renowned for prolific scoring, especially in competition outside the Football League (for instance, 40 in wartime London Combination matches 1916/17, and 57 during Scunthorpe's runaway winning of the Midland League 1926/27). Ernie's style was well depicted as 'firm, dogged and fearless.' Toured Australia with the FA party of 1925, playing 5 times against the national team, and was twice an England reserve in 1920/21. Worked latterly at Vauxhall Motors, hence his connection with their works side.

SIMPSON, John ('Jock')
(Blackburn Rovers, 1911-14, 8)
Born Pendleton, Manchester, 25 December 1885. Died 4 January 1959.
1911: 5ft. 6ins.; 11st.

Career: Schoolboy football in the Falkirk area then assisted two junior clubs there, the second being Laurieston Juniors (joined 1903 and had a trial with Rangers in 1906/07); Falkirk FC later in 1906/07; Blackburn Rovers January 1911 (£1800, then a record); retired through injury during WW1. Other honours: Scottish League (1app). Football League (5 apps). (Blackburn R) FL champions 1912, 1914.

Outside-right. A great wingman able to penetrate the stiffest defence, ball seemingly tied to his toe, moving at speed and then centering with immaculate precision. No mean goal scorer either. Truly a 'Jock': born of Scottish parents who moved back to Scotland when he was 6 weeks old. On leaving school first worked as an iron moulder and then as driver of an omnibus plying between Falkirk and Laurieston. After leaving the game was employed as a licensee in Falkirk.

SLATER, William John
(Wolverhampton Wanderers, 1955-60, 12)
Born Clitheroe, Lancs. 29 April 1927.
1957: 6ft.; 12st 7lbs.

Career:Lancashire junior football; Blackpool amateur 1944, also assisting Yorkshire Amateurs and Leeds University; Brentford amateur December 1951; Wolverhampton Wanderers amateur August 1952, turning professional February 1954; Brentford May 1963-cs 1964; subsequently made occasional appearances for Northern Nomads. Other honours: England amateur international (21 apps). (Blackpool) FA Cup finalist 1951. (Wolves) FL champions 1954, 1958, 1959. FA Cup winner 1960.

Inside-left originally, later a wing/centre-half. A leading amateur who took the professional plunge at 27, long after becoming an established League player: an elegant, composed performer with excellent ball control. Bill, a graduate of Leeds University, held an appointment as deputy Direc-

tor of the Crystal Palace Sports Centre, subsequently taking in turn the posts of Director of Physical Education to the universities of Liverpool and Birmingham.

SMALLEY, Tom
(Wolverhampton Wanderers, 1937, 1)
Born Kinsley nr. Hemsworth, Yorks. 13 January 1912. Died 1 April 1984.
1938: 5ft. $7^1/_2$ins.; 11st. 7lbs.

Career: South Kirkby Colliery; Wolverhampton Wanderers May 1931; Norwich City August 1938 (£4500); Northampton Town October 1945 – cs 1951.

Wing-half. Chiefly on the right flank at Molineux and on the left for Norwich. Had played at inside-forward during junior days and latterly was full-back for Northampton, so obviously a utility man of value. Tom was also ultra-reliable, a hard worker and durable, continuing in the first-class game until well into his 40th year.

SMART, Thomas
(Aston Villa, 1921-30, 5)
Born Blackheath, Staffs. 20 September 1896. Died June 1968.
1927: 5ft. 10ins.; 13st. 4lbs.

Career: Blackheath Town; Army football during WW1; Halesowen; Aston Villa January 1920 (£300); retired cs 1934 but later assisted Brierley Hill Alliance. Other honours: Football League (1 app). (Villa) FA Cup winner 1920; finalist 1924.

Right-back. Quickly into the honours, winning a Cup-winners' medal 3 months after turning senior and his first cap just a year later. 'A muscular and masterly defender, he kicks with force and judgement,' observed a commentator of the early 'Twenties. First choice at Villa Park for a dozen campaigns, partnered in most of them by Tom Mort (q.v.). During the Great War enlisted in 1915 when only a youngster and served with the South Staffs Rgt. and the Field Artillery.

SMITH, Albert
(Nottingham Forest, 1891-93, 3)
Born Nottingham, 23 July 1869. Died 18 April 1921.

Career: Notts Rangers; Long Eaton Rangers; Derby County; Nottingham Forest February 1889; Notts County February 1890; Nottingham Forest again later in 1890; Blackburn Rovers November 1891; Nottingham Forest for third spell early 1892; retired April 1894. Other honour: (Forest) Football Alliance champions 1892.

Right-half. An amateur throughout his career. In 1893 the Athletic News said Smith is 'one of the most forcible halves we have. Is always working, and is a heavy but fair tackler. His great fault is not playing to his forwards.' Albert, a Nottingham boot factor, certainly made the rounds of the local soccer circuit.

SMITH, (Revd.) Arnold Kirke
(Oxford University, 1872, 1)
Born Ecclesfield nr. Sheffield, 23 April 1850. Died 8 October 1927.

Career: Cheltenham College; Oxford University (captain in 1872 – this was prior to the institution of the 'varsity match); Sheffield Club. Also represented the Sheffield FA.

Forward. Powerful, lively attacker with a taste for continuous action, a trait that meant that he was at times pulled out of position. Ordained 1875 and had curacies at Biggleswade (1875-77), East Socon, Beds. (1877-81) and Somersham, Cambs. (1881-82) before becoming Vicar of the last-named parish (1883-89) and of Boxworth, Cambs. (1889-1927).

SMITH, Bert
(Tottenham Hotspur, 1921-22, 2)
Born Higham, Kent, 7 March 1892. Died September 1969.
1921: 5ft. $7^1/_2$ins.; 11st. 4lbs.

Career: Vanbrugh Park; Crawford United; Metrogas FC (London); Huddersfield Town cs 1913; Army football; Tottenham Hotspur cs 1919; Northfleet coach May 1930; Sheppey United briefly October 1931; Young Boys (Berne, Switzerland) player/coach November 1931 – 1934; Harwich and Parkeston manager/coach later in 1934, then held an appointment with Stevenage Town before a long spell as Hitchin Town's trainer/coach and groundsman from 1937 to his retirement in 1966. Other honours: Football League (1 app). (Spurs) FL Div. 2 champions 1920. FA Cup winner 1921.

Right-half summed up in 1921 as 'a strong, virile player, he is full of energy, and his tackling is deadly and certain.' Smith had, until his White Hart Lane days, been a forward, netting 26 goals for Huddersfield's reserves in his first term there. There being no room in Spurs' attack, he was tried at half-back and was an instantaneous success.

SMITH, Charles Eastlake
(Crystal Palace, 1876, 1)
Born Colombo, Ceylon, 1850. Died 10 January 1917.

Career: Rossall School (XI 1869-70, captain 1870); Crystal Palace (the original club); Wanderers. Also represented Surrey. served on the FA Committee 1875-76.

Forward. Like so many of the early attackers was a dribbler of fine dexterity. This asset was made the more valuable by Smith's keen eye for an opening. He was a cousin of the great Corinthian, G O Smith (below), and earned a reputation as an above-average club cricketer.

SMITH, Gilbert Oswald
(Oxford University and Corinthians, 1893–1901, 20)
Born Croydon, 25 November 1872. Died 6 December 1943.
1901: 5ft. 9ins.; 10st. 9lbs.

Career: Charterhouse School (XI 1889–92, captain 1890–92); Oxford University (Blue 1893–4–5–6, captain 1896); Old Carthusians; Corinthians 1892–1903 (joint secretary 1898–1902). Other honours: (Old Carthusians) FA Amateur Cup winner 1897; finalist 1895.

Centre-forward. The greatest of his era. On the light side for the position but adroit footwork, accurate shooting and skill in combination made him outstanding. G O was a fine cricketer too for Oxford University (Blue 1895–96), Surrey (3 matches, 1896) and Hertfordshire. A schoolmaster by profession (MA, (Oxon.) joint head of the Ludgrove preparatory school together with W J Oakley (q.v.). He also shared with Oakley the Corinthians' secretaryship and they were joint authors of the book, 'Association Football'. He is the main figure in Edward Grayson's admirable 'Corinthians and Cricketers' (Naldrett Press, 1955). Cousin of C E Smith above.

SMITH, Herbert
(Reading, 1905–06, 4)
Born Witney, Oxon. 22 November 1879. Died 6 January 1951.
1905: 6ft.; 12st. 10lbs.

Career: Oxford Schools; Witney FC; Reading 1901–08; Oxford City both during and after Reading spell. Also assisted Derby County (1 FL app 1906/07), Stoke (1 FL app 1907/08), Richmond Association and Oxfordshire. President of the Oxfordshire FA from 1919 to his death. Other honours: England amateur international (17 apps). (Oxford C) FA Amateur Cup finalist 1903.

Left-back. Distinguished amateur reported by one authority to be 'a famous full-back with a legendary left-foot drive.' Was brilliant in his general play too, never used his powerful physique unfairly and maintained a high degree of fitness. Captained Reading when the only unpaid member of the side. A major figure in the Thames Valley soccer scene for half a century.

SMITH, J(ames) C(hristopher) Reginald
(Millwall, 1939, 2)
Born Battersea, London, 20 January 1912.
1938: 5ft. 9ins.; 11st. 8lbs.

Career: Hitchin Town (during which spell he represented Herts and the Spartan League, and, cs 1932, signed amateur forms for Tottenham Hotspur); Millwall as a professional August 1935; Dundee March 1946; Corby Town player/manager 1948; Dundee trainer/coach early 1949; Dundee United manager September 1954; Falkirk manager January 1957–May 1959; Millwall manager July 1959–January 1961; returned briefly to South Africa and held appointments with Addington FC and Durban City before appointment as Bedford Town manager late 1961–September 1963; again returned to South Africa December 1963 and held managerial appointments with Addington again and Cape Town City. In the early 1970s was back in England and had managerial appointments with Bedford Town and Stevenage Town. Other honours: England wartime international (1 app). (Millwall) FL Div. 3 (South) champions 1938.

Outside-left. With inside-left capability also. Reg was a gem of a winger – incisive, strong, fast and carrying a lethal shot in either foot. His surname was actually Schmidt, and he was son of a South African rugger international who came to Britain with the first Springboks touring side.

SMITH, John William
(Portsmouth, 1932, 3)
Born Whitburn, Co. Durham, 28 October 1898. Died 19 January 1977
1934: 5ft. 7ins.; 11st. 10lbs.

Career: Whitburn FC; North Shields Athletic; South Shields cs 1919 (£5); Portsmouth December 1927; Bournemouth and Boscombe Athletic May 1935; Clapton Orient October 1936; retired February 1937. Other honours: Football League (2 apps). (Portsmouth) FA Cup finalist 1929, 1934.

Inside-right. Of exceptional talent: clever, resourceful and a tactician of a very high order. Enjoyed a long first-class career, playing in 18 of the 20 inter-war seasons (570 League games, 157 goals). Joined Pompey not long after his South Shields manager, Jack Tinn, went to Fratton Park to start a distinguished tenure there. Jack Smith had 3 brothers also well known pros: Septimus (England), W H (Portsmouth 1928–38) and Tom (Leicester City etc). Jack was later a licensee.

SMITH, Joseph
(Bolton Wanderers, 1913–20, 5)
Born Dudley Port, Staffs. 25 June 1889. Died 11 August 1971.
1922: 5ft. $7^{1}/_{4}$ins.; 12st. 8lbs.

Career: Newcastle Parish Schools Association (North Staffs Sunday School League); Bolton Wanderers May 1908 (£10) (guest player for Chelsea during WW1); Stockport County March 1927 (around £1000); Darwen cs 1929; Manchester Central June 1930; Hyde United September 1930. Reading manager July 1931-August 1935 when he became Blackpool's manager until April 1958, when he retired. Other honours: England 'Victory' international 1919 (3 apps). (Bolton W) FA Cup winner 1923, 1926.

Inside-left. A great Bolton servant who twice skippered them to FA Cup triumphs (including the first Wembley final) and had a long famed partnership with the Welsh international, Ted Vizard. Joe himself was a forceful player, packing one of the hardest shots ever, which brought him 254 goals in some 450 League appearances for the Trotters. His 38 in the 1920/21 season equalled the then FL record. Toured South Africa with the FA team in 1920, playing 3 times against the national side and netting 6 goals against the Frontier club. Subsequently a successful manager.

SMITH, Joseph
(West Bromwich Albion, 1920-23, 2)
Born Darby End nr. Dudley, Worcs. 10 April 1890. Died 9 June 1956.
1922: 5ft. 7ins. 11st.

Career: Netherton St. Andrew's; Darby End Victoria; Cradley Heath St. Luke's; West Bromwich Albion May 1910; Birmingham May 1926; Worcester City as player/manager May 1929 – 1932. Other honours: England 'Victory; international 1919 (1 app). (WBA) FL champions 1920. FL Div. 2 champions 1911.

Right-back. Remarkably consistent, logging up nearly 500 senior appearances for West Brom. He missed only 5 League games in the first six post-WW1 campaigns. Joe was a fast mover sound in tackling (but not rash in committing himself) and discriminating in the use of the long clearance kick.

SMITH, Leslie George Frederick
(Brentford, 1939, 1)
Born Ealing, Middlesex, 13 March 1918.
1938: 5ft. 8ins.; 11st.

Career: West London schools football; Petersham 1932; Wimbledon 1933; Hayes July 1935; Brentford on amateur forms 1935, turning professional March 1936 (he had worked in the club's office from 1933); (guest player for Chelsea during WW2); Aston Villa October 1945 (about £7500); Brentford again June 1952 (£3000); Kidderminster Harriers player/manager August 1953 for 1 season; Wolverhampton Wanderers scout 1954-56. Other honours: England wartime international (10 apps). (Wimbledon) FA Amateur Cup finalist 1935.

Outside-left. A precocious discovery of the 'Thirties – very possibly the youngest player, at 17, ever to appear in an Amateur Cup final, and making his First Division debut at 18. Always had confidence in his own innate ability with the beating of most defenders and hard shooting. Proprietor of a radio/TV business at Aston, Birmingham.

SMITH, Lionel
(Arsenal, 1951-53, 6)
Born Mexborough, Yorks. 23 August 1920.
1951: 6ft. 1in.; 11st. 12lbs.

Career: Yorkshire Tar Distillers FC; Arsenal on amateur forms August 1939, turning professional the following November; Watford June 1954; Gravesend and Northfleet as player/manager May 1955-April 1960. Other honours: Football League (3 apps). (Arsenal) FL champions 1953. FA Cup finalist 1952.

Left-back. Joined Arsenal as a centre-half and, largely due to the war, made his senior debut in the last match of season 1947/48. A stylist with an acute positioning sense, height enabled him to win the great majority of his aerial contests. It is interesting to note his Arsenal colleague, Leslie Compton, made a transition in the other direction – from full-back to pivot.

SMITH, Robert Alfred
(Tottenham Hotspur, 1961-64, 15)
Born Lingdale, North Yorks. 22 February 1933.
1962: 5ft. 9ins.; 12st. 11lbs.

Career: Redcar Boys Club; Redcar United; Tudor Rose; Chelsea ground staff May 1949, turning professional May 1950; Tottenham Hotspur December 1955 (£17,000); Brighton & Hove Albion May 1964 (£5000); Hastings United October 1965-March 1967; Banbury United for a spell from cs 1968. Other honours: (Spurs) European Cup Winners' Cup, winner 1963. FL champions 1961. FA Cup winner 1961, 1962. (Brighton) FL Div. 4 champions 1965.

Centre-forward. Powerful bustling leader ideally suited to capitalise on the chances provided by the likes of John White & Co in

Spurs' celebrated 'Double' side. Bobby's aggregate League figures were 217 goals in 376 matches, which illustrate his degree of opportunism. Was employed as a van driver after leaving the senior game.

SMITH, Septimus Charles
(Leicester City, 1936, 1)
Born Whitburn, Co Durham, 13 March 1912.
1936: 5ft. 11ins.; 12st. 8lbs.

Career: Sunderland Schools; Whitburn FC; Leicester City March 1929; retired May 1949, remaining on the club's training staff until cs 1950. Other honours: England schoolboy international (1 app). Football League (1 app). (Leicester) FL Div. 2 champions 1937.

Right-half was the position in which he made his reputation – hitherto he had been a reasonably successful inside-forward. Strong in tackling, adept in control and distribution, and, above all, perspicacious. Youngest of 4 soccer-professional brothers, a quartet that also included Jack Smith (Portsmouth & England). After leaving the game Sep worked in Leicester as a fitter.

SMITH, Stephen
(Aston Villa, 1895, 1)
Born Abbots Bromley, Staffs. 14 January 1874. Died 19 May 1935.
1895: 5ft. 4ins.; 11st. 6lbs.

Career: Cannock Town; Rugeley; Ceal FC (Hednesford); Aston Villa cs 1893; Portsmouth May 1901; New Brompton cs 1906, serving as player/manager November 1906-cs 1908. Other honours: Football League (2 apps). (Villa) FL champions 1894, 1896, 1897, 1899, 1900. FA Cup winner 1895. (Portsmouth) Southern League champions 1902.

Outside-left. Squat in build and no doubt hardened by previous labours at Hednesford Colliery. 'With great speed he also passes very accurately and is further a safe shot at goal,' was an early verdict. Played a 'blinder' in his international but, even so, was never picked again. Partnered his brother, William, while at Pompey; and his son, Stephen jnr., also a left-winger, assisted 4 London clubs as well as Southend during the 'Twenties. An Oxfordshire shopkeeper for the last 3 years of his life.

SMITH, Thomas
(Liverpool, 1971, 1)
Born Liverpool, 5 April 1945.
1971: 5ft. 10½ins.; 13st.

Career: Liverpool schoolboy football; Liverpool FC ground staff May 1960, turning professional April 1962; Swansea City August 1978, player/coach August 1979 leaving 2 months later following medical report on his injured knee. Subsequently had spell coaching Liverpool's young players before finally leaving the game. Other honours: England Youth international. England Under-23 international (10 apps). Football League (1 app). (Liverpool) European Cup winner 1977. European Cup Winners' Cup finalist 1966. UEFA Cup winner 1973, 1976. FL champions 1966, 1973, 1976, 1977. FA Cup winner 1965, 1974; finalist 1971, 1977. FL Cup finalist 1978.

Utility player starting at inside-left, afterwards appearing in midfield and defence on either flank. A noted toughie who tackled like a tank, but this was by no means the sum total of his football. For Tommy could produce the clever touches with the best of 'em. Was skipper at Anfield for some time.

SMITH, Trevor
(Birmingham City, 1960, 2)
Born Quarry Bank nr. Brierley Hill, Staffs. 13 April 1936.
1960: 6ft. 1ins.; 13st. 7lbs.

Career: Brierley Hill Schools, subsequently representing Staffordshire & District Youth and Birmingham & District Youth; Birmingham City ground staff July 1952, turning professional April 1953; Walsall October 1964 (£17,000); retired through injury February 1966. In season 1967/68 became a permit player for a Lichfield Sunday side, and during the close season of 1970 took over the managership of Mile Oak Rovers FC. Other honours: England Under-23 international (15 apps). England 'B' international (2 apps). Football League (2 apps). (B'ham C) FL Div. 2 champions 1955. FA Cup finalist 1956. FL Cup winner 1963.

Centre-half. A mature talent from the start, as a teenager translating to the senior game with aplomb. Ideally built, of course, using these natural advantages to telling effect, and was finely constructive as well. Later a licensee in the Lichfield district.

SMITH, William Henry
(Huddersfield Town, 1922-28, 3)
Born Tantobie, Co Durham, 23 May 1895. Died 13 April 1951.
1928: 5ft. 10ins.; 11st.

Career: Hobson Wanderers (Northern Alliance); Huddersfield Town October 1913; Rochdale player/manager July 1934, retiring cs 1935 and continuing as manager only until the following November. Other honours: Football League (3 apps). (H'field T) FL champions 1924, 1925, 1926. FA Cup winner 1922; finalist 1928, 1930.

Outside-left on Huddersfield Town's books for over 20 years and rewarded with 4 benefits for such footballing longevity. A fine wingman, exceptionally fast and employing blistering shooting, his partnership with Clem Stephenson (q.v.) was famous. Billy was the first player to score direct from a corner-kick (a few months after the law changed). Father of Conway Smith (post-WW2 of Huddersfield, QPR and Halifax Town), the pair were the first father and son duo to each score 100 Football League goals.

SORBY, Thomas Heathcote
(Sheffield Club, 1879, 1)
Born Sheffield, 16 February 1856. Died 13 December 1930.

Career: Cheltenham College; Thursday Wanderers (Sheffield); Sheffield Club. Also represented the Sheffield FA.

Forward. Keen attacker particularly strong in dribbling. Acknowledging this quality, Alcock's Annual (with its customary candour) went on to say '. . . but too selfish; should play more for his side.' Another Sorby – R A of that ilk – was Sheffield Club's goalkeeper at the time, and may well have been a kinsman. T H Sorby settled in Scarborough and was in business there for many years.

SOUTHWORTH, John
(Blackburn Rovers, 1889-92, 3)
Born Blackburn, December 1866. Died 16 October 1956.

Career: Blackburn Olympic when a teenager; Blackburn Rovers during the 1880s; Everton August 1893 (£400); retired through injury 1895. Other honours: Football League (1 app). (Blackburn R) FA Cup winner 1890, 1891.

Centre-forward among the greatest of the early-professional era and unfortunate to be a contemporary of John Goodall and G O Smith. An unusually prolific scorer from the outset (once notching 6 for Blackburn Olympic when only 16). And for Everton scored 15 out of the 22 registered in 4 matches, this including a 6 against West Brom. Some early critics thought him the best English centre while the author of the first Rovers history recorded he '. . . led the forward line with even greater judgment (than James Brown, the club's previous international centre) and was a more successful marksman.' A professional violinist, Southworth from 1896 played in the famous Hallé Orchestra of Manchester.

SPARKS, Francis John
(Herts Rangers and Clapham Rovers, 1879-80, 3)
Born Billericay, Essex, 4 July 1855. Died 13 February 1934.

Career: St Albans Pilgrims 1873; Brondesbury 1873-74; Upton Park 1876-78; Herts Rangers; Clapham Rovers. Also represented Essex and London. Served on the FA Committee 1878-80. Other honour: (Clapham Rovers) FA Cup winner 1880.

Forward operating in the centre at the time when 6-forward attacks were normal. 'Capital shot at goal,' said a commentator of 1881, 'but did not play as well last season' (i.e. in 1880/81). And the player certainly did seem to drift into obscurity after 1880. Besides shooting ability, Sparks worked hard and, although somewhat slow, was a good team man.

SPENCE, Joseph Walter
(Manchester United, 1926-27, 2)
Born Throckley, Northumberland, 15 December 1898. Died 31 December 1966.
1925: 5ft. 8ins.; 11st.

Career: Newcastle area schoolboy football; Bluchers Juniors; Throckley Celtic; Scotswood cs 1918; Manchester United March 1919; Bradford City June 1933; Chesterfield May 1933; retired cs 1938. Scouted for Chesterfield later. Other honours: Football League (1 app). (Chesterf'd) FL Div. 3 (North) champions 1936.

Outside-right/centre-forward. The reason for the Old Trafford chant, 'Give it to Joe,' that became famous country-wide. What is less well known is that by turning out (mostly as a 'regular') in 19 of the 20 between-the-wars seasons, Joe established an inter-war record. Spence, a speedy, skilled and strong-shooting attacker, grossed 613 League appearance (194 goals), 481 of them for Manchester United, which stood as a club record for 30 years. Father of Joe Spence jnr. (York City 1950-54) and cousin of George Brown (England). Worked for the Chesterfield Tube Co until retiring in 1965.

SPENCE, Richard
(Chelsea, 1936, 2)
Born Platt's Common nr. Barnsley, 18 July 1908. Died March 1983.
1938: 5ft. 6ins.; 9st. 2lbs.

Career: Thorpe Colliery; Platt's Common WMC; Barnsley February 1933; Chelsea October 1934 (£4000); retired cs 1950 and joined Chelsea's training staff, continuing in this appointment until the mid-1970s. Other honour: (Barnsley) FL Div. 3 (North) champions 1934.

Outside-right. Two-footed, tricky little forward, possessor of a blistering shot. His 19 League goals of 1934/35 established a Chelsea record for a wingman. Dicky's length of service at Stamford Bridge – over 40 years – was outstanding.

SPENCER, Charles William
(Newcastle United, 1924-25, 2)
Born Washington, Co Durham, 4 December 1899. Died 9 February 1953.
1924: 5ft. 10ins.; 11st. $7^1/_2$lbs.

Career: Glebe Rovers (Washington); Washington Chemical Works; Newcastle United October 1921; Manchester United July 1928 (£3250); Tunbridge Wells Rangers as player/manager May 1930; Wigan Athletic as player/manager August 1932-March 1937. Grimsby Town manager March 1937-May 1951, when he resigned through ill-health; York City manager November 1952 to his death. Other honours: Football League (2 apps). (Newcastle) FL champions 1927. FA Cup winner 1924.

Centre-half effective in changing circumstances. Early on had been noticeably creative and attack-minded. Then, with the changed offside rule of 1925, developed a defensive role, but was by no means a mere 'stopper'. Reliable always. Toured Australia in 1925 with the FA party, playing against the national team on 5 occasions.

SPENCER, Howard
(Aston Villa, 1897–1905, 6)
Born Edgbaston, Birmingham, 23 August 1875. Died 14 January 1940.
1905: 5ft. 10½ins.; 12st. 12lbs.

Career: Birmingham schoolboy football; Stamford FC (Birmingham); Birchfield Trinity; Aston Villa 1894; retired November 1907. Aston Villa director June 1909 – May 1936. Other honours: Football League (9 apps). (Villa) FL champions 1896, 1897, 1900. FA Cup winner 1895, 1897, 1905.

Right-back. A classic defensive talent of the pre–1914 era bracketed with the great Scots, Walter Arnott and Nick Ross. Spencer was a model player: sporting, resourceful and consummate in judgment. Became managing-director of a coal and coke contracting firm and died a rich man.

SPIKSLEY, Fred
(Sheffield Wednesday, 1893–98, 7)
Born Gainsborough, Lincs. 25 January 1870. Died 28 July 1948.
1903: 5ft. 7ins.; 10st.

Career: Jubilee Swifts; Gainsborough Trinity 1887 (3 apps for Lincolnshire); Sheffield Wednesday January 1891; Glossop October 1904; Leeds City early in 1905; Southend United cs 1905; Watford during season 1905/06 to cs 1906. Subsequently a coach in Nuremberg, Germany, and interned on outbreak of war, August 1914. Post-war had coaching engagements in Mexico (from December 1923), with Fulham FC to cs 1926 when he went back to Nuremberg, eventually returning to England in 1932. Other honours: Football League (2 apps). (Wednesday) FL champions 1903. FL Div. 2 champions 1900. FA Cup winner 1896.

Outside-left. A 'Nineties star possessing pace, dribbling capability and the virtue of invariably being available to colleagues. Suffered WW1 internment like many other soccer celebrities, fellow England caps such as Bloomer, Pentland and Sam Wolstenholme among them. A prize-winning runner over 440 yards and an oarsman of note. Was once a printer and later a bookmaker (he died at Goodwood).

SPILSBURY, Benjamin Ward
(Derby County, 1885–86, 3)
Born Findern nr. Derby, 1 August 1864. Died 15 August 1938.

Career: Repton School (XI 1881–83, captain 1883); Cambridge University (Blue 1884-5-6-7, captain 1887); Corinthians 1885–88; Derby County 1884–88; Derby County 1884–88.

Outside/inside–right. One of those spirited amateurs whose infectious enthusiasm often made up for an odd lapse in technique. Middled the ball excellently from the wing and he could deliver a telling shot – he scored 4 against Ireland, March 1886, and also shot Derby's first-ever goal. Represented his public school at cricket and athletics (long jump) in addition to soccer. Emigrated to Canada circa 1888, working as a land agent in Vancouver, where he died.

SPINK, Nigel P.
(Aston Villa, 1983, 1)
Born Chelmsford, 8 August 1958.
1983: 6ft. 1ins.; 13st. 10lbs.

Career: Junior football; Chelmsford City, Aston Villa January 1977 (£6000). Other honour: (Aston Villa). European Cup winner 1982 (sub).

Goalkeeper. Came to general notice as a substitute in Villa's European Cup triumph of 1982, taking over as the club's first choice 'keeper from veteran Jimmy Rimmer the following December. Nigel, with an impressive physique, moves lithely, is brisk in action and often brilliant in execution.

SPOUNCER, William Alfred
(Nottingham Forest, 1900, 1)
Born Gainsborough, Lincs. 1 July 1877. Died 31 August 1962.
1903: 5ft. 8ins.; 10st. 7lbs.

Career: Gainsborough Grammar School (XI 1889); Gainsborough Trinity 1893/94 season; Sheffield United October 1895; Nottingham Forest May 1897 – 1910 (£125). Subsequently a coach in Europe including Barcelona in the 1920s. Other honours: (Forest) FL Div. 2 champions 1907. FA Cup winner 1898.

Outside-left who gave Forest fine service, aggregating 338 League and FA Cup appearances in which he scored 51 goals for the Nottingham club. A wily winger skilled in accurate centering. Was the last surviving member of Forest's Cup-winning side of '98.

SPRINGETT, Ronald D.G.
(Sheffield Wednesday, 1960–66, 33)
Born Fulham, 22 July 1935.
1963: 5ft. 10ins.; 12st. 1lb.

Career: Victoria United (London); Queen's Park Rangers February 1953; Sheffield Wednesday March 1958 (fee variously reported between £9 and £15,000); Queens Park Rangers again May 1967 (£16,000); Ashford Town September 1970. Other honours: Football League (9 apps). (Wednesday) FL Div. 2 champions 1959. FA Cup finalist 1966.

Goalkeeper, agile and daring and possessing great anticipation. Was England's undisputed first choice for $3^1/_2$ seasons – he was absent only once between November 1959 and February 1963, and eventually became Wednesday's most capped player. Ron's younger brother Peter, and England Under-23 goalkeeper, also had notable runs with QPR and Sheffield Wednesday. In fact the brothers' careers dovetailed uniquely. Later involved in a gardening business.

SPROSTON, Bert
(Leeds United, Tottenham Hotspur and Manchester City, 1937–39, 11)
Born Elworth nr. Sandbach, Cheshire, 22 June 1915.
1936: 5ft. $7^1/_2$ins.; 11st. 2lbs.

Career: Sandbach Ramblers (trial with Huddersfield Town); Leeds United May 1933; Tottenham Hotspur June 1938 (£9500); Manchester City November 1938 (£9500); retired cs 1950. Bolton Wanderers trainer from July 1951, later scouting for that club, an activity he was still enjoying in the mid-1980s. Other honours: Football League (4 apps). (Man. City) FL Div. 2 champions 1947.

Right-back. A star of the late 'Thirties – cool, a grand tackler and exceptionally quick to recover. Was playing in good class Cheshire League soccer at 17, supplanting an elder brother in the process. Bert's short stay at Tottenham was through failing to settle in London. The fees paid by Spurs and Manchester City were close to the then record.

SQUIRE, Ralph Tyndall
(Old Westminsters, 1886, 3)

Born Marylebone, London, 10 September 1863. Died 22 August 1944.

Career: Westminster School (XI 1880–82); Cambridge University (Blue 1884, 1886: unable to play in the 'varsity match in '85 when he acted as secretary of the CUFC). Old Westminsters; Corinthians 1886–92 (Treasurer for many years from 1903); Clapham Rovers. Also represented London. Served on the FA committee 1884–87.

Full-back/half back of some versatility, equally capable in either role. 'Strong and not lacking in pace he is a sure kick, and with any amount of dash sticks to his opponent unflinchingly,' wrote a 'Nineties critic. A fine oarsman too, rowing at Henley in the 1883 Ladies' Plate for his college's first boat (Trinity Hall). MA (Cantab).

STANBROUGH, M(aurice) Hugh
(Old Carthusians, 1895, 1)
Born Cleobury North, Salop, 2 September 1870. Died 15 December 1904.

Career: Charterhouse School (XI 1889); Cambridge University Blue 1890-1-2, captain 1892); Old Carthusians; Corinthians 1890–1904; Eastbourne; retired through a knee injury. Other honours: (Old Carthusians) FA Amateur Cup winner 1894; finalist 1895.

Outside-left.; 'Having plenty of pace and clever with it, he is quite one of the best outside-lefts, at least in the South,' said an 1895 writer who had earlier reported that the Old Carthusians and Corinthians counted him among their most reliable players. Stanbrough was a schoolmaster by profession, holding a succession of appointments in Southern England. At the time of his untimely death he was teaching at St. Peter's, Broadstairs.

STANIFORTH, Ronald
Huddersfield Town, 1954–55, 8)
Born Newton Heath, Manchester, 13 April 1924.
1957: 5ft. $10^3/_4$ins.; 11st.

Career: Manchester Schools 1937/38; Newton Albion (Manchester Amateur League); Stockport County 1946; Huddersfield Town May 1952 (£1000 including another player); Sheffield Wednesday July 1955 (a deal in which 2 players from each club were exchanged); Barrow as player/manager October 1959 (about £1000), retiring from playing 1961 and continuing as manager until July 1964; Sheffield Wednesday assistant coach July 1970, chief coach March 1971, subsequently having spell as youth coach to January 1976. Other honours: England 'B' international (3 apps). (Wednesday) FL Div. 2 champions 1956, 1959.

Right-back. A polished stylist, clean and confident in his kicking and calm under the severest pressure. Maintained a consistent level of performance too: an aggregate League match total of 473 gives a good average of 31 per season.

STARLING, Ronald William
(Sheffield Wednesday and Aston Villa, 1933-37, 2)
Born Pelaw, Co. Durham, 11 October 1909.
1937: 5ft. $9^3/_4$ins.; 11st. 7lbs.

Career: Durham Schools; Washington Colliery; Hull City on amateur forms 1925 and worked in the club's office until signing as a professional 1927; Newcastle United May 1930 (£3750); Sheffield Wednesday June 1932 (£3250); Aston Villa January 1937 (£7500); retired July 1948 and then was Nottingham Forest coach until June 1950. Other honours: (Wednesday) FA Cup winner 1935. (Villa) FL Div. 2 champions 1938.

Inside-forward. A precocious talent from the start – in his school team at 8 and goal scoring in men's soccer at 16. His scintillating ball jugglery delighted spectators for a dozen of the inter–war campaigns. After leaving football ran a newsagency in Sheffield.

STATHAM, Derek James
(West Bromwich Albion, 1983, 3)
Born Whitmore Reams, Wolverhampton, 24 March 1959.
1983: 5ft. 5½ins.; 11st. 1lb.

Career: Wolverhampton schoolboy football; West Bromwich Albion apprentice July 1975, turning professional April 1976; Southampton August 1987 (£100,000). Other honours: England Youth onternational. England 'B' international. England Under-21 international (6 apps).

Left-back. His all-action style, ability to outjump much taller adversaries and mazy runs down the left flank were noted at an early stage. Full England honours were confidently predicted by critics. Unfortunately serious injuries interfered with a consistent flowering of Derek's exceptional talent. High priced moves to Glasgow Rangers and Liverpool were called off. And it is certain Sansom's long tenure of the England left-back berth would have been under much greater threat with a usually fit Statham around.

STEELE, Frederick Charles
(Stoke City, 1937, 6)
Born Hanley, Stoke-on-Trent, 6 May 1916. Died 23 April 1976.
1938: 5ft. 10½ins.; 11st. 12lbs.

Career: Downing's Tileries (Stoke); Stoke City 1931 (originally on amateur forms); Mansfield Town as player/manager July 1949 (£750); Port Vale as player/manager December 1951, retiring from playing May 1953, remaining as manager until January 1957; Port Vale manager again October 1962-February 1965. Other honours: Football League (2 apps).

Centre-forward. Made his senior debut at inside-right when 18, revealing a craft mature beyond his years. Switched to centre in 1935/36 and the goals began to flow: a remarkable 33 in 35 League outings during 1936/37, for instance. This is still a Stoke record, as is his aggregate peacetime haul of 142, 1934-49. Netted 5 against Derby County, September 11, 1937. Freddie was a licensee between spells as Port Vale's manager and uncle of David Steele, the England cricketer.

STEIN, Brian
(Luton Town, 1984, 1)
Born Cape Town, South Africa, 19 October 1957.
1984: 5ft. 10ins.; 11st. 8lbs.

Career: North London schoolboy football; North Paddington Boys Club; Sudbury Court; Crouch End Vampires (a Sunday side); Edgware Town; Luton Town October 1977 (£1000); Caen (France) cs 1988. Other honours: England Under-21 international (3 apps). (Luton T) FL Div. 2 champions 1982. FL Cup winner 1988.

Strike-forward. Fast and elusive, able to turn quickly at speed and possessor of a class 'touch'. Thought by one Luton manager to be the finest header of a ball in the First Division. Came to this country when 8 years old. Older brother of Mark Stein, the England Youth international and a colleague at Kenilworth Road.

STEPHENSON, Clement
(Huddersfield Town, 1924, 1)
Born New Delaval, Co Northumberland, 6 February 1890. Died 24 October 1961.
1922: 5ft. 7½ins.; 12st. 3lbs.

Career: New Delaval Villa; West Stanley; Blyth Spartans; Aston Villa March 1910 (£165) (Stourbridge for development cs 1910-February 1911) (guest player for Leeds City during WW1); Huddersfield Town March 1921 (£3000); retired and became Huddersfield manager May 1929–June 1942. Other honours: Football League (3 apps). (Villa) FA Cup winner 1913, 1920. (H'field T) FL champions 1924, 1925, 1926. FA Cup winner 1922; finalist 1928.

Inside-left. A brilliant strategist whose signing by Huddersfield was a master-stroke, transforming the side into the greatest of the 'Twenties. Methodically constructive, Clem's partnership with left-winger W H Smith became famous. His brothers, Jim and George, also played for Aston Villa, the latter also being capped by England.

STEPHENSON, George Ternent
(Derby County and Sheffield Wednesday, 1928-31, 3)
Born New Delaval, Northumberland, 3 September 1900. Died 18 August 1971.
1930: 5ft. 10ins.; 12st.

Career: Northumberland Schools; New Delaval Villa; Leeds City August 1919; Aston Villa November 1919 (£300) (Stourbridge for development, during which time he played in a 'junior international' for the Birmingham FA vs. Scotland); Derby County November 1927; Sheffield Wednesday February 1931; Preston North End July 1933; Charlton Athletic May 1934 (£200); retired through injury May 1937 and joined Charlton's staff later becoming their assistant manager. Huddersfield Town manager August 1947 – March 1952. Other honour: (Charlton) FL Div. 3 (South) champions 1935.

Inside-forward, mostly inside-left. Cultured forward, youngest of three well known footballers another of whom was Clem (above). George's brainy promptings were a feature of his performance and he scored regularly himself. His son, Bobby, played professionally during the 1960s besides being a county cricketer for Derbyshire and Hants, 1967-80.

STEPHENSON, J(oseph) Eric
(Leeds United, 1938-39, 2)
Born Bexleyheath, Kent, September 1914. Killed in action 8 September 1944.
1938: 5ft. 6½ins.; 10st. 2lbs.

Career: Leeds schoolboy and junior football; Harrogate; Leeds United on amateur forms January 1933, turning professional September 1934.

Inside-left, craftsman of constructive merit whose bent was towards providing scoring chances for fellow forwards. On his own account he netted 22 goals in 115 peacetime League and FA Cup games. Lost his life in Burma while serving as a major in the Gurkha Rifles.

STEPNEY, Alexander Cyril
(Manchester United, 1968, 1)
Born Mitcham, Surrey, 18 September 1942.
1968: 6ft.; 11st. 9lbs.

Career: Surrey Schools; London Schools (trial for Fulham); Tooting and Mitcham 1958; Millwall amateur March 1963, turning professional May 1963; Chelsea May 1966 (£50,000); Manchester United September 1966 (£55,000); Dallas Tornado (USA) January 1979 (£50,000); Altrincham as player/coach September 1979. Other honours: England Under-23 international (3 apps). Football League (2 apps). (Man. Utd.) European Cup winner 1968. FL champions 1967. FL Div. 2 champions 1975. FA Cup winner 1977; finalist 1976, 1979.

Goalkeeper. Passed on by Chelsea after but 1 League outing to win glory at Old Trafford. Described as 'solid, secure and un-

spectacular', Stepney could nevertheless pull off instinctive, nerve-tingling saves. In aggregate played 535 senior games for Manchester United (and converted 2 penalties), and his grand total was around the 700 mark.

STEVEN, Trevor McGregor
(Everton, 1985-88, 24)
Born Berwick-upon-Tweed, 21 September 1963.
1986: 5ft. 8ins.; 10st. 9lbs.

Career: Junior football; Burnley apprentice, turning professional September 1981; Everton June 1983 (£300,000). Other honours: England Youth international. England Under-21 international (2 apps). (Burnley) FL Div. 3 champions 1982. (Everton) European Cup Winner's Cup, winner 1985. FL champions 1985, 1987. FA Cup winner 1984; finalist 1985, 1986.

Midfield. (Right-sided). One of the best talents to emerge in the early 'Eighties, adept at close control and taking on defenders (like a good oldfashioned outside-right). A helpmeet to his own defence as well, returning quickly when need arises. Attended a rugger-playing school (Berwick High) but received good soccer coaching all the same.

STEVENS, Gary Andrew
(Tottenham Hotspur, 1985-86, 7)
Born Hillingdon, Middlesex, 30 March 1962.
1985: 6ft.; 12st.

Career: After an early association with Ipswich Town became a Brighton and Hove Albion apprentice, turning professional October 1979; Tottenham Hotspur June 1983 (£350.000). Other honours: England Under-21 international (8 apps). (Brighton) FA Cup finalist 1983. (Spurs) UEFA Cup winner 1984. FA Cup finalist 1987 (sub).

Defender-midfield. An invaluable utility player capable of performing well almost anywhere. Made name during Brighton's 1983 FA Cup run, especially in the final and its re-play, when his tenacity and never-say-die spirit took the eye of many experts. And he has the skills too. Has been unlucky with injuries since transferring to White Hart Lane.

STEVENS, M(ichael) Gary
(Everton, 1985-88, 26)
Born Barrow-in-Furness, 27 March 1963.
1986: 5ft. 11ins.; 10st. 11lbs.

Career: Schoolboy football; Everton apprentice July 1979, turning professional March 1981; Rangers August 1988 (£1m.). Other honours: (Everton) European Cup Winners' Cup, winner 1985. FL champions 1985, 1987. FA Cup winner 1984; finalist 1985, 1986. FL Cup finalist 1984.

Right-back. An integral part of Everton's defence during the club's successful rise in the mid-1980s. Very fast, his speed in recovery an important asset, and tenancious when challenging the opponent in possession. Specialises in long throws that have brought many a goal.

STEWART, James ('Tadger')
(Sheffield Wednesday and Newcastle United, 1907-11, 3)
Born Newcastle-upon-Tyne, 1883. Died 23 May 1957.
1907: 5ft. 9ins.; 11st. 4lbs.

Career: Todds Nook; Gateshead NER; Sheffield Wednesday May 1902; Newcastle United August 1908 (4-figure fee); Rangers September 1913 (£600); North Shields Athletic player/manager May 1914. Other honours: Football League (4 apps). (Wednesday) FA Cup winner 1907. (Newcastle) FL champions 1909 FA Cup finalist 1911.

Inside-forward taking either flank with equal facility. Had subtle control, his craft delighting the crowds, and he could slot home the goals too. Known as Tadger from boyhood. After WW1 lived at Gateshead and worked as a commercial traveller.

STILES, Norbert Peter ('Nobby')
(Manchester United, 1965-70, 28)
Born Collyhurst, Manchester, 18 May 1942.
1967: 5ft. 6ins.; 10st. 10lbs.

Career: Manchester Schools; Lancashire Schools; Manchester United ground staff September 1957, turning professional June 1959; Middlesbrough May 1971 (£20,000); Preston North End August 1973 (£20,000)–1975, becoming that club's chief coach and then was manager July 1977–June 1981; Vancouver Whitecaps (Canada) coach until appointed West Bromwich Albion assistant manager early in 1984, serving as manager October 1985-February 1986, after which he joined the club's coaching staff. Other honours: England schoolboy international. England Youth international. England Under-23 international (3 apps). Football League (3 apps). (Man. Utd) European Cup winner 1968. FL champions 1965, 1967.

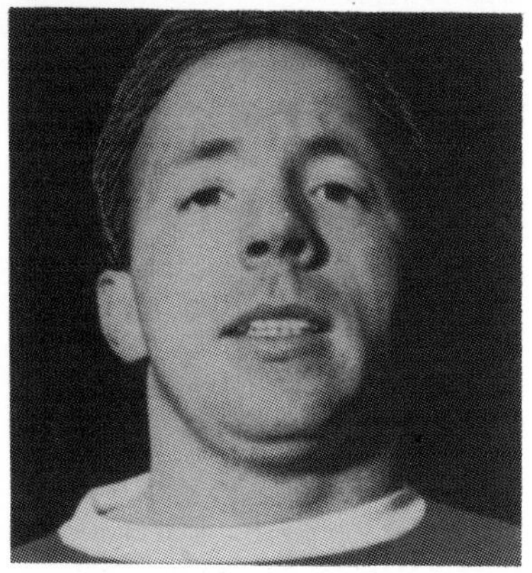

Left-half. Always associated with England's 1966 World Cup triumph, when his perkiness, ferocious tackling and toothless grin became national topics. The tackling seemed to involve any part of an opponent's anatomy, a fact due, it was said, to defective vision. Nobby had been knocked down by a bus when a child and had to wear contact lenses when playing. Awarded a FA Cup winners' medal in 1963 although he did not appear in the final. Brother-in-law of Johnny Giles of Leeds United fame.

STOKER, Lewis
(Birmingham, 1933-34, 3)
Born Wheatley Hill, Co. Durham, 31 March 1910. Died 1979.
1934: 5ft. $8^1/_2$ins.; 10st. 6lbs.

Career: Durham schoolboy football; Brandon Juniors; Esh Winning Juniors; Bearpark; West Stanley; Birmingham September 1929 (originally on a month's trial); Nottingham Forest May 1938. Other honour: Football League (1 app).

Right-half. Curiously did not command a regular place in his school team. Progressed well enough later, however, to become a class wing-half, tackling and passing in fine style. On leaving his Bearpark school – which , incidentally, also produced the Derby County and England outside-right, Sammy Crooks – he worked as an electrician.

STORER, Harry
(Derby County, 1924-28, 2)
Born West Derby, Liverpool, 2 February 1898. Died 1 September 1967.
1925: 5ft. 9ins.; 11st. 10lbs.

Career: Heanor schools football; Ripley Town; Eastwood FC (Notts County as an amateur 1918/19); Grimsby Town as an amateur February 1919, turning professional the following April; Derby County March 1921 (£4500, a record for Grimsby); Burnley February 1929 (£4250); retired cs 1931. Coventry City manager May 1931; Birmingham City manager May 1945; Coventry City manager for a second spell November 1948–December 1953; Derby County manager June 1955; retired May 1962 but later scouted for Everton.

Left-half/inside-left. A valuable player converted to left-half by the Mariners. Derby fielded him at inside-left for long periods from 1923/24 in deference to his shooting and dribbling qualities, but half-back was his best berth. An extremely hard worker, a trait that brought much publicity in managerial days as a renowned disciplinarian. A Derbyshire cricketer 1920-36, following in the footsteps of his father and uncle, both of whom were professional footballers also.

STOREY, Peter Edwin
(Arsenal, 1971-73, 19)
Born Farnham, Surrey, 7 September 1945.
1972: 5ft. $9^1/_2$ins.; 11st. 7lbs.

Career: Aldershot Schools; Arsenal apprentice May 1961, turning professional September 1962; Fulham March 1977 (£10,000); retired November 1977. Other honours: England schoolboy international. Football League (2 apps). (Arsenal) Inter-Cities Fairs Cup winner 1970. FL champions 1971. FA Cup winner 1971; finalist 1972. FL Cup finalist 1968, 1969.

Right-back. Later right-half. Well known as an aggressive spoiler who owned a tackle that rivalled Norman Hunter's in severity. Was a regular member of the Arsenal line-up that won a clutch of honours after many years of club anonymity.

STOREY-MOORE, Ian
(Nottingham Forest, 1970, 1)
Born Ipswich, 17 January 1945.
1970: 5ft. 10ins.; 12st. 7lbs.

Career: Scunthorpe Schools; Ashby Juniors (Scunthorpe) (trial with Blackpool); Nottingham Forest amateur August 1961, turning professional May 1962; Manchester United March 1972 (£200,000); retired through injury December 1973. Made a come-back in Non-League soccer with Burton Albion September 1974 and there some years, becoming player/manager. Later (circa 1981) assisted Shepshed Charterhouse. Other honours: England Under-23 international (2 apps). Football League (2 apps).

Outside-left. Capable of performing more than adequately on the extreme right. Unusually well proportioned for a wingman, this making him even more dangerous. Around 1970 was reckoned the most menacing in the position, hard shooting bringing a fine return of 105 goals in 236 League outings for Forest. It was an ankle injury that brought the premature end to Ian's senior career.

STRANGE, Alfred Henry
(Sheffield Wednesday, 1930-34, 20)
Born Marehey, Derbys. 2 April 1900. Died October 1978.
1930: 5ft. 8ins.; 11st.

Career: Marehey Colliery; Portsmouth December 1922; Port Vale October 1924; Sheffield Wednesday February 1927 (in exchange for another player); Bradford May 1935; retired cs 1936. Other honours: Football League (3 apps). (Wednesday) FL champions 1929, 1930.

Right-half, after spending the first third of his first-class career as a centre-forward. Though useful enough leading the attack, Strange really blossomed as a wing-half with his quick tackling and fine distribution. Subsequently a poultry farmer in the Ripley area.

STRATFORD, Alfred Hugh
(Wanderers, 1874, 1)
Born Kensington, London, 5 September 1853. Died 2 May 1914.

Career: Malvern College (XI 1871-2-3-4, captain 1874); Old Malvernians; Wanderers; Swifts. Also represented Middlesex. Other honours: (Wanderers) FA Cup winner 1876, 1877, 1878.

Full-back. 'A first-rate back,' recounted a critic in 1874, 'with an extraordinary power of kicking off. With a little more 'head' will make a most useful player.' (Presumably 'power of kicking off' denotes a strong kick, and 'head', thought). Stratford played cricket for Middlesex 1877-80 (18 matches) and Herefordshire. Emigrated to the States circa 1890 and played cricket there. He died at Newark, New Jersey.

STRETEN, Bernard R.

(Luton Town, 1950, 1)

Born Gillingham, Norfolk, 14 January 1921. 1955: 5ft. 9½ins.; 11st. 10lbs.

Career: Norfolk junior football; Notts County amateur; Shrewsbury Town amateur; Luton Town amateur January 1947, turning professional January 1948; King's Lynn July 1957; Wisbech Town cs 1959; Cambridge City early in 1961, later a permit player with North Walsham FC, Norfolk. Other honours: England amateur international (6 apps).

Goalkeeper. Daring, extremely agile and often brilliant, not least in the saving of point-blank range shots. Had strong competition for the first team spot at Kenilworth Road with another England cap, Ron Baynham, but still ran up a total of 276 League outings in his decade there. Bernard eventually went back to live in his native Norfolk.

STURGESS, Albert

(Sheffield United, 1911-14, 2)

Born Etruria, Stoke-on-Trent, 21 October 1882. Died 16 July 1957.

1914: 5ft. 10ins.; 12st.

Career: Tunstall Cresswells; Stoke 1903; Sheffield United June 1908; Norwich City July 1923; retired cs 1925. Other honour: (Sheffield Utd.) FA Cup winner 1915.

Wing-half. (His England appearances were made on both flanks.) He played mostly at left-back in the two Norwich campaigns. A hard performer – said to be addicted to cold winter baths! – Albert was industrious and showed good anticipation. At one stage was somewhat irreverently known as 'Hairpin'. After leaving football ran an Eccleshall (Staffs) crockery shop, which was, of course, a highly appropriate occupation for a Potteries native.

SUMMERBEE, Michael George

(Manchester City, 1968-73, 8)

Born Preston, Lancs, 15 December 1942.

1970: 5ft. 10½ins.; 12st. 4lbs.

Career: Cheltenham Schools; Swindon Town amateur August 1959, turning professional the following December; Manchester City August 1965 (£32,000); Burnley June 1975 (£25,000); Blackpool December 1976; Stockport County October 1977 (originally on loan), serving as player/manager March 1978-October 1979; had spell with Mossley from November 1980. Other honours: England Under-23 international (1 app). Football League (1 app). (Man. City) FL champions 1968. FL Div. 2 champions 1966. FA Cup winner 1969. FL Cup winner 1970; finalist 1974.

Outside-right/centre-forward whose resolve and gritty endeavour had much to do with Manchester City's successes during his decade at Maine Road. Opponents treated him with respect, and with reason. Son of a well known professional and nephew of another, Mike was awarded a winners' medal in the European Cup Winners' Cup tourney of 1970. He had missed the final through injury.

SUNDERLAND, Alan
(Arsenal, 1980, 1)
Born Conisbrough, Yorks. 1 July 1953.
1980: 5ft. 9ins.; 11st. $6^1/_4$lbs.

Career: Don & Dearne Schools; Yorkshire Schools; Wolverhampton Wanderers apprentice, turning professional June 1971; Arsenal November 1977 (£240,000, a then Wolves record); Ipswich Town on loan February 1984, signing permanently July 1984 (Cambridge United on loan, March 1987). Other honours: England 'B' international. England Under-23 international (1 app). England Under-21 international (1 app). (Wolves) FL Div. 2 champions 1977. FL Cup winner 1974. (Arsenal) European Cup Winners' Cup finalist 1980. FA Cup winner 1979; finalist 1978, 1980.

Strike forward capable of playing anywhere - originally a midfielder and played full-back when a sub in an Under-23 international. A quick performer, an excellent controller of the ball and fine at headwork.

SUTCLIFFE, John William
(Bolton Wanderers and Millwall Athletic, 1893-1903, 5)
Born Shibden nr. Halifax, 14 April 1868.
Died 7 July 1947.
1901: 6ft.; 12st. 10lbs.

Career: After a distinguished career in rugby football joined Bolton Wanderers September 1889; Millwall Athletic April 1902; Manchester United May 1903; Plymouth Argyle January 1905; Southend United 1911/12. Arnhem (Holland) coach 1914 and had spell as Bradford City's trainer from May 1919. Other honours: Football League (5 apps). (Bolton W) FA Cup finalist 1894.

Goalkeeper with claims to being the best of the 'Nineties and a place among England's greatest. Strong in all aspects and said to be unsurpassed in handling low shots. Played rugger for Bradford (2 seasons). Heckmondwike and Yorkshire before gaining an England cap against New Zealand in 1889. Eldest of a large family – the youngest, C S Sutcliffe, was goalkeeper of Sheffield United's 1925 FA Cup-winning side.

SWAN, Peter
(Sheffield Wednesday, 1960-62, 19)
Born South Elmsall, Yorks. 8 October 1936.
1961: 6ft. $0^1/_4$in.; 12st.
Career: Doncaster Schools; Sheffield Wednesday amateur May 1952, turning professional November 1953, banned May 1965, returning June 1972; Bury August 1973; Matlock Town player/manager cs 1974; Worksop Town manager July 1976; Buxton manager cs 1977; later was Matlock Town manager again, leaving during season 1981/82. Other honours: England Youth international. England Under-23 international (3 apps). Football League (6 apps). (Wednesday) FL Div. 2 champions 1959.

Centre-half among the best stoppers of his day, strong on the ground and his height usually providing natural dominance in headwork. Was particularly noted for speed of recovery. From the mid-1960s employed as a licensee in the Sheffield area.

SWEPSTONE, Harry Albemarle
(Pilgrims, 1880-83, 6)
Born in the Stepney district of London, 1859. Died 7 May 1907.

Career: Chigwell School; Clapton; Pilgrims; Ramblers; Swifts 1887-88. Also represented Essex and London. Founder member of the Corinthians (and responsible for giving the club its name), playing twice in season 1885/86. Served on the FA Committee 1883-84.

Goalkeeper. Brilliant and agile, ranked the best 'keeper of his day. Resourceful also – '. . . has a peculiar aptitude for striking the ball away with his arm . . .' (which must have been well worth seeing). A solicitor by profession (admitted 1881), he first practised at Bethnal Green, 1881-92, and then Bishopsgate.

SWIFT, Frank Victor
(Manchester City, 1947-49, 19)

Born Blackpool, 24 December 1913. Died 6 February 1958.

1949: 6ft. 2ins.; 14st.

Career: Blackpool schoolboy football; Blackpool Gasworks; Fleetwood 1931/32; Manchester City on amateur forms 1931/32, turning professional October 1932 (guest player for Hamilton Academicals during WW2); retired cs 1949 but returned and played in 4 FL matches early in season 1949/50. Other honours: England wartime international (8 apps). England 'B' international (1 app). Football League (3 apps). (Man. City) FL champions 1937. FL Div. 2 champions 1947. FA Cup winner 1934.

Goalkeeper apt to hit the headlines throughout his career, starting with fainting at the conclusion of the 1934 Cup final (presumably overjoyed). Immensely popular, formidable physically – besides the above dimensions he had a hand span of $11^1/_2$ inches – graceful in action and a natural humorist. Originally worked part-time at Blackpool gasworks and with the family pleasure boat on the beach; was a Manchester licensee after the War and later a soccer journalist. Lost his life in the Munich air crash while engaged in the last-named capacity. Frank's brother, Fred, kept goal for Oldham Athletic and other League clubs during the 1930s.

TAIT, George
(Birmingham Excelsior, 1881, 1)

Born 1859. Died 1882.

Career: Junior football to Birmingham Excelsior.

Centre-forward. 'Altogether outclassed in an international team, but is useful to his club,' said an 1881 handbook with the frankness usual at the time. Tait had proved a dangerous raider in club football, leading his line well. His inclusion for England was in line with the then policy of spreading honours around in matches other than those against Scotland.

TALBOT, Brian Ernest
(Ipswich Town and Arsenal, 1977-80, 6)

Born Ipswich, 21 July 1953.

1979: 5ft. 10ins.; 12st.

Career: Junior football; Ipswich Town apprentice July 1970, turning professional August 1972; Arsenal January 1979 (£450,000); Watford June 1985 (£150,000); Stoke City October 1986 (£25,000); West Bromwich Albion January 1988, player/manager November 1988. Other honours: England 'B' international. England Under-21 international (1 app). (Ipswich T) FA Cup winner 1978. (Arsenal) European Cup Winners' Cup finalist 1980. FA Cup winner 1979; finalist 1980.

Midfield (right side). One for those who like their footballers to be full blooded. As one commentator defined his qualities: '. . . driving enthusiasm, stout heart and rugged commitment . . . gutsy, no-surrender attitude.' Equalled Lord Kinnaird's century-old record of collecting FA Cup winners' medals in successive seasons in the colours of two different clubs. Became a qualified FA coach in 1980 to be one of the youngest holders of this distinction. Had spell as chairman of the PFA, resigning the position after his elevation to managerial status.

TAMBLING, Robert Victor
(Chelsea, 1963-66, 3)

Born Storrington, Sussex, 18 September 1941.

1965: 5ft. 8ins.; 11st. 8lbs.

Career: East Hampshire Schools; Chelsea ground staff July 1957, turning professional September 1958 (Crystal Palace on loan January-February 1970); Crystal Palace June 1970 (£40,000); Cork Celtic October 1973, having spells as player/manager while there; Waterford 1977; Shamrock Rovers 1978. Other honours: England schoolboy international. England Under-23 international (13 apps). Football League (1 app.). (Chelsea) FA Cup finalist 1967. FL Cup winner 1965.

Forward happy anywhere in the attack but especially so on the left, the better berths for his favourite left-foot shooting. A noted scorer, Bobby once netted 5 for Chelsea and hit 4 on 4 different occasions. In all for Chelsea and Palace scored 176 goals in 365 League matches and 5 substitutions. Became proprietor of a sports outfitting business at Havant, Hants.

TATE, Joe Thomas

(Aston Villa, 1931-33, 3)

Born Old Hill, Staffs. 4 August 1904. Died 18 May 1973.

1934: 6ft. 1in.; 12st. 7lbs.

Career: Round Oak; Cradley Heath (Birmingham League); Aston Villa April 1925; Brierley Hill Alliance as player/manager cs 1935. Other honour: Football League (1 app).

Left-half. Joined Villa as an inside-left, moving to half-back circa 1927. Then, together with Alec Talbot and Jimmy Gibson, for some years formed an awesome trio of halves all standing over 6ft. Joe's was a commanding presence, an ideal link between defence and attack, though his career was marred by injury. He had earlier represented the Birmingham FA in a so-called junior international. A good cricketer, he was once on Warwickshire's ground staff and later an assistant coach at Rugby School.

TAYLOR, Edward

(Huddersfield Town, 1923-26, 8)

Born Liverpool, 7 March 1887. Died 5 July 1956.

1922: 5ft. 9ins.; 12st 7lbs.

Career: Marlborough Old Boys (Liverpool); Liverpool Balmoral (England amateur trial 1912); Oldham Athletic as a professional February 1912 (guest player for Liverpool and Fulham during WW1); Huddersfield Town June 1922 (£2500); Everton February 1927; Ashton National September 1928; Wrexham November 1928; retired cs 1929. Other honours: Football League (2 apps). (H'field T) FL champions 1924, 1926. (Everton) FL champions 1928.

Goalkeeper of quality, certainly among the very best of the 'Twenties. Quick thinking and quick moving, his perceptions heightened by a study of opponents' strengths and weaknesses. A cousin of Charlie Hallows, the Lancashire and England cricketer, Taylor later went into the cotton trade in Manchester.

TAYLOR, Ernest

(Blackpool, 1954, 1)

Born Sunderland, 2 September 1925. Died 9 April 1985.

1955: 5ft. $5^1/_2$ins.; 10st. 4lbs.

Career: Hylton Colliery Juniors; Newcastle United September 1942; Blackpool October 1951 (£25,000); Manchester United February 1958 (£7500); Sunderland December 1958 (£7500); Altrincham cs 1961; Derry City November 1961; retired February 1962. Coach to New Brighton FC (Christchurch, New Zealand) February 1964-1965. Other honours: England 'B' international (1 app). (Newcastle) FA Cup winner 1951. (Blackpool) FA Cup winner 1953. (Man. Utd) FA Cup finalist 1958.

Inside-right, obviously something of a Cup fighter. A speedy ball player, packing a surprisingly hard shot for a small man. On his return to England from New Zealand worked for Vauxhall Motors at Hooton, Cheshire, keeping actively in touch with soccer as adviser to Heswall FC (West Cheshire League).

TAYLOR, James Guy
(Fulham, 1951, 2)
Born Hillingdon, Middlesex, 5 November 1917.
1951: 5ft. 11ins.; 11st. 10lbs.

Career: Hillingdon Town; Fulham March 1938; Queen's Park Rangers April 1953; Tunbridge Wells Rangers as player/manager May 1954; Yiewsley FC manager June 1958-March 1959; coach to Uxbridge FC (Corinthian League) cs 1959. Other honours: Football League (3 apps). (Fulham) FL Div. 2 champions 1949.

Centre-half finally after joining Fulham as an inside-right and appearing at wing-half just after the War. He quickly became one of the best pivots in the country, strong in tackling and judicious when parting. A rangy build proved advantageous too. During WW2 Jim served in the Royal Navy.

TAYLOR, Peter John
(Crystal Palace, 1976, 4)
Born Rochford nr. Southend-on-Sea, Essex, 3 January 1953.
1976: 5ft. 9ins.; 11st. 7lbs.

Career: South-East Essex Schools; Canvey Island FC; Southend United apprentice 1969, turning professional January 1971; Crystal Palace October 1973 (£80,000); Tottenham Hotspur September 1976 (around £200,000); Orient November 1980 (£150,000) (Oldham Athletic on month's loan January 1983); Maidstone United later in 1983; Exeter City September-December 1983. Other honours: England Under-23 international (4 apps).

Winger described as 'a left-footed right-winger', doing duty on both flanks. At his peak an assured performer with ball control, the capacity to go past defenders on either side, a stunning shot and finely accurate in centering. Had been a midfielder in his schooldays, after which he worked as a storekeeper before turning professional.

TAYLOR, Philip Henry
(Liverpool, 1948, 3)
Born Bristol, 18 September 1917.
1949: 5ft. $9^3/_4$ins.; 11st. 2lbs.

Career: Bristol Schools; Bristol Rovers ground staff cs 1932, turning professional 1935; Liverpool March 1936 (around £5000); retired July 1954 thereupon joining Liverpool's coaching staff; acting manager May 1956 and manager April 1957-November 1959. Other honours: England schoolboy international. England 'B' international (2 apps). Football League (4 apps). (Liverpool) FL champions 1947. FA Cup finalist 1950.

Right-half post-war after gaining a youthful reputation as an inside-right during the 'Thirties. Composed, very polished and an excellent skipper at Anfield after his removal to wing-half. A capable cricketer, Phil made one appearance for Gloucestershire (1938). Employed as a sales representative after leaving the game.

TAYLOR, Thomas
(Manchester United, 1953-58, 19)
Born Barnsley 29 January 1932. Died in the Munich air crash, 6 February 1958.
1957: 6ft.; 12st. 11lbs.

Career: Smithies United; Barnsley July 1949; Manchester United March 1953 (£29,999). Other honours: England 'B' international (2 apps). Football League (2 apps). (Man. Utd) FL champions 1956, 1957. FA Cup finalist 1957.

Centre-forward who could take an inside berth as well. Reckoned by many to be England's finest centre since Lawton, his early demise came at the height of his powers. Tommy was a superb opportunist and his quick eye was aided by shooting and heading skills. Scored 138 goals in 212 League matches for Barnsley and Manchester United.

TEMPLE, Derek William
(Everton, 1965, 1)
Born Liverpool, 13 November 1938.
1965: 5ft. 7½ins.; 11st. 3½lbs.

Career: Liverpool Schools; Everton ground staff 1955, turning professional August 1956; Preston North End September 1967 (£35,000); Wigan Athletic July 1970 (£1000). Other honours: England schoolboy international. England Youth international. Football League (2 apps). (Everton) FA Cup winner 1966.

Outside-left was perhaps his best position but he could make a good show anywhere in the attack. He possessed great speed, deft footwork and goal scoring nous (he had scored more than 100 in representative schoolboy soccer). Temple started running a business in Wigan while serving the local club as a part-time professional.

THICKETT, Henry
(Sheffield Unitd, 1899, 2)
Born Hexthorpe nr. Doncaster, 1873. Died 15 November 1920.
1901: 5ft. 8½ins.; 14st. 7lbs.

Career: Hexthorpe FC; Sheffield United 1890, leaving for Rotherham Town after one season, returning to United December 1893; Bristol City as player/manager May 1904, retired cs 1905, continuing as manager only until 1910. Other honours: Football League (2 apps). (Sheffield U) FL champions 1898. FA Cup winner 1899, 1902; finalist 1901.

Right-back. Swift-moving – despite his bulk – fearless, and the exploiter of a lovely kick. The flaw lay in occasional indifferent tackling. Managed Bristol City when they won the Second Division championship (1906) and reached the FA Cup final (1909), later becoming a Trowbridge licensee to his death. Latterly, too, he tipped the scales at 26st. (shades of his Bramall Lane colleague, Tiny Foulke (q.v.)!).

THOMAS, Daniel Joseph
(Coventry City, 1983, 2)
Born Worksop, 12 November 1961.
1983: 5ft. 7ins.; 11st.

Career: Worksop Schools; Coventry City apprentice, turning professional December 1978; Tottenham Hotspur June 1983 (£250,000); retired through injury December 1987. Other honours: England schoolboy international. England Under-21 international (8 apps). (Spurs) UEFA Cup winner 1984.

Right-back. Had a glittering career as a youngster, playing in all 9 of England's internationals at schoolboy level in season 1976/77. Quickly took to the first-class game, gaining Under-21 caps and displaying the modern full-back facets of speed and clever dribbling down the wing. Sustained a serious leg injury during the 1986/87 campaign.

THOMAS, David
(Queen's Park Rangers, 1975-76, 8)
Born Kirkby-in-Ashfield, Notts. 5 October 1950.
1975: 5ft. 8ins.; 9st. 13lbs.

Career: Co Durham Schools; Burnley apprentice February 1966, turning professional October 1967; Queen's Park Rangers October 1972 (165,000); Everton August 1977 (£200,000); Wolverhampton Wanderers October 1979 (£325,000); Vancouver Whitecaps (Canada) 1981; Middlesbrough March 1982; Portsmouth June 1982-1985. Other honours: England Youth international. England Under-23 international (11 apps).

Forward was his 'broad brush' designation but Thomas could more precisely be described as an outside-right. For he patrolled the right flank and, on gaining possession, would speed away eventually to middle the ball with consummate accuracy. Had been a great prospect, making his senior debut when 16. Considering the roll-call above, it is surprising to find he won no medals at club level.

THOMPSON, Peter
(Liverpool, 1964-70, 16)
Born Carlisle, 27 November 1942.
1967: 5ft. 8ins.; 11st. 6lbs.

Career: Carlisle Schools; Preston North End ground staff August 1958, turning professional November 1959; Liverpool August

1963 (£37,000); Bolton Wanderers January 1974, after 6 weeks on loan (£18,000); retired March 1978. Other honours: England schoolboy international. England Under-23 international (4 apps). Football League (5 apps). (Liverpool) European Cup Winners' Cup finalist 1966. FL champions 1964, 1966. FA Cup winner 1965; finalist 1971 (sub).

Outside-left among the cleverest of individualist ball players, his feinting, darting runs a major feature at Anfield during the decade there. A brilliant entertainer. Became director of a garage business, also having interests in Blackpool caravan parks.

THOMPSON, Philip Bernard
(Liverpool, 1976-83, 42)
Born Kensington, Liverpool, 21 January 1954.
1980: 6ft.; 11st. 8lbs.

Career: Kirkby Schools (Liverpool); Liverpool FC apprentice, turning professional February 1971; Sheffield United on loan December 1984, signing permanently March 1985; Liverpool again as player/coach July 1986. Other honours: England Under-23 international (2 apps). England Youth international. England 'B' international. (Liverpool) European Cup winner 1978, 1981. UEFA Cup winner 1976. FL champions 1976, 1977, 1979, 1980, 1982. FA Cup winner 1974. FL Cup winner 1981, 1982; finalist 1978.

Central defender; earlier had played on the right side of the defence. Something of a paradox in that despite a frail appearance (with legs unflatteringly referred to as 'matchsticks' – shades of Joe Mercer!), Phil had a tackle disconcertingly hard and true. And his continuous resolve could never be questioned. Was the Reds' skipper at one juncture.

THOMPSON, Thomas
(Aston Villa and Preston North End, 1952-57, 2)
Born Fence Houses, Co Durham, 10 November 1928.
1950: 5ft. 5½ins.; 10st. 4lbs.

Career: Lumley YMCA (Durham); Newcastle United August 1946 (£15); Aston Villa September 1950 (£12,500); Preston North End June 1955 (£28,500); Stoke City June 1961 (£1500); Barrow March 1963-1964. Other honours: England 'B' international (1 app). Football League (2 apps).

Inside-right. Not very big yet by thrust and speed off the mark contrived the extremely respectable League record of 224 goals in 442 League appearances. Tommy's best return was at Preston (117 in 188 outings), flourishing in the company of the great Tom Finney. He had a delicate touch too when such was called for.

THOMSON, Robert Anthony
(Wolverhampton Wanderers, 1964-65, 8)
Born Smethwick, Staffs. 5 December 1943.
1964: 5ft. 11½ins.; 11st. 6lbs.

Career: Birmingham Schools; Wolverhampton Wanderers ground staff cs 1959, becoming an apprentice 1960/61 and professional July 1961; Birmingham City March 1969 (£55,000) (Walsall on loan November 1971-February 1972); Luton Town July 1972-1976; subsequently ran Connecticut Bi-Centennials, USA, assisting Port Vale (signed October 1976) and Stafford Rangers between spells in the States. Other honours: England Under-23 international (15 apps). Football League (4 apps).

Left-back. A prospect from the start, a trialist for the England schoolboy team and joining Wolves before his 16th birthday. Played in mature fashion when introduced to the senior game (his debut was in a FA Cup-tie, January 1962). A polished back, quick to intervene and possessing a clean kick.

THORNEWELL, George
(Derby County, 1923-25, 4)
Born Romiley, Cheshire, 8 July 1898. Died 6 March 1986.
1925: 5ft. 6ins.; 10st. 5lbs.

Career: Rolls-Royce FC (Derby), where he was apprenticed during WW1 (guest player for Nottingham Forest 1917/18); Derby County May 1919; Blackburn Rovers December 1927; Chesterfield August 1929; Newark Town 1932. Other honours: (Blackburn) FA Cup winner 1928. (Chesterfield) FL Div. 3 (North) champions 1931.

Outside-right. Capital little winger, neat in style, employer of a fund of tricks and high consistency. In a career aggregate of exactly 400 League games, George scored 36 goals. Moved to Derby with his newly-widowed mother when 8 months old, the youngest of 8 children. For many years a licensee at Duffield near Derby.

THORNLEY, Irvine
(Manchester City, 1907, 1)
Born Hayfield, Derbys. 1883. Died 24 April 1955.
1919: 5ft. 9ins.; 11st.

Career: Glossop Villa; Glossop St James; Glossop North End 1901/02; Manchester City March 1904; South Shields August 1912; Hamilton Academicals cs 1919; Houghton (North-Eastern League) cs 1920. Other honours: Football League (2 apps). (Man. City) FL Div. 2 champions 1910.

Centre-forward. Thrustful, lively leader apt to give opposing defences the run around should their concentration lapse. Immensely popular at Hyde Road (Manchester City's then ground), his benefit, which realised £1036, being a record at the time.

TILSON, S(amuel) Frederick
(Manchester City, 1934-36, 4)
Born Barnsley, 19 April 1904. Died 21 November 1972.
1938: 5ft. 9ins.; 11st. $9^1/_2$lbs.

Career: Barnsley Schools; Regent Street Congs. (Barnsley); Barnsley FC March 1926; Manchester City March 1928 (£4000 including Eric Brook, q.v.); Northampton Town March 1938; York City cs 1939; retired during WW2. Manchester City coach post-war, then their assistant manager to July 1965 after which he was appointed chief scout. Other honours: Football League (3 apps). (Man. City) FL champions 1937. FA Cup winner 1934.

Centre-forward/inside-left first coming to prominence in the latter position. Fred was a quick thinker, a marksman and performer of a demoralising body swerve. Suffered many injuries and was out of action for the 1933 Cup final. Made up for it the following year, however, scoring 4 times in the semi-final and twice in the final. Nicknamed 'Old Dryasdust' according to the 1950 FA Year Book.

TITMUSS, Frederick
(Southampton, 1922-23, 2)
Born Pirton, Herts. 15 February 1898. Died 2 October 1966.
1925: 5ft. $8^1/_2$ins.; 11st.

Career: Pirton United (Luton Alliance) 1914/15; Hitchen Town; Army football (he served with the RGA and Lancashire Fusiliers during WW1) and played for his battn. team in France; Southampton cs 1919; Plymouth Argyle February 1926; retired cs 1932 but later assisted St Austell FC (Cornwall) as a part-time professional. Other honours: (Soton) Div. 3 (South) champions 1922. (Plymouth) Div. 3 (South) champions 1930.

Left-back. 'A sound tackler who kicks with excellent judgment,' was a comment during his cap-winning period, and these qualities were maintained for another decade or so. Complemented admirably Tom Parker (q.v.) at The Dell and another international at Home Park, Moses Russell of Wales. After leaving Argyle was a Plymouth licensee until his death.

TODD, Colin
(Derby County, 1972-77, 27)
Born Chester-le-street, County Durham, 12 December 1948.
1975: 5ft. 9ins.; 11st. 6lbs.

Career: Chester-le-street Schools; Sunderland apprentice when 15, turning professional December 1965; Derby County February 1971 (£175,000); Everton September 1978 (£300,000); Birmingham City September 1979 (£250,000); Nottingham Forest August 1982 (£65,000); Oxford United February 1984; Vancouver Whitecaps, Canada May 1984; Luton Town October 1984-1985; Middlesbrough reserve team coach May 1986, first team coach September 1986. Other honours: England Youth international. England Under-23 international (14 apps). Football League (3 apps). (Derby County) FL champions 1972, 1975.

Defender (nominated left-half in his early years), sometimes full-back. A class performer over many seasons: a crisp, sure tackler and fast, able to take the spectators' attention as few in his position do. As well, in fact, as a favoured ball-juggling forward. Colin's ability to send long accurate passes over a long distance could scarcely be bettered. The PFA 'Player of the Year' for 1975.

TOONE, George
(Notts County, 1892, 2)
Born Nottingham, 10 June 1868. Died 1 September 1943.
1890s: 5ft. $7^1/_2$ins.; 11st. 2lbs.

Career: Nottingham Jardine's; Notts Rangers; Notts County 1889; Bedminster August 1899; Bristol City cs 1900; Notts County again cs 1901; retired 1902. Other honour: (Notts Co) FL Div. 2 champions 1897. FA Cup winner 1894.

Goalkeeper figuring prominently in Notts County's ups and downs of the 'Nineties. His displays were marked by coolness, assured handling and smart clearances. Missed the 1891 Cup final because of injury. For some years a Nottingham licensee after leaving the game, and father of George jnr., a half-back with Notts County, Sheffield Wednesday and Watford 1913-25.

TOPHAM, Arthur George
(Corinthians, 1894, 1)
Born Ellesmere, Salop, 19 February 1869. Died 18 May 1931.

Career: Oswestry School; Oxford University (Blue 1890); Casuals; Eastbourne; Chiswick Park; Corinthians 1893-97. Other honour: (Casuals) FA Amateur Cup finalist 1894.

Half-back able to take on any of the three berths (he was, for example, left-half in his international and centre-half for the '94 Amateur Cup final). Had a tackle of marked effectiveness but flawed his performances sometimes by misplacing passes. He was a schoolmaster, first as co-proprietor of a school at Eastbourne and then, from 1912, at Ascham St Vincent's School, another Eastbourne academy. Elder brother of Robert Topham (below).

TOPHAM, Robert
(Wolverhampton Wanderers and Casuals, 1893-94, 2)
Born Ellesmere, Salop, 3 November 1867. Died 31 August 1931.

Career: Oswestry School; Oxford University (no Blue); Oswestry FC; Wolverhampton Wanderers 1891-96; Casuals; Chiswick Park; Corinthians 1894-98. Other honours: (Oswestry) Welsh Cup finalist 1885. (Wolves) FA Cup winner 1893. (Casuals) FA Amateur Cup finalist 1894.

Outside-right earning high praise in the 1893 Athletic News Annual. 'Was the mainstay of the Cup-holders' forwards. Is very speedy, dribbles well, and centres in a most dangerous fashion. Is bad to get off the ball, and often carries it through by sheer energy.' Was invited in 1885 to play for Wales against Scotland, but declined. A master at Brighton College 1892-1905 after which he was a hop grower in Kent. Brother of A G Topham (England).

TOWERS, M(ark) Anthony
(Sunderland, 1976, 3)
Born Manchester, 13 April 1952.
1976: 5ft. 9ins.; 11st.

Career: Manchester Schools; Lancashire Schools; Manchester City apprentice July 1967, turning professional April 1969; Sunderland March 1974 (£100,000 and another player); Birmingham City July 1977

(£140,000); Montreal Manic, Canada, early in 1981 (£30,000). Other honours: England schoolboy international. England Youth international. England Under-23 international (8 apps). (Man. City) European Cup Winners' Cup winner 1970. FL Cup finalist 1974. (Sunderland) FL Div. 2 champions 1976.

Midfield. A committed player but cool – 'ever at the heart of things' as one scribe put it. Performed with a mature assurance from the start, winning a major European competition medal when only 15 days past his 18th birthday. (Judging from his Christian names, Tony's parents must have been devotees of the immortal bard).

TOWNLEY, William
(Blackburn Rovers, 1889-90, 2)
Born Blackburn, 14 February 1866. Died 30 May 1950.
1891: 5ft. 10ins.; 10st. 12lbs.

Career: Blackburn junior football and Blackburn Olympic to Blackburn Rovers; Stockton July 1892; Darwen July 1894; Manchester City September 1896-cs 1897. Coach on the continent from 1909-34, mainly in Germany but also in Holland, Sweden and Switzerland around the mid-1920s. Other honours: (Blackburn R) FA Cup winner 1890, 1891.

Outside-left with a penchant for goal scoring, not least from long range, while he had a talent for heading. The first of only 3 players to register 3 goals in a FA Cup final, Townley's feat occurring in 1890. Worked as a school teacher from 1890 until his coaching career started. Father of John C Townley, who was on the books of Spurs, Brighton and Clapton Orient between the wars.

TOWNROW, John Ernest
(Clapton Orient, 1925-26, 2)
Born West Ham, 28 March 1901. Died 11 April 1969.
1925: 5ft. $11^1/_2$ins.; 13st.

Career: West Ham Schools; Fairbairn House; Clapton Orient August 1919; Chelsea February 1927 (£5000); Bristol Rovers May 1932-1933. Other honour: England schoolboy international.

Centre-half, constructive, of ideal pivotal physique and possessing a cogent tackle. Did not entirely curb an attacking inclination when the 'third back' idea came into vogue following the offside law change in 1925. During his playing career continued working as an engineer at Becton Gasworks and was later in the licensed trade. Jack's younger brother, Frank, an Eastville colleague, was also an English schoolboy cap.

TREMELLING, R(ichard) Daniel
(Birmingham, 1928, 1)
Born Burton-on-Trent, 12 November 1897. Died 1970.
1927: 5ft. 10ins.; 10st. 12lbs.

Career: Langwith Colliery Junction Wagon Works; Shirebrook; Lincoln City during WW1; Birmingham June 1919; Bury May 1933-1936. Had spell as Birmingham's assistant trainer from June 1936 to the War. Other honours: Football League (3 apps). (Birmingham) FL Div. 2 champions 1921.

Goalkeeper, regular guardian of the Birmingham net for a decade, especially noteworthy for his clean handling. A measure of his worth is that the great Harry Hibbs had been on the books some 5 years before taking over as first choice. Dan's brother Bill, a centre-half, won honours with Blackpool and Preston North End during the 'Thirties.

TRESADERN, John
(West Ham United, 1923, 2)
Born Leytonstone, Essex, 26 September 1890. Died 26 September 1959.
1923: 5ft. 6ins.; 10st. 1lb.

Career: Barking Town; West Ham United July 1913 as an amateur, turning professional 1913/14; Burnley October 1924; Northampton Town as player/manager May 1925-cs 1927, remaining as manager only until 1930. Crystal Palace secretary/manager October 1930; Tottenham Hotspur manager June 1935; Plymouth Argyle manager April 1938-November 1947; Aston Villa scout 1948/49; Chelmsford City manager June 1949-November 1950; Hastings United manager December 1951; Tonbridge manager April 1958 to his death. Other honour: (WHU) FA Cup finalist 1923.

Left-half remarkably robust for a small man though, of course, possessed of other facets as well. These included consistency and all-round quality. Spent most of his adult life in football, wide managerial experience taking in first-class and non-League levels. During WW1 held a commission in the Royal Garrison Artillery.

TUEART, Dennis
(Manchester City, 1975-77, 6)
Born Newcastle-upon-Tyne, 27 November 1949.
1976: 5ft. 8ins.; 11st. 2lbs.

Career: Newcastle Schools; Newcastle junior football; Sunderland August 1967; Manchester City March 1974 (£250,000); New York Cosmos, USA, February 1978 (£250,000); Manchester City again January 1980 (£150,000); Stoke City July 1983; Burnley December 1983-May 1984. Other honours: England Under-23 international (1 app). Football League (2 apps). (Sunderland) FA Cup winner 1973. (Man. City) FA Cup finalist 1981 (sub). FL Cup winner 1976.

Forward (more precisely an outside-left in earlier designation). His style was rightly termed 'hyper-active' and this activity combined with ready skills made for a dangerous marauder. Scored some spectacular goals, his creativity in tight situation leading to colleagues scoring too.

TUNSTALL, Frederick Edward
(Sheffield United, 1923-25, 7)
Born Gravesend, 29 March 1900. Died 18 November 1965.
1925: 5ft. $7^1/_2$ins.; 11st. 6lbs.

Career: Darfield St George's; Scunthorpe United 1920; Sheffield United December 1920 (£1000); Halifax Town February 1933; Boston United August 1936 and, after retiring from playing, continued to serve this club into the post-war years in various capacities as trainer, manager and coach.

Other honours: Football League (4 apps). (Sheffield U) FA Cup winner 1925.

Outside-left. Formed a celebrated wing with the renowned Irish cap, Billy Gillespie. Tunny, as he was popularly known, was fast, direct and liable to launch shots of the thunderbolt variety. Scored the goal ('a masterpiece of quick thinking,' says one report) that gave the Blades their 1925 Cup triumph. His fee to Bramall Lane seems a likely record receipt for a non-League club at that time, though this cannot be proven. Brother-in-law of George Briggs (Birmingham 1923-33).

TURNBULL, Robert
(Bradford, 1920, 1)
Born South Bank, Middlesbrough, 17 December 1895.
Died 18 March 1952.
1922: 5ft. 7½ins.; 12st. 3lbs.

Career: South Bank Schools; South Bank East End; Army football; Bradford January 1918; Leeds United May 1925; Rhyl Athletic September1932; retired 1933. Other honours: England 'Victory' international 1919 (3 apps).

Outside-right. Described as fast, direct and orthodox, to which may be added brilliant footwork and accurate centring when in form. First starred in a renowned school side, one season personally notching 80 goals. Twice toured South Africa with FA parties, playing twice in 1920 and thrice in 1929 against the national teams. A steel worker before and after his football career.

TURNER, Arthur
(Southampton, 1900-01, 2)
Born Farnborough, Hants. 1877. Died 4 April 1925.
1903: 5ft. 8ins.; 11st. 10lbs.
Career: Aldershot North End 1892-94; South Farnborough; Camberley St Michael's; Southampton 1899; Derby County May 1902; Newcastle United January 1903; Tottenham Hotspur February 1904 (£150); Southampton again cs 1904; retired cs 1905. Other honours: (Soton) Southern League champions 1901. FA Cup finalist 1900, 1902.

Outside-right very much the opportunist type. He would pounce on the slimmest of chances eventually parting with the ball to the most advantageously placed colleague. Left the first-class game early – when only 28 – and returned to his native Farnborough, there joining his father's business.

TURNER, Hugh
(Huddersfield Town, 1931, 2)
Born Wigan, 6 August 1904.
1930: 5ft. 10ins.; 12st 8lbs.

Career: Felling Colliery (Darlington on amateur forms cs 1924); High Fell FC (Gateshead) cs 1925; Huddersfield Town April 1926; Fulham May 1937-1946. Other honours: Football League (1 app). (H'field T) FA Cup finalist 1930.

Goalkeeper. An unspectacular performer (and none the worse for that) but one possessing in plentitude the cardinal goalkeeping virtues of soundness and confidence. Maintained a high consistency level too – 394 League and FA Cup matches for Huddersfield and first choice at Craven Cottage in his two peacetime campaigns there.

TURNER, James Albert
(Bolton Wanderers, Stoke and Derby County, 1893-98, 3)
Born Blackbull nr. Goldenhill, Staffs. 1866. Died 9 April 1904.

Career: Black Lane Rovers; Bolton Wanderers early in 1889; Stoke cs 1894; Derby County June 1896 (£70); Stoke again August 1898-1900. Other honours: Football League (1 app). (Derby Co) FA Cup finalist 1898.

Left-half was the position occupied in his 3 England appearances and '98 Cup final, but was actually a valuable utility player. His 30 League outings in 1899/1900, for example, were made up of 28 at outside-left and 2 at outside-right, and he had earlier taken other roles in attack and defence. Turner was utterly reliable too, exploiting an effective tackle and excellent judgment generally. Worked as a clerk for a commercial firm.

TWEEDY, George Jacob
(Grimsby Town, 1937, 1)
Born Willington, Co Durham, 8 January 1913. Died 23 April 1987.
1938: 6ft.; 13st.

Career: Durham Schools; Willington Town; Grimsby Town August 1931; retired cs 1950 and appointed Grimsby's assistant manager the following September; returned as a player late in 1951, finally retiring April 1953.

Goalkeeper unfortunate in being the contemporary of Hibbs and Woodley. Ideally proportioned, he had all the required qualities, especially a marvellous sense of anticipation and in assured handling. George's first-class career spanned an abnormally long period. Settled in the Grimsby area and later engaged in the furniture trade.

UFTON, Derek Gilbert
(Charlton Athletic, 1954, 1)
Born Crayford, Kent, 31 May 1928.
1957: 5ft. 11½ins.; 12st. 4lbs.

Career: Borough United (Kent); Dulwich Hamlet (Cardiff City amateur); Bexleyheath & Welling; Charlton Athletic as a professional September 1948; retired through injury cs 1960. Tooting & Mitcham FC coach January 1962; Plymouth Argyle coach September 1964, caretaker manager April 1965 becoming manager the following month until January 1968. Charlton Athletic director August 1984.

Centre-half who had a lot of exposure at left-half too. A cool player especially strong in the tackle. Suffered a recurring shoulder injury that eventually forced his retirement. Ufton was an excellent cricketer for Kent (148 matches, 1949-62). His other activities outside football have included photographic modelling and managing a West End club.

UNDERWOOD, Alfred
(Stoke, 1891-92, 2)
Born Newcastle-under-Lyme, Staffs. 1869. Died 8 October 1928.
1890s: 'about 6ft.; 13st.'.

Career: Hanley Tabernacle; Etruria FC (Stoke-on-Trent); Stoke in the mid-1880s; retired through injury cs 1893 but made isolated appearances afterwards. Other honour: (Stoke) Football Alliance champions 1891.

Left-back. 'A most consistent back,' remarked the Athletic News, 'a big kick, but occasionally rather wild in tackling.' Member of Stoke's famous defensive trio (Rowley, Clare and Underwood) that flourished until the latter's knee injury in season 1892-93. Like his partner, Tommy Clare, Alf was extremely mobile for a big man. A potter by trade, he was an invalid from the early 1900s onwards.

URWIN, Tom
(Middlesbrough and Newcastle United, 1923-26, 4)
Born Haswell nr. Sunderland, 5 February 1896. Died 7 May 1968.

1922: 5ft. 6ins.; 10st. 10lbs.

Career: Sunderland Schools; Fulwell FC (Sunderland Nonconformist League); Lambton Star; Shildon as an amateur 1913, turning professional February 1914; Middlesbrough May 1914; Newcastle United August 1924 (£3200); Sunderland February 1930 (£525); retired cs 1936. Later became coach to Sunderland's junior players. Other honours: Football League (1 app). (Newcastle) FL champions 1927.

Outside-right/outside-left. Lasted a long time in the first-class game, a sprightly little wingman showing much pace and exceptional ability in pinpoint centering. One of only 4 players to turn out for the North-East's 'Big 3' and, uniquely, he received benefits from each. Worked latterly as a clerk in a Sunderland hospital, retiring in February 1962.

UTLEY, George
(Barnsley, 1913, 1)
Born Elsecar nr. Barnsley, 1887. Died 8 January 1966.
1911: 5ft. $10^1/_2$ins.; 13st.

Career: Elsecar FC; Wentworth FC; Sheffield Wednesday on amateur forms cs 1906 but through an injury did not play for them and, after a knee operation, returned to Elsecar; Barnsley 1907; Sheffield United November 1913 (for a record £2000); Manchester City September 1922. Bristol City trainer November 1923; Sheffield Wednesday trainer/coach May 1924; Fulham trainer July 1925 to circa 1928. Other honours: Football League (1 app). (Barnsley) FA Cup winner 1912; finalist 1910. (Sheffield U) FA Cup winner 1915.

Left-half. A battler imbued with all the competitive qualities the word 'Barnsley' conjures up. A fine general, too, and one especially noted for his long throws. In 1914 took over the sports outfitting business that had for long been run by the Sheffield United trainer, George Waller. Also for many years Utley was cricket coach at the Lancashire public school, Rossall, this appointment commencing some considerable time before the Great War.

VAUGHTON, O(liver) Howard
(Aston Villa, 1882-84, 5)
Born Aston, Birmingham, 9 January 1861. Died 6 January 1937.

Career: Waterloo FC (Birmingham); Birmingham FC (not the present club); Wednesday Strollers; Aston Villa 1880-circa 1888. Aston Villa's Vice-President 1923, President June 1924, leaving the office September 1924 to become a director until December 1932, elected a life member February 1933. Other honour: (Villa) FA Cup winner 1887.

Inside-left. 'Very unselfish,' said Alcock, 'and plays well for his side; not a good shot at goal.' Erratic shooting was, however, the only chink in Vaughton's armour, for he had the remaining necessary skills. From boyhood adept at all sports – cycling, roller and ice skating (winning national awards for both), a county hockey player, a class golfer and he played cricket for Warwickshire and Staffordshire. For many years on management and ground committees of Warwickshire CCC. A silversmith by vocation: his firm manufactured the second FA Cup.

VEITCH, Colin Campbell McKechnie
(Newcastle United, 1906-09, 6)
Born Newcastle-upon-Tyne, 22 May 1881.
Died 26 August 1938.
1906: 5ft. 7½ins.; 12st. 5lbs.

Career: Newcastle Schools; Rutherford College (Newcastle); Newcastle United as an amateur January 1899, turning professional 1903; retired during WW1. Post-war was secretary of Newcastle Swifts (United's nursery side) to cs 1926; Bradford City secretary/manager August 1926-January 1928. Other honours: Football League (4 apps). (Newcastle) FL champions 1905, 1907, 1909. FA Cup winner 1910; finalist 1905, 1906, 1908, 1911.

Half-back by preference but actually a player of extraordinary versatility. In the above medal-winning line-ups he occupied 3 different positions (mostly as pivot despite his height) and, for Newcastle, actually turned out in 8 outfield berths. A master of all the playing techniques. Chairman of the Players' Union 1909-12. Very much a man of parts outside the game too. Chairman, producer and actor for Newcastle's People's Theatre; and a professional journalist for the last 9 years of his life.

VEITCH, John Gould
(Old Westminsters, 1894, 1)
Born Kingston Hill, Surrey, 19 July 1869.
Died 3 October 1914.

Career: Westminster School (XI 1887); Cambridge University (Blue 1888-9-90-1); Old Westminsters; Corinthians 1889-98.

Inside/outside-left. Not the most consistent of forwards yet, when in form, he could be a potent force. Tall and strong, adept at dribbling and a marksman to be reckoned with. This last quality is well borne out in an examination of his Corinthians' statistics: in 72 matches for the club he scored a remarkable total of 63 goals.

VENABLES, Terence Frederick
(Chelsea, 1965, 2)
Born Bethnal Green, London, 6 January 1943.
1965: 5ft. 8¼ins.; 11st. 8lbs.

Career: Dagenham Schools; Chelsea amateur July 1958, turning professional August 1960; Tottenham Hotspur May 1966 (£80,000); Queen's Park Rangers June 1969 (£70,000); Crystal Palace September 1974 (in part exchange for another player)-1975. Crystal Palace coach 1975, manager/coach June 1976; Queen's Park Rangers manager October 1980, director also (and second largest shareholder) November 1981; Barcelona manager May 1984-September 1987 and appointed Spurs' manager later that month. Other honours: England schoolboy international. England Youth international. England amateur international (1 app). England Under-23 international (4 apps). Football League (1 app). (Chelsea) FL Cup winner 1965. (Spurs) FA Cup winner 1967.

Right-half/inside-left, diverse positions revealing utility value. An incisive tackler, immaculate in distribution. Established a record by being capped at five different levels. Has been just as successful in the managerial field, steering Palace and QPR to 2nd Division championships and Barcelona to their first Spanish League title for 11 years. The latter feat earned him the

'World Manager of the Year' award for 1985, the first Briton to receive this accolade. Is also a writer (co-author of 'They Used to Play on Grass', Hodder & Stoughton, 1971) and of TV scripts. Known to the tabloid press as 'El Tel'.

VIDAL, (Revd.) Robert Walpole Sealy
(Oxford University, 1873, 1)
Born Cornborough nr. Bideford, Devon, 3 September 1853.
Died 5 November 1914.

Career: Westminster School (XI 1870-72, captain 1872); Oxford University (Blue 1874-75, captain 1875); Old Westminsters; Wanderers. Served onthe FA Committee 1872 and 1874. Other honours: (Oxford University) FA Cup winner 1874; finalist 1873. (Wanderers) FA Cup winner 1872.

Forward. Shrewd, fast and (thanks in no small measure to consummate ball control) a renowned dribbler. Equally famed for his marksmanship. So far as can be ascertained, the only player to win a FA Cup winners' medal while still at school. An Oxford rugger Blue 1873, and later shone at golf. Ordained 1877 and Vicar of Abbotsham, Devon, 1881 to his death. Was later known as 'R W Sealy'.

VILJOEN, Colin
(Ipswich Town, 1975, 2)
Born Johannesburg, South Africa, 20 June 1948.
1975: 5ft. 8ins.; 10st. 10lbs.

Career: Southern Transvaal FC; Ipswich Town amateur 1965/66, turning professional August 1967; Manchester City August 1978 (£100,000); Chelsea March 1980 (£45,000)-cs 1982. Other honour: (Ipswich Town) FL Div. 2 champions 1968.

Midfield. Summed up as '. . . a player of outstanding perception, a quick reader of situations with ability to flight the ball cunningly into space and create havoc in crowded goalmouths.' His 11-year service at Portman Road took in 367 senior matches (and 5 substitutions), in which he scored 54 goals. Became a British subject in 1971. After leaving football took employment as a licensee near the airport at Heathrow.

VIOLLET, Dennis S.
(Manchester United, 1960-62, 2)
Born Manchester, 20 September 1933.
1961: 5ft. 8ins.; 11st.

Career: Manchester Schools; Manchester United amateur cs 1949, turning professional September 1950; Stoke City January 1962 (£25,000); Baltimore Bays, USA, May 1967-September 1968 (£10,000); Witton Albion January 1969; Linfield player/manager July 1969; Preston North End coach 1970; Crewe Alexandra coach February 1971, manager cs-November 1971; later returned to the States as manager/coach of Washington Diplomats, resigning June 1977. Other honours: England schoolboy international. Football League (3 appearances). (Man. Utd) FL champions 1956, 1957. FA Cup finalist 1958. (Stoke C) FL Div. 2 champions 1963. FL Cup finalist 1964. (Linfield) Irish Cup winner 1970.

Centre/inside-forward. Belied his appearance, lasting the hardest of games, playing with a captivating grace and skill. Particularly good with the measured pass. Holder of Manchester United's FL scoring record of 32 in 1959/60, registered in 36 matches – a splendid feat.

VON DONOP, Pelham George
(Royal Engineers, 1873-75, 2)
Born Southsea, Hants. 28 April 1851. Died 7 November 1921.

Career: Somerset College, Bath; Royal Military Academy, Woolwich; Royal Engineers. Other honours: (Royal Engineers) FA Cup winner 1875; finalist 1874.

Forward among the fleetest of the early practitioners indulging his clever dribbling wiles to splendid effect. Served with the Royal Engineers 1871-99, retiring with the rank of Lt-Colonel. He was an Inspecting

Officer of Railways 1899-1913 and Chief Inspecting Officer 1913-16.

WACE, Henry
(Wanderers, 1878-79, 3)
Born Shrewsbury, 21 September 1853. Died 5 November 1947.

Career: Shrewsbury School; Cambridge University (Blue 1874-5); Wanderers; Clapham Rovers; Shropshire Wanderers. Other honours: (Wanderers) FA Cup winner 1877, 1878.

Forward. 'A very good and dangerous 'centre'; plays pluckily and sticks to the ball,' relates an Alcock's Annual. A notable in other fields too, getting a Blue for rugger as well as soccer in 1874 and '75, and achieving outstanding distinctions at Cambridge. Son of Shrewsbury solicitor, Wace became a barrister (called to the Bar 1879) and was subsequently an acknowledged authority on bankruptcy law.

WADDLE, Christopher Roland
(Newcastle United and Tottenham Hotspur, 1985-88, 36)
Born Heworth nr. Gateshead, 14 December 1960.
1986: 6ft.; 11st. 5lbs.

Career: Pelaw Juniors; Clarke Chapman (works side); Tow Law Town cs 1979; Newcastle United July 1980 (£1000); Tottenham Hotspur July 1985 (£590,000). Other honours: England Under-21 international (1 app). (Spurs) FA Cup finalist 1987.

Forward. A most deceptive player, looking gangling and with a somewhat lumbering gait, but turning out to have the rare ability to run at defences, beating opponents by sheer ball jugglery. Able, too, to score goals from 'impossible' angles often inducing a pronounced swerve in so doing. Really came into his own during 1986-87 as a performer of acknowledged international class. Cousin of Alan Waddle, the well known much-travelled centre-forward of Swansea City etc.

WADSWORTH, Samuel John
(Huddersfield Town, 1922-27, 9)
Born Darwen, Lancs. 13 September 1896. Died 1 September 1961.
1922: 5ft. 9ins.; 11st. 7lbs.

Career: Darwen FC; Blackburn Rovers 1914; Nelson May 1919; Huddersfield Town March 1921 (£1600); Burnley September 1929; Lytham 1931; retired through injury and subsequently coached in Holland, one of his appointments being with PSV Eindhoven. Other honours: Football League (6 apps). (H'field T) FL Champions 1924, 1925, 1926. FA Cup winner 1922.

Left-back. Thought by a Huddersfield Town historian to be world class and this is far from a fanciful notion. For Wadsworth had all the qualities a back of his time needed – calmness, tackles perfectly timed and clearances perfectly placed. After going to Holland, spent the rest of his life there apart from the War years.

WAINSCOAT, W(illiam) Russell
(Leeds United, 1929, 1)
Born: East Retford, Notts. 28 July 1898. Died July 1967.
1929: 5ft. 11ins.; 12st. 7lbs.

Career: Maltby Main Colliery (Yorks) before and after WW1; Barnsley March 1920; Middlesbrough December 1923

(£3750); Leeds United March 1925 (£2000); Hull City October 1931 – 1934. Other honour: (Hull City) FL Div. 3 (North) champions 1933.

Inside-left, with a deal of experience at centre-forward also. Big and strong. Russell possessed the brand of crafty footwork more often the prerogative of Scottish forwards. Was in the 1926 FA Touring team to Canada, in one game netting 5 goals. A consistent scorer throughout his first-class career (e.g. 48 in 86 first team matches for Hull City). Held a variety of jobs outside the game – they included at different times railway clerk, licensee and shopkeeper both footwear and drapery.

WAITERS, Anthony Keith
(Blackpool, 1964-65. 5)
Born Southport, 1 February 1937.
1965: 6ft. 2ins.; 13st. 12lbs.

Career: RAF football (Middlesbrough amateur); Loughborough College; Bishop Auckland; Macclesfield; Blackpool amateur July 1959, turning professional the following October; retired May 1967 on appointment as FA North-West regional coach; Liverpool coach January 1969; Burnley player/coach July 1970; Coventry City director of coaching December 1971-March 1972; Plymouth Argyle manager October 1972–April 1977; Vancouver Whitecaps manager later in 1977; coach to the Canadian Olympic games team 1984. Has also had spells as Tranmere Rovers coach and as a Chelsea scout. Other honours: England amateur international (1 app). Football League (5 apps).

Goalkeeper. Heavily built yet noticeably agile, his keen reflex action the reason for a competent dealing of close-range shooting. The 3 year lay off, 1967-70, did not affect unduly earlier brilliance. Became a widely experienced coach and was the North American Soccer League's 'Coach of the Year' for 1978.

WALDEN, Frederick Ingram ('Fanny')
(Tottenham Hotspur, 1914-22, 2)
Born Wellingborough, 1 March 1888. Died 3 May 1949.
1914: 5ft. 2$^1/_2$ins.; 10st.

Career: Wellingborough schoolboy football and then assisted 3 clubs of that town (White Cross, All Saints and Redwell – who paid him 5 shillings per week) before joining Northampton Town cs 1909; Tottenham Hotspur April 1913 (£1750); Northampton Town again May 1926; retired cs 1927. Other honours: Football League (1 app). Southern League (3 apps). (Spurs) FL Div. 2 champions 1920.

Outside-right. This most diminutive of footballers enjoyed a popularity in inverse proportion to his size. Crowds revelled in his capacity to wriggle past bigger opponents outwitted by uncanny control and left floundering by smart acceleration. Unluckily was on the injured list at the time of the 1921 Cup final. Played cricket for Northants 1910-29 (258 matches) - Fanny was one of the smallest-ever county cricketers too. He later became a first-class umpire and stood in several Test matches. Originally worked as a moulder in an iron foundry.

WALKER, William Henry
(Aston Villa, 1921-33, 18)
Born Wednesbury, Staffs. 29 October 1897. Died 28 November 1964.
1925: 5ft. 11$^1/_2$ins.; 12st. 5lbs.

Career: West Midlands schoolboy football; Hednesford Town (3 matches circa 1912); Darlaston; Wednesbury Old Park; Aston Villa as a part-time professional 1915 (assisted Wednesbury Old Park and guested for Birmingham during WW1), Villa as a full pro May 1919; retired December 1933 on appointment as Sheffield Wednesday manager to November 1937; Chelmsford City manager January 1938 – October 1938; Nottingham Forest manager March 1939–July 1960 when he retired on health grounds but served on Forest's committee until his death. Other honours: Football League (6 apps). (Villa) FA Cup winner 1920; finalist 1924.

Inside-left, after making his mark as a centre-forward. A great and much respected player of the 'Twenties, as the Villa programme related on his retirement. 'His artistry was superb; his skill in ball control unsurpassed. No player was more likely to head the ball into the net than he.' Son of a well known former Wolves' player, George Walker, who did not want Billy to join the paid ranks. He had his managerial successes too, steering both Wednesday and Forest to FA Cup wins.

WALL, George
(Manchester United, 1907-13, 7)
Born Boldon Colliery, Co. Durham, 20 February 1885. Died 1962.
1909: 5ft. 6ins.; 10st. 11lbs.

Career: Boldon Royal Rovers: Whitburn for 1 season; Jarrow cs 1902; Barnsley November 1903; Manchester United March 1906 (£175); Oldham Athletic March 1919 (£200); Hamilton Academicals June 1921; Rochdale cs 1922; Ashton National September 1923. Other honours: Football League (5 apps). (Man. Utd.) FL champions 1908,1911. FA Cup winner 1909.

Outside-left, enjoying a long career that took in well ove r 500 first-class appearances. Had the usual winger attributes of speed and centring ability plus a left-foot drive of fierce velocity. Toured South Africa with the 1910 FA party, thrice appearing against the national team. After leaving football worked for many years on the Manchester docks.

WALLACE, Charles William
(Aston Villa, 1913-20, 3)
Born Sunderland 20 January 1885. Died 7 January 1970.
1919: 5ft. 8½ins.; 11st. 12lbs.

Career: Sunderland Schools; Southwick FC (Co. Durham); Crystal Palace cs 1905; Aston Villa May 1907; Oldham Athletic May 1921; retired cs 1923. Later was in charge of Villa's junior team and for many years after WW2 was a steward and dressing-room attendant at Villa Park. Other honours: Football League (5 apps). (Villa) FL champions 1910. FA Cup winner 1913, 1920.

Outside-right showing a blistering turn of speed, consistently middling the ball with goal-producing accuracy. Always unselfish. Reputedly the only player to have missed a penalty in a FA Cup final (which he did in 1913). Worked as a painter and decorator in Birmingham.

WALLACE, David L. ('Danny')
(Southampton, 1986, 1)
Born London, 21 January 1964.
1986: 5ft. 4ins.; 9st. 13lbs.

Career: Junior football; Southampton apprentice 1980, turning professional January 1982. Other honours: England Youth international. England Under-221 international (14 apps).

Forward. Wingman short in stature but considerable in skills. Combines pace and dribbling ability – a crowd pleasing amalgam. His first senior outing occured at 16 years 10 months, making the Saints' youngest debutant for several decades (and possibly of all time).

WALSH, Paul Anthony
(Luton Town, 1983-84, 5)
Born Plumstead, London, 1 October 1962.
1983: 5ft. 8ins.; 10st. 1lb.

Career: Junior football to Charlton Athletic as an apprentice, turning professional October 1979; Luton Town July 1982 (£250,000 and another player); Liverpool May 1984 (£700,000); Tottenham Hotspur February 1988 (£500,000). Other honours: England Youth international. England Under-21 international (4 apps). (Liverpool) European Cup finalist 1985. FL champions 1986. FL Cup finalist 1987.

Forward. The possessor of great dribbling skills aided by bursts of acceleration and marksmanship. As a youth his exciting play attracted many scouts to The Valley, even-

tually to warrant a quarter-million fee when still only 19. 'Young Player of the Year' for 1984.

WALTERS, Arthur Melmoth
(Old Carthusians, 1885-90,9)
Born Ewell, Surrey, 26 January 1865. Died 2 May 1941.

Career: Charterhouse School (XI 1882-83); Cambridge University (Blue 1884-5-6-7); Old Carthusians; Corinthians 1885-93; East Sheen. Also represented Surrey. Other honours: (Old Carthusians) FA Amateur Cup winner 1894; finalist 1895.

Right-back. Fast moving and strong kicking. Famous, of course, as member of a great full-back pairing with his brother, P M Walters below. Given their initials the pair were inevitably referred to as 'Morning' and 'Afternoon' Walters. MA (Cantab) and a solicitor by profession (admitted November 1889). Also distinguished himself in athletics and swimming when at Charterhouse.

WALTERS, Percy Melmoth
(Old Carthusians,1885-90, 13)
Born Ewell, Surrey, 30 September 1863. Died 6 October 1936.

Career: Learned the game at Charterhouse School but was not in the XI; Oxford University (Blue 1885); Old Carthusians; Corinthians 1885-92; East Sheen; Epsom. Also represented Surrey. FA committee 1886 and a Vice-President 1891-92. Other honour: (Old Carthusians) FA Amateur Cup finalist 1895.

Left-back, perfectly complementing his brother and partner above, he did not take up the game seriously until his last year at Oxford. Strong, courageous and able to clear from any angle. Retired temporarily in 1893, as did A M Walters, because of a fatal accident to a younger brother. In 1885 represented Oxford University at cricket. MA (Oxon) and a barrister by profession (called to the Bar 1888).

WALTON, Nathaniel
(Blackburn Rovers, 1890, 1)
Born Preston, Lancs. 1867. Died 3 March 1930.
1891: 5ft. 8ins.; 10st. 12lbs.

Career: Witton FC (Blackburn); Blackburn Rovers 1885; Nelson cs 1893; retired cs 1898. Blackburn Rovers; trainer 1898-1906. Other honours: (Blackburn R) FA Cup winner 1886, 1890, 1891.

Inside-forward positions were thought to show off his talents to best effect, but his versatility was such he could cope anywhere. His 3 Cup finals found him at outside-right and in both inside-forward berths, and he even appeared as an emergency goalkeeper at one stage. Nat, notable for foraging powers and as a link man, became a Blackburn licensee.

WARD, James Thomas
(Blackburn Olympic, 1885, 1)
Born Blackburn, 28 March 1865.

Career: Blackburn schoolboy football; Little Harwood 1879; Blackburn Olympic 1881; Blackburn Rovers 1886. Other honour: (Blackburn Olympic) FA Cup winner 1883.

Full-back on the left for England and the right for his Cup-winning medal, thus demonstrating he had two good feet. Moved quickly to the ball, was sure in his kicking and generally presented an appreciable barrier. Employed as a cotton mill operative originally, Ward later became a Blackburn licensee.

WARD, Peter David
(Brighton & Hove Albion, 1980, 1)
Born Lichfield, Staffs. 27 July 1955.
1980: 5ft. 7ins.; 10st. 3lbs.

Career: Burton Albion; Brighton and Hove Albion May 1975 (£4000); Nottingham Forest October 1980 (£400,000, a Brighton record) – 1983 (Brighton and Hove Albion on loan October1982-February 1983).

Subsequently went to the States and played in indoor soccer there. Other honours: England 'B' international. England Under-21 international (2 apps).

Strike-forward. Slightly built but at his zenith a first-rate opportunist taking chances by means of speed in electrifying short bursts. This zenith can be pinpointed at season 1976/77 when Brighton won promotion to Division 2 and Peter established a new club League scoring record (32 goals). Broke another club record – the fee paid by Forest – but this, unlike the '76/77 goals total, has been surpassed.

WARD, Timothy Victor
(Derby County, 1948-49, 2)
Born Cheltenham, 17 September 1917.
1951: 5ft. 9ins.; 11st. 9lbs.

Career: Cheltenham Schools; Cheltenham Town; Derby County April 1937 (£100); Barnsley as player/coach March 1951, retiring from playing 1952/53, manager March 1953 (after being Exeter City's manager for a mere 14 days); Grimsby Town manager February 1960; Derby County manager June 1962-May 1967; Carlisle United manager June 1967-September 1968. Had spell as a Nottingham Forest scout from August 1969.

Wing–half. Was an outside-right in his school days and converted to wing-half by Cheltenham Town. Broke into Derby's first team not long before the War at left-half, succeeding Errington Keen (q.v.). After WW2 switched to the other flank and won his England caps there. Tim was a stylist with pace, sagacity and a yen for attacking football. Employed as representative for an engineering firm after leaving the game, he also undertook coaching junior sides.

WARING, Thomas ('Pongo')
(Aston Villa, 1931-32, 5)
Born High Tranmere, Birkenhead, 12 October 1906. Died 20 December 1980.
1932: 6ft. $1^1/_4$ins.; 12st.

Career: Birkenhead Schools; Tranmere Celtic; Tranmere Rovers early in 1926; Aston Villa February 1928 (£4750); Barnsley November 1935; Wolverhampton Wanderers July 1936; Tranmere Rovers again October 1936; Accrington Stanley November 1938; Bath City July 1939. Continued to play well into middle-age with various local sides in the Merseyside area: Ellesmere Port Town, Grayson's FC (a shipyard club), Birkenhead Dockers and Harrowby. Other honour: (Tranmere R) Div. 3 (North) champions 1938.

Centre–forward. A colourful character from the inter-war period. The stories about him, apocryphal and otherwise, had a wide circulation. Aside from this, Pongo was a fine footballer – a tall, long striding opportunist who scored freely (he notched 6 in an 11-1 Tranmere win over Durham City, January 7, 1928). His later essays into junior soccer coincided with employment at Merseyside docks.

WARNER, Conrad
(Upton Park, 1878, 1)
Born Cripplegate in the City of London, 19 April 1852. Died 10 April 1890.

Career: Upton Park for some years (was captain and President in the mid-1880s). Played for London and Middlesex in representative matches.

Goalkeeper. 'A capital goalkeeper, always cool, and very quick at getting rid of the ball,' the Football Annual for 1881 succinctly relates. At that time he was not devoting so much of his leisure to the game, but a few years before was reckoned the country's best custodian. He was a games' allrounder, assisting Chestnut RUFC in the early 1870s, captaining Southgate hockey club and was sometime secretary of the Winchmore Hill Cricket and Lawn Tennis Club. Came from a wealthy Quaker family and educated at a Quaker school: Grove House School, Tottenham. Warner was by vocation a stationer (with Partridge & Cooper, a firm still in existence). He died of pneumonia in New York while on a business trip there.

WARREN, Benjamin
(Derby County and Chelsea, 1906-11, 22)
Born Newhall, Derbys. 1879. Died 15 January 1917.
1906: 5ft. 8ins.; 12st.

Career: Swanlincote junior football; Newhall Town; Newhall Swifts; Derby County May 1899; Chelsea August 1908 (£1250-1500); retired on health grounds February 1912. Other honours: Football League (5 apps). (Derby Co) FA Cup finalist 1903.

Right-half. Rich in representative honours by pre-'14 standards, won by being the best in his position for half a dozen years. A touch slow but yet brave, splendid in ball control and crisp in tackling. His son, Harry, also played professionally, later becoming far better known as a manager.

WATERFIELD, George Smith
(Burnley, 1927, 1)
Born Swinton nr. Rotherham, 2 June 1901.
1929: 5ft. $8^1/_2$ins.; 11st.

Career: Swinton FC; Mexborough; Burnley October 1923; Crystal Palace June 1935 – 1936.

Left-back. Signed by Burnley as an outside-left but tried as a back during the 1924/25 season with remarkable results. 'Speed is his greatest asset,' reported a 1925 Lancashire handbook, going on to praise the player's powers of recovery. These qualities were complemented with well timed tackles and a good kick. Formerly a miner, George had 373 League outings with the Turf Moor club.

WATSON, David
(Norwich City and Everton, 1984-88, 12)
Born Liverpool, 20 November 1961.
1986: 11st. 12lbs.

Career: Liverpool Schools; first associated with Liverpool FC when 15, first assisting their 'A' team and turning professional May 1979; Norwich City November 1980 (£200,000); Everton August 1986 (£900,000). Other honours: England Under-21 international (7 apps). (Norwich C) FL Div. 2 champions 1986. FL Cup winner 1985. (Everton) FL champions 1987.

Central-defender. No League outings for Liverpool and spotted by Norwich in the Anfielders' reserve side. Norwich appeared to have possibly paid an exhorbitant fee for one with scant experience (it was made up of £50,000 plus a similar sum after 25 senior appearances, with a possible further £100,000 if capped). In the event Watson proved a fine investment. He is an authoritative player, well disciplined and a key defensive figure accomplished in every aspect.

WATSON, David Vernon
(Sunderland, Manchester City, Werder Bremen, Southampton and Stoke City, 1974-82, 65)
Born Stapleford, Notts. 5 October 1946.
1978: 5ft. $11^1/_2$ins.; 11st. 7lbs.

Career: Nottingham Schools; Stapleford Boys FC; Notts County amateur 1965/66, turning professional January 1967; Rotherham United December 1967 (£8000 and another player); Sunderland December 1970 (£100,000); Manchester City June 1975 (£175,000 and another player); Werder Bremen, Germany, June 1979 (£200,000); Southampton October 1979 (£200,000);

Stoke City January 1982 (£50,000); Vancouver Whitecaps, Canada, 1983; Derby County September 1983; Fort Lauderdale, USA, cs 1984; Notts County again as player/coach September 1984, later assisting Kettering Town. Other honours: (Sunderland) FA Cup winner 1973. (Man. City) FL Cup winner 1976.

Centre-half, who had success also leading the atttack. Remarkably long lasting, commanding big fees when in his 30s. Magnificent in the air (and not lacking in ground operations either) and very sharp, thanks to consistent fitness. In 1979 created a record by appearing in 3 consecutive internationals when on the books of 3 different clubs.

WATSON, Victor Martin
(West Ham United, 1923-30, 5)
Born Chesterton, Cambs. 10 November 1897. Died 3 August 1988.
1923: 5ft. 9½ins.; 11st. 2lbs.

Career: Girton FC; Cambridge Town; Peterborough and Fletton United; Brotherhood Engineering Works (Peterborough); Wellingborough Town; West Ham United March 1920 (£50); Southampton June 1935; retired cs 1936. Other honour: (WHU) FA Cup finalist 1923.

Centre-forward. Dashing, harassing, free-scoring leader whose record stands comparison with the best. Scored 326 goals in 505 League and FA Cup games for the Hammers. Still holder of the club's League seasonal and aggregate records, his tally including a 6 (vs. Leeds, February 1929), three 4s and 13 hat-tricks. The only centre-forward to represent England before and after the 1925 offside law change. After leaving football worked as a market gardener and small-holder.

WATSON, William
(Burnley, 1913-20, 3)
Born Birkdale, Southport, 11 September 1890. Died 1 September 1955.
1914: 5ft. 7½ins.; 11st. 2lbs.

Career: Southport schoolboy football; Blowick Wesleyans (Sunday school side); Southport Central 1907, turning professional the following year; Burnley March 1909 (£200); Blackburn Rovers for a spell November 1926 as coach and captain of the club's 'A' team. Other honours: England 'Victory' international 1919 (1 app). Football League (5 apps). (Burnley) FL champions 1921. FA Cup winner 1914.

Left-half, of polish and high consistency, studied in his approach with precise, thoughtful distribution. Skippered Burnley at one juncture and was also captain for one of his inter-league matches. Created a Burnley record by playing in 112 consecutive games to March 22, 1913. After leaving football worked as an ironmonger and, later, as a decorator. Served two spells as a Liberal councillor on the Southport local authority.

WATSON, Willie
(Sunderland, 1950-51, 4)
Born Bolton-upon-Dearne, Yorks. 7 March 1920.
1950: 5ft. 8½ins.; 11st. 4lbs.

Career: Huddersfield schoolboy and junior football; Huddersfield Town October 1937; Sunderland April 1946 (£7 or £8000); Halifax Town as player/manager November 1954 (£4000)-April 1956. Halifax Town manager again September 1964; Bradford City manager April 1966-January 1968. Other honours: England 'B' international (3 appearances).

Right-half, after a considerable and successful period at outside-left. Wing-half was undoubtedly his métier, however, with his ability in winning the ball and the perceptive use of it afterwards. A distinquished and long-serving cricketer for Yorkshire (1939-57), Leicestershire (1958-64) and England (23 Test matches), Willie was a test selector 1962-64. Son of Wm. Watson, Huddersfield Town 1912/13-1926/27, a left-half who won 3 League championship and 2 Cup final medals with that club.

WEAVER, Samuel
(Newcastle United, 1932-33, 3)
Born Pilsley, Derbys. 8 February 1909. Died 15 April 1985.
1932: 5ft. 10ins.; 11st. 5lbs.

Career: Pilsley Red Rose (Sutton Junction on trial); Sutton Town 1926; Hull City March 1928 (£50); Newcastle United November 1929 (£2500); Chelsea August 1936 (£4166) (guest player for Leeds United during WW2); Stockport County December 1945; retired cs 1947. Leeds United coach 1947-49; Millwall trainer/coach June 1949 – January 1954; Mansfield Town coach September 1955 – June 1958 when appointed that club's manager to January 1960; Mansfield Town assistant trainer February 1960 – 1967 when he became chief scout before finally retiring. Other honours: Football League (2 apps). (Newcastle) FA Cup winner 1932.

Left-half, sometimes inside-left. Leapt to fame by reason of his 35 plus yd. throws. (Length of throws was not at the time much regarded. The art since, of course, is extensively practised). Sam had other skills, too, in tackling, distribution and so on. A good cricketer, he played twice for Somerset in 1939 and was masseur to Derbyshire CCC for a time from 1956.

WEBB, George William
(West Ham United, 1911, 2)
Born Poplar, London, 1888. Died 28 March 1915.
1911: 5ft. $9^1/_2$ins.; 11st. 10lbs.

Career: Ilford schoolboy football; Ilford Alliance; Ilford FC; Wanstead (during which time he made occasional appearances for West Ham); West Ham United 1908/09; Manchester City cs 1912; retired cs 1913. Other honours: England amateur international (7 apps). Southern League (1 app).

Centre-forward, sometimes inside-left. 'He is of fine physique, speedy, and a great shot, and has played an important part in the Hammers' success during the present campaign,' wrote a commentator in 1911. Webb was a leading amateur of that time, two full caps showing he could hold his own in the best professional company too.

WEBB, Neil John
(Nottingham Forest, 1988, 9)
Born Reading, 30 July 1963.
1988: 6ft.; 13st.

Career: Reading schools and junior football to Reading FC as an apprentice, turning professional November 1980; Portsmouth June 1982 (£87,500); Nottingham Forest June 1985 (£250,000). Other honours: England Under-21 international (3 apps). England Yough international (10 apps). (Portsmouth) FL Div. 3 champions 1983.

Midfield. A fine all round player with the ability to win tackles, pass and shoot accurately, and employ a marked positional sense. Holds the distinction of being chronologically the 1000th man to be capped by England. Son of Doug Webb (Reading 1955-67).

WEBSTER, Maurice
(Middlesborough, 1930, 3)
Born Blackpool, 13 November 1899. Died February 1978.
1930: 5ft. 8ins.; 11st. 8lbs.

Career: Bloomfield Villa (Blackpool); South Shore Wednesday (Blackpool); Fleetwood circa 1920; Lytham October 1921; Stalybridge Celtic October 1921; Middlesborough March 1922; Carlisle United June 1935; retired cs 1936. Middlesbrough training staff 1936/37; Carlisle United trainer May 1937. Other honours: Football League (1 app). (Middlesbro') FL Div. 2 champions 1929.

Centre-half, sometimes wing-half. Apparently handicapped as a pivot because lacking in inches, but constructive ability and quickness of recovery more than atoned. Particularly good at feeding his attack. Was 13 years at Ayresome Park but aver-

aged only 20 League outings per season due mainly to long periods on the injured list. A plumber by trade.

WEDLOCK, William John ('Fatty')
(Bristol City, 1907-14, 26)
Born Bedminster, Bristol, 28 October 1880. Died 24 January 1965.
1909: 5ft. 4$^1/_2$ins.; 10st. 7lbs.

Career: Masonic Rovers; Bristol Melrose; Arlington Rovers for 4 years, during which time he signed amateur forms for Bristol City and represented Gloucestershire; Aberdare FC as a part-time professional 1899/1900; Bristol City cs 1905; retired cs 1921. Other honours: Football League (3 apps). (Aberdare) Welsh Cup finalist 1904, 1905. (Bristol C) FL Div. 2 champions 1906. FA Cup finalist 1909.

Centre-half. One of England's greatest pivots, his small stature no bar to heading the ball. Amazing powers of recovery earned him the title of 'the india-rubber man'. An extremely fair player too – it was said only one penalty was ever awarded against him. Was not offered a professional engagement by Bristol City and so joined Aberdare, the former thus losing 5 seasons of a unique talent. At one time Billy held the record for consecutive international appearances (18). A stone mason by trade, after leaving football he was for many years licensee of a hostelry near the Ashton Gate ground.

WEIR, David
(Bolton Wamderers, 1889, 2)
Born Aldershot. Died November 1933 aged 70.

Career: Maybole FC (Ayrshire); Glasgow Thistle; Halliwell; Bolton Wanderers cs 1888; Ardwick May 1890; Bolton Wanderers again January 1893; retired cs 1895 and returned to Scotland, there coaching (and occasionally playing for) his original club, Maybole. Glossop manager 1909; coach in Stuttgart, Germany, April 1911.

Utility player – his international appearances were at centre-half and inside-left and he turned out for Bolton in several forward positions. Forceful in attack and individualistic by inclination. Son of an officer's batman (hence, presumably, the Aldershot birth place), David spent his youth from the age of 12 in Scotland, which explains the early Maybole FC connection.

WELCH, Reginald de Courtenry
(Old Harrovians, 1873-74, 2)
Born Kensington, London, 1851. Died 4 June 1939.

Career: Harrow School (XI 1871); Old Harrovians; Harrow Chequers; Wanderers; Remnants. Also represented Middlesex. Served on the FA Committee 1873-75 and 1879-80. Other honours: (Wanderers) FA Cup winner 1872, 1873.

Goalkeeper/full-back (which sounds an unusual combination to modern ears!) Be that as it may, Welch was a hard working back, accurate in his kicking. Perhaps less good between the posts, not rising much above the average. All the same he was England's custodian in the 1874 Scotland match. Employed as an Army tutor 1883-95, subsequently becoming Principal of the Army College, Farnham, Surrey.

WELLER, Keith
(Leicester City, 1974, 4)
Born Islington, London, 11 June 1946.
1974: 5ft. 10ins.; 12st. 1lb.

Career: Played for the representative schools' sides of Islington, Hackney and Middlesex; Arlington Boys Club; Tottenham Hotspur amateur August 1963, turning professional January 1964; Millwall June 1967 (£18,000); Chelsea May 1970 (£100,000); Leicester City September 1971 (£100,000); New England Teamen (USA) February 1979 (£40,000). Other honour: Football League (1 app).

Forward. Could make a show in any of the classical 5 attacking positions but was found in the No. 7 shirt as often as not. 'Immense skills on the ball and good at coming through from behind and pinching surprise goals,' was one typical summing-up. Scored 90 in 434 League outings (and 8 subs). Keith worked as a floor layer before turning professional. Interested in aviation, he qualified as a pilot.

WELSH, Donald
(Charlton Athletic, 1938-39, 3)
Born Manchester, 25 February 1911.
1938: 5ft. 11½ins.; 12st. 5½lbs.

Career: Manchester Schools; Lancashire Schools; Royal Navy football; Torquay United on amateur forms early in 1933, turning professional July 1934; Charlton Athletic February 1935 (£3250); retired November 1947 on appointment as Brighton & Hove Albion secretary/manager; Liverpool manager March 1951-May 1956; Bournemouth & Boscombe Athletic manager July 1958-February 1961; Wycombe Wanderers professional coach July 1963-November 1964; briefly on Charlton Athletic's administrative staff from December 1964. Other honours: England wartime international (8 apps). Football League (1 app). (Charlton) FL Div. 3 (South) champions 1935. FA Cup winner 1947; finalist 1946.

Utility player. Master of four positions: centre and left-half, centre-forward and inside-left. Put an excellent physique to good use, being bold and strong-shooting in attack and resourceful in defence. Between managerial appointments he had worked as a Devon licensee and youth centre manager.

WEST, Gordon
(Everton, 1969, 3)
Born Darfield nr. Barnsley, 24 April 1943.
1969: 6ft. 1in.; 14st.

Career: Don & Dearne schools; Blackpool amateur 1958, turning professional April 1960; Everton March 1962 (£27,500, then a British record for a goalkeeper); left the game for a short spell before joining Tranmere Rovers October 1975 and was also reserve team coach with that club before retiring in 1978. Other honours: England Youth international. England Under-23 international (3 apps). Football League (1 app). (Everton) FL champions 1963, 1970. FA Cup winner 1966; finalist 1968.

Goalkeeper, of doughty physique which he would 'put about' in spectacular fashion. A real spectator pleaser, his acrobatics were utilised for Everton's cause in 399 senior matches. Created a sensation by turning down an opportunity to join the 1970 England World Cup squad, preferring to stay with his family. Gordon was married to a concert pianist, by the way.

WESTWOOD, Raymond William
(Bolton Wanderers, 1935-37, 6)
Born Brierley Hill, Staffs. 14 April 1912.
Died January 1982.
1935: 5ft. 7ins.; 10st. 2lbs.

Career: Brierley Hill Schools; Stourbridge; Brierley Hill Alliance when only 15; Bolton Wanderers February 1930; Chester December 1947; Darwen late in 1949. Other honours: Football League (5 apps).

Inside/outside-left. Soon made a mark at Bolton, playing on the extreme left until a developed physique enabled him to move inside. Being a smart mover famed for direct, straight-through bursts, he could finish the operation with a deadly shot. It would appear he could have joined Aston Villa, but opted for Bolton because his uncle, David Stokes, an inter-league medalist, had graced the Burnden scene from 1902 – 1920.

WHATELEY, Oliver
(Aston Villa, 1883, 2)
Born Birmingham, 1862. Died October 1926.

Career: Gladstone Unity (Coventry); Aston Villa 1880 – circa 1888.

Inside-forward. Did not maintain an even level of performance though, on song, was very formidable indeed. Reckoned the hardest shot of his time, Olly (as he was popularly known) could and would shoot from any angle. By vocation an artist, designer and draughtsman, in 1911 he underwent a severe operation. Nonetheless, although too old for military service, he served in Rouen, France, with the YMCA during the 1914/18 War. In the 1920s, in poor health, he fell on hard times, and so straitened were his circumstances that, in 1923, Aston Villa set up a fund to help their old star.

WHEELER, John E.
(Bolton Wanderers, 1955, 1)
Born Crosby, Liverpool, 26 July 1928.
1958: 5ft. 9ins.; 12st 2lbs.

Career: Carlton FC (Liverpool Combination); Tranmere Rovers as an amateur 1944, turning professional April 1946; Bolton Wanderers February 1951 (fee plus another player valued @ £8000); Liverpool September 1956 (about £9000); appointed New Brighton's player/manager May 1963 but did not take up the post, later that close season becoming Bury's assistant trainer, promoted to head trainer cs 1967 and trainer/assistant manager September 1969, leaving the club September 1970. Other honours: England 'B' international (5 apps). Football League (2 apps). (Bolton W) FA Cup finalist 1953.

Right-half. Played inside-right on occasion. Sturdy physically, possessed lots of stamina and went into tackles positively. Scored 48 goals in the course of a 454 League match aggregate, the first figure illustrating a natural attacking flair.

WHELDON, George Frederick
(Aston Villa, 1897-98, 4)
Born Langley Green, Worcs. 1 November 1869. Died 13 January 1924.
1903: 5ft. 8ins.; 11st. 7lbs.

Career: Rood End White Star; Langley Green Victoria (West Bromwich Albion on trial 1888); Small Heath 1890; Aston Villa June 1896; West Bromwich Albion June 1900; Queen's Park Rangers December 1901; Portsmouth cs 1902; Worcester City cs 1904; Coventry City cs 1905; retired January 1907. Other honours: Football League (4 apps). (Small Heath) FL Div. 2 champions 1893. (Villa) FL champions 1897, 1899, 1900. FA Cup winner 1897.

Inside-left. A brilliant dribbler whose intricate pattern-weaving could create havoc, and who specialised in the making of opportunities. Wheldon was an excellent cricketer as well, playing regularly for Worcestershire 1899-1906 and later for Carmarthenshire. Said to be nicknamed "Diamond"

WHITE, Tom Angus
(Everton, 1933, 1)
Born Manchester, 29 July 1908. Died 13 August 1967.
1933: 5ft. 9ins.; 11st.

Career: Southport Schools; Trinity Old Boys; Southport September 1925; Everton February 1927; Northampton Town on trial October 1937; New Brighton February 1938, retiring the following close season. Other honours: (Everton) FL champions 1932. FA Cup winner 1933.

Centre-half, when capped and in the 1933 Cup final, but actually a performer of outstanding versatality. Played centre-half at school, then started scoring goals in any and every forward berth. There is no doubt that he would have been at home anywhere in the defence as well for he proved to be a positive sheet anchor at pivot. Died following a fall at Liverpool Docks, where he had worked from leaving football.

WHITEHEAD, James
(Accrington and Blackburn Rovers, 1893-94, 2)
Born Church, Lancs. Died August 1929 aged 59.

Career: Peel Bank; Accrington cs 1890; Blackburn Rovers cs 1893; Manchester City September1897; retired cs 1899.

Inside-right. Earned the encomiums of Rovers' 1925 historian, Charles Francis, who probably saw him in action. Whitehead "... was short and stocky, but he tackled the biggest backs with a zest that was refreshing. Crafty and skilful, he often toyed with opponents, and sometimes stood head and shoulders over his colleagues. He was such a powerful shot that with one of his drives he knocked Rowley, the Stoke custodian, clean into the net at Blackburn." In his second international Jimmy was inside to his Blackburn partner, Harry Chippendale.

WHITFELD, Herbert
(Old Etonians, 1879, 1)
Born Lewes, Sussex, 15 November 1858. Died 6 May 1909.

Career: Eton College (XI 1877); Cambridge University (Blue 1879-80-81); Old Etonians. Other honours: (Old Etonians) FA Cup winner 1879; finalist 1881.

Forward. Writing in 1881 a scribe reported Whitfeld to be" ...a very good player" who "dribbles well and works unceasingly" and who is "much improved in pace." Whitfeld was a sporty all-rounder – an Oxford Cricket Blue, 1878-81 inclusive, he represented the University at athletics and real tennis also. He played for Sussex CCC 1878-85 (captain 1883 and '84), as did his brother and a nephew. In professional life held a high appointment with Barclays Bank.

WHITHAM, Michael
(Sheffield United, 1892, 1)
Born Ecclesfield nr. Sheffield, 6 November 1867. Died 6 May 1924.

Career: Ecclesfield FC; Rotherham Swifts as a professional for a year; Sheffield United early in 1890 – 1898. Subsequently held several appointments as a trainer, these including Gainsborough Trinity (2 spells), Rotherham County, Huddersfield Town and finally, up to the date of his death, Brentford.

Right-back, usually for Sheffield United although he figured at left-half in his solitary international. Could also play a fair game at centre-half. "Very fast, and standing a good height his heading is a great feature," recorded one scribe in the 1890s. Represented the Sheffield FA against both Glasgow and London.

WHITWORTH, Stephen
(Leicester City, 1975-76, 7)
Born Ellistown nr. Coalville, Leics., 20 March 1952.
1975: 6ft.; 11st. 9lbs.

Career: Leicestershire schools football to Leicester City as an associate schoolboy when 14, later becoming an apprentice and turning professional November 1969; Sunderland March 1979 (£180,000); Bolton Wanderers October 1981; Mansfield Town July 1983 to cs 1985. Other honours: England schoolboy international. England Youth international. England Under-23 international (6 apps). (Leicester) FL Div. 2 champions 1971.

Right-back, of whom one discerning critic said was a lot more skilful than his determined, tenacious style indicated. Steve's obvious qualities included pace, composure and the wish to get the ball away gainfully without applying a big boot. Moreover, he rarely had a bad game.

WHYMARK, Trevor John
(Ipswich Town, 1978, 1)
Born Burston, Norfolk, 4 May 1950.
1978: 5ft. 10ins.; 10st. 8lbs.

Career: Diss Town; Ipswich Town May 1969; Vancouver Whitecaps (Canada) November 1978 (£150,000) (Sparta Rotterdam September 1979 and Derby County December 1979, on loan); Grimsby Town December 1980 (£80,000, a Grimsby record); Southend United January 1984 – 1985. Other honours: England Under-23 international 7 apps).

Forward. From his junior days excellent in headwork. Later became proficient on the ground also, developing the ability to turn and beat opponents. His Grimsby period included a year as player/coach (1982-83). Up to the end of season 1984/85 Trevor's FL record reads 352 matches and 22 substitutions, 92 goals.

WIDDOWSON, Sam Weller
(Nottingham Forest, 1880, 1)
Born Hucknall Torkard, Notts. 16 April 1851. Died 9 May 1927.
Circa 1880: 5ft. $8^1/_2$ins.; 11st. 7lbs.

Career: Notts. schoolboy and junior football; Nottingham Forest 1878-85 and was that club's chairman 1879-84. Twice served on the FA Committee, 1888-92 and 1893-94.

Centre-forward. Described by Tityrus (J A H Catton) as "that splendid Herculean player". Besides strength he also had quickness off the mark and marksmanship. Captained Forest for several seasons and was the inventor and patentee of shinguards (1874). It is said Widdowson owed his Pickwickian first names to his father being an avid Dickensian. A noted athlete (hurdles and sprints), played three times for Notts CCC 1878-79 and employed in the lace trade.

WIGNALL, Frank
(Nottingham Forest, 1965, 2)
Born Blackrod nr. Chorley, Lancs. 21 August 1939.
1965: 5ft. $10^1/_2$ins.; 12st.

Career: Blackrod FC (Lancashire Combination); Horwich RMI; Everton May 1958; Nottingham Forest June 1963 (£20,000); Wolverhampton Wanderers March 1968 (£50,000); Derby County February 1969 (£20,000); Mansfield Town November 1971 (£8000); King's Lynn player/manager July 1973-July 1974; Burton Albion August 1974. National coach to Qatar, Persian Gulf, October 1974 for 5 years; on his return became manager of Shepshed Charterhouse. Other honours: Football League (2 apps).

Centre/inside-forward, of all round competence, blending well into the several forward-lines that enjoyed his membership. Equally good in the air or on the ground. In a total 299 League games (and 22 substitutions) Frank scored 106 goals. Besides the Shepshed managership was employed as a car salesman.

WILKES, Albert
(Aston Villa, 1901-02, 5)
Born Birmingham 1874. Died 9 December 1936.
1902: 5ft. $7^1/_2$ins.; 12st. 7lbs.

Career: West Bromwich schoolboy football; Oldbury Town; Walsall; Aston Villa cs 1898; Fulham cs 1907; retired July 1909 in order to concentrate on his business. Later a FL referee. An Aston Villa director from September 1934. Other honour: (Villa) FL champions 1900.

Wing-half, able to take both left-wing forward positions too. A tremendously hard grafter staunch in defence and a formidable tackler. Founder of the famous West Bromwich firm of photographers that bears his name and specialises in soccer material, and a prominent worker for the Baptist Church.

WILKINS, Raymond Colin
(Chelsea, Manchester United and AC Milan 84)
Born Hillingdon, Middlesex, 14 September 1956.
1980: 5ft. $7^1/_2$ins.; 10st. 11lbs.

Career: Middlesex Schools; London Schools; Chelsea apprentice when 15, turning professional October 1973; Manchester United August 1979 (£825,000); AC Milan June 1984 (£1.5m); Saint-Germain (Paris) July 1987; Rangers November 1987 (£250,000). Other honours: England Youth international. England Under-23 international (2 apps). England Under-21 international (1 app) Football League (1 app). (Man. Utd.) FA Cup winner 1983. FL Cup finalist 1983.

Midfield. A precocious talent, becoming Chelsea's youngest-ever skipper at 18 (he later captained Manchester United and England.) From this early start, a leading player: composed, superb in distribution and no mean shot. His, however, has not been a career without criticism. At one stage it was widely thought he indulged in lateral play in preference to going forward, for instance. Son of George Wilkins (Brentford 1936-47) and brother of Graham (Chelsea 1972-82). Ray was known as "Butch" Wilkins in his initial seasons.

WILKINSON, Bernard
(Sheffield United, 1904, 1)
Born Thorpe Hesley, Yorks. 12 September 1879. Died 28 May 1949.
1904: 5ft. 6ins.; 11st.

Career: Thorpe Hesley junior football; Shiregreen; Shefield United July 1899; Rotherham Town June 1913. Other honour: (Sheffield Utd) FA Cup winner 1902.

Centre-half, short for the job but described as "a veritable pocket Hercules." Quite tireless, good at heading with an inclination to attack and shoot. Member of a renowned athletic family (a brother, W H

Wilkinson, was a colleague at Bramall Lane), he played Yorkshire Council cricket and rejected an offer from the Yorkshire CCC. Subsequently a successful Sheffield business man.

WILKINSON, Leonard Rodwell
(Oxford University, 1891, 1)
Born Highgate, London, 15 October 1868. Died 9 February 1913.

Career: Charterhouse school (XI 1887); Oxford University (Blue 1889-90-91); Old Carthusians; Corinthians 1890-93. Other honours: (Old Carthusians) FA Amateur Cup winner 1894, 1897; finalist 1895.

Goalkeeper. A top-class amateur 'keeper, lithe in movement and capable of brilliance. Shared with fellow full internationalists, Wreford-Brown and Stanborough, the distinction of appearing in all three of Old Carthusians' Amateur Cup finals of the 'Nineties. Wilkinson also gained a Blue for athletics (1890-91). By calling a barrister (called to the Bar 1893).

WILLIAMS, Bert Frederick
(Wolverhampton Wanderers, 1949-56, 24)
Born Bilston, Staffs. 31 January 1920.
1950: 5ft. 10ins.; 12st. 2lbs.

Career: Bilston Schools; Thompson's FC (Wolverhampton Works League); Walsall on amateur forms 1935/36, turning professional April 1937; Wolverhampton Wanderers September 1945 (£3500); retired cs 1957. Other honours: England wartime international (1 app). England 'B' international (1 app). Football League (5 apps). (Wolves) FL champions 1954. FA Cup winner 1949.

Goalkeeper of spectacular persuasion treating the crowds to countless thrills. Bert's perfectly timed leaps and dives could be quite breath-taking. Engaged with a sports outfitting business in Bilston, he also started a goalkeeping school in 1969.

WILLIAMS, Owen
(Clapton Orient, 1923, 2)
Born Ryhope, Co. Durham, 23 September 1896. Died 9 December 1960.
1923: 5ft. 8ins.; 11st. 2lbs.

Career: Sunderland Schools; Ryhope Colliery (trial with Sunderland and signed amateur forms for Manchester United); Easington Colliery; Clapton Orient July 1919; Middlesbrough February 1924 (£3000); Southend United July 1930; Shildon September 1931. Other honours: (Middlesbrough) FL Div. 2 champions 1927, 1929.

Outside-left. "One of the speediest outside-lefts in the country, with good ball control," a critic concisely observed in 1923 of this sturdy performer. He enjoyed first-team football for practically the whole of his dozen League campaigns (361 matches, 77 goals). Fitted in well at Middlesbrough with star forwards such as Camsell, Pease and Jackie Carr to play with. Owen's brother, T H Williams, a colleague at Orient, assisted several other FL clubs during the 'Twenties.

WILLIAMS, Steven Charles
(Southampton, 1983-85, 6)
Born London, 12 July 1958.
1984: 5ft. 11ins.; 10st. 11lbs.

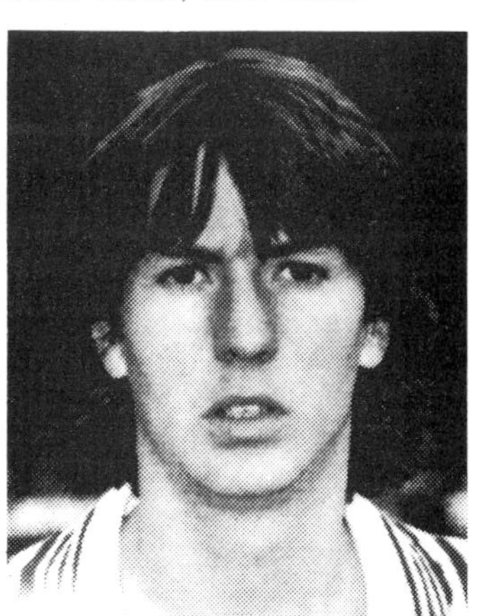

Career: Romford Schools (Crystal Palace on schoolboy forms); Southampton apprentice, turning professional September 1974; Arsenal December 1984 (£550,000); Luton Town July 1988 (£300,000). Other honours: England 'B' international. England Under-21 international (15 apps). (Soton) FL Cup finalist 1979. (Arsenal) FL Cup winner 1987.

Midfield. Actually appeared in the Saints' first team straight from their youth side without first playing for the reserves. A natural talent: incisive, intelligent in distribution and aggressive. The aggression has sometimes brought trouble.

WILLIAMS, William
(West Bromwich Albion, 1897-99, 6)
Born West Smethwick, Staffs. 20 January 1876. Died 22 January 1929.

Career: Smethwick schoolboy football: Hawthorn Villa; West Smethwick FC; Old Hill Wanderers; West Bromwich Albion May 1894; retired through injury June 1901, then becoming Albionn's trainer and, later, scout. Other honours: Football League (5 apps). (WBA) FA Cup finalist 1895.

Right/left-back forced to retire in his mid-twenties because of cartilage trouble. A loss to football as may be gauged from an 1895 summing-up:"...a safe and reliable kick, he is in addition a very effective tackler, and as he is fast and possesses no end of pluck, he is very difficult to pass, and even when passed has not done with his opponents to whom he sticks to the last." Latterly, and for quarter of a century, a West Bromwich licensee.

WILLIAMSON, Ernest Clarke ("Tim")
(Arsenal, 1923, 2)
Born Murton Colliery, Co Durham, 24 May 1890. Died 30 April 1964.
1923: 5ft. 10ins.; 12st. 12lbs.

Career: Murton Red Star (Wearside League); Wingate Albion (North Eastern League); Croyden Common June 1913; Army Football; Arsenal cs 1919 after assisting that club during WW1; Norwich City June 1923; retired 1925. Other honour: England 'Victory' international 1919 (1 app).

Goalkeeper. Apparently nicknamed Tim after the great Middlesbrough custodian below. This Tim was an effiecient performer displaying agility and sureness in his handling. From around 1924 for many years a Norwich licensee and he also had a spell as groundsman to a local bowling club.

WILLIAMSON, Reginald Garnet ("Tim")
(Middlesbrough, 1905-13, 7)
Born North Ormesby, Yorks. 6 June 1884. Died 1 August 1943.
1911: 5ft. 9ins.; 12st. 8lbs.

Career: Coatham Grammar School; Redcar Crusaders; Middlesbrough 1903; retired cs 1924.

Goalkeeper. An Ayresome Park institution for over 20 years. Tim was also a man of character and deservedly popular everywhere. A great 'keeper, a contemporary wrote of his "...keen perception and remarkable agility, and his advice and instruction to the young players with whom he is surrounded (that) has proved a big asset to the North-Eastern club." He was an engineering draughtsman by vocation.

WILLINGHAM, C(harles) Kenneth
(Huddersfield Town, 1937-39, 12)
Born Sheffield, 1 December 1912. Died May 1975.
1938: 5ft. 7½ins.; 11st. 4lbs.

Career: Yorkshire Schools; Ecclesfield; Worksop Town; Huddersfield Town ground staff 1930, turning professional November 1931; Sunderland December 1945; Leeds United as player/coach March 1947; retired May 1948 from playing, remaining on the Leeds' coaching staff for a further 2 years; had a spell as Halifax Town's coach from 1952. Other honours: England wartime international (3 apps). Football League (6 apps). (H'field T) FA Cup finalist 1938.

Right half. A notability of the 'Thirties, an exuberant, tireless half likely to take the ball through at speed any time. This speed had always been present: besides skippering Yorkshire Schools at soccer, Ken was the county's schoolboy half-mile champion and ran for England. Latterly a licensee in Leeds. Represented England at shinty.

WILLIS, Arthur
(Tottenham Hotspur, 1952, 1)
Born Denaby nr. Doncaster, 2 February 1920.
1950: 5ft. 7ins.; 11st. 2lbs.

Career: Junior football to Tottenham Hotspur as an amateur 1938, developing with Finchley until signed as a professional January 1944; Swansea Town September 1954, player/assistant trainer November 1957-cs 1958 when he ceased playing and remained as assistant trainer; Haverfordwest FC player/manager cs 1960. Other honour: (Spurs) FL champions 1951. (Swansea T) Welsh Cup finalist 1956.

Right/left-back. Looked upon as a right-back originally but moved to the left flank after Alf Ramsey arrived from Southampton. Neat in style, he had an acute positional sense and blended well with the clever Ramsey. Arthur's career at White Hart Lane was notable for the struggle with the England 'B' internationalist, Charlie Withers, for the left-back spot. A comparison between their respective records shows something of an 'even Stephen' situation.

WILSHAW, Dennis J.
(Wolverhampton Wanderers, 1954-57, 12)
Born Stoke-on-Trent, 11 March 1926.
1957: 5ft. 101/4ins.; 11st. 8lbs.

Career: Potteries schools football; Packmoor Boys Club; Wolverhampton Wanderers March 1944 (Walsall on loan May 1946 - September 1948); Stoke City December 1957 (about £12,000); retired July 1961, subsequently doing some coaching for the club. Other honours: England 'B' international (2 apps). (Wolves) FL champions 1954.

Centre-forward/inside and outside-left. Played on the extreme left originally, in his first season after recall from Walsall netting 10 goals in 11 FL outings, mostly from centre-forward. This prolificacy was rewarded by his first 'B' cap. A thrustful utility forward, Dennis totalled 172 goals in a League career that encompassed 378 matches. A schoolmaster by profession.

WILSON, Charles Plumpton
(Hendon, 1884, 2)
Born Roydon, Norfolk, 12 May 1859. Died 9 March 1938.

Career: Cambridge University (no Blue); Hendon; Casuals; Corinthians.

Wing-half. A strong half possessing the stamina to last throughout the most gruelling match. Shone especially at headwork. Wilson was a prime example of the gifted games all-rounder. A rugger star (he started at his schools, Uppingham and Marlborough) who was a Blue (1878-9-80-1, captain 1881) and played for England. A cricket Blue 1880-81, who assisted Norfolk 1881-85. And he cycled for Cambridge Univer-

sity. One of only 3 men capped for England at both soccer and rugger (the others were J W Sutcliffe and R H Birkett). A schoolmaster by a profession: master at Elstree School 1881-98, and Joint Headmaster of Sandroyd School, Cobham, Surrey, 1898-1920. Brother of G P Wilson (below).

WILSON, Claude William
(Oxford University, 1879-81, 2)
Born Banbury, Oxon. 9 September 1858. Died 7 June 1881.

Career: Brighton College (XI 1876-77, captain 1877); Oxford University (Blue 1879-80-1); Old Brightonians. Also represented Sussex. Other honour: (Oxford University) FA Cup finalist 1880.

Full-back. 'A splendid back; strong kick; very fast and active; his unexpected demise, in June, was deeply regretted by all who knew him,' summerised Alcock in 1881. Wilson was also a cricketer of note, challenging for a blue at the time of his death and making an appearance for Surrey in 1881.

WILSON, Geoffrey Plumpton
(Corinthians, 1900, 2)
Born Bourne, Lincs. 21 February 1878. Died 30 July 1934.

Career: Rossall School (XI 1894-96, captain 1896); Corinthians 1897/98-1901/02; Southampton (3 matches 1901/02); Casuals; London Hospital.

Inside-left. A noted amateur expert in ball control, a main factor in his neat and effective dribbling. This dribbling ability was not selfishly indulged for his team work was first class. Scored 8 goals in his first 26 matches for the Corinthians. A physician and surgeon by profession (qualifed 1902) and a much younger brother of the England 'double' internationalist, C P Wilson (q.v.).

WILSON, George
(Sheffield Wednesday, 1921-24, 12)
Born Blackpool, 14 January 1892. Died 25 November 1961.
1925: 5ft. 9ins.; 11st.

Career: Preston schoolboy football; Willow's Rovers (Kirkham Sunday school team); Fleetwood; Morecambe (West Lancs. League); Blackpool February 1912; Sheffield Wednesday March 1920 (£3000); Nelson July 1925 (£2000, a then record fee paid by a Third Division club); retired cs 1930. Other honours: Football League (4 apps).

Centre-half, reckoned the best in the UK in the years immediately following the Great War. A hard worker and fast mover, Wilson excelled at headwork - at which art he can have had few superiors - and was a stylist. A Blackpool licensee for 30 years to his retirement in May 1961.

WILSON, Ramon
(Huddersfield Town and Everton, 1960-68, 63)
Born Shirebrook, Derbys. 17 December 1934.
1964: 5ft. 8ins.; 11st. 6lbs.

Career: Langwith Boys Club; Langwith Junction Imps; Huddersfield Town ground staff May 1952, turning professional the following August; Everton June 1964 (£25,000 and another player); Oldham Athletic June 1969; Bradford City as player/coach July 1970; retired from playing May 1971 and served as Bradford City's assistant manager until the end of that year. Other honours: Football League (10 apps). (Everton) FA Cup winner 1966; finalist 1968.

Left-back of world class, a virtuoso in every phase of his craft. A stern tackler quick in recovery, a superb kicker and an overlap specialist, he was a member of England's 1966 World Cup winning team. Ray left football to go into business as an undertaker.

WILSON, Thomas
(Huddersfield Town, 1928, 1)
Born Seaham, Co Durham, 16 April 1896. Died 2 February 1948.
1928: 5ft. $10^{1}/_{2}$ins.; 12st. 7lbs.

Career: Sunderland Schools; Seaham Colliery; Sunderland 1913/14; Seaham Colliery again 1918/19; Huddersfield Town June 1919; Blackpool November 1931; retired June 1932 when appointed Huddersfield Town's assistant trainer, serving in this capacity up to the War; Barnsley trainer 1945 to his death. Other honours: Football League (3 apps). (H'field T) FL champions 1924, 1925, 1926. FA Cup winner 1922; finalist 1920, 1928, 1930.

Centre-half thought by the Sunderland management after WW1 to be over-weight and allowed to depart, a happening that brought Huddersfield an exceptional servant. Tom was at Leeds Road throughout Town's momentous 'Twenties, magnificent in head work and probing ground passing to both centre field and wing. During WW2 continued to assist with Huddersfield's training sessions while working for British Dyes.

WINCKWORTH, William Norman
(Old Westminsters, 1892-93, 2)
Born London, 9 February 1870. Died 9 November 1941.

Career: Westminster School (XI 1888); Old Westminsters; Corinthians 1890-94.

Right-half. Approved of by an Athletic News writer (1893 Annual) with a not-unusual admontion at the end: 'One of the best tackling half-backs of the day. He heads well, and kicks strongly when necessary. He does not, however, feed his forwards well.' Winckworth's soccer career actually ended in 1894 when he went to Calcutta and was in business there until 1914. He later lived in Devonshire, near Exeter.

WINDRIDGE, James Edwin
(Chelsea, 1908-09, 8)
Born Small Heath, Birmingham, 21 October 1882. Died 23 September 1939.
1908: 5ft. 7ins.; 11st. 7lbs.

Career: Small Heath Alma; Small Heath FC during the 1902/03 season; Chelsea April 1905 (£190); Middlesborough November 1911; Birmingham (formerly named Small Heath) again April 1914; retired during WW1.

Inside-left rising to stardom in the late 1900's. Expert in close dribbling, a feared marksman and proficient at passing. A useful cricketer, he made 7 first-class appearances for Warwickshire spread over the period 1909-13. Became a licensee in the Birmingham area.

WINGFIELD-STRATFORD, Cecil Vernon
(Royal Engineers, 1877, 1)
Born West Malling, Kent, 7 October 1853. Died 5 February 1939.

Career: Royal Military Academy, Woolwich; Royal Engineers. Also represented Kent. Other honour: (Royal Engineers) FA Cup winner 1875.

Forward. Played on the left-wing and was mainly noted for remarkable speed that often left opponents trailing. He was, though, apt to tire during the later stages of a hard-fought match. Served with the Royal Engineers 1873-1910, when he retired holding the rank of brigadier. Was recalled for service in WW1. Awarded the CMG 1916 and CB 1918.

WITHE, Peter
(Aston Villa, 1981-85, 11)
Born Liverpool, 30 August 1951.
1983: 6ft. 2ins.; 12st.

Career: Smiths Coggins FC (Liverpool); Southport amateur cs 1970, turning professional August 1971; Barrow on trial December 1971; Port Elizabeth, South Africa early 1972, subsequently assisting another

South African club, Arcadia Shepherds; Wolverhampton Wanderers on loan October 1973, signing permanently February 1974 (£10,000); Portland Timbers, USA; Birmingham City August 1975 (£40,000); Nottingham Forest September 1976 (£42,000); Newcastle United August 1978 (£200,000); Aston Villa May 1980 (£500,000, a Villa record); Sheffield United June 1985 (Birmingham City on loan September 1987). Other honours: (Forest) FL champions 1978. FL Cup winner 1978. (Villa) European Cup winner 1982. FL champions 1981.

Centre-forward. A varied career that really took off 5 years after becoming a professional, thereafter earning major club honours in addition to 11 England caps. Strong and tall, expert at shielding the ball and quite unselfish. A hundred per cent trier too and consistent.

WOLLASTON, Charles Henry Reynolds
(Wanderers, 1874-80, 4)
Born Felpham, Sussex, 31 July 1849. Died 22 June 1926.

Career: Lancing College (XI 1864-68, captain 1867 and '68); Oxford University (before institution of 'Varsity match); Lancing Old Boys; Clapham Rovers; Wanderers. Also represented Middlesex. Other honours: (Wanderers) FA Cup winner 1872, 1873, 1876, 1877, 1878.

Forward. A contemporary comment - 'very pretty and effective' - referred to his consummate dribbling skills. In addition, his accurate shooting and stamina were memorable. Shares with J H Forrest (q.v.) and the Scotland cap, the Hon. A F Kinnaird, the record of earning 5 FA Cup winners' medals. A solicitor by calling (admitted 1875), he was in the employ of the Union Bank of London 1878-98, first as assistant secretary and then as secretary.

WOLSTENHOLME, Samuel
(Everton and Blackburn Rovers, 1904-05, 3)
Born Little Lever, Lancs, 1876.
1904: 5ft. 9½ins.; 12st.

Career: Darley Vale; Farnworth FC; Farnworth Alliance; Horwich; Everton late in 1897; Blackburn Rovers May 1904; Croydon Common cs 1908; Norwich City cs 1909; retired cs 1913. Went to Germany as a coach and was interned at the outbreak of the 1914/18 War. Other honours: Football League (2 apps).

Right-half with a keen sense of what the other man was going to do and a dab hand at placing passes to maximum advantage. It occasioned some surprise when Everton allowed him to go while still in his mid-twenties. Fellow internees in Germany were the England caps, Steve Bloomer and Fred Spiksley, and the trio organised soccer for the camp.

WOOD, Harry
(Wolverhampton Wanderers, 1890-96, 3)
Born Walsall, 26 June 1868. Died 5 July 1951.
1903: 5ft. 10ins.; 12st. 10lbs.

Career: Walsall Town Swifts; Wolverhampton Wanderers 1887; Walsall cs 1891, returning to Wolves during the ensuing season; Southampton cs 1898; retired cs 1905 and became Portsmouth's trainer. Other honours: Football League (4 apps). (Wolves) FA Cup winner 1893; finalist 1889, 1896. (Soton) Southern League champions 1899, 1901, 1903, 1904. FA Cup finalist 1900, 1902.

Inside-forward. A model player, sporting to a degree. Exercised fine ball control, spraying out passes with impressive precision. Settled in Portsmouth on taking up his final soccer appointment and, on leaving the game, was a licensee there. Father of the noted goalkeeper, Arthur Wood (Clapton Orient, 1921-31).

WOOD, Raymond E.
(Manchester United, 1955-56, 3)
Born Hebburn, Co Durham, 11 June 1931.
1957: 5ft. 11ins.; 11st. 12lbs.

Career: Newcastle junior football (Newcastle United amateur); Darlington September 1949; Manchester United December 1949 (£5000); Huddersfield Town December 1958 (£1500); Bradford City October 1965; Barnsley October 1966 (after trial)-1967. Los Angeles Wolves manager early in 1968, later coaching in Cyprus, Greece, Kuwait and Kenya. From 1978 was coach to the Emirites Sports Club, Abu Dhabi and their national side. Other honours: England 'B' international (1 app). England Under-23 international (1 app). Football League (3 apps). (Man. Utd) FL

Champions 1956, 1957. FA Cup finalist 1957.

Goalkeeper, a good handler, excellent in anticipation and very courageous. His courage was never better demonstrated than in the 1957 Cup final when his cheek bone was broken by a controversial charge after only 6 minutes. Wood bravely stayed on the field at outside-right despite suffering intense pain.

WOODCOCK, Anthony Stewart
(Nottingham Forest, FC Cologne and Arsenal, 1978-86, 42)
Born Nottingham, 6 December 1955.
1983: 5ft. 10ins.; 11st.

Career: Schoolboy football; Nottingham Forest apprentice 1972, turning professional January 1974 (Lincoln City on loan February-March 1976, Doncaster Rovers on loan September-October 1976); FC Cologne November 1979 (£650,000, a German record); Arsenal June 1982 (£500,000); FC Cologne again July 1986 (£200,000). Other honours: England 'B' international. England Under-21 international (2 apps). (Forest) European Cup winner 1979. FL Champions 1978. FL Cup winner 1978, 1979.

Forward (left-sided). Made his name as a member of Forest's highly successful late 1970s side. Skilful, a rare taker of chances when close in and the possessor of shattering acceleration. Able, too, in passing the ball when off balance.

WOODGER, George ('Lady')
(Oldham Athletic, 1911, 1)

Born Croydon, 3 September 1883. Died 1961.
1907: 5ft. 71/2ins.; 11st.

Career: Thornton Heath Wednesday; Croydon Glenrose; Croydon Wanderers; Crystal Palace as an amateur during the 1905/06 season turning professional cs 1906; Oldham Athletic September 1910 (£800); Tottenham Hotspur cs 1914; retired during WW1.

Inside/outside-left. 'A player possessing a neat, clever, polished style which has earned for him the peculiar title of 'Lady',' wrote a commentator in 1907 by way of explanation. Woodger's delicate subtleties were not such, however, as to prevent him being extremely dangerous on occasion. Represented Surrey during the mid-1900s in his amateur period.

WOODHALL, George ('Spry')
(West Bromwich Albion, 1888, 2)
Born West Bromwich, 5 September 1863. Died 29 September 1924

Career: West Bromich All Saints; Churchfield Foresters; West Bromwich Albion May 1883; Wolverhampton Wanderers October 1892; Berwick Rangers (Birmingham League) late in 1893; Oldbury Town 1894; retired 1898. Other honours: (WBA) FA Cup winner 1888; finalist 1886, 1887.

Outside/inside-right. Well nicknamed for Woodhall was indeed spry - an alert attacker, consistant in performance and according to one report, 'unerring in centring the ball.' Was on the wing for his two losing Cup finals, then 'third time lucky' on moving inside with the celebrated Billy Bassett manning the touch-line. Spry worked for the Salter firm that has historic ties with the Throstles.

WOODLEY, Victor Robert
(Chelsea, 1937-39, 19)
Born Slough, Bucks. 26 February 1910. Died 23 October 1978.
1936: 5ft. 11½ins.; 11st. 10lbs.

Career: Bucks area junior football; Windsor & Eton (Spartan League); Chelsea May 1931; Bath City December 1945; Derby County March 1946; Bath City again, this time as player/manager, May 1947 - December 1949. Other honours: Football League (4 apps) (Derby Co) FA Cup winner 1946.

Goalkeeper. Burgeoned as a major 1930s figure, playing for his country 19 times on the trot before war intervened. He had no pretensions towards showiness, meeting all demands with impressive assurance. His clean handling may be specially mentioned. Became a licensee at Bradford-on-Avon, Wilts, where he died.

WOODS, Christopher Charles Eric
(Norwich City and Rangers, 1985-88, 13)
Born Swineshead nr. Boston, Lincs. 14 November 1959.
1986: 6ft. 2ins.; 12st. 8lbs.

Career: Boston Schools; Nottingham Forest apprentice, turning professional December 1976; Queen's Park Rangers June 1979 (£250,000); Norwich City on loan March 1981, joining permanently May 1981 (£225,000); Rangers July 1986 (£600,000, a record fee for a Scottish club at the time, and the British record for a 'keeper). Other honours: England Youth international. England 'B' international. England Under-21 international (6 apps). (Forest) FL Cup winner 1978. (Norwich C) FL Div.2 champions 1986. FL Cup winner 1985. (Rangers) Scottish League champions 1987. Scottish League Cup winner 1987.

Goalkeeper with an aptitude for creating records: no League games for Forest yet won a major medal, kept 13 consecutive 'clean sheets' during '86/87, a British first-class record and the fee paid by Rangers is a British record for a' keeper. Highly skilled in all aspects of a custodian's craft, Chris has worked hard for his success. A great uncle is Eric Houghton (q.v.) . As a boy represented Lincolnshire at basketball.

WOODWARD, Vivian John
(Tottenham Hotspur and Chelsea, 1903-11, 23)
Born Kennington, London, 3 June 1879. Died 31 January 1954.
1903: 5ft. 101/2ins.; 11st.

Career: Ascham College, Clacton; Clacton FC; Harwich & Parkeston; Chelmsford; Tottenham Hotspur 1901; Chelsea November 1909 - cs 1914; retired during WW1. Tottenham Hotspur director 1908-09; Chelsea director July 1922 - 1930. Represented Essex while engaged in junior football there. Other honours: English amateur international (44 apps). Football League (3 apps).

Centre/inside-forward. A celebrated amateur among the finest forwards ever, whether from the paid or unpaid ranks. A brilliant dribbler, expert at ground passing and invariably on target when shooting or heading. And always the complete sportsman. Holder of the aggregate record for full and amateur caps. Originally worked as an architect, later taking up farming. Played cricket for Essex 2nd XI and rose to the rank of major during WW1.

WOOSNAM, Maxwell
(Manchester City, 1922, 1)
Born Liverpool, 6 September 1892. Died 14 July 1965.
1923: 5ft. 10$^1/_2$ins.; 12st. 6lbs.

Career: Winchester College (XI 1908-11); Cambridge University (Blue 1912-13-14, captain 1914); Corinthians 1913-21; Chelsea 1914; Manchester City October 1919; Northwich Victoria cs 1925. Other honours: England amateur international (2 apps).

Centre-half. Another of the great amateurs, his play the archetypal amateur approach - brave, hard, glorying in a shoulder charge and the open game. Must be ranked with C B Fry (q.v.) as a multi-master of sport. He won Blues for golf, lawn tennis and real tennis and was the 12th man in the 'Varsity cricket match of 1914. Won the Wimbeldon doubles (with R Lycett) 1921 and was mixed doubles finalist that year. Represented Britain at lawn tennis in the 1920 (gold medalist) and '24 Olympic Games. Later was president of both the Isthmian and the Corinthian-Casuals FC. Held an appointment with ICI for 31 years. Uncle of the Welsh internationalist, Phil Woosnam.

WORRALL, Fred
(Portsmouth, 1935-37, 2)
Born Warrington, 8 September 1910. Died 13 April 1979.
1934: 5ft. 6½ins.; 11st. 2lbs.

Career: Witton Albion; Nantwich; Oldham Athletic December 1928; Portsmouth October 1931; Crewe Alexandra during WW2; Stockport County September 1946; Chester coach July 1948 and later trained the players of Warrington RLFC before having a spell as Stockton Heath FC (Cheshire) manager from cs1953. Other honours: Football League (2 apps). (Portsmouth) FA Cup winner 1939; finalist 1934.

Outside-right. Fast, spry, direct winger able in spite of a moderate height to jump high when heading. Signed for Bolton Wanderers December 1928 but, because of a technical breach, that club was forbidden to sign him at any time. Fred, consistent and remarkably injury-free, had a curious League appearance record for Pompey. In 6 of his 7 whole peacetime seasons he made 41 out of a possible 42 appearances.

WORTHINGTON, Frank Stuart
(Leicester City, 1974-75, 8)
Born Shelf nr. Halifax, 23 November 1948.
1975: 6ft.; 12st.

Career: Schools football; Huddersfield Town apprentice 1963, turning professional November 1966; Leicester City August 1972 (£80,000); Bolton Wanderers October 1977 (£90,000) after a month on loan; Birmingham City November 1979 (£150,000); Tampa Bay Rowdies, USA, March 1981 (£100,000), returning to Birmingham the following season before joining Leeds United March 1982 (in exchange for another player); Sunderland December 1982 (£50,000); Southampton June 1983 (£25,000); Brighton & Hove Albion May 1984; Tranmere Rovers player/manager July 1985-February 1987, a little later joining Preston North End, and subsequently assisted Stalybridge Celtic and Chorley. Other honours: England Under-23 international (2 apps). Football League (1 app). (H'field T) FL Div.2 champions 1970. (Bolton) FL Div.2 champions 1978.

Strike forward prominent on the FL circuit for over two decades. Very skilful, deft both on the ground and in the air, and a hard shot. Always seemed to have a tincture of arrogance, perhaps engendered by innate confidence. Frank's brothers, David and Bob, were well known professionals too.

WREFORD-BROWN, Charles
(Corinthians and Old Carthusians, 1889-98, 4)
Born Clifton, Bristol, 9 October 1866. Died 26 November 1951.

Career: Charterhouse School (XI 1884-5-6); Oxford University (Blue 1888-9, captain '89); Corinthians 1887-1903; Old Carthusians; Casuals. Also represented London on occasion. Served on the FA committee 1892-93, 1895-1902 and 1903-04; the FA Council 1919-41 and was a Vice-President from 1941. For many years on the FA's selection committee for international matches. Other honours: (Old Carthusians) FA Amateur Cup winner, 1894, 1897.

Centre-half in the classic mould, as a 'Nineties writer tells us. 'A half-back of many parts, he plays the game thoroughly. A sure kick with either foot, he is clever in stopping the opposite forwards. He passes out to his own men with great judgement, and is always playing for his side, never to the gallery.' Played cricket for Oxford University (Blue 1887) and Gloucestershire (5 matches over the period 1886-98). A solicitor by profession (admitted 1895). Is said to have given the game its popular name, 'soccer'.

WRIGHT, E(dward) Gordon D(undas)
(Cambridge University, 1906, 1)
Born Earlsfield Green, Surrey, 3 October 1884. Died 5 June 1947.
1907: 5ft. 10 1/2 ins.; 11st.

Career: St. Lawrence School, Ramsgate; Cambridge University (Blue 1904-5-6). During the period 1905-13 assisted a number of clubs: Corinthians 1905-07; Portsmouth September 1905-1906; Hull City 1905-13; Leyton 1909/10 season; Worthing; Reigate Priory. Other honours: England amateur international (20 apps).

Outside-left. An impressive amateur wingman able to both exercise control and middle the ball from any angle when travelling at high speed. A tactician too, well demonstrated in his 152 League outings with Hull City (he was that club's first internationalist). Son of an East Riding clergyman, Wright first worked as a schoolmaster and then qualified as a mining engineer. He practised in South Africa, then in the States and finally South Africa again, where he died.

WRIGHT, J(ohn) Douglas
(Newcastle United, 1939, 1)
Born Rochford nr. Southend-on-Sea, 29 April 1917.
1949: 6ft.; 11st. 7lbs.

Career: Southend junior football to Southend United during the 1936/37 season; Newcastle United May 1938 (£3250); Lincoln City December 1948 (£600); Blyth Spartans as player/coach December 1954, becoming player/manager cs 1955 and then served as secretary May 1957-November 1960. Other honour: (Lincoln City) FL Div.3 (North) champions 1952.

Wing-half of willowy build and a cultured brand of footwork that was quite captivating. An outstanding case of the war taking vintage years from a major talent. The sole blemish one critic could find was Doug's fondness for dribbling in the vicinity of his own goal. Set a splendid example when captaining the Imps to promotion in '52.

WRIGHT, Mark
(Southampton and Derby County, 1984-88, 22)
Born Dorchester-on-Thames, Oxon. 1 August 1963.
1985: 6ft. 3ins.; 12st. 1lb.

Career: Junior football; Oxford United August 1980; Southampton March 1982 (£140,000 including another player); Derby County August 1987 (£760,000, a record for both Derby and Southampton). Other honours: England Under-21 international (4 apps).

Central defender. Had made less than a dozen FL appearances for Oxford before moving to Southampton as part of a complicated deal involving three players (the reputed fee, £220,000, included one from Southampton valued at £80,000). Wright has height to dominate in the air and is highly skilled in his groundwork as well. A broken leg in 1986 prevented his selection for the World Cup journey of that year, but he has made an excellent recovery to perform as efficiently as ever.

WRIGHT, Thomas James
(Everton, 1968-70,11)
Born Liverpool, 21 October 1944.
1969: 5ft. 8ins.; 11st. 3lbs.
Career: Liverpool Schools; Everton ground staff 1961, turning professional March 1963; retired through injury February 1974. Other honours: England Under-23 international (7 apps). (Everton) FL champions 1970. FA Cup winner 1966; finalist 1968.

Right-back after winning schoolboy honours at inside-forward and a subsequent conversion to wing-half. Noted as one of the game's most constructive defenders, especially good at heading and ultra-reliable. Loved to surge down the flank in the modern manner. Uncle of Billy Wright (Everton & England Under-21)

WRIGHT, William Ambrose
(Wolverhampton Wanderers, 1947-59, 105)
Born Ironbridge, Salop, 6 February 1924.
1950: 5ft. 8ins.; 11st. 6lbs.

Career: Staffs schools football; Wolverhampton Wanderers ground staff 1938, turning professional 1941 (Leicester City guest player during WW2); retired August 1959. Manager/coach of England's Youth team October 1960; Arsenal manager March 1962-June 1966. Other honours: England 'B' international (1 app). Football League (21 apps). (Wolves) FL champions 1954, 1958, 1959. FA Cup winner 1949.

Left-half and then centre-half after initially playing inside-forward. A great player from the 1940s and '50s, an inspiring captain of club and country, incisive in tackling and a consummate passer of the ball. Billy was a model professional, never sent off or even cautioned, and the first to make a century of international appearances (for which he was elected a hon. life member of the FA). 'Footballer of the Year' 1952, and awarded the CBE 1959. Member of the Pilkington Commission on broadcasting 1960. Became a sports reporter for a Midlands TV company after relinquishing the Arsenal managership.

WYLIE, John George
(Wanderers, 1878, 1)
Born Shrewsbury, 1854. Died 30 July 1924.

Career: Shrewsbury School; Wanderers; Sheffield Club. Also represented the Sheffield FA. Other honour: (Wanderers) FA Cup winner 1878.

Forward who would later have been depicted as a centre or inside-forward. Had strength and pace and was successful with his shooting. His performances, however, were often flawed by excessive individualism. Wylie was a solicitor by vocation (admitted 1878) practising in London.

YATES, John
(Burnley, 1889, 1)
Born Blackburn 1861. Died 1 June 1917.

Career: Accrington1879; Blackburn Olympic 1880; Accrington again February 1886; Burnley cs 1888-1894. Also represented Lancashire. Other honour: (Blackburn Olympic) FA Cup winner 1883.

Outside-left both positive and forceful. Burnley's first internationalist, he had been in what was then the first-grade game a full decade before this signal honour. Responded by scoring a hat-trick but, nevertheless, was not selected again. Enjoyed a fruitful partnership at Burnley with Pat Gallocher, a schemer who could capitalise on Jack's thrustful play. He (Jack Yates) was a cotton weaver by vocation.

YORK, Richard Ernest
(Aston Villa, 1922-26, 2)
Born Birmingham, 25 April 1899. Died 9 December 1969.
1924: 5ft. 91/2ins.; 11st.

Career: Birmingham Schools 1910-13; RAF football during WW1; Aston Villa cs 1918; Port Vale June 1931; Brierley Hill Alliance cs 1932. Other honours: England schoolboy international (2 apps). Football League (2 apps). (Villa) FA Cup finalist 1924.

Outside-right. Joined Villa as a right-half, moving to the wing and succeeding Charlie Wallace (q.v.). 'Besides being one of the cleverest wingers in the country, he is also an expert amateur runner,' recorded a 1926 scribe, and indeed speed was York's most obvious trait. His centres and passing generally had accuracy too. Commissioned in the Army during WW1, he transferred to the Air Force and served as a pilot. More prosaically, he ran a Birmingham decorating and plumbing business later.

YOUNG, Alfred
(Huddersfield Town, 1933-39, 9)
Born Sunderland, 4 November 1905. Died 30 August 1977.
1938: 5ft. 11$^1/_2$ins.; 12st. 11lbs.

Career: Durham City 1926; Huddersfield Town January 1927; York City November 1945; retired 1946 and then coached in Denmark until 1948; Huddersfield Town coach July 1948-May 1952. Returned to the game as Bradford's manager December 1957; Esbjerg FC (Denmark) coach November 1958; Huddersfield Town coach again December 1960 and then their chief scout 1964-July 1965. Other honours: Football League (2 apps). (H'field T) FA Cup finalist 1938.

Centre-half. Something of a slow developer - a process partially engendered by several years in the shadow of a long-reigning Tom Wilson (q.v.). Once established, however, Alf won a clutch of caps in the 1930s. A prime example of a 'stopper' pivot: strong, dominating and unstinting in effort.

YOUNG, Gerald Morton
(Sheffield Wednesday, 1965, 1)
Born Harton, South Shields, 1 October 1936.
1965: 5ft. 10$^1/_2$ins.; 11st. 10lbs.

Career: Jarrow schools football; was on Newcastle United's books when 16 but, getting no opportunity, returned to junior football; Hawthorn Leslie (works side); Sheffield Wednesday May 1955; retired 1971. Appointed Wednesday's second team trainer/coach April 1971 with effect from the following July, he was later chief coach until October 1975; subsequently on Barnsley's staff for a short while. Other honour: (Wednesday) FA Cup finalist 1966.

Left-half eventually after senior outings at centre and inside forward and outside-left. A fine club man-dedicated and quite reliable, giving of his best at all times. Made 335 first team appearances for the Wednesday in which he scored 16 goals. Completed an electrician's apprenticeship before joining the paid ranks.

AN ENGLAND MISCELLANY

ENGLAND'S MANAGERS

Three of England's managers – the alliterative trio of Ramsey, Revie and Robson – had been England players and so appear in the body of this book. The others were:

SIR WALTER WINTERBOTTOM, born 1914 in Lancashire. Educated at Oldham Grammar School and became a school master. After assisting the Cheshire League side, Mossley, joined Manchester United in 1936. His chances as a centre-half at Old Trafford were limited due to the presence of the talented George Vose and he grossed only 25 League and 2 FA Cup appearances before the outbreak of war. He played in wartime soccer while serving as a commissioned officer in the RAF until injury ended his career in 1945. He was a full time FA Director of Coaching in 1948. The post carried the job of England manager, though not with the supreme command his successors enjoyed (he had to report to the FA's Selection Committee). Winterbottom left in 1963 and then had a distinguished career with the Sports Council. He was awarded a knighthood in 1978 not long before his retirement.

RON GREENWOOD, born Burnley 1921. Played centre-half for Bradford (Park Avenue), Brentford, Chelsea and Fulham during the initial post-war decade, 1946-56. The highlights were winning a League championship medal when with Chelsea (1955) and an England 'B' cap. He qualified as a coach while still a player. After managing Eastbourne United and successfully running England's Youth team, Greenwood was appointed Arsenal's chief coach and he also managed the England Under-23 side. Enjoyed a notable and lengthy spell as West Ham's manager 1961-75 and then was their general manager 1975-77. He was England's manager for 5 years, 1977-82.

OLDEST AND YOUNGEST DEBUTANTS

Without every full birth-date it cannot be stated with absolute assurance that any particular player holds these palms. It is generally thought, however, that the oldest debutant (at 38 years, 65 days) is L H COMPTON and (at 18 years, 183 days) the youngest is DUNCAN EDWARDS.

Frank Hudspeth is a likely runner-up in the 'oldest' category, but it is noticeable that England selectors had few, if any, qualms about picking players on the wrong side of 30. This was especially so in the inter-war period. During the first two post-war seasons Knight, Bagshaw, Longworth, Chedgzoy, Downs and Fred Bullock, all born in the 1880's, received first caps. And before World War 2 we find more 'Over 30s' in the persons of Wainscoat, Bestall, Harrow, Pym, Bliss, Tom Wilson, Clem Stephenson, George Shaw, Tresadern, Ernest Coleman, Joe Peacock, Nuttall, Pantling, Harry Jones, Vincent Mathews and Harry Hardy. Earlier Brittleton, born 1879, was first honoured in 1911/12, while in the 1950s Willis, Medley and Syd Owen come into the category. (The list is not intended to be exhaustive).

Teenage debutants were perhaps – as with Scotland – more liable to crop up before the Great War (e.g. A S and James Brown, Forrest, R D Anderson and M P Betts with 'possibles' such as Moon, Maynard and Morse). Between the wars there were Geldard and Lawton, while in post-WW2 days, besides Duncan Edwards, there was Tony Allen. With the evolution of the squad system examples at either end of the age range are rarer, at any rate for outfield players.

RELATIONSHIPS

Brothers

3 brothers: A L, E C and E H Bambridge

2 brothers:
J and R Charlton
J C and W E Clegg
B O and R Corbett
A W and H A Cursham
A T C and C F Dobson
Frank and F R Forman
F W and J Hargreaves
C F W and G H H Heron
A and E Lyttelton
F R and R Osbourne
C and T Perry
H E and W S Rawson
A and C Shelton
J W and S C Smith
C and G T Stephenson
A G and R Topham
A M and P M Walters
C P and G P Wilson

Father and Son

G R and G E Eastham

Uncle and Nephew

C Granger and E Holliday

Cousins

H Adcock and J Bradford
S Barkas and W Felton
G Brown and J W Spence
A and E W Chadwick
A Cowell and A E Houlker
A and J N Cunliffe
J and R Froggatt
C E and G O Smith

Father-in-law and Son-in-law

S Bloomer and A E Quantrill

Brothers-in-law

Frank and F R Forman, and JH Linacre

ENGLAND SCHOOLBOY INTERNATIONALISTS WHO BECAME FULL CAPS

C D Allen
S Anderson
A F Barrett
J W Barrett
C S Bastin
B J Bridges
T D Brooking
H S Carter
M V Chamberlain
H Chambers
R Charlton
H E Clamp
W Cresswell
N V Deeley
R W Dix
S G J Earle
D Edwards
W Ellerington
A Geldard
L A Goulden
A Grimsdell
J Hagan
J N Haynes
E I L Kail
C Lawler
W McGuinness
S Matthews
L D Medley
J Melia
J Mullen
R A Parry
D Pegg
S J Perryman
M S Peters
A Quixall
J R Richardson
K G Sansom
L F Shackleton
P L Shilton
S C Smith
N P Stiles
P E Storey
R V Tambling
P H Taylor
D W Temple
D J Thomas
Peter Thompson
M A Towers
J E Townrow
T F Venables
D S Viollet
S Whitworth
R E York

In additon, J H Baker and C Crowe were capped by Scotland at schoolboy international level.

FOOTBALLER/CRICKETERS

Until the respective seasons overlapped considerably and, for leading players, each became an almost all-year activity, it was common for many to play both games at professional level. These included a significant number of England soccer internationalists who are listed below. In these cases of some early caps, they assisted counties before those counties attained first class or Minor Counties status. Service with Scottish counties has also earned a mention.

'Double internationals' (those who have represented England at both soccer and cricket) are indicated by an asterisk.

*J ARNOLD	Oxfordshire and Hampshire
C T ASHTON	Essex
S R BASTARD	Essex
H BETMEAD	Lincolnshire
M P BETTS	Middlesex and Kent
F H BIRLEY	Lancashire, Surrey and Cheshire
G BRANN	Sussex
C M BUCHAN	Durham
C J BURNUP	Kent
J CARR (Newcastle U)	Northumberland
H S CARTER	Durham and Derbyshire
L H COMPTON	Middlesex
T E R COOK	Sussex
N C COOPER	Surrey
F N S CREEK	Wiltshire
A W CURSHAM	Nottinghamshire and Derbyshire
H A CURSHAM	Nottinghamshire
H B DAFT	Nottinghamshire
S H DAY	Kent
J H G DEVEY	Warwickshire
J A DIXON	Nottinghamshire
A G DOGGART	Durham and Middlesex
E J DRAKE	Hampshire
*A DUCAT	Surrey
H J FLEMING	Wiltshire
*R E FOSTER	Worcestershire
W H FOULKE	Derbyshire
*C B FRY	Surrey, Sussex and Hampshire
*L H GAY	Hampshire and Somerset
W GEORGE	Warwickshire, Wiltshire and Shropshire
W E GILLIAT	Buckinghamshire
J GOODALL	Derbyshire and Hertfordshire
R C GOSLING	Essex
L GRAHAM	Essex
A GRIMSDELL	Hertfordshire
*W GUNN	Nottinghamshire
*H T W HARDINGE	Kent
S S HARRIS	Gloucestershire, Surrey and Sussex
F HARTLEY	Oxfordshire
E B HAYGARTH	Gloucestershire, Hampshire and Berkshire
M S HELLAWELL	Warwickshire
A G HENFREY	Northamptonshire
J. HILLMAN	Forfarshire
G HODGSON	Lancashire and Forfarshire

W E HOUGHTON	Lincolnshire and Warwickshire
L S HOWELL	Surrey
J H A HULME	Middlesex
G C HURST	Essex
J IREMONGER	Nottinghamshire
W S KENYON-SLANEY	Shropshire
R K KINGSFORD	Surrey
A E KNIGHT	Hampshire
J LEE	Leicestershire
T LINDLEY	Nottinghamshire
W LINDSAY	Surrey
L V LODGE	Durham and Hampshire
*Hon A LYTTELTON	Worcestershire and Middlesex
Hon E LYTTLETON	Middlesex, Hertfordshire and Worcestershire
*J W H MAKEPEACE	Lancashire
*C A MILTON	Gloucestershire
C MITCHELL	Kent
W R MOON	Middlesex
E NEEDHAM	Derbyshire
C J OTTAWAY	Kent and Middlesex
P J de PARAVACINI	Middlesex and Buckinghamshire
J PAYNE	Bedfordshire
T M PIKE	Worcestershire
G B RAIKES	Norfolk and Hampshire
H E RAWSON	Kent
L F SHACKLETON	Northumberland
*J SHARP	Lancashire and Herefordshire
G O SMITH	Surrey and Herefordshire
H STORER	Derbyshire
A H STRATFORD	Middlesex and Herefordshire
PHILIP H TAYLOR	Gloucestershire
D G UFTON	Kent
F I WALDEN	Northamptonshire
*W WATSON (Sunderland)	Yorkshire and Leicestershire
G F WHELDON	Worcestershire and Carmarthenshire
H WHITFELD	Sussex
S W WIDDOWSON	Nottinghamshire
CHARLES P WILSON	Norfolk
CLAUDE W WILSON	Surrey
J E WINDRIDGE	Warwickshire
M WOOSNAM	Cheshire
C WREFORD-BROWN	Gloucestershire

DOUBLE INTERNATIONALS

Besides those who have represented England at soccer and cricket, as indicated above, there are English soccer internationalists who have played for England at other sports. They include R H Birkett, C P Wilson and J W Sutcliffe at Rugby Union, at which sport R C Osman captained England Schools. C K. Willingham was an English shinty international as was L A Page at baseball.

PLAYED FOR TWO COUNTRIES

In addition to representing England, J Reynolds appeared for Ireland, J H Edwards and R E Evans for Wales, and K Armstrong for New Zealand.

CLUB CONTRIBUTIONS

It has been interesting to calculate the number of players individual clubs have contributed to England teams. (Note: The numbers add up to a far higher figure than the 1003 Who's Who entries, due to so many appearing when on the playing strengths of more than one club).

Aston Villa	51
Everton	50
West Bromwich Albion	42
Tottenham Hotspur	41
Arsenal	39
Blackburn Rovers	38
Liverpool	37
Derby County	36
Manchester United	35
Sheffield United	34
Sheffield Wednesday	32
Wolverhampton Wanderers	32
Manchester City	31
Nottingham Forest	30
Chelsea	29
Bolton Wanderers	25
Burnley	24
Stoke City	22
Huddersfield Town	21
Middlesbrough	21
Sunderland	21
West Ham United	21
Leeds United	20
Newcastle United	20
Southampton	20
Corinthians	19
Oxford University	18
Notts County	17
Birmingham City	14
Old Etonians	14
Preston North End	14
Wanderers	14
Blackpool	13
Leicester City	13
Cambridge University	12
Ipswich Town	11
Portsmouth	11
Queen's Park Rangers	11
Luton Town	10
Old Carthusians	10
Fulham	9
Old Westminsters	8
Swifts	8
Charlton Athletic	7
Millwall	7
Bury	6
Clapham Rovers	6
Royal Engineers	6
Sheffield Club	6
Crystal Palace (present day)	5
Norwich City	5
Old Harrovians	5
Bristol City	4
Casuals	4
Crystal Palace (original)	4
Darwen	4
Accrington	3
Bradford City	3
Brighton & Hove Albion	3
Clapton	3
Grimsby Town	3
Old Brightonians	3
Oldham Athletic	3
Upton Park	3
Brentford	2
Clapton Orient	2
Coventry City	2
Dulwich Hamlet	2
Herts Rangers	2
Old Foresters	2
Old Malvernians	2
Reading	2
Walsall Town Swifts	2
Watford	2
Barnes	1
Barnsley	1
Birmingham Excelsior	1
Blackburn Olympic	1
Bradford (Park Avenue)	1
Bristol Rovers	1
Crewe Alexandra	1
1st Surrey Rifles	1
Gillingham	1
Great Lever	1
Hendon	1
Leyton	1
Liverpool Ramblers	1
New Brighton Tower	1
Notts Rangers	1
Oxford City	1
Pilgrims	1
Saltley College	1
Sheffield Albion	1
Sheffield Heeley	1
Shropshire Wanderers	1
South Shields	1
Stafford Road	1
Stockport County	1

CLUB CONTRIBUTIONS (continued)

Swindon Town	1
The Army	1
Tufnell Park	1
Uxbridge	1
Wednesbury Old Athletic	1
Wednesbury Strollers	1

From Scottish and European clubs:

Scotland	Hibernian	1
	Rangers	2
Germany	FC Cologne	1
	SV Hamburg	1
	Werder Bremen	1
Italy	AC Milan	2
	Bari	1
	Inter Milan	1
	Sampdoria	1
Spain	Barcelona	1
	Real Madrid	1

BIRTH PLACES

Including the three possibilities, 997 of the entries contain a birth place. They divide as follows:

From the largest cities

London	106
Birmingham	28
Liverpool	38
Manchester	28
Sheffield	27
Leeds	6
Bristol	13

From the traditional counties (i.e. within the boundaries obtaining from time immemorial until the lamentable changes of 1974)

Bedfordshire	2
Berkshire	9
Berwickshire	1
Buckinghamshire	5
Cambridgeshire	4
Cheshire	24
Cornwall	2
Cumberland	6
Devonshire	8
Derbyshire	35
Dorset	2
Durham	74
Essex	17
Gloucestershire	2
Hampshire	19
Herefordshire	1
Hertfordshire	6
Kent	19
Lancashire	132
Leicestershire	12
Lincolnshire	14
Middlesex	12
Norfolk	7
Northamptonshire	6
Northumberland	33
Nottinghamshire	37
Oxfordshire	9
Shropshire	16
Somerset	1
Staffordshire	79
Suffolk	4
Surrey	18
Sussex	11
Warwickshire	4
Wiltshire	5
Worcestershire	11
Yorkshire	78

Born outside England

Belgium	1
Canada	1
Ceylon (Sri Lanka)	2
French Guiana	1
India	7
Jamaica	2
Malaya	1
Mauritius	1
Mexico	1
Scotland	2
South Africa	7

APPEARANCES, 1872-1988

The following players had appeared on 20 or more occasions in the period:

Player	Apps	Matches
ANDERSON, V.A. (Nottingham Forest, Arsenal and Manchester United)	30	Czechoslovakia 1979; Sweden, 1979, '87; Bulgaria 1980; Spain 1980, '87; Norway and Wales 1981; Rumania and Scotland 1981, '85; N. Ireland 1982, '84, '85, '87 (2); Iceland 1982; Turkey 1985, '87; Finland and USA 1985, Mexico 1985, '86; Russia 1986; Yugoslavia 1987; W. Germany, Hungary and Colombia 1988.
ARMFIELD, J.C. (Blackpool)	43	Brazil 1959, '62, '64; Peru 1959, '62; Mexico 1959, '61; USA 1959; Scotland 1960-64 inc.; Yugoslavia 1960, '66; Spain 1960, '61; Hungary 1960, '62; N. Ireland and Wales 1961-64 inc.; Portugal, Luxembourg and Austria 1961, '62; Italy 1961; Switzerland 1962, 1963; Argentina and Bulgaria 1962; France (2) and East Germany 1963; FIFA 1964; Finland 1966.
BALL, A.J. (Blackpool, Everton and Arsenal)	72	Yugoslavia 1965, '68, '73; W. Germany 1965, '66 (2), '68, '70, '72 (2), '75; Sweden 1965; Scotland 1966-72 inc., '73 (2), '75; Spain 1966, '67, '68 (2); Finland and Denmark 1966; Uruguay 1966, '69; Argentina 1966; Portugal 1966, '70, '74 (sub); Poland 1966 (2), '73; Wales 1967-70 inc., '73 (3), '75; N. Ireland 1967, '69, '71, '73, '75; Austria 1967, Czechoslovakia 1967, '70 (sub), '73; Russia 1968; Rumania 1969 (2), '70; Mexico 1969; Brazil 1969, '70; Colombia, Ecuador and Belgium 1970; Malta (2: 1 sub) and E. Germany 1971; Greece 1971, '72; Switzerland 1972; Cyprus 1975 (2).
BANKS, G. (Leicester City and Stoke City)	73	Scotland 1963-72 inc.; Brazil 1963, '69, '70; Czechoslovakia 1963, '67, '70; E. Germany 1963; Wales 1964, '67, '68, '70, '72; FIFA and USA 1964; N. Ireland 1964-71 inc.; Uruguay 1964, '66, '69; Portugal 1964 (2), '66; Argentina 1964, '66; Hungary and Sweden 1965; Yugoslavia 1965, '66, '68; W. Germany 1965, '66 (2); '68, '72 (2); Spain 1966, '68; Poland (2), Finland and Mexico 1966; France 1966, '69; Russia 1968 (2); Rumania 1969 (2), '70; Holland, Belgium, Colombia and Ecuador 1970; Malta 1971 (2); Greece 1971, '72; Switzerland 1972.
BARNES, J.C.B. (Watford and Liverpool)	42	N. Ireland 1983 (sub), '85; Australia 1983 (3 inc. 1 sub); Denmark, Luxembourg (sub), France (sub), Uruguay and Chile 1984; Russia 1984, '88; Scotland 1984, '85, '88; Brazil 1984, '87; E. Germany, Finland (2), Italy (sub), and USA (sub) 1985; W. Germany 1985 (sub), '88; Turkey 1985, '87 (sub); Rumania 1985, '86 (sub); Mexico 1985, '86 (sub); Israel 1986 (sub) '88; Canada (sub) and Argentina (sub) 1986; Sweden 1987; Yugoslavia, Holland (2), Switzerland, Colombia and Eire 1988.
BARNES, P.S. (Manchester City, West Bromwich Albion and Leeds United)	22	Italy, W. Germany and Hungary 1978; Brazil 1978, '81; Wales 1978, '80, '81; Scotland 1978, '79; Denmark 1979, '80; Eire, Czechoslovakia, N. Ireland (2), Bulgaria and Austria 1979; Spain

		1981 (sub); Switzerland 1981 (sub); Norway 1982 (sub); Holland 1982 (sub).
BASTIN, C.S. (Arsenal)	21	Wales 1932, '34, '36, '37; Italy 1933, '35; Switzerland 1933, '38; N. Ireland 1934, '35, '37, '38; Scotland 1934, '35, '36, '38; Hungary and Czechoslovakia 1934; Germany 1936, '38; Austria 1936; France 1938.
BEARDSLEY, P.A. (Newcastle United and Liverpool)	26	Egypt (sub), Russia, Mexico, Canada (sub), Portugal (sub), Poland, Paraguay and Argentina 1986; Israel 1986, '88; N. Ireland (2) Spain and Brazil 1987; Yugoslavia and Scotland 1987, '88; W. Germany, Turkey, Holland (2), Hungary, Colombia, Switzerland and Eire 1988.
BELL, C. (Manchester City)	48	Sweden 1968; W. Germany 1968, '70 (sub), '72 (2), '75; Wales 1969, '72, '73 (3), '74; Bulgaria 1969, '74; France and Uruguay 1969; Brazil 1969, '70 (sub); N. Ireland 1970 (sub), '72-'75 inc.; Holland 1972 (2); Portugal 1970, '75; Czechoslovakia 1970, '73, '75; Greece 1972; Scotland 1972, '73 (2), '74, '75; Yugoslavia and Poland 1973, '74; Austria, Italy, Argentina and E. Germany 1974; Cyprus 1975 (2), '76; Switzerland 1976.
BLENKINSOP, E. (Sheffield Wednesday)	26	France and Belgium 1928, '29, '31; N. Ireland, Wales and Scotland 1929-'33 inc.; Spain 1929 '32; Germany 1930; Austria 1930, '33
BLOOMER, S. (Derby County and Middlesbrough)	23	Ireland 1895, '96, '97, '99, 1901, '02, '05; Scotland 1895, '97-1902 incl.,'04, '05, '07; Wales 1896, '97, '99, 1902, '05, '07.
BROOKING, T.D. (West Ham United)	47	Portugal 1974, '75, '76; Argentina 1974, '80 (sub); E. Germany and Yugoslavia 1974; Bulgaria 1974, '79; Czechoslovakia 1975 (sub); Wales 1976, '77 '78, '79 (sub), '80; Brazil 1976; Italy 1976, '77, '78; Finland 1976, '77, '82; Eire 1977, '79; Holland 1977, N. Ireland 1977, '79, '80 (2); W. Germany 1978; Scotland 1978 (sub), '79, '80, '82; Hungary 1978, '81, '82; Denmark 1979, '80, Sweden (sub) and Austria 1979; Belgium 1980; Spain 1980, '81 '82 (sub); Switzerland and Rumania 1981.
BUTCHER, T.I. (Ipswich Town and Rangers)	52	Australia 1980, '83 (3); Spain 1981, '82, '87; Wales 1982, '83; Scotland 1982, '83, '85, '86, '87; France 1982, '84; Czechoslovakia 1982; W. Germany 1982, '83, '85; Denmark, Luxembourg and Hungary 1983, '84; Greece 1983; N. Ireland 1983, '84, '85, '87 (2); E. Germany, Finland (2) Eire, Rumania, Italy and USA 1985; Turkey 1985, '88; Israel, Russia, Mexico, Canada, Portugal, Morocco, Poland, Paraguay and Argentina 1986; Sweden and Brazil 1987; Yugoslavia 1987, '88
BYRNE, R.W. (Manchester United)	33	Scotland 1954-'57 inc.; Yugoslavia 1954, '57; Hungary, Belgium, Uruguay and Switzerland 1954; N. Ireland and Wales 1955-'58 inc.; W. Germany and Spain 1955, '56; France 1955, '58; Portugal 1955; Denmark 1956, '57 (2); Brazil, Sweden and Finland 1956; Eire 1957 (2).
CHANNON, M.R. (Southampton and Manchester City)	46	Yugoslavia 1973, '74; Scotland 1973 (2)-'77 inc.; N. Ireland 1973, '74, '75 (sub), '76, '77; Wales 1973-

		'77 inc.; Czechoslovakia 1973, '75, '76 Russia 1973; Italy 1973, '74, '76, '77; Austria, Poland, E. Germany and Bulgaria 1974; Portugal 1974, '75 '76; Argentina 1974, '77; W. Germany and Cyprus (2) 1975; Switzerland 1976, '78; Brazil 1976, '77; (sub); Finland 1976, '77; Luxembourg and Uruguay 1977.
CHARLTON, J. (Leeds United)	35	Scotland 1965, '66, '67; Hungary and Sweden 1965; Yugoslavia 1965, '66; W. Germany 1965, '66 (2); Wales 1966-'69 inc.; Austria, Poland (2), Finland Denmark, Uruguay, Mexico and Argentina 1966; N. Ireland 1966, '67; Spain 1966, '68; France 1966, '69; Portugal 1966, '70; Czechoslovakia 1967, '70; Rumania 1969; Holland 1970 (2).
CHARLTON, R. (Manchester United)	106	Scotland 1958-'69 inc.; Portugal 1958, '61, '62, '64, '66, '70; Yugoslavia 1958, '60, '66, '68; N. Ireland 1959, '61, '62, '64-'70 inc.; Russia 1959, '68 (2); Wales 1959-'62 inc.; '64, '66-'70 inc.; Italy 1959, '61; Brazil 1959, '62, '63, '64, '69, '70; Peru 1959, '62 Mexico 1959, '61, '66, '69; USA 1959, '64 (sub); Sweden 1960, '68; Spain 1960, '61, '66, '68 (2); Hungary 1960, '62; Luxembourg 1961, '62; Austria 1961, '62, '66; Switzerland 1962, '63; Argentina 1962, '64, '66; Bulgaria 1962, '69; France 1963 '66; Czechoslovakia 1963, '67, '70; East Germany 1963; FIFA and Eire 1964; Uruguay 1964, '66; Holland 1965, '70 (2); W. Germany 1966 (2), '70; Finland, Noray and Poland 1966; Rumania 1969 (2), '70; Colombia and Ecuador 1970.
CHERRY, T.J. (Leeds United)	27	Wales 1976, '78, '79, '80; Scotland 1976 (sub), '77 (sub), '80; Brazil 1976, '77, '78, Finland 1976; Eire 1977, '80; Italy and Uruguay 1977; Luxembourg 1977, '78; N. Ireland 1977, '78, '80; (sub); Switzerland 1978; Czechoslovakia and Sweden 1979; Australia and Spain (sub) 1980.
CHIVERS, M.H. (Tottenham Hotspur)	24	Malta 1971 (2); Greece 1971, '72; N. Ireland 1971, '72 (sub), '73 Scotland 1971, '72, '73 (2); Switzerland 1972 (2 inc. 1 sub); W. Germany 1972 (2); Wales (3), Czechoslovakia, Russia and Italy 1973; Poland 1973, '74; Austria 1974.
CLAYTON, R. (Blackburn Rovers)	35	N. Ireland 1956-'60 inc.; Spain, Finland and W. Germany 1956; Brazil 1956, '59; Sweden 1956, '60; Wales and Scotland 1957-'60 inc.; Yugoslavia 1957, '58, '60; Denmark (2) and Eire (2) 1957; France and Portugal 1958; Russia 1958, '59; Italy Peru, Mexico and USA 1959.
CLEMENCE, R.N. (Liverpool and Tottenham Hotspur)	61	Wales 1973 (2), '75, '76 (2), '80; East Germany and Yugoslavia 1974; Bulgaria 1974, '79, '80; Czechoslovakia and Portugal 1975, '76; W. Germany 1975, '78; Cyprus 1975; N. Ireland 1975, '76, '78, '79 (2), '82; Scotland 1975-'80 inc.; Switzerland 1976, '78, '81; Brazil 1976, '77, '81; Finland 1976 '77, '82; Eire 1977, '79, '80; Italy 1977, '78; Holland and Uruguay 1977; Luxembourg 1977, '78 83, '84; Argentina 1977, '80; Denmark 1979, '80; Austria 1979 (sub); Belgium 1980; Spain 1980, '81;

		Rumania and Hungary 1981; Norway 1982.
COHEN, G.R. (Fulham)	37	Uruguay and Portugal 1964, '66; Eire, USA and Brazil 1964; N. Ireland and Wales 1965-68 inc.; Belgium, Holland, Hungary, Yugoslavia and Sweden 1965; Scotland 1965, '66, '67; W. Germany 1965, '66 (2), Austria, Poland (2), Norway, Denmark, Mexico, France and Argentina 1966; Spain 1966, '67; Czechoslovakia 1967.
CONNELLY, J..M. (Burnley and Manchester United)	20	Wales 1960, '62, '63, '66; Sweden 1960, '65; N. Ireland and Scotland 1960, '66; Portugal and Switzerland 1962, Austria 1962, '66; France 1963; Hungary and Yugoslavia 1965; Norway, Denmark and Uruguay 1966.
COOPER, Terence (Leeds United)	20	France and Mexico 1969; Wales and Scotland 1969, '71; Holland, Belgium, Columbia, Ecuador, Rumania, Brazil, Czechoslovakia and W. Germany 1970; E. Germany, Malta and N. Ireland 1971; Switzerland 1972 (2); Portugal 1975.
COPPELL, S.J. (Manchester United)	42	Italy 1978, 80; W. Germany 1978, '82; Brazil 1978, '81; Wales 1978, '79 (sub), '80, '81; N. Ireland 1978, '79 (2), '80; Scotland 1978-82 inc.; Hungary 1978, '81, '82; Denmark 1979, '80; Eire 1979, '80 (sub); Czechoslovakia 1979, '82; Bulgaria and Austria 1979; Spain, Argentina and Belgium 1980; Rumania 1981 (2 inc. 1 sub); Switzerland 1981 (2); France, Finland and Kuwait 1982; Luxembourg and Greece 1983.
COPPING, W. (Leeds United and Arsenal)	20	Italy 1933, '35; Switzerland 1933; N. Ireland 1934, '35, '38; Wales 1934, '38, '39; France 1934; Scotland 1934, '38; Austria and Belgium 1936; Norway, Sweden and Finland 1937; Czechoslovakia 1938; FIFA and Rumania 1939.
CROMPTON, R. (Blackburn Rovers)	41	Wales 1902, '03, '04, '06-'14 inc.; Ireland 1902, '04, '06-'09 inc.; '11-'14 inc.; Scotland 1902, '03, '04, '06-'14 inc.; Austria 1908 (2), '09; Hungary 1908, '09 (2), '09 (2); Bohemia 1908.
CROOKS, S.D. (Derby County)	26	Scotland 1930, '31, '32, '34, '36; Germany 1930; Austria 1930, '33; N. Ireland 1931-35 inc.; Wales 1931-'33 inc.; '36, '37; France 1931, '34; Belgium 1931; Spain 1932; Hungary 1934, '37; Czechoslovakia 1934.
DICKINSON, J.W. (Portsmouth)	48	Norway and France 1949; Eire 1950; Wales 1950-'54 inc.; '56, '57; Scotland 1950, '52, '53, '54, '56; Portugal 1950, '55; Belgium 1950, '53, '54; Chile and USA 1950, '53; Spain 1950, '55, '56; N. Ireland 1951-54 inc.; '56; Yugoslavia 1951, '54, '57; Austria (2) and Italy 1952; Switzerland 1952, '54; Argentina 1953; Uruguay 1953, '54; FIFA and Hungary (2) 1954; Denmark 1956, '57.
DOUGLAS, B. (Blackburn Rovers)	36	Wales, N. Ireland and Portugal 1958, '61, '62; France 1958; Scotland 1958, '59, '61, '62, '63; Yugoslavia 1958, '60; Russia 1958 (2), '59; Brazil 1958, '62, '63; Austria 1958; '61; Hungary 1960, '62; Luxembourg 1961, '62; Spain, Mexico and Italy 1961; Peru, Argentina and Bulgaria 1962; Switzerland 1963.

FENWICK, T.W. (Queen's Park Rangers and Tottenham Hotspur)	20	Wales (sub), Russia, Brazil, Uruguay and Chile 1984; Scotland 1984, '85; Finland and USA 1985; Mexico 1985, '86; Rumania, Turkey, N. Ireland, Egypt, Portugal, Morocco, Poland and Argentina 1986; Israel (sub) 1988.
FINNEY, T. (Preston North End)	76	N. Ireland 1974-50 inc.; '52, '53, '56, '59; Eire 1947, '50, '57 (2); Wales 1947-54 inc.; '56, '57, '58; Holland 1947; France 1947; '49, '52, '58; Portugal 1947, '50, '51, '58; Belgium 1948, '50, '53, '54; Sweden 1948, '49; Scotland 1948-54 inc.; '56, '57, '58; Italy 1948, '50, '52; Norway 1949; Chile and USA 1950, '53; Spain 1950, '56; Argentina 1951, '53; Austria 1952; Switzerland 1952, '54; Uruguay 1953, '54; Yugoslavia 1954, '57, '58; Hungary 1954; W. Germany 1955; Denmark 1956, '57 (2); Russia 1958 (2), '59.
FLOWERS, R. (Wolverhampton Wanderers)	49	France 1955, '63 (2); Wales 1959-63 inc.; '65; Scotland 1959-63 inc.; Italy 1959, '61; Brazil and Peru 1959, '62; Mexico 1959 (sub), '61; USA 1959, '64; Sweden and Yugoslavia 1960; N. Ireland 1960-63 inc.; Spain 1960, '61; Hungary 1960, '62; Austria and Luxembourg 1961, '62; Portugal 1961, '62, '64; Switzerland 1962, '63; Argentina and Bulgaria 1962; Eire 1964; Holland and Germany 1965; Norway 1966.
FRANCIS, T.J. (Birmingham City, Nottingham Forest, Manchester City and Sampdoria)	52	Holland 1977; Luxembourg and Brazil 1977; '78; Scotland 1977, '78, '81 (sub), '82 (sub), '83, '85, '86; Switzerland 1978, '81; Italy 1978 (sub), '85; W. Germany 1978 (sub), '82; Wales 1978, '82; Hungary 1978, '83; Bulgaria 1979 (sub), '80; Sweden and Austria (sub) 1979; N. Ireland 1980, '82, '83, '84, '85 (sub); Spain 1980, '81, '82; Rumania 1981, '85; Norway, France, Czechoslovakia and Kuwait 1982; Finland 1982 (sub), '85; Denmark 1983, '84; Greece and Australia (3) 1983; Russia 1984; E. Germany (sub), Turkey (sub) and Mexico 1985.
FRANKLIN, C. (Stoke City)	27	N. Ireland, Wales and Scotland 1947-'50 inc.; Eire 1947, '50; Holland and Portugal 1947; France and Switzerland 1947, '49; Belgium 1948; Sweden 1948, '49; Italy 1948, '50; Denmark and Norway 1949.
GOODALL, F.R. (Huddersfield Town)	25	Scotland 1926, '27, '28, '30, '31; Belgium 1927, '28, '31; Luxembourg 1927; France 1927, '28, '34; Wales 1928, '31, '33, '34; Germany 1930; Austria 1930, '33; N. Ireland 1931-'34 inc.; Italy and Switzerland 1933.
GREAVES, J.P. (Chelsea and Tottenham Hotspur)	57	Peru 1959, '62; Mexico 1959, '66; USA 1959; Wales 1960, '61, '63, '64, '66; Sweden 1960; Yugoslavia 1960, '65, '66; Spain 1960, '61, '67; N. Ireland 1961, '63, '64, '65; Italy and Luxembourg 1961; Scotland 1961, '62, '63, '65, '67; Portugal 1961, '64 (2); Austria 1961, '66, '67; Switzerland 1962, '63; Hungary 1962, '65; Argentina 1962, '64; Bulgaria 1962; Brazil 1962, '63, '64; France 1963 (2), '66; Czechoslovakia

		1963; FIFA 1964; Uruguay 1964, '66; Eire 1964; Belgium and Holland 1956; Norway, Denmark and Poland 1966.
HAPGOOD, E.A. (Arsenal)	30	Italy 1933, '35, '39; Switzerland 1933, '38; N. Ireland and Wales 1934, '35, '36, '39; Scotland 1934, '35, '36, '38, '39; Hungary and Czechoslovakia 1934; Holland 1935; Germany 1936, '38; Austria and Belgium 1936; Finland 1937; France 1938; FIFA, Norway and Yugoslavia 1939.
HARDY, S. (Liverpool and Aston Villa)	21	Ireland 1907, '09, '10, '12, '14, '20; Wales 1907, '09, '10, '14, '20; Scotland 1907-'10 inc., '13, '14, '20; Hungary (2) and Austria 1909.
HATELEY, M.W. (Portsmouth, A.C. Milan and Monaco)	31	Uruguay and Chile 1984; Russia 1984, '88 (sub); Brazil 1984, '87 (sub); E. Germany (sub), Finland (2), N. Ireland and Italy 1985; Eire 1985, '88 (sub); Scotland 1985, '86, '87; Mexico 1985, '86; Rumania, Egypt, Canada, Portugal, Morocco and Paraguay (sub) 1986; Turkey 1986, '87 (sub); W. Germany (sub), Holland (2 subs), Hungary (sub), and Colombia (sub) 1988.
HAYNES, J.N. (Fulham)	56	N. Ireland 1955, '56, '58-'62 inc.; Spain 1956, '60, '61; Scotland 1956, '58, '59, '61, '62; Brazil 1956, '58, '59, '62; Sweden, Finland and W. Germany 1956; Wales 1957, '58, '61, '62; Yugoslavia 1957, '58, '60; Eire (2) and Denmark 1957; France 1958; Portugal and Austria 1958, '61, '62; Russia 1958 (3), '59; Italy and Mexico 1959, '61; Peru 1959, '62; USA 1959; Hungary 1960, '62; Luxembourg 1961; Switzerland, Argentina and Bulgaria 1962.
HIBBS, H.E. (Birmingham)	25	Wales 1930-'36 inc.; Scotland 1930, '31, '33, '35; Germany 1930, '36; Austria 1930, '33; N. Ireland 1931-'35 inc.; Spain 1932; Italy and Switzerland 1933; France 1934; Holland 1935.
HODDLE, G. (Tottenham Hotspur)	53	Bulgaria and Australia 1980; Wales 1980, '81, '82; Spain 1980, '81, '87; Scotland 1981, '83, '85, '86, '87; Norway, Iceland, Czechoslovakia (sub) and Kuwait 1982; N. Ireland 1982, '83, '86, '87; Luxembourg 1983 (sub), '84; France 1984; Hungary 1984, '88 (sub); Eire 1985 (sub), '88 (sub); Italy (sub) and USA 1985; W. Germany 1985, '88; Mexico 1985, '86; Rumania, Israel, Canada, Portugal, Morocco, Poland, Paraguay and Argentina 1986; Russia 1986, '88; Turkey 1986, '87, '88 (sub); Sweden 1987; Yugoslavia 1987, '88 (sub); Holland (2 inc. 1 sub) 1988; Colombia (sub) 1988.
HOWE, D. (West Bromwich Albion)	23	Wales and N. Ireland 1958, '59, '60; France, Portugal, Yugoslavia and Austria 1958; Scotland and Brazil 1958, '59; Russia 1958 (3), '59; Italy, Peru, Mexico and USA 1959; Sweden 1960.
HUGHES, E.W. (Liverpool and Wolverhampton Wanderers)	62	Wales 1970, '71, '72, '73 (3), '74, '77, '79; N. Ireland 1970, '72, '74, '75, '78, '79, '80; Scotland 1970, '72, '73 (2), '74, '77, '78, '80 (sub); Holland and Belgium 1970; Portugal 1970,

		'75; E. Germany 1971, '74; Malta 1971 (2); Greece 1971, '72; Switzerland 1972, '78; W. Germany 1972 (2), '78; Poland 1973, '74, Russia 1973; Italy 1973, '74, '77, '78; Austria, Bulgaria and Yugoslavia 1974; Argentina 1974, '77; Czechoslovakia and Cyprus (sub) 1975; Luxembourg 1977, '78; Brazil and Uruguay 1977; Hungary 1978; Denmark, Eire and Sweden 1979; Spain (sub) 1980.
HUNT, R. (Liverpool)	34	Austria 1962, '67; E. Germany 1963; Scotland and Portugal 1964, '66; USA 1964; Wales 1965, '67, '68; Poland and W. Germany 1966 (2); Spain 1966, '67, '68 (2); Finland, Norway, Uruguay, Mexico, France and Argentina 1966; N. Ireland 1967, '68; Czechoslovakia 1967; Russia (2), Sweden and Yugoslavia 1968; Rumania 1969 (2).
HUNTER, N. (Leeds United)	28	W. Germany 1966, '68, '70 (sub), '72 (2); Yugoslavia 1966, '68; Finland 1966; Spain 1966 (sub), '68; Austria 1967, '74; Sweden 1968; Russia 1968, '73 (sub); Rumania 1969; Wales 1969, '72, '73 (2); Holland 1970; Malta 1971; N. Ireland 1972, '74 (sub); Scotland 1972, '74; Poland 1974; Czechoslovakia 1975.
HURST, G.C. (West Ham United)	49	W. Germany 1966 (2), '68, '70, '72; Scotland 1966, '67, '69, '70, '71; Yugoslavia 1966, '68; Finland, Denmark, Argentina and Portugal 1966; N. Ireland 1967-'70 inc.; Czechoslovakia, Spain and Austria 1967; Wales 1967, '68, '70, '71; Russia (2) and Sweden (sub) 1968; Rumania 1969 (2), '70; Bulgaria, France, Mexico and Uruguay 1969; Brazil 1969, '70; Holland (2 inc. 1 sub), Belgium, Colombia and Ecuador 1970; E. Germany 1971; Greece 1971, '72; Switzerland 1972 (2).
KEEGAN, J.K. (Liverpool, SV Hamburg and Southampton)	63	Wales 1973 (2), '74, '76 (2), '77, '79; N. Ireland 1974, '75, '76, '79, '80, '82; Argentina 1974, '77, '80; E. Germany and Yugoslavia 1974; Bulgaria 1974, '79; Czechoslovakia 1975, '76, '79; W. Germany 1975, '78; Cyprus 1975 (2); Scotland 1975, '76, '79, '82; Portugal 1976; Switzerland 1976, '78, '81; Brazil 1976, '77, '78; Finland 1976, '77, '82; Eire 1977, '79, '80; Italy 1977, '78, '80; Holland, Luxembourg and Uruguay 1977; Hungary 1978, '81, '82; Denmark 1979, '80; Sweden and Austria 1979; Spain 1980 (2), '81, '82 (sub); Belgium 1980; Norway 1982.
LABONE, B.L. (Everton)	26	N. Ireland 1963, '69; Wales 1963, '70; France 1963; Spain 1967, '68; Austria 1967; Scotland 1968, '69, '70; Sweden, Yugoslavia and Russia 1968; W. Germany 1968, '70; Rumania and Brazil 1969, '70; Bulgaria, Mexico and Uruguay 1969; Belgium, Colombia and Ecuador 1970.
LAWTON, T. (Everton, Chelsea and Notts County)	23	Wales, N. Ireland and Scotland 1939, '47, '48; FIFA, Norway, Yugoslavia and Rumania 1939; Italy 1939, '48; Eire, Holland, France, Switzerland and Portugal 1947; Belgium and Sweden 1948; Denmark 1949.

LEE, F.H. (Manchester City)	27	Bulgaria, France, Mexico and Uruguay 1969; N. Ireland and Scotland 1969, '71; Wales 1969, '70, '71; Holland (2), Portugal, Belgium, Colombia, Ecuador, Rumania and Brazil 1970; W. Germany 1970, '72; E. Germany and Malta 1971; Greece 1971, '72; Switzerland 1972 (2).
LINEKER, G.W. (Leicester City Everton and Barcelona)	35	Scotland 1984 (sub), '85 (sub), '88; Eire and W. Germany 1985, '88; Italy (sub) and USA 1985; Rumania 1985 (sub), '86; Turkey 1986, '87, '88; N. Ireland 1986, '87 (2); Egypt, Canada, Portugal, Morocco, Poland, Paraguay and Argentina 1986; Russia 1986, '88; Spain and Brazil 1987; Yugoslavia 1987, '88; Holland (2), Hungary, Colombia and Switzerland 1988.
LOFTHOUSE, N. (Bolton Wanderers)	33	Yugoslavia 1951; Wales 1952, '53, '54, '56, '59; N. Ireland 1952-'55 inc.; Austria (2), Italy and Switzerland 1952; Scotland 1952, '53, '55, '56; Belgium and Uruguay 1953, '54; Chile, Argentina and USA 1953; FIFA 1954; France and Portugal 1955; Spain 1955, '56; Denmark and Finland (sub) 1956; Russia 1959.
McDERMOTT, T. (Liverpool)	25	Switzerland 1978, '81 (2 inc. 1 sub); Luxembourg 1978; N. Ireland 1979, '80 (2 inc. 1 sub); Wales 1979, '82 (sub); Sweden 1979; Denmark, Eire, Belgium (sub) and Spain 1980; Scotland 1980, '82 (sub); Norway and Hungary 1981, '82; Rumania (2 inc. 1 sub) and Brazil 1981; Holland and Iceland 1982.
McFARLAND, R.L. (Derby County)	28	Greece 1971, '72; Malta 1971 (2); N. Ireland 1971, '73, '74; Scotland 1971, '72, '73, '76; Switzerland and W. Germany 1972; Wales 1972, '73 (3), '74; Czechoslovakia 1973, '76; Poland 1973, '74; Russia 1973; Italy 1973, '74, '77; Austria 1974; Eire 1977.
MADELEY, P.E. (Leeds United)	24	N. Ireland 1971; Switzerland (2), Greece, W. Germany (2) and Wales 1972; Scotland 1972, '73; Czechoslovakia 1973, '75, '76; Poland and Italy 1973, '74; Russia 1973; Austria 1974; Portugal 1975, '76; Cyprus 1975; Finland 1976; Eire and Holland 1977.
MANNION, W.J. (Middlesbrough)	26	N. Ireland and Wales 1947, '48, '51; Eire 1947, '50; Holland and Switzerland 1947; Scotland 1947, '50, '51; France 1947, '49, '52; Portugal 1947, '50; Belgium 1948, '50; Sweden and Italy 1948; Norway 1949; Chile and USA 1950; Yugoslavia 1951.
MARINER, P. (Ipswich Town and Arsenal)	35	Luxembourg 1977 (sub), '78, '84; N. Ireland 1977, '80 (sub); Wales 1978 (sub), '80, '83; Scotland 1978, '80, '82; Australia and Italy (sub) 1980; Spain 1980 (sub), '81, '82; Norway 1981, '82; Switzerland 1981 (2); Hungary 1981, '82, '84; Holland, Kuwait, France, Czechoslovakia and Finland 1982; W. Germany 1982, '83; Denmark 1983, '84; Greece 1983; E. Germany and Rumania 1985.
MATTHEWS, S. (Stoke City and Blackpool)	54	Wales 1935, '38, '39, '48, '49, '55, '56, '57; Italy 1935, '39, '48; Germany 1936, '38; Scotland 1937,

		'38, '39, '47, ''48, '49, '51, '55, '57; Czechoslovakia 1938; Switzerland 1938, '47, '49; France 1938, '55; FIFA 1939, '54; Norway 1939; N. Ireland 1939, '48, '49, '51, '54, '55, '57; Yugoslavia 1939, '57; Portugal 1947, '55; Belgium 1948, '54, '56; Denmark 1949, '57 (2); Spain 1950, '55; Hungary and Uruguay 1954; W. Germany 1955; Eire 1957.
MERRICK, G.H. (Birmingham City)	23	N. Ireland and Scotland 1952, '53, '54; Austria (2) and Italy 1952; Switzerland 1952, '54; Wales, Belgium and Uruguay 1953, '54; Argentina and Chile 1953; FIFA, Hungary (2) and Yugoslavia 1954.
MILLS, M.D. (Ipswich Town)	42	Yugoslavia 1973; Wales 1976 (2), '77, '78; N. Ireland 1976, '77, '78, '79 (2), '80; Scotland 1976-'89 inc., '82; Brazil 1976, '78; Italy 1976 (sub), '77; Finland 1976, '77 (sub), '82; W. Germany 1978, '82; Hungary 1978, '81, '82; Denmark 1979, '80; Eire, Bulgaria and Austria 1979; Spain 1980 (2), '82; Switzerland 1981 (2); Norway, France, Czechoslovakia and Kuwait 1982.
MOORE, R.F.C. (West Ham United)	108	Peru 1962; Hungary 1962, '65; Argentina 1962, '64, '66; Bulgaria 1962, '69; Brazil 1962, '63, '64, '69, '70; Wales 1963, '64, '66-'70 inc., '72, '73 (3); N. Ireland 1963-'71 inc., '73; Scotland 1963-'72 inc., '73 (2); France 1963 (2), '66, '69; Czechoslovakia 1963, '67, '70, '73; E. Germany 1963, '71; Switzerland 1963, '72 (2); Rest of World, Uruguay and Eire 1964; Portugal 1964 (2), '66, '70; Belgium 1965, '70; Yugoslavia 1965, '68, '73; W. Germany 1965, '66 (2), '68, '70, '72 (2); Sweden 1965, '68; Austria 1966, '67; Spain 1966, '67, '68 (2); Poland 1966 (2), '73; Norway and Denmark 1966; Uruguay and Mexico 1966, '69; Russia 1968 (2), '73; Rumania 1969, '70; Holland, Colombia and Ecuador 1970; Greece 1971, '72; Malta 1971; Italy 1973, '74.
MORTENSEN, S.H. (Blackpool)	25	Portugal 1947, '50; Belgium and Italy 1948, '50; Wales and N. Ireland 1948, '49, '50; Sweden 1948, '49; Norway 1949; Scotland 1948-'51 inc.; Chile USA and Spain 1950; Argentina 1951; FIFA and Hungary 1954.
MULLERY, A.P. (Tottenham Hotspur)	35	Holland 1965, '70 (2 inc. 1 sub); Spain 1967, '68 (2); Austria 1967; Wales 1968, '70; N. Ireland 1968, '69, '70; Russia, Sweden and Yugoslavia 1968: Scotland 1968, '69, '70 (sub); Rumania and Brazil 1969, '70; Bulgaria, France, Mexico and Uruguay 1969; Portugal, Colombia, Ecuador, Czechoslovakia and West Germany 1970; E. Germany, Malta and Greece 1971; Switzerland 1972.
NEAL, P.G. (Liverpool)	50	Wales 1976, '77, '80, '82, '83; Italy 1976, '78, '80; Scotland 1977, '78, '79, '83; Brazil 1977, '81;

		Argentina 1977, '80; Uruguay 1977; Switzerland 1978, '81; W. Germany 1978; N. Ireland 1978, '79 (2), '80, '83; Hungary 1978, '81, '82, '83; Denmark 1979, '80, '83, '84; Eire, Bulgaria and Austria 1979; Spain 1980, '81; Belgium 1980; Rumania 1981; Norway, Holland, Iceland, France (sub) and Kuwait 1982; Greece (2), Luxembourg and Australia (2) 1983.
NEWTON, K.R. (Blackburn Rovers and Everton)	27	W. Germany 1966, '68, '70; Scotland 1966, '68 '69, '70; Spain 1967, '68; Austria 1967; Wales 1968, '69; Sweden and Yugoslavia 1968; Rumania and N. Ireland 1969, '70; Bulgaria, France, Mexico, Uruguay and Brazil 1969; Holland, Colombia, Ecuador and Czechoslovakia 1970.
NORMAN, M. (Tottenham Hotspur)	23	Peru, Hungary and Bulgaria 1962; Argentina 1962, '64; Brazil 1962, '63, '64; France, Czechoslovakia and E. Germany 1963; Scotland 1963, '64; Wales, FIFA, Uruguay, Portugal (2) and USA 1964; Belgium and Holland 1965; N. Ireland 1964, '65.
PENNINGTON, J. (West Bromwich Albion)	25	Wales 1907-'13 inc.; '20; Scotland 1907-'14 inc., '20; Ireland 1908, '11, '12, '14; Austria 1908, '09; Hungary 1909 (2).
PETERS, M.S. (West Ham United and Tottenham Hotspur)	67	Yugoslavia 1966, '68; Finland and Argentina 1966; Poland 1966, '73, '74; Mexico and France 1966, '69; Portugal 1966, '70 (sub), '74; W. Germany 1966, '70, '72 (2 inc. 1 sub); N. Ireland 1967-'71 inc., '73; Wales 1967, '68, '70, '71, '72 (sub), '73; Scotland 1967-'71 inc., '73 (2), '74; Czechoslovakia 1967, '70, '73; Russia 1968 (2), '73; Spain (2) and Sweden 1968; Rumania and Brazil 1969, '70; Bulgaria and Uruguay 1969; Holland (2), Belgium, Colombia and Ecuador 1970; E. Germany and Malta (2) 1971; Greece 1971, '72; Switzerland 1972; Italy 1973, '74; Austria 1974.
RAMSEY, A.E. (Southampton and Tottenham Hotspur)	32	Switzerland 1949, '52; Italy 1950, '52; Scotland 1950-'53 inc.; Portugal 1950, '51; Belgium, Chile and USA 1950, '53; Spain 1950; N. Ireland and Wales 1951, '52, '53; Yugoslavia 1951; Argentina 1951, '53; France and Austria (2) 1952; Uruguay 1953; FIFA and Hungary 1954.
ROBSON, B. (West Bromwich Albtion and Manchester United)	69	Eire 1980, '85; '88; Australia 1980; Norway and Wales 1981, '82; Rumania 1981 (2), '85, '86; Switzerland 1981 (2), '88; Spain 1981, '82, '87; Brazil 1981, '84, '87; Scotland 1981-'85 inc., '87 '88; Hungary 1981, '82, '84, '88; N. Ireland 1982, '84, '87 (2); Holland 1982, '88 (2); Czechoslovakia 1982; Finland 1982, '85 (2); France 1982, '84; W. Germany 1982, '85; Denmark and Greece 1983; Luxembourg 1983, '84; Russia 1984, '88; Uruguay and Chile 1984; E. Germany, Italy and USA 1985; Turkey 1985-'88 inc.; Mexico 1985, '86; Israel, Portugal and Morocco 1986; Yugoslavia and Colombia 1988.
ROBSON, R.W. (West Bromwich Albion)	20	France, Russia (2), Brazil and Austria 1958; Spain 1960, '61; Hungary 1960; N. Ireland, Luxembourg,

		Wales and Portugal 1961, '62; Scotland, Mexico and Italy 1961; Switzerland 1962.
SANSOM, K.G. (Crystal Palace and Arsenal)	86	Wales 1979, '80 (sub), '81, '82; Bulgaria and Belgium 1980; Eire 1980, '85, '88; Italy 1980, '85; Argentina 1980, '86; N. Ireland 1980, '82, '83, '85, '86, '87 (2); Scotland 1980-'86 inc., '88; Switzerland 1981 (2), '88; Norway 1981; Rumania 1981 (2), '85, '86; Spain 1981, '82, '87; Brazil 1981, '84; Holland 1982, '88 (2); Czechoslovakia 1982; Finland 1982, '85 (2); France 1982, '84; W. Germany 1982, '83, '85, '88; Denmark, Luxembourg and Hungary 1983, '84; Greece 1983 (2); Russia 1984, '86, '88; Uruguay and Chile 1984; E. Germany and USA 1985; Turkey 1985-'88 inc.; Mexico 1985, '86; Egypt, Israel, Canada, Portugal, Mexico, Poland and Paraguay 1986; Sweden 1987; Yugoslavia 1987, '88; Colombia 1988.
SHILTON, P.L. (Leicester City, Stoke City, Nottingham Forest, Southampton and Derby County)	100	E. Germany 1971, '85; Wales 1971, '73, '74, '77, '78, '83, '84; Switzerland 1972, '81, '8; N. Ireland 1972, '73, '74, '77, '80, '83, '87 (2); Yugoslavia 1973, '88; Scotland 1973 (2), '74, '82-'86inc., '88; Czechoslovakia 1973, '79, '82; Poland 1973, '74, '86; Russia 1973, '84, '86; Italy 1973, '74, '80, '85; Austria 1974, '79; Argentina 1974, '86; Cyprus 1975; Hungary 1978, '82, '83, '84; Sweden 1979, '87; Spain 1980, '82, '87; Norway 1981; Rumania 1981, '85, '86; Holland 1982, '88 (2); Kuwait 1982; France 1982, '84; W. Germany 1982, '83, '85, '88; Denmark 1983, '84; Greece (2) and Australia (3) 1983; Brazil 1984, '87; Uruguay and Chile 1984; Finland 1985 (2); Turkey 1985, '86, '88; Egypt, Israel, Mexico, Canada, Portugal, Morocco and Paraguay 1986; Colombia and Eire 1988.
SMITH, G.O. (Oxford University and Corinthians)	20	Ireland 1893, '96-1900 inc.; Wales 1894-1900 inc.; Scotland 1894; '96-1901 inc.
SPRINGETT, R.D.G. (Sheffield Wednesday)	33	N. Ireland 1960-63 inc.; Scotland 1960, '61, '62; Yugoslavia 1960; Spain 1960, '61; Hungary 1960, '62; Luxembourg and Portugal 1961, '62; Mexico and Italy 1961; Austria 1961, '62, '66; Wales 1962, '63, '66; Switzerland 1962, '63; Peru, Argentina, Bulgaria and Brazil 1962; France 1963 (2); Norway 1966.
STEVEN, T.M. (Everton)	24	N. Ireland, Eire, Rumania, Finland, Italy and USA (sub) 1985; Turkey and Russia 1986 (sub), '88; Mexico (sub), Egypt, Poland, Paraguay and Argentina 1986; Sweden and Spain (sub) 1987; Yugoslavia 1987 (sub), '88; Holland (2), Hungary, Scotland and Switzerland 1988.
STEVENS, M.G. (Everton)	26	Italy and W. Germany 1985; Rumania, N. Ireland, Egypt, Canada, Portugal, Morocco, Poland, Paraguay and Argentina 1986; Israel and Turkey 1986, '88; Scotland 1986, '87, '88; Brazil 1987; Yugoslavia, Holland (2), Hungary (sub), Switzerland, Eire and Russia.
STILES, N.P. (Manchester United)	28	Scotland 1965, '66, '67, '70; Hungary, Yugoslavia

		and Sweden 1965; Wales 1966, '67; Austria, Spain, Poland (2), West Germany (2), Norway, Denmark, Uruguay, France, Argentina and Portugal 1966; N. Ireland 1966, '67, '70; Czechoslovakia 1967; Russia 1968; Rumania 1969.
STRANGE, A.H. (Sheffield Wednesday)	20	Scotland 1930-'33 inc.; Germany 1930; Austria 1930, '33; N. Ireland 1931-'34 inc.; Wales 1931, '32, '34; France 1931, '34; Belgium 1931; Spain 1932; Italy and Switzerland 1933.
THOMPSON, Philip B. (Liverpool)	42	Wales 1976 (2), '80, '82; N. Ireland 1976, '79, '80; Scotland 1976, '79, '80, '82; Brazil 1976; Italy 1976, '80; Finland 1976, '77, '82; Eire 1979 (sub), '80; Czechoslovakia 1979, '82; Bulgaria 1979, '80; Sweden (sub) and Austria 1979; Denmark, Argentina and Belgium 1980; Spain 1980 (2), '82; Norway and Hungary 1981, '82; Rumania 1981; Holland, France and Kuwait 1982; W. Germany 1982, '83; Greece 1983.
TODD, C. (Derby County)	27	N. Ireland 1972, '74-'77 inc.; Portugal 1974, '75 (sub), '76; Wales 1974, '75; Scotland 1974, '75, '76; Argentina, E. Germany, Bulgaria and Yugoslavia 1974; W. Germany and Cyprus (2) 1975; Switzerland, Czechoslovakia and Brazil 1976; Finland 1976, '77; Eire and Holland (sub) 1977.
WADDLE, C.R. (Newcastle United)	36	Eire and W. Germany 1985, '88; Finland (sub), Italy and USA 1985; Rumania and Mexico 1985 (sub), '86; Scotland 1985 (sub), '86, '87, '88 (sub); Turkey 1986, '87; N. Ireland 1986, '87 (2); Israel 1986, '88; Russia, Canada, Portugal, Morocco, Poland (sub) and Argentina (sub) 1986; Sweden (sub), Yugoslavia, Spain and Brazil 1987; Hungary, Colombia, Switzerland (sub) and Holland (sub) 1988.
WARREN, B. (Derby County and Chelsea)	22	Ireland, Wales and Scotland 1906-'09 inc., '11; Austria 1908 (2), '09; Hungary 1908, '09 (2); Bohemia 1908.
WATSON, David V. (Sunderland, Manchester City, Werder Bremen, Southampton and Stoke City)	65	Portugal 1974, '75, '76; Scotland 1974 (sub), '75, '77-'81 inc.; Argentina 1974, '77, '80; E. Germany and Yugoslavia 1974; Bulgaria 1974, '79, '80; Czechoslovakia 1975, '76 (sub), '79; W. Germany 1975, '78; Cyprus 1975 (2); N. Ireland 1975, '77, '78, '79 (2), '80 (2), '82; Wales 1975, '77, '78, '79, '81; Switzerland 1976, '78, '81 (2); Holland and Uruguay 1977; Luxembourg and Brazil 1977, '78; Italy 1978, '80; Hungary 1978, '81; Denmark and Eire 1979, '80; Sweden and Austria 1979; Spain (2) and Belgium 1980; Norway and Rumania (2) 1981; Iceland 1982.
WEDLOCK, W.J. (Bristol City)	26	Ireland and Scotland 1907-'12 inc.; Wales 1907-'12 inc., '14; Austria 1908 (2), '09; Hungary 1908, '09 (2); Bohemia 1908.
WILKINS, R.C. (Chelsea, Manchester United and AC Milan)	84	Italy 1976, '78, '80, '85; Eire 1977, '79, '85; Finland 1977, '82, '85 (2); N. Ireland 1977-'80 (2) inc., '82, '84, '85, '86; Brazil 1977, '81, '84; Argentina 1977, '80; Uruguay 1977, '84;

		Switzerland 1978 (sub), '81; Luxembourg 1978; W. Germany 1978, '82, '83; Wales 1978, '79, '80 (sub), '81, '82, '84; Scotland 1978-'82 inc., '84, '85 '86; Hungary 1978, '81 (sub); Denmark 1979, '80, '83, '84; Czechoslovakia 1979, '82; Bulgaria 1979, '80; Sweden 1979 (sub), '87; Austria 1979; Spain 1980 (2), '81 (sub), '82; Belgium 1980; Rumania 1981, '85; Holland, France and Kuwait 1982; Russia 1984, '86; Chile 1984; E. Germany 1985; Turkey and Mexico 1985, '86; Israel, Egypt, Canada, Portugal and Morocco 1986; Yugoslavia (sub) 1987.
WILLIAMS, B.F. (Wolverhampton Wanderers)	24	France 1949, '52, '55; Eire, Italy, Belgium, Chile and USA 1950; Wales 1950, '51, '52, '56; Scotland and Portugal 1950, '51, '55; Spain 1950, '55, N. Ireland, Argentina and Yugoslavia 1951; West Germany 1955.
WILSON, R. (Huddersfield Town and Everton)	63	Scotland 1960, '62, '64, '65, '67, '68; Yugoslavia 1960, '65, '66, '68; Spain 1960, '66, '68 (2); Hungary 1960, '62, '65; Wales 1962, '64, '66, '67; Portugal 1962, '64 (2), '66; N. Ireland 1962, '63, '66, '67, '68; Austria 1962, '66, '67; Switzerland 1962, '63; Peru and Bulgaria 1962; Argentina 1962, '64, '66; Brazil 1962, '63, '64; France 1963, '66; Czechoslovakia 1963, '67; E. Germany 1963; FIFA and Eire 1964; Uruguay 1964, '66; W. Germany 1965, '66 (2 inc. 1 sub); Sweden 1965; Poland (2), Finland, Denmark and Mexico 1966; Russia (2) 1968.
WOODCOCK, A.S. (Nottingham Forest, FC Cologne and Arsenal)	42	N. Ireland 1978, '80, '82 (sub), '84, '85; Eire and Bulgaria 1979 (sub), '80, Czechoslovakia and Sweden 1979; Spain 1980 (2), '82; Argentina, Belgium and Italy 1980; Norway and Switzerland 1981; Rumania 1981 (2), '86 (sub); Wales 1981 (sub), '84; Scotland 1981, '84; Holland 1982; Finland 1982 (sub), '85; W. Germany 1982 (sub), '83 (sub); Greece 1983 (2); Luxembourg 1983, '84; France (sub), Brazil and Uruguay (sub) 1984; E. Germany 1985; Turkey 1985, '86 (sub); Israel 1986 (sub).
WOODWARD, V.J. (Tottenham Hotspur)	23	Ireland 1903, '04, '05, '08, '09, '10; Wales 1903, '05, '08, '09, '11; Scotland 1903, '04, '05, '07, '08; Austria 1908 (2), '09; Hungary 1908, '09 (2); Bohemia 1908.
WRIGHT, M. (Southampton and Derby County)	22	Wales 1984; E. Germany, Finland, Italy and W. Germany 1985; Eire 1985, '88; Turkey and Rumania 1985, '86; N. Ireland 1986, '87; Egypt and Russia 1986; Yugoslavia and Scotland 1987; Israel, Holland (2 inc. 1 sub), Colombia and Switzerland 1988.
WRIGHT, W.A. (Wolverhampton Wanderers)	105	N. Ireland and Scotland 1947-'59 inc.; Eire 1947, '50, '57 (2); Wales 1947-'50 inc., '52-'59 inc.; Holland 1947; France 1947, '49, '52, '55, '58; Switzerland 1947, '49, '52, '54; Portugal 1947, '50, '55, '58; Belgium 1948, '50, '53, '54; Sweden 1948, '49, '56; Italy 1948, '50, '52, '57; Denmark

and Norway 1949; Chile 1950, '53; USA 1950, '53, '59; Spain 1950, '55, '56; Argentina 1951, '53; Austria 1952 (2), '58; Uruguay 1953, '54; FIFA and Hungary (2) 1954; Yugoslavia 1954, '57, '58; W. Germany 1955, '56; Denmark 1956, '57 (2); Brazil 1956, '58, '59; Finland 1956; Russia 1958 (3), '59; Peru and Mexico 1959.